D0523229

CANADIAN
DEMOCRACY
a concise introduction

Stephen Brooks · Marc Ménard

OXFORD
UNIVERSITY PRESS

OXFORD

UNIVERSITY PRESS

Oxford University Press is a department of the University of Oxford.
It furthers the University's objective of excellence in research, scholarship,
and education by publishing worldwide. Oxford is a registered trade mark of
Oxford University Press in the UK and in certain other countries.

Published in Canada by
Oxford University Press
8 Sampson Mews, Suite 204,
Don Mills, Ontario M3C 0H5 Canada

www.oupcanada.com

Copyright © Oxford University Press Canada 2013

The moral rights of the authors have been asserted

Database right Oxford University Press (maker)

All rights reserved. No part of this publication may be reproduced, stored in
a retrieval system, or transmitted, in any form or by any means, without the
prior permission in writing of Oxford University Press, or as expressly permitted
by law, by licence, or under terms agreed with the appropriate reprographics
rights organization. Enquiries concerning reproduction outside the scope of the
above should be sent to the Permissions Department at the address above or through
the following url: www.oupcanada.com/permission/permission_request.php

Every effort has been made to determine and contact copyright holders.
In the case of any omissions, the publisher will be pleased to make
suitable acknowledgement in future editions.

Library and Archives Canada Cataloguing in Publication
Brooks, Stephen, 1956–
Canadian democracy : a concise introduction / Stephen Brooks & Marc Ménard.

Includes bibliographical references and index.
ISBN 978–0–19–544374–5

1. Canada—Politics and government—Textbooks.
2. Democracy—Canada—Textbooks. I. Ménard, Marc,
1956– II. Title.

JL75.B76 2013   320.971   C2012-906482-3

Cover image: Ingram Publishing/Getty Images

This book is printed on permanent (acid-free) paper ∞ which
contains a minimum of 10% post-consumer waste.

Printed and bound in the United States of America.

1 2 3 4 — 16 15 14 13

Brief Contents

Contents

PART I INTRODUCTION 1

1 | An Introduction to Political Life 2

PART II THE SOCIETAL CONTEXT OF POLITICS 29

2 | Political Culture 30

3 | The Social and Economic Setting   77

4 | Regionalism and Canadian Politics   104

PART III THE STRUCTURES OF GOVERNANCE   129

5 | The Constitution   130

6 | Rights and Freedoms   170

7 | Federalism   191

8 | How Parliamentary Government Works in Canada   226

PART IV PARTICIPATION IN POLITICS 275

9 | Parties and Elections 276

10 | Interest Groups 314

11 | The Media   343

PART V CANADIAN POLITICAL ISSUES   369

12 | Language, Diversity, and Aboriginal Politics   370

13 | Canada in the World   419

Figures, Tables, and Boxes

FIGURES

TABLES

BOXES

Democracy Watch

CANADIAN SPOTLIGHT

INSIDE POLITICS

MEDIA BEAT

Preface

I often wonder if Canadian politics wouldn't be easier to teach if our system of government was not a parliamentary democracy. Indeed, Canadian politics is difficult for most students or citizens to understand without some sort of theoretical training. To the untrained eye, it appears to be an odd amalgamation of laws, institutions, and accommodations that are either inherited, borrowed, or invented by Canadians for Canadians. By contrast, totalitarian regimes seem to be easier to grasp, perhaps because of the simplified arrangements, the efficient and blunt use of power, and the general lack of accommodation. Even the American democratic system of government, with its constitutional separation of powers and system of checks and balances, seems prettier to look at and easier to explain. Yet, for all its complexity and occasional inelegance, Canadian democracy has allowed Canadians for almost a century and a half to manage their differences, share their resources, protect their rights, and regularly and peacefully change their governments.

This concise version of Stephen Brooks's *Canadian Democracy* is written mainly for those who are new to Canadian politics. As a long-time teacher of politics, I have discovered that students learn politics best when the instructor and the textbook offer early, clear, and frequent explanations of the "why" of politics, followed immediately by theoretical models, examples, and illustrations. This is what first enticed me to use *Canadian Democracy* in my classroom. Therefore, the concise version has been structured with the same treatment of the key components of Canada's political system around such themes as equality, freedoms, rights, and access. The five-part structure of the original text has also been kept.

Part I, the introduction, begins with an explanation of why politics is best studied using certain definitions and scientific methodology. This is followed with explanations of fundamental concepts such as power, the state, and democracy that continue to be used throughout the book.

Political scientists often refer to political systems as though they were living and breathing organisms, constantly evolving eco-systems. Part II of the textbook, which includes Chapters 2 to 4, is devoted to understanding the societal context in which Canadian democracy has evolved and continues to evolve. The reader will notice that comparisons with the United States are frequent and woven into many chapters. Notwithstanding the obvious historical and geographic relationship to the United States, the use of comparisons (one democracy to another) can be very useful in understanding the evolution of a democracy. Chapter 2 discusses political culture with particular attention to the values, ideologies, and institutions of Canadian society, as well as the role that culture, in addition to history and geography, has played in shaping the Canadian political system.

Economics, which is discussed in Chapter 3, is also an important determinant of any political system, and is a good place to begin our understanding of the forces that shape the laws, institutions, and policies of a country. Chapter 4 examines regionalism as a constant theme in Canadian politics. Canadian democracy has had to adapt to its unique historical and geographic circumstances. But one of the more fascinating aspects of Canadian politics is how it has managed to overcome significant internal political divisions such as regional conflict and disparities.

Part III deals with the structural elements, the heart of Canadian democracy: its Constitution, institutions, and political arrangements and accommodations.

Newcomers to Canadian politics are often fascinated to learn that much of our Constitution, the fundamental rules of the game, is unwritten. Chapter 5 is first and foremost an introduction to the elements of the Canadian Constitution that form the basis for the way Canadians are governed, which includes the power relationships between different government institutions as well as the limits citizens place on their politicians and their governments. Chapter 6 expands on the discussion started in Chapter 5 by familiarizing the reader with the language of rights and freedoms, looking at how citizens express their demands in a democracy as well as discussing the effects of the 1982 Canadian Charter of Rights and Freedoms on Canadian society.

The idea of sharing power between a central government and smaller regional governments—federalism—was considered by the Fathers of Confederation to be a great compromise without which there would be no Canada. Chapter 7 shows the reader that while many Canadians feel a deep sense of commitment to Canada as a country, strong ties to their region continue to exert a tremendous influence on Canadian politics. The issue of who should play the dominant role, the provinces or the federal government, continues to be asked and debated.

Another surprise for students of Canadian politics is how very different the Canadian system of government is from the American system, in spite of them both being democracies. As such, the comparison made in Chapter 8 between the two countries' machinery of government is often illustrative and educational. It is also interesting to see, in a democracy, the extent to which the machinery of government is shaped by the values and the expectations of its citizens.

Part IV is an exploration of how Canadians participate in the democracy. If Canadians live in a democracy, what is the nature of their participation in the country's politics, and how do they access politicians and the levers of government? Chapter 9 discusses these matters as well as the role that elections and political parties play in the democratic process.

Organizations such as interest groups also have a role to play in a democracy, and Chapter 10 is devoted to an analysis and breakdown of the interest-group system in Canada. Chapter 10 also looks at different theories that help political scientists explain interest-group activities and their tactics, and which segments of Canadian society benefit the most from interest-group activities.

Most Canadians have an opinion about government and how well or poorly it works. Chapter 11 looks at some important questions about the role of the media as an agent of change. The quality of the information provided by the media and the images portrayed therein can significantly affect how people interact with each other and the political system.

Part V, which includes Chapters 12 and 13, is an analysis of contemporary issues in Canadian politics. Chapter 12 looks at long-standing issues in Canadian politics: language politics and the Quebec question; diversity, immigration, and gender politics; and Aboriginal politics. And finally, Chapter 13 closes the book with a brief look at Canada's international presence and the perceptions, values, and expectations that Canadians have about its role on the world stage.

What Stephen Brooks wrote in the preface of the seventh edition of *Canadian Democracy* is worth repeating: the title of the book is neither a judgment nor a conclusion. It is, rather, a focus. And the approach is neither an uncritical celebration of Canadian politics nor a lopsided condemnation of its shortcomings and failures. By looking at the complex and contested concept of democracy, we hope to encourage the readers to think about Canadian politics in ways that will enable them to assess fairly and realistically the performance of Canada's political system.

ACKNOWLEDGEMENTS

There was no way of knowing, when I was first asked by OUP, what a personal challenge this particular project would be. I liked using *Canadian Democracy* in the classroom. And I was happy and proud to work on a project that would make the text more accessible and make it fit into a fourteen-week semester. Nevertheless, the process of abridging any textbook, like a home renovation, is never as easy as one initially thinks. Countless hours went into ensuring that the quality of the textbook would not be affected by the reduction in size.

I would like to thank Stephen Brooks and Katherine Skene, Oxford University Press, for giving me the opportunity to work on *Canadian Democracy: A Concise Introduction* in spite of my general lack of experience in the field of writing and editing. They were taking a risk, and I was surprised at how much leeway and patience I was granted. That being said, I had a tremendous amount of support and assistance from editor Jodi Lewchuk and copy editor Leslie Saffrey.

Support and assistance also came from Claire Moane, Chair of the School of English and Liberal Studies, Seneca College of Applied Arts and Technology, as well as the library staff at Seneca Libraries. I also received countless suggestions and thoughtful comments from my colleagues, Mark Rubinstein and Ken Sproul, both social science professors at Seneca College.

And finally, I would like to acknowledge the contributions and encouragement from my wife, Liz, daughters, Laura, Catherine, and Carolyn, and the members of our extended family. Our dinnertime conversations and heated debates over politics are a constant reminder of the importance of being clear, factual, and succinct.

Marc Ménard, Professor, School of English and Liberal Studies,
Faculty of Business, Seneca College, Toronto, Ontario

Highlights of the Concise Edition

Canadian Democracy: A Concise Introduction presents a succinct overview of Canadian government and politics without sacrificing depth and breadth of coverage. Key features of the concise edition include:

- **UNIQUE STRUCTURE AND HALLMARK WRITING STYLE.** The country's social values are covered in parts I and II, giving readers a foundation for understanding Canada's governmental institutions and political structures, covered in parts III and IV. Throughout, clear writing and accessible language guide readers through the sometimes complex world of political process.

- **SPECIAL FEATURES GEARED TOWARDS STUDENT ENGAGEMENT.** Inviting students into debate, shining the light on uniquely Canadian issues, and taking a behind-the-scenes look at the daily world of politics and the media, the following features capture readers' interest and involve them with content.

  » **"Democracy Watch"** boxes focus on controversial events, processes, and situations related to Canadian democracy and end with debate-style questions.

  » **"Canadian Spotlight"** boxes provide timelines on important themes in Canadian democracy and highlight events, people, and places that have played a role in the evolution of Canadian government.

  » **"Inside Politics"** boxes feature special issues and provide commentary on key concepts.

  » **"Media Beat"** boxes feature news and other media stories related to politics.

- **STRIKING PRESENTATION OF KEY TERMS AND THEIR DEFINITIONS.** Both key terms and their definitions are highlighted directly in the narrative, giving readers in-context understanding of important concepts and taking the guesswork out of studying.

32   II | The Societal Context of Politics

VALUES, IDEOLOGIES, AND INSTITUTIONS

Ideas assume various forms in political life. When they take the form of *a set of interrelated values and beliefs about how society is organized and ought to function*—an interpretative map for understanding the world—they constitute an **ideology**. An ideology spills beyond the boundaries of politics to embrace beliefs and judgments about other social relationships,

YEAH, WE'RE PUNKUINS, SO WHAT!
WE DON'T HAVE TO LIVE BY YOUR
CONFORMIST IDEOLOGY

Youth are sometimes drawn to a very different set of values and beliefs than was the generation before them. What is your vision of how society should be org function? Is this ideology similar to that of your parents is beliefs are different from theirs?

2 | Political Culture   53

...king groups in the United States, rates of cultural assimilation have been high. Moreover, Canadian governments have shown themselves to be as capable as ...th counterparts of discriminating against ethnic and religious communities. For ...oth countries many people of Japanese origin were deprived of their property and ...camps during World War II. The religious practices of Doukhobors, Hutterites, ...s, and Jehovah's Witnesses have at various times brought them into conflict with ...awa or provincial governments. And in both Canada and the United States immi-...olicy has historically discriminated against non-white, non-European peoples—...h this is no longer a fair characterization of policy in either country. ...spite evidence that also in Canada tolerance of cultural diversity has known limits, ...limits have been less restrictive than in the United States. The treatment of Canada's ...original peoples, for example, has been less harsh and less violent than that of America's ...original minorities. And there is nothing in Canada's history that compares to the offi-...l discrimination and the physical violence directed against American blacks for much of ...at country's history. An official policy of multiculturalism has existed in Canada since 1971 ...d was entrenched in the Constitution in 1982.[37] **Multiculturalism is *the idea that cul-tural diversity is not only good for society, it should also be encouraged***. Moreover, Canada's ...Constitution appears to provide a firmer basis for affirmative action programs and other state activities that have as their goal "the amelioration of conditions of disadvantaged individuals

(Left) BC Doukhobors commemorate the anniversary of leader Peter Lordly Verigin's death on 29 October 1927. Verigin and his people clashed with the government over their aversion to private ownership of land, which led the Crown to reclaim more than a third of Doukhobor land in 1907. (Right) Japanese Canadians arrive at an internment camp in BC's interior in 1942. In the wake of the Japanese attack on Pearl Harbor in the United States, the Canadian government speculated that Japanese living in Canada were engaged in espionage and confined them to segregated camps and sold off their possessions and assets at auction.

38   II | The Societal Context of Politics

TABLE 2.1 | KAY LAWSON'S SUMMARY OF IDEOLOGIES

General Issues	Communism and Some Forms of Socialism	Social Democrats/ Feminism	Liberalism	Conservatism	Fascism
1. Means of Change	Revolution	Persuasion and democratic elections			Coup/coercion
2. Human Nature	Unselfish and social	Selfish and social			Selfish and unsocial
3. Role of the State	Economic redistribution	Protect individual liberty			Control
4. Values	Economic equality	Freedom and political equality			Social order
5. Positions	Far left	Left	Centre	Right	Far right

This table shows how the values of most present-day ideologies are very similar.

Source: Adapted from Kay Lawson, *The Human Polity: A Comparative Introduction to Political Science* (New York: Wadsworth, 2002).

that governments can and should act to alleviate hardships experienced by the poor and the oppressed. They are more likely to worry about minority group rights than individual free-doms, in the sense that they see protecting disadvantaged minorities as a necessary step in achieving real freedom for the members of these groups. Modern liberalism has also become associated with support for multiculturalism and openness toward non-traditional lifestyles and social institutions.

The doctrine of classical conservatism has disappeared from contemporary democracies, leaving what has been called the conservative outlook or "conservative mind."[72] Modern conserv-atives tend to embrace the economic beliefs that once were characteristic of liberals. Like classical liberals, they defend the principle of equality of opportunity and are more likely to place the protection of personal freedoms before the advancement of minority rights. As in earlier times, conservatism is generally viewed as the ideology of the privileged in society. It is worth noting, however, that conservative politicians and political parties receive much of their support from middle-class voters whose hands are far from the levers of economic power and social influence.

Of the three classical ideologies, the meaning of "socialism" has changed the least. There is today, however, much less confidence among socialists that state ownership of the means of economic production and distribution is desirable. Modern socialists, or *social democrats* as they often call themselves, temper their advocacy of an egalitarian society with an accept-ance of capitalism and the inequalities that inevitably are generated by free-market economies. Defending the rights of society's least-well-off elements is today carried out largely under the banner of other "isms" including feminism, multiculturalism, and environmentalism. These collectivist–egalitarian belief systems have more impact on Canadian and American politics than does socialism.

A second reason why the traditional trio of "isms" is no longer a reliable guide to politics has to do with the character of political divisions in modern society. The aristocracy of land and title and the deferential social norms that nurtured classical conservatism belong to the

- **ART PROGRAM WITH EMPHASIS ON VISUAL LEARNING.** A host of images, political cartoons, and figures and tables in each chapter bring a visual dimension to learning about key ideas and concepts.

Online Support

- INTEGRATED ONLINE MATERIAL AND A FULL SUITE OF ANCILLARIES. With online material integrated with the text and a robust suite of supplements, *Canadian Democracy: A Concise Introduction* offers one-stop shopping for all student and instructor needs.

  - » **Podcasts** providing mini-lectures focused on important issues of the day. An icon in the text's margin indicates where a relevant podcast is available online.

  - » **Links** featuring audio and visual material from the CBC archives and TVO's politics-focused roundtable forum *The Agenda*.

  - » **Appendices**, including the Constitution Act, 1867, and the Constitution Act, 1982, as well as instruction on how to write an essay.

  - » **"Get Involved" section** for students, featuring a history of Canada's major political parties; Q&As with members of parliament; and links to political websites of interest, including *Democracy Watch*, *Elections Canada*, *The Democracy Project*, and many more.

  - » **Student study guide**, offering short-answer questions; self-testing quizzes; glossary flashcards; and suggestions for books, articles, and media resources highlighting political issues in Canada.

  - » **Test generator**, **instructor's manual**, and **PowerPoint presentations** for instructors, offering a comprehensive array of teaching supports.

Part I

Introduction

We all have an idea of what politics involves. But the term "political science" may be less familiar and, in some ways, more puzzling. The problem may arise from the word "science" and images of hard facts, measurements, and laboratories. The problem may also arise from the fact that some experts consider politics an art, which defies experimentation and measurement. The study and understanding of politics, as for all forms of human behaviour and organization, seems to lack the hard edge and to rely on techniques quite different from those used in the natural and applied sciences such as physics and biology. Can there be such a thing as political science?

The answer is: yes, within limits. Political science is considered a "soft" rather than a "hard" science. Like the natural and applied sciences, political science rests on a bedrock of empirical analysis—analysis that seeks to formulate laws about the world of politics and government based on verifiable observation and, in some cases, experimentation. Like the practitioners of the hard sciences, those who study politics and government seek to do so objectively, attempting to understand the way things are and how they may be changed. Political scientists' analysis of politics may not always look like the activities and results of those in the hard sciences, but the aspiration to produce objective, empirical knowledge is the same. Political scientists generally have to make do with observing behaviour and the functioning of institutions in less controlled circumstances than might be found in laboratories or computer simulations.

No matter where politics and government are studied, the core concepts and analytical methods are the same. Power, authority, identity, participation, bureaucracy, integration, stability, and equality are just some of the core concepts that are relevant to understanding the politics of any country. In Part I of *Canadian Democracy: A Concise Introduction* we examine some of the concepts that are crucial to understanding politics and government in Canada.

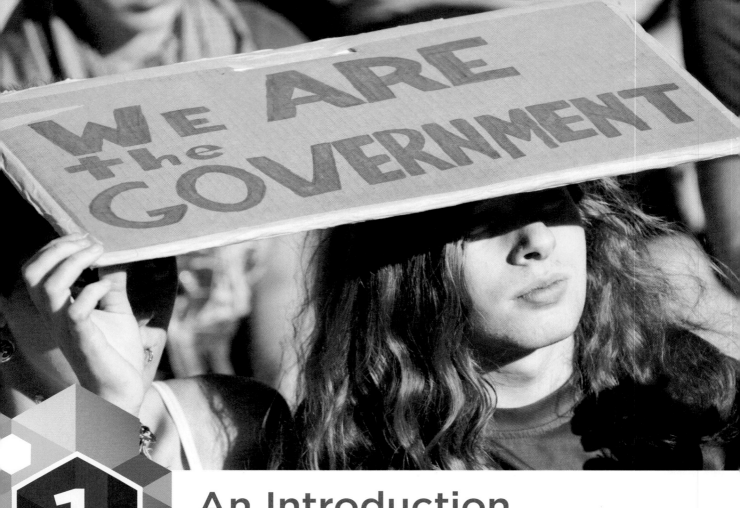

An Introduction to Political Life

An understanding of politics and government requires a tool kit of fundamental concepts and terms that are useful in analyzing political life. This chapter will equip you with such tools by examining the following concepts:

- Politics
- Power
- The state
- Government
- Authority
- Legitimacy
- Democracy

POLITICS AS A VOCATION

If you want a job that earns you the respect of your fellow citizens, become a firefighter, a nurse, a teacher, or a police officer, but do not become a politician. This is the conclusion that seems to emerge from Leger Marketing's annual survey of Canadians, asking them which professions they trust most.[1] Firefighters had the trust of 97 per cent of Canadians in 2007; nurses, 94 per cent; teachers, 89 per cent; and police officers, 84 per cent. Politicians were second-last at 15 per cent. Based on this survey, one might say that politicians have an image problem.

The image of politicians as untrustworthy, and of their calling as low and dishonest, is not entirely fair. There is no hard evidence that politicians are more likely to be dishonest or have lower moral standards than those in other occupations. Indeed, many, if not most, people who run for and are elected to public office are motivated by a desire to serve and to improve the lives of those they represent. Many politicians make significant financial and personal sacrifices by holding public office. Yet Canadians do not trust them.

To understand why, we need to think about the nature of the politician's craft in societies with democratic forms of government. In liberal democracies such as Canada, not everyone shares the same opinions or has identical interests. To win elections, politicians and political parties need to appeal to a range of interests and values. Once elected, politicians and parties

In the 2011 Canadian federal election, the voter turnout was just 61.4 per cent. Why do you think nearly 40 per cent of eligible voters chose not to cast ballots? What qualities are voters looking for that they are not finding in today's politicians?

must do the same: balance competing demands and points of view. Moreover, politicians may find that their ability to do certain things—things that may be popular or that they believe are the right thing to do—is limited by circumstances beyond their control. Promises that politicians make cannot be kept, or perhaps are kept, but not quite in the form or according to the timetable that was expected. And perhaps politicians knew or suspected this all along, saying things and making promises with a reckless disregard for the truth or the realistic likelihood of achieving those goals, in the hope of being elected.

It is the messy activity of politics—the compromises, the occasional evasiveness, the failure to deliver on promises made, and the sense that those elected to public office do not faithfully represent those who put them there—that leads to cynicism about politicians and political parties. This may also help explain why Canadians lack confidence in their politicians, and why most Canadians do not participate in political life or follow politics very closely. Canadians are not alone in their negativity. A World Values Survey in 2000 indicated that people in established democracies have little confidence in political parties.[2] Canadian surveys also show that younger voters tend to be the least interested in politics and are less likely to participate than middle-aged and older citizens.

A healthy dose of cynicism about politics is probably a good thing, at least if the cynicism is fuelled by knowledge. But cynicism based on ignorance or coupled with apathy may not be healthy for democracies. Whether you are a hardened cynic or an enthusiastic fan of Canadian politics, no judgment about how well the political system works is helpful unless it is informed.

POLITICS AND THE MANAGEMENT OF POWER AND CONFLICT

As indicated earlier, politics is considered by many to be both an art and a science. Politics is the messy business of managing power and conflict within a society. It arises from the fact of scarcity and involves skills in the use of *power* and the resolution of *conflicts*. There are limits to wealth, privacy, clean air and water, social recognition, and so on. In the real world, it is not possible to fully satisfy every person's needs and desires. Conflicts take place between rival claimants and generally occur for two reasons: over **values** (***personal beliefs in what is right or wrong, important or not important, valuable or not valuable***); and over **resources** (***things we need for survival or desire for comfort***). These conflicts explain why politics exists. But more than this, politics is also about how rival claims are settled. **Politics**, then, is ***the activity by which rival claims are settled by public authorities***.

What distinguishes politics from the conflicts, struggles, and rivalries in such settings as the family, the workplace, social organizations, and the marketplace is the public nature of political disputes and the use of public authority—embodied in the state—to deal with them. The boundary of what is considered to be political is located in the limits of the state's authority. Political philosophers sometimes call this the *public realm*. Beyond this line is the *private realm*, where the state's authority does not extend.

Political theorists agree that politics is about the exercise of power. However, as Box 1.1 shows, theorists disagree about what *power relations* count as political ones. Michel Foucault, Karl Marx and Friedrich Engels, and the feminist movement define politics in ways that would include, for example, the relations between bosses and workers in a corporation, between parents and children in a family, or between teachers and students in a school. And in a sense they are right. In the words of American political scientist Charles Merriam, "obviously there is governance everywhere—government in heaven; government in hell; government and law among outlaws; government in prison."[3] John Locke and David Easton both offer a more limited definition of politics, one that goes back to Aristotle's conception of the Greek polis. They argue that what is distinctive about politics is its association with a system for settling disputes that is both public and binding on the whole community. At the centre of this system is the state, or government.

These definitions disagree in another important way. Marxist, postmodernist, and feminist definitions associate politics with a pervasive pattern of oppression. For them, politics is

INSIDE POLITICS

BOX 1.1 | Some Important Definitions of Politics and Power

A political system can be designated as those interactions through which values are authoritatively allocated for a society.

—David Easton, *A Systems Analysis of Political Life*, 1965

Political power, then, I take to be a right of making laws with penalties of death and, consequently, all less penalties for the regulating and preserving of property, and of employing the force of the community in the execution of such laws and in the defense of the commonwealth from foreign injury; and all this only for the public good.

—John Locke, *The Second Treatise of Government*, 1690

Political power, properly so called, is merely the organized power of one class for oppressing another.

—Karl Marx and Friedrich Engels, *The Communist Manifesto*, 1848

Basically power is less a confrontation between two adversaries or the linking of one to the other than a question of government. This word must be allowed the very broad meaning which it had in the sixteenth century. "Government" did not refer only to political structures or to the management of states; rather it designated the way in which the conduct of individuals or of groups might be directed: the government of children, of souls, of communities, of families, of the sick. It did not cover only the legitimately constituted forms of political or economic subjection, but also modes of action . . . which were destined to act upon the possibilities of action of other people. To govern, in this sense, is to structure the possible field of action of others.

—Michel Foucault, *The Subject and Power*, 1982

The personal is political.

—Slogan of the feminist movement

fundamentally about how inequalities are generated and reinforced through the power relations that exist between classes and gender groups at all levels of society.

Does it matter, in the end, how we define politics? We would argue that there is a very practical reason for rejecting those definitions of politics that confer on all power relations, wherever they may be located and however limited they may be, the label "political." If politics is viewed as being everywhere and in all social interactions, we lose sight of the boundary that separates the public and private realms. This boundary may not be very distinct, but it is crucial for understanding the politics of any society. Moreover, such a boundary is necessary in order to protect the freedoms that most of us believe to be important features of a democratic society. Political conflict is largely about where exactly this boundary between public and private should be drawn: what should be public matters and state decisions, and what should remain private. We can agree that power relations are ubiquitous without taking the next step to claim that politics, therefore, has no bounds.

But there is, perhaps, another reason for adopting the more limited definition of politics that we have put forward. Only those power relations that take place in the public realm can legitimately be associated with the use of force in its most naked, punitive forms. Compulsion, punishment, and violence do, of course, take place in all sorts of social settings. It is clear, however, that only the public authorities—those who wield the power of the state—have the *legitimate right* to back up their decisions with the full power of society. All other power relations are more limited. The reason for this difference is that the state is the only institution that can reasonably claim to speak and act on behalf of the entire community, and its unique function is to ensure the conditions for some degree of *social order*. This social order is necessary for all other social activities; without order there is no peaceful basis for reconciling conflicts in society.

POWER

In order to understand both politics and society, one must also understand power. Philosopher and Nobel Prize laureate Bertrand Russell wrote that "the fundamental concept in social science is Power, in the same sense in which Energy is the fundamental concept in physics." We are all attracted to power because **power** is ***the ability to influence what happens***. According to Russell, power holds a greater attraction for people than wealth.

> When a moderate degree of comfort is assured, both individuals and communities will pursue power rather than wealth: they may seek wealth as a means to power, or they may forgo an increase of wealth in order to secure an increase in power, but in the former case as in the latter, their fundamental motive is not economic . . .[4]

As indicated in Table 1.1, power is an agent of social change that takes many forms and is found in all sorts of settings, not just political ones. Social scientists like to unpack the concept of power, breaking it down into species that are distinguished from one another according to the reason why the compliant party obeys. Compliance may result from the ***threat or use*** *of force* (**coercion**); from *the ability of A to convince B that a particular action is reasonable or otherwise in B's best interests* (**influence**); or from *the recognition by the compliant party that the person or organization issuing a command has the right to do so and should be obeyed* (**authority**). Politics involves all these faces of power—coercion, influence, and authority—at various times and in different circumstances. Table 1.1 shows us some of the many forms power can take, ranging from the "softer" forms of power—influence and authority—to its "harder" forms—coercion.

Democratic politics relies primarily on the two softer, non-coercive species of power. But coercion is also used, and no democracy is without its system of courts, police, and prisons. How far coercion and democracy are compatible, however, is an open question. This point is illustrated by a famous and timeless exchange between then Prime Minister Pierre Trudeau and CBC journalist Tim Ralfe in October 1970,[5] a few days after the Liberal government had suspended civil liberties by invoking the War Measures Act because of the Front de libération du Québec (FLQ) crisis in Quebec. Ralfe asked "Sir, what is it with all these men with guns around here?" and said that he was ". . . worried about living in a town that's full of people with guns running around." Trudeau responded:

> Why? Have they done anything to you? Have they pushed you around or anything? . . . there are a lot of bleeding hearts around who just don't like to see people with helmets and guns. All I can say is, go on and bleed, but it is more important to keep law and order in the society than to be worried about weak-kneed people. . . . I think the society must take every means at its disposal to defend itself against the emergence of a parallel power which defies the elected power in this country, and I think that goes to any distance.

Was Trudeau right? One of the great ironies of democracy is that, unlike other political systems, it requires that dissenting points of view and opposition to those in power be respected. Whether the issue is invocation of the War Measures Act in 1970 or the measures

TABLE 1.1 | VARIANTS OF POWER

Type of Power	Influence	Authority	Coercion
Examples of Power	Diplomacy	Profession	Verbal threat
	Persuasion	Hereditary position	Weapons
	Argument	Election	Blackmail
	Knowledge	Marital status	Extortion
	Media	Family order	Physical size
	Beauty	Ownership	Fines
	Charisma	Credentials	Prison
		Permits	Torture
Degree of Power	Soft		Hard

taken to combat terrorism since 11 September 2001, the eternal trade-off is the same. Arresting people suspected of terrorist acts is, most would agree, necessary to protect democratic government. At some point, however, protecting law and order may exact a high cost in terms of personal freedoms. For example, since the 9/11 terrorist attacks on the World Trade Center and the Pentagon, access to public buildings became more restricted, border crossings became more time-consuming and stressful, airport security was tightened, and measures were taken to curb the rights of immigrants. Some of these changes proved to be temporary, but many—such as the new air travel security tax imposed on all Canadian travellers since 2002; the Anti-terrorism Act, which came into effect in December 2001; and the "no-fly list," which came into effect in 2007—have been enduring. In a democracy, those in power must justify use of coercion as necessary to maintain such values as freedom, equality, justice, and the rule of law. Inevitably, however, people will disagree over the meaning and relative importance of these values and over how much coercion is acceptable.

Alleged protesters at the June 2010 G20 summit in Toronto, Ontario are arrested on the University of Toronto campus and await transport to a holding facility. Security measures at the summit, including a five-tier screening process and a temporary extension of police powers, were criticized by some as excessive infringement on citizens' personal freedoms such as the right to peaceful assembly.

THE STATE

The existence of the state, we argued earlier, is a necessary condition for the existence of politics. But what is the "state"? To this point we have used the terms "state" and "government" as though they meant the same thing. This lack of distinction is often harmless, but it can lead to serious confusion. For example, to argue that the government is corrupt or wasteful, or that its policies are undesirable, does not necessarily call into question the state's legitimacy. It does, however, challenge the authority of the particular people who control the levers of the governmental system. In an established democracy, political activity is far more likely to be directed at influencing and changing the government than at reforming the state.

Canadian political scientist Leo Panitch provides this definition of the **state**:

> [The state is] a broad concept that includes government as the seat of legitimate authority in a territory but also includes bureaucracy, judiciary, the Armed Forces and internal police, structures of legislative assemblies and administration, public corporations, regulatory boards, and ideological apparatuses such as the education establishment and publicly owned media. The distinguishing characteristic of the state is its monopoly over the use of force in a given territory.[6]

According to this definition, the state has three main characteristics. First, it involves territorial boundaries. Beyond its borders, a state has limited or no legal authority. Second, the state consists of a complex set of institutions that wield public authority such as the courts, the police, and the educational system, as well as the elected legislature and the bureaucracy. Third, the state has what Max Weber called a "monopoly of the legitimate use of physical force in the enforcement of its order." As we see in Box 1.2, there are many other definitions of "state," which raise important questions about the purposes and the interests of those who wield the power of the state.

Some definitions of the state offer answers to these questions. The Marxist and Leninist definitions in Box 1.2 characterize the state as an instrument of class oppression. Marx argued that the end of class conflict would sound the death knell for the state. It would "wither away," no longer having any function. Contemporary Marxists, except for a few diehards, no longer predict the state's demise and the ascent of a social utopia. Feminists view the state as a patriarchal institution, reinforcing and perpetuating the social superiority of men over women. Many political scientists, and probably most economists, would argue that the state is responsive to any group with enough political clout to persuade policy makers that it is in their interest to meet the group's demands for public actions on private wants.

Theoretical Approaches to Understanding the Role of the State

Contemporary political science offers four main approaches to answering the question: On whose behalf and in whose interests is the state's authority exercised? These approaches include: pluralism, class analysis, feminism, and postmodernism.

INSIDE POLITICS

BOX 1.2 | Alternative Definitions of the State

The executive of the modern State is but a committee for managing the common affairs of the whole bourgeoisie.

—Marx and Engels, *The Communist Manifesto*

The state is that fiction by which everyone seeks to live at the expense of everyone else.

—French economist Frédéric Bastiat, *c.* 1840

L'Etat, c'est moi. [I am the state.]

—Attributed to Louis XIV of France, 1638–1715

[The state is that institution which] successfully upholds a claim to the monopoly of the legitimate use of physical force in the enforcement of its order . . . within a given territorial area.

—Max Weber, *The Theory of Social and Economic Organization*

All state-based political systems are patriarchal—that is, in no country in the world are women equal participants in the institutions of the state or equal beneficiaries in its distribution of power or in the norms and values sanctioned in law and enforced by those institutions.

—Jill Vickers, *Reinventing Political Science*

Pluralism Approach

Some political theorists espouse **pluralism**, and ***see politics as being fundamentally a competition between different interests***. They believe that the state responds chiefly to the demands of those groups that are best organized, have superior financial resources, can claim to speak on behalf of large segments of the population, and are successful in associating their special interests with the general interests of society. The pluralist model assumes various forms. The *society-centred* variants emphasize the impact of groups in society on the state, while the *state-centred* variants place greater emphasis on the ability of public officials to act on their own preferences and according to their own interests. Those who work within this perspective argue that groups do not compete on a level playing field, and cite business interests as occupying a privileged position within this competition.

Class Analysis Approach

According to the **class analysis** approach, economics shapes politics. Beginning with Karl Marx, class analysis theorists ***see the state in capitalist societies as an instrument through which small minorities control most of society's wealth to maintain their social and economic dominance***. They may disagree on how this dominance is achieved, but they all seem to agree that the state is complicit in perpetuating inequalities rooted in the economic system. They note that the state decision makers are influenced by the demands and interests of certain classes more than others. They cite as examples the state's vulnerability to declines in business confidence, the control of the dominant class over the mass media and popular culture, and a lack of class consciousness among even the least-privileged groups in society, which they argue stems from the widespread acceptance of capitalist and individualistic values.

Feminism Approach

In the **feminism** approach *the state is seen as an inherently patriarchal institution, where politics are not neutral or gender-free*. This means that the state, its structures, and its laws all serve to institutionalize male dominance. Feminists see the need to increase the representation of women in elected legislatures, the bureaucracy, and the courts, and to create governmental bodies and programs that recognize women as a group with interests and needs that are not identical to those of men. Feminists also indicate that power relationships between men and women differ greatly in poorer and richer economies. Most feminist political theorists insist that a state-centred political system will continue to be patriarchal unless there is a change in the hierarchical nature of authority embodied in the state. Like Karl Marx's famous prediction that the state would "wither away" once classes were abolished, many feminists argue that eliminating gender discrimination would cause the state, as we know it, to disappear.

Postmodernism Approach

In **postmodernism** *the state is viewed as an essentially oppressive and even repressive institution*. But unlike class analysis and feminism, postmodernism is much more eclectic in the forms of oppression that it associates with the state and public authority. Groups may be oppressed based on their race, gender, ethnicity, sexual preference, or some other trait. This trait excludes them from the dominant group that controls the levers of state power and whose values and identity are reflected in the institutions, language, and mores of the society. Postmodernists view the state as repressive in that its structures, laws, and activities repress the expression of some values while they legitimize and nurture others. Those who embrace this approach constitute what is sometimes called the New Left. The Old Left wished to see the overthrow of the capitalist state and its transformation into a socialist utopia without property, money, or status. Postmodernists, however, are more dubious about the revolutionary visions associated with class analysis and the Old Left, believing that the problem of the state is not simply its relationship to economic power but, as well, to forms of oppression and repression more generally.

GOVERNMENT

A distinction should now be made between the state and the government. The **government** is *the organization of the state and the system of institutions and agencies used to exercise its authority*. In a democratic political system, where governments are chosen and removed through elections, the term "government" usually refers to those who have been elected to power. In a democracy, a government is seen as more personal than the state, being associated with a particular group of people and, usually, with a political party. In an election, the rules and procedures by which a government is formed are part of the state system. And like the rest of the state, they are less likely to generate political controversy and to undergo change than are the current government and its policies.

CANADIAN SPOTLIGHT

BOX 1.3   Timeline: Important Dates in the Evolution of Canadian Democracy up to Confederation

1759   The gradual conquest of New France by the British culminates in a victory at the Plains of Abraham outside Quebec City.

1763   The Treaty of Paris ends French rule in Canada. The British Royal Proclamation of 1763 creates the colony of Quebec and recognizes Aboriginal land rights.

1774   The Quebec Act recognizes the French civil code of law and the Roman Catholic religion in the colony. This is the first significant instance of "accommodation" in Canadian history.

1776   The American War of Independence prompts a flood of Loyalist refugees. An estimated one-third of the American colonies' population moves north and settles in what are now Nova Scotia, New Brunswick, Prince Edward Island, Quebec, and Ontario.

1791   The Constitution Act of 1791 creates Lower Canada (Quebec) and Upper Canada (Ontario). *Representative government* is established in both colonies. The colonies are also given permission to keep their taxes.

1837 and 1838   Armed rebellions occur in both Upper and Lower Canada because of corruption, poverty, social divisions, and disaffection with the ruling elites.

1839   Lord Durham releases a report that analyzes the causes of the rebellions and recommends implementing a parliamentary style of government similar to Britain's; his model includes the concept of *responsible government* wherein the government executive is drawn from the elected assembly. To reduce political conflict between English and French Canadians, he also recommends a policy of assimilation of the French-Canadian population, and that Upper Canada and Lower Canada be united so that the assembly can be dominated by the English-Canadian majority.

1841   Upper and Lower Canada are united through the Act of Union.

1856   Ottawa becomes Canada's capital.

1867   The Dominion of Canada is created under the British North America Act (BNA Act) passed by the British Parliament. Sir John A. Macdonald becomes Canada's first prime minister. Initially, the Dominion includes Ontario, Quebec, Nova Scotia, and New Brunswick, but within six years, Prince Edward Island, Manitoba, and British Columbia join.

Underlying this distinction between state and government is an important practical difference in how each compels the obedience of the citizens, corporations, and associations within its jurisdiction. The willingness of individuals and groups to obey the decisions of government—decisions they may vigorously disagree with, and may not have voted for—is based on their view that the state's authority is legitimate. By **legitimacy** we mean that *the rules and institutions that constitute the state, and which determine how governments are chosen, are accepted by most people as being reasonable*. The legitimacy of the state, therefore, is based on the *consent* of those who are governed. Legitimacy depends not on coercion—an ever-present fear of penalties for disobeying the law—but rather on an implicit acceptance of the rules of the political game.

Government popularity and state legitimacy are not the same. Democracy requires some measure of stability and respect for rules, including those rules that determine who has the right to govern and how and when that right ends. A particular government or prime minister may be deeply unpopular, but people continue to obey the law and refrain from storming the legislature (although they may organize protests and even throw some tomatoes) because of their implicit acceptance of the state's legitimacy. Government may be upheld by consent or by force. In fact, it is usually upheld by both.

What sets Canada's political system apart from many around the world is that Canadians have a peaceful opportunity to change the government at least every five years. Some states, such as Haiti, Zimbabwe, or Syria, are considered failed states precisely because changes of government are either very difficult, or, when they do occur, violent.

The state's authority is sometimes questioned by individuals or by organized interests. When this happens, as Trudeau argued in October 1970 regarding the FLQ's apparent disregard for that authority, the public authorities may resort to force in order to maintain their ability to govern or to crush civil disobedience.

The question of when citizens may be justified in resisting the law, through either passive disobedience of public authority or violence, is an old one. Two of the world's greatest democracies, the United States and France, trace their modern origins to bloody revolutions undertaken in defence of principles that the revolutionaries believed warranted violence against the state. Some, such as American writer and libertarian thinker Henry David Thoreau, India's Mahatma Gandhi, and American civil rights leader Martin Luther King Jr, developed a philosophy of non-violent civil disobedience that has been influential around the world. Others, like American Malcolm X, some leaders of the 1960s American student movement, and the French students whose 1968 demonstrations helped end the Charles de Gaulle presidency, acted on the premise that fighting oppression and injustice through violent opposition to the law and its enforcers is consistent with democracy.

The debate over civil disobedience—when is it justified and what forms may it take in a democracy?—has resurfaced in recent years, principally around issues associated with globalization and income inequality. Since what the media dubbed the "Battle in Seattle," when 1999 meetings of the World Trade Organization were disrupted by thousands of protesters, and scenes of violent confrontations with the police were broadcast live around the world, organized protest is expected near any meeting of policy makers from the world's wealthiest countries. The street tactics used at anti-globalization protests in Seattle, Genoa, Quebec City, and more recently during the G20 meeting in Toronto have produced, somewhat ironically, a service industry that specializes in providing activist groups with advice and training on confrontations with the police, effective use of the media, and general strategies and tactics for gaining influence through civil disobedience. The oppression and violence that the state may inflict on members of the society, the argument goes, warrant self-defence on the part of victims.

Government that relies primarily on threats and violence to maintain its rule is generally unstable. Even the most repressive political authorities usually come to realize that popular consent is a firmer basis on which to govern. In some societies, the popular consent that legitimizes political rule may emerge from the uncoordinated activities of the various social institutions that influence the values and beliefs of citizens: the media, the schools, the family, and governments. In other societies, the state's legitimacy is deliberately and assiduously cultivated through official propaganda.

Mahatma Gandhi (left) and Malcolm X (right) had very different approaches to protest and resisting the law. What are the pros and cons to each approach—Gandhi's civil disobedience and Malcolm X's engaged opposition?

The active mobilization of society by the state, the deliberate manipulation of public attitudes, and the ruthless suppression of dissent by the public authorities are not features that most of us associate with democracy. The calculated fostering of consent through propaganda is a characteristic feature of totalitarian rule. **Totalitarianism** is *a system of government that suppresses all dissent in the name of some supreme goal*. This goal may be tied to the destiny of the "race," as it was in Nazi Germany, or to "class struggle," as it was in the Soviet Union under Stalin. Distinctions between the state, government, and society lose all meaning—indeed, they are considered to be subversive—under totalitarianism.

The way in which legitimacy is generated in political democracies is more subtle than under totalitarian rule, and depends primarily on social institutions—the mass media, the churches, the educational system—that are not directly under the control of the state. For example, even public broadcasters and public educators in democracies enjoy a measure of free choice not experienced by their counterparts in totalitarian regimes. Thus legitimacy appears to be based on the free choice of individuals: an appearance that some argue is an illusion. For example, both Marxists and feminists believe government by "popular consent" is a sham that conceals the fundamentally undemocratic character of society and politics. Some Marxist critics use the term **cultural hegemony** to signify *the ability of society's dominant class to have its values and beliefs accepted as the conventional wisdom in society at large*.

DEMOCRACY

"Democracy is like pornography," says classical historian and political commentator Victor Davis Hanson, "we know it when we see it."[7] Hanson's observation seems commonsensical. Most of us would agree that a country in which free elections are held is almost certainly more democratic than one where they are not. *Freedom* seems to be an important element of democracies. Where we see a lack of freedom and egregious and persistent violations of human rights, or a serious lack of accountability on the part of those who govern, we are unlikely to believe that such a country is democratic. Many countries including Canada, the United States, the Democratic People's Republic of Korea, the People's Republic of China, and the Islamic Republic of Iran claim to be democracies. "Democracy" is a label to which regimes throughout the world try to lay claim. Obviously they cannot all be democratic unless they meet certain requirements; otherwise the concept of democracy is diluted to the point of becoming meaningless.

Defining democracy is not an easy task. The word "democracy" comes to us from two words in ancient Greek: "demos"—"people (the many)" and "kratos"—"rule". In the simplest terms, therefore, "democracy" means "rule by the people." In a book published at the height of the Cold War, Canadian political philosopher C.B. Macpherson argued that there are in fact three different types of democracy in the modern world.[8] Only one, *liberal democracy*, is characterized by competition between political parties. What Macpherson calls the *developmental* and *communist* versions of democracy do not have competitive elections, and probably would not be considered democratic by most Canadians. But they both claim to attach greater importance to the social and economic equality of individuals than do liberal democracies, in addition to recognizing the formal political equality of citizens. If democracy is about equality, Macpherson argues, the developmental and communist versions are at least as democratic as the liberal version of democracy found in the capitalist world.

As Table 1.2 shows us, there are many words in politics that end with "-cracy." Each word refers to a political system where different groups and/or group sizes control the state and the levers of government.

If we accept Macpherson's argument that there are not one but three types of democracy, each with a legitimate claim to the label, the world looks like a very democratic place. Leaving aside personal and military dictatorships, and the odd monarchy like the Kingdom of Saudi Arabia or the Sultanate of Brunei, most of what is left would seem to qualify. While common sense suggests that democracy is not so widespread, Macpherson challenges us to reflect on what makes politics and society democratic or not. Is democracy a system of government? Or does democracy connote a type of society? Was Canada democratic before the female half of the population received the vote? Do the persistence of poverty and the clear evidence of large inequalities in the economic condition and social status of different groups in Canada mean that Canadian society is less than democratic?

About the only thing that everyone can agree on is that democracy is based on equality. Agreement breaks down over how much equality in what spheres of life is necessary for a society to qualify as democratic. Majority rule, government by popular consent, "one person–one vote," and competitive elections are the political institutions usually associated with democratic government. But it has long been recognized that the operation of democratic political institutions can result in oppressive government unless there are ways to safeguard some freedoms. In order to safeguard the rights and freedoms of individuals and minorities against what Alexis de Tocqueville called "democratic despotism," constitutional limits on the state's power over its citizens may be set or the political status of particular social groups may be entrenched in the formal rules and informal procedures of politics. Democracies have

TABLE 1.2 | TYPES OF POLITICAL SYSTEMS

Political System or Regime	Number of Participants in Control	Definition	
Autocracy	One	Absolute control of the state by one person—monarchy, despotic regime, or dictatorship	
Plutocracy	A few	Control of the state by the wealthy	
Oligarchy	A few	Control of the state by the powerful	
Aristocracy	A few	Control of government by an elite class of citizens (the best) or by a hereditary class (nobility)	
Ochlocracy	Many	Rule by the mob—rule or tyranny of the majority (majoritarianism)	
Democracy	Many	Control of the state by the people (direct democracy) or with the consent of the people (representative democracy)	

Democracy Watch

BOX 1.4 **Is Canada's Democracy Broken?**

In 2009, *Maclean's* magazine hosted a round-table discussion on the topic "Our Democracy Is Broken," with low voter turnout given as one piece of evidence that all is not well with Canada's democratic system.

Up for Debate

Is democracy possible when only 61.4 per cent of eligible voters cast ballots, as in the 2011 Canadian federal election? Why or why not?

police forces, courts, and jails. But unlike other forms of government, they do not depend on coercion and violence, and they give citizens an opportunity to choose who will govern them.

Perhaps even more important than constitutional guarantees and political practices are a society's social and cultural values. Tocqueville argued that the best protection against the *tyranny of the majority* is the existence of multiple group identities in society. When individuals perceive themselves as belonging to particular social groups—such as religious denominations, ethnic or language groups, or regional communities—in addition to sharing a common citizenship with everyone else, the democratic state is less likely to be turned to oppressive ends. After all, everyone has a personal interest in the tolerance of social diversity because the rights and status of his or her own group depend on it. As is discussed later in this book, the existence of multiple group identities (diversity and multiculturalism) is an important feature of Canadian democracy.

Some twentieth-century writers argue that cultural values represent the main bulwark against the tyranny of the majority. Democratic government, they suggest, depends on popular tolerance of diversity. In *The Civic Culture*, American political scientists Gabriel Almond and Sidney Verba contend that democratic government is sustained by cultural attitudes.[9] According to this *political culture* approach, determining a society's degree of democracy involves examining the population's attitudes and beliefs. This, rather than the existence of apparently democratic political institutions, is argued to be the true test of democracy and the key to sustaining it.

The civic culture thesis has recently enjoyed a renaissance through work on what is called **social capital**: *norms of interpersonal trust, a sense of civic duty, and a belief that one's involvement in politics and in the life of the community matters.* Where levels of social trust are low, public authorities must invest more in institutions and policies that rely on repression and force to maintain social order. Social capital is argued to have an economic value, but the main argument for policies, practices, and institutions that promote social capital is that citizens will be happier and have greater control over their own lives.

Not everyone agrees. Socialists argue that a society in which the poor are excluded from full participation in political life because they are preoccupied with the problem of feeding and housing themselves decently cannot be described as democratic. The formal equality of citizens that democratic government confers and even most people's endorsement of democratic values do not alter the fact that social inequalities produce inequalities in political power. Some critics go even further in dismissing the democratic claims of capitalist societies. They argue that inequality results simply from a very small proportion of the population—the capitalist class—controlling the vast majority of the means of economic production and distribution. This inequality in property ownership, Marxists have long argued, far outweighs the importance of "one person–one vote" and competitive elections in determining the real political influence of different classes in society.

Inequalities such as those between bosses and workers, parents and children, men and women, and one ethnic or language community over another, it is often claimed, undermine the democratic character of societies whose formal political institutions are based on the equality of citizens. Indeed, if we use any of the all-inclusive definitions of politics examined earlier in this chapter, it is impossible to resist the logic of this argument. Inequalities confront us wherever we turn, and true democracy seems elusive. Even if we define politics more narrowly to include only those activities that focus on the state, it is obvious that even in the most egalitarian societies a small portion of all citizens dominates public life. For most of us, participation in politics takes the form of short bursts of attention and going to the polls at election time. Is it reasonable to speak of democratic government when the levers of state power are in the hands of an elite?

Direct Democracy and Representative Democracy

The short answer to the question above is, "It depends on what we expect from democracy." If we expect that all citizens should have the opportunity to participate in the law-making process, we are bound to be disappointed. With some historical exceptions like the Greek polis and the township democracies of seventeenth- and eighteenth-century America, examples of **direct democracy**—*government of the citizens by the citizens*—are scarce. Direct democracy survives in some isolated pockets such as the couple of Swiss cantons where the *Landsgemeinde*—citizens gathering outdoors each spring to vote on important public questions—still exists. Modern technology, however, creates the possibility of direct democracy from people's living rooms in all advanced industrial societies. Recent television programs such as *Canadian Idol* or *So You Think You Can Dance Canada* show us how participatory democracy could work. There is no physical or technological reason why making popular choices by pressing telephone keys or clicking your computer's mouse could not be adapted to political decision making. There may, however, be other reasons for rejecting what modern technology makes possible.

Perhaps the most commonly advanced reason for rejecting direct democracy via the Internet, and for being skeptical about the value of public opinion polls, is that many citizens are poorly informed about important public issues. Does it make sense, therefore, to ask citizens about a particular government policy when the majority of people may know little about it or be grossly misinformed?

Thomas Jefferson provided a famous answer to this question. "Every government degenerates when trusted to the rulers of the people alone. The people themselves therefore are [democracy's] only safe depositories."[10] Members of the public, Jefferson acknowledged, are often poorly informed or wrong in their opinions on public matters. However, Jefferson believed the solution lay not in excluding the public from determining public affairs but in educating the public. Jefferson placed great stress on the roles of the press and of public education in producing an informed citizenry.

We often hear that the information explosion generated by satellite communication, television, and the Internet has made us the best-informed generation of all time. But as Neil Postman observes, this conceit fails to address why most people are unable to explain even the most basic elements of issues that have received saturation coverage in the media. This ignorance does not prevent pollsters from asking people for their opinion on matters that they may barely understand and clearly deprives poll results of any meaning other than the signals they send to politicians looking for waves to ride. Postman blames modern education, and especially the media, for this ignorance. Television, the defining medium of the last half-century, is singled out for particular blame.

> What is happening here is that television is altering the meaning of "being informed" by creating a species of information that might properly be called *disinformation*. . . . Disinformation does not mean false information. It means misleading information—misplaced, irrelevant, fragmented or superficial information—information that creates the illusion of knowing something but which in fact leads one away from knowing. . . . when news is packaged as entertainment, that is the inevitable result.[11]

The pillars that Jefferson counted on to support democratic government have rotted, according to Postman. The irony is that this has happened in an age when more information from more corners of the world is available to the average person than ever before.

All modern democracies are **representative democracies**, where *government is carried out by elected legislatures that represent the people*. Citizens delegate law-making authority to their representatives, holding them responsible for their actions through periodic elections. Representative democracies sometimes include decision-making processes that provide opportunities for greater and more frequent citizen participation. Examples of democratic institutions that allow for citizen participation in public affairs include **plebiscites** and **referendums** (*direct votes of citizens on important public questions*), frequent elections, electing judges and administrative officials, and formal procedures for removing elected officials before the end of their term (through voter petitions and "recall" elections).

The appearance of increased participation may be deceiving. In countries like the United States and Switzerland, where referendums are a normal part of the political process, voter turnout is usually very low. Partly because of this, and partly because vested interests are quick to spend money on advertising and mobilizing their supporters, critics charge that referendums may produce outcomes that are far from democratic.[12]

Respect for rights and freedoms is generally considered a distinguishing feature of democratic government. Which rights and freedoms warrant protection and in what circumstances they may legitimately be limited by government are matters of dispute. Many argue that government that levies heavy taxes on citizens is undemocratic. Their reasoning is that individual choice is reduced when government, representing the collectivity, decides how a large share of people's income will be spent. Others argue that the same levels of taxation actually promote freedom by paying for policies that give disadvantaged groups opportunities that they would not have in a "free" market. Even a value as central to democracy as freedom of speech is sometimes argued to have undemocratic side effects. For example, some believe that any person or organization should have the right to spend money on advertising a particular political point of view during an election campaign. Others argue that unlimited freedom of speech in these circumstances is undemocratic, because some individuals and groups are financially better endowed than others, and therefore, the points of view of the affluent will receive the greatest exposure.

Measuring Democracy

Rights and freedoms are believed by most of us to be important in democracies, but everyone except extreme libertarians believes that protecting these rights or freedoms can sometimes produce undemocratic outcomes. There is no surefire test that will tell us when democracy is promoted or impaired by protecting a right or freedom. Indeed, this quandary is one of the greatest sources of conflict in modern democracy, sometimes portrayed as a struggle between the competing pulls of *individualism* (the private realm) and *collectivism* (the public realm). A private realm that is beyond the legitimate reach of the state is a necessary part of what is sometimes called a free society. Democracy does not exist where the individual's right to be protected from the state is obliterated by the state's right to impose its will on the individual.

So how democratic is Canada? According to Freedom House's World Democracy Audit[13] Canada is one of the most democratic countries in the world, but trails slightly behind some of the Scandinavian and Northern European democracies. In ranking countries, Freedom House *operationalizes* the concept of democracy, defining it in measurable ways so that scores can be assigned to each country. The criteria used in the Freedom House survey of the world's political systems combine measures of political rights, civil liberties, press freedom, public corruption, and the rule of law to arrive at a country's democracy ranking (see Box 1.5).

A country may claim to be a democracy having free elections, a constitution that protects rights and freedoms, and a media system that permits the expression of diverse points of view and criticism of the powerful. But if corruption is pervasive, allowing individuals and organizations to buy special treatment; nepotism is rampant; or the law applies to different people in different ways depending on who they are and who they know, a society's claim to be democratic is undermined. In a democracy, however, such behaviours are considered unlawful or at least unethical, depending on how egregiously they violate the rule of law. The **rule of law** may truly be said to be the foundation of democratic government, on which all else rests. "It means," said Eugene Forsey (1904–91), one of Canada's foremost constitutionalists of the

INSIDE POLITICS

BOX 1.5 | Measuring Freedom

Freedom House uses certain criteria in its "democracy index" to determine how well countries respect and protect political rights and civil liberties.

Political Rights Criteria

A. **Electoral Process**

- Free and fair elections of heads of government and representatives
- Fair electoral laws and fair electoral framework

B. **Political Pluralism and Participation**

- The right to organize competing political parties as well as the opportunity for the opposition to gain power through elections
- People's choices free from external or internal domination or threats
- Full rights and participation of minorities

C. **Functioning of Government**

- Elected representatives and heads of government freely determine government policies
- Decision making is transparent, free from pervasive corruption, and accountable to the electorate between elections

Civil Liberties Criteria

D. **Freedom of Expression and Belief**

- Free and independent media and other forms of cultural expression
- Free religious institutions and practice in public and in private

- Academic freedom
- Open and private discussion

E. **Associational and Organizational Rights**

- Freedom of assembly, demonstration, and open public discussion
- Free non-governmental organizations
- Free professional and private organizations
- Free trade unions, peasant organizations, or equivalents, as well as collective bargaining

F. **Rule of Law**

- Independent judiciary
- Rule of law in civilian and criminal matters
- Police under direct civilian control
- Protection from political terror including unjustified imprisonment, exile, or torture
- Freedom from war and insurgencies
- Equality of treatment

G. **Personal Autonomy and Individual Rights**

- Free choice of residence, employment, and education
- Property rights
- Private business rights
- Social freedoms including gender equality, marriage partnership, and family size
- Equal opportunity and freedom from economic exploitation

Source: Adapted from Freedom House, Checklist Questions http://freedomhouse.org/report/freedom-world-2012/checklist-questions.

twentieth century, "that everyone is subject to the law; that no one, no matter how important or powerful, is above the law."[14] It means that **no public official has the legitimate right to exercise any powers other than those assigned to his or her office by the law.** And if someone in a position of public trust attempts to go beyond his or her legal authority, then it is up to the courts to check that abuse of power. An independent judiciary is, therefore, necessary to democratic governance.

This is all fine theory, but inequalities and circumstances can sometimes undermine democratic values and processes. There is also an ever-present tension between **majoritarianism—*the belief that the opinion of the majority should almost always be considered in decision making*—**and competing visions of democracy. Let us consider the following questions: In a democracy, who gets heard and why? Is democracy a process or an outcome?

Who Gets Heard and Why?

Access to political decision makers and the ability to influence public opinion are not equally distributed in society. If the president of the Royal Bank of Canada places a telephone call to the federal minister of finance, this call will be returned. Your call or mine probably will not (try it!). Since the beginning of elections in Canadian politics, individuals and organizations have made financial contributions to political parties and their candidates. For the relatively modest sum of $1100 per year (or $550 if you are 35 years of age or under), you can join the Liberal Party's Laurier Club. Among other things, this contribution buys an invitation to party functions across the country, where you might be able to speak directly with the party leader. Corporations are banned from buying memberships, but their CEOs, presidents, board members, and so on are not, and many members of the Laurier Club have corporate connections.

Between election campaigns, interest groups of all sorts are active in many ways, trying to influence the actions of government and the climate of public opinion. Much of this activity costs money—often a lot of money. The services of a high-powered, well-connected lobbying firm can easily run into hundreds of thousands of dollars. A public relations campaign that uses polling and focus groups, followed by some combination of electronic and print media advertising, may cost as much or more. Although there is no guarantee that spending money on such activities will produce favourable political outcomes, there is a widespread and probably well-founded belief that such an investment may yield impressive returns.

But it is not as simple as spending money. The issues that get onto the **public agenda—*the matters that have been identified by opinion leaders in the media and in government as ones that warrant some policy response*,** even if that response is a decision not to act—are not determined by the spending of self-interested groups alone. The American journalist H.L. Mencken once said that the proper role of his profession was to "bring comfort to the afflicted and afflict the comfortable." Some in the media, in Canada and elsewhere, take Mencken's counsel to heart. But whether what they report and how they report it "afflicts the comfortable" or not, it is undeniably the case that the values and beliefs of those who shape public opinion—including teachers, journalists, and writers—influence the stories they tell and how they are told.

In Canada, as in other capitalist democracies, there is a long-standing and ongoing debate over whether the media—an important segment of the opinion-shaping class—do better at afflicting or at comforting the privileged and the powerful. On one point, however, the evidence is clear: interests and points of view that are not those of the wealthy and the well-connected do find their way into the public conversation.

In the lead-up to the 2011 spring federal election, Canadian prime minister Stephen Harper limited his daily encounters with the media to just five questions. Some speculated that he was minimizing the risk of making any public gaffes during the campaign, while others felt he was shunning reporters who held different social values than those of his Conservative government. What are the advantages and disadvantages of the press having unrestricted access to the country's top politicians?

Is Democracy a Process or an Outcome?

Tocqueville warned about the tyranny of the majority: that the multitude might show little concern for the rights and interests of minorities and see little wrong in imposing the force of their superior numbers on people whose values and behaviour differ from those of the majority. Most people agree that majoritarianism needs to be tempered by protections for individual and group rights. That is why constitutions like Canada's include express guarantees of rights and freedoms.

But when the rights claims of a minority are upheld by the courts, despite unsympathetic or divided public opinion, and when elected officials are unwilling to legislate such protection, often some argue that this situation is undemocratic. What is undemocratic, these critics charge, is that unelected public officials—judges in this case—have usurped policy-making prerogatives that in a democracy should be exercised by the people's elected representatives. For example, when Ottawa and the provincial governments agreed to the Charter of Rights and Freedoms in 1981, its equality section (s. 15) did not include sexual orientation among the banned grounds for discrimination. This omission was deliberate. The case for including a reference to sexual orientation had been made during the hearings on the Charter, but had been almost unanimously rejected by representatives of the federal and provincial governments. Several years later, however, the Supreme Court of Canada decided that discrimination on the basis of sexual orientation was *analogous* to that based on religion, race, or colour—forms of discrimination that are expressly prohibited by section 15 of the Charter. The Court ruled that sexual orientation should have the same protection under the equality rights provision of the Charter as those characteristics that were expressly mentioned in this important part of Canada's Constitution.

Whether you agree or disagree with the Supreme Court's decision, the point is that cases like this raise contentious issues about what processes in Canadian society are democratic and undemocratic. Even if many people support such decisions, should citizens consider it a problem when unelected officials—like judges, who cannot be removed from office no matter how unpopular the decision—make decisions that could significantly alter their society? Are there some issues that by their very nature or importance should be resolved only by those who have been elected to govern? Does democracy involve a particular process, and if so, what is that process? Or is democracy more about producing socially desirable outcomes regardless of whether elected or appointed officials make the decisions?

Defining Democracy

On reflection, most of us would probably agree that democracy involves both a legitimizing process for resolving rival claims and a means of producing socially desirable outcomes, whether through appointed officials or elected representatives. Throughout this book we argue that formal institutions are only part of what makes a society's politics democratic or not. The activities of the media, interest groups, and political parties are at least as crucial to the quality of democracy. Likewise, the socio-economic and ideological backgrounds of democratic government have important effects on how the formal and informal aspects of the political system operate.

Democracy, then, can be reduced neither to a simple constitutional formula nor to some particular vision of social equality. Several complex elements come into play, so that defining the term "democracy" is a perilous task. Someone is bound to disagree either with what is included in the definition or with what has been left out. In full recognition of these hazards, we offer the following definition. **Democracy** is *a political system based on the formal political equality of all citizens, in which there is a realistic possibility that voters can replace the government, and in which certain basic rights and freedoms are protected*.

In the chapters that follow, we will discuss some of the prominent features of Canadian democracy, including political fault lines such as the rift between French- and English-speaking Canada, the relationships with the United States and the United Kingdom, and regionalism. Other political fault lines of Canadian politics, such as class conflict, religious conflict, the rural–urban split, ethnicity, age, Aboriginal rights, gender, and others will also be examined.

Listen to the "Nouveau Politics" podcast on parties, branding, and political ideology, available at www.oupcanada.com/BrooksConcise.

SUMMARY

This chapter had two purposes: first, to introduce concepts that are essential to the study of politics in general, including the concepts of politics, power, the state, government, authority, legitimacy, and democracy; and second, to lay the groundwork for the study of Canadian political life and democracy in particular. We saw that politics arises from the fact of scarcity and is the activity by which rival claims are settled. Not surprisingly, the two constant features of politics are power—the ability to influence what happens—and conflict—conflict over values and conflict over resources. Throughout Canadian history, Canadians have devised particular institutions and processes to settle rival claims. Whether these institutions and processes can properly be called democratic and whether they work are some of the things political scientists seek to understand.

We also defined and discussed the role of the state and the difference between the terms "state" and "government," particularly in the context of democracies. Theoretical approaches to explaining the state were discussed: pluralism, class analysis, feminism, and postmodernism. Specific characteristics that set democracy apart from other forms of government were examined, as well as some of the issues typically debated in democratic societies, and in particular, Canadian society. We differentiated between direct democracy and representative democracy. And, finally, for the purposes of this book, "democracy" was defined.

STARTING POINTS FOR RESEARCH

Bernard Crick, *Democracy: A Very Short Introduction* (New York: Oxford, 2002).

Mark O. Dickerson, Thomas Flanagan, and Neil Nevitte, *Introductory Readings in Government and Politics*, 4th edn (*Toronto*: ITP Nelson, 1995).

Robert Jackson and Doreen Jackson, *An Introduction to Political Science: Comparative and World Politics*, 5th edn (Toronto: Pearson, 2008).

C.B. Macpherson, *The Real World of Democracy* (Toronto: CBC Enterprises, 1965).

Jill Vickers, *Reinventing Political Science: A Feminist Approach* (Halifax: Fernwood, 1997).

CBC ARCHIVES AND TVO'S *THE AGENDA*

Visit the companion website for *Canadian Democracy: A Concise Introduction* to follow links to audio and video footage related to the main themes of the chapter: www.oupcanada.com/BrooksConcise.

RELEVANT WEBSITES

Visit the companion website for *Canadian Democracy: A Concise Introduction* to browse a collection of websites featuring material related to the key themes of the chapter, an excellent starting point for research.

REVIEW EXERCISES

1. Which country is more democratic, Canada or the United States? Canada or Sweden? What criteria have you used in arriving at your conclusions and how would you set about measuring whether a society has more or fewer of the attributes that you associate with democracy? In order to guide your thinking about how the concept of democracy can be operationalized, go to the website for Freedom House: www.freedomhouse.org. Does Freedom House's ranking of Canada seem reasonable to you?

2. This chapter introduced some concepts and issues relevant to Canadian political life. An easy way to tell what political issues are current in Canada is to look at the political cartoons included in Canadian print journalism. Find a Canadian political cartoon that relates to a political issue with which you are familiar. One of the best sources is www.artizans.com.

Click on "Political Cartoons—CDN." What message do you think each cartoonist is trying to communicate? Do you think the cartoonist's treatment of the subject is fair or biased? In what ways and why?

3. Debate: Do you agree or disagree that elected representatives should always follow the will of the majority?

Part II

The Societal Context of Politics

In every society certain issues and divisions, or fault lines, are more prominent and are more fundamental to an overall understanding of its politics and government than are others. Canadian society and its democratic system of government have had to manage a broad range of social fault lines including ideologies, the French–English split, regionalism, economic class, ethnicity, and age and gender differences, as well as external influences from other countries and from globalization. For example, the fact that English and French are spoken by large portions of the population and that the French-speaking population is concentrated largely in one region, with a history that predates the anglophone majority in Canada, continues to influence the politics of the country. Another example is the relatively recent arrival of millions of immigrants from countries outside of Europe, which has changed Canadian demography and is having a significant impact on Canadian politics. Yet another influence on Canadian politics and government is the country's long-standing relationship to the United States, a relationship that involves a complex web of interconnections through trade, investment, population, culture, and foreign policy. In short, the societal context within which political life unfolds is crucial to understanding both the nature of any country's politics and the distribution of power and influence.

Some argue, however, that the actions of the state and their impacts on society are at least as important as, if not more so than, the effects of societal forces on the policies and institutions of government. State actors, including key political leaders and bureaucrats, often have a powerful influence on what happens in politics, shaping the contours of the political conversation, determining which interests and voices are listened to, and thus steering the outcomes that ensue. But only rarely are elected and appointed officials able to ignore the pressure of values, ideas, and interests from the society around them. These values, ideas, and interests, including a society's significant *political identities*, its economic structure, and the major fault lines that cut across its landscape, provide the broader context within which political behaviour and policy making take place. These societal factors are the subject of Part II of the book.

Political Culture

Ideas and the values they stem from constitute an important element of political life. **Values**, which are one's *personal beliefs about what is good or bad, right or wrong, important or trivial, valuable or worthless, and so on*, are at the root of the ideas citizens have about their society and their expectations of their system of government. This chapter surveys some key issues pertaining to the role of values and ideas in Canadian politics, and discusses the main political ideas and political culture of Canadians. After reading this chapter, you will be able to

1. Analyze and explain the relationship between values, ideologies, and institutions
2. Differentiate between the main ideologies in Canadian politics by using specific models and concepts
3. Define and explain the role political culture plays in Canadian democracy
4. Use the fragment theory approach, the role of formative events approach, and/or the class analysis (economic theory) approach to explain the basis of Canadian political ideas and political institutions
5. Outline the values, attitudes, and expectations of Canadians with respect to the ideas of community, freedom, equality, and the role of the state
6. Differentiate between the values, ideas, and expectations of Canadians and those of Americans

CANADIAN VALUES AND CANADIAN CULTURE

There is no greater Canadian pastime than reflecting on what it means to be Canadian. Unlike the Chinese, the Russians, and the Americans, to name a few, Canadians have long been obsessed with the values and beliefs that make them distinctive. In fact, this perennial search for the cultural essence of the Canadian condition has most often been about explaining the ways in which the values and beliefs of Canadians are different from those of Americans.

Various answers about what Canadians value have been given over the years. Until the latter half of the twentieth century, these answers essentially boiled down to this: Canadians believed in a more orderly, less individualistic society than that of the United States. The Canadian state was expected to engage in activities that promote the welfare of society and the development of an independent Canada. The affective tie to Great Britain remained strong well into the middle of the century, and indeed many Canadians, particularly in English-speaking Canada, thought of themselves as British and of their country as more British than American in its values, institutions, and heritage.

This answer to the question of what it means to be a Canadian has seemed less plausible as Canada has become less British over the last couple of generations. Many still believe, however, that Canadian values continue to be less individualistic and less hostile to government than those of the United States. Such words as "tolerant," "compassionate," and "caring" are often used in comparisons between the two countries, always suggesting that Canadians have more of these qualities than Americans. And it is not just Canadians who make this claim. For the American left, Canada has for about a generation now served as a sort of "Nirvana to the north": a place that shows what is possible in public policy and social relations and a model to be emulated.[1] As the bonds joining Canada to the United States economically and culturally have multiplied and deepened, the question of what it means to be a Canadian continues to be a sort of national obsession.

This is not true, however, in French-speaking Canada, whose centre of gravity is Quebec, where over 90 per cent of Canadian francophones live. Insulated from American cultural influences by language, and for much of their history by the strongly Catholic character of their society, French Canadians have been less likely to define themselves and their history with reference to the United States. They have long worried about assimilation and the anglicizing influences on their language and culture. But they have tended to see the challenge as coming chiefly from within Canada, with its English-speaking majority, rather than from the United States. This perceived challenge has provided the basis for the rise of, first, French-Canadian nationalism and, more recently, of Quebec nationalism. Lately, as non-traditional sources of immigration have become increasingly important in Quebec, the question of what it means to be Québécois has received greater attention. But in answering it, few French-speaking Canadians would think of using as a starting point the United States and what are believed to be American values and beliefs.

VALUES, IDEOLOGIES, AND INSTITUTIONS

Ideas assume various forms in political life. When they take the form of *a set of interrelated values and beliefs about how society is organized and how it ought to function*—an interpretative map for understanding the world—they constitute an **ideology**. An ideology spills beyond the boundaries of politics to embrace beliefs and judgments about other social relationships,

Youth are sometimes drawn to a very different set of values and beliefs than was the generation before them. What is your vision of how society should be organized and function? Is this ideology similar to that of your parents? Why might your values and beliefs be different from theirs?

including economic ones. This holistic character of ideologies distinguishes them from more limited political value systems. People tend not to be aware of their own ideological leanings, and might be puzzled or even startled at being labelled a "conservative," "liberal," or "socialist." However, this does not mean that ideology is irrelevant to their political beliefs and actions. In fact, ideologies are sometimes used to justify political action such as a peaceful protest, a new piece of legislation, or even a revolution. When the politics of a society is described as "pragmatic" and "non-ideological," these terms may simply indicate that a particular ideology dominates to such a degree that it has become the conventional wisdom. Someone who regularly and consciously thinks about political matters and other social relationships in ideological terms is an ideologue: a person who is consciously committed to a particular interpretive map of society. Most people are not ideological in this sense of the word.

If ideology is the currency of the political activist, political culture is the medium of the general population. A **political culture** consists of *the characteristic values, beliefs, and behaviours of a society's members in regard to politics*. The importance that people place on such values as personal freedom, equality, social order, and national prestige is one aspect of political culture. Citizens' expectations of their government, their participation in public life, patterns of voter turnout, party activism, social movement activities, and other politically relevant forms of behaviour are all part of political culture. So is the pattern of knowledge about political symbols, institutions, actors, and issues. Obviously, people do not hold identical views on these matters, nor does their participation in politics conform to a single template. It is reasonable, nevertheless, to speak of a society, even one with a number of significant political fault lines, as having certain core values or a belief system that is shared by most of its members.

In Canada, research on political culture has focused primarily on the differences between the politically relevant values, attitudes, and beliefs of French-speaking and English-speaking Canadians, and on the question of whether English-speaking Canada is characterized by regional political cultures. To determine whether these differences are significant, political scientists have attempted to measure such things as levels of political knowledge and participation, feelings of **political efficacy** (*people's sense of whether their participation in politics matters*) and **alienation** (variously defined as *apathy, estrangement from the political system, or the belief that politics is systematically biased against one's interests and values*), attitudes toward political authority and government, and the sense of belonging to a particular regional or linguistic community.

Another way in which ideas are relevant for politics is through individual *personality traits* and *attitudes* about things political. One of the most often repeated claims about Canadians—one that we examine later—is that they are more deferential and less likely to question and challenge authority than are Americans. Several questions used in studies of political culture, such as those dealing with political efficacy and trust in public officials, tap politically relevant dimensions of personality. Research on the political consequences of individual personality traits has often focused on the relationship between a person's general attitudes toward authority and non-conformity, as well as their political attitudes on issues like the protection of civil liberties and tolerance of minority rights. The main conclusion of this research is that personality traits show up in an individual's political ideas and actions.

Left-Wing and Right-Wing Values, Ideas, and Ideologies

One popular way of categorizing political ideas is to describe them as being left wing, right wing, or centrist/moderate. **Right wing** and **left wing** are *labels often used to classify the political ideas that lie behind an action, opinion, or statement*. These labels are also used to group ideas and/or political parties that are in opposition to each other. **Left** *refers to collectivist and social justice ideas and ideologies, and political parties that advocate social reform*; whereas **right** *refers to ideas and ideologies that advocate social order, protection of private property, economic freedom, and support for capitalism* (see Figure 2.1). For example, newspaper editorials proposing tax cuts for the affluent or the elimination of public funding for abortions are often characterized as right-wing. Alternatively, editorials advocating increasing the minimum wage, banning the use of replacement workers during a strike or lockout, or increasing spending on assistance for developing countries are likely to be described as left wing. Centrist or moderate positions, as these terms suggest, fall between the right and left wings of the political spectrum. They attempt to achieve some middle ground between the arguments and principles of left and right. The **centre** is, virtually by definition, *the mainstream of a society's politics*, and those who occupy this location on the political spectrum are likely to view themselves as being non-ideological and pragmatic.

"Right" and "left" are shorthand labels for conflicting values and belief systems. These beliefs include basic notions about how society, the economy, and politics operate, as well as ideas about how these matters should be dealt with by government and by society. To be on the right in Anglo-American societies generally means that one subscribes to an *individualistic* belief system (see Figure 2.1). Such a person is likely to believe that their achievements in life are principally due to their own efforts—that the welfare of society is best promoted by allowing individuals to pursue their own interests, and that modern government is too expensive and intrusive. To be on the left, however, is to prefer a set of beliefs that may be described as *collectivist*. A leftist is likely to attribute greater weight to social and economic circumstances as determinants of one's opportunities and achievements. Those on the left have greater faith in the ability of government to intervene and promote the common good and have doubts about the economic efficiency and social fairness of free markets. Although those on the left may be critical of government actions or institutions, they reject the claim that government needs to be smaller and less influential. Smaller government, they argue, works to the advantage of the affluent and privileged at the expense of the disadvantaged.

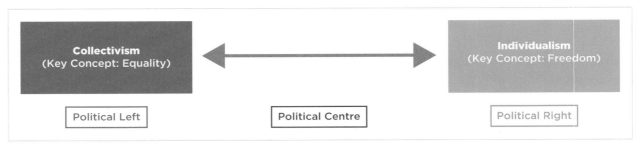

FIGURE 2.1 LEFT/RIGHT SOCIO-ECONOMIC SPECTRUM

In reality, the politics of left and right is more complicated than these simplified portraits suggest. Perhaps this is complicated by the fact that, in addition to socio-economic issues, there are also issues pertaining to how much freedom individuals should have and how much control (power) governments should maintain (see Figure 2.2). For example, opposition to abortion, same-sex marriage, and assisted suicide is generally viewed as a right-wing position, and many who subscribe to all the elements of right-wing politics may support these policies. Such people, sometimes labelled **libertarians** (such as many members of the Tea Party in the United States), *believe that individuals should be allowed the largest possible margin of freedom in all realms of life, including moral choices*. They also believe that government should be much smaller and less intrusive. The libertarian right has been, until recently, smaller and less of a political force than the socially conservative right. Social conservatives are distinguished by such stands as opposition to abortion and same-sex marriage, support for capital punishment and stiffer jail sentences, and rejection of forms of pluralism, which they believe corrode traditional values and social order. The wellsprings of their conservatism are quite different from those of libertarianism, but their shared antipathy for certain aspects of the modern welfare state cause libertarians and social conservatives to be grouped together on the right. The fissures in this alliance and the limitations of the right–left categorization of political ideas become apparent when the issue is personal morality (e.g., abortion, homosexuality, religious teachings in public schools).

Despite these limitations, and the fact that labels like "right" and "left" are more often used to discredit one's political opponents than to inform in a dispassionate way, the right–left spectrum taps a crucial and enduring truth of modern politics. This involves the character of the good society and how best to achieve it. We have said that the underlying struggle is essentially one between collectivist and individualist visions of the good society. These visions differ in how they view the conditions that promote the social good and how much power is exercised by the state. This difference is illustrated in Figure 2.2, where we see that too much oppression can lead to totalitarian regimes, in which citizens may be asked to sacrifice a great

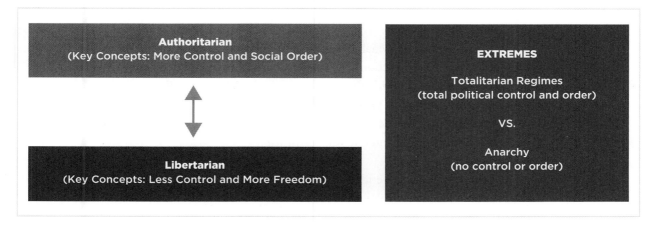

FIGURE 2.2 POLITICAL POWER SPECTRUM
This model shows us that ideologies are also about how much political power the state should have.

deal, even their lives, for the sake of a social goal or social order, or the opposite situation, whereby too little control by the state can lead to anarchy.

Ideologies in Canadian Democracy

Until the recent adoption of a publicly oriented health-care system in the United States in 2010, Canada's health-care system was often invoked whenever Canadian–American cultural differences were discussed. It is commonly said that one of the cultural characteristics that distinguishes Canadians from Americans is Canadians' propensity to sacrifice individual self-interest for the good of the community. Canadian nationalists often feared that privatization of health-care services would lead Canada to slide down the slope toward American values and public policies. What the watchdogs of Canadian-style health care were really saying was that the more collectivist Canadian health-care model provided greater dignity for individuals and was fairer than the more individualistic pre-2010 American health-care system. The idea that Canada's health-care model both reflects Canadian values and is vital to their protection frequently finds its way into election campaign advertising, particularly to attack parties and candidates who appear to favour reforms to the system. These are portrayed as being un-Canadian and, worse, pro-American in their sympathies and values. Defenders of the American privately oriented health-care system would retort that Canadian health policy was a form of socialism.

Socialism, liberalism, and conservatism are the trio of ideologies that have greatly influenced the politics of Western societies since the American and French revolutions:

- **Socialism** is ***an ideology based on the collective or state ownership of the means of production and the belief in the state's ability to provide social justice, redistribute wealth, and fix social problems***. Concepts usually associated with socialism include equality, redistribution of wealth, left-wing politics, complete or partial ownership of the means of production, social programs, and bigger government.
- **Liberalism** is ***based on the belief that the state must protect individual liberty, personal choice, and the right to private property***. Concepts usually associated with liberalism include inalienable rights, individualism, constitutional protection for rights and freedoms, protection of private property, and liberal democracy.
- **Conservatism** is ***an ideology based on the belief that traditions and social order are important and that gradual change is best***. Concepts usually associated with conservatism include social stability, family values, continuity, right-wing politics, and maintaining social and religious institutions.

The importance of these ideologies in defining the contours of political life is seen in major and minor political parties in many Western democracies, including Canada, continuing to use the names "liberal," "conservative," and "socialist."

In Canada, the two parties that have dominated national politics for most of the country's history are the Liberal Party and the Conservative Party. They have their roots in the ideological divisions of the nineteenth century. Over time, however, the labels have lost much, if not all, of their informative value. Today, the ideological distance between a Liberal and a Conservative seems small. Both parties and their supporters share in the dominant liberal tradition that pervaded Canada and the United States. It may be said of all Canadian political parties, including the New Democratic Party (NDP), the Bloc Québécois, and the Green Party, that they traditionally believed in similar core liberal values. At the heart of this tradition was the primacy of individual freedom. **Classical liberalism**—*liberalism as understood until the middle of the nineteenth century—was associated with freedom of religious choice and practice, free enterprise and free trade in business and economics, and freedom of expression and association in politics.* These liberal values constituted a sort of national ethos in the United States, where they were enshrined in the Declaration of Independence during the American Revolution (1776) and in the Bill of Rights (1791). In the colonies of British North America, which would become Canada in the late nineteenth century, liberalism's dominance was somewhat more tentative. This was due to the streak of conservatism kept alive by some elites in colonial society, notably officials of the Catholic Church and the Church of England, and the British colonial authorities.

Classical conservatism was an ideology rooted in the ideas of the Irish statesman and political philosopher Edmund Burke, whose writings were a reaction to the disorder caused by the French and American Revolutions; he *emphasized the importance of tradition and social order. Classical conservatism accepted human inequality—social, political, and economic—as part of the natural order of things.* Conservatives believed in the importance of continuity with the past and the preservation of law and order. They were wary of innovation and opposed to such basic liberal reforms as equal political rights for all men (even liberals did not come around to the idea of equal political rights for women until the twentieth century). Unlike liberals, who located the source of all just rule in the people, conservatives maintained that God and tradition were the true founts of political authority. Consequently, they supported an established church and were strong defenders of the Crown's traditional prerogatives against the rival claims of elected legislatures.

Although no party having the label "socialist" has ever achieved the status of even an important minor national party in either Canada or the United States, socialist ideology has been influential in various ways. **Classical socialism** was *based on the principle of equality of condition and radical egalitarianism* that distinguished socialist doctrine from liberalism's advocacy of equality of opportunity. Socialists supported a vastly greater role for the state in directing the economy, providing better working conditions and greater rights for workers vis-à-vis their employers, and instituting reforms like public health care, unemployment insurance, income assistance for the indigent, public pensions, and universal access to public education, which became the hallmarks of the twentieth-century welfare state.

The usefulness of these three "isms" as benchmarks for reading the political map is disappearing (see Table 2.1), for two main reasons. First, the labels of all three classical ideologies, and especially liberalism and conservatism, mean something quite different today from what they meant 100–200 years ago. For example, contemporary liberalism does not place individual freedom above all else. Instead, modern liberals are distinguished by their belief

TABLE 2.1 | KAY LAWSON'S SUMMARY OF IDEOLOGIES

General Issues	Communism and Some Forms of Socialism	Social Democrats/ Feminism	Liberalism	Conservatism	Fascism
1. Means of Change	Revolution	Persuasion and democratic elections			Coup/coercion
2. Human Nature	Unselfish and social	Selfish and social			Selfish and unsocial
3. Role of the State	Economic redistribution	Protect individual liberty			Control
4. Values	Economic equality	Freedom and political equality			Social order
5. Positions	Far left	Left	Centre	Right	Far right

This table shows how the values of most present-day ideologies are very similar.

Source: Adapted from Kay Lawson, *The Human Polity: A Comparative Introduction to Political Science* (New York: Wadsworth, 2002).

that governments can and should act to alleviate hardships experienced by the poor and the oppressed. They are more likely to worry about minority group rights than individual freedoms, in the sense that they see protecting disadvantaged minorities as a necessary step in achieving real freedom for the members of these groups. Modern liberalism has also become associated with support for multiculturalism and openness toward non-traditional lifestyles and social institutions.

The doctrine of classical conservatism has disappeared from contemporary democracies, leaving what has been called the conservative outlook or "conservative mind."[2] Modern conservatives tend to embrace the economic beliefs that once were characteristic of liberals. Like classical liberals, they defend the principle of equality of opportunity and are more likely to place the protection of personal freedoms before the advancement of minority rights. As in earlier times, conservatism is generally viewed as the ideology of the privileged in society. It is worth noting, however, that conservative politicians and political parties receive much of their support from middle-class voters whose hands are far from the levers of economic power and social influence.

Of the three classical ideologies, the meaning of "socialism" has changed the least. There is today, however, much less confidence among socialists that state ownership of the means of economic production and distribution is desirable. Modern socialists, or *social democrats* as they often call themselves, temper their advocacy of an egalitarian society with an acceptance of capitalism and the inequalities that inevitably are generated by free-market economies. Defending the rights of society's least-well-off elements is today carried out largely under the banner of other "isms" including feminism, multiculturalism, and environmentalism. These collectivist–egalitarian belief systems have more impact on Canadian and American politics than does socialism.

A second reason why the traditional trio of "isms" is no longer a reliable guide to politics has to do with the character of political divisions in modern society. The aristocracy of land and title and the deferential social norms that nurtured classical conservatism belong to the past. They live on in the folklore of castles and estates in the once rigidly hierarchical societies of Europe, in the continuing pomp of hereditary royalty, and in Great Britain's House of Lords. Otherwise, classical conservatism has no legitimacy in the middle-class cultures of Western societies. In the United States the structures and values that supported classical conservatism never existed, and in Canada they achieved only a precarious and passing toehold.

The struggles of liberalism in the eighteenth and nineteenth centuries, and of socialism in the nineteenth and twentieth, have largely been won. Liberals fought for free-market reforms and the extension of political rights and freedoms first to the new propertied classes created by the Industrial Revolution and then more widely to the (male) adult population. They fought against conservatives who dug in to protect the political privileges of a hereditary aristocracy and the economic dominance of the traditional landowning classes. Socialists fought for more government control over the economy, for workers' rights like collective bargaining and limits on the hours of work, and for the welfare state. They fought against both the vestiges of conservatism and liberalism's emphasis on individualism. Today, Canadians, Americans, and Western Europeans live in affluent, middle-class societies that bear little resemblance to those of the nineteenth century.

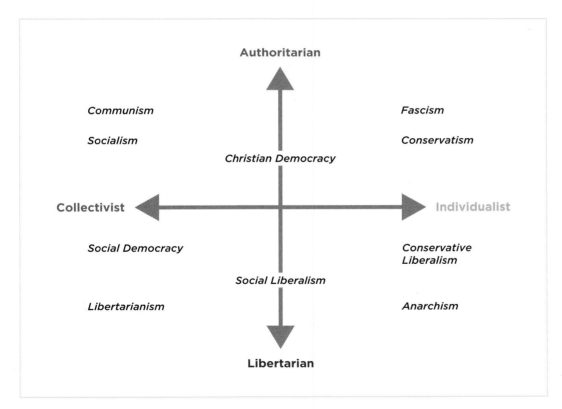

FIGURE 2.3 THE POLITICAL COMPASS
When Figure 2.1 and Figure 2.2 are combined as they are here, we get a fairly sophisticated model for categorizing ideologies and political parties according to their values, ideas, and policies.

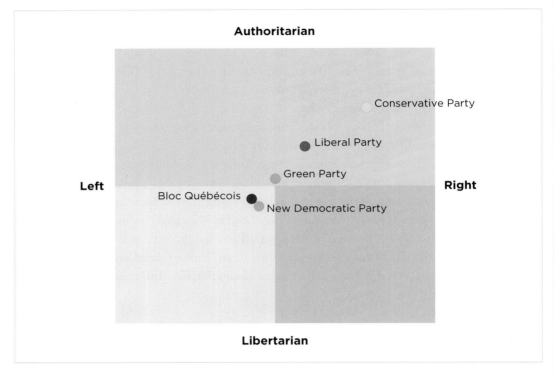

FIGURE 2.4 POLITICALCOMPASS.ORG AND THE IDEOLOGICAL POSITIONS OF CANADIAN POLITICAL PARTIES IN 2011

Politicalcompass.org interprets the ideological position of Canadian political parties during the 2011 general election as follows:

> While the Liberals and the Conservatives accuse each other of reckless spending policies, their real differences are a little more significant on the social scale of The Political Compass. Ethical issues play well for the Liberals at the present time, while the Conservatives' winning card is family values. Identity politics make for a more comfortable debate between parties of relatively little economic distinction. Both of the big two, after all, talk of lower taxes, jobs and growth.
>
> Perhaps because Canada has emerged in better shape from the financial crisis than most other industrialised countries, the Canadian left has not enjoyed the reinvigoration of progressive parties in other democracies. The NDP has further lost its radical edge, sounding increasingly like one of the milder European Social Democratic parties; keen to be all things to more voters, perhaps presenting a safe pair of hands for coalition with the Liberals. The Greens, with their promises on labour rights and childcare, have moved slightly to the left, countering the otherwise rightward drift of the major national parties.
>
> Bloc Québécois continues to pose difficulties for The Political Compass. The diversity of conflicting views within the party are transcended by its core cause.

How does this interpretation of the ideological positions of Canadian political parties mesh with your understanding of each party's values and policies? Are you surprised to see any of the parties fall where they do on this grid?

Source: http://www.politicalcompass.org/canada2011.

Does this mean, as some have argued, that the traditional ideologies are obsolete, unsuited to the realities of modern society? Some commentators dismiss the traditional "isms" and the left–centre–right ideological grid as outmoded ways of thinking about politics. It is a great mistake, however, to underestimate the continuing importance of ideology in politics. Although the traditional ideologies now must jostle with feminism, environmentalism, multiculturalism, and other "isms" on a more crowded playing field, and despite the changes in the meanings of the classical ideological labels, they continue to be useful, though certainly not infallible, guides to understanding political ideas.

There are those who would argue that the individualism–collectivism dichotomy has become obsolete and that politics has become largely a debate about means rather than ends. But such thinking underestimates the continuing vitality of the struggle between competing images of the moral order. Many of the deepest differences of opinion on important issues in contemporary public life, such as abortion, same-sex marriage, free trade, and taxation, are based on people's different ideas about good government, personal dignity, justice, economic and social order, and the good society. Those on the right of the modern ideological divide are less likely than those on the left to look to state intervention as a preferred solution to social and moral problems. This may be seen in the ongoing debate over the consequences of globalization—a debate in which moral considerations are seldom far from the surface.

EXPLAINING CANADIAN IDEAS, POLITICAL CULTURE, AND INSTITUTIONS

Explanations of Canadians' political ideas, and of the institutions that embody them, can be grouped into three main approaches: the fragment theory approach, the role of formative events approach, and the economic (class analysis) approach. Each of these perspectives stresses a different set of causes and forces in the origins and shaping of Canadians' political ideas and institutions.

The Fragment Theory Approach: European Parents and Cultural Genes

Canada, along with other New World societies, was founded by immigrants from Europe. Aboriginal communities already existed, of course, but the sort of society that developed in Canada had its roots and inspiration in the values and practices of European civilization. Those who chose or were forced to immigrate to the New World did not represent a cross-section of the European society from which they came. They were unrepresentative in terms of their social class, their occupations, and in some cases their religion. Moreover, immigration tended to occur in waves, coinciding with historical and ideological developments in Europe. New World societies were "fragments" of the European societies that gave birth to them. They were fragment societies because they represented only a part of the socio-economic and cultural

Despite the victory of the "No" side in the 1995 Quebec sovereignty referendum, the ideological differences between French and English Canada can be traced back to the eighteenth century. Do you think it is possible for descendants of different societies to build a nation together based on a single vision?

spectrum of the European society from which they originated, and also because their creation coincided with particular ideological epochs.

According to this approach, the timing of settlement is crucial. Along with their material possessions, immigrants brought their *cultural baggage*: values, beliefs, and practices acquired in Europe and transplanted into the New World. As David Bell and Lorne Tepperman observe, "the 'fragment theory' sees the culture of founding groups as a kind of *genetic code* that does not determine but sets limits to later cultural developments."[3]

Canada has been characterized as a two-fragment society. French Canada was founded by immigrants from France who brought with them their Catholicism and *feudal* ideas about social and political relations. Feudal society is characterized by fairly rigid social classes connected by a web of traditional mutual rights and duties, and by the exclusion of most people from the full right to participate in politics. According to French-Canadian historian Fernand Ouellet, this was the ideological and social condition of New France when the colony was conquered by British forces in 1759.[4] Cut off from the social and political developments unleashed by the French Revolution in 1789, when emigration from France, except for some priests, virtually dried up, French Canada's ideological development was shaped by its origins as a feudal fragment of pre-revolutionary France. Institutions, chiefly the Catholic Church, the dominant social institution in French Canada until well into the twentieth century, maintained this pre-liberal inheritance.

The "cultural genes" of English Canada are very different. English Canada was originally populated by immigrants from the United States. These were the so-called "Loyalists" who found themselves on the losing side of the American War of Independence (1776). They migrated north to British colonies that were overwhelmingly French-speaking. Although there is some debate about their "cultural baggage," the general view seems to be that Loyalists held predominantly eighteenth-century liberal political values and beliefs centred on individual freedom in politics, religion, and economic relations. A crucial political tenet of this liberalism was the idea that government was based on the consent of the people. So why did the Loyalists leave the United States, a society whose political independence was founded on liberal beliefs?

The defenders of fragment theory offer different answers. Some argue that the liberalism of the Loyalists was diluted by conservative or **Tory** political beliefs: ***deference toward established authority and institutions, acceptance of inequality between classes as the natural condition of society, and a greater stress on preserving social order than on protecting individual freedoms.***[5] Others reject the view that Tory values were ever a legitimate part of English Canada's political culture, arguing that this belief system had no roots in the pre-revolutionary Thirteen Colonies and therefore could not have been exported to English Canada through the Loyalist migration.[6] The Loyalists were "anti-American Yankees" who rejected American independence because of their loyalty to the British Empire and to the monarchy, and their dislike of republican government (or, as they were more likely to put it, "mob rule"). Their support for liberal ideas was shown by the fact that they immediately clamoured for elected assemblies and the political rights they had been used to in America. Bell and Tepperman argue that

"The typical Canadian," an Englishman observed a hundred years ago, "tells you that he is not, but he is a Yankee—a Yankee in the sense in which we use the term at home, as synonymous with everything that smacks of democracy." The

> Loyalist in Canada is thereafter always a paradox, an "anti-American Yankee."
> Only one path leads out of his dilemma: creating a myth that helps him survive.
> In this myth, he insists that he is British.[7]

The debate over how important non-liberal values were among the Loyalists is not merely academic. Contemporary analyses of English Canada as a more deferential and conservative society than the United States often trace this alleged difference back to the original ideological mixtures of the two societies. A second reason why the debate matters involves the explanation for Canadian socialism. Some who contend that conservative values were an important and legitimate component of English Canada's original cultural inheritance go on to argue that socialism emerged in Canada first because liberalism failed to achieve the status of an unchallenged national creed (as it did in the United States), and second because social class was not a foreign concept in English Canada.[8] According to this view, conservatism and socialism are two varieties of collectivism.

The Formative Events Approach: Counter-Revolution and the Conquest

Societies, like human beings, are marked by certain major events at critical periods in their development. These events are "formative" in the sense that they influence a society to evolve along particular lines. In politics, these formative events are associated both with ideas and with institutions. For example, the American Revolution was fought in the name of liberal values and was followed by the adoption of a constitution and government structures that enshrined a preference for dispersed political power, a weak executive, and guarantees for individual rights. The institutions embodied eighteenth-century liberal values of individual freedom and limited government that shaped the subsequent pattern of American politics.

Formative events theorist and American sociologist Seymour Martin Lipset argued that the political development of the United States has been shaped by its *revolutionary origins*, while that of English Canada has been shaped by its *counter-revolutionary origins*. Lipset writes

> Americans do not know but Canadians cannot forget that two nations, not one, came out of the American Revolution. The United States is the country of the revolution, Canada of the counterrevolution. These very different formative events set indelible marks on the two nations. One celebrates the overthrow of an oppressive state, the triumph of the people, a successful effort to create a type of government never seen before. The other commemorates a defeat and a long struggle to preserve a historical source of legitimacy: government's deriving its title-to-rule from a monarchy linked to church establishment. Government power is feared in the south; uninhibited popular sovereignty has been a concern in the north.[9]

The Loyalists thus were the founders of an English-speaking society that originated in its rejection of the American republic. This rejection would be repeated several times: in the War of 1812; in the defeat of the American-style democratic reforms advocated by the losers in the 1837–8 rebellions in Lower and Upper Canada; and in the 1867 decision to establish a new country with a system of government similar to that of Great Britain. The political history of Canada, including many of its major economic and cultural policies, reads largely as a series of refusals in the face of Americanizing pressures.

Is rejection of American political values and institutions proof of the greater strength of conservative values in English Canada? Some who agree with Lipset do not agree that counter-revolutionary gestures signify *ideological conservatism*. Bell and Tepperman argue that the Loyalists were not anti-government, and that Canadians ever since appear to have been more willing to use the state for social, economic, and cultural purposes than were their American neighbours. But, they claim, a fondness for government is not inconsistent with liberal values. It is only in the United States, where the Revolution was about the tyranny of government, that liberalism acquired an anti-government character.[10]

What 1776 represents for English Canada's political development, the British Conquest of New France in 1759 represents for that of French Canada. The Conquest has always occupied a central place in French-Canadian nationalism, testifying to French Canadians' own awareness of its significance. The motto on Quebec licence plates, "Je me souviens" ("I remember"), is in fact a reference to the time before the Conquest, when French-speaking Canadians presumably were free from the oppression of Ottawa and English Canadians. Particularly under Parti Québécois governments in Quebec it has been common for the Conquest to be mentioned in official government documents on subjects ranging from language to the economy and constitutional reform.

History did not, of course, stop at the Conquest. The crushed 1837 rebellion in Lower Canada (Quebec) signalled the defeat of the politically liberal *patriotes* and consolidated the dominance of the conservative ideology in French Canada. This ideology would ultimately collapse by the end of the 1950s, finally brought down by the weight of the enormous social and economic transformations that the conservatives had ignored and even denied. Since then, conservative ideology has had little credibility in Quebec, but the memory of the Conquest continues to be a favourite starting point for Quebec nationalists. The protests generated in 2008 by plans (later cancelled) to re-enact the 1759 Battle of the Plains of Abraham, as part of Quebec's four hundredth anniversary celebration showed how raw this nerve remains.

The Class Analysis Approach: Economic Structure and Political Ideas

From a class analysis perspective, both fragment theory and the formative events explanation are "hopelessly idealistic."[11] This is because these two approaches suggest that political values and institutions are primarily based on ideas—the "cultural baggage" of fragment theory and the cultural mindset and symbols associated with the notion of formative events. An economic interpretation, by contrast, explains a culture and its institutions as the products of class relations. These class relations are rooted in the particular system of economic production and distribution—the *mode of production* as Marxists call it—that is found in a society at any point in time. Ideas and institutions change in response to transformations in the economic system and in the class relations associated with this system. The dominant ideas and political arrangements of a society are not, however, merely the shadows cast by economic phenomena. But what sets this explanation apart from the other two is the belief that culture and institutions are the embodiments of power relations whose sources lie in the economic system.

By whom, for whom, and how is political culture produced? And what are the effects? Those who approach political values and institutions from the angle of economically determined class relations argue that a society's dominant ideas are inevitably those of its most powerful class (those who control the system of economic production and distribution). The important means of forming and spreading ideas and information, such as the privately owned mass media, are controlled by the dominant class. Others, including the schools, mainstream religious organizations, and the state, accept and spread the values of this class for reasons

In fall 2011, the international Occupy Movement, which had a significant presence in Halifax, Toronto, Calgary, and Vancouver, emerged to protest economic and social inequality. "We Are the 99%" became the movement's slogan, referring to the concentration of wealth and power among 1 per cent of American income earners. One of the goals of the mass movement was to bring an end to the corrupting influence of money on politics. What examples can you think of that indicate your federal government is acting in the public's, versus the corporate world's, best interests?

more subtle than ownership. Chief among these reasons is their support for *social order* and their rejection of tendencies and ideas that fundamentally challenge the status quo. The predominant institutions and social values are not class-neutral.

Why would the members of subordinate classes embrace the values and beliefs of a self-interested dominant class? The class analysis perspective offers a two-part answer. First, those who do not belong to the dominant class—essentially most people—may be the victims of *false consciousness*. This concept, first used by Karl Marx, describes the inability of the subordinate classes to see where their real interests lie. In feudal societies, for example, deference to established authority and belief in a hereditary aristocracy's "natural right to rule" are ideas that uphold the privileges of the dominant class. In liberal societies, the widespread belief that hard work opens socio-economic opportunities is another example of an idea promoted to reinforce the dominance of a small wealthy minority who control the economy. We learn in school, in the media, and in other ways, that equality of opportunity is a characteristic feature of our society. And yet, abundant empirical evidence shows that significant barriers to socio-economic mobility exist, that poverty is often passed on from generation to generation, and that those at the top of the socio-economic pyramid constitute a largely self-perpetuating elite.

The second reason why members of subordinate classes accept the ideas of the dominant class as "common sense" is that to some extent these ideas conform to their personal experience. For instance, democratic claims about the fundamental equality of all persons have a false ring in societies where some people are denied a share of this equality because of ethnicity. However, claims about equality may appear to be valid in a society in which, under the constitution, citizens enjoy equal protection under the law, there is universal suffrage, and there are no second-class citizens. Or, consider the liberal belief, discussed earlier, that opportunities to acquire wealth and social standing are relatively open. While some people never escape the socio-economic circumstances they are born into, many others do. The 2008 election of Barack Obama as president of the United States—the son of a Kenyan goatherd!—is evidence in mythic proportions. There is enough proof that hard work and/or intelligence results in material success to make liberalism's claims credible. As Patricia Marchak observes, "the propagation of an ideology cannot occur in a vacuum of experience; there must be a fair amount of congruence between personal experience and ideological interpretation for the propaganda ['dominant ideology'] to be successful."[12] Where this congruence is either weak or totally absent, the dominant class must rely on force to uphold its rule.

This idea is important: a society's dominant values and beliefs must be compatible with the experience of most of its members; otherwise the ideas of the dominant class will be exposed as pure self-interest. It means that what some have called "false consciousness" cannot be totally false. We can understand this better by looking at Quebec and the ideological changes associated with its "Quiet Revolution" of the 1960s.

As recently as the 1950s, the dominant ideology in French-speaking Quebec was conservatism. It was an ideology based on the concept of ***la survivance*** (survival): ***conserving French Canada's religious and linguistic heritage in the face of assimilationist pressures***. While possessing the formal structures of political democracy, Quebec's political life was dominated by autocratic politicians, rampant patronage, and social institutions—notably the Roman

Catholic Church and conservative newspapers—that encouraged submission to established authority.[13] Functions like education and social services that in virtually all industrial democracies were already under state control were still in the hands of the Church in Quebec. Even the province's francophone labour unions were predominantly "confessional"—linked to a church whose ideas about industrial relations were shaped largely by its concern for preserving social harmony.

This conservatism, linked to the Church's social dominance and to a sharply limited role for the provincial state, was increasingly out of step with the industrial society that had been evolving in Quebec throughout the twentieth century. Those who advocated reforms that entailed a more interventionist role for the Quebec state (such as public control over education and social assistance) and saw Quebec as a secular industrial society necessarily found themselves in conflict with the spokespersons for the conservative ideology. By the 1950s, however, the typical Québécois was a city-dweller who worked in a factory, store, or office,[14] and a new middle class of university-educated francophone professionals was becoming larger.[15] This new middle class was the leading force behind the expansion of the state in the early to mid 1960s. Ultimately, the lack of congruence between the values of the conservative ideology and the personal experience of most Québécois brought about the collapse of the one dominant ideology. It was replaced by one in tune with the new and growing groups like the middle class and the francophone business community, which have dominated Quebec politics since the Quiet Revolution.

THE VALUES, IDEAS, AND ATTITUDES OF CANADIANS

What do Canadians believe about politics? Is it true that they value social order more, and individual freedom less, than do their American counterparts? Does French Canada, and more particularly French-speaking Quebec, constitute a "distinct society" in terms of its values and beliefs? Is it reasonable to talk about the political ideas of English-speaking Canadians, or are the regional differences in political culture too great to warrant such an approach?

In the following pages we will organize our analysis of political culture and public attitudes and expectations under five themes: community, political violence, freedom, equality, and expectations of the state. These tap crucial dimensions of political culture while allowing us to explore the differences and similarities between French- and English-speaking Canadians, between different regions, and between Canadians and Americans.

Community

"Canadians," someone has said, "are the only people who regularly pull themselves up by the roots to see whether they are still growing." This search for a national identity unites successive generations of Canadians. Indeed, as the above remark suggests, the obsessive and often insecure introspection of Canadians may be one of the chief characteristics of the Canadian identity (in English Canada, at least).

The roots of this preoccupation with national identity go back to the Conquest and the American War of Independence. The Conquest laid the basis for a society in which two main ethnolinguistic communities would cohabit—communities whose values and aspirations would frequently be at cross-purposes. The American War of Independence, as explained earlier, was followed by the emigration of Loyalists from the United States to the British colonies that would become Canada. Founded by those who rejected the republican democracy to the south, English Canada would constantly compare itself to that society and seek to explain and justify its separate existence.

More recently these two historical strands of Canada's identity "crisis" have been joined by newer challenges to the political community. These have come from Aboriginal Canadians and from some ethnic minorities who reject their perceived marginalization. Lacking a confident unifying sense of national identity, Canadian society has been buffeted by identity politics and the often irreconcilable definitions of Canada.

The term **political community** implies, quite simply, *a shared sense of belonging to a country whose national integrity is worth preserving*. This is something less than **nationalism**, which *defines a community by its language, ethnic origins, traditions, or unique history*. And it is not quite the same as patriotism, which one associates with a more fervent and demonstrative love of country and its symbols than is usually considered seemly in Canada. Political community is, rather, what historian W.L. Morton once described as "a community of political allegiance alone."[16] National identity is essentially political—a sense of common citizenship in a country whose members have more in common with one another than with the citizens of neighbouring states and who believe that there are good reasons for continuing to live together as a single political nation. The term "political nationality" is used by Donald Smiley to refer to precisely this sort of non-ethnic, non-racial sense of political community.[17]

The importance in politics of national identity and a sense of political community is illustrated in the breakup of the Soviet Union and of Yugoslavia after the end of the Communist Party's monopoly over power. Nationalist aspirations and bitter animosities that had been kept in check under totalitarian rule were unleashed; there was no popular basis for political community, undermining any possibility of countries or retaining their pre-reform boundaries. Breakup was inevitable in these formerly communist political systems once more democratic institutions were in place.

The image of Canadian troops laying siege to Gatineau, Quebec or of armed barricades where the Trans-Canada Highway crosses the border between Ontario and Quebec, probably seems like a lurid fantasy to most Canadians. The great national bust-up, if Quebec were to declare its independence, would almost certainly be acrimonious, but many believe that civil war such as was seen in the breakup of Yugoslavia is unlikely. Not everyone agrees, however. In public statements in late 1991, Gordon Robertson, former Chief Clerk of the Privy Council (under Pierre Trudeau) and a rather conservative person by temperament, raised precisely the spectre of the strife in the former Yugoslavia in arguing that a breakup of Canada could very well be violent.

Prediction is perilous. What is clear, however, is that Canada's sense of community often seems fragile, threatened by French–English tensions, western grievances against central

Canada, and most recently, conflicts between Aboriginal Canadians and the federal and provincial governments. But this apparent fragility needs to be viewed alongside evidence that suggests that the country has been relatively successful in managing such tensions. The Constitution dates from 1867, making it one of the oldest and most durable in the world. Moreover, the country's territorial integrity has (so far) remained unshaken by either civil war or secession. This is not to understate the importance of the rifts in Canada's sense of community. But the problems of Canadian unity and identity should be viewed from a broader perspective.

There are four major challenges to the Canadian political community: French–English relations, Aboriginal demands for self-government, American influence on Canadian culture, and regional tensions. The first two are occasionally associated with political violence and calls for redrawing territorial boundaries. They represent clear challenges to the Canadian political community. The challenge of American influence assumes forms that are less territorial; nevertheless, its impact on the Canadian political community has been great. We will examine American influences separately in Chapter 3.

The fourth challenge, regional tensions, has been an important factor in Canadian politics from the country's inception. We would argue, however, that regional grievances and conflicts have never threatened Canada's territorial integrity. Westerners and, less stridently, Atlantic Canadians have long complained about policies and institutions that favour the interests of Ontario and Quebec. But their resentment has never boiled over to produce politically significant separatist movements, nor popular defection from the idea of Canada. The importance of regionalism will be discussed in Chapter 4.

For most of Canada's history, relations between the francophone and anglophone communities have not posed a threat to the political community. The differences and tensions between Canada's two major language groups have been managed through political accommodations between their political elites. This practice of accommodating differences arguably goes back to the Quebec Act of 1774. Official protection was extended to the Roman Catholic Church and Quebec's civil law system just when the British authorities were worried about the prospect of political rebellion in the American colonies spreading north. The tradition of deal making between French and English Canada acquired a rather different twist in the couple of decades prior to Confederation, when the current provinces of Ontario and Quebec were united with a common legislature. The practice of dual ministries—having a leader from each of Canada East (Quebec) and Canada West (Ontario)—quickly developed, as did the convention that a bill needed to be passed by majorities from both East and West in order to become law. The federal division of powers that formed the basis of the 1867 Confederation continued this deal-making tradition. Provincial jurisdiction over education, property, civil rights, and local matters was shaped by Quebec politicians' insistence on controlling matters involving cultural differences.

This tradition of elitist deal making has continued throughout Canada's history at two different levels. Nationally, the federal cabinet and national political parties, particularly the Liberal Party of Canada, have been important forums where Quebec's interests could be represented. But as a more aggressive Quebec-centred nationalism arose in the 1960s, the ability to represent the interests of French and English Canada within national institutions became less important than whether compromises could be reached between the governments of Canada and Quebec.

The political arrangements and circumstances that for a couple of centuries had prevented French–English conflicts from challenging the idea of a single Canada seemed to come unstitched during the 1960s. Quebec independence, which had been a marginal idea that surfaced sporadically, became a serious proposition advocated by many French-speaking intellectuals and apparently supported by a sizable minority of Québécois. The independence option spawned several organized political groups. In 1968, most of them threw their support behind the pro-independence Parti Québécois (PQ). Since then, the debate over whether the province should remain in Canada, and if so, on what terms, has been a chief dimension of Quebec political life.

There have been many political arrangements between First Nations communities and the Canadian community since the arrival of the European settlers some four hundred years ago. However, two issues have figured prominently in defining these arrangements: property rights and the relationship of the First Nations to the state. For instance, under French colonial rule, France did not recognize Aboriginal rights to the land, but Aboriginals who converted to Christianity were given the status and rights of French citizens. When the French territories were taken over by the British, a new relationship ensued. The Royal Proclamation of 1763 and subsequent treaties sought to organize and stabilize the relationship of the British state and the Aboriginal North Americans in matters of trade and land use. There were also two underlying assumptions embedded in these documents. First, First Nations were under the protective stewardship of the British. And second, First Nations had some rights to the land, with some right to compensation for land taken by European settlers. In order to ensure that colonial growth was not impeded, the British Crown "reserved" lands for Aboriginal populations. To this day, the Royal Proclamation of 1763 is still important in settling land-claims disputes between First Nations and a provincial or the federal government.

The notion of protective stewardship, as well as the practice of reserving land for First Nations, continued after Confederation, and the passing of the Indian Act in 1876. The Indian Act gave First Nations on the reserves control over their economy and society, but very limited powers of self-government. For almost a century after Confederation, it was assumed that the First Nations would be absorbed into mainstream Canadian society. Indeed, there were many attempts through government practices, laws, and policies, including the extension of voting rights to First Nations peoples, to speed up this integration. Nevertheless, the First Nations remain distinct in respect of their culture, legal and social status, and civil rights. And the issues of land claims and self-government continue to capture most of the headlines when it comes to coverage of First Nations' issues in the news.

In attempting to understand how great a threat Quebec separatism and Aboriginal claims have posed to the Canadian community, we will consider two measures: political violence and public attitudes.

Political Violence

Canadians are not accustomed to the violent resolution of political disputes. There have been only two political assassinations since Confederation; the first was in 1868 when D'Arcy McGee was shot down in Ottawa, and the second in 1970 when Quebec's minister of labour, Pierre Laporte, was kidnapped and strangled to death by members of the FLQ. *The World Handbook of Social and Political Indicators* ranks Canada well down the list of countries in terms of political violence. And even though non-violent protest is more common in Canadian politics than violence (as one would expect in any genuine democracy), protest demonstrations historically have been much rarer in Canada than in most other advanced industrialized democracies.[18]

Violence, however, has been neither absent nor unimportant in Canadian politics. Much of that violence has involved labour disputes or workers' protests where the police or military were called in to protect the interests of employers and the capitalist social order. Examples include the violent suppression of the Winnipeg General Strike in 1919 and the use of the Royal Canadian Mounted Police in Regina in 1935 to break up the "On to Ottawa Trek" of unemployed workers during the depth of the *Great Depression*. The forcible detention of many Japanese, German, and Italian Canadians during World War II is another instance of state political violence. Indeed, in most of these cases it was the state that decided to use violence to settle some conflict or deal with some perceived menace. The most significant instances of political violence instigated by groups or individuals against the state have been related to the French–English conflict and, more recently, the status of Canada's Aboriginal population.

As indicated in Box 2.1, tribal animosities that have existed between French and English Canadians have crystallized around violent events on several occasions.

The 1970 October Crisis, as the affair came to be called, is unique in Canada's political history. It is the only occasion when the War Measures Act was invoked during peacetime. The government of Pierre Trudeau, which acted on the urging of the Quebec Liberal government of Robert Bourassa, argued that civil order was teetering on the verge of collapse in Quebec, and that there existed a state of "apprehended insurrection." Most commentators argue that, even with the kidnappings and the uncertainty, Ottawa's reaction was excessive. Excessive or not, the October Crisis needs to be placed in proper perspective. The political kidnappings were the work of a tiny band of political extremists whose tactics enjoyed little support among Quebec nationalists. Although there was some sympathy for the goals of the FLQ, it evaporated after their murder of Pierre Laporte.

In recent years political violence has been linked most often to unresolved disputes between groups of Aboriginal Canadians and public authorities. During the summer and autumn of 1990—a time now known as the "Indian summer of 1990"—a group of Mohawk Warriors protested the planned expansion of a golf course on land they claimed as their own near Oka, Quebec by barricading a road leading to the golf course. The confrontation eventually escalated, resulting in the death of one Quebec police officer, a sympathy blockade by Mohawks at Kahnawake of the Mercier Bridge leading into Montreal, and similar blockades by other First Nations bands in communities across the country. Eventually, the standoff at Oka

CANADIAN SPOTLIGHT

BOX 2.1   Timeline: Major Violent Confrontations between French Canadians and English Canadians

1885   The hanging of the francophone Métis leader Louis Riel after the defeat of the Northwest Rebellion; government's unwillingness to commute the death sentence was seen by the francophones as anti-French prejudice

1917   The World War I anti-conscription riots in Quebec; French Canadians believed Canada's participation was motivated by colonial attachments

1955   Montreal riots when Maurice "Le Rocket" Richard was suspended by Clarence Campbell, the president of the National Hockey League. French-Canadian supporters

saw the suspension as motivated by discrimination on the part of *les maudits anglais* ("the damned English").

1960s   The spate of bombings and vandalism in the 1960s directed at symbols of the federal government's authority and anglophone domination in Quebec

October 1970   The kidnapping of British trade commissioner James Cross and kidnapping and assassination of Quebec cabinet minister Pierre Laporte. The federal government reacted by invoking the War Measures Act, under which normal civil liberties were suspended.

(Left) Montrealers take to Victoria Square on 24 May 1917 to protest compulsory service enacted by anglophone prime minister Sir Robert Borden in World War I. (Right) A man is arrested by two Montreal policemen during the 1955 riot over the suspension of Maurice Richard at the Montreal Forum.

led to riots involving the non-Aboriginal townspeople and members of the local Mohawk band of Kanesatake, the intervention of thousands of Canadian troops and even visits by United Nations observers.[19]

Fears of another Oka were raised in 1995 when small groups of Aboriginals occupied land that they claimed was sacred at Gustafsen Lake, British Columbia, and at Ipperwash Provincial Park in Ontario. Violence broke out in both cases and an Aboriginal was shot dead at Ipperwash. Since then a number of violent episodes, but no deaths, have occurred in New Brunswick, Ontario, and Quebec (see Box 2.2). Although the circumstances of each case were unique, they all had one element in common: resistance by Aboriginal Canadians against laws, policies, or property claims that violated what they maintained to be their distinct status and rights. In the standoff at Caledonia, Ontario, from 2006 to 2008, some spokespersons for the Six Nations Reserve stated bluntly that the rulings of Canadian courts do not apply to their people. Some non-Aboriginal Canadians agree.

Public Attitudes and Challenges to the Canadian Community

Disagreements and disputes both between French- and English-speaking Canadians and between Aboriginals and non-Aboriginals represent significant challenges to the notion of a single Canadian political community.

Égalité ou indépendance! ("Equality or independence!") is a familiar phrase to any contemporary Quebec-watcher. This slogan did not, however, originate with the Parti Québécois, but is the title of a booklet written by Daniel Johnson, leader of the Union Nationale and Premier of Quebec between 1966 and 1968. Even though neither Johnson nor the Union Nationale was committed to separatism, the phrase also served as his party's campaign slogan in the 1966 election. With the birth of the Parti Québécois in 1968, the province acquired a political party whose leader, René Lévesque, and platform were committed to taking Quebec out of Canada. Johnson's rhetoric and Lévesque's commitment represented and helped catalyze an important change in Quebec politics: the idea of Quebec independence. Before the mid 1960s independence was a marginal idea in the province's politics, supported by many Québécois intellectuals but not taken seriously by the main political parties or by the public. But since that time, independence has attracted the support of a sizable minority of Québécois.

Although its level has varied over time, there appears to be a durable core of support for the idea of Quebec independence. According to public opinion polls, it has ranged from a low of about 20 per cent to a high of nearly 60 per cent over the last few decades.[20] Support is always higher for **sovereignty-association**—a term generally understood to mean *a politically sovereign Quebec that would be linked to Canada through some sort of commercial union or free trade agreement*—than for outright political and economic separation. It is clear that many Québécois are conditional separatists, and that even among PQ supporters there has always been much less enthusiasm for complete separation than for separation with economic association.

When the PQ was first elected as government in 1976, it was clear that Quebec voters were not casting their ballots for separatism. The PQ was committed to holding a referendum on

Quebec independence, so non-separatists and soft separatists could vote for the party without fear that a PQ government would necessarily bring about Quebec independence. Indeed, a 1976 survey revealed that only about half of those intending to vote for the PQ actually favoured independence.[21] The PQ government held its promised referendum on sovereignty-association in 1980. When the PQ sought re-election in 1981, it ran on its governing record and promised not to hold another referendum during its next term. As in 1976, the PQ's 1981 victory could not be interpreted as a vote for separatism. Similarly, in 1998 the PQ won re-election after a campaign in which such issues as unemployment and health-care reform clearly overshadowed independence. At that time, Premier Lucien Bouchard felt constrained to admit that the 43 per cent of votes cast for the PQ, versus 44 per cent for the Quebec Liberal Party, could in no way be viewed as a mandate for independence or a referendum in the near term.

The first direct challenge to the Canadian political community came in the May 1980 referendum on sovereignty-association. The referendum question was very carefully—some would say trickily—worded. It stressed that the proposal was not a radical break from Canada but a negotiated political independence for Quebec that would maintain economic ties to Canada.

Despite the PQ's careful strategy, Quebec voters rejected the sovereignty-association option 59.6 per cent ("Non") to 40.4 per cent ("Oui"). Even a majority of francophones voted against Quebec independence.[22] Advocates of Quebec separatism noted that sovereignty-association was more popular among younger voters. Time, they argued, would turn the tide in favour of independence. Others argued that the greater popularity of the "Oui" option among those who entered adulthood in the nationalist 1960s and early 1970s—Quebec's "baby boomers"— reflected the exceptional politically formative experiences of this generation, and that subsequent generations, not raised in the intensely nationalist ferment that characterized the 1960s in Quebec, would find separatism less appealing.

It does not appear, however, that Quebec separation is less popular today among young francophone Québécois than it was among their counterparts in the 1960s and 1970s. On the contrary, support for separatism is stronger among younger cohorts of Quebec's francophone electorate than among other voters. Support for separatism is especially strong among young, highly educated Québécois, as it was in the 1960s. Separatists believe that support for independence will grow over time, as older cohorts of the electorate are replaced by younger, pro-independence ones. Skeptics note, however, that political preferences often change as one grows older and that there is no reason to assume that the younger generation's support for Quebec sovereignty will remain firm. This certainly seems to have been the case in the 2011 federal election, when support in Quebec shifted dramatically from the Bloc to the NDP. The NDP were offering a slate of much younger and inexperienced candidates. Only 2 of the 49 Bloc MPs were returned to Ottawa, while the NDP went from one Quebec seat in 2008 to an astounding 59 seats in 2011.

Accustomed to the challenge that Quebec separatism poses to the political community, many Canadians were surprised when the Oka crisis revealed another challenge to the idea of a single Canada. In fact, however, the armed confrontation at Oka discussed in the previous section had several precedents. Violent confrontations between Aboriginals and non-Aboriginals punctuate Canadian history, going back to before the extermination of the Aboriginal

Beothuk of Newfoundland in the 1700s (the last Beothuk died in 1829). Some major episodes of violence between Aboriginals and non-Aboriginals are described in Box 2.2, including the recent events described in the previous section.

These violent clashes are linked by a common thread: the struggle between the traditional independence of Aboriginal communities and the authority first of the European colonial authorities and then of the Canadian state. Aboriginal resistance to the rule of Canadian authorities and the authorities' efforts to establish their rule and crush Aboriginal resistance span over three centuries. But the struggle between Aboriginal aspirations and the authority of the majority community has only occasionally produced flashpoints of violence. Long periods of apparent peace have been more characteristic of Aboriginal–non-Aboriginal relations. We say "apparent peace," because even during these periods the conflict between the aspirations

CANADIAN SPOTLIGHT

BOX 2.2 Timeline: Major Violent Confrontations between Aboriginals and Non-Aboriginals and/or Political Authorities

1700s Many Beothuk Aboriginals were killed by European settlers to Newfoundland.

1763 Led by Odawa war chief Pontiac, a confederation of tribes (Seneca, Ojibwa, and other tribes in the Detroit area) rebelled against British rule in several bloody confrontations.

circa **1794** Shawnee and other tribes in the Ohio River Valley, led by war chief Tecumseh, attempted unsuccessfully to resist non-Aboriginal settlement.

1869–70 In the Red River Rebellion, Manitoban Métis fought for provincial status and guaranteed land and cultural rights.

1885 In the Northwest Rebellions, a series of battles took place between Métis and First Nations forces on one side and non-Aboriginal militia volunteers and soldiers on the other.

1990 An armed confrontation at Oka, Quebec resulted in the death of a police officer and riots against Aboriginals protesting the expansion of a golf course on land that Mohawks claimed was theirs by historical right.

1995 Armed confrontations took place at Gustafsen Lake, British Columbia, and Ipperwash Provincial Park in Ontario. In both cases a small group of Aboriginals (Shuswap in BC and Chippewa in Ontario) occupied land they claimed was sacred. An Aboriginal protester was killed at Ipperwash.

2000 Conflict between Aboriginal Mi'kmaq and non-Aboriginals erupted at Burnt Church, New Brunswick, over fishing rights.

2004 Anti-police riots took place when 67 Aboriginal officers of Kanesatake, Quebec, who were authorized by the local band council and financed by the federal government, were trapped in the police station for three days by armed protesters from the local Mohawk community.

of many Aboriginal communities and the demands and restrictions imposed by the Canadian state was alive but dormant, waiting for the catalyst of some issue or incident. The confrontation at Oka turned out to be such an incident, galvanizing Aboriginal groups and throwing into sharp relief the issues of Aboriginal land claims and demands for self-government.

The land-claims issue is essentially about who has the right to control territory to which various Aboriginal communities claim a historical right. Treaties signed by British authorities prior to Confederation and by Ottawa after Confederation—which were intended to extinguish Aboriginal claims to these territories in exchange for reserves, money, and other benefits—do not cover all of Canada. In fact, enormous areas encompassing much of the North and both the western and eastern extremities of the country were not covered by treaties. Moreover, about 40 per cent of status Indians[23] are members of bands that have not signed

2006–8 At Caledonia in Southern Ontario, police arrested 16 Aboriginal protesters who claimed that land being developed for houses rightfully belonged to them, dating back to the Haldimand Grant of 1784, although an Ontario court had ruled otherwise. Other protesters responded to the arrests by setting fires and blockading a major highway.

(Left) In a now-famous image, Canadian soldier Patrick Cloutier and Saskatchewan Aboriginal Brad Larocque come face to face in the tense standoff at the Kanesatake Reserve in Oka, Quebec on 1 September 1990. (Right) Aboriginal protesters stand their ground on a blockade erected near Caledonia, Ontario on 22 May 2006.

treaties with Ottawa. Having never been vanquished militarily or given up their territorial rights through a treaty, they claim that the land their ancestors inhabited still belongs to them.

Until the Oka confrontation, land-claims negotiations progressed at a snail's pace, leading most Aboriginal groups to conclude that Ottawa was not serious about settling these claims, many of which related to government misuse and misappropriation of lands that had been reserved for Aboriginal groups who had signed historic treaties. The Mohawk warrior claim to be a sovereign nation outside the authority of Canadian law was more extreme than most Aboriginal demands for self-government, and this claim was steadfastly rejected by the federal government and most Canadians. "Native self-government," Progressive Conservative Prime Minister Brian Mulroney declared "does not now and cannot ever mean sovereign independence. Mohawk lands are part of Canadian territory, and Canadian law must and does apply."[24] A few years later, Liberal Prime Minister Jean Chrétien also rejected the claims of some Aboriginals that they stand outside the authority of Canadian law.

Recent land-claim settlements that include structures for Aboriginal self-government, notably the creation of Nunavut in the eastern Arctic and the Nisga'a Treaty in British Columbia, state explicitly that laws of general application continue to apply to those who inhabit these Aboriginal lands and that the Charter of Rights and Freedoms applies to their governments. Nevertheless, a sort of de facto acceptance of separate communities, defined by their Aboriginal ethnicity and heritage, now exists within Canada.

Freedom

Individual freedom is said to be central to the American political creed, symbolized in such icons as the Declaration of Independence, the Bill of Rights, and the Statue of Liberty. Canadians, it is usually claimed, are more willing than Americans to limit individual freedom in pursuit of social order or group rights. Is this true?

The greater stress on individual freedom and suspicion of government control in the United States compared to Canada is corroborated by many types of evidence. One of these is literature. Writers like Henry David Thoreau, Jack Kerouac, and Allen Ginsberg embody a powerfully individualistic current that runs through American literature. There is no Canadian equivalent to Thoreau, whose writings about civil disobedience and the need to resist the demands of society as the price to be paid for a life of virtue and freedom have significantly influenced the libertarian tradition in American politics. Individualism and freedom are also powerful themes in American popular culture. Hollywood's portrayal of the "loner," whose virtue and appeal lie in indifference to laws and social conventions, has long been one of the most successful and popular film genres. Clint Eastwood, Harrison Ford, Bruce Willis, and Denzel Washington are among those actors whose film characters embody this against-the-grain individualism.

Americans' passionate love affair with freedom is evident in the very different character of the gun control debate in Canada and in the United States, as was depicted with considerable irony in Michael Moore's Academy Award–winning documentary *Bowling for Columbine*

(2002). When Liberals proposed tougher restrictions on gun ownership and a national registry for all firearms in 1993, opposition in Canada focused on such matters as whether the legislation would really reduce the use of guns in committing crimes and whether the legislation reflected urban Canada's insensitivity and even hostility to the values and lifestyles of hunters and rural communities. Even during the 2010 debate over the Conservative government's proposal to dismantle it, few Canadians have argued that a fundamental freedom was jeopardized by a long-gun registry.

In the United States, however, proposals to restrict the sale and ownership of firearms invariably face objections from those who see these restrictions threatening individual freedom. These objections are not merely the cynical ravings of National Rifle Association devotees and of white supremacists who wrap themselves in the guarantee of the Bill of Rights' Second Amendment of the "right to bear arms." Many Americans believe gun ownership is a right, not a privilege. One sometimes hears the argument that restrictions on gun ownership would leave citizens helpless to defend themselves, not simply against criminals but against the state! This argument would be met with blank stares of incomprehension in Canada. Americans are more likely than Canadians to believe that gun ownership is part of their right to protect themselves and their property instead of relying on the state to do this for them.

Mistrust of the state is as old as the American War of Independence. It is woven into the American Constitution's systems of political checks and balances; it was behind the adoption of a Bill of Rights, which amended the Constitution; and it was also part of the case for federalism, which, as James Madison argued in the famous *Federalist Papers*, no. 51, would help prevent the emergence of any political majority large enough to threaten individual and minority rights. In the US political culture, Americans' pride in their system of government and patriotism exceeding that of most other democracies have coexisted with a mistrust of government rooted in both the revolutionary experience and in the individualistic spirit. Thus, many Americans—and not just those who participate in the civilian militias that are a distinctly American phenomenon—understand the argument that government may be the problem and the enemy, and that citizens have a right to defend themselves without relying on government.

In Canada, where the state is viewed as more benign, Canadians are less likely to share these views. As Seymour Martin Lipset observes, "If [Canada] leans towards **communitarianism—** ***the public mobilization of resources to fulfill group objectives***—the [United States] sees individualism—private endeavour—as the way an 'unseen hand' produces optimum, socially beneficial results [emphasis added for definition]."[25] Canadian writer Pierre Berton makes the same point in maintaining that "We've always accepted more governmental control over our lives than . . . [Americans] have—and fewer civil liberties."[26]

Statistical data measuring people's attitudes can also help us comment on or generalize about the value attached to freedom in each society. When asked in a 1980 survey to choose between the protection of individual liberty and the defence of social order, Americans consistently gave more freedom-oriented responses than Canadians.[27] This pattern has persisted. The 1991 World Values Survey found that Americans were considerably more likely than

Canadians to say that they would opt for liberty over equality (75 per cent versus 61 per cent). Unfortunately, this question was not asked of Americans and Canadians in the 2001 surveys.

Americans' greater stress on individual freedom is often credited to their individualist culture. Canadians, on the other hand, are frequently portrayed as less assertive about their rights as individuals and more concerned than Americans with social order. Attitudinal data provide some support for these claims. Some people object to these characterizations on the grounds that Americans' understanding of "freedom" as "the absence of restraint on individual behaviour"—what is sometimes called "negative freedom"—actually denies real freedom to many people. Canadians' greater willingness to permit government restrictions on individual behaviour means not that they value freedom less, but that they are more likely than Americans to believe that real freedom often requires that government interfere with individual property rights and economic markets. Moreover, Canadians tend to believe that governments should guarantee access to such things as public education and universal health care to help equalize the opportunities available to both the well off and the less privileged. Canadians, some argue, have what might be characterized as a positive conception of freedom, one that requires that government act rather than get out of the way.

The somewhat weaker attachment of Canadians to what might be characterized as an individualistic notion of freedom is corroborated by the words and symbols that political parties use to win support. If we think of these words and symbols as a sort of connective tissue between citizens and those who wish to represent them, it is clear that the key to electoral success lies in using ideas, images, words, and symbols that resonate positively with many voters. A study of the campaign rhetoric used by parties and party leaders during each country's elections in 2000 found that the core values and unifying themes expressed in the George W. Bush/

Democracy Watch

BOX 2.3 The Meaning of Freedom

I am a Canadian, free to speak without fear, free to worship in my own way, free to stand for what I think right, free to oppose what I believe wrong, or free to choose those who shall govern my country. This heritage of freedom I pledge to uphold for myself and all mankind.

—*John Diefenbaker, when introducing the Canadian Bill of Rights in Parliament, 1 July 1960*

Up for Debate

Would you characterize the freedoms outlined in the Canadian Bill of Rights (a precursor to the Charter of Rights and Freedoms) as the same as the freedoms enjoyed and protected by Americans? How might the freedoms enjoyed by citizens of Canada and United States be different?

Republican Party message were clearly more individualistic than those of any national leader and party in Canada.[28] From this example, and from the attitudinal data and other evidence about cultural values, one gets the sense that the defence of individual freedom can be a harder sell in Canada than in the United States.

In the wake of the terrorist attacks of 11 September 2001, the American and Canadian governments both passed laws that placed greater restrictions on individual rights and freedoms. Public opinion surveys showed that Canadians were considerably less likely than Americans to believe that such restrictions were necessary, but at the same time polls showed that Canadians and Americans almost equally accepted security measures that involved some loss of privacy safeguards.[29] The post-9/11 spike in American support for measures that appeared to purchase security at the cost of reduced freedoms and rights for some has dissipated over time. Moreover, opposition to limitations on freedoms and rights existed in the United States from the moment the Patriot Act was passed in 2001; this opposition gained strength and won victories in both Congress and the courts as time went on. Although it is arguable that 9/11 produced a short-term gap between Canadian and American attitudes toward the security/freedom trade-off, it is not certain that the core beliefs of Americans became less freedom-oriented as a result of these terrorist attacks.

Equality

If the Loyalists had left a Tory imprint on Canadian politics, we would expect to find that Canadians place a lower value on equality than do Americans. Tories, after all, believed that the organization of society along class lines was a natural and desirable state of affairs. They were apt to sneer at American democracy as "mobocracy." A long line of sociologists, political scientists, and historians, going back to Alexis de Tocqueville and other Europeans who visited North America in the nineteenth century, have generally agreed that America's political culture is more egalitarian and Canada's more hierarchical.

Whether or not this characterization was ever accurate, it is no longer obviously true. As Neil Nevitte showed in *The Decline of Deference* (1996), Canadians appear to value equality more than do Americans. They are much more likely to support public policies, such as a publicly funded health-care system and a guaranteed minimum income, that are intended to narrow the gap between the poor and the well off. A comparative study of the development of the welfare state in Canada and the United States corroborates this difference. Robert Kudrle and Theodore Marmor argue that ideological differences between the two societies are the main reasons for the earlier enactment and more generous character of welfare-state policies in Canada, observing that "in every policy area it appears that general public as well as elite opinion . . . [has been] more supportive of state action in Canada than in the United States."[30] At the same time, some observers caution that too much is often attributed to cultural differences in explaining differences between social policies in these countries. Gerard Boychuk argues that the significance of race politics in the United States and of territorial politics in Canada better explains the difference in the health policies of the two countries than does political culture.[31]

Canadians are more likely than Americans to value equality of results, whereas Americans are more likely than their northern neighbours to value equality of opportunity. Numerous cross-national attitudinal surveys confirm this observation.[32] In Canada, egalitarianism has its roots in a more collectivist tradition; in the United States it draws on a more individualistic tradition. This seems to be the conclusion of Michael Ignatieff, a former journalist and academic, and then leader of the Liberal Party of Canada, when he writes

> I like market society because I like its freedoms and freedom is a very chilly thing. It doesn't give you a metaphysics. It doesn't give you a community. But it gives you freedom. And then you have to decide which of these values in life you want. . . America and Canada are both free nations. But our freedom is different: There is no right to bear arms north of the 49th parallel, and no capital punishment either; we believe in collective rights to language and land, and in our rights and culture; these can trump individual rights. Not so south of the border. Rights that are still being fought over south of the border—public health for example—have been ours for generations.[33]

The value differences between the two societies are not starkly contrasting. Nevertheless, they help to explain Canadians' apparently greater tolerance—at least historically—for state measures targeted at disadvantaged groups and regions. Lipset's conclusion seems a fair one: "Canadians are committed to redistribution egalitarianism, while Americans place more emphasis on meritocratic competition and equality of opportunity."[34]

This difference between the two societies, however, should not be pushed too far. If Americans care more about equality of opportunity and Canadians about equality of condition, then we would expect to find greater acceptance of economic inequalities among Americans. But the evidence is unclear. Although the average CEO-to-worker earnings ratio is about twice as great in the United States as in Canada—44 to 1 compared to 21 to 1 in the manufacturing sector, as of 2001[35]—Canadians and Americans are almost identical in their beliefs about what would constitute a "fair" ration of maximum-to-minimum earnings: respondents from both countries say that it should be about 10 to 1.[36]

In Canada, more than in the United States, debates over equality historically have been about group rights and equality between different groups in society, not about equality between individuals. This difference goes back to the founding of the two societies. While the American Constitution made no distinction between groups of citizens, the Quebec Act of 1774 incorporated protection for religious rights, and the British North America Act of 1867 provided protections for both religious and language rights.

A by-product of Canada's long tradition of recognizing group rights, many have argued, is greater tolerance of *cultural diversity* than one finds in the United States. This is the familiar, if exaggerated, theme of the Canadian "mosaic" versus the American "melting pot." Although there is considerable historical evidence to suggest that non-French, non-British groups have felt less pressure to abandon their language and customs in Canada than have non-English-speaking groups in the United States, rates of cultural assimilation have been high in both societies. Moreover, Canadian governments have shown themselves to be as capable as their American counterparts of discriminating against ethnic and religious communities. For example, in both countries many people of Japanese origin were deprived of their property and confined to camps during World War II. The religious practices of Doukhobors, Hutterites, Mennonites, and Jehovah's Witnesses have at various times brought them into conflict with either Ottawa or provincial governments. And in both Canada and the United States immigration policy has historically discriminated against non-white, non-European peoples— although this is no longer a fair characterization of policy in either country.

Despite evidence that also in Canada tolerance of cultural diversity has known limits, these limits have been less restrictive than in the United States. The treatment of Canada's Aboriginal peoples, for example, has been less harsh and less violent than that of America's Aboriginal minorities. And there is nothing in Canada's history that compares to the official discrimination and the physical violence directed against American blacks for much of that country's history. An official policy of multiculturalism has existed in Canada since 1971 and was entrenched in the Constitution in 1982.[37] **Multiculturalism** is *the idea that cultural diversity is not only good for society, it should also be encouraged*. Moreover, Canada's Constitution appears to provide a firmer basis for affirmative action programs and other state activities that have as their goal "the amelioration of conditions of disadvantaged individuals

(Left) BC Doukhobors commemorate the anniversary of leader Peter "Lordly" Verigin's death on 29 October 1927. Verigin and his people clashed with the government over their aversion to private ownership of land, which led the Crown to reclaim more than a third of Doukhobor land in 1907. (Right) Japanese Canadians arrive at an internment camp in BC's interior in 1942. In the wake of the Japanese attack on Pearl Harbor in the United States, the Canadian government speculated that Japanese living in Canada were engaged in espionage and confined them to segregated camps and sold off their possessions and assets at auction.

or groups including those that are disadvantaged because of race, national or ethnic origin, colour, religion, sex, age or mental or physical disability."[38]

The thesis of the Canadian mosaic versus the American melting pot should not be pushed too hard. Despite the fact that cultural assimilation seems historically to have been part of the American ethos, a combination of government policies and court decisions in that country has steered it away from the melting pot and toward a mosaic society. An extensive system of Spanish-language schools has been created in parts of the United States, particularly California, over the last two decades. Affirmative action policies such as university admission quotas and redrawing congressional boundary lines to maximize the proportion of minority voters began earlier and arguably have been taken further in the United States. Universities and other schools in the United States also pioneered the concept and practice of minority-oriented curricula (African-American studies, for example), and this dimension of cultural pluralism is well established there, even while some other aspects of multicultural policy appear to be under assault. Indeed, the very intensity of controversy over multiculturalism, affirmative action, and ascription-based policies in the United States is to some degree a reflection and a testament of just how successful the mosaic model has been in influencing American society.

At the same time, the idea of multiculturalism and the programs and structures that seek to implement the mosaic model have tended to go unchallenged in Canada. Neil Bissoondath's best-selling book *Selling Illusions: The Cult of Multiculturalism in Canada*[39] and Reginald Bibby's *Mosaic Madness: The Poverty and Potential of Life in Canada*[40] are two of the salvoes launched against official multiculturalism (as opposed to tolerance of diversity and pluralism that are not sponsored and reinforced by the state).

In view of how deeply the distinction between the Canadian mosaic and the American melting pot is embedded in the collective Canadian psyche, it may be surprising that there has been little effort to test empirically this article of faith. But this is not so surprising if we consider that articles of faith are assumed to be self-evident. Moreover, Canadians may see something sacrilegious in questioning a belief central to their ideas of what distinguishes their society from that of the United States.

In *The Illusion of Difference*, Jeffrey Reitz and Raymond Breton risk this sacrilege by testing the proposition that Canadians are more tolerant of diversity than their allegedly more assimilationist neighbours to the south. They review existing studies of the mosaic versus melting pot thesis and examine a number of comparative surveys and census data from the two countries. They conclude that the differences between Canada and the United States are "more apparent than real." The Canadian style, they argue, "is more low-key than the American; moreover, Canadians have a conscious tradition of 'tolerance' that Americans do not have." These differences in the way multiculturalism and ethnic diversity have been thought of in the two societies "have not produced less pressure towards conformity in Canada, or less propensity to discriminate in employment or housing."[41] Comparing rates of language retention, ethnic group identification, participation in ethnically based social networks, and attitudes and behaviour toward racial minorities, Breton and Reitz conclude that there is almost no empirical basis for Canadians' cherished self-image of their society as being more tolerant and less assimilationist than that of the United States.

Perhaps in response to the public's growing sense that cultural mosaic policies have contributed to national disunity, in late 1998 the federal government proposed changes to the Immigration Act that would require prospective immigrants to Canada, other than those in the family and refugee classes, to speak either French or English. This proposal was criticized for discriminating against prospective immigrants from countries—mainly less developed ones—where the likelihood of knowing either English or French is relatively low.

Gender equality is another dimension of group rights that has acquired prominence in recent decades. In both Canada and the United States attitudes concerning the appropriate roles and behaviour of men and women have changed sharply in the direction of greater equality. The visible signs of this change are everywhere, including laws on pay equity, easier access to abortion, affirmative action to increase the number of women employed in male-dominated professions, more positive portrayal of females in the media, and greater female participation in politics. While these are all indirect measures of attitudes toward gender equality, we might reasonably infer from the actions of governments and private organizations that these values do exist. Comparing Canada to the United States using such measures, we come up with a mixed scorecard. The differences between the two societies tend not to be very large, Canada being "more equal" on some counts, and the United States on others. The percentage of female elected officials in each country's legislature is not very different: in 2009, 22.4 per cent of Members of Parliament in Canada were female, compared to 17.2 per cent of those in the United States' House of Representatives. According to the data collected by the World Values Survey, public opinion is almost identical in the two countries regarding relations between the sexes and the roles appropriate to each.

As with other dimensions of equality, there is no evidence to support the claim that Canadians value equality less than Americans do. Indeed, in terms of recognizing group rights, it is fair to say that Canadian governments have gone at least as far as their American counterparts. In one important respect, however, Canadians are unequivocally more committed to an egalitarian society: racial equality. The World Values Survey 2000 suggests that racist sentiments are somewhat more pervasive in the United States than in Canada. Although it is tempting to infer from the statistics on such matters as racial segregation, income differences associated with race, and crime and sentencing data that Americans tend to be more racist than Canadians, such an inference may not be warranted. For example, should one infer from the election of a black American as president in 2008, while no black has ever been the leader of a Canadian political party, that Americans are more tolerant of racial difference? Or does the fact that a much higher percentage of blacks hold public office or are CEOs of the largest companies in the United States than in Canada, suggest that the United States is the more racially tolerant society? The answer, most would agree, is no. The enormous differences in the historical circumstances shaping race relations in the two societies and the much greater relative size of the black population in the United States are reasons to be wary of drawing such conclusions. And these two factors ensure that race and racism are far more central to American than to Canadian political life.

Before we jump to conclusions about current attitudes toward race in both societies, we should keep in mind that the average incomes of black Canadians are about 80 per cent of those for white Canadians, roughly the same as in the United States, and that the likelihood of blacks and whites intermarrying is about the same (5 per cent) in both societies. As well, if our focus is the degree of racial and ethnic tolerance in majority populations (and these "majorities" are dwindling), we also would need to examine other groups—South Asians, Aboriginal peoples, Chinese, Hispanics, etc.—using numerous demographic variables.

Canadians' Expectations of the State

It is often argued that Canadians are more likely than Americans to look to government to meet their needs. They are also more likely to accept, rather than mobilize against, government actions they dislike. Thomas Jefferson's declaration, "That government is best which governs least," has an oddly foreign tone to Canadians. The mistrust of government and implicit celebration of individualism that inspired Jefferson's aphorism are not sentiments that have resonated in Canada the way they have throughout American history.

This view of Canadians as more demanding of the state and more passive toward it appears to be well founded. On the expectations side, Canadian governments do more than American ones to redistribute wealth between individuals and regions of the country. They have resisted the expansion of a private presence in health care and post-secondary education. They own corporations whose activities range from electricity generation to television broadcasting, while American governments have generally been content to regulate privately owned businesses in these same industries. And they are much more actively involved in promoting particular cultural values, especially those associated with bilingualism and multiculturalism, than are most governments in the United States. In Canada, the state accounts for a larger share of gross national expenditure than in the United States—and spends more on redistributive social programs and also takes a larger share of citizens' incomes in taxes. Overall, government appears to be more intrusive in Canadian society.

What about the evidence for Canadians' alleged deference to authority and passivity in the face of government actions that they dislike? It was once fairly common to hear Canadian political experts intone that "freedom wears a crown," meaning that the more orderly society and the stability that Canadians experienced through this country's parliamentary system and titular monarchy, compared to the rather chaotic "mobocracy" to the south, provided a sort of protective mantle under which citizens were better able to enjoy their democratic rights and freedoms. "We've always accepted more governmental control over our lives than . . . [Americans] have—and fewer civil liberties," argued Pierre Berton, Canada's foremost popular historian. But, he added, "the other side of the coin of liberty is license, sometimes anarchy. It seems to us that . . . Americans have been more willing to suffer violence in . . . [their] lives than we have for the sake of individual freedom."[42]

Canadians' apparent greater faith in government, compared to the more skeptical attitudes of Americans, owes a good deal to a collectivist ethos that sets Canadians and their history apart from the United States. It is this ethos that Canadian nationalists are invoking when they argue that Canada's public health-care system and more generous social programs reflect the "soul" of this country, and that their dismemberment would send Canadians down the allegedly mean-spirited path of American individualism. Some of Canada's most prominent

INSIDE POLITICS

BOX 2.4 | What Architecture Says about a Nation's Politics

Canadians' preference for *neo-gothic* rather than *Greco-roman* architecture in their government buildings may also reflect a preference for the ideas of *conservatism* such as tradition and social order over *liberalism* and the ideas of individualism and democratic values. The columns found in the Greco-Roman architecture of many American political buildings suggests a reliance of the society and of the state on individuals, whereas the keystones and arch architecture found in Canada's Parliament buildings suggests a reliance on institutions such as the monarchy in maintaining the integrity of the state.

(Top left) United States Capitol Building. (Top right) United States National Archives, column detail. (Bottom left) Doorway to the Canadian Parliamentary Library. (Bottom right) Hallway in the interior of the Canadian Parliament buildings.

thinkers, including George Grant and Charles Taylor, have argued that the collectivist ethos and greater willingness to use the state to achieve community goals are central to the Canadian political tradition.

In *Lament for a Nation*, Grant argues that the Canadian political tradition is marked by a communitarian spirit that rejects the individualism of American-style liberalism. He traces the roots of this spirit to the influence of conservative ideas and the British connection, which helped to keep alive a benign view of government as an agent for pursuing the common good. This distinctive national character is, Grant believes, doomed to be crushed by the steamroller of American liberalism and technology, which, he maintains in later works, would ultimately flatten national cultures throughout the capitalist world.

Grant's "lament" is in the key of what has been called **red Toryism**. Red Tories are *conservatives who believe that government has a responsibility to act as an agent for the collective good, and that this responsibility goes far beyond maintaining law and order.* Grant and others in this tradition favour state support for culture through the Canadian Broadcasting Corporation. They are comfortable with the welfare state and the principle that government should protect the poor and disadvantaged. Critics claim that Red Toryism is a rather paternalistic philosophy of state–citizen relations. Defenders, however, maintain that it is compassionate and a true expression of a collectivist national ethos that distinguishes Canadians from their southern neighbours.

Charles Taylor is not a red Tory. Canada's most internationally acclaimed living philosopher is firmly on the left of the political spectrum. He agrees with Grant about the importance of collectivism in Canada's political tradition. Taylor has always been extremely critical of what he calls the "atomism" of American liberalism, a value system that he believes cuts people off from the communal relations that nurture human dignity. Like most Canadian nationalists, he believes implicitly in the moral superiority of Canada's collectivist political tradition. Taylor is one of the leading thinkers in the contemporary movement known as **communitarianism**, which is based on *the belief that real human freedom and dignity are possible only in the context of communal relations that allow for the public recognition of group identities and that are based on equal respect for these different identity-groups.* Taylor argues that the key to Canadian unity lies in finding constitutional arrangements that enable different groups of Canadians to feel that they belong to Canada and are recognized as constituent elements of Canadian society. "Nations . . . which have a strong sense of their own identity," says Taylor, "and hence a desire to direct in some ways their common affairs, can only be induced to take part willingly in multinational states if they are in some ways recognized within them."[43] He calls this the recognition of "deep diversity." The realization of deep diversity would require, at a minimum, official recognition of Quebec as a distinct society and probably constitutional acknowledgement of an Aboriginal right to self-government. To some this might sound like a recipe for dismantling whatever fragile sense of Canadian community already exists. Taylor insists, however, that one-size-fits-all notions of community do not work in the modern world.

Deference and Changing Canadian Values

The characterization of Canadians as more deferential and less likely to question authority than Americans has been challenged in recent years. In *The Canadian Revolution*, Peter C.

Newman argues that the historically elitist tenor of Canadian life collapsed between 1985 and 1995 under the pressure of developments in Canada and in the world at large. Newman speaks of the rise of a "new populism" and of what he calls the "breakdown of trust between the governors and the governed."[44] The growth of the underground cash economy in reaction to the GST, the breakdown of the old two-party dominance in the 1993 election, Canadian citizens' rejection of the elite-supported Charlottetown Accord, the violent clash between Aboriginals and non-Aboriginal authorities at Oka in 1990, and the near-victory of Quebec separatists in 1995 are, Newman argues, indications of Canadians' passage from deference to defiance. He attributes this transition to a constellation of factors that includes the arrogance of politicians, the more competitive global economy, the inability of Canadian government to continue financing the system of entitlements that Canadians came to take for granted in the 1960s and 1970s, and the decline in religious faith, among other things.

A more quantitative treatment of the same phenomenon is offered by Neil Nevitte in *The Decline of Deference*.[45] Nevitte agrees that Canadians are less deferential today than in the past. He attributes this change to the post-materialist values of those born following World War II. **Post-materialism** is *an ideology that attaches comparatively greater importance to human needs for belonging, self-esteem, and personal fulfillment* than does **materialism**, which *places greater stress on economic security and material well-being.* Such issues as employment and incomes matter most to materialists, whereas post-materialists are likely to place higher value on so-called quality-of-life issues such as the environment, human rights, and group equality. Materialists are less likely than post-materialists to have confidence in public institutions and to trust in the judgments of elites.

CANADIAN SPOTLIGHT

BOX 2.5 Changing Canadian Values

Canadian "baby boomers'" values were influenced by historical events such as

- World War I
- The Great Depression
- World War II

Recent generations of Canadians have had their values shaped by

- The bombing of the World Trade Center on 11 September 2001
- Global warming
- Self-actualization and better education
- Globalization

The "new Left" in Canada is less concerned with traditional moral standards (for example, it is in favour of same-sex marriage) and more concerned with tolerance and the environment. There is less attachment to hierarchies and traditional parties, and, as a result, Canadians are considered by some to be more "difficult to govern."

Source: Neil Nevitte, *The Decline of Deference* (1996), discussed in Robert J. Jackson and Doreen Jackson, *Politics in Canada*, 7th edn (Toronto: Pearson Education Canada, 2009), 67.

Nevitte shows that Canadians' confidence in government institutions, including the armed forces, police, Parliament, and public service, declined during the 1980s, and that high levels of confidence are much less likely to be expressed by those between the ages of 25 and 54 than by older citizens. He also finds that Canadians are, if anything, slightly more skeptical of government institutions than are Americans—not the traditional stereotype of deferential Canadians and defiant Americans one would expect to find.

We should not be too quick to conclude, however, that the old characterization of Canadians as more deferential of authority and trusting of government than Americans is no longer accurate. What Nevitte and others call post-materialism may be more pervasive in Canada than in the United States. But data from the 2000 World Values Survey show that only with respect to the armed forces do Americans express much more confidence than Canadians. Levels of confidence in the police, Parliament/Congress, the public service, and government are about the same in the two countries. This example suggests that perhaps we should be cautious in our interpretation and the significance of data collected at a single point in time.

These attitudes are also evident when we examine another way of measuring deference, which involves looking at peoples' defiant actions toward authority. When Canadians and Americans are asked whether they have attended or might attend a lawful demonstration, join an unofficial strike, or occupy a building or factory, Canadians are somewhat less likely to answer "yes." The differences between the two populations are small—and have decreased from 10 years earlier—but this piece of evidence does not support the claim by some that Canadians, emboldened by the experience of life under the Charter, have become less deferential than Americans.

Canadians and the Notion of Social Capital

Citizens' expectations of government can also be examined by looking at **social capital—*the fabric of connections between members of a community*.** Social capital is made up both of norms, such as trust in one's neighbours, and of behaviours, such as voting and participating in community organizations. The roots of this concept can be found in Alexis de Tocqueville's observations on the propensity of mid-nineteenth-century Americans to join voluntary associations in order to achieve communal goals. Tocqueville believed that these voluntary associations were the connective tissue of American democracy. They reminded citizens that they belonged to a community and depended on one another.

Many commentators on American society argue that social capital in that country has been in serious decline for years. While the evidence for this claim is not rock solid, it is clear that Americans continue to be more likely than the citizens of Canada and other rich democracies to belong to and participate in voluntary associations such as religious, youth, sports and recreation, educational, and cultural groups.[46] These are activities that in Canada are more likely to be publicly funded and the responsibility of state agencies. One might conclude here that Americans are more likely than Canadians to believe that private citizens and the voluntary associations they create—not the state—should be responsible for meeting many of society's needs.

Canadians and Religious Values

Some significant part of the civic and communal engagement of Americans is due to the far greater strength of traditional religious values in the United States compared to Canada. Canada is, quite simply, a more secular society than the United States, though not nearly as secular as some Western European democracies. **Secularization** involves *a decline in the belief that religion and religious authorities should be looked to for guidance about behaviour and an increase in the social, cultural, and political influence of elites whose expertise is not based on religious faith*.

For most of their respective histories, Canada and especially French-speaking Canada were generally considered more traditionally religious than the United States. Religious elites certainly appeared to have more influence in Canada, at least until the 1960s. Since then, the process of secularization has advanced more rapidly in Canada and other Western democracies than in the United States. A number of measures have shown that Americans tend to be more traditionally religious than Canadians.

The more secular character of Canada's political culture helps to explain why issues with moral dimensions, such as abortion and embryonic stem cell research, are more controversial in the United States, and why Canadian legislation recognizing same-sex marriage was passed in 2005, while this particular battle still rages on in the United States. The more secular nature of Canadian culture also helps to explain why Canadian politicians, unlike their American counterparts, infrequently invoke religious references or even mention God in their public statements. Being perceived as too religious can even be a liability in Canadian politics, as Canadian Alliance leader Stockwell Day discovered in the 2000 federal election when his born-again Christianity made him a target of sniping by the media and rival parties.

HOW DIFFERENT ARE CANADIAN AND AMERICAN VALUES?

Observing English Canada and the United States about 100 years ago, the French sociologist André Siegfried argued that the differences between them were relatively small and certainly insignificant by European standards. Siegfried was one of the first to weigh in on a question that has been at the centre of the comparative study of political culture in Canada and the United States: Which are politically more significant, the similarities or the differences in the values and beliefs of these two societies?

One hundred years after Siegfried, Michael Adams[47] and Philip Resnick[48] are among those who argue that these value differences are significant and growing. Adams goes so far as to conclude that Canada and the United States are fundamentally different and maintains that this has always been the case. Resnick is more cautious. He acknowledges the undeniable similarity between Canadian and American culture but argues that, in many important ways, Canadians have more in common with Western Europeans, such as the French, than they do with Americans. Moreover, Resnick believes that this affinity with Europeans and the gap between Canadians and Americans have been growing in recent years.

A. God is very important in my life. (percentage agreeing)

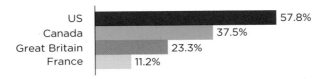

US   57.8%
Canada   37.5%
Great Britain 23.3%
France   11.2%

B. I do unpaid voluntary work for a religious or church organization. (percentage agreeing)

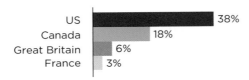

US   38%
Canada   18%
Great Britain 6%
France   3%

C. I agree that marriage is an outdated institution. (percentage agreeing)

US   10%
Canada   22%
Great Britain 26%
France   36%

D. It would be better for the country if more people with strong religious beliefs held public office. (percentage disagreeing)

US   25%
Canada   50%
Great Britain 54%
France   68%

E. There are absolutely clear guidelines about what is good and evil. (percentage agreeing)

US   49%
Canada   42%
Great Britain 42%
France   25%

F. I believe in sin. (percentage agreeing)

US   89%
Canada   74%
Great Britain 72%
France   43%

FIGURE 2.5 STRENGTH OF TRADITIONAL RELIGIOUS VALUES: CANADA, UNITED STATES, FRANCE, AND GREAT BRITAIN, 2000

Sources: World Values Survey, 2000 (B–F) and 2006 (A)

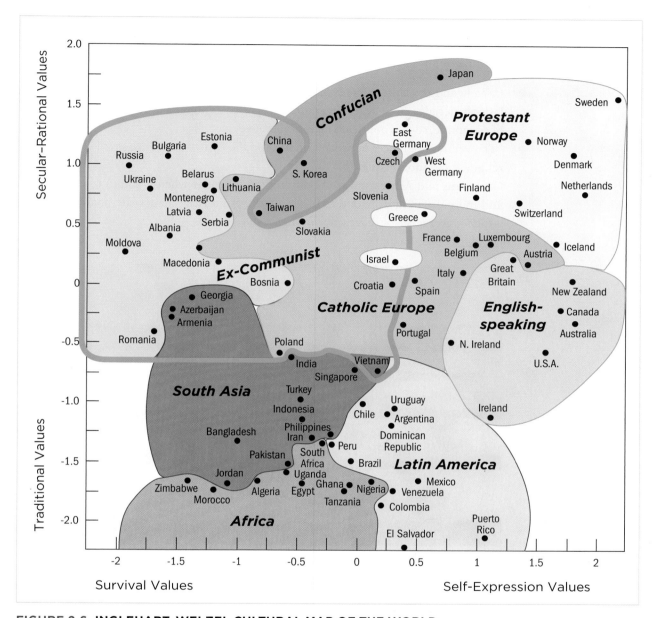

FIGURE 2.6 INGLEHART-WELZEL CULTURAL MAP OF THE WORLD

This map shows that many basic values are closely correlated. The scale on the vertical axis represents a continuum from traditional to secular values; the horizontal scale, ranging from survival values to self-expression values, reflects the fact that increasing wealth in many societies since the 1960s has meant that, as Ronald Inglehart puts it, "priorities have shifted from an overwhelming emphasis on economic and physical security toward . . . subjective well-being, self-expression and quality of life."

Source: Adapted from World Values Survey, 2000.

Drawing on data from the three rounds of the World Values Survey (1981, 1990, and 2000), Christian Boucher tests Adams's and Resnick's hypotheses. Boucher arrives at the following conclusions:

- Canada and the United States have each undergone substantial value change over the last two decades, both becoming more "progressive and secular regarding some aspects of economic, social, political and moral issues."
- "The values differences between Canada and the United States are small . . . except for religious and moral issues."[49]
- Canadians and Americans are becoming more similar when it comes to some values and more different in regard to others. There is no clear, across-the-board pattern of either convergence or divergence in their value systems.

The "Canadian Keyboard" identifies a few stereotypes that Canadians use to differentiate themselves from Americans.

TABLE 2.2 | AMERICAN VERSUS CANADIAN NATIONALISM

American "Flags and Fears" Nationalism	Canadian "Hopes and Holidays" Nationalism
• Thrill and terror	• Shared civic ideas and values
• Bound together against a common enemy	• Celebrate common events/sports
• Patriotic	• Nationalistic but not patriotic
• Grand symbolism	• Subtle symbols
• Ideal country	• Not an ideal country
• Already invented	• Continually re-invented every few generations

Source: Based on "Canada: Nation or Notion?," an Adam Gopnik and Malcolm Gladwell debate, *Ideas*, CBC Radio 1, Toronto, 30 July 2008.

SUMMARY

As we saw in this chapter, the choices that a society makes with respect to its governance, and the institutions and constitutional arrangements it uses to govern itself, stem from the values, attitudes, and expectations of its citizens. While history and geography may have played a part in shaping Canadian democracy, Canadians and their political leaders have also made choices leading to the development of democratic institutions of government that are different from those of other countries, including the United States. Early in the chapter, we saw how important it is to look at a society's values and how those values shape the ideas and ideologies that drive government policies, political actions, and social change. We used the fragment theory approach, the role of formative events approach, and/or the class analysis (economic theory) approach to explain the basis of Canadian political ideas and political institutions. Certain models such as the left- and right-wing concept and the political compass continue to be useful for those who study politics. In particular they help us differentiate between the main ideologies and political parties in Canadian democracy. Later in the chapter, we looked at Canadians' values, attitudes, and expectations surrounding their notions of community, freedom, equality, and the role of the state.

Much of the chapter was dedicated to explaining the role that political culture plays in Canadian democracy, and the similarities and the differences between Canadian and American political culture. In the end, the most significant aspects of the debate over the value differences between Canada and the United States may be that it has gone on for so long and that it continues to generate controversy among those who study Canadian politics. The differences are relatively small, certainly, compared to those between Canada and most other Western democracies. But this debate is rooted not in the reality of large or growing value differences, but rather in the precariousness of the national identity of English-speaking Canada. This identity has always been based on the premise of significant value differences between Canada and the United States, a premise used to explain why these two countries are not and should not be united under one constitution.

STARTING POINTS FOR RESEARCH

David Bell, *The Roots of Disunity*, rev. edn (Toronto: Oxford University Press, 1992).

Seymour Martin Lipset, *Continental Divide: The Values and Institutions of the United States and Canada* (Toronto: C.D. Howe Institute, 1989).

Neil Nevitte, *The Decline of Deference: Canadian Value Change in Cross-National Perspective* (Peterborough, Ont.: Broadview Press, 1996).

Philip Resnick, *The European Roots of Canadian Identity* (Peterborough, Ont.: Broadview Press, 2005).

David Thomas and Barbara Boyle Torrey, eds, *Canada and the United States: Differences That Count*, 3rd edn (Peterborough, Ont.: Broadview Press, 2008).

Nelson Wiseman, *In Search of Canadian Political Culture* (Vancouver: University of British Columbia Press, 2007).

CBC ARCHIVES AND TVO'S *THE AGENDA*

Visit the companion website for *Canadian Democracy: A Concise Introduction* to follow links to audio and video footage related to the main themes of the chapter: www.oupcanada.com/BrooksConcise.

RELEVANT WEBSITES

Visit the companion website for *Canadian Democracy: A Concise Introduction* to browse a collection of websites featuring material related to the key themes of the chapter, an excellent starting point for research.

REVIEW EXERCISES

1. Using Table 2.1 and the political compass in Figure 2.3, where would you place each party represented in the federal or provincial legislatures? Where would you place yourself and why?

2. Choose any three organizations from the following list. From the information included in their websites, decide whether each organization advocates mainly collectivist or individualistic ideas.

   Fraser Institute: www.fraserinstitute.ca
   Centre for Social Justice: www.socialjustice.org
   Canadian Centre for Policy Alternatives: www.policyalternatives.ca
   Canadian Labour Congress: www.clc-ctc.ca
   Sierra Club Canada: www.sierraclub.ca
   C.D. Howe Institute: www.cdhowe.org
   National Citizens Coalition: www.morefreedom.org
   Council of Canadians: www.canadians.org

3. Canadians often compare their values and beliefs to those of Americans. In 2005 the Dominion Institute published a series of five articles on "American Myths" (www.dominion.ca/americanmyths/), which argue that the beliefs that many Canadians hold about Americans and how Canadians differ culturally from their southern neighbours are fundamentally wrong. Are you convinced by the arguments and evidence in this series? Why or why not?

3

The Social and Economic Setting

Canadians commonly view the United States as a benchmark against which we compare ourselves and our achievements. After President George W. Bush's 2004 re-election, for example, many Canadians were gratified to read stories about Americans inquiring into the possibility of moving to Canada. This seemed to be the surest confirmation of the typical Canadian belief that Canada is superior in important ways to the powerhouse to the south. The Canadian self-image is one of compassion, tolerance, and prosperity. Our southern neighbours may be richer, but we tend to believe that our country's prosperity is more equally shared. The resilience of the Canadian banking system compared to the near-collapse of the American banking system during the 2008 economic *meltdown* provided another example of how our economic and political systems might have their advantages.

Canadians are indeed fortunate. But politics unfolds against a backdrop of social and economic conditions, and not all Canadians share in that good fortune. In 2005, approximately 11 per cent of Canadians were below what is conventionally called the "poverty line." In recent years, there have been many criticisms of the conditions for the poor in Canada and our government's performance in this regard. As we discussed in Chapter 1, politics is often about conflict over values and over the allocation of resources. Just as the values of a society and the institutions of the state establish boundaries to political life, so do the social and economic settings. They do so by determining the sorts of problems a society faces, what resources are available for coping with these problems, the nature and intensity of divisions within society, and the distribution of politically valuable resources between societal interests.

This chapter focuses on specific socio-economic aspects of Canadian society such as material well-being, equality, discrimination, poverty, and quality of life, as well as political and economic sovereignty. After reading this chapter, you will be able to

1. Explain the social and economic settings of Canadian politics
2. Make socio-economic comparisons of regions within Canada, as well as comparisons with other countries
3. Discuss poverty and the distribution of income in Canada
4. Explain the nature and characteristics of socio-economic mobility in Canada
5. Explain how the Canadian democratic political system copes with the socio-political divisions created by scarcity and how the economy affects the ideals and aspirations of Canadians and the problems faced by policy makers
6. Measure the quality of life in Canada and compare it to that of other states
7. Identify some of the economic and cultural factors that limit Canada's independence

MATERIAL WELL-BEING

Canada is an affluent society. This simple fact is sometimes obscured by bad news such as plant closings, slipping competitiveness, and growing poverty. For most of the last generation, the average real purchasing power of Canadians was the second-highest in the world, topped only by that of Americans. While Canada has slipped several notches in the last decade, it remains among the top ten wealthiest countries in the world.[1] Degrees of affluence affect both the opportunities and problems faced by policy makers. For example, the problems of poverty in an affluent society like Canada differ from those of poverty in a poorer society like Mexico or a destitute one like Sudan. Not only do Canada's poverty problems look enviable from these countries' perspectives, but the available means for Canadian governments to deal with the problems are far greater. The very definition of what constitutes a public problem in need of government attention is also influenced by a society's material conditions. For instance, environmental pollution, which can be a prominent issue on the public agendas of affluent societies, tends to be a less pressing socio-economic problem in poorer societies.

Within affluent societies, cultural and institutional differences are probably more important as determinants of the public agenda and government response than are differences in material well-being. For example, societies in Western democracies tend to have a high regard for the rule of law and for the role of the judiciary. The values and the institutions associated with these often affect the public agenda and government responses, even though they have little to do with material well-being. But the characteristics of a national economy, factors upon which material affluence depends, significantly influence the politics and public policies of any society. These characteristics include the sectoral and regional distribution of economic activity, the level and distribution of employment, the characteristics of its labour force, the profile of its trade with the rest of the world, and so on.

The frequent mention of the issue of employment in the news should indicate just how important it is to Canadians. Despite their high standard of living, Canadians have seldom been complacent about their affluence. Fears that Canada's material well-being may rest on fragile footings have long been expressed. As Canadians grapple with globalization and what this economic restructuring means for their future, these fears have become increasingly urgent. Most people want a secure job at a decent rate of pay; it enables one to plan for the future and achieve the goals that one has for oneself and one's family. Unemployment can be personally and socially devastating, and governments react with rhetoric, gestures, and policies. These policies may or may not succeed in reducing unemployment, but no government would pass up an opportunity to express its commitment to increasing jobs and its sympathy for the unemployed.

What does Canada's employment record look like? Compared to other advanced industrialized democracies, Canada has done fairly well. Over most of the past 30 years the national level of unemployment has averaged between 7 and 9 per cent. This may not impress Americans, whose unemployment rate has typically been a few percentage points below Canada's. This

"When America sneezes, Canada catches a cold." This saying from the world of finance and economics indicates just how closely the two countries' economies are intertwined. Should it make Canadians nervous, then, to look through their binoculars and see the American economy struggling? Even if the Canadian economy is currently outperforming America's, is that performance sustainable over the long term? Why or why not?

situation changed recently, however, beginning with the 2008 recession. As of December 2010 Canada's overall unemployment rate was 7.6 per cent[2] compared to 9.8 per cent in the United States.[3] Canadians, however, are used to dismissing the superior employment record of the United States as being bought with lower wages and greater income inequality than most Canadians would tolerate (the claim about lower wages is simply not true, however, if one compares real wages and net after-tax incomes).

When we look beyond the United States for comparisons, we see that Canada's unemployment rate has been close to the average for the more affluent OECD countries. Moreover, the economy's ability to create new jobs has been among the best—an important point, because Canada's labour force has grown faster than those of most other advanced industrial democracies.

The distribution of employment across sectors of the Canadian economy closely resembles that of the world's other major capitalist economies. More than three-quarters of workers are in service industries (sales, communications, transportation and warehousing, tourism, finance, public administration, etc.). In June 2012 approximately 10 per cent were employed in the manufacturing sector, less than 4 per cent worked in primary industries like farming, fishing, forestry, and mining, and 7 per cent worked in construction.[4] These proportions are similar to those in our major trading partner, the United States. Over time, the service sector's share of total employment has grown dramatically, from about 40 per cent in the mid twentieth century to the current level of over 7 in 10 jobs. The shares in the primary and secondary sectors have obviously declined, more sharply in primary industries than in manufacturing. These employment trends have led many to worry that the Canadian economy is "deindustrializing." In fact, however, these employment trends are broadly similar to those that have characterized all the world's major capitalist economies over the last several decades.

In the last two decades, a debate has emerged over the relative value to an economy of service versus manufacturing jobs. Some argue that service industries, particularly in generating knowledge and distributing information, also produce value, and so there is no reason to worry about a shrinking manufacturing base. Others argue that the manufacturing sector is especially important and that a point can be reached in Canada and the United States where further decline of the manufacturing base undermines the economy's overall competitiveness and drags down real incomes.[5] Much of this argument hinges on the often-heard claim that new jobs in the burgeoning service sector tend to be unskilled and low-paying—"McJobs." These jobs, it is said, have increasingly replaced better-paying manufacturing jobs that have been exported to low-wage economies. The belief, however, that the new economy primarily creates McJobs is false. The new economy also creates better-paying jobs in information technology, communications, financial services, and other service industries that require education and skills. What have been lost in the new economy are the low-skill/high-paying manufacturing jobs that characterized the factory economy of the 1950s to the 1970s. Their disappearance has heightened the importance of education and skills as necessary qualifications for well-paying jobs. While instances of PhDs driving taxis or flipping burgers will always be reported by the media, studies of education and income in developed and developing economies show that education and training generally translate into higher incomes and better job security.

Fears over the export of low-skill manufacturing jobs have been replaced by worries that more highly skilled jobs in areas such as computer programming and financial services are moving abroad to some developing countries like India. Unlike the earlier movement of repetitive low-skill jobs, for example, in textile and footwear manufacturing, to developing countries like China, *outsourcing* also includes the loss of more highly skilled and highly paid jobs in areas such as financial services and software development. These fears are probably unfounded. Canada's job creation rate has been one of the best in the developed world for over a decade, and projections suggest that as the country's population continues to age, the supply of workers, including those needed to fill highly skilled and well-paying jobs, will not meet the demand. But even if it could be shown that outsourcing has and will continue to result in a hemorrhage of jobs, one could still make the case that sharing employment opportunities with people in less affluent parts of the world is preferable to providing them with foreign aid. If Canadians truly believe, as polls suggest, that the world's wealth should be shared more equally, then they should applaud the redistribution of economic activity from the rich countries to the poorer ones. But most do not.

BOX 3.1 | The Best of Times?

As the American economy sank deeper into the quagmire of the subprime mortgage crisis in financial markets that began around 2006, dragging down Canada and other Western economies, and the price of a barrel of oil and a number of other natural resources reached vertiginous levels in 2007–8, Brookings Institution policy analyst Gregg Easterbrook made a startling claim: "Most are, right now, the best-off they have ever been."[6] His analysis and supporting data concerned the United States, but could be applied to Canada as well.

- The real income of a typical person or household has never been higher.
- The percentage of people attending and graduating from university has never been greater.
- The amount of space per person in the average home is at an all-time high.
- The likelihood of being a crime victim has been falling steadily.
- All forms of pollution, with the exception of greenhouse gases, are in decline.
- Rates of cancer, heart disease, and stroke have fallen.

Despite Easterbrook's claims and the overwhelming evidence of improvement in most people's lives, the public mood is often downcast and pessimistic. This is what Easterbrook calls *The Progress Paradox*, the title of a book he published in 2005. He blames the media, arguing that the incentive system within which most reporters, producers, writers, and other media personnel operate tends to reward bad news stories and to discourage covering good news. You may be dubious about Easterbrook's argument, but his "progress paradox" encourages us to open our minds to the possibility that the diet of doom and gloom we are fed by much of the media may reflect something other than the facts.

EQUALITY

> One of the most persistent images that Canadians have of their society is that it has no classes. This image becomes translated into the assertion that Canadians are all relatively equal in their possessions, in the amount of money they earn, and in the opportunities which they and their children have to get on in the world. . . .
>
> That there is neither very rich nor very poor in Canada is an important part of the image. There are no barriers to opportunity. Education is free. Therefore, making use of it is largely a question of personal ambition.[7]

This may well have been the image held by most Canadians when sociologist John Porter wrote these words in *The Vertical Mosaic* (1965). It is doubtful whether Canadians today are as confident that their society is without serious inequalities. Stories about homelessness, food banks, poverty, and growing income inequality have become routine. Moreover, charges of discrimination made by women's groups, Aboriginal Canadians, visible minorities, gays and lesbians, and other marginalized groups are more commonly heard today. The passage of provincial human rights codes and of the Charter of Rights and Freedoms and the proliferation of human rights officers (e.g., ombudspersons and race relations or equity officers) have increased the awareness of inequality. These reforms were inspired by a sense that existing policies and institutions did not adequately protect the equality of citizens and that, in some cases, laws and institutions actually perpetuated social and economic inequality.

Despite the heightened awareness of inequalities, Canadians generally cling to the belief that their society is basically middle class. This belief, which is not totally false, springs from the dominant liberal ideology. Individualism and a belief that opportunities to get ahead in life are open to those with the energy and talent are at the core of this ideology. To say that society is basically middle class means, from this ideological perspective, that the barriers to upward mobility are relatively low for the vast majority of people. The fact that some people are extraordinarily wealthy and others are quite destitute needs to be set alongside an even more prominent fact: most Canadians occupy a broad middle band in terms of their incomes and lifestyles.

Wealth is unevenly divided in all societies. Few people believe that the sort of levelling implied by Karl Marx's comment "From each according to his abilities, to each according to his needs" is desirable. But many people are disturbed by the jarring contrast between eye-popping luxury and destitution. The gap between rich and poor is not as great in Canada as in some other industrialized democracies, but it is persistent and, according to recent reports, growing.[8]

Some groups bear the brunt of poverty more than others. According to Statistics Canada, until recently the distribution of income remained essentially unchanged for decades. The richest one-fifth of the population receives about 47 per cent of all income, while the poorest one-fifth accounts for about 4 per cent. If social security benefits are left out of the picture, the inequality gap is much wider: the bottom fifth of Canadians accounts for barely 1 per cent of earned income. Canada is fairly typical when its income distribution is compared to that of other advanced capitalist societies. Its distribution of income is more equal than in countries such as the United States, but less equal than in others such as Japan and Sweden.

Recent news stories and academic studies purporting to show a growing gap between the rich and the poor in Canada contribute to a widespread belief that inequality has worsened. For example, a 2010 performance report by the Conference Board of Canada notes that income inequality grew faster in Canada than all but one of the seventeen industrialized countries.[9] And in December 2010, the World Socialist Web Site reported that Canada's richest 1 per cent

TABLE 3.1 | MEASURING CLASS

Class and Income	Education	Occupations	Communities and Percentages
Upper class and corporate elite	Post-secondary		3–5 per cent of the population
Upper upper class • Much of the wealth is inherited ("old money")	Private school and post-secondary	Owners and directors of large Canadian companies such as Bell Canada, Bell Media, Bombardier, and Power Corporation of Canada	Wealthiest 1 per cent of the population • The "Rich 100" (e.g., Rogers, Thomson, Desmarais, and Weston families) • Lobby groups and organizations: Canadian Council of Chief Executives, political parties
Lower upper class • Salaries in excess of $100,000		• Self-employed professionals (lawyers, doctors, etc.) • Affluent farmers	2–4 per cent of the population
Middle class • Good education • White-collar and professional jobs • Own their own home • Salaried wages • Families earning about $50,000–100,000 per year	Post-secondary	• Small business people • Self-employed professionals • Middle managers, civil servants, teachers, nurses, and other salaried professionals	40–50 per cent of the population
Working class • Manual or routine work • Earning hourly wage • Families earning below $50,000; almost no accumulated wealth	High school or less	Working in • Resource exploitation • Assembly • Clerical, sales, and service jobs • Crafts and trades	33 per cent of the population
Working poor and poor • More than 55 per cent of income (20 percentage points above the national average) is spent on food, clothing, and shelter • Live in subsidized or low-income housing, or are homeless	High school or less	Working for minimum wages and at seasonal and temporary jobs or on welfare	20 per cent of the population; 16 per cent of this group have insufficient income to cover the basic necessities like food, clothing, and shelter.

Source: Canadian Council on Social Development, *The Canadian Fact Book on Poverty 2000*, 14, http://www.ccsd.ca/pubs/2000/fbpov00/chapter2.pdf

grabbed one-third of all income growth since 1987.[10] Statistics Canada research shows that every income group experienced an increase in real income between 1996 and 2006, but the wealthiest Canadians benefited from the greatest percentage increase in their average incomes. Some household types have done better than others in improved average incomes over time, but every family type experienced improvement in average real incomes between 1976 and 2006.

An assessment of equality involves analyzing both the extent of poverty and the distribution of income. "Poverty" is to some degree a relative concept, meaning something different in an advanced industrialized society than in a developing country. In Canada, poverty is usually measured using Statistics Canada's definition of an income so low that an individual or household lives in "straitened circumstances." Statistics Canada's low-income cut-offs (LICOs) are generally referred to by the media, academics, politicians, and others as the **poverty line**, currently defined to mean that ***more than 55 per cent of income (20 percentage points above the national average) is spent on food, clothing, and shelter.*** The term "poverty line" has become an established part of Canada's political vocabulary and for many Canadians evokes images of need and destitution. However, according to a study of poverty lines by the National Council of Welfare,[11] there are limitations to measuring poverty in this way:

- Poverty lines are relative and arbitrary.
- Poverty lines measure the incomes of groups of people, not individual's need.
- Some poverty line definitions are better than others, but none of them are perfect.

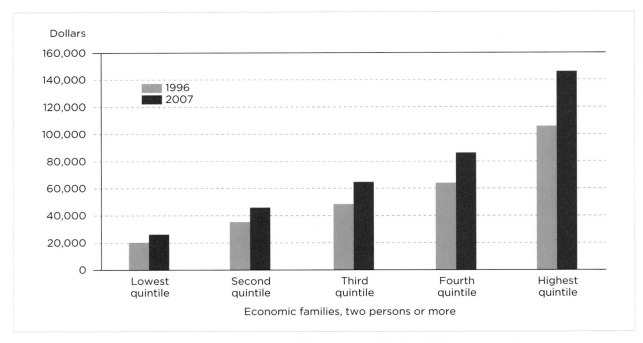

FIGURE 3.1 AVERAGE AFTER-TAX INCOME QUINTILES, CANADA, 1996 AND 2007

Source: Statistics Canada, *Income in Canada, 2007*, Catalogue no. 75-202-X, adapted from chart 9, p. 17.

Although the number of Canadians whose incomes fall below the poverty line varies from year to year, the figure has fluctuated over the past few decades between a high of about 16 per cent (1996) and a low of 10–11 per cent in 2007–8. The likelihood of being poor is not, however, evenly distributed across the population. Two of the groups most at risk are Aboriginal Canadians and women. Consider the facts in Table 3.2.

Why are these groups particularly susceptible to poverty? There is no single or simple answer, but a few contributing causes are clear. In the case of Aboriginal Canadians, discrimination can partly explain the higher jobless rate and lower incomes. Lower levels of education also are a factor. But as John Price notes, these causes are considerably less important than "cultural heritage, choice of occupation and residence far from the main centres of the economy."[12]

Likewise, poverty among women results from a complex set of causes. Most of the difference in the poverty levels of women and men is due to the comparatively high poverty rates of single-parent mothers with children under 18, and unattached women. The lower incomes of women are chiefly due to their segregation in lower-paying occupations and the greater number of women than men who work part-time. Of course, these conditions also have causes, some of which we examine in Chapter 12.

Regionalism and Inequality

Inequality also has an important regional dimension in Canada. Income levels and employment rates vary dramatically and persistently between provinces, as well as between regions within provinces. Personal incomes in what have traditionally been the poorest provinces (Newfoundland and Labrador, New Brunswick, and Prince Edward Island) are about 80–85 per cent of the Canadian average. These citizens have been more dependent than Canadians in wealthier provinces on transfer payments from government. For example,

TABLE 3.2 | TWO GROUPS MOST AT RISK FOR POVERTY

Aboriginal Canadians	Women
• The employment rate for Aboriginal Canadians is the lowest of any ethnic group, at about two-thirds of the national level. To put this a bit differently, the unemployment rate among Aboriginal people is usually between two and two and one-half times the national level. • The employment rate for Aboriginals living on reserves is only half the Canadian rate. • About one-half of all status Indians obtain most of their income from employment, compared to roughly 70 per cent of all Canadians. • Aboriginal incomes are about two-thirds the Canadian average. • Close to half of Aboriginal Canadians living off reserve fall below the poverty line, a figure that is about three times greater than for the general population.	• Women are more likely than men to be poor. • The poverty rate for women is about one-third higher than that for men. • Elderly women are about three times more likely than elderly men to fall below the poverty line. • Over 40 per cent of single-parent families headed by women fall below the poverty line (post-tax income), a rate several times higher than for two-parent families and three times greater than for single-parent families headed by men. • The poverty rate among single-parent families headed by young mothers is absolutely crushing. For mothers under 25 it is close to 70 per cent (post-tax income). Among those aged 25–44 it is roughly 40 per cent.

Source: National Council of Welfare, *A New Poverty Line: Yes, No or Maybe?* (Ottawa: Minister of Public Works and Government Services Canada, 1999), 1.

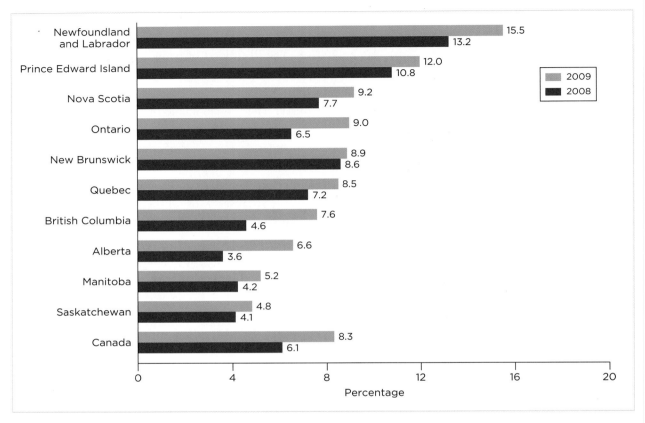

FIGURE 3.2 PERCENTAGE OF UNEMPLOYED BY PROVINCE IN 2009 AND 2010

Table source: Government of Alberta. Government of Alberta material has been used and referenced by permission of the Government of Alberta under the conditions outlined in the disclaimer as follows: © 1995–2012 Government of Alberta – Disclaimer http://www.finance.alberta.ca/copyright.html#disclaimer.

the median government transfer to a family of two persons or more was slightly more than $12,000 in Newfoundland and Labrador in 2006, compared to about $3,000 in Alberta and $4,000 in Ontario.[13] Statistics Canada studies show that inter-regional variation in average personal incomes has narrowed over the last few decades but is still quite wide. This change is due mainly to government transfers that provide greater income benefits to the residents of the poorer provinces. On the other hand, the gap between the highest and lowest regional rates of unemployment has widened.

Socio-Economic Mobility

One of the important dimensions of equality, and one of the chief influences on it, is **socio-economic mobility**. This refers to *the ability of individuals, families, and groups to move from one social or economic position to another.* Socio-economic mobility implies the existence of hierarchically arranged differences in society, such as those that exist between income groups and occupations. These differences exist to varying extents in all societies. In an *open society*, where socio-economic mobility is high, movement up and down the social ladder is

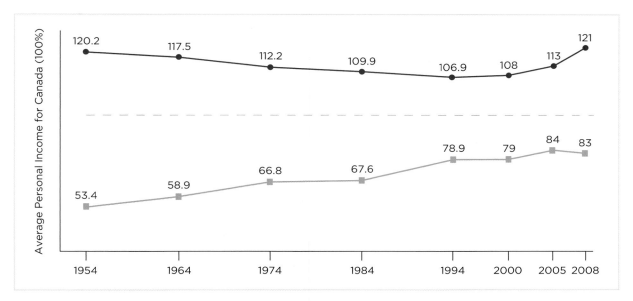

FIGURE 3.3 THE GAP BETWEEN THE RICHEST AND POOREST PROVINCES, 1954–2008

Note: The two provinces used in this comparison are Ontario and Newfoundland and Labrador, for all years except 2005, when Alberta was the wealthiest province, and 2008, when Alberta was the wealthiest province and Nova Scotia was the poorest province.

Source: Statistics Canada, *Provincial Economic Accounts*.

common and the barriers to entry into high-paying occupations, prestigious groups, or elites are low. In a *closed society*, there is relatively little intergenerational movement on the social ladder, and barriers into these privileged groups are high.

Most Canadians believe that theirs is a relatively open society, and compared to many it is. But an enormous amount of evidence shows that social stratification in Canada remains high and that socio-economic mobility is lower than the conventional wisdom suggests. The vertical mosaic that John Porter analyzed over four decades ago has been opened up, but several studies show that gender, ethnicity, race, and family background continue to exert a tremendous downward pull on mobility.

A national survey of social mobility and status achievement in Canada indicates that individuals' socio-economic backgrounds explain about one-third of the differences in people's level of educational attainment.[14] Educational attainment is strongly related to the educational achievements of the parents and the occupation of the father. Education is highly correlated with income, and several years of post-secondary education are, of course, necessary to qualify for some of the most prestigious and high-paying professions in Canada. The sons and daughters of professionals with higher-status occupations and higher incomes are more likely to graduate from university. Likewise, those born into a relatively poor family, where the parents' educational level and occupational status are low, are far less likely to achieve higher incomes and higher-status occupations as adults. These claims are corroborated by two 1994 studies carried out by Statistics Canada.[15]

The good news is that intergenerational social mobility in Canada appears to be higher than in the United States, the United Kingdom, and some other wealthy democracies.[16] Moreover, Canada does a better job than many other societies in terms of how quickly immigrants and their children are able to climb the socio-economic ladder.[17] Despite the fact that the Canadian economy has needed highly skilled immigrants for decades, smooth integration by immigrants into the labour force often does not happen immediately. Indeed, evidence shows that their skills are frequently underutilized, at least for a few years after their arrival. A 2003 Statistics Canada study found that 6 in 10 immigrants were working in occupational fields different than those for which they had been trained in their first country.

Immigrants' job prospects do, however, improve over time. The employment rate of those between the ages of 25 and 44 arriving in Canada between 1991 and 1996 was 61 per cent, but increased to 74 per cent by 2001. Although this figure was still several percentage points below the employment rate for those born in Canada, it clearly was a significant improvement over a relatively short time. Some immigrants simply need to spend some time in school, upgrading their education, acquiring language skills, or becoming certified in their occupational field. The fact that an increasing number of immigrants in Canada's labour force are of non-European descent and are members of what in Canada are called *visible minorities* raises the issue of whether some barriers that immigrant workers face are due to discrimination.

The problems of assessing foreign credentials, lack of Canadian work experience, and language and cultural barriers may be more significant in explaining the underemployment and underutilization of skilled and educated immigrants. Indeed, in some parts of Canada, foreign-born are as common as Canadian-born. As of the 2006 census, foreign-born people made up about 46 per cent of the population of the Greater Toronto Area and about 40 per cent of that of the Vancouver metropolitan region. Visible minorities constitute significant shares of the population in these cities, and although few would claim that prejudice has disappeared from their workplaces, cultural diversity is now firmly anchored in these and other major urban centres in Canada.

The Canadian Elite and Socio-Economic Mobility

What about the political and economic elite in Canadian society? John Porter argued that these classes were largely self-perpetuating, recruiting new members chiefly from those groups that already dominated them. Does this continue to be true? Academic and journalistic opinion on Canada's *corporate elite* agrees that this group is highly unrepresentative of the general population and that access to it appears to be much easier for those from certain backgrounds than from others. The most systematic studies of the corporate elite's social characteristics have been carried out by sociologists John Porter and Wallace Clement. Porter's study was based on 1951 data and Clement's on 1972 data.[18] They both found that of this elite (which they defined as the directors of Canada's dominant corporations)

- Most were male
- About a third had attended private schools like Upper Canada College or Ridley College

- Many had upper-class backgrounds (50 per cent in 1951 and 59.4 per cent in 1972)
- Those of non-Anglo-Saxon ethnic origin were under-represented (13.8 per cent of Clement's 1972 group, compared to 55.3 per cent of the Canadian population)
- About half (51.1 per cent in 1972) belonged to one or more of the six most prominent private clubs in Canada

The picture they sketched was one of a self-perpetuating group whose social backgrounds and adult activities set them sharply apart from the general population (see Box 3.2).

Access to the political elite is certainly more open today than in the past. Traditionally, the major political parties were dominated by males of either British or French ethnic origins. They still are, but the representation of females and Canadians of non-British, non-French origins has increased sharply over the last couple of decades. The election of Audrey McLaughlin as

"A ceiling? All this time I thought it was a floor."

The "glass ceiling" is an invisible form of job discrimination that excludes large numbers of women from the higher-paying and more prestigious jobs that have historically been held by men. Do you think that representation quotas—that is, requiring organizations, including political parties, to employ a proportional number of women or other marginalized minority groups—is an effective way for women to break through the glass ceiling? Why or why not?

NDP leader in 1989 marked the first time a woman had been chosen to lead a national political party, followed by the 1993 selection of Kim Campbell as leader of the Progressive Conservative Party and of Alexa McDonough as leader of the NDP in 1994. A handful of women have led provincial political parties and one, Catherine Callbeck of Prince Edward Island, was elected premier. Several of Canada's major cities have had female mayors. The continuing domination of Canada's political elite by males of British and French ethnic origins, albeit less strikingly than in the past, thus seems to be the result of systemic rather than deliberate discrimination.

THE ROOTS OF INEQUALITY

Why do inequalities like those described in the preceding pages exist? And what are the consequences for Canadian politics and society? These are complex questions that cannot be fully dealt with here. However, several factors seem to contribute to inequality, including deliberate discrimination, systemic discrimination, choice, and politics.

CANADIAN SPOTLIGHT

BOX 3.2 Canada's Corporate Elite: Where Everyone Looks the Same

These are the leaders of Canada's biggest companies by market cap [the investment community's assessment of a company's net worth, calculated by multiplying its share price by the number of shares in circulation], ranked from one to 50. . . . With one exception, they're all white, middle-aged males. If corporate Canada was an ice cream, it would be vanilla—make that two scoops. That in itself shouldn't be surprising, but what is rather shocking is the almost complete absence of any kind of diversity. Not one woman heads up a Top 50 company, despite women making up half the workforce. Only one visible minority—John Lau at Husky Energy—found his way to the top, even though at least 13.4 per cent of the population identifies themselves as such. . . .

Aside from being white, the men at the top of Canada's corporate food chain are middle-aged, with the typical exec being almost 53, and very well educated. Oddly enough, though, it turns out a business degree isn't the path to fame and fortune: turns out your average Canadian CEO is more likely to have a bachelor of science degree. Roughly a fifth of them reported having an MBA. Roughly half have multiple degrees. . . .

Hard work, and biding your time while rising through the ranks, can also pay off. Telus's Darren Entwistle started out a telephone lineman for Bell Canada; Canadian National Railway's Hunter Harrison's first job was crawling under box cars to oil wheel bearings; and Canadian Pacific Railway's Fred Green has been with the company since 1978. Clearly, this group is bright and hard-working—positive signs of meritocracy at work. Now, the challenge is to get that culture of meritocracy to extend beyond white middle-aged men.

Source: Excerpted from Andy Holloway, "The Big 50: The CEOs of Canada's Largest Companies," *Canadian Business* 22 May–4 June 2006.

Deliberate Discrimination

The prejudice that one person feels toward the members of some group or groups becomes *deliberate discrimination* when it is acted upon. Deliberate discrimination is characterized by the intent to treat the members of some group in an unequal manner. For example, the landlord who refuses to rent to someone he suspects of being homosexual is discriminating against that person and against all members of that group. The intent that underlies social prejudice and bigotry is, however, often hard to prove. While there is no doubt that this sort of discrimination still exists in Canadian society and is exercised against the members of some groups more than others, it is probably much less important in explaining inequality than the following three causes.

Systemic Discrimination

Systemic discrimination is discrimination without conscious individual intent. It is ***the discrimination inherent in traditions, customary practices, rules, and institutions that have the effect of favouring the members of one group over another.*** For example, in 1999 the British Columbia Human Rights Commission ruled that the section of the province's Highway Act requiring motorcyclists to wear helmets unintentionally discriminated against male Sikhs, whose religion requires them to wear a turban. Other examples are the height and/or weight requirements for certain jobs that discriminate against women, because women are typically smaller than men. Everyone recognizes, however, that some job requirements may be reasonable, even if they have the effect of discriminating against certain groups.

Yet another example of how deeply rooted systemic discrimination may be is the way in which our society often assumes that child-rearing is primarily a female function. This assumption is deeply embedded in our culture and social practices, and is even reinforced through the law (why else would about 85 per cent of child custody orders in cases of separation and divorce assign sole custody to the mother?). The result is a situation where the opportunities effectively open to men and women are not equal. It may appear that individual choice entirely determines what opportunities are pursued, particularly since the Constitution proclaims the equality of men and women. But these individual choices are shaped by the weight of social practices and cultural values that have the effect of discriminating between males and females.

Choice

Individual *choice* can, however, contribute to inequality. For example, a status Indian who decides to stay on the reserve reduces his or her opportunities of finding a job, and if employment is found, it will probably pay less than a job in the city. First Nation reserves are usually far from centres of population and economic activity, so an economic cost accompanies the choice of life on the reserve. Likewise, if one decides to live in Cape Breton in Nova Scotia, northern Ontario, or many other regions of Canada, there is a greater probability that one will be unemployed or earn less than someone else who moved to Toronto or Calgary.

Mobility choices like these are not always easy. A person who grows up in the poverty and deprivation that characterize most First Nation reserves may not perceive the choices or have the resources to make some choices. For example, some First Nation reserves are geographically remote. Therefore, the cost of transportation and lodging can have a significant impact on people's education and career choices. Nevertheless, individual choice affects inequality.

Politics

How much inequality is socially acceptable? How much equality is enough? Are some forms of discrimination necessary to protect or promote other values? Which groups should be targeted for affirmative action schemes? Although debates over equality generally use the language of civil rights and social justice, they are essentially struggles over *politics*.

Fairness and equality are cultural notions. And as values and beliefs change, a society's notions of what is fair may also be transformed. A century ago only a small minority of Canadians regretted the fact that women were without most rights that are taken for granted today. Poverty was once believed to be primarily the fault of those experiencing it—an explanation that absolved society, the economic system, and governments from blame for the suffering of the many unfortunate people who had been born into poverty.

Value shifts are almost certain to be accompanied and influenced by political struggles. If Canadians are more conscious today of the discrimination that has been practised against the country's Aboriginal peoples it is because of Aboriginal groups who have struggled to bring these inequalities to the public's attention and to influence government policy. The social policies that redistribute wealth from more affluent to less affluent Canadians did not emerge overnight: they were built up over time in response to struggles between conflicting interests and values. Political parties, interest groups, individuals, and various parts of the state may all participate in such struggles.

The structure of the state also affects what sorts of inequalities are dealt with by governments and influences the opportunities and resources available to different interests. The fact that Canadian governments have long targeted more money at regional economic inequalities than have American governments is likely due to the particular division of powers between Ottawa and the provinces under Canada's Constitution, and the relatively greater leverage of the provincial governments than of the state governments in the United States. For example, the entrenchment of the Charter of Rights and Freedoms in the Canadian Constitution has had an enormous impact on the prominence of equality rights issues, the strategies that groups use to achieve their goals, and the treatment of certain groups. The interplay of interest, ideas, and institutions that is politics plays a key role in determining what inequalities get on the public agenda and how they are dealt with.

MEASURING QUALITY OF LIFE

The United States, the world's wealthiest society, has one of the world's highest homicide rates and a drug problem that costs thousands of lives and billions of dollars annually. In spite of its wealth, the United States suffers from a number of social pathologies such as a high rate of alcoholism, many thousands of homeless people, and a high level of marriage breakup, which creates numerous single-parent families, usually headed by women, and leads to a high incidence of child poverty. Racism, urban blight, and the environmental and other costs associated with suburban sprawl are a few of the other problems with which it must cope.

Canadians often take smug pride in being less afflicted by these problems. But Canada's high standard of living is also tarnished by problems that undermine the **quality of life** (**QOL**) experienced by millions. The QOL index *measures social and economic prosperity using a combination of objective and subjective determinants*. Social problems often become politicized as groups demand government action to deal with them. In some cases, government policies are blamed for causing or contributing to QOL problems. For example, Aboriginal groups and sympathizers argue that the appallingly bad quality of life experienced by many Aboriginal Canadians is due to unjust and discriminatory policies. While the QOL in Canada is comparatively high, the picture is not uniformly bright for all groups. Aboriginal Canadians, in particular, experience conditions far below what most Canadians would consider decent and acceptable in a wealthy society.

One way to measure the QOL in a society is to ask people how happy they are. Pollsters have done this for decades. They find that generally Canadians are relatively happy most of the time. However, they are much less likely to say that they are very happy compared to people with shorter life expectancies in much poorer countries such as Nigeria, Tanzania, or Mexico.[19]

People in comparatively rich countries such as Italy, Spain, and Finland report being much less happy with their lives. Thus it seems that there is no particular correlation between the happiness of national populations and material well-being.

There is, however, a correlation between material well-being and the level of satisfaction with life expressed by a nation's population. Canadians and citizens of other wealthy countries are far more likely to express a high degree of satisfaction with their lives than to say that they are very happy. Indeed, in the 2000 World Values Survey four out of five Canadians said they were highly satisfied. But a persistent and significant minority of Canadians are not satisfied. Attitudinal data like these tell us nothing about the causes of dissatisfaction or the problems that undermine a society's QOL. For this, we must rely on objective measures such as mortality, crime, suicide, alcoholism, and destitution.

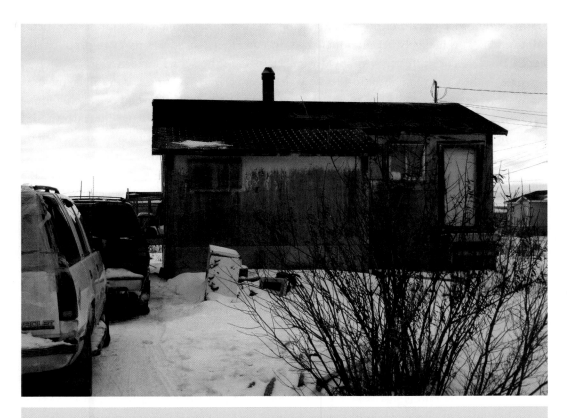

In late 2011, the leadership of the Attawapiskat First Nation, a Cree community in the Kenora region of Northern Ontario, declared a state of emergency—the third in three years—in response to dropping temperatures and a concern for residents living in inadequate housing. Dilapidated structures like this one, common in the community, house large families and suffer from serious problems such as mouldy, substandard insulation, no running water, and no access to sanitation systems. Why do you think the issues of substandard socio-economic conditions on reserves keep resurfacing? And why do you think there is not more public demand to improve the quality of life faced by many of Canada's First Nations?

Compared to other advanced industrialized societies, Canada does relatively well on these measures. Its mortality rate of about 7 per 1000 members of the population and the infant mortality rate of just under 6 per 1000 are about average for such societies. Life expectancy is above average, at about 75 years for males and 81 years for females. In terms of violent crime, Canada is unexceptional. Canada's current homicide rate is somewhat below 2 homicides per 100,000 population, compared to a rate of about 9 per 100,000 in the United States. Although rates vary marginally from year to year, the statistics do not support the popular assumption that murders in Canada have become more common; Canada's homicide rate has actually declined since the mid 1970s.

Crime, Suicide, and Drug Abuse

Statistics on other violent crimes, such as rape, domestic violence, and assault, are difficult to interpret. This is partly because of changes in reporting procedures that can produce statistical increases or decreases without any real changes in the actual incidence of the offence. Changes to the law and public attitudes may also affect crime statistics. For example, the dramatic increase in the number of rape charges and convictions from several decades ago may be due to victims' greater willingness to come forward, resulting from changed social attitudes and reforms to the law on sexual assault. Comparisons between countries are complicated by variations in policing practices, the definition of offences, and the manner in which crime statistics are collected. Interpretation problems aside, the data do not suggest that Canada is an exceptionally dangerous place to live. At the same time, the widespread belief that Canada is much less crime-ridden than the United States is not supported by the empirical evidence. While it is true that Americans are more likely to be the victims of homicide, victimization rates for other violent offences and crimes against property are not lower in Canada; in some cases they are even higher. Moreover, only about one-quarter of Canadians, roughly the same as Americans, say that they feel very safe on the street after dark.[20]

Suicide, alcoholism, and other forms of drug abuse are social pathologies symptomatic of a low QOL. Suicide accounts for about 5 per cent of deaths among Canadians between the ages of 15 and 69, compared to 36 per cent for cancer, 30 per cent for circulatory system malfunctions, and 10 per cent for accidents. There is enormous international variation even when levels of national wealth are controlled for, suggesting that suicide is closely related to culture. For example, Mexico's rate is just over 1 per 100,000; Italy and the United Kingdom have rates around 8 per 100,000; Switzerland's rate is about 18 per 100,000 and Hungary and Austria top the list at about 40 and 25, respectively. Canada's rate of about 13 per 100,000 falls in the middle.

It is conservatively estimated that about 4–5 per cent of adult drinkers in Canada, or over 600,000 people, are alcoholics.[21] This figure is based on the mortality rate from cirrhosis of the liver, national cirrhosis rates being highly correlated with alcohol consumption levels. Alcoholism in Canada is about average for Western industrialized countries. The level is dramatically lower than in such countries as Hungary, Germany, Italy, and France. Abuse of other non-medical drugs generally is not considered to be a major problem in most of Canadian society, although particular cities, including Vancouver and Toronto, and some isolated

Aboriginal communities have been exceptions. While the lack of hard data makes it difficult to reliably assess the costs inflicted on society by drug abuse, the social and economic costs associated with illegal drug use in Canada are probably less than those caused by alcohol and tobacco consumption.

Homelessness and the Welfare Gap

Advanced industrial societies all have in place a "safety net" of social programs intended to protect individuals and households from destitution. Examples of such programs include social welfare, public housing, employment insurance, public health insurance, and workers' compensation. Nevertheless, some people do not or cannot get the help they need. When the safety net fails to catch a significant number of those who cannot make ends meet, surely the QOL for some people is falling below acceptable standards. Homelessness and the demands placed on food banks are two indicators of holes in the social safety net.

The extent of homelessness is difficult to pin down for the obvious reason that the homeless do not have fixed addresses or telephone numbers, and cannot be tracked with any accuracy. The 2008 Senate report *Poverty, Housing and Homelessness* acknowledges the difficulties and does not even attempt to attach a number to this problem. Statistics Canada's first attempt to count the homeless came up with the implausibly low figure of 14,145, based on the number of people nationwide sleeping in emergency shelters on the night of 15 May 2001. As Canada's largest city, where the cost of accommodation is relatively high, Toronto experiences homelessness on a scale and with a visibility probably greater than elsewhere in Canada. The problem also exists in other cities like Vancouver, where the price of housing is high.

The number of Canadians who rely on food banks also increased. Food Banks Canada estimates that Canada's more than 800 food banks provided food to roughly 850,000 people during a typical month. About half of food bank users rely on social assistance (such as welfare or Old Age Security) as their main source of income. The disabled and those with no income account for another 18 per cent. Six per cent are homeless. Immigrants and refugees make up 11 per cent of food bank users, rising to 18.5 per cent in large cities. Eighteen per cent of users have employment income, and 4 per cent are post-secondary students. According to Food Banks Canada, the number of food bank users has roughly doubled since 1989, and is 20 per cent higher than in 2001.[22]

While demands on food banks are largely cyclical, increasing during periods of high unemployment, there appears to be a permanent component. Even when the rate of unemployment has fallen in recent years, demand has grown. This demand, many argue, is created by the **welfare gap**, *the gap that exists between the income that social assistance provides and the cost of living.* The size of this gap varies across the country, first because social assistance benefits are determined by the individual provinces and second because of regional variations in the cost of living. But the gap is wide in all provinces.[23] As social assistance benefits fail to keep pace with increases in the cost of living, the demand on food banks inevitably increases. Given the growth in the "normal" use of food banks, increasing unemployment pushes an already strained system to the breaking point.

Not everyone agrees that a welfare gap exists or that it is widening. We have already alluded to the limitations of Statistics Canada's low-income cut-offs (LICOs or "poverty lines") as measures of poverty. Some researchers have proposed alternative measures of poverty that would be based on the actual spending needs of Canadians. For example, economist Chris Sarlo of the Fraser Institute has developed "basic needs lines" (BNLs). These measures are based on the cost of maintaining long-term physical well-being, including shelter, a nutritious diet, clothing, personal hygiene, health care, transportation, and a telephone. BNLs are considerably lower than Statistics Canada's LICOs, and unlike LICOs they do not automatically rise as average personal income increases. If BNLs are used to measure poverty instead of LICOs, a very different picture emerges. When all forms of income assistance are included, the welfare gap narrows and virtually disappears in some provinces.

Aboriginal Canadians

Canada is an affluent society whose social pathologies are similar to those of other advanced industrial societies. Based on the QOL measures, the United Nations is certainly right in rating Canada as one of the world's best countries in which to live. But the QOL is sharply lower for one group, namely, Aboriginal Canadians. Consider these facts:

- Life expectancy for status Indians is about 10 years less than that of Canadians in general.
- Infant mortality rates are twice as high among Aboriginals as non-Aboriginals.
- Aboriginal death, illness, and accident rates are about three times greater than national levels.
- Most deaths of status Indians under 45 are caused by violence. Also, almost one-fifth of all murder victims and over one-fifth of all murder suspects in Canada are Aboriginal.
- Although Aboriginal Canadians make up less than 3 per cent of the population, about 18 per cent of those in prisons are Aboriginal.
- The suicide rate among Aboriginal Canadians is well over twice the Canadian rate; among Inuit, suicide occurs at about six times the national rate.
- Alcoholism is much more prevalent among Aboriginals than non-Aboriginals. An estimated 50–60 per cent of accidents and deaths among status Indians are alcohol related.
- Compared to the general Canadian population, Aboriginals are several times more likely to live in overcrowded conditions.

POLITICAL, ECONOMIC, AND CULTURAL SOVEREIGNTY

Political Sovereignty

In most contexts, **sovereignty** is understood to mean *the ability of a person or entity to act independently without outside interference*. A democracy requires sovereignty and self-government. This means that public policies affecting the lives of citizens should be formulated by people elected by and accountable to these same citizens. The first major step toward self-government in Canada was taken in 1848, when the principle of **responsible government** was recognized in the colonies of Nova Scotia and United Canada (today's Ontario and Quebec). *Responsible government meant that the governor, himself chosen by the British Colonial Office, was obliged to select cabinet ministers who were members of the elected legislature*. A cabinet unable to keep the support of a majority in the legislature would be required to resign.

Self-government advanced another step with Confederation. The British North America Act of 1867 created a new country out of the colonies of Nova Scotia, New Brunswick, and United Canada, and transferred to its federal and provincial legislatures the exclusive right to make laws for Canada and its provinces. Full self-government was almost achieved. We say "almost" because certain powers were withheld from Canadian governments and, therefore, from the voters who elected them. These included

- The power to enter into foreign treaties, which was formally transferred from the United Kingdom to Canada in 1931 by the Statute of Westminster
- The power to amend the Constitution. Even with Confederation in 1867, the power to amend our Constitution remained in the hands of the British Parliament until the BNA Act, with all its amendments, was patriated in 1982. Patriation ended the United Kingdom's authority to pass laws applying to Canada, and a procedure for amending the Constitution in Canada was established (see Chapter 5).
- The power to interpret the Constitution. At Confederation, the highest court for British North America was the Judicial Committee of the Privy Council (JCPC), which was a committee comprising members of the British House of Lords. The JCPC's authority over Canada continued until 1949, when the Supreme Court of Canada became the final appellate court in the country and, as such, its constitutional umpire.

Step by step the Canadian state achieved the full powers of self-government that it exercises today. With the passage of the Constitution Act, 1982, the last formal impediment to political sovereignty was removed. But political sovereignty has been far less controversial in the modern politics of Canada than economic and cultural sovereignty. The real limitations on Canadian independence, many have argued, have not come from the vestiges of colonialism that have gradually been removed from Canada's Constitution, but have been and are imposed by economic *dependence* on, first, Great Britain and then the United States, and by the "colonization" of Canada by American cultural industries. Formal political sovereignty, according to Canadian nationalists, is meaningless so long as the country's economic and cultural destinies are controlled by others.

Economic Sovereignty

No self-governing democracy is totally independent of external influences—especially in this era of globalization. Trade, military alliances and animosities, and contemporary mass media are some of the chief factors that have created a web of interdependence between modern societies. The question as to whether the nature and extent of these external influences undermine a country's political independence has become increasingly important to Canadians. If one looks at Canada's economic relations with the rest of the world, both historically and today, there is no denying our enormous dependence on foreign sources of investment capital, imports, and markets for Canadian exports. Some of the main features of Canada's international economic relations are listed in Box 3.3.

This dependence must, however, be put into perspective. Several advanced industrial democracies like Canada, including the Netherlands, Belgium, Sweden, the United Kingdom, and Germany, rely on trade for much of their national income. These countries are members of the European Union, which imposes considerably greater limitations on the policy makers of its member states than the North American Free Trade Agreement (NAFTA) imposes on the Canadian, American, and Mexican governments. What is unique about Canada is the extent to which our trading relations depend on a single partner—the United States. Among

CANADIAN SPOTLIGHT

BOX 3.3 Canada's Economic Links to the United States and the Rest of the World

Past

- Much of the money used to build the roads, railways, and canals of Canada's early commercial economy was borrowed from foreign, mainly British, investors.
- At Confederation, Canada was already heavily in debt to foreign investors.
- An estimated 450 American companies had established subsidiaries in Canada by 1913.
- By the 1920s, the United States had surpassed the United Kingdom as the major source of foreign investment.
- The level of foreign ownership in Canada peaked in 1971 at 37 per cent of corporate non-financial assets. The level was close to 60 per cent for manufacturing industries.

Present

- Foreign investors, mainly American, control about one-fifth of corporate non-financial assets in Canada.
- Over half of all American investment in Canada is located in Ontario, although with the dramatic escalation in the world price of petroleum from 2005 to late 2008, the rate of new American investment in Alberta has been greater than in any other region of Canada.
- About one-third of Canada's gross domestic product (GDP) comes from trade, of which roughly 80 per cent is with the United States (close to 80 per cent of our export trade and about 75 per cent of our import trade).
- Canada went from being a net importer of investment capital to a net exporter around 1996. As of 2005, the estimated market value of foreign direct investment in Canada was $771 billion compared to $808 billion Canadian direct investment abroad. Canada is one of the top 10 sources of foreign investment in the American economy.[24]

advanced industrialized economies, only Japan comes close to this level of dependence on a single trading partner (close to half of Japan's exports are purchased by the United States).

In terms of investment, Canada remains heavily dependent on foreign capital. But this dependence has weakened over the last couple of decades as Canadian investment abroad has increased. Indeed, as a result of the increasing globalization of business and investment, Canada has come to look more like several other advanced industrial economies with respect to foreign ownership. Again, however, Canada is rather unusual in the degree to which it is dependent American foreign investment. Following the global crisis in financial markets that started in late 2008, it is difficult to predict the future of foreign investment in Canada and Canadian investment abroad.

Cultural Sovereignty

Culturally, Canada, especially English-speaking Canada, has always lived in the shadow of the United States (see Box 3.5). Physical proximity, a common language, and shared values have facilitated the flow of cultural products such as books, magazines, films, television programs, and music recordings between the two countries, but mostly from the United States to Canada. This largely one-way flow exists because greater domestic audience/readership is available to American producers, which better enables them to produce high-quality, low-cost, mass-appeal products that are attractive to advertisers. Advertising revenue is the main or sole source of income for most privately owned media businesses (producers of films, compact discs, DVDs, video games, and books are the chief exceptions). It thus makes economic sense for Canadian broadcasters, for example, to buy a product that is demonstrably popular with viewers, at a fraction of the cost of production in Canada.

Predictably, American-made films, television programs, video games, popular music, and magazines dominate Canada's English-language market. American books also do very well in the English-Canadian market, with authors like John Grisham, Stephen King, Stephenie Meyer, and Ken Follett featuring on the bestseller lists in both countries. Newspapers are the main exception to the rule of American dominance, partly due to provisions in Canada's Income Tax Act that heavily favour Canadian-owned newspapers, and partly because, for most people, newspapers are primarily sources of local information.[25]

With respect to sovereignty, questions arise: Is Canada's political independence undermined by its economic dependence on the United States and by the enormous influence of American mass media? How so? And is the Canadian predicament so different from other industrialized democracies in the face of globalization?

Magazines Canada is the national trade association representing Canadian-owned and Canadian-content magazines in English and in French. Would seeing the organization's logo on a publication at the newsstand make you more inclined to buy it? Do you think it is important to distinguish Canadian content in this way? Why or why not?

The answer to the first question is clearly "yes." Canadian policy makers must be sensitive to the actions and possible reactions of governments in the United States. Moreover, numerous public policy matters, from transboundary pollution to interest rates, are affected by circumstances in the United States—circumstances over which Canadians and their governments can exert little, if any, control. Canada's economic and cultural linkages with the United States affect us in too many ways to be listed here. The fact that roughly 80 per cent of our export trade is with the United States obviously means that our economy is highly vulnerable to the state of the American economy and to changes in the exchange rate between the Canadian and American dollars. The fact that Canadians are raised on a heavy diet of Hollywood films, television, magazines, and an Internet dominated by American websites certainly affects the images and ideas in our heads. To the extent that these American cultural imports erode distinctively Canadian values (whatever these may be or might have been), one may argue that they also erode the cultural basis for a Canadian society and for public policies that are different from those of the United States.

Faced with challenges from a larger, more powerful economy and a predatory mass culture, governments typically respond with protectionist policies. They attempt to protect domestic industries or local culture through import restrictions, subsidies to domestic producers, regulations affecting business practices and cultural industries, and so on. Canadian policy

Democracy Watch

BOX 3.4 CRTC: Protector or Punisher?

Since 1999, commercial radio licences in Canada require stations to program 40 per cent Canadian content, defined as meeting at least two of the following criteria:

- **M** (music): composed solely by a Canadian
- **A** (artist): a Canadian performs the music or the lyrics
- **P** (performance): recorded in Canada or performed and broadcast in Canada
- **L** (lyrics): written by a Canadian

While established to promote Canadian arts, these rules raise difficult situations. Homegrown stars such as Avril Lavigne and Drake can be forced to record in Canadian studios, even if they are living elsewhere, in order to meet the Canadian content requirements. In a famous 1991 case, Bryan Adams clashed with the CRTC over his international hit "(Everything I Do) I Do It for You," which was deemed "not Canadian" because it was co-written by a British producer. (It was following this case that the "L" was added to the list of criteria to allow more songs to be considered Canadian.)

Up for Debate

Are the CRTC's Canadian content rules outmoded? Do artists deserve air time based on MAPL criteria or on the merits of their work? Should it be part of the government's mandate to promote Canadian culture in this way?

MEDIA BEAT

BOX 3.5 | The Long Shadow of American Culture

American magazines account for close to two-thirds of magazine sales in English Canada.

About two-thirds of television viewing time in English Canada is spent watching American programs. This increases to about 90 per cent in the case of dramas and comedies.

During a fairly typical week in May 2010, 23 of the 30 most-watched television programs (excluding newscasts) in English Canada were American. The exceptions included two Stanley Cup hockey games, a hockey game pre-game show, and four newscasts. In contrast, only 2 of the top 30 in the French-language market for that week (*Criminal Minds* and *Desperate Housewives*) were American.

Canada's feature film and television production industries depend on a life-support system of government subsidies channelled through the Income Tax Act and Telefilm Canada, and through the production activities of the Canadian Broadcasting Corporation and the National Film Board. Despite this support, few genuinely Canadian films reach the box office.

makers have resorted to all these measures. To cite but one example, Canadian cultural policy is determined largely by the rules that the Canadian Radio-television and Telecommunications Commission (CRTC) imposes on broadcasters. The CRTC establishes and enforces a dense thicket of regulations governing Canadian content on radio and television, and these regulations have a very simple bottom line: to ensure that more Canadian music and television programming reaches the airwaves than would be the case if market forces were allowed to operate without restriction. In some areas, particularly the music industry, Canadian content rules have nurtured a very successful English-Canadian music industry known domestically and internationally. In 2005, sales of Canadian music accounted for 21 per cent of all sales.[26]

Finally, is the Canadian situation really so different from that of other small and middle-sized democracies? After all, Hollywood's *Harry Potter and the Deathly Hallows: Part 2* and *Transformers: Dark Side of the Moon* were the box office hits of 2011 throughout much of the world, just as they were in North America. McDonald's restaurants span the globe, so much so that the standardized cost of a "Big Mac" is used by the respected business newspaper *The Economist* as a measure of the cost of living in different countries. As of the summer of 2012 there were 69 Starbucks locations in Toronto, but 39 in Paris and over 750 in China. The United States–dominated Internet, direct broadcast satellites, cable news networks, international credit cards, and multinational corporations have shrunk the globe, so that no country is free from some other's cultural or economic incursions.

By late 2011, many economists and political pundits, particularly in central Canada, were wondering why Canada did not have an industrial strategy. Labour economist Jim Stanford noted that in 1999 finished goods made up almost 60 per cent of our exports, but by July 2011, two-thirds of our exports were in unprocessed or semi-processed goods.[27] In other words, Canada seemed to be losing much of its industrial base, and its economy seemed to be specializing in resource extraction rather than the exportation of finished goods. Other analysts, particularly in the resource-rich West, were arguing that imposing an industrial strategy would harm the one area of the economy that has been doing well—resource extraction—and hinder trade with other nations. And while this debate seemed to be about which economic approach is best for Canada, a number of questions address the kind of society Canada ought to be. How much dependence on another economy is too much? Is a diversified economy preferable? Has Canada had alternatives to relying on first the British economy and then the American economy? On the cultural front, if most Canadians prefer American films, television programs, magazines, and music over homegrown alternatives, should their governments interfere? Obviously the protectionist measures such as the Canadian content quotas imposed on radio stations are not a response to listener demands. And anyway, what are the distinctive elements in Canadian culture that policy makers want to preserve? Does protectionism preserve these values or just the industries that depend on the state's cultural life-support system? The answer to these many questions are inevitably coloured by one's own values.

SUMMARY

Has Canada lived up to its self-image and idealized standards of compassion, tolerance, and prosperity? In this chapter we have tried to explain how Canadian society and its politics are influenced by its socio-economic setting. Canada is an affluent society that arguably has managed, perhaps because of a wealth of resources, government policies, and good fortune, to overcome some of the socio-economic problems that plague governments in other countries. In fact, Canadians have prided themselves on overcoming several of the socio-economic problems that afflict their powerful neighbour to the south.

The Canadian economy is changing rapidly because of a worldwide rationalization of manufacturing and services. We have witnessed job losses in some sectors, especially manufacturing, but job gains in the service sector, including high-paying, skilled jobs. In spite of these economic changes, and in many ways, Canada continues to be a caring and sharing society. When QOL measures are examined and compared with other countries, Canada continues to be a good place to live. Nonetheless, the distribution of income in Canada has changed over the last several decades with some groups in Canadian society, namely women and Aboriginals, more likely to live in poverty.

With respect to cultural and economic sovereignty, Canada is not unique in its struggle with external influences that limit the sovereignty of its elected governments. These influences seem to be felt somewhat more powerfully in Canada because of its proximity to the United States. However, it might be too much to claim, as have some Canadian nationalists, that economic and cultural ties to the United States undermine Canadian democracy. A self-governing democracy does not require freedom from external influence; but the nationalist arguments are based on an outdated ideal of national autonomy that bears increasingly little relevance to today's globalized economies and interdependent states.

STARTING POINTS FOR RESEARCH

Patrick James and Mark Kasoff, *Canadian Studies in the New Millennium* (Toronto: University of Toronto Press, 2008).

Ernie Lightman, *Social Policy in Canada* (Toronto: Oxford University Press, 2003).

Stephen McBride, *Globalization and the Canadian State*, 2nd edn (Halifax: Fernwood, 2005).

Julie McMullin, *Understanding Social Inequality: Intersections of Class, Age, Gender, Ethnicity and Race in Canada* (Toronto: Oxford University Press, 2004).

Michael Ornstein and H. Michael Stevenson, *Politics and Ideology in Canada: Elite and Public Opinion in the Transformation of the Welfare State* (Montreal and Kingston: McGill-Queen's University Press, 1999).

William Watson, *Globalization and the Meaning of Canadian Life* (Toronto: University of Toronto Press, 1998).

CBC ARCHIVES AND TVO'S *THE AGENDA*

Visit the companion website for *Canadian Democracy: A Concise Introduction* to follow links to audio and video footage related to the main themes of the chapter: www.oupcanada.com/BrooksConcise.

RELEVANT WEBSITES

Visit the companion website for *Canadian Democracy: A Concise Introduction* to browse a collection of websites featuring material related to the key themes of the chapter, an excellent starting point for research.

REVIEW EXERCISES

1. Education is one of the principal ladders for upward socio-economic mobility. How accessible is post-secondary education in Canada compared to other wealthy democracies?

2. How many homeless people are in your community? How much food bank use is there?

3. Make a list of the most influential people in your town or city. Are they politicians, business people, journalists, or activists?

4. Debate: Do the economic elite owe their wealth and power to hard work, creativity, and intelligence, or to inherited position, exploitation of workers, deceiving consumers, and/or manipulating the laws?

4 Regionalism and Canadian Politics

"Canada has too much geography," declared the country's longest-serving prime minister, William Lyon Mackenzie King. By this he meant that the country's vastness and the diversity in natural endowments and interests of its regions produced conflicts that would likely not exist in a more compact country. Canadians have always accepted the truth of King's dictum, believing that the challenges of *regionalism* and inter-regional conflict are central to the Canadian story. Indeed, one of the most astute Canadian political observers, Donald Smiley, identified regionalism as one of the three fundamental axes of Canadian politics—the other two being the rift between English Canadians and French Canadians, and Canada's long-standing relationship with the United States. As Smiley indicated, regionalism has been the source of major political divisions and controversies in Canadian history, and continues to be a defining feature of its political landscape.

This chapter looks at several important aspects of regionalism in Canadian politics, including the following topics: predicting the demise of regionalism; the persistence of regionalism; the boundaries of Canada's regions; regional political cultures; regional grievances and western alienation; and western versus central Canadian "visions" of the country. After reading this chapter, you should be able to

1. Describe the six different regions in Canada and how their different economies affect their political aspirations
2. Discuss the tensions between any two regions of Canada
3. Name three national structures or policies intended to accommodate regional interests and perspectives
4. Discuss the history of western alienation in Canada and the western Canadian conception of equality

Along with King, most Canadians have viewed regionalism as a problem. Aside from occasional patriotic celebrations of Canada's regional diversity and sheer size, few have argued that size and regional diversity are positive attributes in political life. Students of American politics will know, however, that some founders of the United States believed size and diversity were positive characteristics of a political system that respects freedom. For example, in the *Federalist Papers*, James Madison argued that a larger territory encompassing a greater diversity of regional interests was more likely to provide protection for personal freedoms, group rights, and sectional interests than would a smaller, more homogeneous country. Madison reasoned that as a country's physical size increased, and the scope of its social, and especially its economic interests, grew, it became less likely that any particular group or coalition of interests could dominate others. Small countries with comparatively homogeneous populations were, he thought, unable to maintain respect for individual and minority rights, and the majority would inevitably exercise a form of tyranny by using their superior numbers to oppress the rights of others.

Despite some agreement in western Canada, Madison's argument that vast republics help protect rights has never resonated very positively in Canada. The debates on Confederation contain no echoes of this argument. Canada's expansion was seen by most as a necessary pre-emptive action to reduce the possibility that the vast western territories would be annexed by a United States where the ideas of territorial expansion and **manifest destiny**, *a nineteenth-century American belief that the United States was destined to expand and include all North America*, were riding high. Surprisingly, perhaps, one of the few Canadians to theorize about regionalism's consequences in the style of Madison was Pierre Trudeau, usually considered a prime minister with a strong preference for centralized federal power. Trudeau's thoughts on the political virtue of regionalism were, however, formulated before he entered federal politics in 1965. Aside from the early Trudeau and some disgruntled westerners, few Canadians have disagreed with Mackenzie King's assessment that regionalism has been primarily a burden.

THE UNEXPECTED PERSISTENCE OF REGIONALISM

In the last few decades there has been an upsurge in regionalism in Canada, a trend mirrored in many other parts of the world. The signs of this upsurge can be seen in the *party system*, *western alienation*, *regional economic disparities*, and *intergovernmental conflict*.

The Party System

For most of Canada's history, the two dominant parties have been the Liberals and Conservatives (called Progressive Conservatives between 1942 and 2003). Although they did not draw equally well from all regional segments of the electorate—the Liberals did much better than the Conservatives in Quebec for most of the twentieth century and the Conservatives tended to be stronger than the Liberals in the West for most of the second half of that century—both were very clearly national political parties with significant support across Canada.

Since the 1993 general election, the character of Canada's party system has appeared to be based more regionally than nationally. This is most obvious in the case of the Bloc Québécois, which runs candidates only in Quebec; it elected more MPs from that province than any other party in the 1993, 1997, 2004, 2006, and 2008 elections and ran a strong second to the Liberals in the 2000 election. The Canadian Alliance, formerly the *Reform Party*, won almost all its seats west of Ontario and received the greatest share of the popular vote of any party in the four combined western provinces in the 1993, 1997, and 2000 federal elections. The Progressive Conservative Party, long a truly national party in terms of the regional breadth of its support, elected more of its MPs from the Atlantic provinces in these same three elections than from any other part of the country. The Alliance and the Progressive Conservatives merged into the Conservative Party of Canada in 2003, a union that delivered fewer than a quarter of the seats in Ontario and none from Quebec in the 2004 election. Only the Liberal Party appeared able to claim significant support in all regions of the country over the four national elections between 1993 and 2004, although even its regional support was very uneven.

In the 2006 and 2008 elections, Liberal support continued to be very weak west of Ontario, but Conservative support rebounded in Ontario and even in Quebec. There was an expectation that the trend of fragmentation along regional lines would continue in the 2011 general election, but the election surprised many and may have signalled a political shift. It was an unprecedented disaster for the Liberal party, which lost support to the Conservatives and NDP in many of its traditional strongholds. The Conservative party could now claim that it was truly Canada's new "natural governing party"—a label once given to the Liberal party. The Bloc Québécois was all but annihilated in Quebec and the NDP made unprecedented gains in that province, and gained enough seats to become the Official Opposition. It remains to be seen if the 2011 trends hold in subsequent elections.

Western Alienation

Western grievances against both Ottawa and the Ontario–Quebec axis that has dominated the national political scene have existed ever since the western provinces joined Canada. But in the 1970s there was a sharp upward ratcheting in the rhetoric associated with these grievances, and the term "western alienation" entered the lexicon of Canadian politics. As always, economics was at the root of this discontent. Spokespersons for the western provinces argued that Ottawa treated the resources with which the West was well endowed, and which formed the basis for western prosperity, differently and less favourably than those located primarily in provinces like Ontario and Quebec. Although Albertans were the most vocal in making this case, politicians and industry leaders in British Columbia and Saskatchewan provided a supportive chorus.

Economic Disparities

In terms of real prosperity, the gap between Canada's richest and poorest provinces has not narrowed. Indeed, if the federal government transfers intended to narrow this gap are excluded, the disparity has increased between wealthy provinces like Alberta and Ontario and the less affluent provinces like New Brunswick and Nova Scotia. (Although, since the 2009–10 fiscal year, Ontario has become a "have-not" province, meaning it received equalization payments from the federal government to make up a shortfall in the tax the province was able to collect). Such a disparity does not necessarily mean greater inter-regional conflict if the central

Every province is interested in acquiring the greatest share of resources for its population. One often hears of provincial premiers wanting more power in matters such as natural resources and constitutional jurisdiction or wanting a greater share of federal equalization payments. A province's citizens may consider competing with the federal government about the right thing to do, but is there a downside to practising this kind of self-interest?

government is able to subsidize incomes and public services in the poorer regions, and if taxpayers in the wealthier regions are willing to pay for this redistribution of wealth. However, these conditions have been eroded in the last two decades as the political will to maintain these redistributive transfers has weakened.

Intergovernmental Conflict

The pendulum of federal–provincial power has swung back and forth between Ottawa to the provinces since Confederation. Sir John A. Macdonald's hope and expectation that the provincial governments would become little more than "glorified municipalities," deferring to Ottawa on all matters of national importance, was stymied from the beginning by provincial politicians who had other ideas and by judges whose interpretation of the division of powers in Canada's Constitution did not accord with Macdonald's. Today, regionalism and intergovernmental conflict in areas such as environmental policy, health care, taxation, cities, and post-secondary education are part of the Canadian political landscape.

PREDICTING THE DEMISE OF REGIONALISM

The persistence and even resurgence of regionalism in Canada and elsewhere surprised most twentieth-century social and political observers. They had agreed that as the conditions of people's lives became more similar, their values, beliefs, and behaviour would likewise converge. As modern transportation, mass media, public education, and consumer lifestyle habits broke down the barriers that previously separated regional communities and nurtured their distinctiveness, regionalism would become a weaker force in social and political life. Even theorists on the left predicted that region, like religion and ethnicity, would be replaced by class as the main fault line in the politics of modernized societies.

Contrary to these expectations, and despite the undeniable fact that in many important ways the lives of people throughout the world's rich industrialized societies are more alike today than a generation or two ago, regionalism and nationalism continue to be important forces in political life. This certainly is true in Canada, as the signs of regionalism's vitality and the persistence of a nationalist movement in Quebec demonstrates. Three principal factors help to explain the attraction and persistence of regionalism: the continued strength of regionally based elites, the failure of national institutions, and the persistence of differences in regional economic interests and social characteristics.

Regionally Based Elites

First, traditional thinking underestimated the degree to which regionally based states and elites may invest in regionalism—and regionally based nationalism, too, as in Quebec—when this investment either serves their own interests or promotes their vision of the regional

CANADIAN SPOTLIGHT

BOX 4.1   Modernization and Regionalism

The expectation . . .

In . . . modernizing societies, the general historical rec-ord has spelled centralization. . . . the main reasons for this change, the major grounds of centralization and decentralization are to be found not in . . . "ground rules" [the Constitution and court rulings] . . . [or] in the personal, partisan or ideological preferences of officeholders, but in the new forces produced by an advanced modernity.

—Samuel Beer, *The Modernization of American Federalism, 1973*

The Canadian reality . . .

Modernization had led not to centralization in the Canadian federal system but rather to the power, assertiveness, and competence of the provinces. Furthermore, the provinces where modernization has proceeded most rapidly are insistent about preserv-ing and extending their autonomy.

—Donald Smiley, *"Public Sector Politics, Modernization, and Federalism: The Canadian and American Experiences," 1984*

community that they purport to represent. During the 1970s Canadian political scientists began to use the term **province building** to describe *the phenomenon of powerful provincial governments using the constitutional, legal, and taxation levers to increase their control within their provincial borders and, consequently, their stature vis-à-vis Ottawa.* Alberta and Quebec were most often cited as examples of provincial state elites seeking to extend the scope of their authority.

But the phenomenon of province building has not been limited to Alberta and Quebec. Alan Cairns argues that regionalism's strength in Canada is primarily due to a Constitution that gives Canada's provincial governments considerable law-making and revenue-raising powers, reinforced by what he sees as the natural tendency of those who control, work for, or depend on provincial states to protect and extend their control. We will have more to say about this later in the chapter.

The Failure of National Institutions

A second factor not anticipated by those who predicted the demise of regionalism is the fail-ure of Canadian political, cultural, and economic institutions to produce levels of national integration and identity that would overcome regionally based thinking and acting. Many Canadians, particularly in Quebec and the West, remain unconvinced that the institutions of the national government and its policies have their best interests in mind. Students of federal-ism make a distinction between *inter-state federalism*, where conflict and co-operation play out between the national and regional governments, and *intra-state federalism*, where these forces are contained within the institutions of the national state. There certainly is no shortage of national structures and policies designed to accommodate regional interests. A short list of these, past and present, includes the following:

Structures

- The Senate incorporates the principle of regional representation, with Ontario, Quebec, the four western provinces, and the three Maritime provinces all having the same number of seats.
- The Supreme Court Act requires that at least three of the nine justices be members of the Quebec bar. Moreover, the custom has developed over time whereby it is expected that three judges will be from Ontario and at least one from each of western and eastern Canada.
- The federal cabinet has always been at the centre of attempts to ensure regional representation in federal decision making. Every prime minister has given careful consideration to including representatives from each region and province in his or her cabinet.
- Section 36 of the Constitution Act, 1982 commits the federal government to the principle of "making equalization payments to ensure that provincial governments have sufficient revenues to provide reasonably comparable levels of taxation." Although the practical significance of this constitutional commitment is far from clear, its spirit clearly involves a federal obligation to assist the less affluent provincial governments.

Policies

- For about two decades, and in response to criticism that the Canadian media system and federal cultural policy has a strong central Canada bias, Ottawa has attempted to "regionalize" its cultural activities in various ways. One way involves regional programming through the Canadian Broadcasting Corporation (CBC), and another involves the programs and spending activities of the Canadian Heritage department, which, like the CBC, has a mandate to express Canada's diversity.
- Federal support for regional economic development has a long and much-criticized history in Canada. These activities were given an organizational focus and a major spending boost through the 1968 creation of the Department of Regional Economic Expansion, which has morphed into departments and agencies by other names over the years. Today, Ottawa's support for the economies of the less affluent provinces is channelled mainly through the Atlantic Canada Opportunities Agency and Western Economic Diversification Canada, both under Industry Canada.
- Ottawa is always sensitive to the probable reactions of citizens and their spokespersons when making decisions that have important regional spending and employment implications.

While these structures and policies have not been complete and abject failures, it is nevertheless clear that they have not succeeded in neutralizing regionalism. It is always possible, of course, that Canadian regional grievances and acrimony might have been worse without these efforts at intra-state federalism.

Regional Economic Interests and Social Characteristics

A third factor to thwart the predicted demise of regionalism is the persistence of differences in the economic interests and social characteristics of regions. In many respects, how people in Ontario and Saskatchewan live, the sorts of jobs they are likely to do, what they watch on television, and the cultural milieu in which they live are more alike today than two generations ago. But differences persist and their political importance, often fanned by politicians or other regional spokespersons, is considerable. For example, about one-quarter of Alberta's GDP derives from the petrochemical industry, a level of dependence on a particular industry that is unrivalled in Canada. Ontario's economy depends on the automobile industry, with automotive vehicles and parts accounting for close to 40 per cent of all exports—about

Nunavut (which means "Our Land"), with an Aboriginal population of more than 85 per cent, is a unique region of the country. Its distinctive character is visible in the design of its legislative building—called "The Ledge" by locals in Iqaluit—which incorporates Inuit themes in its architecture (for instance, the entrance is shaped like a dog sled) and uses local symbols and resources in its décor (e.g., the assembly's seats and benches are upholstered in sealskin and the ceremonial mace is carved from walrus tusk and adorned with precious metals and stones found in the region). Also noteworthy is the assembly's circular seating area. How might this round configuration, quite different from other government houses in which parties sit opposite each other across aisles, affect the debates, discussions, and negotiations that take place within it?

12 per cent of Ontario's GDP. Almost all the exported automotive goods go to the United States, a fact that injects a great deal of urgency into the uncertainty surrounding the industry's future in Ontario.

We also find some significant differences in the demography of provinces and regions. On the whole, and with one major exception, these demographic differences tend to have considerably less political impact than do Canada's different regional economic interests. The major exception is Quebec, which is the only majority francophone province, with over 80 per cent of the provincial population claiming French as their mother tongue and a majority having French ancestry. Another region whose ethnic character is dramatically different from the rest of Canada is Nunavut, where about 85 per cent of the population is Aboriginal. This is not to say that there are not enormous differences in the demographic character of provinces like British Columbia, with its large non-European and Asian immigrant population, and Nova Scotia, where people of British Isles ancestry predominate. But the ethnic characters of British Columbia and Nova Scotia do not get expressed in our politics the way that Quebec's francophone character does.

MAPPING REGIONALISM IN CANADA

How many regions does Canada have? The answer depends on our definition of "region." A map with boundaries drawn along economic lines will look different from one drawn along lines of demography or history. Some argue that the only sensible way to conceive of Canada's regions is along provincial lines, such that each province constitutes a separate region. More commonly, however, political observers tend to combine certain provinces into the same region, particularly the western and eastern provinces. But here, too, there are difficulties. The justification for lumping Manitoba and British Columbia into a common region designated "the West" is unclear. Aside from both being west of Ontario they may appear to have no more in common than do Manitoba and Nova Scotia. Difficulties aside, it has been common to speak of four or five main regions in Canada: the West (or British Columbia and the Prairies), Ontario, Quebec, and the Atlantic provinces. In terms of both physical and cultural geography, as well as economics, the Canadian North is another significant region.

There are three principal ways to determine the boundaries of regions: economics, values, and identity.

Listen to the "Is It Time to Redraw the Regional Map of Canada?" podcast, available at www.oupcanada.com/BrooksConcise.

Canada's Economic Regions

Common economic interests, often linked to physical geography, may provide a basis for classifying regions. Atlantic Canada's greater dependence on fisheries, Ontario and Quebec's greater manufacturing base, and the West's comparatively greater reliance on grain production and natural resources are economic interests that provide a basis for considering these parts of Canada as constituting distinctive regions. As Table 4.1 shows, the economic characteristics of Canada's provinces vary considerably.

The regional variation that exists in Canada's industrial structure is often at the root of major political conflicts between regions and between Ottawa and the provinces. The Kyoto Protocol, which requires policies that would reduce the use of carbon-based fuels, pitted Ottawa against Alberta for about a decade. Albertans and their government knew that the environmental gains of the protocol would be achieved at the expense of the industry that is central to their economy. The federal government was able to point to public opinion polls showing that a clear majority of Canadians favoured ratifying the Kyoto agreement. As it turned out, the Conservative Party's victory in the 2006 national election rendered the issue moot, given the party's lack of sympathy for the Kyoto guidelines and its less interventionist approach to global warming.

Historically, the federal government's major economic policies have been slanted toward the interests of central Canada. On occasion the discrimination against and even exploitation of other regions, particularly the West, has been egregious. Examples include tariffs, each province's terms of entry into Confederation, and the National Energy Policy.

Tariffs

For most of Canada's history a cornerstone of economic policy was high tariffs on manufactured imports, whose costs and benefits were distributed unequally between regions. The cost for western farmers to ship grain by rail to the Fort William railhead (today's Thunder Bay), despite federal subsidies, always seemed greater than it should have been. And the costs of shipping eastern manufactured goods to the West made prices higher than they might have been if trade—protected by the high tariffs of the National Policy beginning in 1879—had followed more natural north–south lines with American states and regions. The Canadian Pacific Railway's control over extensive prime lands (part of its original agreement with the government in the nineteenth century) also rankled western sensitivities.

Terms of Entry into Confederation

Outside Alberta and Saskatchewan, few Canadians know that when these provinces entered Canada in 1905 they did not immediately receive all the law-making powers and control over natural resources that the other provinces enjoyed. This discriminatory treatment was due to Ottawa's desire to retain control over the economic development of the Prairies, then being settled rapidly, and whose expansion was essential to the National Policy goal of building a larger domestic market for Quebec and Ontario manufacturers.

The National Energy Program (1981)

A generation after it was abolished by Brian Mulroney's Progressive Conservative government in 1984, the *National Energy Program (NEP)* remains vivid in the memory of Albertans. It involved, they reasonably believed, an enormous transfer of wealth from Alberta to the rest of Canada, and chiefly to the consumers and industries of Canada's industrial heartland, perpetrated by a Liberal government that they considered hostile to western, and especially

Alberta's, interests. The NEP placed a limit on the price (considerably below the world price) that could be charged in Canada for oil and gas from Canadian sources. Canadian producers' ability to export their petroleum at the world price was limited because energy exports had to be approved by the National Energy Board. Albertans thus saw the NEP as a subsidy to central Canada. These fears were rekindled when the price of oil and gas rose dramatically in 2005, leading to proposals from some eastern Canadian politicians that Alberta's energy "windfall" be shared more equitably with the rest of Canada.

When world oil prices doubled in 2007–8, there was less talk about the rest of Canada getting a slice of Alberta's growing revenue pie. One reason for this change was probably the fact of a Conservative government in power, holding all 28 Alberta seats in the House of Commons,

TABLE 4.1 | SELECTED ECONOMIC AND POPULATION CHARACTERISTICS, BY PROVINCE

Province	Median Family Income (2007)* ($)	Unemployment Rate (May 2010) (%)	Percentage of Labour Force in Manufacturing (2008) (%)	Most Important Industries	Average Annual Population Growth, 2004–2009 (%)	Median Government Transfers to Families (2007) ($)
NL	61,750	14.0	6.4	Fishing, mining, oil & gas, newsprint	–0.3	11,500
PEI	64,880	9.6	8.7	Fishing, mining, oil & gas, newsprint	0.5	9,000
NS	66,670	9.1	8.6	Forestry, agriculture, tourism, fishing	0.0	5,800
NB	63,230	9.9	9.6	Forestry, mining, agriculture	0.0	7,800
Que.	67,430	7.8	14.0	Manufacturing, mining, hydroelectric power	0.8	7,200
Ont.	76,510	9.3	13.5	Motor vehicles & parts, manufacturing, finance	1.1	4,500
Man.	69,490	5.6	11.3	Manufacturing, agriculture	0.8	4,500
Sask.	73,830	5.0	6.0	Agriculture, mining	0.6	3,400
Alta	89,720	7.0	7.2	Oil & gas, agriculture	2.6	1,700
BC	71,880	7.7	8.1	Forestry, tourism, mining	1.4	3,700
Canada	73,420	8.3	11.5		1.1	4,900

*Households consisting of a couple living together, with or without children.

Sources: Various online publications of Statistics Canada, www.statcan.gc.ca.

and led by a prime minister from that province. But another reason was that the issue of energy costs was now framed largely in environmental terms. How to reduce consumer and industry dependence on fossil fuels and reduce CO_2 emissions had become more important than whether some provinces should share their wealth.

Canada's Cultural Regions

In a widely cited and disputed study of regional political cultures in Canada, conducted in 1974, Richard Simeon and David Elkins conclude that "there are strong differences among the citizens of Canadian provinces and those of different language groups in some basic orientations to politics."[1] They argue that these regional variations cannot be totally explained by demographic and socio-economic differences between Canada's regions. They maintain that the sources of these differences are unclear, but that their existence is undeniable.

Other researchers have arrived at very different conclusions about regional political cultures in Canada. There is a shaky consensus that regional variations in basic and enduring political values and beliefs are not very great in English-speaking Canada, and that the differences between French-speaking Quebec and the rest of Canada are not enormous.

A 2002 survey by Environics Research Group appears to support this consensus, which notes, for example, the "lack of any significant regional differences of opinion on the Charter's legitimacy or the relationship between Parliament and the courts"[2] (see Figure 4.1). Moreover, there does not appear to be any difference in support across Canada's regions for such Charter principles and values as bilingualism and minority language, education rights, multiculturalism, the appropriateness of "reasonable limits" on freedom of expression, and the rights of the accused.

The one outlier, however, is Quebec, which shares with other Canadian regions support for the Charter and its general principles, but which is considerably more likely to value equality over personal freedom and consistently more likely to support the extension of equality rights to disadvantaged groups (see Figures 4.2 and 4.3). These findings seem to confirm the widely held view that Quebec is a more collectivist society than other regions of Canada.

One of the most thorough examinations of popular ideology in Canada, the large national survey by Michael Ornstein and Michael Stevenson in 1999, corroborates the conclusion that, Quebec aside, the regional variations in Canada's political culture are not very great.[3] The survey confirms Canadians' support for social programs, redistributive policies, foreign investment, labour unions, and large corporations. Ornstein and Stevenson's examination of provincial variation in ideology reveals that the differences are, for the most part, small and that Quebec stands out as the one province that is clearly to the left of the others. Moreover, contrary to the findings of Simeon and Elkins 25 years earlier, Ornstein and Stevenson did not find any significant variation between the provinces, Quebec included, in levels of political efficacy or political participation. "Not one province," they argue, "differs significantly from the national mean for the measure of efficacy."[4]

The existence of several regional political cultures in English-speaking Canada seems clearer if one looks at how regional populations view Ottawa and its policies rather than at ideologies or values. Albertans stand out as those least likely to believe that the federal

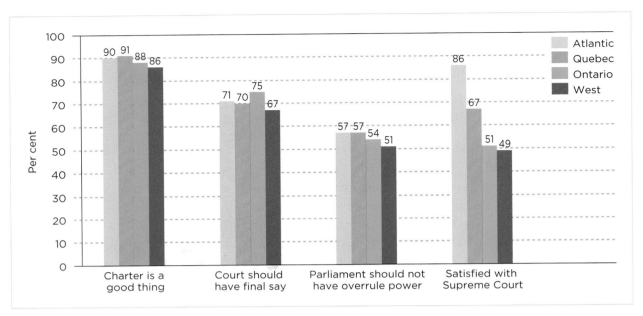

FIGURE 4.1 OPINION ON THE CHARTER AND THE COURTS, BY REGION, 2002

Source: Centre for Research and Information Canada (CRIC), *The Charter: Dividing or Uniting Canadians*, Apr. 2002, 30, www.ccu-cuc.ca.

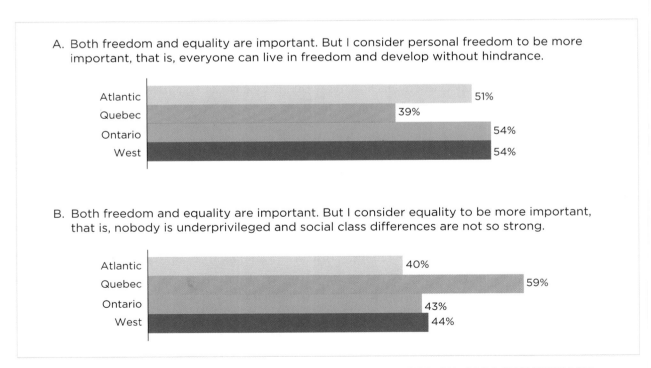

FIGURE 4.2 SUPPORT FOR FREEDOM VERSUS EQUALITY, BY REGION, 2002 (PERCENTAGE AGREEING WITH THE STATEMENT)

Source: Adapted from CRIC, *The Charter*, Table 6, 30.

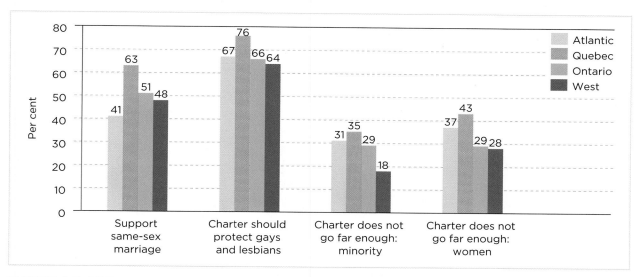

FIGURE 4.3 ATTITUDES ON EQUALITY, BY REGION, 2002
Source: CRIC, *The Charter*, 31.

government deserves their trust and confidence or that Ottawa gives them value for their tax money. They also appear to be less committed than other Canadians to the long-standing policy of equalization payments to the poorer provinces. And they are the least likely to believe that their province is treated with the respect it deserves. Atlantic Canada, on the other hand, displays greater trust and confidence in the federal government and is the only part of the country where citizens are more likely to name Ottawa than their provincial government as providing them with value for their money (see Figures 4.4–4.7).

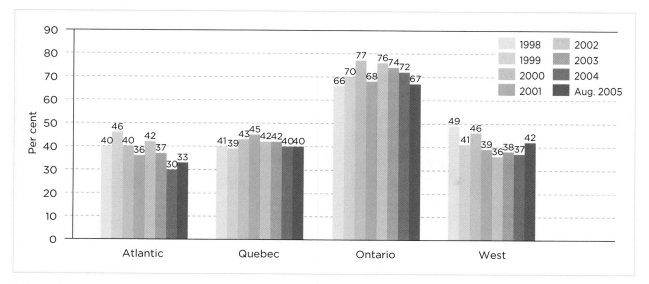

FIGURE 4.4 PROVINCE IS TREATED WITH RESPECT IT DESERVES, BY REGION, 1998–2005
Source: CRIC, www.ccu-cuc.ca

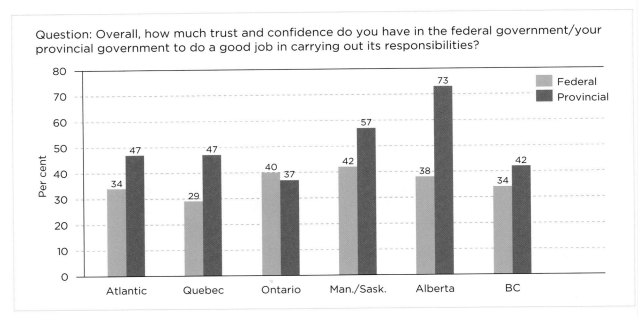

Question: Overall, how much trust and confidence do you have in the federal government/your provincial government to do a good job in carrying out its responsibilities?

FIGURE 4.5 TRUST AND CONFIDENCE IN FEDERAL AND PROVINCIAL GOVERNMENTS, BY REGION, 2004 (PERCENTAGE SAYING THEY HAVE A GREAT DEAL OR A FAIR AMOUNT)

Source: CRIC, Canada–US–Mexico Comparative Federalism Survey (June 2004).

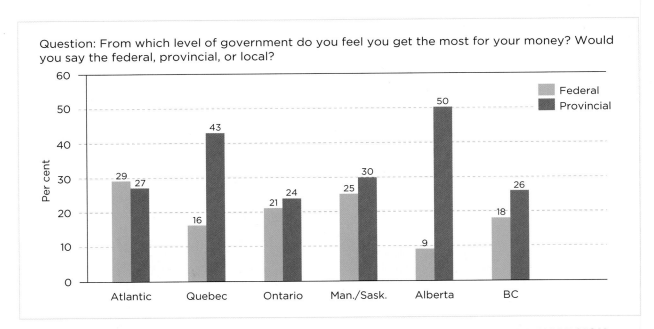

Question: From which level of government do you feel you get the most for your money? Would you say the federal, provincial, or local?

FIGURE 4.6 LEVEL OF GOVERNMENT THAT GIVES YOU MOST FOR YOUR MONEY, BY REGION, 2004

Note: Responses for "local government" not shown.
Source: CRIC, Canada–US–Mexico Comparative Federalism Survey (June 2004).

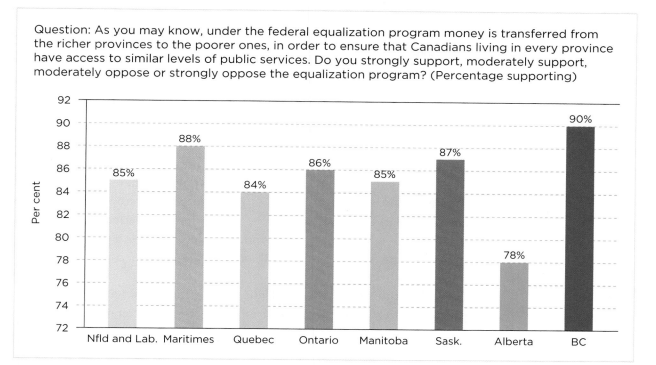

Question: As you may know, under the federal equalization program money is transferred from the richer provinces to the poorer ones, in order to ensure that Canadians living in every province have access to similar levels of public services. Do you strongly support, moderately support, moderately oppose or strongly oppose the equalization program? (Percentage supporting)

FIGURE 4.7 SUPPORT FOR EQUALIZATION, BY REGION, 2004

Source: CRIC, *Portraits of Canada*, 2004, www.ccu-cuc.ca.

Cross-Border Regions

A more recent method of mapping regions is suggested by Debora VanNijnatten and her colleagues in their work on **cross-border regions (CBRs)**. They define a CBR as *a distinct grouping of neighbouring and nearby provinces and states whose economic, cultural, and institutional linkages create commonalities between the members of this binational (Canada–US) grouping and set it apart from other regions.* Based on an analysis of the density of economic, institutional, and socio-cultural ties between adjacent and nearby provinces and states, VanNijnatten and her colleagues propose a rather different regional map (see Figure 4.8). It includes the following regions:

- *The West*, which includes British Columbia, Alberta, and Yukon in Canada, and Alaska, Washington, Idaho, Oregon, and Montana in the United States. It is characterized by a sense of remoteness from each country's central government, a strong regional identity, and similar values. A dense network of private and public institutional linkages spans the Canada–US border and more emphasis is placed on shared environmental issues than in other regions.

- *The Prairie–Great Plains.* This CBR includes Alberta, Saskatchewan, and Manitoba in Canada, and Montana, Wyoming, North Dakota, South Dakota, and Minnesota in the United States. Although the institutional linkages between these relatively sparsely populated and natural resource–dependent provinces and states are less entrenched than in other CBRs, the region features extensive economic ties and strong linkages based on shared management of common watersheds.

- *The Great Lakes–Heartland.* The shared waters of the Great Lakes and the enormous volume of trade and daily flow of vehicles and people across the Canada–US border are the most obvious features of this CBR. A dense network of cross-border institutions, public and private, link its states—Michigan, Indiana, and Ohio—and province—Ontario. But unlike in the West, there is no strong sense of shared regional identity.
- *The East.* Although Quebec and Canada's Atlantic provinces have some significant trade and institutional linkages, their ties to adjacent and nearby American states are rather different. Quebec is part of a CBR that includes Vermont, Maine, New Hampshire, and New York, while the Atlantic provinces belong to a CBR that includes Maine, New Hampshire, Massachusetts, Rhode Island, and Connecticut. The Quebec–New England CBR is characterized by strong ties of history, trade, transportation, and institutions, but little shared regional identity. The Atlantic–New England grouping is based on ties of history, trade, environmental and energy co-operation, a rich network of institutional linkages, and a strong sense of regional identity.

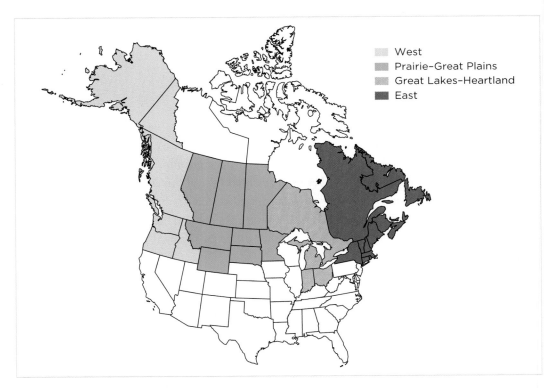

FIGURE 4.8 CROSS-BORDER REGIONS

Source: Adapted from Debora VanNijnatten, "Canada–US Relations and the Emergence of Cross-Border Regions," Government of Canada, Policy Research Initiatives, 2006, www.policyresearch.gc.ca.

Democracy Watch

BOX 4.2 **Canada: All Things to All People?**

Canada will be a strong country when Canadians of all provinces feel at home in all parts of the country, and when they feel that all of Canada belongs to them.

—Pierre Elliott Trudeau

Up for Debate

How true do you believe former Prime Minister Pierre Elliott Trudeau's statement to be? Given the distinct regional identities that exist all over the country, can Canada ever be all things to all its people? Should it be all things to all its people?

Thinking about Canadian regions while taking into account these cross-border linkages is useful in various ways. First, we can better understand the causes and nature of integration between Canada and the United States and more accurately describe the integration between the states and provinces in each of these four CBRs. As VanNijnatten puts it, North American integration is a bottom-up phenomenon.[5] Second, the significant powers held by provincial or state and local governments on both sides of the border, and the fact that transportation, the environment, security, energy supply and distribution, and many other matters tend to be regional, ensure that these subnational governments and private regional organizations and institutions are important players in managing cross-border issues.[6]

REGIONAL IDENTITIES AND WESTERN ALIENATION

What if, instead of looking for significant and enduring regional differences in fundamental political values and beliefs, we asked whether citizens of Canada's regions view their history in different ways or hold different aspirations for their country and their region's role in it? We find then compelling evidence for the existence of regional political cultures. In particular, we find that the West has long been characterized by sentiments of resentment toward and alienation from Ottawa and by what westerners perceive to be the political preoccupations of central Canada. Roger Gibbins and Sonia Arrison argue that it is reasonable to speak of "national visions" in the West that, in their words, "address not simply the place of the West within the Canadian federal state, but also the nature of *Canada* as a political community."[7] These national visions are more than feelings of being unfairly treated and marginalized within Canadian politics—the resentment captured in the Reform Party's slogan, "The West wants in"—they are deeply rooted in regional histories that have forged a collective conscious-ness and memories that are different from those of central and eastern Canada.

Starting in a major way in the 1950s with W.L. Morton, western Canadian historians began to react against what they saw as a narrative of Canadian history told from a central Canadian perspective. This perspective, said Morton,

> fails to take account of regional experience and history and makes coherent Canadian history seem an "imperialist creed," an imposition on Maritime, French-Canadian, Western and British Columbian history of an interpretation which distorted local history and confirmed the feeling that union with Canada had been carried out against local sentiment and local interest.[8]

Morton and many others have attempted to counter the centralist bias of Canadian history writing, but the belief lives on that the West's stories are not given fair weight by a Canadian academic and cultural establishment centred in the Toronto–Ottawa–Montreal tri-angle (see Box 4.3).

Writing during the height of the struggle between Pierre Trudeau, who championed a bilingual vision of Canada, and René Lévesque, who advocated Quebec independence, George Woodcock fulminated about the "betrayal" of Confederation, which he argued was based on

CANADIAN SPOTLIGHT

BOX 4.3 The West as Canada's Internal Colony

To trace the decreasing sensitivity of the national gov-ernment to influences which are specifically provincial or regional would be to write the history of Canadian political institutions over more than a century.

—*Donald Smiley, Canada in Question: Federalism in the Seventies, 1976*

Unfortunately, federal policies, the attitudes of Central Canadian governments and the biases of so-called national institutions, such as the Canadian Broadcasting Corporation, have painted regionalism with the brush of divisiveness, disunity and even trea-son. Influences tending to strengthen regional power are "balkanizing," while those working to increase the central power are "in the national interest." But this

is true only if what is good for Central Canada is also good for Canada.

—*David Jay Bercuson, Canada's Burden of Unity, 1977*

Western Canada has paid for the development of Canadian nationality, and it would appear that it must continue to pay.

—*Harold Innis, History of the C.P.A., 1923*

The West has never felt in control of its own destiny. None of the wealth of recent years has eased this feeling. In fact, the tremendous wealth of the region merely sharpens the contrast with the political power-lessness that exists on the national level.

—*Doug Owram, "Reluctant Hinterland," 1981*

"the long campaign of the centralists in Ottawa to recover the power that in recent decades has rightfully flowed to the regions."[9] Woodcock accused "centralizers" like Trudeau of having no appreciation of or sympathy for the West's distinctive history and consciousness.

In a similar vein Barry Cooper, a Calgary-based political scientist, argues that a distinctive history and political tradition exists in western Canada:

> . . . dualism is not the political issue in the West that it is in central Canada. Moreover, multiculturalism does not mean the same thing to a third or fourth generation non-French, non-British Westerner as it does to someone from the Azores or Calabria living on College Street in Toronto.[10]

What is referred to as **western alienation**, Cooper argues, is not in fact a psychological, sociological, or economic condition. Rather, it is *the awareness that the public realm—whose voices are heard and what counts as legitimate political discourse—belongs to others*. These "others" are the citizens of central Canada and the elites who purport to speak on their behalf.

Of course, the evolution of the West's history and the political traditions are not disconnected from those of the rest of Canada. Likewise, as Gibbins and Arrison observe, "western visions" of the nature of the Canadian political community and their region's place in it are not restricted to the West. They identify a set of core values that they believe are more solidly anchored in the West than in other regions of Canada; the same values also find support, but to a lesser degree, among Canadians in other regions, including French-speaking Quebec. Western visions of Canada are more likely to embrace the individual equality of all Canadians, the equal status of all provinces, and a populist style of doing political business.

Individual Equality

Gibbins and Arrison rightly note that opposition to the official recognition and even constitutionalization of multiculturalism and to a group-rights concept of Canada has come largely from such popular western spokespersons as John Diefenbaker, Preston Manning, and Stephen Harper.

The argument that westerners are more receptive to a so-called classically American conception of equality is corroborated by the election of ideologically conservative provincial governments (Ralph Klein and Ed Stelmach, in Alberta) and Gordon Campbell (British Columbia), and the impressive support in the West for Reform/Alliance and the Conservative Party in federal elections. These core values include treating all individuals equally regardless of group membership and ensuring formal equality of opportunity. On the other hand, it must be said that there is little data to support the claim that westerners are significantly different from their compatriots when it comes to equality. Moreover, generalizations about the western conception of equality are difficult in light of the very different histories of Saskatchewan and Alberta.

Provincial Equality

According to Gibbins and Arrison, provincial equality has two components. One is the sense that Canadian federalism would operate more fairly if the West had more influence on decisions taken by Ottawa. The idea of an elected Senate in which each province has an equal number of senators has been spearheaded by western spokespersons since the 1980s. The other component of this core value involves opposition to any arrangement that treats Quebec differently from and more favourably than the western provinces. Opposition to the Charlottetown Accord in the 1992 referendum was significantly higher in the four western provinces than in the rest of English-speaking Canada. Constitutional recognition of Quebec as a *distinct society* and provisions that might be interpreted as providing special status for Quebec were among the most controversial sections of the Accord. The West's enthusiasm for the idea that the provinces are all equal in their rights and powers clashes with Quebecers' preference for a binational vision of the country in which French-speaking Quebec and the rest of Canada are equal partners. Observers of the western political scene know that westerners have often felt resentment against Quebec, believing it to be the "spoiled child" of Confederation.

Toronto is Canada's largest city. But in the 2006 election the party that formed the government did not elect a single MP from Toronto, leaving Torontonians to experience the sort of exclusion that some western provinces came to regard as normal under Liberal governments.

Populism

The third component of the western vision involves a populist style of politics. In its simplest form, **populism** is ***an ideology that seeks to return power to the common people***. It arose in the American West and Midwest in the late 1800s out of the perception that economic and political elites were too powerful and unsympathetic to the people's interests. It sees elected politicians as delegates of those who elected them and therefore is hostile to party discipline and aspects of parliamentary government. Populists favour recall votes to remove unfaithful public officials from office, plebiscites and referendums to give people a more direct say in the decisions that affect them, short terms of office, and term limits for public officials.

The western Canadian version of populism is a combination of imported ideas and homegrown conditions that made the American message resonate in a farm- and resource-based economy where people were constantly reminded by the railroads, the grain elevator companies, the tariffs, and the banks that they did not control their own destiny. In a study of referendums in Canada, Patrick Boyer shows that this instrument of populist democracy has been used far more extensively in the West than in other parts of Canada.[11] The Reform Party's original platform placed a heavy emphasis on referendums and recall votes, although these became less prominent in the subsequent Alliance Party's platform. After Alliance morphed into the Conservative Party, with a broader national membership, it would seem that such an emphasis had lost the cachet it formerly had among the western conservative elite. For example, when former Liberal cabinet minister David Emerson switched from the Liberals to the Conservatives immediately after the 2006 election in order to take a plum cabinet position in the new Harper government, both Emerson and his new Conservative colleagues quickly dismissed any possibility of recall or a by-election despite popular protest.

At the provincial level, British Columbia has been in the forefront of populist democracy in Canada. It has held four referendums since 1991, including one in 2002 on the highly contentious question of Aboriginal land claims and treaty negotiations in the province. In 1995 it passed a recall and citizen initiative law—the first province to do so. In 2011, this legislation was used to abolish the unpopular Harmonized Sales Tax (HST) in British Columbia. All four western legislatures have laws requiring that proposed constitutional amendments be submitted to the people in a referendum, although Canada's Constitution does not require this. Thus, there have been strong indications that populist values are more solidly rooted in the West than in the rest of Canada. On the other hand, even though the Conservative Party has been shaped and led by westerners, its commitment to egalitarian populism has waned since coming to power.

THE ATLANTIC PROVINCES

As Canada's poorest region, with its own list of grievances toward the federal government and central Canada, one might expect the Atlantic provinces to generate an eastern version of western alienation. The easternmost provinces have produced occasional leaders such as Newfoundland premiers Joey Smallwood (1949–72), Brian Peckford (1979–89), and Danny Williams (2003–2010) who have been outspoken critics of what they saw as Ottawa's unjust treatment of their province. A radical-populist Maritime rights movement—the Antigonish Movement—swept the region in the 1930s, and proposals for Maritime union have existed since before Confederation; both of these ideas continue to surface occasionally, though with little political support. However, the dissatisfaction of Atlantic Canadians has never produced the vehicles for expressing alienation and resentment such as those found in western Canada, including the Progressive movement of the 1920s, the Social Credit Party from the 1930s to the 1970s, and the Reform Party in the late 1980s and 1990s. Why not?

The answer is complex, but two elements are crucial. First, the populist values linked to western alienation have been comparatively weak in the Atlantic provinces. This is due to the demographic and economic differences between the eastern and western regions, as well as the differences in their political histories. As noted earlier, Alberta and Saskatchewan did not achieve provincial status until 1905 and did not have control of their natural resources for 25 years, whereas Nova Scotia and New Brunswick (and soon afterward PEI), despite some loud and articulate anti-Confederation voices, were full members of the original Confederation pact. The historically dominant parties of Canada also have deep roots in the Maritimes stretching back to Confederation. *Protest parties* have always found it difficult to break through the two-party domination in the East. The Progressives failed to win a single seat from the region even in 1921, when they formed the official opposition. The Social Credit Party and the Reform Party did no better. The NDP won a seat in Nova Scotia in 1962, but did not win another in Atlantic Canada until 1974. And while NDP fortunes have improved recently, its status as a protest party for the East is dubious.

Economically and demographically the Maritimes have been in decline relative to the rest of Canada since the late nineteenth century. The region's population as a share of the national population has plummeted since Confederation; and the economies of the eastern provinces are among the weakest in Canada. This remains true, despite Newfoundland and Labrador's impressive resource-fuelled growth of recent years. It may be important to note that in spite of ongoing economic and political problems, and strong encouragement by the British government, Newfoundlanders and Labradorians were never enthusiastic about joining Confederation. Support for the idea remained weak until the economy began to decline again after a period of prosperity during World War II. The promise of improved incomes and government services convinced a small majority to vote for Confederation in a 1949 referendum. Most eastern provinces depend on money redistributed by Ottawa from more prosperous regions in order to pay for public services. These conditions stand in stark contrast to the prosperity that Alberta and British Columbia have experienced during most of the last half-century, and that Saskatchewan now enjoys as a result of higher world prices for its natural resources, and to the dramatic population growth experienced in the two westernmost provinces.

The much more assertive attitude of western Canadians compared to their eastern cousins and their greater willingness to reject the traditional political parties in favour of protest parties surely is linked to some degree to confidence in their region's economic future. "The West wants in" slogan of the Reform Party was not the plea of a weak and supplicant region, but rather the demand of a region whose population believed that Canadian politics needed to adjust to the reality of their economically powerful and growing provinces.

SUMMARY

Regionalism continues to cut deep grooves across Canada's political landscape due to political and bureaucratic rivalries, different economic interests, and inequalities between the provinces in their political and economic clout. The importance of these factors has not diminished over time, ensuring that regional conflict remains, as Donald Smiley once described, one of the three major axes of Canadian politics. With varying degrees of success there have been attempts at accommodating regional interests and perspectives through national structures and policies. We have discussed the history of western alienation in Canada and the western Canadian conception of equality, and how the grievances of the Atlantic provinces have not led to the kind of alienation and political fallout seen in western Canada. However, in spite of these attempts at accommodation, western provinces' and Atlantic provinces' grievances against Ottawa and the Ontario–Quebec axis—fuelled by the party system, western alienation, regional economic disparities, and intergovernmental conflict—continue to dominate the national political scene.

STARTING POINTS FOR RESEARCH

Keith Archer and Lisa Young, eds, *Regionalism and Party Politics in Canada* (Toronto: Oxford University Press, 2002).

Christopher Dunn, ed., *Provinces: Canadian Provincial Politics*, 2nd edn (Toronto: University of Toronto Press, 2006).

Roger Gibbins and Loleen Berdahl, *Western Visions, Western Futures* (Peterborough, Ont.: Broadview Press, 2003).

Nelson Wiseman, *In Search of Canadian Political Culture* (Vancouver: University of British Columbia Press, 2007).

CBC ARCHIVES AND TVO'S *THE AGENDA*

Visit the companion website for *Canadian Democracy: A Concise Introduction* to follow links to audio and video footage related to the main themes of the chapter: www.oupcanada.com/ BrooksConcise.

RELEVANT WEBSITES

Visit the companion website for *Canadian Democracy: A Concise Introduction* to browse a collection of websites featuring material related to the key themes of the chapter, an excellent starting point for research.

REVIEW EXERCISES

1. Compare media coverage in three different regions of the country. Do this by consulting three daily papers in three different provinces—one from the West, one from Ontario, and one from an eastern province.

2. Who were Amor de Cosmos, Henry Wise Wood, Louis Robichaud, and Joseph Howe? What is the significance of each for his region of the country?

3. Debate: Should a politician follow his or her conscience or the will of the people?

Part III

The Structures of Governance

The root of the word "government" is the Latin verb "gubernare," meaning "to guide or direct." And, indeed, government does provide direction for a society through the management of the public's business. This general function is performed through a number of specialized institutions, including a legislature, a head of state and head of government (executive), a bureaucracy, and a court system (judiciary). The authority and roles of these institutions within a country's governmental structure depend in large part on its constitution. Laws are made, implemented, and enforced, and redress is provided to aggrieved citizens, on the basis of written and unwritten rules embodied in a country's constitution. This is the ideal of democratic governance.

Constitutions and structures of government reflect the societies in which they are embedded. In the case of Canada, the Constitution adopted in 1867 and the country's parliamentary system of government may be understood as responses to particular societal and historical circumstances. The same is true for the revisions in the Constitution Act, 1982. But once in place, constitutions and government institutions tend to have what political scientists call an *independent effect* on political outcomes. In other words, the issues that get onto the political agenda, how they are framed, what voices are listened to, and what ultimately happens is to some degree influenced by the structures of government. Societal factors are important—the environment of ideas and interests that press on those who exercise public authority—but political outcomes depend to some degree on the nature of the constitutional and governmental systems through which they are processed.

One of the most difficult challenges in political analysis is to distinguish between the influence of *societal factors* and that of *structural factors* (constitutions and institutions) on politics and policy. The balance between structural and societal factors depends on the issue in question; however, governmental structures almost always play a role in determining political outcomes.

The Constitution

Constitutions are at the heart of democratic politics. A **constitution** is *a set of fundamental rules that govern political life in a particular territory*. It is an essential ingredient of democratic politics. A constitution is no guarantee that human rights will be respected, that group rights will be protected, or that political opposition to those who govern will be tolerated. South Africa, for example, for decades had a constitution that denied its black majority equal rights. Closer to home, a well-established constitutional government deprived thousands of Japanese Canadians of their rights as citizens during World War II. And in Alberta in the 1950s, the provincial government allowed the forced sterilization of people deemed to be mentally retarded.

Without a constitution, however, the concepts of rights and limited government have no secure protection. It is "fundamental" because all other laws must conform to the constitution in terms of both how they are made and their substance. A constitution is a necessary condition for democratic politics. Without it there is no civilized way to resolve conflicts and no way to predict either the powers of government or the rights of citizens.

After reading this chapter, you should be able to

1. Differentiate between constitutional law and constitutional conventions and give examples of each

2.   Outline some functions performed by a constitution
3.   Identify the categories of rights and freedoms protected by the Canadian Charter of Rights and Freedoms
4.   Identify and discuss the relationships created and governed by constitutional rules in Canada
5.   Discuss the principal characteristics of parliamentary government in Canada
6.   Distinguish between the procedures used to amend the Constitution before and after 1982, and discuss whether or not citizens should participate in the process of amending the Constitution
7.   Explain the major changes proposed by the Meech Lake Accord and the Charlottetown Accord, and discuss the reasons for the failure of these two attempts to amend the Constitution
8.   Discuss the importance of the following sections of the Constitution Act, 1982: 15, 24, 33, 40, and 52

CONSTITUTIONS AND CONSTITUTIONALITY

A constitution is expected to establish order, allowing for the peaceful settlement of differences. Early liberal thinkers like Thomas Hobbes, John Locke, and Jean-Jacques Rousseau all used the concept of the "state of nature" to illustrate the impulse behind constitutional government. The state of nature, wrote Hobbes, was one of chaos in which no one could feel secure in the possession of one's property or life. *Insecurity* is sometimes called the root of all evil; it is insecurity that leads people to accept the necessity of a constitution, and demand that it provide greater security, even if agreement on its precise components is difficult.

In modern societies the alternatives to constitutional government are anarchy or totalitarianism. Where **anarchy** reigns, such as the ***chaos and civil strife*** that broke out in some of the new republics created after the dissolution of the Soviet Union in the 1990s, there are no generally accepted rules for resolving the differences between factions of the population. The state does not exist.

Under **totalitarianism**, *in which all dissent is suppressed in the name of some supreme goal*, the state exists, but because its powers are unlimited, and all realms of social and economic life are subordinate to it, it makes no sense to talk of a constitution. The constitution ceases to be one when the rules of the political game can be changed for convenience, or if its terms are purely arbitrary.

The rules that make up a constitution deal with two sets of relations. The first involves the relationship between citizens and the state. A constitution empowers the state to act—to pass laws on the community's behalf—but it also limits the state's power by identifying those individual and group rights that the state cannot infringe. The second set of relations involves the distribution of functions and powers between different parts of the state. This mechanism is often analyzed under three main functional headings: the *legislature* (making the law); the *executive* (implementing the law); and the *judiciary* (interpreting the law). But the reality of the modern state is more complicated than this tripartite division of powers suggests.

In a **federal system** of government like Canada's, there is also a third set of relations: *a constitutional division of law-making powers between a national government and regional governments*. This third aspect of the Constitution has overshadowed the other two for most of Canada's history. Indeed, before 1982, when the Charter of Rights and Freedoms was entrenched in the Constitution, the relations between individuals and the state in Canada were defined by the courts mainly in terms of federal and provincial legislative powers.

A constitution's rules may take three forms: written documents (e.g., the BNA Act of 1867), the decisions of courts (called the *common law*), or unwritten conventions.

Constitutional conventions are those *practices that emerge over time and are generally accepted as binding rules of the political system*. An example would be the convention that the leader of the party that captures the most seats in a House of Commons election is called on to form a government. In Canada the first two components of the Constitution—written documents and the common law—together make up *constitutional law*. Conventions, while part of the Constitution, do not have the status of constitutional law, at least not in Canada. This distinction was made by the Supreme Court of Canada in a 1981 ruling (*Attorney General of Manitoba et al. v. Attorney General of Canada et al.*) It should not be interpreted to mean that constitutional law is more important than constitutional conventions. What it does mean, however, is that the rules of constitutional law are enforceable by the courts, whereas constitutional conventions are not.

Constitutional Functions

A constitution does more than provide a basis for non-violent politics. As discussed below, it also performs several specific functions that involve representation, power sharing, rights, community identity, and national purpose.

Representation

All modern democracies are representative democracies, in which politicians make decisions on behalf of those who elect them. But this still leaves enormous room for variation in how the population is represented, who is represented, and how representatives are selected.

A constitution describes both the basis of political representation and the method by which representatives are chosen. The basis of democratic representation may be by population, by territory, or by group. **Representation by population** is based on *the principle of "one person—one vote," where all elected members of the legislature should represent approximately the same number of voters*. This arrangement is most likely to allow the preferences of a simple majority of the population to be translated into law. Although virtually all modern democracies incorporate some form of "rep by pop" in their constitutions, many temper majority rule by requiring regional representation as well. For example, the American Constitution gives each state the right to two senators. Representation in Canada's Senate is also by region: Ontario, Quebec, the West, and the Maritimes each have 24 seats, Newfoundland has six, and the northern territories one each. Federalism is a form of government that embodies the principle of territorial representation. It does so by giving regional governments the exclusive right to pass laws on particular subjects.

A constitution may also accord representation to groups. Suggestions for Senate reform in Canada have included proposals to guarantee seats for women and for First Nations. The defeated 1992 Charlottetown Accord would have ensured that Quebec, whose share of Canada's population has been falling, would maintain one-quarter of all seats in the House of Commons, which is about its current share. This was, one might argue, a thinly disguised guarantee of francophone group representation.

A constitution also establishes how public office holders are selected. Election and appointment are the two basic methods, but each allows for a wide variety of procedures that affect who is represented and their responsiveness to the popular will. For example, members of the judiciary are typically appointed for life, a practice that is expected to insulate them from popular passions and the influence of elected governments. An elected legislature is a standard feature of democratic political systems and, for that matter, of non-democratic ones. But many constitutions divide the legislative power between an elected chamber and an appointed one, as in Canada, the United Kingdom, and Germany.

Finally, the electoral process itself has a crucial influence on representation. The **single-member constituency** system used in Canada, *in which each constituency (riding) gets one representative in the House of Commons and/or provincial legislature*, discourages political parties from directing their appeals at a narrow segment of the national electorate. Unless that segment happens to be concentrated in a particular region, such a strategy will not pay off in elected members. A case in point is the Green Party's failure to win a seat in the 2008 federal election despite gaining 6.8 per cent of the popular vote. A system of **proportional representation**, whereby *a party's percentage of the popular votes translates into a corresponding share of seats in the legislature*, has a very different effect. It promotes a splintering of the party system and allows for the direct representation of much narrower interests, as is sometimes seen in countries like Germany, Israel, and Belgium. In a system like Canada's, groups with narrower interests must often rely on whatever influence they can achieve within one of the larger political parties or turn to non-electoral political strategies.

Power

Constitutional government means that the state is empowered to act and that its actions may be backed up by the full weight of public authority. A constitution, therefore, provides the basis for the legitimate exercise of state power including coercion and use of force. But a democratic constitution also limits and divides power. For example, a requirement that elections be held periodically restrains state power by making politicians accountable to, and removable by, the electorate. The existence of separate branches of government, or of two levels of government as in the case of federalism, divides state power between different groups of public officials. How power is divided among the various parts of the state, or between the national and regional governments, is not determined solely by the constitution. But constitutional law and conventions affect the extent and distribution of state power.

Rights

A **right** is *something that a person is entitled to*, like the right to vote or the right not to be arrested without a reason. Constitutions vary in the particular rights that they assign to individuals or to groups. At a minimum, a democratic constitution establishes the basic right of citizens to choose their government. But most constitutions also guarantee—although not without limit—such rights as the individual's right to *free speech, freedom of association*, and *freedom of religion and conscience*, as well as legal rights such as *freedom from arbitrary detention and illegal search and seizure*. These rights limit the state's power vis-à-vis the individual either by making that power dependent on popular consent (democratic rights) or by establishing an individual's right not to be interfered with by the state (personal liberty).

Rights may also empower individuals by requiring the state to either protect or promote their interests. For example, a right to equal treatment under the law provides a constitutional remedy for individuals who have been discriminated against because of their sex, race, ethnic background, or whatever other basis prohibited by the constitution. The state is obliged to protect their interests. As a practical matter this may involve judicial decisions that remedy a private wrong (for example, requiring a minor hockey association to permit females to play in the same league with males). But the protection of equality may also entail the state being involved in broader activities like affirmative action or racial desegregation.

Constitutions may also recognize the special status of particular groups, giving special rights to their members that are not enjoyed by others. For example, Canada's Constitution declares that both French and English are *official languages* with "equality of status and equal rights and privileges as to their use in all institutions of the Parliament and government of Canada."[1] This is a positive right, in the sense that it obliges the state to assume particular linguistic characteristics and to protect the rights of both French- and English-speakers in matters that fall under Ottawa's jurisdiction. A constitution that recognizes the special status of particular religious denominations, as the Israeli constitution recognizes the Jewish religion, the Iranian Constitution the religion of Islam, or the British constitution the Church of England, empowers certain groups and gives them state-protected rights that are not held by other denominations.

It may be helpful to note that some constitutions, such as Iran's, are **codified**, which means that Iran has *a formal, written, unified document*, whereas some countries, such as Britain and Israel, do not. Canada has both a codified and an **uncodified constitution**. Many of *the powers of government, as well as the limits to government power, are unwritten or based on precedents, or embedded in the country's laws, conventions, and traditions*—many of them borrowed from the system of government in the United Kingdom.

Community and Identity

When Pierre Trudeau wrote that "A nation is no more and no less than the entire population of a sovereign state,"[2] he was arguing that a constitution establishes a community. And in an obvious sense it does. A constitution establishes rules within a given territory and establishes a shared condition—a constitutional community and legal membership—for those who live in

"I think Trudeau's proposed new constitution is a credit to our profession
. . . devious, full of loopholes, escape clauses, obscurities. . . ."

Most Canadians have not read our country's Constitution, assuming it is written largely in legal jargon, which can sometimes be difficult for the average person to interpret. Is it? Visit the companion website at www.oupcanada.com/BrooksConcise to read the Constitution Act, 1867 and the Constitution Act, 1982 for yourself. Do you find the documents easy to understand? If not, which parts are most difficult to grasp? Should these Constitution documents be "translated" into everyday language so that all Canadians can consider them carefully?

that territory. Individuals in Rimouski, Quebec, and in Kitimat, British Columbia, are part of the same constitutional system and share a formal political status as Canadians.

Carrying the same national passport and being eligible to vote in the same elections may, however, seem a rather weak basis for a *sense of community*. The fact of being citizens of the Soviet Union, for example, did not erase the strongly nationalist sentiments of Ukrainians, Estonians, and other ethnic communities; for these groups the Soviet constitution and the political community it created were things to regret. Likewise in Canada, a significant minority of the population—Quebec separatists—rejects the Canadian political community and would prefer to live under a different constitution creating an independent Quebec.

A constitution, therefore, may inspire negative, positive, or indifferent feelings among the members of a political community. These feelings may be associated with the political community that a constitution creates, or with the particular institutions, values, and symbols embedded in a constitution. The monarchy and other institutions and symbols of Canada's colonial past have historically been aspects of our Constitution that have divided Canadians of French origin from those of British origin.

In general, a constitution may generate a shared identity and unity among a country's citizens, and sometimes people have positive feelings toward the political community it creates and the values it embodies. On these counts, Canada's Constitution has had a mixed record of successes and failures. On the one hand, there has been overwhelming support in all regions and social groups for the Charter of Rights and Freedoms. However, official bilingualism and constitutional proposals to recognize Quebec as a "distinct society" within Canada have been two of the most divisive constitutional issues in recent years.

National Purpose

The Constitution Act, 1867 not only created Canada but also included provisions that embodied a national purpose. This purpose was building a new country stretching from the Atlantic to the Pacific Oceans, and an integrated economy tying together this vast territory.

A communal goal—a constitutional sense of purpose and direction for society—is not so rare. When the first permanent non-Aboriginal settlement was established at what today is Quebec City in the early seventeenth century, it operated under a royal charter that proclaimed the Catholic mission of the French colony. The colony was an outpost of a political and economic empire, but it was also a beachhead of Christianity, from which Catholicism would spread to the rest of the continent. Many countries' constitutions have a national purpose. The Constitution of the People's Republic of China includes references to building a socialist society. And those of the Islamic Republics of Iran and of Pakistan both declare that society should conform to Muslim religious teachings.

Canada's nation-building goal in 1867 is evident in the anticipation that other parts of British North America would eventually join it,[3] in the prohibition of barriers to trade between provinces,[4] and in the constitutional commitment to build the Intercolonial Railway—a project described as "essential to the Consolidation of the Union of British North America, and to the assent thereto of Nova Scotia and New Brunswick."[5] The Constitution Act, 1982 commits Ottawa and the provinces to promoting equal opportunities for all Canadians and reducing economic disparities between the country's regions.[6]

The most controversial part of the failed **Meech Lake Accord** of 1987, an attempt to reform Canada's Constitution *was the recognition of Quebec as a "distinct society."* This would have transformed Quebec nationalism from a political movement to a constitutionally entrenched fact. The Quebec legislature and government would have been constitutionally required to "preserve and promote" the distinct character of the province, which the distinct society proposal made clear was the French-speaking character of Quebec.

FEATURES OF THE CANADIAN CONSTITUTION

As constitutional documents go, Canada's is fairly long. In fact, it is not one document but a series of laws passed between 1867 and 1982. Together these form a body of law both longer and more detailed than the United States Constitution. Even so, the written documents of Canada's Constitution provide a fragmentary and even misleading picture of how the Constitution actually works. Many of the Constitution's most basic features—including many that deal with the democratic accountability of government to the people—are not in these documents. On the other hand, some of what is included in the written Constitution would, if acted upon, probably result in a constitutional crisis! For instance, the Queen is formally the head of state in Canada and has the authority to make decisions such as when an election will take place and who will be appointed to cabinet. No one, however, expects our head of state to actually make such decisions.

Canada's Constitution embodies values and principles that are central to the political life of the country. In its 1998 decision on the constitutionality of Quebec separation, the Supreme Court of Canada referred to these values and principles as the "internal architecture" of the Constitution.[7] Although not necessarily part of the written Constitution, these principles, which include federalism, democracy, constitutionalism and the rule of law, and respect for minority rights, "form the very foundation of the Constitution of Canada."[8]

Federalism

"The principle of federalism," declares the Supreme Court, "recognizes the diversity of the component parts of Confederation, and the autonomy of provincial governments to develop their societies within their respective spheres of jurisdiction."[9] In other words, provinces are not constitutionally subordinate to the federal government, nor is Ottawa dependent on the provinces for the exercise of those powers assigned to it by the Constitution. The written Constitution distributes law-making and revenue-raising authority between the central and regional governments. This reflects the underlying federal principle that some matters properly belong to the provinces to decide, while others are national in scope and properly decided by the federal government.

Democracy

Democracy has always been one of the fundamental, if unwritten, "givens" of Canada's constitutional system. In fact, aside from a written requirement for periodic elections under the Constitution Act, 1867, there were few other explicit indications that the Constitution adopted by the founders was democratic. And while the authority of governments was detailed painstakingly, the Constitution was remarkably silent when it came to the rights of citizens. Why was this so?

In explaining this silence of the Constitution before the 1982 Charter, the Supreme Court noted that to have declared explicitly that Canada was a democracy and what that meant would have seemed to the founders redundant and even silly: "The representative and democratic nature of our political institutions was simply assumed."[10] In the preamble to the Constitution Act, 1867, the framers wrote that Canada had adopted "a constitution similar in Principle to that of the United Kingdom." Democratic principles would be the baseline against which our government would operate.

But the precise meaning of the democracy principle, as we saw in Chapter 1, is not obvious and has evolved over time. For example, women did not have the vote for more than 50 years

CANADIAN SPOTLIGHT

BOX 5.1   Timeline: Canada's Constitutional History

1867   The British North America (BNA) Act (Constitution Act, 1867) is passed in Britain and creates Canadian Confederation by joining Ontario and Quebec (the province of Canada) with Nova Scotia and New Brunswick.

1870   The province of Manitoba is established.

1871   British Columbia joins Canada.

1873   Prince Edward Island joins Canada.

1905   The provinces of Saskatchewan and Alberta are established.

1926   The Imperial Conference: the colony of Canada is proclaimed "autonomous."

1927   The process of finding ways of amending the Constitution begins.

1931   The Statute of Westminster proclaims that Canada is a sovereign country.

1949   Most of the Constitution can now be amended in Canada. The Supreme Court of Canada replaces the Judicial Committee of the British Privy Council as the final court of appeal for Canada. Newfoundland joins Canada.

1960–6   Quebec seeks to change the Constitution.

1967–71   Negotiations to amend the Constitution fail.

1976   The Parti Québécois is elected as Quebec's government.

1980   The Quebec government loses a referendum on sovereignty-association.

1982   The BNA Act is patriated to Canada, and the Constitution Act, 1982, along with the Charter of Rights and Freedoms, is adopted. All parts of the Constitution can now be amended in Canada.

1987   The prime minister and premiers agree to make constitutional changes through the Meech Lake Accord.

1990   The Meech Lake Accord fails to pass in the Newfoundland and Manitoba legislatures.

1992   The prime minister, premiers and Aboriginal leaders reach agreement with the Charlottetown Accord. The Accord fails to pass in a national referendum.

1995   A Quebec referendum on sovereignty is narrowly defeated.

2000   The conditions for a province to achieve sovereignty are laid out in the federal Clarity Act.

after Confederation. Even when the meaning of democracy is written and defined, as it was in the United States Constitution, expectations and understandings change over time. What meaning do we attribute to the democratic principle of Canada's Constitution today?

The Supreme Court's 1998 decision on separation answers this question by distinguishing between process and outcomes. On the process side, the Court observed that majority rule is a basic premise of constitutional democracy in Canada. The fact that Canada has a federal Constitution means, however, that "there may be different and equally legitimate majorities in different provinces and territories and at the federal level."[11] In other words, a nationwide majority does not trump a provincial majority if the matter in question (e.g., most constitutional amendments) belongs constitutionally to the provinces or requires the approval of some number of provincial legislatures.

In a 1986 Charter decision,[12] the Supreme Court had expressed the view that the democratic principle underlying the Charter and the rest of Canada's Constitution is also linked to substantive goals: respect for the inherent dignity of every person; commitment to equality and social justice; and social and cultural diversity, including respect for the identities of minority groups' social and political institutions that enhance the opportunities for individuals and

The crafting of a constitution and implementation of constitutional reforms are processes that require participation, co-operation, and compromise among many stakeholders. Can you think of any unique challenges that Canada might face if it wanted to undertake any changes to its current Constitution?

groups to participate in society. This view was echoed in the Supreme Court's 1998 ruling in words that were directly relevant to the issue of Quebec separation. The Court said "The consent of the governed is a value that is basic to our understanding of a free and democratic society."[13] Democratic government derives its necessary legitimacy from this consent. Moreover, the legitimacy of laws passed and actions taken by a democratic government rests on "moral values, many of which are imbedded in our constitutional structure."[14] The Supreme Court did not expand upon these moral values.

The Principles of the Rule of Law and of Constitutionalism

"At its most basic level," declares the Supreme Court, "the rule of law vouchsafes to the citizens and residents of the country a stable, predictable and ordered society in which to conduct their affairs."[15] The **rule of law** *guarantees that all public authority must be exercised in accordance with the law and that there will be one law for all persons*. We are often offended when we hear that a public official has overstepped the bounds of his or her office, regardless of his or her intentions, or that someone has been accorded preferred treatment because of personal connections. We see these actions as violating the rule of law: ours is a government of laws, not of individuals, and everyone is entitled to equal treatment under the law.

The **constitutionalism** principle involves *predictable governance that has its source in written rules rather than the arbitrary wills of individuals*. For example, section 52(1) of the Constitution Act, 1982 states that the Constitution is the supreme law of the land and that all government action must conform to the Constitution. Until the constitutionalism principle was expressly stated and the Charter entrenched in 1982, the final authority of the Constitution was less certain. The pre-Charter era was one of **parliamentary supremacy**: *Parliament's authority was considered superior to that of all other institutions of government*. Constitutionalism, by contrast, places certain matters (rights and guarantees) beyond the reach of government.

Constitutionalism and the rule of law temper and modify the principle of majority rule in a democracy. Together, they constitute a sort of bulwark against what Tocqueville called the "tyranny of the majority"; even if an overwhelming majority supports a particular government action, the action can be carried out only if it is either lawful or constitutional.

Protection of Minorities

Canada has a history of recognizing group rights that goes back to early British colonial rule. The Royal Proclamation of 1763 included details on the rights of the "several Nations or Tribes of Indians . . . who live under our protection." The Quebec Act of 1774 recognized the rights of Catholics in Quebec and guaranteed the overwhelmingly French-speaking population the enjoyment of their "Property and Possessions, together with all Customs and Usage's relative thereto, and all other their Civil Rights." Most historians agree that these concessions were intended to ensure the support of the Catholic Church in Quebec at a time when rebellion was simmering in the American colonies. Group rights were recognized again through the "double majority principle" that operated when Canada East (Quebec) and Canada West (Ontario) were united through a common legislature from 1841 to 1867. Under this principle any bill touching on language or religion in either Canada East or Canada West had to be approved by majorities of legislators from both Canada East—mainly French and Catholic—and Canada West—mainly English and Protestant. This gave a veto to each ethnolinguistic community on legislation affecting minority rights.

The Constitution Act, 1867 entrenched the principle of minority rights through the section 93 guarantee of minority religious education rights and the section 133 declaration that French and English were to have official status in the Parliament of Canada, the legislature of Quebec, and courts created by either of those bodies. "The protection of minority rights," declares the Supreme Court, "was clearly an essential consideration in the design of our constitutional structure even at the time of Confederation."[16] The principle acquired a new level of prominence as a result of the Charter of Rights and Freedoms. The Charter enlarges the scope of official-language minority rights, explicitly recognizes Aboriginal rights, opens the door to a multitude of group-rights claims through its equality section (s. 15), and provides a basis for a variety of minority-rights claims through other sections, including its legal rights and democratic rights provisions.

UNDERSTANDING THE RELATIONSHIPS IN THE CONSTITUTION

A useful way of analyzing a constitution is to approach it from the relationships governed by constitutional rules:

A. Rules between individuals and the state (the Charter of Rights and Freedoms)
B. Rules between the various institutions of government (the machinery and process of parliamentary government)
C. Rules that establish what procedures must be followed to bring about constitutional change
D. Rules between the national and regional governments (federalism)

The first three constitutional relationships are dealt with in this chapter. The federal relationship will be dealt with in Chapter 6.

A. The Charter of Rights and Freedoms

Since 1982, the Charter of Rights and Freedoms has included formal distinctions between fundamental political freedoms, democratic rights, mobility rights, legal rights, equality rights, language rights, and Aboriginal rights. Most categories of rights and freedoms set down in the Charter were already part of Canada's Constitution before 1982 (see Table 5.1). Some can be found in the Constitution Act, 1867. Others were established principles of the common

TABLE 5.1 | HUMAN RIGHTS AND THE CHARTER

Rights Category	Pre-Charter Protections	Charter Protections	Examples of Charter Cases (See Table 6.1 in Chapter 6 for a brief explanation of each case.)
1. Political rights/ fundamental freedoms	Common-law protections implied in the preamble of the Constitution Act, 1867	s.2	*R. v. Oakes*
2. Democratic rights	Constitution Act, 1867, ss. 41, 50, 84, 85	ss. 3–5	*Reference Re Provincial Electoral Boundaries*
3. Legal rights	Common law; Criminal Code	ss. 7–14	*R. v. Morgentaler* *Re BC Motor Vehicle Act* *Hunter v. Southam Inc.* *Andrews v. Law Society of British Columbia* *R. v. Collins* *R. v. Stinchcombe* *R. v. Askov*
4. Economic rights	Common-law rights re contracts, property, mobility, etc.	s. 6 (and implied under some other sections)	
5. Equality rights	Common law, s. 93 of Constitution Act, 1867, guaranteeing educational rights of religious denominations	ss. 15, 28	*Law v. Canada* *Vriend v. Alberta*
6. Language rights	Constitution Act, 1867, s. 133	ss. 18–23	
7. Aboriginal Rights	Treaties	ss. 25, 35	*R. v. Sparrow*
8. Social rights	None	Although not mentioned directly, some court rulings suggest that some social rights are implied	

law. The setting down of rights and freedoms in a Charter, however, has made an important difference in Canadian politics. First, groups and individuals are more likely now than in the pre-Charter era to seek protection for their rights through the courts. Second, these rights and freedoms are now more secure because of the courts' willingness to strike down laws and practices on the grounds that they contravene the Charter.

Fundamental Freedoms

The **fundamental freedoms** guaranteed in section 2 of the Charter are *basic individual political rights (or liberties) that include freedom of religion, belief, expression, the media, assembly, and association.* In the pre-Charter era these freedoms were part of the common law and of Canada's British parliamentary tradition. Individual freedoms were part of the British constitution, and thus became part of Canada's. However, before the Charter the protection of political freedoms by the courts was rather tenuous. Except in a few instances, the courts were unwilling to rule that a freedom was beyond the interference of government. Instead, political liberties were defended using the federal division of legislative powers as the basis for striking down a particular government's interference with individual freedom.

Democratic Rights

Democratic rights include *the right of citizens to vote in periodically held elections and to stand for public office*. This right to vote predated Confederation and was embodied in the Constitution Act, 1867 through those sections that establish the elective basis of representation in the House of Commons and in provincial legislatures (ss. 37 and 40), through the requirement that the legislature meet at least once a year (ss. 20 and 86), through the right of citizens to vote (s. 41), and through the five-year limit on each term of both the House of Commons and provincial legislatures, thereby guaranteeing regular elections (ss. 50 and 85). All these sections are now superseded by sections 3–5 of the Charter.

Mobility Rights

Mobility rights, which are *the rights of citizens to move freely within a country's borders*, were not explicitly mentioned in Canadian constitutional law before 1982, nor was there any mention of restrictions on people's movement. However, Ottawa feared that some provincial governments were undermining the idea and practice of Canadian citizenship by discriminating in favour of their own permanent residents in some occupational sectors and by imposing residency requirements as a condition for receiving some social services. Therefore mobility restrictions were prohibited by section 6 of the Charter. But the Charter does allow "reasonable residency requirements as a qualification for the receipt of publicly provided social services"[17] and permits affirmative action programs favouring a province's residents "if the rate of employment in that province is below the rate of employment in Canada."[18]

Legal Rights

Legal rights are mostly *procedural rights intended to ensure the fair and equal treatment of individuals under the law*. These include the right to a fair trial, the right not to be held without a charge being laid, and the right to legal counsel. Before these rights were entrenched in the Constitution through the Charter, they were recognized principles of the common law and constitutional convention. For example, the field of administrative law was based largely on the principles of *natural justice*: hear both sides of a case, and no one should be a judge in his own case. These were accepted parts of Canada's democratic tradition and Constitution even before they were entrenched in section 7 of the Charter. And along with other freedoms and rights, legal rights were included in the 1960 Canadian Bill of Rights. In addition, the rights of accused parties were set forth in Canada's Criminal Code. The constitutional entrenchment of legal rights, however, has made an important difference and expanded the legal rights of the accused, convicted criminals, and immigrants. In the post-Charter era, the courts have been much bolder in striking down parts of laws and in overturning administrative and police procedures. For example, a successful legal challenge to Canada's abortion law became possible only when the right to "security of the person" was explicitly recognized in section 7 of the Charter.[19]

Equality Rights

Equality rights *embody the rule of law principle that everyone should be treated equally under the law.* These are now entrenched in the Constitution through section 15 of the Charter. But the Charter extends this principle to expressly prohibit discrimination based on race, national or ethnic origin, colour, religion, sex, age, or mental or physical disability.[20]

The terms in this list are important, given that Canadian courts historically have preferred to base their rulings on the precise text of laws and the Constitution. Women's groups and those representing the disabled fought successfully to have the original wording of section 15 changed. The 1960 Canadian Bill of Rights, which applied only in areas of federal jurisdiction, did not include age or disability as prohibited grounds of discrimination.

The equality rights section of the Canadian Constitution is designed to cut two ways. The Charter explicitly declares that affirmative action is constitutional[21] in order to improve the condition of disadvantaged individuals or groups, and it provides individuals with grounds for redress if they believe that the law discriminates against them.

Equality rights are also important features of provincial bills or charters of rights. Since 1975 every province has had such a bill. These rights are administered and enforced by provincial human rights commissions.

Language Rights

Language or **linguistic rights** are *guarantees by the state that an individual or a group has the right to choose a particular language for use in private or in public, and to use that language in a given jurisdiction, for example in the educational system, in the government, or in the courts of a given territory.* At Confederation, the Constitution Act, 1867 dealt with language rights in three ways. First, section 133 declared that both English and French were official languages in the Parliament of Canada and in the Quebec legislature, and in any court established by either the national or the Quebec government. Second, section 93 declared that rights held by denominational schools when a province joined Canada could not be taken away. In fact, Catholic schools in Manitoba or even Ontario were often French-speaking, and most English-language schools in Quebec were Protestant—what were formally denominational rights in section 93 were effectively language rights as well. Third, section 92 puts forth the most important language rights provision and assigns provincial jurisdiction over "all Matters of a merely local or private Nature in the Province" (s. 92.16). When combined with exclusive provincial jurisdiction over education (s. 93), the provincial governments have the power to promote or deny the language rights of their anglophone or francophone minorities.

The Constitution Act, 1982 extends language rights in four ways. First, the declaration of the official equality of English and French found in section 133 of the Constitution Act, 1867 is repeated and broadened to encompass "their use in all institutions of the Parliament and government of Canada" (s. 16.1) and services to the public (s. 20). Second, the New Brunswick legislature's earlier decision to declare the province officially bilingual was entrenched in 1982. Third, the official status of English in the legislature and courts of Quebec and Manitoba is reaffirmed (s. 21). And finally, subject to sufficient demand to warrant services, the right of anglophones and francophones to have their children educated in their mother tongue is entrenched (s. 23).

Language rights would have been given an additional twist if the Meech Lake Accord (1987) or Charlottetown Accord (1992) had become constitutional law (see Chapter 7). The most controversial feature of both accords was the recognition of Quebec as a "distinct society" (clearly, "distinct" referred to the predominantly French-speaking character of Quebec). The "distinct society" clause went on to oblige Quebec's legislature and government to "preserve and promote the distinct identity of Quebec." Critics argued that this would promote the concentration of French in Quebec, with harmful consequences for the status of the French-speaking minorities in other provinces and for the English-speaking minority in Quebec.

In an article called "Say Goodbye to the Dream of One Canada," Pierre Elliott Trudeau indicated what he felt would happen to linguistic minorities in the rest of Canada if the "distinct society" clause of the Meech Lake Accord were to be entrenched in the Constitution.

> Those Canadians who fought for a single Canada, bilingual and multicultural, can say goodbye to their dream: we are henceforth to have two Canadas, each defined in terms of its language. . . .
>
> [The] Government of Quebec must take measures and the Legislature must pass laws aimed at promoting the uniqueness of Quebec. And the text of the accord specifies at least one aspect of this uniqueness: "French-speaking Canada" is "centred" in that province. Thus Quebec acquires a new constitutional jurisdiction that the rest of Canada does not have, promoting the concentration of French in Quebec. It is easy to see the consequences for French and English minorities in the country, as well as for foreign policy, for education, for the economy, for social legislation, and so on.[22]

Aboriginal Rights

In very general terms, **Aboriginal rights** refers to *a recognition and a set of guarantees by the state that Indigenous peoples have certain rights such as civil rights and the rights to land, to preservation of culture, and to self-government*. The explicit recognition of Aboriginal rights in the Constitution dates from the passage of the Charter in 1982. Section 25 declares that the rights and freedoms set forth in the Charter shall not be construed so as to "abrogate or derogate" from whatever rights or freedoms the Aboriginal peoples of Canada have as a result of any treaty or land-claim settlement. It also entrenches in the Constitution "any rights or freedoms that have been recognized by the Royal Proclamation [of 1763]." Section 35(1) appears to limit Aboriginal rights to the status quo that existed in 1982, stating that "The *existing* aboriginal and treaty rights of the aboriginal peoples of Canada are hereby recognized and affirmed" [emphasis added]. In fact, however, this clause has been less a limit than a boost for Aboriginal rights, which have been effectively constitutionalized by the 1982 Constitution Act.

B. The Machinery of Parliamentary Government

British parliamentary government was exported to Canada during the colonial period. Its main features have remained largely unchanged since the middle of the nineteenth century, when the British North American colonies achieved the right to self-government in their domestic affairs. While the declaration that Canada has adopted "a Constitution similar in Principle to that of the United Kingdom" might appear nebulous, Canada's founders understood very clearly what it meant. The constitution of the United Kingdom was, and remains today, a set of political traditions rather than a series of constitutional documents. Those who founded Canada took these traditions as their starting point and grafted onto them certain institutions and procedures—particularly federalism—for which British parliamentary government provided no guide.

The Constitution is silent on the most fundamental principles of democracy and on practices that are essential to the functioning of government. Matters such as the selection of the prime minister, which party has the right to form a government, the relationships between the Crown and the government and between the government and the legislature, the rights of the political opposition, and the role of the judicial branch of government cannot be understood from a simple reading of the Constitution. Nevertheless, in all these matters certain rules are generally agreed upon and are vital parts of the Constitution—so vital, in fact, that when they are challenged the political system faces a crisis, such as in the parliamentary impasse and resulting prorogation, or suspension, that occurred over the government's budget update shortly after the October 2008 general election.

Listen to the "Perspectives on Proroguing" podcast, available at www.oupcanada .com/BrooksConcise.

Parliament

The distinguishing feature of British-style parliamentary government is the relationship between the various institutions that together make up Parliament. Parliament comprises the monarch and the legislature. The monarch, currently Queen Elizabeth II, is Canada's head of state. While the role is primarily a ceremonial one, and almost entirely symbolic, according to the Constitution the monarch wields formidable powers in these areas:

- Choosing which party will be called upon to form the government
- Dissolving Parliament and calling for a new election
- Signing all federal and provincial legislation, into law (giving royal assent)

When the monarch is not in Canada (which is most of the time), her powers are exercised by the Governor General, and at the provincial level, the lieutenant-governors.

TABLE 5.2 | CANADA'S HYBRID POLITICAL SYSTEM

Political System	Federation	Unitary State
Parliamentary	Canada	United Kingdom
Republic	United States	France

This table illustrates the hybrid nature of the Canadian political system. The founders of the Canadian Constitution adopted the British parliamentary democracy model and an American-style federal arrangement.

The ***power that resides formally in the monarchy is in practice held by the Crown's advisers***, the **Privy Council**, which includes all members of the present and past cabinets. However, only present members of cabinet exercise the powers of the Privy Council, and these people are usually elected members of the legislature. At the head of the cabinet is the prime minister. The structure of Canada's Parliament is shown in Figure 5.1.

Parliament comprises, then, both the *executive* and *legislative* branches of government. Those who actually exercise the executive power are drawn from the legislature. In deciding who among those elected Members of Parliament (MPs) and appointed senators will become members of the government, the rule is quite simple. The leader of the political party with the most seats in the elected House of Commons has the right to try to form a government that will be supported by a majority of MPs.

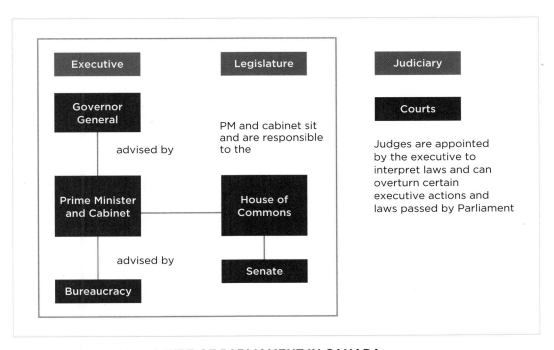

FIGURE 5.1 **THE STRUCTURE OF PARLIAMENT IN CANADA**

Responsible Government

If at any time the government loses its majority support (confidence) in the House, tradition requires that it resign. At this point, and in most cases, a fresh election would be called. However, if another party can put together a government that would be supported by a majority of MPs, the Governor General may call on the leader of that party to try to form a government.

The constitutional principle that the prime minister and cabinet require the confidence of the elected House of Commons in order to govern is called **responsible government**. If a government loses the confidence of the House—through either a defeat on an important piece of legislation (i.e., the annual budget or legislation related to government spending) or on a motion of non-confidence proposed by an opposition party—it loses the right to govern. This may appear to place enormous power in the hands of MPs, but it does not. The reason why responsible government does not translate into fearful governments is **party discipline**; *another tradition of British parliamentary government, according to which a party's* MPs *generally vote as a unified block in the legislature.*

In Canada, however, party discipline is more rigidly practised than in the British Parliament. Of the 38 governments that were elected between 1867 and 2006 only six fell because of a defeat in the legislature. All six were **minority governments**: *those that depended on the support of another party's MPs in order to win votes in the legislature.* But even in these circumstances, it is usually the government that finally determines when an election occurs.

On only one occasion has a government been defeated in the Commons and then had its request for *dissolution* of Parliament and an election denied by the Governor General. This was the 1926 "King–Byng affair," and the denial provoked a constitutional crisis over the appropriate role of the Governor General. There was at least the chance of history repeating itself when the Progressive Conservative government's budget was defeated in 1979. The government had been in place a mere nine months, and the possibility of a minority Liberal government supported by the NDP was not totally outrageous. As it happened, however, Governor General Ed Schreyer granted Prime Minister Joe Clark's request for a new election, although Schreyer claimed afterward that he seriously considered asking the leader of the official opposition to try to form a government. In December 2008, when Prime Minister Stephen Harper faced a non-confidence vote in the House of Commons over a mini-budget, he asked the Governor General, Michaëlle Jean, for a prorogation of Parliament even though there had been a general election less than two months earlier.

Responsible government, then, is part of the living Constitution. It operates today, but not in the narrow sense of legislatures making and defeating cabinets. And while disciplined political parties and dominant prime ministers ensure that cabinets seldom are defeated at the hands of uncooperative legislatures, the practice of cabinet government that is accountable to the elected legislature remains a central feature of Canadian democracy. *Responsible government* suffuses the parliamentary process in the form of the *rights of the legislature* and the corresponding *obligations of the government.* The legislature has the right to scrutinize, to debate, and to vote on policies proposed by the government. In order to carry out these activities the legislature has the general right to question the government and to demand explanations for its actions and for those of bureaucratic officials who act in the government's name. The government, for its part, has a constitutional obligation to provide opportunities for legislative scrutiny of its policies and to account for its actions before Parliament. These rights and obligations are largely codified in the *standing orders*—the rules that govern parliamentary procedure.

Ministerial Responsibility

The accountability of the government to the legislature is the reason behind another principle of British parliamentary government, **ministerial responsibility**. It *entails the obligation of a cabinet minister to explain and defend policies and actions carried out in her or his name*. This individual accountability of cabinet ministers rests on a combination of constitutional law and parliamentary tradition. Section 54 of the Constitution Act, 1867 gives to cabinet the exclusive right to put before the legislature measures that involve the raising or spending of public revenue. The Constitution also requires that any legislation that involves raising or spending public money must originate in the elected House of Commons. In practice, such measures are introduced by particular members of the government. For example, changes to the tax system are proposed by the minister of finance. This reflects the liberal-democratic principle of no taxation without representation, whereby only the people's elected representatives should have the right to propose laws that affect voters' pocketbooks. The accountability of ministers is, therefore, to the people's elected representatives.

Two fundamental principles of British parliamentary government, i.e., strong executive authority and democratic accountability, come together in the concept of ministerial responsibility. Strong executive authority is a tradition that dates from an era when the monarch wielded real power, and the principle that these powers depended on the consent of the legislature was not yet established. When the legislature finally gained the upper hand in the seventeenth century, the tradition of strong executive power was not rejected. Instead, it was tamed and adapted to the democratic principle that government is based on the *consent of the governed*. Since then, individual ministers and cabinet as a whole have exercised the powers that, symbolically, continue to be vested in the Crown. But they do so in ways that enable the people's elected representatives to vote on their proposals and to call them to account for their policies (see Figure 5.2).

In recent times the constitutional principle of ministerial responsibility has come under increasing pressure because of the enormous volume of decisions taken in a minister's name. In fact, no minister can

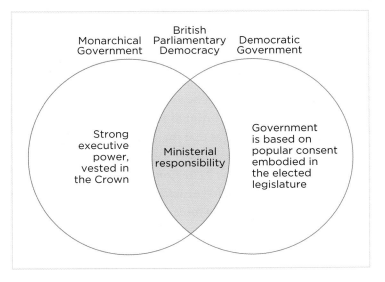

FIGURE 5.2 THE CONSTITUTIONAL ROOTS OF MINISTERIAL RESPONSIBILITY

be well informed about all the policies and actions undertaken in his or her name, and consequently, much decision-making power has passed into the hands of unelected officials. Some have suggested that accountability should be located where decision-making power really lies, but that elected members of the government remain directly accountable for the general lines of policy and for major decisions; otherwise, a vital link in the chain of accountability that joins the people to those who govern them is lost.

Parliamentary Supremacy versus Constitutional Supremacy

Another central feature of British parliamentary government is **parliamentary supremacy**. This means that *the courts will not second-guess the right of Parliament to pass laws on any subject.* Parliament embodies the popular will, and unpopular laws can always be defeated by changing the government at the next election. In a federal system like Canada's, the division of law-making powers between the national and provincial governments complicates matters. But so long as Ottawa and the provinces act within their own spheres of authority, both the federal and provincial parliaments are supreme.

This was the situation in Canada until 1982. When called on to determine whether a law was constitutional or not, the courts almost always referred to the federal division of powers set down in the Constitution Act, 1867. If a legislature was not intruding onto the constitutional territory of the other level of government, its actions were deemed "constitutional." Exceptions to this rule were cases in which laws or actions ran afoul of procedural rules of the common law, like the principles of natural justice. The substance of laws, on the other hand, would not be questioned.

Those who opposed the Charter argued that entrenching rights and freedoms in the written Constitution would result in a transfer of power from legislatures to the courts. This is indeed what has happened. Since 1982, the Supreme Court has struck down numerous federal and provincial laws on the grounds that they violated the guarantees set forth in the Charter. The defenders of parliamentary supremacy claim that a system of court-protected rights and freedoms is fundamentally undemocratic. Their reasoning is that it substitutes the decisions of non-elected judges for those of the people's elected representatives.

What is beyond doubt is that parliamentary supremacy has been replaced in Canada by **constitutional supremacy**. The Constitution Act, 1982 makes this very clear. Section 32 declares that the Charter applies to both the federal and provincial governments and to all matters under their authority. Section 52(1) of the Charter is even more categorical. It states that *"The Constitution of Canada is the supreme law of Canada, and any law that is inconsistent with the provisions of the Constitution is, to the extent of the inconsistency, of no force or effect."* A vestige of Parliament's former superiority is retained, however, through section 33 of the Charter: the so-called **"notwithstanding clause."** *It enables either Parliament or a provincial legislature to declare that a law shall operate even if it violates the fundamental freedoms, legal rights, or equality rights sections of the Charter. Such a declaration must be renewed after five years; otherwise the Constitution reasserts its supremacy.*

Judicial Independence and the Separation of Powers

The role of the judicial branch of government is based on constitutional convention rather than law. The fundamental principles that underlie that role are judicial independence and separation of powers. The Constitution Act, 1867 includes several sections that deal with the system of provincial courts, including how judges shall be selected, how they may be removed, when provincial Superior Court judges must retire (age 75), and who will determine judicial salaries.[23] However, Canadian constitutional law is silent on the powers and the existence and composition of this country's highest court of appeal, the Supreme Court of Canada. Nor is the relationship between the judicial and other branches of government described in much detail. This stands in sharp contrast to the American Constitution, in which there are lengthy descriptions of the powers and separate roles of the legislative, executive, and judicial branches of government. Instead, section 101 authorizes Parliament to establish a "General Court of Appeal for Canada," which it did in 1875 with the Supreme Court of Canada and again in 1970 with the Federal Court of Canada.

It is essential that judges be protected from interference by the government. **Judicial independence** means that *judges are to be free from any and all interference in their decision making*. According to former Chief Justice Brian Dickson, this principle involves "the complete liberty of individual judges to hear and decide the cases that come before them."[24] The principle of judicial independence is deeply embedded in Canada's political culture and enshrined in laws on contempt of court and in guidelines for ministerial conduct. However, doubts have been raised over whether these protections are adequate when, for example, court budgets are determined by governments.[25]

The principle of *separation of powers* guarantees the special role of the judiciary. This role is to interpret the law and the Constitution when disputes arise. As does judicial independence, this principle relies more on cultural norms, statute law, and constitutional convention than it does on constitutional law. There is at least one important reference to the role of the judicial branch in section 24 of the Constitution Act, 1982, which declares that the Charter shall be enforced through the courts.

The perception that the courts represent a check on the powers of Parliament and the provincial legislatures—a perception that has taken hold since the Charter's passage in 1982—reflects an Americanizing trend in Canadian politics. However, the concept of checks and balances between the three branches of government, which is basic to the American Constitution, is not part of British parliamentary democracy.

The ability of the federal and provincial governments to refer a resolution or draft legislation to the courts for a decision on its constitutionality does not, strictly speaking, respect the principle of separation of powers. Constitutional reference cases enable governments to use the provincial and Canadian supreme courts to receive advisory opinions before acting or to thrust a politically volatile issue into the hands of judges. The separation of powers may also be breached when judges step outside their role as interpreters of the law's meaning to advocate some position or reform. Since the mid 1980s, Supreme Court justices, in public speeches and interviews, have occasionally weighed in on matters of public controversy, including the funding of bilingualism, gender bias in the law and the justice system, multiculturalism, and the appropriate role of the judicial branch in Canada's parliamentary system. For example in 2004, Chief Justice Beverley McLachlin weighed in on the matter of Canadian identity in a speech called "Globalization, Citizenship and Identity" when she remarked

> We have achieved a common national space, a space that reflects our history and our shared values. But it has not been easy. Our shared history is not one of continuous bliss and harmonious interaction between diverse groups. Viewed from the perspective of Aboriginal peoples, ethnic minorities, disabled people or women, it is a history marked by profound mistakes. Despite the dark chapters of our history, an ethic of respect and inclusion has been part of Canada's fabric from its beginnings. Canadian history is replete with the efforts of men and women who sought to define their identity in terms that included the other.

After a judicial career in city and provincial courts in British Columbia, Beverley McLachlin was appointed Chief Justice of the Supreme Court of Canada in 2000, the first woman to hold that position. Her reputation for trying to reach out and actively engage Canadians with their highest court can be seen in the excerpt from her speech "Globalization, Citizenship and Identity." Why might it be appropriate for a judge to start such a conversation with the public about an issue so central as Canadian identity?

I believe that this distinctively Canadian ethic of inclusion and tolerance, this distinctively Canadian definition of self and of citizenship is what continues to help us overcome the feelings of loss and alienation that can readily emerge in communities transformed by immigration. . . .

This recognition of the intrinsic diversity of all Canadians provides an avenue for sustainable public discourse within a political community marked by cultural pluralism. In terms of governance, in terms that matter to you as public servants, the task is to uphold communities and institutions where the overlapping commitments of participants are fostered. In a country of diversity, successful communities are those that serve both as refuge and as springboard—those communities that are the "anchor for self-identification and the safety of effortless secure belonging," but also the catalyst of broader civic duties to larger communities. Much like a family, successful communities and institutions should push us to encounter the world, while remaining shelters of comfort and warmth.[26]

Relations between the House of Commons and the Senate

When the founders designed Canada's Parliament, they took the bicameral structure of Britain's legislature as their model. Accordingly, the legislative branch comprised two bodies: an elected House of Commons (the lower house) and an appointed Senate (the upper house). A literal reading of the Constitution suggests that their powers are roughly equal, the major difference being that money bills must be introduced in the House of Commons. However, the superiority of the elected House of Commons has always been clear. The unelected nature of the Senate, along with the brazen patronage of most government appointments to the Senate, has significantly undermined its legitimacy.

The superiority of the House of Commons over the Senate is reinforced by several constitutional conventions and is evident in many ways. The prime minister and other members of the government, for example, are almost always drawn from the House of Commons. And it is unthinkable that a prime minister and most cabinet ministers not be elected MPs. Occasionally, a senator or two are appointed to cabinet. This usually occurs when the party in power has few (or no) MPs from a particular region of the country. The appointment of Michael Fortier to the Senate, and subsequently to cabinet as minister of public works, after the Conservatives' 2006 election victory (with the promise that he would run for a seat in the House of Commons in the next federal election) was such a case. Fortier is an influential lawyer and financier from Montreal, a city in which the Conservatives did not win a seat in 2006. And occasionally the prime minister will appoint to cabinet someone who is neither an MP nor a senator. By tradition, however, this person will very soon afterward seek election to the House of Commons. The system of democratic accountability would crumble if the prime minister and members of the government were not elected and removable by the electorate.

Another convention that reinforces the House of Commons's superiority is that all bills must pass both the Senate and the House of Commons before they become law. Moreover, the stages through which a bill must pass are identical in both houses of Parliament. While the Senate might occasionally suggest minor revisions to legislation, it was generally accepted that the Senate did not have the right to obstruct or reject the will of the House of Commons. This thinking has changed recently, however. After the 1984 election of the Progressive Conservative government, the Senate, which was dominated by Liberal-appointed senators, became more recalcitrant. The Senate delayed and in some cases rejected bills on such matters as drug patents, government spending, unemployment insurance, the Goods and Services Tax, and the Canada–United States Free Trade Agreement. Constitutional law gives senators this right; constitutional convention suggests that they should not try to exercise it. In 2010, Prime Minister Harper broke an election promise on Senate reform, and engineered a Conservative majority in the Senate by filling several vacant seats with Conservative appointees.

The Biases of British Parliamentary Government

In discussing ministerial responsibility, we noted that the pre-democratic tradition of strong executive authority was never abandoned under British parliamentary government (Westminster model). Instead, it was adapted to the democratic principle that government is based on the consent of the people, a principle embodied in the powers of an elected legislature and in the doctrine of responsible government. However, this adaptation does not appear particularly revolutionary or democratic when we recall that the legislature that embodied the popular will originally was elected by, and accountable to, only a fraction of the people, i.e., property-owning males. Universal male suffrage did not arrive until the late 1800s, and females were enfranchised early in the twentieth century. And while these changes extended participatory rights to all the people, it did not fundamentally alter the *non-participatory* biases that were inherent in the Westminster model.

In *Parliament vs. People,* Philip Resnick argues that these biases are a form of **statism—*a political tradition characterized by a relatively strong political executive and by a population that tends to be deferential toward those in power*.** The adoption of the Westminster model in Canada mainly reaffirmed the tradition of centralized executive authority that had existed before the elected legislature's approval was needed to pass laws. The reaffirmation of strong executive power is, Resnick argues, apparent throughout Canada's founding Constitution Act. "What our Founding Fathers were doing was consolidating an orderly . . . move from direct colonial rule to House Rule. . . . They had a particular kind of [political] order in mind, the parliamentary system as it had evolved in Britain, combining the interests of monarchs, lords and commoners." And while today's executive may be more responsive to the electorate, it has not become a servant of the electorate.[27]

Resnick makes the point that the more deferential political culture of Canada has been generated to some degree by parliamentary institutions that discouraged popular participation in politics beyond voting. It enshrined a sort of top-down philosophy of governance.[28] Parliament was sovereign, yes, but Parliament was not merely the people. It also included the Crown, the traditional seat of state authority, whose powers came to be exercised by a prime minister and cabinet with few serious checks from the legislature.

The evidence suggests that Resnick is right. There may have been some influential currents of participatory politics in Canadian history, particularly coming out of western Canada, but these populist urges have struggled against a parliamentary tradition that concentrates political power in the hands of the prime minister (or premiers) and cabinet.

The Charter of Rights and Freedoms may have modified the British parliamentary government in Canada by replacing parliamentary supremacy with constitutional supremacy. The Charter has no doubt generated a greater consciousness of rights among members of the public and shifted Canadian politics away from its elitist past toward a more participatory model. Indeed, one often hears that the Charter ushered in a new era in Canadian politics characterized by less deference to elites. Nevertheless, the British parliamentary system that operates in Canada, albeit modified by the Charter and the principle of constitutional supremacy, continues to concentrate power in the hands of the prime minister and cabinet, and does not appear to be challenged by the fact that many groups are now bypassing electoral and legislative politics in favour of resolving political issues in the courts. And many agree that politics waged in the courts is not necessarily more democratic or accessible.

C. Amending the Constitution

Constitutions are meant to last a very long time, but they seldom do. Forty-seven countries were independent prior to 1900; only about a third of them were independent by 1950. Canada's Constitution Act, 1867 is one of the oldest and most durable. Only the United States (1789), Sweden (1809), the Netherlands (1814), and the United Kingdom (1832) have older constitutions.

A **coup d'état**, *the illegal overthrow of a government by violence or threat of violence*, is one way of changing a constitution. More peaceful means may also accomplish dramatic change, including the wholesale replacement of one constitution by a fundamentally different one. But radical alteration of the fundamental rules and structures of government is much less common than constitutional reform. Reforms, or **constitutional amendments**, aim to *change some aspect(s) of the existing constitution, leaving the basic constitutional structure intact*. Limited change of this sort is generally accomplished through a formal procedure set down in the constitution.

It is difficult to pinpoint when constitutional reform becomes constitutional upheaval. The line has certainly been crossed when a constitution is no longer recognizably what it was before. For example, the 1982 Constitution Act did three main things: (1) transformed Canada's written Constitution from a set of British laws into Canadian constitutional law; (2) entrenched the Charter of Rights and Freedoms in the Constitution; and (3) established formal mechanisms for changing the Constitution. These important changes did not amount to a new Constitution. Most features of parliamentary government and of federalism remained the same. On the other hand, the replacement of parliamentary government by American-style congressional government, the elimination of federalism, or the political independence of Quebec, would each represent a radical transformation of Canada's Constitution.

Constitutional change may also come about through the gradual evolution of principles and practices. For example, the principle that the Governor General should accept the advice of the prime minister on the matters of calling elections and on the prorogation of Parliament is one that emerged gradually as Canada shook off the vestiges of its colonial relationship to Great Britain. This principle was breached by Governor General Lord Byng in 1926 when he denied Prime Minister Mackenzie King's request to dissolve Parliament and call an election; it only then became clear that this relationship between the prime minister and the Governor General was part of the Constitution. The superiority of the House of Commons over the Senate on matters of legislation is another constitutional convention that became clearer with the passage of time. Those appointed to the Senate in 1867 were largely prominent politicians from the new provinces. It was during this early period that the Senate became known as the chamber of "sober second thought." Over time, however, the practice of patronage appointments, the emergence of assertive provincial governments as spokespersons for regional interests, and changing ideas about democracy and representation all contributed to the Senate's decline vis-à-vis the Commons.

Amending the Constitution before 1982

The Constitution Act, 1867 gave Ottawa a very modest power to amend Canada's Constitution regarding matters that concerned only the federal government.[29] In practical terms, this power amounted only to the ability to change electoral districts and boundary lines. The Act gave the provincial governments a similar power.[30] Canada's founders, however, provided only very limited amendment powers in sections 91(1) and 92(1) of the Constitution Act, 1867; these did not allow for changing the division of powers and other important matters. The Canadian Constitution was in fact a British law, and the only clear requirement for constitutional change was that a request would have to be made to the British Parliament.

What was not clear, however, was who here in Canada would have to agree before a resolution could be sent to London. Would all provincial governments have to agree on matters that affected their powers? Just how much provincial consent was needed? Did any one province, such as Ontario or Quebec, enjoy a special right to veto amendments? What if all 10 provincial legislatures and the House of Commons agreed to an amendment, but the Senate rejected it?

After decades of uncertainty, the issue was finally decided by the Supreme Court in 1981, when a stalemate in constitutional negotiations had developed between Ottawa and the provinces. The Liberal government of Pierre Elliott Trudeau wanted to patriate the Constitution, entrench in it a Charter of Rights and Freedoms, and establish a formal procedure for future amendments. Only the governments of Ontario and New Brunswick supported Ottawa's proposal. The conflict ended up in the courts when the governments of Manitoba, Newfoundland, and Quebec each asked their provincial supreme courts whether Ottawa's actions were constitutional. The provinces asked: (1) whether Ottawa's proposed amendments affected provincial powers; and (2) if provincial consent was constitutionally required in order to make such changes. Quebec also asked if it had a special veto over amendments. These decisions were then appealed to the Supreme Court of Canada. In its *Reference on the Constitution*[31] the Court made the following points:

- Some level of provincial consent was required for changes affecting provincial powers. This requirement was a constitutional convention, not constitutional law, and could not, therefore, be enforced by the courts.
- The level of required provincial consent was not at all clear. A majority of the provinces had to agree, but unanimous consent was not necessary.
- In constitutional law, no province had a veto over constitutional change. The Court did not opine on whether such a right existed as a matter of constitutional convention.
- Ottawa did not need provincial consent to ask the British Parliament to change Canada's Constitution in ways affecting provincial powers. If the federal government chose to act unilaterally or with the support of only a few provinces, this would be legal, but at the same time unconstitutional!

Not surprisingly, both Ottawa and the dissenting provinces claimed victory. Legally, the way was clear for Ottawa to act with or without the consent of the provinces. Politically, unilateral action remained a very risky option, particularly in light of the Court's acknowledgement that some level of provincial consent was required by constitutional convention. All 11 governments returned to the bargaining table, and in November 1981, 10 of them were able to reach agreement on a compromise document that became the Constitution Act, 1982. Only the Parti Québécois government of Quebec rejected the proposed changes. Despite Quebec's refusal to sign the 1981 agreement, the Constitution Act, 1982 is constitutional law in that province just as it is elsewhere in Canada. A 1982 Supreme Court decision confirmed this.[32]

Amending the Constitution since 1982

The uncertainties surrounding constitutional amendment have been largely dispelled by the Constitution Act, 1982. Part V of the Act establishes four different procedures, each of which applies to certain types of constitutional change. These procedures and when they are used are explained in Table 5.3.

Any of the four amendment procedures may be set in motion by either Ottawa or a provincial government (s. 46[1]). But because intergovernmental agreement is crucial to the success of most amendments, the most likely scenario is that the prime minister and the provincial premiers will first reach an agreement, which will then be submitted to their respective legislatures. This was the procedure that led to the Meech Lake Accord, the first proposal for constitutional amendment under the 1982 rules. The new procedures have not formally expanded the opportunities for public participation, nor have they enlarged the legislature's role in the process.

In addition to the four different procedures for amending the Constitution, the 10 governments also agreed that the 1982 Constitution Act should include an "opting-out" clause. Under section 40, a provincial government that does not agree to an amendment that transfers powers relating to education or other cultural matters from the provinces to Ottawa is not obliged

TABLE 5.3 | AMENDING THE CONSTITUTION

Procedure	Requirement	Application
1. General (ss. 38, 42)	• Resolution passed by the House of Commons and the Senate* • Two-thirds of the legislatures of the provinces that together make up at least half the population of all the provinces	• Reduction or elimination of powers, rights, or privileges of provincial governments or legislatures • Proportionate representation of the provinces in the House of Commons • Senate • Supreme Court of Canada (except its composition) • Extension of existing provinces into the territories • Creation of new provinces
2. Unanimous consent (s. 41)	• Resolution passed by the House of Commons and the Senate* • Resolution passed by every provincial legislature	• Queen • Governor General • Lieutenant-governors • Right of each province to at least as many seats in the House of Commons as it has in the Senate • Use of the English or French language (except changes that apply only to a single province) • Composition of the Supreme Court • Changing the amending procedures of the Constitution
3. Ottawa and one or more provinces (s. 43)	• Resolution passed by the House of Commons and the Senate* • Resolution passed by the legislature of each province where the amendment applies	• Alteration of boundaries between provinces • Use of French or English in a particular province or provinces
4. Ottawa or a province acting alone (ss. 44, 45)	• If Ottawa, a resolution passed by the House of Commons and the Senate* • If a province, a resolution passed by its legislature	• Executive government of Canada, the Senate, and the House of Commons, subject to the limits established by ss. 41 and 42 of the Constitution Act, 1982

*If after 180 days the Senate has not passed a resolution already passed by the House of Commons, Senate approval is not necessary.

to give up this power. Moreover, Ottawa is required to provide "reasonable compensation" to any dissenting province. The Meech Lake and Charlottetown Accords would have expanded the opting-out section, guaranteeing a dissenting province the right to reasonable compensation in the case of any transfer of legislative powers from the provinces to Ottawa. In fact, this would have enshrined a constitutional practice that has existed since 1964.

The Failure of the Meech Lake Accord

The first effort at amending the Constitution, using the 1982 rules, ended in acrimonious failure. The proposed amendment was in fact a group of changes collectively known as the Meech Lake Accord. The Accord was a 1987 agreement between Prime Minister Brian Mulroney and the 10 provincial premiers. It was a response to five demands that the Quebec Liberal government of Robert Bourassa wanted met before signing the 1981 agreement that produced the Constitution Act, 1982. The main changes proposed by the Accord included:

1. Recognition of Quebec as a *distinct society*
2. Constitutional recognition of a province's right to control its own immigration policy (something Quebec had had since 1978)

3. Provincial power to nominate justices for the Supreme Court of Canada
4. Constitutional entrenchment of a province's right to opt out of federal–provincial shared-cost programs and to be reimbursed for running parallel programs of its own
5. Certain changes to constitutional amendment procedures and categories (see Table 5.3).

After three years of wrangling marked by an anti-French backlash in parts of English Canada and a revival of separatist nationalism in Quebec, the Accord expired when the legislatures of Manitoba and Newfoundland failed to ratify it by the constitutionally imposed deadline of 23 June 1990.

Both the birth and the death of the Accord indicated the amendment process is still difficult even though it is formalized. The Accord represented a deal struck by 11 heads of government with no public participation or legislative debate. In fact, the prime minister and some provincial premiers insisted that their agreement could not be altered. It was submitted to their legislatures for ratification, not for modification. Public participation was solicited very late in the process, and only when the Accord seemed destined for defeat. Indeed, it appeared as though the governments saw public participation as nothing more than a resource to use when convenient. Many who opposed the Accord's provisions also denounced the process as undemocratic.

On the other hand, it was also clear that any change to the 1987 first ministers' agreement would have required that a new resolution be submitted to Parliament and all the provincial legislatures, and the ratification process would have to start over again. The chances of reaching an agreement would likely be reduced, and the process prolonged, if debates and participation were allowed after amendment resolutions had been agreed to by governments.

Meech Lake came to grief because of the same obstacle that had blocked previous efforts at constitutional change. The final months leading up to the ratification deadline were marked by acrimonious debate and some ad hoc efforts to salvage the Accord, and finally ended with Quebec being isolated from the other provinces. There was a sense of déjà vu. Quebec had been similarly isolated in 1971 when the first Bourassa government suddenly withdrew its acceptance of the Victoria Charter amendments, and then again in 1981 when René Lévesque claimed

The failure of the Meech Lake Accord is a testament to the difficulty of amending the Constitution.

to have been betrayed by a last-minute deal between the other provinces and Ottawa. In each case, agreement ran aground because the Quebec government and some governments of English Canada were unable to settle their differences on Quebec's status within Canada.

The Failure of the Charlottetown Accord

The **Charlottetown Accord** of 1992 *was a second attempt at constitutional reform* and was the culmination of what the federal government rather misleadingly *called the "Canada round" of constitutional negotiations* (the period leading up to Meech Lake having been labelled the "Quebec round"). However, there were two chief reasons why the constitutional issue dominated Canadian politics between 1990 and 1992: the desire to get the Quebec government's agreement to the constitutional changes of 1982, and the worry over the post–Meech Lake resurgence of separatism. The deal struck at Charlottetown in August 1992 bore a striking resemblance to the Meech Lake Accord in some important respects. There were certain carry-overs from Meech, such as Quebec's "distinct society" status, Supreme Court nominations, and provinces' ability to opt out of shared-cost programs without penalty. The main features included

- A "Canada Clause" listing the fundamental characteristics of Canadian society
- Entrenchment of the right to Aboriginal self-government
- An elected Senate with equal representation from the provinces and, eventually, special seats for Aboriginal representatives
- A francophone veto in the Senate regarding bills affecting the French language or culture
- A guarantee to Quebec of at least 25 per cent of the seats in the House of Commons
- Confirmation of the provinces' exclusive jurisdiction in several policy areas
- Some decentralization of powers to the provinces in immigration and labour policy

To avoid the charges of elitist deal making that had been levelled at the Meech Lake process, over the next two years there were dozens of government-organized public hearings on the Constitution and hundreds of conferences and forums organized by academics, political parties, and interest groups. But the Charlottetown Accord also failed. Although there were opportunities for citizens and groups to express their views, the proposals presented to Canadians in the 26 October 1992 referendum were widely viewed as yet another instance of the elites cutting a deal and trying to foist it on the public.

The potentially far-reaching changes proposed in the Charlottetown Accord are reflected in the Canada Clause (see Box 5.2). Its provisions sought to express the fundamental values of Canadians. Had the Accord been passed, the Canada Clause would have been included as section 2 of the Constitution Act, 1867 and would have given the courts guidance in their interpretation of the entire Constitution. It is impossible to know how judges would interpret many of the provisions of the Canada Clause. However, it certainly would have given to the courts a whole new field of opportunity, on top of that already provided by the Charter, to involve themselves in the policy-making process. It requires little imagination, for example, to predict that subsection (1)f of the proposed Canada Clause, committing Canadians to "respect for individual and collective human rights and freedoms of all people," could become the legal basis for challenges to social spending cuts, or that subsection (1)b on the Aboriginal peoples of Canada could become the basis for legal claims on tax resources and distinctive legal rights for Aboriginal Canadians.

In the national referendum on the Charlottetown Accord, a majority of Canadians (54.5 per cent) rejected the proposed reforms. During the impassioned referendum campaign it was clear that many English Canadians said "no" to the Charlottetown Accord because they thought it gave Quebec too much. A further decentralization of powers to the provinces and special status for Quebec proved to be more than most English Canadians could stomach. Conversely, many francophone Quebecers rejected the deal because they believed it gave them too little! Indeed, the only serious question asked by members of the Quebec media and the province's politicians during the campaign was "Did Quebec get enough in the Charlottetown Accord?" Although it provided the Quebec government with more than had been proposed in the Meech Lake Accord, this was not enough in the nationalist political climate of that time. The failure of the Meech Lake and Charlottetown Accords confirmed that a wide gap existed between the aspirations of francophone Quebecers and those of their compatriots in the rest of the country.

CANADIAN SPOTLIGHT

BOX 5.2 The Canada Clause

(1) The Constitution of Canada, including the *Canadian Charter of Rights and Freedoms*, shall be interpreted in a manner consistent with the following fundamental characteristics:

a) Canada is a democracy committed to a parliamentary and federal system of government and to the rule of law;

b) the Aboriginal peoples of Canada, being the first peoples to govern this land, have the right to promote their languages, cultures and traditions and to ensure the integrity of their societies, and their governments constitute one of three orders of government in Canada;

c) Quebec constitutes within Canada a distinct society, which includes a French-speaking majority, a unique culture and a civil law tradition;

d) Canadians and their governments are committed to the vitality and development of official-language minority communities throughout Canada;

e) Canadians are committed to racial and ethnic equality in a society that includes citizens from many lands who have contributed, and continue to contribute, to the building of a strong Canada that reflects its cultural and racial diversity;

f) Canadians are committed to a respect for individual and collective human rights and freedoms of all people;

g) Canadians are committed to the equality of female and male persons; and,

h) Canadians confirm the principle of the equality of the provinces at the same time as recognizing their diverse characteristics.

CITIZEN PARTICIPATION IN CONSTITUTIONAL REFORM

For most of Canada's history the only direct actors in constitutional reform were governments. This changed during the negotiations and debates that led to the Constitution Act, 1982, when a number of citizens' interest groups played an active role through lobbying government and attempting to influence public opinion. These groups, and many others inspired by the opportunities created by the Charter, were instrumental in bringing about the death of the 1987 Meech Lake Accord, which had been agreed to by the 11 first ministers in the old pre-1982 style. During the two years of consultation and negotiation that preceded the signing of the 1992 Charlottetown Accord these citizens' interest groups were very much part of the process. Informally at least, Ottawa and the provincial governments appeared to have conceded the legitimacy of a more inclusive style of constitution making.

What they did not concede, however, was a direct role for public participation and consent. Under the old elitist policy-making style, popular consent was mediated by the heads of government. Under the more inclusive policy-making style that emerged in the early 1980s, popular consent was mediated by these heads of government plus certain citizens' interest groups claiming to speak on behalf of women, ethnic and racial minorities, Aboriginal Canadians, the disabled, official-language minorities, and so on. But it was not until the decision was made in the late summer of 1992 to submit the Charlottetown reforms to the people in a national referendum that popular consent was unmediated and the public was given a direct role in the constitutional amendment process. This change represented a remarkable break from Canada's elitist tradition of constitution making.

With few exceptions, mainly in western Canada, the idea of a referendum to approve constitutional change had been rejected throughout Canada's history. When a formal procedure for constitutional amendment was being debated in the 1930s, one of the country's most prominent constitutionalists dismissed the suggestion of a referendum as inconsistent with cabinet government and a device for "passing the buck."[33] Frank Underhill, expressing the views of most intellectuals, argued that average citizens were generally incompetent to decide matters of constitutional change and that their elected representatives usually held more advanced views on public affairs. Legislatures, not citizens, he argued, should be required to ratify constitutional reforms.[34]

However, the idea of holding referendums, while initially considered alien to Canadian political tradition, has gradually emerged in the last 40 years as a means of dealing with contentious matters of provincial or national importance. The flood of condemnation that followed the death of the Meech Lake Accord and the Quebec government's commitment to holding a provincial referendum on whatever agreement it reached with Ottawa promoted the view of referendums as an alternative to elitist-style traditional decision making. The decision to hold a national referendum (a legally non-binding popular vote) on the Charlottetown Accord appeared to mark the beginning of a new era in Canadian constitution making. Most commentators believed that governments in the future would find it difficult to ignore the 1992

Democracy Watch

BOX 5.3   **Referendums: Should the Constitution Be Open to Populist Decision-Making?**

Shouldn't all Canadians have a say in the Constitution that determines how their country should be governed?

In a representative democracy like Canada, power is transferred from the people to elected representatives that form the government, who are entrusted with making decisions related to governing the country. However, declining levels of trust in politicians in recent years has made populist political tools such as the referendum attractive to voters.

One theory suggests that Canadians should be consulted via referendum when an issue is of "transcending national importance."[35] But do all Canadians agree on what is a matter of national importance? For instance, is a movement to include environmental rights in the Canadian Constitution (approximately 90 other countries have done so in the last 40 years), as important nationally as, say, a movement to change the number of regional representatives in the House of Commons? Moreover, do all Canadians feel confident casting a vote on matters grounded in legal, rather than social, terms?

Up for Debate

Is the average Canadian qualified to vote on all constitutional matters? Should changes to the Constitution be made via mandatory referendum? What alternatives can you think of to involve the citizenry in constitutional reform?

precedent of a popular ratification vote. In British Columbia and Alberta, which have more of a populist tradition, the political pressure for constitutional referendums may be irresistible. It remains to be seen whether governments will feel obliged to submit future agreements to the electorate for ratification or whether the Charlottetown experience was an aberration that has left no mark on Canada's political culture.

The Right to Secede

On 20 August 1998 the Supreme Court of Canada handed down its much-awaited decision on the constitutionality of Quebec separation. To some, the most remarkable aspect of the ruling was that it was made at all. The separation of Quebec, if and when it comes about, is a political matter that will be determined by politicians and the people, not by nine appointed judges in Ottawa. This was certainly the view of most Quebec nationalists and of Quebec's Parti Québécois government, whose disdain for the process was such that it refused to send lawyers to argue the case for the constitutionality of Quebec secession. Indeed, the Supreme Court's involvement in this matter was widely viewed by francophone Quebecers as unwarranted meddling in the internal affairs of the province.

In 1996, Ottawa decided to refer the issue of the constitutionality of unilateral secession by Quebec to the Supreme Court. There were political risks associated with Ottawa's involvement in a court challenge to Quebec secession. The Liberal government's decision to push forward, despite these risks, was consistent with what had come to be known as the "Plan B" approach to Quebec separatism. Whereas "Plan A" had involved efforts to satisfy moderate Quebec nationalists with promises of distinct society status for Quebec and some decentralization of powers to the provinces, "Plan B" was a hard-line approach that relied on convincing Quebecers that separation would carry significant economic costs and that some parts of Quebec's lands might not fall under the authority of an independent Quebec state (this was the partition threat, made by predominantly anglophone communities and Aboriginal groups in Quebec, and occasionally expressed by Stéphane Dion, the Liberal minister of intergovernmental affairs). The court challenge to Quebec secession became a major component of the "Plan B" strategy.

Ottawa submitted three questions to the Supreme Court:

1. Under the Constitution of Canada, can the National Assembly or government of Quebec effect the secession of Quebec from Canada unilaterally?
2. Does international law give the National Assembly or government of Quebec the right to effect the secession of Quebec from Canada unilaterally? In other words, is there a right to self-determination in international law that applies to Quebec?
3. If there is a conflict between international law and the Canadian Constitution on the secession of Quebec, which takes precedence?

The Court decided that there was no conflict as in question 3, and so only the first two questions were addressed.

The Court's answer to the first question was a model of ambiguity that provided both federalists and separatists with arguments. In strictly legal terms, said the Court, the secession of Quebec involves a major change to the Constitution of Canada that "requires an amendment to the Constitution, which perforce requires negotiation."[36] However, the Constitution of Canada consists of more than the Constitution Acts passed between 1867 and 1982. "Underlying constitutional principles," said the Court, "may in certain circumstances give rise to substantive legal obligations . . . which constitute substantive limitation upon government action."[37] These underlying constitutional principles provided the basis for the Court's argument that if a clear majority of Quebecers voted "yes" to an unambiguous question on Quebec separation, this would "confer legitimacy on the efforts of the government of Quebec to initiate the Constitution's amendment process in order to secede by constitutional means"[38] These underlying constitutional principles also impose on Ottawa and the provincial governments outside of Quebec an obligation to negotiate the terms of secession, if and when Quebecers and their provincial government express the democratic will to separate.

So who wins on the first question? Both federalists and separatists found enough in the Supreme Court's ruling to allow them to claim victory. Federalists emphasized that, legally speaking, Quebec has no constitutional right to secede unilaterally, and that even if separatists were to win a referendum the Court specified that a "clear majority" on an "unambiguous" question would be required before such a vote could be considered an expression of the democratic will of Quebecers on so weighty a matter. Separatists—or at least those who were even willing to acknowledge the Court's ruling—emphasized that the Court had agreed that the democratically expressed will of Quebecers had to be taken into account in determining whether unilateral secession was constitutional, and that if Quebecers were to express their clear support for separation the rest of Canada would be constitutionally bound to respect this decision and negotiate the terms of secession.

The Court's answer to the second question—whether international law gives Quebec the right to secede—was both shorter and less ambiguous. The Court said "no." While acknowledging that the right of self-determination of peoples exists in international law, the Supreme Court held that this right did not apply to Quebec.

The Court did not answer the contentious question of whether the Quebec population or a part of it constitutes a "people" as understood in international law. It argued that such a determination was unnecessary because, however the Quebec people might be defined, it is clear that Quebecers are neither denied the ability to pursue their "political, economic, social and cultural development within the framework of an existing state,"[39] nor do they constitute a colonial or oppressed people (a claim that is a staple of contemporary Quebec historiography). The Court's pronouncements on these matters are found in Box 5.4.

Does the Supreme Court ruling make a difference? Probably not, or at least not much of one, as the Court seemed to acknowledge at various points in its decision. On the issue of what would constitute a "clear majority" and an "unambiguous question" in a referendum on Quebec independence, the Court admitted that "it will be for the political actors to determine what constitutes a 'clear majority on a clear question.'"[40] Likewise, the practical meaning of the Court's ruling is that the constitutional obligation of the rest of Canada to negotiate the terms of separation with Quebec, if Quebecers express the democratic will to secede, would be for political actors to settle. Finally, in response to the argument that a unilateral declaration of independence by Quebec would be effective whether or not the Court's test of a clear majority on a clear question was met, the judges could say only that this might well be true, but the action would be unconstitutional nonetheless. One suspects that separatists would not lose much sleep over the constitutionality of such a declaration, particularly if, as seems possible, France and certain other countries were to immediately recognize the new Quebec state.

The Clarity Act

Ottawa's response to the 1998 Supreme Court ruling was to pass the Clarity Act in 2000. The Act empowers Parliament (1) to review the wording of any future referendum question to determine whether it is "unambiguously worded" and (2) to determine whether the margin of victory for the separatism option constitutes the "clear majority"—both requirements of the Supreme Court ruling. Under this law the Parliament of Canada could, conceivably, refuse to enter into negotiations on separatism with Quebec if it determined that one or both of these conditions were not met. "Conceivably" is the key word here. There are strong reasons to think that Ottawa's rejection of a referendum question designed by a sovereignist Quebec

Surrounded by his Liberal MPs, then Prime Minister Jean Chrétien stands in the House to cast his vote for the Clarity Act (Bill C-20) in 2000. The Act outlines conditions under which the Government of Canada would enter into negotiations with a province attempting to secede. Though the Clarity Act would apply to any province orchestrating a separation from the rest of the country, many Quebecers interpreted the Act as a means to squelch any further forays down the path of separation.

government, or of even a fairly narrow margin of victory for those in favour of independence, could well backfire, playing into the hands of separatists who would be quick to accuse the federal government and the rest of Canada of meddling in Quebec's affairs. The aim of the Clarity Act was doubtless to strengthen the federalists' hand in a future Quebec referendum, but the actual result could prove to be quite the opposite.

SUMMARY

What should we remember about the Canadian Constitution? First, our Constitution has both written and unwritten components, and is an agglomeration of traditions, conventions, statutes, and documents. Second, our constitutional founders borrowed the British parliamentary model of democracy, as well as the American federal model for sharing power between the central and provincial governments. Third, our Constitution establishes a set of important relationships: between the individuals and the state (fundamental rights and freedoms,

CANADIAN SPOTLIGHT

BOX 5.4 International Law and the Self-Determination of Quebec

There is no necessary incompatibility between the maintenance of the territorial integrity of existing states, including Canada, and the right of a "people" to achieve a full measure of self-determination. A state whose government represents the whole of the people or peoples resident within its territory, on a basis of equality and without discrimination, and respects the principles of self-determination in its own internal arrangements, is entitled to the protection under international law of its territorial integrity.

The Quebec people is not the victim of attacks on its physical existence or integrity, or of a massive violation of its fundamental rights. The Quebec people is manifestly not, in the opinion of the *amicus curiae*, an oppressed people.

For close to 40 of the last 50 years, the Prime Minister of Canada has been a Quebecer. During this period, Quebecers have held from time to time all the most important positions in the federal cabinet. During the 8 years prior to June 1997, the Prime Minister and the Leader of the Official Opposition in the House of Commons were both Quebecers. At present, the Prime Minister of Canada, the Right Honourable Chief Justice and two other members of the Court, the Chief of Staff of the Canadian Armed Forces and the Canadian ambassador to the United States, not to mention the Deputy Secretary-General of the United Nations, are all Quebecers. The international achievements of Quebecers in most fields of human endeavour are too numerous to list. Since the dynamism of the Quebec people has been directed toward the business sector, it has been clearly successful in Quebec, the rest of Canada and abroad.

The population of Quebec cannot plausibly be said to be denied access to government. Quebecers occupy prominent positions within the government of Canada. Residents of the province freely make political choices and pursue economic, social, and cultural development within Quebec, across Canada, and throughout the world. The population of Quebec is equitably represented in legislative, executive, and judicial institutions. In short, to reflect the phraseology of the international documents that address the right to self-determination of peoples, Canada is a "sovereign and independent state conducting itself in compliance with the principle of equal rights and self-determination of peoples and thus possessed of a government representing the whole people belonging to the territory without distinction."

—*Excerpt from The Supreme Court of Canada, Reference re the Secession of Quebec (1998).*

guarantees for individuals and groups); between the different institutions of the state (executive, legislature, and judiciary); and between central and regional governments (federalism). And finally, our Constitution embodies certain key principles and concepts (many of them derived from our British parliamentary heritage) that are essential to the proper functioning of our democracy:

- Constitutional monarchy
- Rule of law
- Judicial review
- Representative government
- Responsible government
- Ministerial responsibility
- Federalism

We should also remember that our Constitution has continuously evolved since it was first written in 1867. Failure to achieve constitutional changes in the 1970s led to the first Quebec referendum on separation in 1980 and a promise by Prime Minister Trudeau to patriate and amend the Constitution. One of the most important changes to the Constitution when it was patriated in 1982 was the constitutional entrenchment of the Charter of Rights and Freedoms. The entrenchment of certain rights and guarantees has resulted in a significant shift away from parliamentary supremacy and given our judiciary a greater role in matters that affect ordinary Canadians. The procedures used to amend the Constitution also changed after 1982, and made it possible to amend the Constitution here in Canada. Since 1982 there have been two attempts at amending the Constitution: the Meech Lake Accord and the Charlottetown Accord. Both ended in failure. These failures led to a second Quebec referendum in 1995.

With respect to a province's right to secede from Confederation, our own Supreme Court and international law both suggest that secession is possible, but that certain conditions would have to be met for the act of secession to be considered legitimate.

STARTING POINTS FOR RESEARCH

Alan Cairns, *Constitution, Government, and Society in Canada: Selected Essays* (Toronto: McClelland & Stewart, 1988).

Peter W. Hogg, *Constitutional Law of Canada* (Scarborough, Ont.: Carswell, 2007).

Peter Russell, *Constitutional Odyssey: Can Canadians Become a Sovereign People?*, 2nd edn (Toronto: University of Toronto Press, 1993).

F.R. Scott, *Essays on the Constitution* (Toronto: University of Toronto Press, 1977).

CBC ARCHIVES AND TVO'S *THE AGENDA*

Visit the companion website for *Canadian Democracy: A Concise Introduction* to follow links to audio and video footage related to the main themes of the chapter: www.oupcanada.com/BrooksConcise.

RELEVANT WEBSITES

Visit the companion website for *Canadian Democracy: A Concise Introduction* to browse a collection of websites featuring material related to the key themes of the chapter, an excellent starting point for research.

REVIEW EXERCISES

1. How do you think our constitutional system would change if all votes in the House of Commons were free votes?

2. Draft a "Canada Clause" to be added at the beginning of the Constitution Act, stating in no more than 100 words the values and core principles that Canada stands for. How does this clause compare to the openings of the constitutions of the United States and France?

3. Debate: Examine the model of the Nunavut Legislative Assembly, where the 19 members sit in a circle, and the parliamentary model used in Ottawa where the government and the opposition parties sit across a centre aisle from each other. Which model works best? Would government be better without partisanship?

4. What conditions would have to be met for a province to be allowed to secede from Confederation? And which matters would have to be negotiated for this province to leave Confederation?

6

Rights and Freedoms

In modern democracies political demands are often expressed in the language of rights and freedoms. This chapter examines some of the controversies associated with rights and freedoms, and discusses the impact of the Canadian Charter of Rights and Freedoms on Canadian politics. After reading this chapter, you will be able to

1. Explain the meaning and origins of "rights and freedoms"
2. Compare the pre-Charter era (1867–1981) with the post-Charter era
3. Differentiate between parliamentary supremacy and constitutional supremacy
4. Outline the consequences of the "notwithstanding clause"
5. Explain how the Charter has been applied by the courts with respect to individual rights and freedoms and to equality

Like the Ten Commandments, rights and freedoms are usually expressed in uncompromising language. Those who argue the case for a woman's right to control her body, or a fetus's right to life, or an individual's right not to be discriminated against on the basis of race or gender typically advance their claims as moral absolutes. Moral absolutes, like Biblical injunctions, are non-negotiable. Either a right or freedom exists or it does not. And if it exists, it must be respected in all cases and not simply when governments or the majority find it convenient to do so. The politics of rights tends to reduce the space for and possibility of negotiation and compromise.

In reality, however, no right or freedom is absolute. There are two reasons for this. One is that rights and freedoms may collide, necessitating some compromise. Does freedom of expression, for example, protect the right of an individual to falsely shout "Fire!" in a crowded theatre? Obviously, there must be limits. To guarantee an individual's freedom of expression in such circumstances could jeopardize the right of other individuals to be protected from unreasonable danger. Many other complex issues arise. Should freedom of expression protect people who "willfully promote hatred"[1] against some group? When do national security considerations trump the individual's right to privacy? Is affirmative action a legitimate means for promoting social equality, or is it **reverse discrimination**—*policies that shift the burden of injustice onto the shoulders of the qualified members of advantaged groups who are not personally responsible for the injustices suffered by minority groups*? Who should determine these issues, the courts or the people's elected representatives?

A second reason why no right or freedom can be treated as an absolute is that this is often impractical. If, for example, a constitution guarantees the right of official-language minorities, does that mean that all government services in the whole country should be available in each of the official languages? Common sense suggests that there are limits to how far, and in what circumstances, the principles of linguistic equality and minority rights should apply.

In another example that occurred in 1990, an Ontario Superior Court judge decided to dismiss hundreds of cases that had been on the docket for months, because the time spent by many accused persons in jail or on bail while waiting for their trial date violated section 11(b) of the Charter—the right "to be tried within a reasonable time." Can the bureaucratic procedures and budget constraints that led to these delays and inflicted real hardship on individuals be justified as "practical limitations" on rights? Or are they matters of mere administrative convenience or policy that should not take precedence over individual rights? Dilemmas like this await us at every turn.

Despite such controversies, and despite the passions they usually unleash, rights and freedoms have had a low profile in Canadian politics for most of this country's history. The courts were reluctant to question the authority of elected legislatures to pass laws, except to decide whether the matter in question constitutionally belonged to Ottawa or to the provinces. As a result, civil liberties issues were transformed into squabbles over the federal–provincial division of powers. This situation changed, however, with the passage of the Charter of Rights and Freedoms in 1982. The Charter entrenched various rights and freedoms in the Constitution, and placed these rights more or less beyond the interference of governments, essentially establishing a principle of *constitutional supremacy* over that of *parliamentary supremacy*.

During the first couple of decades after the Charter's passage, the Supreme Court of Canada handed down several hundred Charter rulings at a rate of about 20–30 per year, including many that had major effects on public policy. And while the pace of judicial interventions seems to have slowed recently, the Charter has decisively changed the face of Canadian politics.

The authority of elected legislatures has receded before the authority of the Constitution and the courts, and the venues and the language of Canadian politics have changed. The discourse of "rights," always a part of the political scene, has assumed much greater prominence since passage of the Charter. Individuals, organized interests, and even governments have turned increasingly to litigation as a means of influencing public policy. But what are the consequences of what Michael Mandel has called the legalizing of politics? Is post-Charter Canada more or less democratic? And aside from lawyers, which groups have gained from these changes?

THE MEANING OF RIGHTS AND FREEDOMS

Rights and freedoms are not watertight compartments in practice. Nevertheless, constitutional experts usually reserve the term "rights" for those individual and group *entitlements* that "are considered so fundamental to human dignity that they receive special protection under the law and usually under the constitution of a country."[2] *Freedoms* involve an individual's liberty to do or believe certain things without restraint by government. Whereas the defence of rights often requires some government action, the protection of freedoms requires that government refrain from interfering in certain matters. Rights suggest an active role for government, freedoms a limited one.

Civil liberties or **civil rights** are terms sometimes used to *refer to all the basic rights and freedoms of citizens*. Under the influence of the United Nations' **Universal Declaration of Human Rights** (1948), the term **human rights** is *used to refer to all the basic rights and freedoms of citizens*, and has become more commonly used to refer to this bundle of rights and freedoms. They include

- *Political rights/fundamental freedoms:* freedom of association, assembly, expression, the media, conscience, and religion, and the right to privacy
- *Democratic rights:* rights of all adult persons to vote and stand for public office, the holding of periodic elections, and the application of law equally to those who govern and to the governed
- *Legal rights:* procedural rights intended to ensure the fair and equal treatment of individuals under the law—the right to due process of law, freedom from arbitrary arrest, the right to a fair hearing, the right to legal counsel, and the right not to be subjected to cruel or unusual punishment
- *Economic rights:* the right to own property and not to be deprived of it without fair compensation, the right to withhold one's labour, and freedom of contract. Economic rights are usually not listed as a separate category of entrenched rights, but they are important in all capitalist democracies.
- *Equality rights:* This is the most recent and probably the most controversial category of rights. The American Constitution, the first modern constitution to include an entrenched guarantee of equality rights, refers only to every person's right to "equal

protection of the laws."[3] The more recent tendency, however, has been to enumerate the proscribed bases of legal discrimination, such as race, religion, ethnicity, gender, and age. Canada's Charter includes mental or physical disability in this list, and has been interpreted by the courts to prohibit discrimination based on sexual orientation.

These five categories are not exhaustive. Other rights could include *language rights* or *group rights* (e.g., religious minorities or Native peoples). Some have argued that *social rights* or *entitlements*, including the right to a job, economic security, housing, and health care, should be entrenched in the Constitution. *Environmental rights* have also been advocated. In Canada, many of the main categories of human rights are entrenched in the Charter, which means that they are firmly established in the Constitution, and that changing or removing them is difficult and unlikely.

EMERGENCE OF RIGHTS ISSUES

Rights issues emerge out of political struggles, and this struggle is a necessary condition for rights claims. What may appear to be obvious and uncontroversial rights claims in Canadian society—for example, the right to vote or the right to express one's personal beliefs—are denied in many societies. Only some political conflicts acquire the character of rights issues. For a rights issue to be considered legitimate, a rights claim must be anchored to one or more of a society's core values/beliefs. These fundamental values operate as limits on rights discourse. And a claim made by an individual or a group will be expressed as a right only when it is denied or placed in jeopardy by the words or actions of another group.

Consider the familiar issue of abortion. Those who argue for a woman's right to abort her pregnancy have often linked this rights claim to individual freedom of choice, a fundamental value in liberal-democratic society. Those who oppose abortion, or who favour restrictions on access to it, often argue that the human fetus has a right to life, the most fundamental of rights in any civilized society. Those who favour access to abortion would, of course, object to the imputation that they do not value human life, just as those who oppose abortion would deny that they undervalue individual freedom. Behind these rights, as behind all the rights that are widely recognized in democratic political systems, rests one (or more) fundamental value, such as the equality of human beings, the autonomy of the individual, and, most important, the nature of the good society. The abortion issue illustrates well the way in which rights claims tend to be squeezed into existing ideological and legal categories, and how unconventional political discourses are discouraged by legalized politics. The success of individual women, women's organizations, and abortionists like Dr Henry Morgentaler in challenging legal restrictions on access to abortion has been due to their case being framed in legal arguments and moral claims that fall within the dominant ideology.

The passage of the Charter opened up new legal avenues to abortion advocates. Canada's abortion law was eventually ruled unconstitutional by a 1987 Supreme Court decision in which the majority ruled that the law violated security of the person. But the same majority agreed that the state has an interest in protecting the fetus, although the Court did not specify the circumstances or stage of fetal development in which abortion would be unacceptable. This acknowledgement of fetal rights provided some encouragement to the anti-abortion coalition, whose political strategy focused increasingly on claiming the personhood of the unborn.

THE PRE-CHARTER ERA

In the pre-Charter era, 1867–1981, rights had a low profile. A couple of factors were responsible for this; the most important was federalism. The Constitution Act, 1867 contains very few references to the rights and freedoms of Canadians. It does, however, include a very detailed catalogue of the "rights" of governments, i.e., the legislative and fiscal powers of Ottawa and the provinces. Faithful to the principle of parliamentary supremacy, the courts were unwilling to overrule the authority of elected legislatures. What appeared to be rights issues were often decided as matters of federalism, of which level of government had jurisdiction. To have a chance at success, therefore, rights claims had to be packaged in the constitutional categories of federalism. The resulting jurisprudence was bizarre, to say the least. Very few court decisions were based on a clear-cut rights argument.

A second factor was responsible for the relatively low profile of rights issues until well into the twentieth century. Most Canadians probably felt that rights were best protected by legislatures, the common law, and a vigilant public: the system that Canada had inherited from the United Kingdom. But increasingly, doubts about the adequacy of these guarantees were being expressed during the 1940s and 1950s by apparent rights violations like Quebec's infamous "Padlock Law" (1937), the Alberta government's attempt to censor the press (1937), the threatened deportation of Japanese Canadians in 1945–6, and the arbitrary measures taken during the Igor Gouzenko spy affair of 1946.

The growing concern over civil liberties was shared by influential groups such as the Canadian Bar Association. They argued that a bill of rights—one that reflected the human rights commitments entered into through the UN—should be entrenched in the Constitution. When the Progressive Conservative Party came to power in 1957 under the leadership of John Diefenbaker, an outspoken advocate of entrenched rights, the timing for a Bill of Rights seemed propitious.

But there was a major snag. Constitutionally entrenching a Bill of Rights that would affect the powers of both Ottawa and the provinces seemed to require the consent of the provinces. It was clear that some of the provinces would oppose entrenchment; consequently, the Conservative government chose to introduce the Bill of Rights as a statute, requiring only the approval of the House of Commons and the Senate.

The **Canadian Bill of Rights** was *a statutory declaration of rights passed by the Canadian Parliament on 10 August 1960*. The rights in the Bill of Rights were not entrenched as they were in the 1982 Charter of Rights and Freedoms, and therefore did not carry the same constitutional and legal weight and influence. It proved to be a major disappointment for civil libertarians. As several court cases would show, the Bill seemed to apply only to the federal government. For almost a decade afterward, the Supreme Court decisions on its application were very conservative and merely reaffirmed the status quo of rights and freedoms prior to 1960.

One particular case, though, seemed to buck the trend. Under the Indian Act, it was illegal for an Indian[4] to be intoxicated off a reserve. In the 1970 *R. v. Drybones* case, the Court agreed that the charge of intoxication against Joseph Drybones conflicted with the Canadian Bill of Rights guarantee of "equality before the law," by subjecting Indians to criminal sanctions that other people were not exposed to. By a five-to-three vote, the Supreme Court used the Bill of Rights to strike down section 94 of the Indian Act.[5] The *Drybones* case proved to be an aberration, however. In subsequent rulings, the Supreme Court retreated from this interpretation of the Bill of Rights. The glimmer of hope that the *Drybones* decision had sparked was extinguished during the 1970s, producing renewed calls for constitutionally entrenched rights.

Before passage of the Charter, the only rights entrenched in Canada's Constitution were associated with religion, language, and elections. However, even on those matters the courts tended to defer to governments and the laws they made. In the Constitution Act, 1867, neither section 93, dealing with education as it related to religion, nor section 133, establishing the equal standing of French and English in Parliament and in federal courts, and in Quebec's legislature and courts, proved to be very effective in protecting minority rights.

Despite the provisions of section 93, the Manitoba Public Schools Act was passed in 1890, which eliminated the Catholic and Protestant schools that had existed in the province and replaced them with a single public school system. In two other cases involving section 93, the courts refused to accept the argument that this section also protected the educational rights of language minorities. The argument had at least a ring of plausibility because, historically, the Roman Catholic schools in Manitoba were predominantly francophone, in Ontario they were often francophone, and Quebec's Protestant schools were anglophone. Thus, when in 1913 the Ontario government banned the use of French as a language of instruction in both public and separate (Catholic) schools, this had a negligible impact on public schools but dealt a major blow to the mostly francophone Catholic schools of eastern Ontario. The issue arose again in the 1970s when the Quebec government passed Bill 22, restricting access to the province's English-language schools, most of which were under the control of Protestant school boards. In both instances the courts rejected outright the claim that section 93 should be read as a protection for linguistic rights in addition to denominational ones.[6]

From the standpoint of promoting bilingualism outside of Quebec, the courts' unwillingness to read language rights into section 93 represented a real setback. On the other hand, the "victories" for language rights in a pair of Supreme Court decisions handed down in 1978 and 1979 produced few practical consequences. Both of these decisions involved the limited guarantee of bilingualism established by section 133 of the Constitution Act, 1867. In both cases the Court declared that this guarantee was beyond the interference of governments, thus repudiating the idea that no action lay outside the competence of Parliament or a provincial legislature so long as it did not encroach on the constitutional powers of the other level of government.

In *Attorney General of Quebec v. Blaikie,*[7] the Supreme Court upheld a Quebec Superior Court decision that had ruled unconstitutional those sections of Quebec's Bill 101 that attempted to make French the sole official language in that province. While Bill 101 did not ban the use of English from the legislature and the province's courts, and the Quebec government continued to print and publish laws and legislative documents in both languages, the law's clear intent was to make French the only official language for all government activities and the dominant language in the province's courts. This, the courts decided, violated the spirit—if not the strict letter—of section 133.

LIFE IN THE POST-CHARTER ERA

During the 1980–81 debate on constitutional reform, critics of an entrenched charter of rights warned that entrenchment would lead to the "Americanization" of Canadian politics, and to the regret of many, the prediction has come true. This Americanization has two main aspects. One involves a more prominent policy role for unelected judges and a related decline in the status of elected legislatures. The other has been an explosion in the number of rights cases brought before the courts, with an accompanying shift to the courts solving political disputes. In short, parliamentary supremacy has been replaced by constitutional supremacy and an increased importance of judges in the governmental process.

Those who advocate the American model of entrenched rights prefer to put their faith in the Constitution and the judges who interpret it. Those who prefer the British model of parliamentary supremacy are more dubious about judge-made law and more inclined to place their trust in the prudence and democratic responsiveness of elected governments.

Does the record of rights enforcement in different countries permit us to draw conclusions about whether the American or the British model is "best"? And has the Charter improved how rights are protected in Canada? There are no easy answers to these questions. Rights activists are themselves divided in their assessment. But if definitive answers are elusive, we can at least attempt to understand how rights have been argued and enforced in Canadian politics. From any perspective, the Charter represents an important watershed.

"In a five to four decision today, the Supreme Court said 'Leave us alone, and we'll leave *you* alone.'"

In the post-Charter era, an increased number of rights issues are being handled by the courts rather than the legislatures. What do you think the cartoonist here is saying about that shift in responsibility for maintaining rights?

In terms of "quality," the change produced by the Charter has been no less pronounced. The previous pattern of deciding rights issues as federalism cases, asking only whether a government was trespassing on the jurisdictional turf of the other level of government, has been abandoned. Rights issues are now dealt with head-on, argued by litigants and decided by judges on the basis of the Charter. Moreover, the courts have shed most of their traditional reluctance to question the substance of duly enacted laws and regulations. Emboldened by the Charter's unambiguous declarations that the "Constitution is the supreme law of Canada" and that the courts have exclusive authority to interpret and enforce the Charter's guarantees, judges have struck down provisions in dozens of federal and provincial statutes. Judges are quite aware of the expanded role they play in the political process, but most insist that there is nothing undemocratic in this. Table 6.1 gives a sense of the many important Charter cases that have come before the Supreme Court since 1982.

Reasonable Limits and the Charter

The courts are "invited" to exercise self-restraint, commonly called **judicial restraint**, by the opening words of the Charter. This is *a legal concept expressed in the Charter that judges should defer to the legislature when exercising their judicial power.* Section 1 declares that the guarantees set forth in the Charter shall be "subject only to such reasonable limits prescribed by law as can be demonstrably justified in a free and democratic society." What are these **reasonable limits**? In the case of *R. v. Oakes* (1986)[8] the Supreme Court establish a standard known as the *Oakes* test on what *reasonable legislative limits can be placed on human rights by legislation if it can be established that they are in the best interest of a free and democratic society.* The first part of this test asks whether a government's objective in limiting a right is sufficiently important to warrant such an encroachment. The second part of the

TABLE 6.1 | CLASSIC CHARTER CASES

Landmark Case	Charter Issue
R. v. Oakes	The "*Oakes* test" of "reasonable limits" on civil rights
R. v. Sparrow	Aboriginal rights
Law v. Canada	Equality rights
R. v. Morgentaler	Women's rights
Re BC Motor Vehicle Act	The right to not be arbitrarily detained
Vriend v. Alberta	Gay rights
Hunter v. Southam Inc.	Government use of search warrants
Andrews v. Law Society of British Columbia	Government use of search warrants
R. v. Collins	The "*Collins* test" on admissibility of evidence
R. v. Stinchcombe	Burden of truth
R. v. Askov	Trial in a timely manner
Reference Re Provincial Electoral Boundaries	Clarifying the Right to Vote

CANADIAN JUDGE IDOL

Must I also sing and dance?

sneuro

Some critics have suggested that if judges are going to play an increased political role in our democracy, there should be a public review of the candidates for the Supreme Court, as there is in the United States. How engaged do you anticipate Canadians might be in a discussion around candidates' eligibility for positions as judges on the Supreme Court of Canada?

test asks whether the extent of the limitation is proportionate to the importance of the government's objective. In order to satisfy this second criterion, a limitation must meet three conditions: (1) it must be rationally connected to the government's objective; (2) it should impair the right in question as little as is necessary to meet the government's objective; and (3) the harm done to rights by a limitation must not exceed the good that it accomplishes.

Some might cite the *Oakes* test as a case of judges interfering with parliamentary authority. But why shouldn't judges give legislators an idea of how the law needs to be changed to bring it into line with their interpretation of the Constitution? The point is, however, that means and ends are not neatly separable in the real world of politics. And who should determine how much or little is enough? Is proportionality an appropriate matter for unelected judges to decide, or should this be determined by elected legislatures?

These questions resurfaced with a vengeance when the Supreme Court ruled on 21 September 1995 that the federal ban on tobacco advertising violated the Charter's guarantee of freedom of expression. Many staunch Charter boosters became skeptics overnight. They were awakened by the tobacco advertising decision to a basic truth of constitutionally entrenched rights: the price of entrenchment is that judges assume a more important role in political life.

The Notwithstanding Clause: Section 33

"What the Charter gives, the legislature may take away." This appears to be the meaning of section 33 of the Charter, the **notwithstanding clause**. It states that *either Parliament or a provincial legislature may expressly declare that a law shall operate even if it offends against section 2 or sections 7–15 of the Charter*. This provision was inserted at the insistence of several provinces. The constitutional deal that produced the Charter would have died without this concession.[9]

Although the notwithstanding clause appears to provide governments with a constitutional escape hatch from much of the Charter, it is not clear that it actually has this effect. It has been resorted to on only a handful of occasions. Why have governments generally been reluctant to use section 33 to avoid or reverse court decisions declaring their laws to be in violation of the Charter? In the words of civil libertarian Alan Borovoy, an outspoken critic of the notwithstanding clause, "The mere introduction of a bill to oust the application of the Charter would likely spark an enormous controversy. . . . Without solid support in the legislature and the community, a government would be very reluctant to take the heat that such action would invariably generate."[10] Some civil libertarians have argued that a legislature's decision to invoke section 33 should itself be subject to review by the courts and therefore possibly be overturned. In a 1985 ruling, the Quebec Court of Appeal agreed. This decision was, however, overruled by the Supreme Court of Canada in *Ford v. Attorney General of Quebec* (1988). The Court pronounced in favour of a literal interpretation of section 33—which also happens to correspond to the intentions of those provincial governments that insisted on the notwithstanding clause—requiring only that a legislature expressly declare its intention to override the Charter.

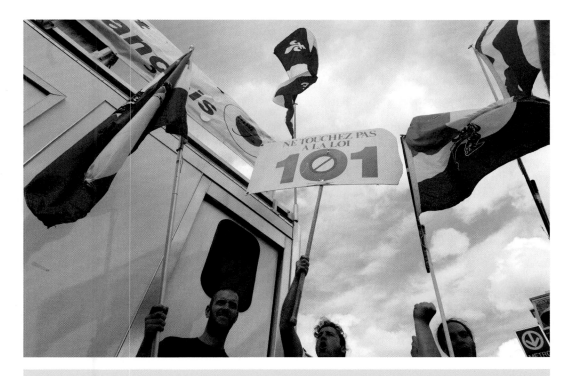

"Don't touch Bill 101." In the case of Bill 101, which protects the French language in Quebec, not using the notwithstanding clause would have been more costly to the Quebec government.

While it appears that there are no serious legal obstacles to a government using section 33 to circumvent the Charter, governments do not want to give the appearance of denying rights to their citizens. In fact, if one does not take into account the PQ's symbolic policy, between 1982 and 1985, of inserting the notwithstanding clause into all laws passed by the Quebec legislature and retroactively into all existing provincial statutes, section 33 has been invoked on only a couple of occasions.

There are, however, circumstances where the denial of rights inflicts little political damage on government and may even produce political dividends. This was certainly true of the Quebec Liberal government's decision to use the notwithstanding clause to re-pass, with some modifications, the provisions of Bill 101 (legislative restrictions on the use of languages other than French) that had been ruled unconstitutional by the Supreme Court. While the government's move precipitated the resignation of three anglophone cabinet ministers and alienated many English-speaking voters, there is no doubt that the political costs of not overriding the Charter would have alienated the much larger French-speaking population and media. The political costs were also negligible when Saskatchewan's Progressive Conservative government inserted section 33 in a 1986 law to force striking public servants back to work.

Democracy Watch

BOX 6.1 To Keep or Not to Keep the Notwithstanding Clause

Those in favour of section 33 say

- In exceptional circumstances, the notwithstanding clause allows elected governments to make policy decisions independent of unelected judges
- This override mechanism is subject to public debate at the time it is enacted and at the time of any reenactment
- The clause acts as a "safety valve" to preserve certain social values and goals if they are threatened by the Charter

Those opposed to section 33 say:

- The clause is inconsistent with the firm establishment of human rights and freedoms guaranteed by the Charter
- The clause may be used in a situation where a principle is only perceived as being, and is not actually, under threat (in other words, it can be used solely as a political tool, perhaps for winning favour with particular special-interest groups)
- The clause can be invoked against those rights and freedoms most in need of protection

Up for Debate

Should section 33 of the Charter of Rights and Freedoms, the notwithstanding clause, be removed? Why or why not?

Do public opinion and vigilant media provide adequate protection against legislative abuses of the notwithstanding clause? This may depend on our expectations for democracy. For some, a law that denies rights to some persons is not a legitimate basis for invoking section 33. They would argue that if the Charter does not protect rights when they are vulnerable, then it fails the real test of its worth: rights are either entrenched against popular passions, the "tyranny of the majority" and legislative assault, or they are not.

But for others, the notwithstanding clause is a mechanism for asserting the *popular will* in exceptional circumstances. For example, some conservative critics of the Charter have argued that governments should be prepared to use the notwithstanding clause more often to reassert the will of the public, particularly on matters like same-sex marriage. The only other way of overcoming an unpopular court decision on the Charter would be to amend the Constitution, a difficult and time-consuming process. The controversy over section 33 is, in the final analysis, nothing less than the familiar debate over parliamentary versus constitutional supremacy.

APPLYING THE CHARTER

News stories on attempts to use the Charter to challenge some law or administrative procedure have become routine. Only a small fraction of the hundreds of trial court rulings on the Charter ultimately reach the provincial superior courts, and fewer still are appealed to the Supreme Court of Canada. Even so, these cases represent a large share of the courts' workload. More than two decades after its passage, it is possible to identify the main tendencies in judicial interpretation of the Charter.

Scope and Authority

With respect to how far would the Court be willing to go in using the Charter to strike down laws passed by elected legislatures, rulings in cases such as *Law Society of Upper Canada v. Skapinker* (1984), indicate that although the Constitution must be considered the supreme law of the land, judges should interpret it in ways that "enable [the legislature] to perform the high duties assigned to it, in the manner most beneficial to the people."[11] In other words, judges should not be too quick to second-guess elected lawmakers.

An additional feature of the Court's approach to the Charter's scope deserves mention. This involves its insistence that the Charter applies only to relationships between the state and citizens, not to private-sector relationships. Thus, the Charter cannot be used by someone who believes that he has been denied a job or an apartment because of his race, or whose private-sector employer requires that she retire at the age of 65. Forms of discrimination like these are pervasive throughout society, but they are not inequalities that can be overcome using the Charter. The Supreme Court has on several occasions articulated this distinction between public (covered by the Charter) and private, as in *Dolphin Delivery* (1986)[12]: "[The Charter] was set up to regulate the relationship between the individual and the government. It was intended to restrain government action and to protect the individual."[13] This position is, in fact, faithful to the intentions of those who framed and agreed to the Charter.

Economic Rights

The Court's refusal to recognize economic rights is related to a public–private distinction. As noted earlier, the Charter is deliberately silent on economic and property rights, except for the qualified protection it extends to the right to live, work, and be eligible for social benefits in any province. Claims that certain economic rights are implied by provisions of the Charter have generally had a cold reception. For example, the courts have expressly rejected business's arguments that a "corporation" should fall within the ambit of section 7 of the Charter, which guarantees the "right to life, liberty and security of the person." The economic rights claims of workers have fared no better. In a 1987 ruling on whether a right to strike exists, the Supreme Court declared "The constitutional guarantee of freedom of association . . . does not include, in the case of a trade union, a guarantee of the right to bargain collectively and the right to strike."[14] The right to bargain collectively and to strike are not, the Court ruled, fundamental rights or freedoms that deserve the constitutional protection of freedom of association under the Charter. "They are," the majority declared, "the creation of legislation, involving a balance of competing interests,"[15] and their scope and limitations are appropriately determined by legislatures. To put it very simply, economic rights were viewed as subordinate to political ones.

But, it is sometimes said that today's dissent becomes tomorrow's law. This appears to be true in the matter of the Supreme Court's interpretation of freedom of association, guaranteed by section 2(d) of the Charter, and worker's rights. In *Dunmore* (2001),[16] the Court struck down as unconstitutional an Ontario law that excluded agricultural workers from collective bargaining rights that were available to other groups of workers.

And it may seem that the courts have not strongly favoured either business or labour in their interpretation of the Charter, but in fact, this appearance of neutrality is deceiving for two reasons. First, business interests have been able to use some of the "political" rights in the Charter to protect property rights, in some cases arguably at the expense of workers, consumers, or other community interests. Second, much of the inequality that exists in society is generated by private economic relations—relations between employers and employees, men and women in the workplace, landlords and tenants, buyers and sellers. To declare that the Charter recognizes only "political" and "democratic" rights but not "economic" ones, as the courts have done, could have the effect of freezing the inequalities that currently exist in society and in the economy. Dominant groups tend to win from this public–private distinction, which places important sources of inequality beyond the authority of the Charter, while subordinate groups lose. The *Dunmore* ruling suggests, however, that the Supreme Court has become less conservative in the matter of economic rights than it was in the past.

Individual Rights and Freedoms

Some individual rights and freedoms are better protected today as a result of the Charter. In fact, the Court's record has been quite mixed. Court decisions have expanded the rights of, among others, those accused of crimes, immigrants, women seeking abortions, and business people wanting to advertise in English in Quebec. On the other hand, Supreme Court decisions

INSIDE POLITICS

BOX 6.2 | Some General Principles of Interpretation that Guide the Courts in Charter Cases

The Charter is designed and adopted to guide and serve the Canadian community for a long time. Narrow and technical interpretation, if not modulated by a sense of the unknowns of the future, can stunt growth of the law and hence the community it serves. It is clear that headings were systematically and deliberately included as an integral part of the Charter for whatever purpose. At the very minimum a court must take them into consideration when engaged in the process of discerning the meaning and application of the provisions of the Charter.

The task of expounding a constitution is crucially different from that of construing a statute. A constitution is drafted with an eye to the future. Its function is to provide a continuing framework for the legitimate exercise of governmental power and, when joined by a bill or a charter of rights, for the unremitting protection of individual rights and liberties. It must be capable of growth and development over time to meet new social, political, and historical realities often unimagined by its framers. The judiciary is the guardian of the constitution and must, in interpreting its provisions, not "read the provisions of the Constitution like a last will and testament lest it become one."

Neither before nor after the Charter have the courts been enabled to decide upon the appropriateness of policies underlying legislative enactments. In both instances, however, the courts are empowered, indeed required, to measure the content of legislation against the guarantees of the Constitution.

It was never intended that the Charter could be used to invalidate other provisions of the Constitution, particularly a provision such as s. 93 of the Constitution Act, 1867, which represented a fundamental part of the Confederation compromise.

In *The Queen v. Big M Drug Mart*, Dickson J. elaborated on how the interests that are intended to be protected by a particular Charter right are to be discovered: "in my view this analysis is to be undertaken, and the purpose of the right or freedom in question is to be sought by reference to the character and the larger objects of the Charter itself, to the language chosen to articulate the specific right or freedom, to the historical origins of the concepts enshrined, and where applicable, to the meaning and purpose of the other specific rights and freedoms with which it is associated within the text of the Charter."

A hierarchical approach to rights, which places some over others, must be avoided, both when interpreting the Charter and when developing the common law. When the protected rights of two individuals come into conflict, as can occur in the case of publication bans, Charter principles require a balance to be achieved that fully respects the importance of both sets of rights.

Source: Excerpted from *Canadian Charter of Rights Decision Digest*, www.canlii.org/en/ca/charter_digest/app-a.html, Canadian Legal Information Institute, 2005. Reproduced with the permission of the Minister of Public Works and Government Services Canada, 2012.

have (1) declared that the Charter's freedom of association does not provide unionized workers with the right to strike; (2) upheld the constitutionality of terribly vague provincial anti-hate laws against claims that they violate freedom of expression; and (3) ruled that secularly worded Sunday closing laws have the effect of being an "indirect and unintentional" violation of freedom of religion, but that they qualify as "reasonable limits" under section 1 of the Charter. Although the courts have not unleashed a torrent of individualism on Canadian society, it is fair to say that individual rights claims tend to do better, and certainly do no worse, under the Charter than previously.

This was certainly true in the *Big M* case, when the Supreme Court decided that the federal Lord's Day Act violated the freedom of religion guarantee set down in section 2 of the Charter. What could not be achieved using the Canadian Bill of Rights became possible under the Charter.

The courts' rulings on legal rights challenges to Canada's criminal law provide another clear illustration of the more liberal treatment of individual rights in the post-Charter era. Charter decisions have produced many important changes in law enforcement practices, including the following:

- "Reverse onus" provisions, requiring a defendant to prove his innocence of a charge, have been ruled unconstitutional.
- Evidence obtained by inappropriate means cannot be used to help convict someone of a crime.
- Writs of assistance, under which the police were able to enter premises without a search warrant, were ruled unconstitutional.
- Search and seizure powers have been restricted.
- Thousands of persons accused of criminal offences have had the charges dismissed because of an Ontario Superior Court ruling that lengthy delays in getting them to trial contravened their section 11(b) right "to be tried within a reasonable time."

In one of the most publicized Charter decisions to date, *Morgentaler* (1988), the Supreme Court struck down Canada's 20-year-old abortion law. Under section 251 of the Criminal Code a woman wanting an abortion required the approval of a hospital's therapeutic abortion committee. However, most local hospitals did not have such a committee, and among the 20 per cent of the hospitals that did perform abortions there were considerable differences in eligibility for the procedure. The majority in *Morgentaler*[17] ruled that the obvious practical inequalities in the application of the law violated section 7 of the Charter, guaranteeing the principles of fundamental justice.

The Court has shown, however, that it is prepared to override individual rights when other values appear to be at stake. This was certainly true when the Supreme Court upheld the hate speech provisions of Canada's Criminal Code in the case of *R. v. Keegstra* (1990).[18] James Keegstra was an Alberta high school teacher who taught his students that the Holocaust was a hoax and an international Jewish conspiracy. He was charged under section 319(2) of the Criminal Code, which makes it a punishable offence to communicate statements, other than in private conversation, that wilfully promote hatred against any identifiable group. In a 4–3 ruling the Supreme Court held that the content of speech, in and of itself, could be considered so offensive as to place it outside the protection of section 2 of the Charter. The ruling in *Keegstra* paid virtually no attention to the question of whether the messages communicated by the accused placed anyone or any group of persons in imminent peril. Such a test was considered to be wholly unnecessary. Instead, the majority accepted the argument that some speech is quite simply inconsistent with the sort of society that Canada is or ought to be, and therefore should be neither tolerated by law nor protected by the Constitution.

There have been a number of important freedom of expression cases under section 2 of the Charter. In *Harper v. Canada* (2004)[19] the Court ruled that the Canada Elections Act's spending limits on third-party election advertising does not violate sections 2(b), 2(d), or 3 of the Charter. The case originated as a challenge brought by Stephen Harper in 2000, when he was president of the National Citizens Coalition, to legislated restrictions on the right of so-called "third parties"—groups and individuals other than registered political parties and their candidates—to spend money on political advertising during election campaigns. The decision is particularly interesting because of the conception of democracy that underpins the majority's ruling, one that sees unfettered freedom of speech as a danger to the equality rights of citizens.

In *WIC Radio Ltd. v. Simpson* (2008), a radio talk-show host and former British Columbia politician, Rafe Mair, in a radio broadcast compared the ideas of a local conservative activist, Kari Simpson, to those of Hitler and the Ku Klux Klan. Simpson claimed that Mair's comments were defamatory and not protected by section 2 of the Charter. Defamation—the impugning of someone's character or actions in a manner that results in real damage being done to that person's reputation, including the impairment of their ability to earn a living—is a private law matter like slip-and-fall accidents on private property. Such matters do not fall directly under the Charter. They are covered by the common law that emerges from judicial rulings on actual cases. However, as the Supreme Court stated in the *Simpson* decision, "the evolution of the common law is to be informed and guided by Charter values."[20] Mair argued that the doctrine of fair comment protected him against the charge of defamation. The Supreme Court agreed. The result of this 2008 ruling is that it is more difficult for public figures or organizations to successfully sue, arguing that their reputation has been damaged, and therefore journalists and broadcasters are less likely to censor themselves out of fear of incurring such lawsuits.

Equality

Any attempt to assess the Charter's overall impact on equality is fraught with difficulties. Some Charter decisions have contributed to greater equality in Canadian society, but others have not.

Section 15 of the Charter deals explicitly with equality rights. Those who drafted this section expected that it would have significant consequences for the laws and administrative practices of governments. For this reason the equality section did not become operative until three years after the Charter was proclaimed. But in fact, section 15 has had less impact on equality in Canada than some other sections of the Charter and less impact than the federal and provincial human rights codes.

First and most important, section 15 does not extend to discrimination in private-sector relationships. We have already discussed the practical consequences of limiting the Charter to abuses of governmental power. As constitutional expert Peter Hogg puts it:

> The real threat to civil liberties in Canada comes not from legislative and official action, but from discrimination by private persons—employers, trade unions, landlords, realtors, restaurateurs and other suppliers of goods or services. The economic liberties of freedom of property and contract, which imply a power to deal with whomever one pleases, come into direct conflict with egalitarian values.[21]

Provincial human rights codes enforced by commissions do, however, cover private-sector relations. In the final analysis the Charter and the courts send out mixed and sometimes confusing signals about equality. The same can be said, of course, about governments. Despite the courts' willingness to go beyond formal legal equality to see whether the effects of a law meet the requirements of the Charter (as the Supreme Court did in *Morgentaler*), the usefulness of the Charter as an instrument for overcoming the most prevalent and deeply rooted forms of social and economic inequality is limited.

Nevertheless, there have been cases where the equality guarantees of the Charter have provided the basis for fairly dramatic and controversial reversals of long-standing public policy. This was true of the Supreme Court's ruling in *M. v. H.* (1999), a case that involved a challenge to the heterosexual definition of spouses in the Family Law Act. The Supreme Court decided that the heterosexual definition of a cohabiting couple under the Family Law Act was unconstitutional, because it denied the same status and rights to homosexual couples.

After a decade and a half of considering equality cases without a systematic and consistent framework for assessing section 15 claims, the Supreme Court developed just such a framework in *Law v. Minister of Human Resources Development*.[22] At the heart of the three-part test is the question of whether the differential treatment of the members of a group under the law is demeaning to human dignity. The interpretive framework articulated in the *Law* decision is another step in the direction of the courts interpreting the Constitution with an eye to its impact on social relationships.

On balance, there is little doubt that what Morton and Knopff call "equality seeking groups," a category that includes women, visible and religious minorities, the mentally and physically disabled, and homosexuals, have won victories using section 15 of the Charter that probably could not have been won without the benefit of constitutionally entrenched equality rights and the judiciary. In their interpretation of section 15 of the Charter, judges have been sensitive to the social and economic context of the inequalities that appear before them as Charter claims. Indeed, many of the major Charter rulings read like sociological or historical treatises.[23] This is precisely what alarms many of the Charter's critics, who recoil at what they see as judicial usurpation of the legislature's function.

Judicial sensitivity to the broader societal and historical context of their interpretations of equality rights was very clear in the Supreme Court's 2008 ruling in *R. v. Kapp*. The Supreme Court ruled that a collective fishing licence given under federal law to three Aboriginal bands did not extend to non-Aboriginal fishers. The non-Aboriginal fishers claimed that the law violated their equality rights under the Charter by making legal distinctions based on race. The Court ruled that the Aboriginal fishing rights were constitutionally protected by the affirmative action clause, section 15(2), of the Charter. In arriving at this decision the Court reiterated its long-held view that section 15 guarantees substantive equality for Canadians, not identical treatment. This opens the door to the judicial consideration of evidence and arguments based on history, economics, and sociology.

What is clear, however, is that the issue of when and how far judges should involve themselves in the determination of public policy has become increasingly prominent. Critics from both the right and the left of the spectrum have attacked what they believe to be an overwillingness on the part of many judges to use the Charter to strike down government policies. Supreme Court justices have discovered that judicial activism is not always received well by the public. In an apparent response to criticisms of being arrogant and indifferent to public sentiment, eight of the nine members of the Supreme Court took the unprecedented step of travelling together to Winnipeg in April 1999. Their trip was widely perceived as a public relations exercise, intended to show that the Court was willing to break out of the cocoon of the nation's capital and get closer to the people. The current Chief Justice, Beverley McLachlin, regularly gives speeches in which she explains the Court's role to a wider public audience.[24]

Criticisms that judges have encroached on the policy-making prerogatives of elected governments are not uncommon in many democracies. This is, of course, a long-standing complaint in the United States, particularly from conservatives. But in fairness to the judges of the Supreme Court, and of all the other courts in Canada, interpreting the Constitution is not supposed to be a popularity contest. If minority rights were to be protected by the courts only when it is popular to do so, these rights would be extremely precarious.

Supreme Court

"I DON'T KNOW ABOUT YOU GUYS, BUT MY MAIL HAS BEEN RUNNING TWO TO ONE AGAINST THE CONSTITUTION."

The entrenchment of rights and freedoms in the Constitution have caused some to wonder if the Charter has resulted in a judiciary that is undemocratic and too powerful. Is this fear a legitimate one? Why or why not?

HAS THE CHARTER "AMERICANIZED" CANADIAN POLITICS?

Early critics of the Charter said that it would "Americanize" Canadian politics. By this they meant that it would do three things. First, it would elevate the importance of unelected judges and the courts, giving them a much more prominent role in determining important policy matters. Second, it would undermine the operation of parliamentary government in Canada and make legislatures accountable to the courts rather than to the people. Third, it would generate a more litigious society in which individuals and groups are more likely to base their claims and political arguments on rights, making compromise more difficult and bypassing such political processes as elections and lobbying in preference for the courts.

Judges are indeed far more prominent in policy making than they were in the pre-Charter era. Parliamentary supremacy has been replaced by constitutional supremacy, with the Supreme Court as chief arbiter, and important issues are often decided in the courts or as a result of court decisions pushing governments in a particular direction. Yet, in spite of these important changes, the Charter has not resulted in a wholesale Americanization of Canadian politics. Judges in Canada have tended to interpret the Charter's guarantees in distinctively Canadian ways, anchored in aspects of Canada's political culture that are different from those of the United States.

This is true in the case of hate speech targeting a particular group, where approaches have been significantly different. The difference boils down to this. In the United States, just because you say something demonstrably false and odious about the members of a group does not mean that you lose the Constitution's protection to speak your mind. If, however, this speech becomes what lawyers call "fighting words," liable to incite violence, then it loses the protection of the First Amendment. But in Canada, some speech is considered to be so nasty that, by its very nature, it promotes hatred and is undeserving of constitutional protection, as is demonstrated by the majority opinion in *Keegstra*. Moreover, the greater willingness of Canadian courts and legislatures to restrict hate speech on the grounds that some ideas and their expression contribute nothing to democratic life, and therefore can be restricted without doing any harm to freedom, is consistent with a cultural difference between these countries that predates the Charter era.

SUMMARY

By 2012, some pundits such as John Ibbitson of *The Globe and Mail* were calling the Charter "Canada's gift to the world."[25] Yet others wondered, in the same edition of *The Globe and Mail*, whether 2012 would see the Conservative government colliding with the judiciary and the Charter in areas such as mandatory minimum sentencing, prostitution, assisted suicide, electronic surveillance, and enhanced police powers.[26]

It is probably fair to say that the changes generated by the Charter have far exceeded the expectations of all but a few of the politicians and experts who presided at its birth. There has been an explosion in the number of rights cases brought before the courts, as well as a shift in the venue of some political conflicts. For the moment, parliamentary supremacy appears to have been replaced by constitutional supremacy, which has increased the importance of judges in the governmental process.

It is true, of course that every major Supreme Court ruling on the Charter serves to clarify the scope and authority of judicial review. We have focused on several early Charter decisions in order to demonstrate that the Court very quickly assumed the mantle of judicial activism. How far judges go in using the Charter to strike down laws and administrative practices is largely up to them. There are, however, two provisions of the Charter that were intended to rein in the courts' authority: the reasonable limits clause (s. 1) and the notwithstanding clause (s. 33). In practice, however, neither of these has been very effective in limiting the scope of judicial activism.

Is there an identifiable pattern in the Court's interpretation of the individual rights guaranteed by the Charter? In essence, and aside from what most commentators characterize as a moderately activist approach, the Court has shown few sharply pronounced tendencies.

STARTING POINTS FOR RESEARCH

Donald Abelson, Patrick James, and Michael Lusztig, eds, *The Myth of the Sacred: The Charter, the Courts and the Politics of the Constitution in Canada* (Montreal and Kingston: McGill–Queen's University Press, 2002).

Alan Cairns, *Disruptions: Constitutional Struggles, from the Charter to Meech Lake* (Toronto: McClelland & Stewart, 1991).

Gerald Kernerman and Philip Resnick, eds, *Insiders and Outsiders: Alan Cairns and the Reshaping of Canadian Citizenship* (Vancouver: University of British Columbia Press, 2005).

Christopher Manfredi, *Judicial Power and the Charter: Canada and the Paradox of Liberal Constitutionalism*, 2nd edn (Toronto: Oxford University Press, 2001).

F.L. Morton and Rainer Knopff, *The Charter Revolution and the Court Party* (Peterborough, Ont.: Broadview Press, 2000).

CBC ARCHIVES AND TVO'S *THE AGENDA*

Visit the companion website for *Canadian Democracy: A Concise Introduction* to follow links to audio and video footage related to the main themes of the chapter: www.oupcanada.com/BrooksConcise.

RELEVANT WEBSITES

Visit the companion website for *Canadian Democracy: A Concise Introduction* to browse a collection of websites featuring material related to the key themes of the chapter, an excellent starting point for research.

REVIEW EXERCISES

1. Find a story in the media that deals with the Charter and answer the following:

    a. What are the circumstances?
    b. Who are the people or organizations involved?
    c. What law/regulation/action/practice is being challenged?
    d. At what stage is the challenge?
    e. Are lawyers or other experts interviewed? Who are they?
    f. What right or freedom of the Charter is at stake in this story?

2. The Conservative government held committee hearings on the 2006 nomination of Justice Marshall Rothstein to the Supreme Court of Canada. Is this model an improvement on the process that existed prior to Rothstein's nomination? Would some other model be preferable?

3. Do an Internet search of constitutions from other countries and compare the Charter of Rights and Freedoms to some of its counterparts in other democracies. What are the main similarities between them? Are there any aspects of these other rights documents that you think should be adopted in Canada?

Federalism

Canada's Constitution establishes two levels of government—national and provincial—both with important law-making and taxation powers. This system of divided jurisdiction is known as federalism. When the proposal to create an independent Canada was discussed at Charlottetown (1864) and Quebec (1867), the main subject of debate was the relationship between the new national and regional governments. Two decades of self-government and the constitutional traditions imported from Britain provided the colonies with ready guideposts for most other features of the Constitution. Federalism, by contrast, was uncharted territory. Most of the founders' practical knowledge of the principles and operation of federalism was based on their observation of the federal system in the United States, which did not inspire much confidence following the secession of the Confederacy and the bloody Civil War of 1861–5. Despite all this, Canada's founders opted for a federal system of government.

After reading this chapter you will be able to

1. Explain the differences between the federal and unitary systems of government
2. Discuss the origins and maintenance of Canadian federalism
3. List the federal division of powers
4. Outline the courts' role in the evolution of Canadian federalism
5. Discuss Quebec's impact on federalism
6. Explain how federalism is financed

WHAT IS FEDERALISM?

In a **federal system** of government *the constitutional authority to make laws and to tax is divided between a national government and some number of regional governments*. Neither the national government acting alone nor the regional governments acting together have the authority to alter the powers of the other level of government. They are coordinate and independent in their separate constitutional spheres. Citizens in a federal state are members of two political communities, one national and the other within the boundaries of a regional unit called a province, state, or canton, depending on the country.

"Federalism" is a legal term, and its existence is based on a constitution. If a single government controls all legislative and taxation powers in a country, then no amount of administrative decentralization or variation in the economic, social, or cultural characteristics of its regions will make it a federal state. Federalism divides political authority along territorial lines, but it is not the only form of government to do so. Important policy-making and administrative powers may be exercised at the regional level even in a **unitary state** where *sovereignty or competence resides exclusively with the central government, and regional or local governments are legally and politically subordinate to it*. The extent to which the activities are *decentralized*, i.e., placed in the hands of regional officials, or remain *centralized* at the national level, is determined by a country's particular social, geographic, and political conditions. This is also true of a federal state, where the constitution provides only a partial and sometimes very misleading guide to the real division of powers between governments. Political authority is also linked to territory in *confederations* and *economic communities*. These are formal groupings of independent states that have agreed to assign certain legislative and administrative

TABLE 7.1 | TERRITORY AND POLITICAL AUTHORITY

Model	Arrangements, Responsibilities, and Relationships	Example
Unitary state	A form of government where sovereignty or competence resides exclusively with the central government, and regional or local governments are legally and politically subordinate to it	France
Federation	A voluntary, power-sharing arrangement where sovereignty or competence is distributed between central and provincial (or state) governments so that, within a single political system, neither order of government is legally or politically subordinate to the other, and each order of government is elected and exercises authority on the electorate	Canada
Confederation	A voluntary arrangement where there is a considerable allocation of responsibilities to central institutions or agencies. Sovereignty is retained by the member-state governments, and the central government is legally and politically subordinate to them. Furthermore, the members of the major central institutions are delegates of the constituent state governments, and changes to the constitution require unanimity.	Switzerland
Economic association	A voluntary political arrangement, with a confederal type of government with common organizing institutions. The functions assigned by the participating states to the common institutions are limited mainly to economic co-operation and coordination.	European Union

Source: Adapted from Canada, Task Force on Canadian Unity, *Coming to Terms: The Words of the Debate* (Hull, QC: Supply and Services Canada, 1979): 21–2.

functions to a common institution or set of institutions. All member states have a say—though not necessarily an equal say—in the decision making of such a body, while retaining their ultimate sovereignty (see Table 7.1).

THE ORIGINS, MAINTENANCE, AND DEMISE OF FEDERAL STATES

Only about two dozen of the 192 member countries of the United Nations have a federal system of government. This is an estimate of the actual number of federal states, because the determination of whether a political system is federal is not an exact science. For example, Mexico, Argentina, and Russia generally are included in the club of federal states, but the central governments of these countries have sometimes interfered with the autonomy of state governments. How many countries actually belong to the federalism club is less important than the fact that the club is a small one, although it does include some of the world's largest and most important countries. Unitary government is far more popular, even in countries where regional political conflicts are strong.

What circumstances lead to the adoption of a federal political system? There is no simple answer. But it is possible to identify a general condition that is present at the birth of all federal states and vital to their continued health: an agreement among the regional components that the benefits of a union exceed the costs of membership. A federal state is essentially a *consensus of regions*. Students of international law and federalism may disagree over the legal right of any part of a federal state to separate from the union, but the political fact is that when a region no longer shares the national consensus upon which federalism is based, its separation becomes a real possibility.

"Federalism," declared Pierre Trudeau, "has all along been a product of reason in politics. . . . it is an attempt to find a rational compromise between the divergent interest groups which history has thrown together; but it is a compromise based on the will of the people."[1] This is why federal unions are often referred to as "pacts," "contracts," or "bargains." The key role of consent may be seen in the case of the former Soviet Union, when, as part of the post–World War II deal between the Soviet Union and the United States–led Western democracies, the countries of Estonia, Latvia, and Lithuania were made members of the Soviet "federal" state against their will. Moscow dominated the regional republics through a Communist party monopoly until the fall of the Soviet Union in 1991.

Trudeau's argument that federalism is the product of reason will not convince Quebec separatists, who view 1867 as a sell-out by an elite of "cannibal kings"[2] willing to collaborate with the Anglo-Saxon oppressor. Nor does reason appear to be the chief factor explaining why disgruntled regions remain part of a federal union when their politicians and their people clearly believe that they are treated unfairly and exploited for the benefit of other regions—a century-old view in western Canada. Some argue that it is the rationale and self-interest of only some groups that lead to federal union, and that federalism may not be reasonable from the standpoint of other groups' self-interest.

Nevertheless, the origins of federal democracies lie in compromise. Some regions may be enthusiastic, while others enter a federal compromise out of despair at the lack of viable alternatives. This does not diminish the fact that the voluntary consent of the regions forms the basis of a federal union. Once established, however, a federal state may achieve a new dynamic. The existence of a national government and the idea of national citizenship can be centralizing factors that offset the decentralizing pull of regional interests. Thus, federalism is sustained by a *sense of political nationality* rather than purely rational calculations on the part of regional populations and politicians.

Federalism and Political Nationality

According to Donald Smiley, an expert on Canadian federalism, political nationality "means that Canadians as such have reciprocal moral and legal claims upon one another that have no precise counterparts in their relations with others, and that Canadians as such have a continuing determination to carry out a significant number of important common activities together."[3] While this sense of political community may not replace or overshadow the other identities that citizens have of themselves, it does transcend regional, ethnic, and linguistic identifications.

Federalism is ultimately sustained by the sense of political nationality—or community—that develops around the national state. By the same token, the breakup of a federal state is sure to be presaged by the deterioration of this sense of community. Sometimes a sense of political nationality is never solidly established in the first place. A fragile political nationality may be destroyed by a particularly divisive regional conflict, as American federalism was split asunder by slavery. The most stable federal systems are those where regional communities share in a sense of political nationality that dampens the decentralizing tendencies produced by regional differences. Switzerland, the contemporary United States, and Austria are good examples of this. The Swiss case in particular demonstrates how regional ethnolinguistic divisions need not prevent the development of a durable political nationality.

What determines the strength of political nationality? And why do regional divisions become independence movements in some federal states but not in others? Several factors come into play, but the most basic is *regional inequality*. If the citizens of a region feel strongly that existing federal structures discriminate against their interests economically and politically, this places a strain on the sense of political nationality. Sentiments like these are very common. For example, a 2005 survey by the Centre for Research and Information Canada found that Ontarians were almost twice as likely as Canadians in most other provinces to believe that their province was treated with the respect it deserved.[4] Studies show, however, no direct correlation between perception of respect for the province and the level of affection and loyalty of provincial populations toward Canada. Nor does a strong provincial identity appear to prevent its people from also identifying with Canada. As Roger Gibbins has observed, with the exception of Quebec, it is probably a mistake to think of national and provincial loyalties as competitive.[5]

Regional grievances are more likely to threaten the stability of federalism when they are linked to a nationalist movement. **Nationalism** becomes a political force ***when the values***

INSIDE POLITICS

BOX 7.1 | A Tale of Two Countries: Language, Nationalism, and Federalism

This country has two major language communities that have coexisted on sometimes uneasy terms since the country achieved independence in the nineteenth century. One of these communities has a significant nationalist movement that includes a couple of political parties committed to independence for their national community. Many of this country's citizens believe that their language community and region has subsidized public services and incomes in the other community for decades, and they feel resentful. This resentment is deepened by long historical memories of social and political inequality between the two communities. As of 2010, the prospects for their continued cohabitation seemed rather bleak.

The country described here is Belgium. Over the years it has often been compared to Canada, facing some rather similar challenges and attempting to manage conflict between its two main language communities, French and Flemish (there is also a very small German-speaking official-language community), through a federal constitution. Unlike that in Canada, however, the nationalist movement aspiring to break up Belgium is associated with the wealthier majority community—the

Flemish-speaking northern region of the country. In the national election of 2010 the most popular political party in that region was the Flemish Nationalist Party, a party committed to independence and led by a multilingual historian whose victory speech began with the words, "Nil volentibus arduum"("For those who have the will, nothing is impossible").

Comparisons between Belgium and Canada can be misleading. Nevertheless, political scientists and constitutionalists from each country have often looked to the other to find answers about what does and does not work in managing inter-community relations in a federal state. If recent developments in Belgium hold any lessons for Canada, the main one is probably this: when the ties of identity and shared cultural values that bridge the language gap between communities are weak, and when one group believes that existing state institutions treat it unfairly, federalism is in trouble. The compromise at the heart of federalism's viability ultimately depends on the sentiment of the people or, more precisely, the peoples who live together under a federal constitution. This is what the French historian Ernest Renan meant when he said that federalism is a daily referendum of the popular will.[6]

and beliefs shared by the people of a territory or a community are translated into a public policy or agenda. Nationalist values and beliefs are usually accompanied by territorial claims. Nationalism is distinguished from regionalism by its demands on behalf of both a territory and a community within that territory that shares some ethnic, linguistic, or other cultural traits. These claims can range from demands for outright independence to more moderate calls for greater autonomy for regions where members of the national community are concentrated. Nationalism is far more difficult to accommodate within a federal state than is a region's complaints of unfair treatment. Indeed, nationalism that is linked to the social and cultural characteristics of a group is fundamentally at odds with the concept of political nationality on which a viable federal state depends.

THE ORIGINS OF CANADIAN FEDERALISM

Canada's federal Constitution was a compromise. Most of the anglophone Fathers of Confederation favoured a unitary system of government similar to Britain's under which all power would be in the hands of a new national Parliament. They were opposed, however, by two groups. The strongest opposition came from the French-Canadian representatives of Canada East (known today as Quebec) led by George-Étienne Cartier. They believed that a federal union with constitutional protections and exclusive provincial jurisdiction over linguistic and cultural matters would protect their interests. Federalism was also the preferred constitutional option of Maritime politicians. Maritimers had developed strong local identities that they were unwilling to see submerged under unitary government. Besides, in an era when politics and patronage were virtually synonymous it was only reasonable that provincial politicians would want to retain control over such important sources of contracts as roads and public works, as well as bureaucratic sinecures.

Some anglophone politicians of Ontario and Quebec saw merit in the idea of dividing legislative powers between two levels of government. For example, Grit politician George Brown expressed the view that conflict between the English Protestant and French Catholic communities—conflict that had produced government instability and political deadlock in the legislature of United Canada and that was one of the reasons behind the Confederation movement—would be reduced by assigning local matters to the provincial legislatures.[7] Ottawa would deal with matters of national interest, such as trade and commerce, immigration, defence, and transportation. The presumption that sectional rivalries and local interests would not enter into deliberations on these national issues was naive, to say the least.

Federalism was a necessary compromise between two contradictory tendencies. The forces that were pushing the British North American colonies toward a political union wanted a strong national government. Commercial interests, particularly railroad promoters, wanted unification to increase their ability to raise investment capital abroad and their creditworthiness. A larger union, with a wider revenue base and an integrated national economy, was crucial to the railroad promoters' interests and to the Canadian financial institutions linked to them. Likewise, a strong central government was needed if British North America was to assume the burden of its own military defence, and if expansion into the sparsely populated region between Ontario and British Columbia was to be accomplished. Tugging in the opposite direction were the forces of cultural dualism as well as the colonial administrations and regional societies that were unwilling to be submerged in a unitary state dominated by Ontario and Quebec.

What sort of federal union did the founders envisage? Expectations varied greatly. Some, such as Canada's first prime minister, John A. Macdonald, anticipated that the provincial governments would be little more than glorified municipalities, subordinate to Ottawa. Others, like Oliver Mowat, did not share this centralist vision and he, Ontario's third premier, led the movement for provincial rights during the 1870s and 1880s.[8]

The agreement the founders reached gave to the federal government what then were the most important legislative powers and sources of public revenue. (For a complete list of federal, provincial, and shared responsibilities, refer to Table 7.2.) When we consider that promoting

The Fathers of Confederation at Charlottetown. Canada's entrance into federalism was far from a unanimous decision; rather, the system of divided jurisdiction was a compromise that made Ottawa the seat of national power to control certain issues while leaving the provinces to oversee others.

economic growth and military defence (also a federal responsibility) were two of the chief functions of the nineteenth-century state—maintaining public order was the third, and responsibility for this was divided between Ottawa and the provinces—there is little doubt that Ottawa was assigned the major legislative powers of that era. The federal government was also assigned the duty to build an intercolonial railway connecting Montreal to Halifax. Responsibility for immigration and agriculture was divided between the federal and provincial governments, but in the event of a conflict Ottawa's legislation would prevail.

Ottawa's superiority was also clear on the taxation front. Donald Smiley notes that customs and excise taxes—indirect forms of taxation—accounted for about three-quarters of colonial revenues prior to Confederation. The provinces were restricted to the less developed field of "direct taxation"(e.g., sales tax), as well as royalties on provincially owned natural resources. These were meagre revenues compared to those of the federal government. The Confederation agreement also established the practice of federal money transfers to the provinces. The dependence of the economically weaker provinces on federal subsidies began in 1867 and continues to this day. Together, the powers and tax revenues appeared to establish Ottawa's clear superiority over the provinces in economic matters (see "Financing Federalism" later in this chapter).

In addition to all this, the Confederation agreement included several provisions that have been described as *quasi-federal*. They appear to establish a nearly colonial relationship between Ottawa and the provinces by permitting the federal government to intervene in a provincial economy on matters of "public works" in the national interest, to disallow laws passed by provincial legislatures, and/or to pass laws protecting rights held by denominational minorities at the time of a province's entry into Confederation. While the disallowance of laws pertaining to the protection of minority rights in education was never used, the other powers were used widely during the first few decades after Confederation and periodically during the first half of the twentieth century. In most instances, Ottawa was reacting to provincial economic policies that challenged its own priorities and jurisdiction.

Do the founders' intentions really matter? Legally, no. In interpreting the federal division of powers the courts have generally been unreceptive to arguments about what the Fathers of Confederation had in mind.[9] Indeed, the Supreme Court of Canada's ruling in the 1981 Patriation Reference, *Re Resolution to amend the Constitution*, declared that "arguments from history do not lead to any consistent view or any single view of the nature of the British North America Act. So, too, with pronouncements by political figures or persons in other branches of public life. There is little profit in parading them."[10]

The Compact and Contract Theories of Canadian Federalism

Politically, however, arguments about intentions can matter. There are two arguments most frequently made about Canadian federalism: (1) that it represents a *compact* between French and English Canada; or (2) that it is a *contract* by the provinces to give up certain powers to a new national government of their creation. Both the compact and contract theories of federalism maintain that the federal "bargain" cannot be changed without the mutual consent of those who agreed to it.

The compact theory suggests that Quebec—the province in which most francophones reside and the only province in which they are in the majority—should have a veto over any constitutional change that affects either the federal distribution of powers or the relative weight of Quebec in Parliament and on the Supreme Court (where three of the nine justices must be members of the Quebec bar). This argument was rejected by the Supreme Court of Canada in the 1981 Patriation Reference.

The proponents of contract theory claim that each province has the right to veto constitutional change that affects provincial powers or national representation. In fact, there are three variants of contract theory. One would restrict the right of veto to the original signatories (Nova Scotia, New Brunswick, Quebec, and Ontario). A second extends it to all provinces, regardless of when they joined Canada. The third maintains that the unanimous consent of the provinces is not required to change the federal distribution of powers, but that "substantial provincial agreement" is necessary. Like compact theory, none of these variants of contract theory has any legal foundation.

The political importance of both compact and contract theories may be seen in the fact that Canadian governments were for nearly 50 years (1935 to 1982) unable to agree on a formula for amending the Constitution. Unanimous provincial consent appeared to be a political requirement for enacting an amendment formula. Moreover, many experts assumed wrongly, it turned out, that unanimity or something close to it was also a legal requirement.

The compact interpretation of Canadian federalism continues to carry political weight. The Quebec government's refusal to agree to the Constitution Act, 1982 was widely viewed as a serious blow to the Constitution's legitimacy. Former prime minister Brian Mulroney regularly, if misleadingly, spoke of bringing Quebec into the Constitution. Legally, of course, the 1982 reforms applied right across Canada. But politically the prime minister had a point. The government of Quebec, whose claim to speak on behalf of one of the country's two founding nations rests on the fact that the province is home to about 90 per cent of Canadian francophones, did not consent to far-reaching constitutional changes. Both of Quebec's major provincial political parties, the Parti Québécois and the Quebec Liberal Party, insist that Canadian federalism must be viewed as a compact between founding nations, a view that enjoys diminishing support in the rest of Canada. Indeed, diminished support for the idea of Canada as a binational compact is precisely the problem, claimed Claude Ryan, former leader of the Quebec Liberal Party.

> If the movement in favour of sovereignty was able to put down its roots and develop itself in Quebec, it is precisely because more and more Quebecers came to the conclusion that this equality, which had been the dream of many generations, will never be realized with the Canadian federation.[11]

The contract theory of Canada lives on politically in the idea of the formal equality of the provinces. Section 2 of the 1997 Calgary Declaration, an agreement among all the provinces except Quebec on the parameters for future constitutional negotiations, states "All provinces, while diverse in their characteristics, have equality of status." The Declaration also states that any constitutional amendment that confers powers on one province must make these powers available to all provinces. This involves a fundamentally different view from that of the compact theory. For example, the contract theory idea that provinces are and ought to remain formally equal is not easily squared with the compact theory notion of Quebec as a "distinct society."

The Federal Division of Powers

Whatever may have been the intentions of the founders in 1867, it is clear today that both levels of government exercise wide-ranging legislative and taxation powers. Canada's founders took exceptional pains to specify the responsibilities of each level of government. But a literal reading of the division of powers drafted in the 1867 Constitution, as well as the formal changes that have been made since, provides a partial and somewhat misleading guide to Canadian federalism. Some policy areas, such as electronic communications, air transportation, and environmental protection, were unimagined when the federal division of powers was framed, and so are not explicitly assigned to either Ottawa or the provinces. In other cases, what were minor responsibilities in the nineteenth and early twentieth centuries have assumed greater importance as a result of economic and societal changes, and of changes to the state itself.

The heart of the federal division of powers is found in sections 91 and 92 of the Constitution Act, 1867. Each of these sections contains a detailed list of enumerated powers that belong exclusively to Parliament (s. 91) or the provincial legislatures (s. 92). Combined with several other sections that also deal with the division of powers, this is the constitutional foundation of Canadian federalism. An examination of who holds what powers reveals that both Ottawa and the provinces have the capacity to act in most of the major policy fields (see Table 7.2).

Some of the constitutional powers listed in Table 7.2 could have been placed under more than one policy heading. The authority to tax, for example, has been used to promote economic growth, redistribute income, and subsidize special interests. Unemployment insurance is both an economic policy that is tied to retraining and job finding, and a social policy that has the effect of redistributing income to less affluent regions. Immigration policy has always been harnessed to the needs of the Canadian economy and has also been tied to cultural policy through citizenship services and language training for immigrants.

At the same time, governments have sometimes found the authority to legislate through powers that are implied rather than stated in the Constitution. The most important example is the federal government's spending power. Ottawa spends billions of dollars annually on programs that fall under the jurisdiction of provincial and municipal governments. These include federal moneys given to universities for research and student scholarships, to school boards for language instruction, and to individuals for purposes that might appear to fall under provincial jurisdiction (e.g., tax benefits for child care). Ottawa's constitutional "right" to spend money for any purpose has never been definitely established in the courts.[12] Nevertheless, the spending power today provides the constitutional basis for such major federal grants to the provinces as the Canada Health Transfer (CHT), Canada Social Transfer (CST), and equalization payments.

TABLE 7.2 | THE FEDERAL DIVISION OF POWERS AND RESPONSIBILITIES

Federal	Provincial	Shared
• Any mode of taxation • National defence • Aboriginal Canadians • Banking and monetary standards • Criminal laws and penitentiaries • Judicial appointments • Interprovincial transportation and communications • Official bilingualism in federal institutions • Protection of denominational education rights • Equalization of provincial public revenues • Treaties • Laws for the "peace, order, and good government" of the country • Matters not enumerated in powers of the provinces	• Direct taxation within province • Natural resources • Hospitals and health care • Education • Property and civil rights • Administration of justice and organization of courts • Municipalities • Public lands	• Immigration • Old-age pensions • Agriculture

THE COURTS AND FEDERALISM

Laypersons might expect constitutional terms such as "trade and commerce," "property and civil rights," and "direct taxation" to have straightforward meanings. For constitutional lawyers, governments, and private interests, however, the federal division of powers is a dense thicket of contradictory and contested meanings and opportunities and is often a matter to haggle over in the courts. The judicial decisions that have resulted from these disputes have played an important role in shaping the evolution of Canadian federalism. Among the many contentious sections of the Constitution, the courts' interpretation of Ottawa's authority to "make laws for the peace, order, and good government of Canada" and the federal government's "trade and commerce" power have had the greatest impact on the division of powers. We will look briefly at each of these.

Peace, Order, and Good Government

The courts have tended to place a narrow interpretation on the federal Parliament's general authority to make laws for the "**peace, order, and good government of Canada**"(POGG). This has been reduced over time to *an emergency power that can provide the constitutional basis for federal actions in special circumstances, but that cannot be used to justify federal laws during "normal" times*. The narrow interpretation of POGG began with the *Local Prohibition* case (1896). The Judicial Committee of the Privy Council (JCPC) ruled that Ottawa could not use POGG to override the enumerated powers of the provinces. The decision also marked the introduction into Canadian constitutional law of the "national dimensions" test. Lord Watson wrote:

> Their Lordships do not doubt that some matters, in their origin local or provincial, might attain such dimensions as to affect the body politic of the Dominion, and to justify the Canadian Parliament in passing laws for their regulation or abolition in the interest of the Dominion.[13]

When does a matter acquire "national dimensions"? This question was addressed in a series of three decisions handed down in 1922, 1923, and 1925. In *Re Board of Commerce Act, 1919, and the Combines and Fair Prices Act, 1919* (1922), the JCPC struck down two federal laws introduced after World War I to prevent business monopoly and hoarding of essential commodities. For the first time the "emergency doctrine" was articulated, according to which Parliament could pass laws under the authority of POGG only in the case of a national emergency. Writing for the majority, Viscount Haldane declared:

> Circumstances are conceivable, such as those of war or famine, when the peace, order and good Government of the Dominion might be imperilled under conditions so exceptional that they require legislation of a character in reality beyond anything provided for by the enumerated heads in either s. 92 or s. 91.[14]

In these and other cases the JCPC essentially ruled that some national crisis, specifically a wartime emergency, had to exist before federal laws could be based on POGG.

In the 1970s the Supreme Court of Canada found that POGG could be used to justify federal laws during peacetime. The Court was asked to rule on the constitutionality of Ottawa's Anti-Inflation Act, 1975. A majority of the Court accepted the federal government's argument that mounting inflationary pressures constituted an emergency justifying legislation that encroached on provincial jurisdiction. Not only was the "emergency doctrine" liberated from war-related circumstances, the Court also indicated its reluctance to challenge Parliament's judgment on when emergency circumstances exist. The result, according to constitutionalists such as Peter Russell, is that Ottawa now appears to have fairly easy access to emergency powers under this doctrine.[15] Constitutionally, this may be so. Politically, however, any federal government would think twice before legislating under this contentious power. In the three decades since Ottawa won this constitutional victory there has not been a single instance where the federal government has relied on POGG as the basis for an alleged intrusion into provincial jurisdiction.

Trade and Commerce

On the face of it, Ottawa's authority over the regulation of trade and commerce (s. 91[2])[16] of the Constitution Act, 1867 appears rather sweeping. However, court decisions have construed the trade and commerce power to be much narrower, limited largely to interprovincial and international trade. At the same time, provincial jurisdiction over property and civil rights in the province (s. 92[13])[17] has been interpreted as the provinces' own "trade and commerce" power. This line of judicial interpretation began with the *Parsons* decision of 1881. Based on its view that a broad, literal interpretation of section 91(2) would leave the provinces powerless to affect business, the JCPC interpreted "regulation of trade and commerce" to include "political arrangements in regard to trade requiring the sanction of parliament, regulation of trade in matters of interprovincial concern, and it may be that they would include general regulation of trade affecting the whole Dominion."[18] To construe Ottawa's trade and commerce power otherwise, the JCPC argued, would be to deny the "fair and ordinary meaning" of section 92(13) of the Constitution Act, 1867, which assigns property and civil rights in the province to the provincial governments.

The legacy of *Parsons* has been that Ottawa's authority to regulate trade and commerce has been limited to interprovincial trade, international trade, and general trade affecting the whole of Canada. But even this definition of federal jurisdiction has presented problems of interpretation. A series of Supreme Court decisions, culminating in *Caloil Inc. v. Attorney General of Canada* (1971), signified a broader interpretation of Ottawa's power to regulate interprovincial trade.[19] Ottawa's authority was given an additional boost by a 1971 reference decision of the Supreme Court. In *Attorney General for Manitoba v. Manitoba Egg and Poultry Association et al.* (1971), the *"Chicken and Egg" Reference*—no kidding—the Court ruled unconstitutional a provincial egg-marketing scheme that restricted imports from other provinces, on the grounds that it encroached on Ottawa's trade and commerce power. Justice Bora Laskin referred to the trend toward a more balanced interpretation of federal and provincial jurisdiction over trade.[20] Laskin argued that "to permit each province to seek its own advantage . . . through a figurative sealing of its borders to entry of goods from others would be to deny one of the objects of Confederation . . . namely, to form an economic unit of the whole of Canada."[21] In *General Motors of Canada Ltd. v. City National Leasing* (1989), the Supreme Court laid down five criteria that must be met before Ottawa may regulate commerce under the "general trade" provision of section 91(2) of the Constitution. They are:

> (1) the impugned legislation must be part of a general regulatory scheme; (2) the scheme must be monitored by the continuing oversight of a regulatory agency; (3) the legislation must be concerned with trade as a whole rather than with a particular industry; (4) the legislation should be of a nature that the provinces jointly or severally would be constitutionally incapable of enacting; and (5) the failure to include one or more provinces or localities in a legislative scheme would jeopardize the successful operation of the scheme in other parts of the country.[22]

THE EVOLUTION OF CANADIAN FEDERALISM

Court rulings seldom put an end to conflicts between Ottawa and the provinces. Instead, they typically become part of the bargaining process between governments. Consider examples such as the *Employment and Social Insurance Act Reference* (1937). The JCPC struck down a federal statute establishing a program to deal with national unemployment, which was followed by negotiations that led to a 1940 constitutional amendment that gave Ottawa authority over unemployment insurance. In *Public Service Board v. Dionne* (1978), the Supreme Court confirmed Ottawa's exclusive jurisdiction over television broadcasting. Immediately afterward, the federal minister of communications announced Ottawa's willingness to negotiate some division of authority with the provinces. Other cases such as *CIGOL v. Government of Saskatchewan* (1978) and *Re Constitution of Canada* (1981), resulted in further negotiations and new arrangements. Or, as in *Reference re Secession of Quebec* (1998), which dealt with Quebec's right to secede from Canada unilaterally, by clarifying some of the constitutional questions associated with Quebec secession the Court provided all sides in this ongoing political struggle with ammunition for future sniping.

Judicial review may have shaped the evolution of federalism in a way that the Fathers of Confederation had not planned, but as Pierre Trudeau observed,

> . . . it has long been the custom in English Canada to denounce the [Judicial Committee of the] Privy Council for its provincial bias; but it should perhaps be considered that if the law lords had not leaned in that direction, Quebec separatism might not be a threat today: it might be an accomplished fact.[23]

Legal disputes over the division of powers are symptomatic of other underlying tensions. These tensions have three main sources:

1. The status of Quebec and the powers of the Quebec state
2. Relations between the more heavily industrialized and populous centre of the country and the outlying western and eastern regions (centre–periphery relations)
3. The political and administrative needs of governments

Quebec's Role in Federalism

"What does Quebec want?" The question has been asked countless times over the years by English Canadians. Some genuinely want to know; others ask it out of exasperation. In order to understand what Quebec wants from Canada it is also necessary to consider what the rest of Canada expects from, and is willing to concede to, Quebec.

Quebec's unique role in Canadian federalism derives from two factors. One is its predominantly French-speaking character. Over 80 per cent of the provincial population claims French as their mother tongue, and about 90 per cent of all Canadian francophones reside in Quebec. The second factor is Quebec's size. In 1867, it was the second most populous province, and Montreal was the hub of Canada's commercial and financial industries. Today, Quebec is still Canada's second most populous province, accounting for approximately one-quarter of Canada's population. Economically, Quebec's gross provincial product is surpassed only by Ontario.

Quebec's distinctive social and cultural fabric explains why it has made special demands on Canadian federalism. Because it is a large province with the second largest bloc of seats in the federal Parliament, and because francophones have always been able to control Quebec's provincial legislature, the demands of Quebec have had a significant impact on the evolution of Canadian federalism. This impact has been experienced on two main fronts: the Constitution and the financial and administrative practices of federalism. We will examine Quebec's impact on the financial and administrative dimensions of federalism later in this chapter.

Quebec and the Constitution

Quebec's influence on the Constitution predates Confederation. Between 1848 and 1867 Ontario and Quebec formed United Canada, governed by a single legislature in which the two colonies held equal representation. To become law, a bill had to be approved by a majority of members on both the Ontario and Quebec sides of the legislature, also known as a *double majority*. This was Canada's first experience with the federal principle of regional representation, and it turned out to be a failure.

Quebec's influence on the Constitution of 1867 was strongly evident. Its representatives were most insistent on a federal constitution where the provincial government would have authority over matters vital to the preservation of the language, religion, and social institutions of Quebec. Indeed, for decades the clerical and political leaders of French Canada viewed Canadian federalism as a pact between two peoples. "Canadian Confederation," declared Henri

Bourassa, "is the result of a contract between the two races in Canada, French and English, based on equality and recognizing equal rights and reciprocal duties. Canadian Confederation will last only as long as this equality of rights is recognized as the basis of the public right in Canada, from Halifax to Vancouver."[24]

The equality Bourassa had in mind did not last very long. It was violated in Manitoba where the status of French in the provincial legislature and the educational rights of francophone Catholics were swept away a couple of decades after that province entered Confederation. It was also violated in Ontario, where Regulation 17 (1913) banned French instruction from the province's public schools. As a result, French Canada began to identify with Quebec as the only province in which the francophone majority could defend its rights and preserve its culture.

The consequences of limiting French Canada to the boundaries of Quebec became apparent by the middle of the twentieth century. As Ottawa became increasingly involved in areas of provincial jurisdiction, particularly through its spending power and its monopolizing of direct taxation between 1947 and 1954, the Quebec government became more and more protective of provincial powers under the Constitution. Indeed, the Quebec government of Maurice Duplessis was the first to reject Ottawa's monopoly over the personal income tax field, imposing its own provincial income tax in 1954. But not until the Quiet Revolution of the 1960s was Quebec's resentment of Ottawa's encroachment onto provincial territory matched by aggressive constitutional demands. The first instance of this occurred during the negotiations on a public old-age pension scheme (1963–5). Premier Jean Lesage stated that his government would agree to a constitutional amendment giving Ottawa the authority to pass pension legislation only if Quebec were able to opt out of the plan. Ottawa agreed, and so was born the Canadian practice of provinces being able to opt out of a federal shared-cost program without suffering any financial loss.

Quebec's constitutional demands appeared to become even more ambitious

Co-operative federalism *revolves around the idea that federalism can be a decentralized and possibly an unequal sharing of power and financial resources.* **What does this editorial cartoon seem to be saying about the co-operative federalism that existed from the 1930s to the 1970s?**

a few years later. In the 1966 provincial election, the Union Nationale party ran on the slogan "Québec d'abord!" ("Quebec first!") The party's leader, Daniel Johnson, called for major constitutional reform that included the transfer of most social and cultural matters to the province, constitutional recognition of Canada's binational character, and exclusive provincial control over the major tax fields then shared with Ottawa. With the exception of international representation for Quebec, however, these demands were not pursued with much vigour during the five years that the Union Nationale was in power (1966–70). As Kenneth McRoberts observed:

> In purely symbolic terms Quebec's demands seemed very significant; Quebec was seeking to assume what many regarded as the trappings of sovereignty. Yet . . . these demands did not directly attack the real distribution of power and responsibilities to the extent that various Lesage demands, such as a separate Quebec Pension Plan, had.[25]

Despite the lack of substantive change in Quebec's constitutional status and powers during this period, the province's nationalist undercurrent was gaining momentum. The creation of the Parti Québécois (PQ) in 1968, under the leadership of René Lévesque, brought under one roof most of the major groups committed to the eventual political independence of Quebec. The Liberal Party of Quebec (LPQ) remained federalist, but advocated what amounted to special status for Quebec within Canadian federalism. "Un fédéralisme rentable" ("profitable federalism") was the passionless way in which Liberal leader Robert Bourassa explained Quebec's commitment to Canada.

Constitutional negotiations between Ottawa and the provinces had been ongoing since 1968. The 1970 election of a Liberal government in Quebec appeared to provide an opportunity to bring these talks to a successful conclusion. But when the 11 heads of government met in Victoria in 1971, it became apparent that Quebec's price for agreeing to a constitutional amendment formula and a charter of rights was higher than Ottawa was willing to pay.[26] Quebec demanded constitutional supremacy, as well as the fiscal means to pay for programs, in social policy areas that Ottawa controlled such as family allowances, unemployment insurance, employment training, and old-age pensions. Ottawa went some way toward meeting these demands. But the Trudeau government refused to concede the principle of provincial supremacy over social policy and would not provide a constitutional guarantee that provinces would receive financial compensation for operating their own programs in these areas. The federal–provincial compromise reached in Victoria fell apart days later in Quebec, where the deal was seen as constitutional entrenchment of the status quo.

After Quebec's rejection of the Victoria Charter, the Bourassa government adopted a piecemeal strategy for changing federalism, negotiating with Ottawa on single issues. It was unsuccessful, however, in extracting any major concessions from a federal government that believed provincial powers were too great and that was opposed to special status for Quebec.

A rather different strategy was followed by the PQ government of René Lévesque after it came to power in 1976. The PQ was committed to holding a provincial referendum on its option of political sovereignty for Quebec, combined with an economic association with the

This editorial cartoon offers an interpretation of the strategies used by Prime Minister Trudeau and his then minister of justice, Jean Chrétien, at a first ministers' conference. Based on the 1971 result, how well would you say Trudeau's tactics worked?

rest of Canada. Instead of simple confrontation with Ottawa, the Lévesque government pursued a gradualist strategy of providing "good government." This required some degree of co-operation with Ottawa, given the intricate network of intergovernmental programs and agreements, while attempting to convince the Quebec population of the merits of **sovereignty-association**—*a term generally understood to mean a politically sovereign Quebec that would be linked to Canada through some sort of commercial union or free trade agreement*. The two governments co-operated on many new capital spending projects, on management of the economy, and on immigration policy. The PQ government even participated in federal–provincial talks on constitutional reform in 1978–9. All this occurred against the background of the looming referendum on the PQ's separatist option.

Sovereignty-association was rejected by Quebec voters in May 1980. But they re-elected the PQ to office in 1981. It was thus a PQ government that participated in the constitutional negotiations on "renewed federalism" that the federal Liberal government had initiated after the Quebec referendum. But it was also a PQ government that refused to sign the 1981 constitutional accord that became the Constitution Act, 1982. The PQ's refusal was hardly surprising given that none of the demands that Quebec governments had made since the 1960s were included in the Accord. Even Quebec Liberals rejected it. Although the legality of the Constitution Act, 1982 was not in doubt, its political legitimacy was. The provincial government of the country's second largest province, and home to 90 per cent of Canada's francophones, had not agreed to the most significant changes to the Constitution since 1867.

The return of Robert Bourassa and the Liberals in the 1985 provincial election appeared to reflect the muted tenor of Quebec nationalism in the post-referendum era. Change had also taken place in Ottawa. Prime Minister Brian Mulroney, who was elected in 1984, did not share Pierre Trudeau's view that the provinces were too powerful. Nor was he opposed to some form of special status for Quebec, as Trudeau was. Conditions seemed propitious, according to Prime Minister Mulroney, for "bringing Quebec into the constitutional family."

It was not to be. The Quebec government put forward a package of five demands that had to be met before it would agree to the 1982 constitutional reforms. These proposals were agreed to by Ottawa and all the provincial premiers on 30 April 1987, forming the basis of what became known as the Meech Lake Accord. As we saw in Chapter 5, these constitutional proposals died on the drawing board in 1990, and two years later, in 1992, the Charlottetown proposals for constitutional reform, which offered Quebec even more and also brought Aboriginal Canadians to the table, were defeated in a national referendum.

In the wake of the Charlottetown Accord's rejection, politicians of all stripes fled from the constitutional issue. It was not an issue in the 1993 federal election campaign, at least not outside Quebec. In Quebec, however, these matters were kept before the voters by the Bloc Québécois, led by Lucien Bouchard. The Bloc's raison d'être was, of course, to achieve political independence for Quebec. Their success in capturing 54 of Quebec's 75 seats in the House of Commons may not have been a vote for separation, but it demonstrated the depth of Quebec voters' dissatisfaction with federalism.

Despite their obvious wish to avoid the constitutional quagmire, the federal Liberals, who formed the government in 1993, were forced to confront the issue of separation following the 1994 election of the PQ in Quebec. The PQ were committed to holding a referendum on Quebec independence within a year of their election. When the referendum campaign began in September of 1995, there appeared to be little enthusiasm among Québécois for the PQ's separatist vision. The federalist campaign relied on messages intended to convince Quebecers that they would suffer economically if the province voted "yes." About halfway through the campaign, however, leadership of the "yes" side passed from Quebec premier Jacques Parizeau to Bloc Québécois leader Lucien Bouchard. Support for independence took off, due largely to Bouchard's charismatic style and ability to connect emotionally with francophone Quebecers, but also due to a terribly uninspired campaign by the federalists. Prime Minister Jean Chrétien stayed on the sidelines until polls showed the "yes" side to be leading. His initial refusal to make any offer to Quebec wavered when he suggested that he supported constitutional recognition of Quebec as a distinct society and a Quebec veto over constitutional reform. On

"Oui" supporters rally on the floor of the Palais de congrès in Montreal as they wait for the results of the 1995 referendum vote (left); "Non" supporters react to poll results as the pro-Canada vote inches up to 50 per cent en route to a slim victory in the 1995 sovereignty referendum (right).

30 October 1995, the "no" side emerged with the narrowest of victories: 49.6 per cent against independence, 48.5 per cent for it.

The federal Liberals' uncertain performance in the referendum campaign, and their reluctance to deal with the issue of Quebec's demands and constitutional reform, may have been due to Canadians' reactions to constitutional issues, which ranged from indifference to deep hostility. But it may also have been due to their inability to formulate a positive response to the sovereignty option proposed by Quebec nationalists. This inability can be traced to the Liberal model of federalism that took shape during the Trudeau era. Although not a centralist model, it assumes that a strong central government is essential to Canadian unity. Moreover, this model is generally opposed to what is called **asymmetrical federalism**, *the constitutional recognition of differences in the status and powers of provincial governments*; in particular, it is against a constitutional entrenchment of special status for Quebec. The Constitution Act, 1982, particularly the Charter and the denial of a right of constitutional veto to any single province, embodies this vision of federalism.

This model is, of course, hotly contested by the separatists, but also by Quebec's nationalist-federalists such as the Liberal Party of Quebec. They argue that to keep Quebecers interested in Canadian federalism, constitutional reforms should include at least the recognition of Quebec's special responsibility for the protection and promotion of the French language in Canada, as well as a veto over constitutional change. Since Trudeau stepped down as party leader in 1984, the federal Liberals have shown a willingness to concede many of those demands. However, their enthusiasm for constitutional reforms has been tempered by mixed feelings among voters in Ontario and downright hostility in western Canada, and by a loyalty among some Liberals to Trudeau's brand of no-special-status-for-Quebec federalism.

In the wake of the close call for federalists in the 1995 Quebec referendum, when a clear majority of francophones voted for the sovereignty option, the federal Liberal Party visibly distanced itself from the Trudeau era. Only weeks after the referendum the Liberal government introduced a motion (1) recognizing Quebec as a distinct society; (2) assigning the province a veto over constitutional change (Ontario and British Columbia were also assigned veto power, as were the prairie and Atlantic regions if at least two provinces representing more than 50 per cent of the regional population opposed a proposed amendment); and (3) transferring to Quebec some authority for job training. The first two of this trio of reforms have clear constitutional implications. While this motion did not change the written Constitution, it did change the Constitution in an informal way. Likewise, the resolution introduced by the Conservative government and passed by the House of Commons in 2006, recognizing Quebec as "a nation within a united Canada," does not change the constitutional status of Quebec in any formal way. But it arguably conferred a sort of de facto special status on Quebec in matters of constitutional reform. In fact, these measures marked a return to a tradition of flexibility in Canadian federalism that predates Pierre Trudeau's entry into federal politics. It is a tradition familiar to students of the British Constitution and of Canadian federalism alike, whereby constitutional change is the result not of formal amendments to the written Constitution but of developments in policy and practice whose status is greater than that of ordinary laws but not quite that of tablets brought down from Mount Sinai by Moses in the Hebrew scriptures.

Centre–Periphery Relations

Canada spans five and a half time zones and occupies the second largest land mass of any country, and yet the narrow belt that runs between Windsor and Montreal—the "industrial heartland" of Canada—is home to over 55 per cent of Canada's population and generates about 60 per cent (2007) of national income and production. Ontario and Quebec together account for just under 60 per cent of the 308 seats in the House of Commons. Despite significant population and economic growth in western Canada, no national political party can hope to form a government without considerable support from the voters of at least one, and usually both, of these provinces. They form Canada's *centre*, in terms of both their political and their economic power.

Predictably, the provincial governments of Ontario and Quebec carry greater weight in Canadian federalism than do those of the other provinces. The other eight provincial governments preside over regions whose interests have usually been subordinated by Ottawa to those of central Canada. In this sense these other provinces constitute Canada's *peripheries*, situated on the edge of national politics. As we have discussed in other chapters, resentment toward central Canada and the federal government has deep roots in the politics of these provinces, particularly in the West. A short list of their historical grievances includes a tariff policy that for a century protected manufacturing jobs and corporate profits in Ontario and Quebec; the perceived insensitivity of the country's Toronto- and Montreal-based financial institutions when it comes to western interests; Ottawa's treatment of the petroleum resources concentrated in the West; investment and spending decisions by the federal government;

official bilingualism; and the perception of Ottawa's favouritism toward Quebec's interests. As Donald Smiley has written, "there are dangers that Canadian problems will be resolved almost entirely within the framework of the heartland of the country with the progressive alienation from national affairs of those who live on the peripheries."[27]

The federal principle of regional representation is embodied in the Canadian Senate and is practised by prime ministers in selecting cabinet ministers and in other federal appointments. And yet, this federal deference to regionalism has not provided these regions with what they believe to be adequate influence in Ottawa. **Intra-state federalism—*the representation and accommodation of regional interests within national political institutions*—**has been an abysmal failure. Deprived of this influence, the peripheral regions have tended to rely on their provincial governments for the protection and promotion of their interests.

The fact that more MPs are elected from Ontario and Quebec than from all other provinces combined has been the root cause of Ottawa's tendency to favour central Canada. This tendency has been reinforced by the ideological bias of Canadian politics to interpret Canadian history and identity in terms of experiences that are more germane to central Canada than to the peripheral regions. The central-Canadian identity is based on a concept of "Canada" that has two sources: a *counter-revolutionary/Loyalist tradition*, which rejected the values and political institutions of the United States; and a *cultural dualism*, which is so important to its political history. Neither of these experiences is central to the identity and political consciousness of western Canadians.[28] In the Maritimes, too, the national myths, symbols, and identities associated with "Canada" often have had little relationship to their experience.[29]

The subordinate status of the interests and cultural values of the peripheral regions of the country have often been reflected in relations between Ottawa and the provincial governments of the peripheries. For example, Ottawa has exercised its constitutional power to disallow provincial laws 112 times,

Newfoundland discusses alienation with other provinces. Given Canada's large geographic size, to what extent do you believe it is possible for the country to practise federalism and not have certain regions feel some degree of alienation?

but only a few of these were Ontario or Quebec laws.[30] When Manitoba joined Confederation in 1870, it did so without control of its public lands. Ottawa retained control to promote its own nation-building strategy relating to railway construction and western settlement.[31] Similarly, when Saskatchewan and Alberta became provinces in 1905, they did not acquire immediate control over their public lands and natural resources.[32] Ottawa argued that this was necessary to accomplish its immigration and settlement objectives for western Canada. Of course, these provinces received subsidies from Ottawa as compensation for the revenue they were deprived of. However, they never considered the compensation adequate for the quasi-colonial status imposed on them by Ottawa.

There is nothing subtle about the disallowance or denial of provincial constitutional powers. Today, grievances against Ottawa are about less blatant forms of policy discrimination against the interests of the peripheries. Among the items perennially on this list are claims that Ottawa does too little to support prairie grain farmers or the east coast fishing industry, and that the federal government's spending decisions unfairly favour Ontario and Quebec. Even in provinces like Alberta, British Columbia, and Saskatchewan, which are wealthy by Canadian standards, a sense of powerlessness is a major component of their provincial politics. "The West," observes Alberta historian Doug Owram, "has never felt in control of its own destiny. None of the wealth of recent years has eased this feeling. In fact, the tremendous wealth of the region merely sharpens the contrast with the political powerlessness that exists on the national level."[33] Having an Albertan, Stephen Harper, as prime minister has taken the edge off this sentiment, but it has not disappeared entirely. The outraged reaction of Albertans, when, several weeks after the 2008 federal election, the opposition parties attempted to dislodge the Conservatives from power and replace them with a coalition government supported by the Bloc Québécois, showed that the region is still very conscious of the long decades when it was on the outside of federal politics, looking in. The West, aware of its economic strength and its growing population, may become less resentful of what it perceives to be the domination of national politics by Ontario and Quebec with the election of a Conservative majority government in May 2011.

State Interests and Intergovernmental Conflict

The fact that Quebec is overwhelmingly francophone gives it a special set of interests that any Quebec government feels bound to defend. Likewise, grain farming and resource extraction in Saskatchewan, petroleum in Alberta, the automotive industry in Ontario, and forestry in British Columbia shape the policies of these provincial governments on taxation, trade, and other policies affecting these interests. Each province comprises a set of economic, social, and cultural interests that together influence the demands each provincial government makes on federalism. Intergovernmental conflict, then, is to some extent the clash of conflicting regional interests.

Governments do not simply reflect societal interests, however. They actively shape these interests through their policies, sometimes deliberately and other times inadvertently. Moreover, governments have their own political and administrative interests, the pursuit of which may have nothing to do with the interests of those they represent. "Canadian federalism," Alan Cairns has argued, "is about governments, governments that are possessed of massive human and financial resources, that are driven by purposes fashioned by elites, and that accord high priority to their own long-term institutional self-interest."[34] The *state-centred* interpretation of federalism maintains that conflicts between governments are likely to be generated or influenced by the "institutional self-interest" of politicians and bureaucrats.

The evidence in support of this view is overwhelming. Intergovernmental turf wars over taxation and over jurisdictions often seem remote from the concerns of Canadian citizens. For example, in 1998 the federal government proudly announced the creation of the Millennium Scholarship to provide financial assistance to university students. Provincial governments immediately cried foul, pointing out that education falls under provincial jurisdiction and that Ottawa had not consulted them. From a potential student recipient's perspective, this provincial grievance was totally irrelevant. But from the state's point of view, the ability to control revenue sources and legislative competence affects the ability of federal and/or provincial politicians to pursue their interests in re-election, in career advancement, and in personal prestige, as well as their own conception of the "public interest." The same may be said of the personal careers, ambitions, and fortunes of bureaucratic officials who have a vested interest in their organizations and programs, and also have their own conception of the public interest.

A concept that has often been associated with the provincial governments of Alberta and Quebec[35] is **province building**. As the term suggests, it occurs ***when the political administrative needs of governments are reinforced by the demands of province-oriented economic interests.*** This is the opposite of the *nation-building* orientation of Sir John A. Macdonald's post-Confederation government, and has been defined as the "recent evolution of more powerful and competent provincial administrations which aim to manage socioeconomic change in their territories and which are in essential conflict with the central government."[36] But the Ontario government is as "powerful and competent" as these other provincial states, and no one would accuse Ontario of "province building." Ontario's pivotal status in Canadian politics, however, based on its large population and economic importance, has meant that it generally has been able to count on a sympathetic hearing in Ottawa. Aside from a few recent instances of complaining about fiscal imbalances in the federal equalization payments to the provinces, aggressive and persistent "fed-bashing" by Ontario provincial politicians has not been a popular tactic because it has not been necessary for the achievement of their goals. In other respects, however, Ontario governments have not lagged behind their more aggressive counterparts.

Intergovernmental Relations

The Constitution, as we have seen, does not establish a neat division of legislative and taxation powers between Ottawa and the provinces. The chief sources of public revenue are shared between the two levels of government. The same is true of their involvement in most major policy fields. Defence and monetary policy come closest to being exclusive federal terrain, although provincial governments do not hesitate to express their views on such issues as the location of armed forces bases, major defence purchases, and interest rates. On the provincial side, local functions such as snow removal, garbage collection, and sidewalk maintenance, are typically free of federal involvement—but not entirely, because the money that Ottawa transfers annually to the provinces affects how much they in turn transfer to their municipalities, thereby affecting the municipalities' ability to carry out these local functions.

Divided jurisdiction has given rise to a sprawling and complicated network of federal–provincial relations. This network has often been compared to an iceberg, only a small part of which is visible to the eye. The "visible" tip of intergovernmental relations involves the much publicized meetings of the prime minister and provincial premiers (first ministers' conferences) as well as meetings of provincial premiers. Less publicized, but far more frequent, are hundreds of annual meetings between federal and provincial cabinet ministers and bureaucrats. Many of these meetings take place in the context of ongoing federal–provincial structures like the Continuing Committee on Fiscal and Economic Matters, established in 1955, and the Economic and Regional Development Agreements negotiated between Ottawa and the less affluent provinces. Others are generated by the wide range of shared-cost activities that link the two levels of government, from major spending programs such as the Canada Health Transfer to smaller federal subsidies such as those for official minority-language education.

Executive federalism is a *term sometimes used to describe the relations between cabinet ministers and officials of the two levels of government.* The lack of input from the public or the legislatures, the lack of distinction between provincial and federal responsibilities, and the secrecy that generally cloaks the negotiations and the decision-making process, have generated accusations that executive federalism is undemocratic, for several reasons. First, it undermines the role of elected legislatures, whose role is usually limited to ratifying *faits accomplis*. Second, an agreement to jointly finance a program or to share responsibilities in a particular field makes it difficult for citizens to determine which level of government should be responsible for specific policies. Third, executive federalism provides no meaningful opportunities for public debate (including political parties, interest groups, and individual Canadians) of important intergovernmental issues that directly affect citizens such as health-care services, welfare, and post-secondary education.

Donald Smiley lists three other concerns about executive federalism.[37]

- *It distorts the political agenda.* Executive federalism has a territorial bias. It reinforces the significance of territorially concentrated interests and of the provincial governments that represent them, at the same time as it undervalues the importance of other interests.
- *It fuels government expansion.* Competitive relations between Ottawa and the provinces have produced inefficient duplication, as each level of government has its own bureaucracy to pursue similar goals.
- *It perpetuates intergovernmental conflict.* The increasing sophistication of executive federalism, conducted through specialized bureaus staffed by intergovernmental affairs specialists, reduces the likelihood of resolving federal–provincial disputes. This happens because specialized intergovernmental affairs bureaus, which exist in all provinces and at the federal level, and the experts who staff them tend to perceive issues in terms

of the powers and jurisdiction of their particular government. Intergovernmental conflict is in a sense institutionalized by the fact that what is perceived to be at stake are the power, resources, and prestige of one's government.

The practitioners of executive federalism argue that this approach is necessary. "Overlapping powers" is an unavoidable fact of life under Canada's federal Constitution. Is it realistic to imagine that complex administrative and financial agreements can be negotiated in public forums? Much policy making is carried on in a closed fashion, dominated by cabinet ministers and bureaucratic elites. Why condemn executive federalism for traits that are deeply embedded in Canadian policy making generally? The fact is, however, that the characteristics of executive federalism are out of sync with the less deferential political culture that has evolved in Canada over the last generation. Governments continue to negotiate behind closed doors, and the constitutional overlap, competition, and ambiguity persist, but public acceptance of executive federalism and elitist policy making is much weaker today than in decades past.

Financing Federalism

From the very beginning, money has been at the centre of intergovernmental relations. The Confederation agreement included an annual per capita subsidy that Ottawa would pay to all provincial governments.[38] Moreover, the new federal government agreed to assume liability for the debts of the provinces as they stood in 1867.[39] Taxation powers were divided between the two levels of government, with Ottawa receiving what were at the time the major sources of public revenue.

These financial arrangements have never been adequate. The root of the problem is that the provinces' legislative responsibilities proved to be much more extensive and expensive than the founders had anticipated. This has been referred to as the *fiscal gap*. Provincial governments attempted to fill this gap between their revenues and their expenditures through an increasing array of provincial taxes. Licence fees, succession duties, and personal and corporate income taxes all were used to increase provincial revenues. In addition, the provinces pressed Ottawa for more money. Indeed, only two years after Confederation the federal subsidy paid to Nova Scotia was increased. An important precedent was thereby established: federal–provincial financial relations are determined by governments, not by the Constitution.

As Ottawa conceded *tax room*—in particular, revenue sources like the personal income tax—the provinces' revenues improved steadily between the 1950s and the 1970s (see Figure 7.1). Today, combined provincial and local revenues exceed those of the federal government. But at the same time, provincial dependence on subsidies from Ottawa remains high in several provinces. In the case of the poorest provinces, money from Ottawa currently accounts for about half of their total revenue. Part of this dependence has been encouraged by Ottawa through **shared-cost programs**, *provincially administered programs where Ottawa's financial contribution is geared to what a province spends*. Until 1995 the major shared-cost program was the Canada Assistance Plan (CAP), which financed welfare and other provincial social services. That year, CAP was replaced with the Canada Health and Social Transfer,

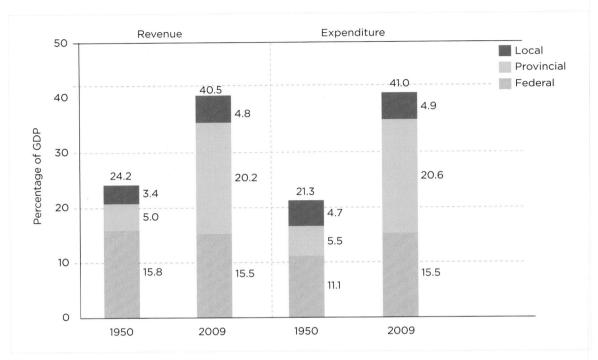

FIGURE 7.1 PUBLIC FINANCE IN CANADA: REVENUE AND EXPENDITURE AS PERCENTAGES OF GDP FOR EACH LEVEL OF GOVERNMENT, 1950 AND 2009

Source: Based on data from Canada, Department of Finance, Fiscal Reference Tables, 2009; Statistics Canada, *Canadian Economic Observer*, Historical Statistical Supplement 1994–5, Catalogue no. 11-210.

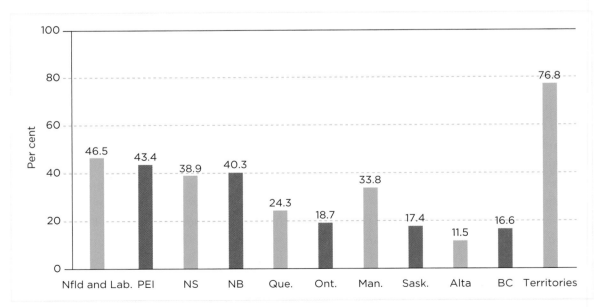

FIGURE 7.2 FEDERAL CASH TRANSFERS AS PERCENTAGE OF PROVINCIAL GOVERNMENT EXPENDITURES, 2008–9

Source: Canada, Department of Finance, Fiscal Reference Tables, 2009.

which was not geared to provincial spending. Federal grants for health care and post-secondary education also were launched on a shared-cost basis, but were converted by Ottawa into **block funding** programs where *Ottawa's financial contribution is geared to the previous year's subsidy plus an amount calculated on the basis of growth in the recipient province's gross product*. The federal government argued that the shared-cost formula did not encourage the provinces to control program costs. Under block funding, Ottawa is not obliged to match provincial spending, and indeed the effect of the switch to block funding has been to transfer an increasing share of the burden of health care and post-secondary education costs onto the provinces.

Not surprisingly, provincial governments have made several criticisms about the shift in financial burden. First, they claim that it is unfair for Ottawa to encourage them to spend more on social services by offering to share program costs on a matching basis, and then for Ottawa to back out of the financial arrangement. Second, the provinces' ability to increase their own sources of revenue to compensate for reduced federal transfer payments is limited by the fact that they share all the major tax fields with Ottawa. Unless the federal government is willing to give up some tax room to the provinces, provincial governments face the hard choice of increasing the total tax burden on their citizens. Third, any reduction in Ottawa's commitment to financing provincial social services hurts the poorer provinces more than it does the wealthier ones. As Figure 7.2 shows, the Maritime provinces in particular depend on federal transfers for maintaining the level of social services at comparable levels to other provinces.

Some of the money that Ottawa transfers to the provinces carries conditions as to how it must be spent. These are called conditional grants. Transfers with no strings attached are called unconditional grants. Important examples of both include the following:

- Previous residency in the province should not be a condition for receiving benefits from provincial social assistance programs: need should be the only requirement.
- The block transfer that Ottawa makes to the provinces under the CHT and the CST must be spent on health care, post-secondary education, and social services previously covered under CAP.
- The Canada Health Act, 1984 allows Ottawa to reduce its payment to provincial governments that permit physicians to extra-bill their patients. The terms of the CHT and

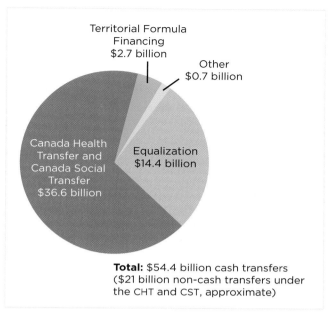

FIGURE 7.3 FEDERAL CASH TRANSFERS TO PROVINCES AND TERRITORIES, 2010–11 (ESTIMATED)

Source: Department of Finance, "Government of Canada Support to Provinces and Territories at All-Time High," 18 Dec. 2009, at: www.fin.gc.ca/n08/09-119-eng.asp.

CST also specify that provinces must respect the principles of the Canada Health Act, 1965 (portability of coverage between provinces, comprehensiveness of provincial plans, universality, public funding, and public administration).

According to a complex negotiated formula, **equalization payments** are *paid to provincial governments whose per capita tax revenues fall below the average of the two most affluent provinces.* Equalization accounts for about one-quarter of all federal cash transfers to the provinces, and about a quarter of the total revenue of the poorest provincial governments. It carries no conditions as to how it must be spent. Figure 7.3 provides a breakdown of federal transfers to the provinces.

The adequacy of federal transfers is not the only issue that has set Ottawa against the provincial governments. Another long-standing complaint of the provinces is that shared-cost programs distort provincial spending priorities because of the enticement of matching federal grants. Ottawa's spending power also permits undue federal interference in matters of

Democracy Watch

BOX 7.2 **Making a Case for Federalism**

Pros of Federalism

- *Promotes loyalty.* Residents of provinces become attached to their regional identities, and giving these regions power fosters a sense of belonging.
- *Makes running the country easier.* Canada is a large geographic region, and its population is diverse; giving power to regional authorities makes the federal government's job easier.
- *Fosters pluralism.* By giving provincial and municipal governments power, the federal government allows the diverse populations in each region to interact with their local officials and tackle issues unique to each area.
- *Prevents tyranny.* With provinces responsible for specific programs and services, there is protection against the federal government dictating how things should be run.

Cons of Federalism

- *Inhibits national cohesion.* Allowance for provincial independence can make it difficult for various regions to see eye-to-eye.
- *Inhibits accountability.* A blurring of the boundaries between provincial and federal jurisdiction can make it difficult to sort out what went wrong when policies and/or programs fail.

Up for Debate

Given these pros and cons of federalism, what would be your recommendation and rationale to a government of a currently non-federalist country that is contemplating this style of governance?

provincial jurisdiction. The government of Quebec has been most insistent about this. Indeed, there are several instances since the 1950s of Quebec governments declining moneys or declining participation in shared-cost programs. Both the Meech Lake and Charlottetown Accords included a provision that would have obligated Ottawa to provide "reasonable compensation" to provinces choosing not to participate in a new national shared-cost program, so long as the province's own program was "compatible with the national objectives." Critics argued that this opened the door for an erosion of **national standards** in social policy. By linking federal moneys to *Canada-wide standards in the delivery of social programs, the federal government hoped to have uniformity of service for all Canadians and create a " national social union."* Defenders claimed that this particular section merely constitutionalized a long-standing practice in Canadian federalism.

THE FEDERAL SPENDING POWER, NATIONAL STANDARDS, AND THE SOCIAL UNION

In the 1990s it became popular to vilify certain provincial governments, such as the Progressive Conservative governments of Ralph Klein in Alberta and Mike Harris in Ontario, for having undermined national standards in social programs. One of the major threats to national standards, however, came from Ottawa's shrinking financial commitment to provincially administered social programs. Federal transfers as a share of provincial program spending fell from 21 per cent in 1986–7 to 16 per cent in 1996–7.[40] Wealthier provinces, including Ontario, Alberta, and British Columbia, faced the largest burden of these cuts.

Ottawa's retreat from financing provincial social programs became unmistakable with the 1995 federal budget. Liberal finance minister Paul Martin's "new vision of Confederation" replaced the shared-cost programs that paid for welfare and social services, as well as the funding for health and post-secondary education, with a single block transfer called the Canada Health and Social Transfer (CHST). The CHST institutionalized the ad hoc freezes and caps on transfers that had been imposed from the early 1980s. It did so, in Ottawa's words, by ensuring that "the amounts transferred will not be determined by provincial spending decisions (as under cost-sharing)."[41] The transition to block funding under the CHST was argued to have the following beneficial effects:

- Provinces will no longer be subject to rules stipulating which expenditures are eligible for cost-sharing or not.
- Provinces will be free to pursue their own ... approaches to social security reform.
- The expense of administering cost-sharing will be eliminated.
- Federal expenditures will no longer be driven by provincial decisions on how, and to whom, to provide social assistance and social services.[42]

Provinces would not, however, be free to do whatever they pleased under the new fiscal arrangements: health care and social assistance were two areas where national standards would

INSIDE POLITICS

BOX 7.3 | Two Former Premiers and Two Views on Federal Transfers

For

No Canadian should have his or her life chances determined solely by geography. Canadians enjoy a political culture much like a family; we are all responsible for each other. These principles, enshrined in our Constitution, differentiate us from our friends in the United States where no such program exists. The vehicle for leveling the national playing field is the country's equalization program. Because of equalization, the gap between richer and poorer provinces has been reduced. The Canadian people understand the principle. [Polls demonstrate] that overwhelming majorities in each province support equalization.

Still, ideological opponents of equalization argue that such a program is wrong; they claim that it interferes with the operation of market forces and perpetuates poverty in some regions of the country. These claims are demonstrably wrong. Equalization has never prevented provinces from developing their own natural resources. Saskatchewan's oil and natural gas industries were developed even though that province's equalization payments declined as a result. Equalization did not obstruct the mining of potash in Saskatchewan, nickel in Manitoba, and hydroelectric development in Quebec, Manitoba, and Newfoundland and Labrador. There is no reason for it to be otherwise in the future. Furthermore, Ontario has always supported equalization, recognizing as it does that a strong Canada also strengthens that province.

—Howard Pawley, former Premier of Manitoba (1981–8) and Adjunct Professor, University of Windsor, in *Opinion Canada* 7, 10 (17 March 2005). Reprinted with permission of the author.

Against

I think it was Karl Marx who once said that religion is the opiate of the masses. Well, I can tell you that federal dependency is the opiate of this region, Atlantic Canada. Dependency—unemployment insurance, welfare cheques, transfer payments—have all become a narcotic to us to which we have become addicted. And there is not a person in this room that can tell you and me that we have not been influenced and affected, and had our behaviour modified by being part of that culture, because it shaped everything that we are. We know it to be true. We know it better than anybody else in Canada.

Looking at experience from all over the world, I can tell you that those jurisdictions which establish low and predictable corporate tax regimes end up resulting in much better growth, and long-term growth, and a much better environment for business to prosper.

What we need to do is get rid of all of the make-work projects and the money we spend transferring people to federal unemployment. We need to get rid of all those programs and either get rid of the taxes low-income people pay or offer income supplementation so they are always better off working in a job. If we do that, if we change that incentive system, it will have a powerful impact on Atlantic Canada.

I despise the people who whine and snivel about their lot in life within this country. People who tell us that, unless they get their lighthouses saved, they're going to separate from Canada, have no time in my book. We may not like base closures in Atlantic Canada, and we certainly don't like transfer payment cuts . . . but we will not—we will not—consider that an act of alienation or humiliation.

—Frank McKenna, former Premier of New Brunswick (1987–97), in a speech to the Atlantic Vision Conference of Atlantic Canadian Premiers in Moncton, NB, 9 October 1997. Reprinted by permission.

be maintained. Critics noted that even if Ottawa were able to enforce national standards, the lumping together of Ottawa's transfer for health care, social assistance, and post-secondary education under the CHST would permit provinces greater room to shift spending from politically unpopular welfare programs to more popular health care and education spending.

The CHST appeared to decisively end the notion of shared-cost programs and thus to mark a retreat from Ottawa's commitment to maintaining national standards in social policy, a commitment that has always depended on the federal spending power. In 2004 the CHST was divided into the Canada Health Transfer and the Canada Social Transfer, a change that provided greater transparency in identifying how much money was being transferred for specific provincial purposes.

Appearances may deceive, however. The Liberals' determination to rein in federal transfers to the provinces was not matched by corresponding decentralization. On the contrary, the Liberal government refused to make concessions on national standards, particularly in regard to the health-care system. Essentially, their message was this: we will give you fewer and fewer dollars to pay for your health-care services, but we will continue to set conditions on how those services must operate.

The Liberals' resolve was put to the test by the Progressive Conservative government of Alberta, which allowed the establishment of private clinics for certain health services like cataract operations, where patients, for a price, could jump the queue of the publicly funded system. In the end, all Ottawa could do was withhold some of the health-care dollars that Alberta would normally receive. For a wealthy province like Alberta, this was not much of a penalty.

Ottawa's retreat from its financial commitment to provincially administered social programs was not well received by provincial governments. Ottawa's success in transforming budget deficits into surpluses was largely due to cuts in transfers to the provinces, the use of Employment Insurance fund

In a 2004 initiative on health care struck between then Liberal prime minister Paul Martin and the provincial premiers, Quebec negotiated a separate deal in acknowledgement of its unique health-care system. Some Canadians felt this "special treatment" was unfair, especially since attempts by Alberta to introduce new elements into its system, such as limited private care, had previously been opposed by the federal government. Is allowing each province to strike its own deals with the federal government an advantage or disadvantage of federalism?

surpluses as general revenue, and increased federal tax revenues during the mid to late 1990s. Very little of this transformation was due to cuts in Ottawa's own program spending. From the provinces' point of view, Ottawa's deficit-cutting strategy left them to deal with the politically difficult choices of raising taxes, cutting services, or both. Moreover, the Liberal government's insistence that national standards for health care and welfare would have to be respected was particularly galling.

This was the background to the idea of a Canadian *social union*, a concept that emerged in the wake of the transfer cuts announced in Ottawa's 1995 budget. The social union involves some new set of arrangements for funding and determining program standards in health, welfare, and post-secondary education. Provinces like Alberta and Ontario, who receive the lowest per capita payments under the CHT and CST, tend to see the social union as a commitment to national standards that are negotiated with Ottawa. This is a decentralized version of the social union, under which the control over social programs and the money to fund them would shift to the provinces. Ottawa and some of the more transfer-dependent provinces insist on a central role for the feds in financing and maintaining the uniformity of social program standards, limiting provincial barriers against citizens from other provinces when it comes to social services. Quebec governments have kept their distance from the social union negotiations, and have insisted that neither Ottawa nor the other provinces have any constitutional authority to interfere with Quebec's autonomy.

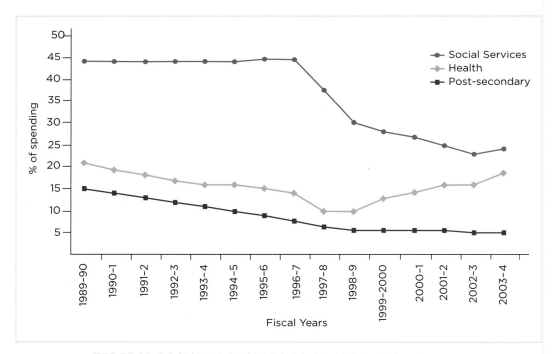

FIGURE 7.4 FEDERAL SOCIAL TRANSFERS AS A PERCENTAGE OF PROVINCIAL PROGRAM SPENDING, 1989–2003

Source: France St-Hilaire, "Fiscal Gaps and Imbalances: The New Fundamentals of Canadian Federalism," 20 May 2005, www.irpp.org.

Until the recession that began in late 2008, which sent many national economies into a tailspin, the federal government experienced large annual budget surpluses for several years, totalling over $61 billion between 1997 and 2005. But anyone who expected that this would lead to a return to the older model of fiscal federalism, whereby Ottawa helped the provinces to achieve their social policy objectives, has been disappointed. "Since 1997," observes France St-Hilaire, "[Ottawa] has clearly preferred to reinvest in direct spending initiatives over which it is able to maintain full control and gain visibility."[43] This has been so, St-Hilaire notes, in the fields of post-secondary education and social services where most federal spending now takes the form of federal programs. The exception has been health care. As Figure 7.4 shows, the federal share of provincial spending on health care rebounded after the trough experienced in the late 1990s. This rebound has continued under the Conservative government. The 2002 report of the Romanow Commission on the Future of Health Care suggested that in order to retain certain standards in health-care delivery, Ottawa's contribution would have to be at least 25 per cent, and in 2005, Parliament legislated an automatic escalator of six per cent per year—an increase that was slated to continue until 2014. Between 2006 and 2008 Ottawa's contribution to provincial health care increased by roughly 13 per cent. Even so, Ottawa's contributions to health care is estimated to be only 20 per cent of the cost to the provinces.[44]

SUMMARY

As we said earlier, federalism is a consensus of regions, wherein the regional governments agree to give up some of their sovereignty to a central governing authority with a constitutional purpose: economic, political, or both. In this chapter, we outlined the origins of Canadian federalism and discussed the initial division of powers, which has regularly caused disputes between Ottawa and provincial governments. The Canadian federal arrangement is essentially a great compromise: a sharing of power between competing regional interests and values. And the federalism we see in Canada today is likely very different from what the Fathers of Confederation had in mind. This great compromise, and the resulting constitutional power-sharing arrangement, has continuously evolved through precedents, through negotiations between Ottawa and the provinces, and through the interpretation of the Constitution by the courts during disputes over jurisdiction.

Many Canadians may feel a genuine sense of political nationality; however, regional differences continue to exercise significant political influence on the debates over provincial and federal jurisdiction, and on policies at both levels. Particularly in Quebec, nationalism has sometimes become a competing force within the federation and has often influenced the nature of federalism. For instance, many Canadians do not accept that Ottawa should be the dominant partner in the federal relationship. In fact, there seem to be two streams of interpretation about the nature and the origin of federalism in Canada that sees the relationship otherwise. Some, particularly in French Canada, see federalism as a compact between English and French Canada, while others see federalism as a contract in which the provinces agree to give up some powers to the federal government in a spirit of equality. The compact/contract approach to understanding federalism is certainly helpful in appreciating the stance that some provinces have taken in their relationship with Ottawa.

That being said, much of the relationship between Ottawa and the provinces has had to do with money. Under the Constitution, the provinces have certain responsibilities, such as health care, education, and social services, that have increased in importance and in costs since 1867. A significant portion of provincial budgets is dedicated to programs in these areas. And for mostly political reasons, the federal government has gradually agreed to take on a size-able share of the fiscal burden for these programs. This has been done through cost-sharing agreements and equalization payments to the poorest provinces, which are designed to ensure that Canadians receive a certain standard of care and service across the country.

In post-secondary education and social services, Ottawa has been able to create and administer its own programs, but this has not always been the case in health care. In order to maintain some leverage over health policy, Ottawa has had no choice but to increase its financial contribution to provincial health-care programs. Nonetheless, because of financial constraints, the scale of federal transfers is today significantly less than it was in the decades when the public health-care system was based on the 50/50 financing formula.

STARTING POINTS FOR RESEARCH

Herman Bakvis and Grace Skogstad, eds, *Canadian Federalism: Performance, Effectiveness, and Legitimacy*, 2nd edn (Toronto: Oxford University Press, 2008).

Alan Cairns, *Charter versus Federalism: The Dilemmas of Constitutional Reform* (Montreal and Kingston: McGill–Queen's University Press, 1992).

Alan Maslove, ed., *How Ottawa Spends 2008–2009: A More Orderly Federalism?* (Montreal and Kingston: McGill–Queen's University Press, 2008).

Michael Murphy, ed., *Canada: The State of the Federation 2005* (Kingston, Ont.: Institute of Intergovernmental Relations, Queen's University, 2005).

Ian Peach, ed., *Constructing Tomorrow's Federalism: New Perspectives on Canadian Governance* (Winnipeg: University of Manitoba Press, 2007).

Richard Simeon, *Political Science and Federalism: Seven Decades of Scholarly Engagement* (Kingston, Ont.: Institute of Intergovernmental Relations, Queen's University, 2002).

Donald Smiley, *The Federal Condition in Canada* (Toronto: McGraw-Hill Ryerson, 1987).

Pierre Elliott Trudeau, *Federalism and the French Canadians* (Toronto: Macmillan, 1968).

CBC ARCHIVES AND TVO'S *THE AGENDA*

Visit the companion website for *Canadian Democracy: A Concise Introduction* to follow links to audio and video footage related to the main themes of the chapter: www.oupcanada.com/BrooksConcise.

RELEVANT WEBSITES

Visit the companion website for *Canadian Democracy: A Concise Introduction* to browse a collection of websites featuring material related to the key themes of the chapter, an excellent starting point for research.

REVIEW EXERCISES

1. Visit the primary website for the government of Canada (www.gc.ca). Click on "About Government" and then "Provinces and Territories." Click on a province or territory. Make a list of the main issues discussed at the site. What information is provided about the relationship of the province's/territory's finances and programs to Ottawa?

2. Draw up a list of issues that would have to be resolved if Quebec were to separate from the rest of Canada. Attach a level of difficulty to each, ranging from 1 (easily resolved) to 10 (impossible to resolve).

3. Does it matter which level of government pays for what share of health-care costs and which level or levels set the rules for health policy? In answering this question be sure to address the issues of constitutionality, political accountability, Canadian values, and taxpayer interests.

How Parliamentary Government Works in Canada

Modern government is a complicated affair. Many of its parts seem to perform no useful function, and it appears to have been assembled piece by piece, without much planning and without discarding old parts to make room for new ones. The purpose of the machinery of government is easily lost, and it seems certain that there must be a more efficient way of governing. But for all its inelegance and appearance of muddling, parliamentary government does produce results. Laws are passed, regulations are applied, applications are dealt with, cheques are issued, and the innumerable other specific tasks performed by government are carried out. How well these tasks are done, whether some of them should be done at all, and what other things should be done by public authorities are important questions. But before we can answer them, we need an understanding of the machinery itself— the individual parts, the functions they perform, and the relations between them.

This chapter focuses on state institutions at the national level; but Canadians also encounter the machinery of government at the provincial and local levels, where the state's activities affect their lives in ways that often seem more direct and significant. Hospitals, schools, police, garbage collection, transit, roads and water treatment: these are primarily the responsibilities of provincial and local governments. Together, provincial and local governments out-spend and out-tax the federal government.

After reading this chapter on the key components of the machinery of government, you will be able to

1. Explain the roles, and the relationships between, the major institutions of government within Canadian parliamentary democracy
2. Outline the role of the monarch and the Governor General
3. Outline and discuss the powers, responsibilities, and functions of the prime minister and the cabinet
4. Discuss the role of central agencies, the bureaucracy, and the regulatory agencies
5. Discuss the functions of the legislature and explain how a law is passed
6. Describe the influence and the activities of MPs
7. Outline how a law is passed
8. Describe the role of the judiciary within Canadian democracy

THE ORGANIZATION OF GOVERNMENT

The formal organization of the government of Canada, as portrayed in Figure 8.1, seems deceptively simple. The three branches of government coincide with three major functions of democratic governance: the legislature makes the laws; the executive implements the laws; and the judiciary interprets the laws.

Unlike the American system of government, where the three branches of government are clearly demarcated and constitutionally separated, the Canadian parliamentary government does not have a clear *separation of powers* or a clear system of *checks and balances* to prevent any one branch of government from abusing power. There are many examples. For instance, legislative and executive functions are fused in the office of the prime minister (PM), who is both head of the legislature and, informally, the head of the executive. The legislature, in fact, is dominated by a small group of its members—the prime minister and the cabinet— who oversee the executive branch. Laws may be debated and passed in the legislature, but these laws typically originate in the executive branch as bills that are seldom expected to change much. In the case of the judicial branch of government, the courts do not, strictly speaking, involve themselves in the making of laws. In recent times, however, Canadian courts have played a major role in the determination of policy on important matters such as Sunday shopping, abortion, Aboriginal landownership, the collective bargaining rights of workers, same-sex pension benefits, and the legal definition of marriage. And finally, in the case of the bureaucracy, the bureaucrats whose job it is to implement the laws passed by their political masters in the executive branch often have enormous discretion in determining the actual meaning of laws that provide them with only vague guidelines about what they are expected to do.

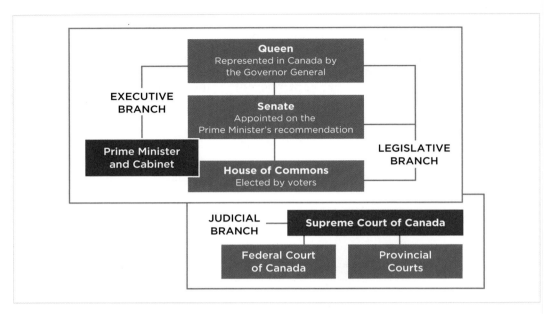

FIGURE 8.1 THE FORMAL ORGANIZATION OF THE CANADIAN PARLIAMENTARY SYSTEM OF GOVERNMENT

In this system of government, which is based on the Westminster model from the United Kingdom, there is no clear separation of the branches of government as there is in the republican model shown in Figure 8.2.

Source: "At Work in the House of Commons," *The House of Commons Report to Canadians 2008*, http://www.parl.gc.ca/About/House/ReportToCanadians/2008/rtc2008_05-e.html.

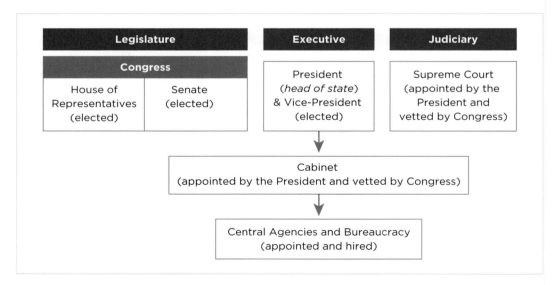

FIGURE 8.2 THE REPUBLICAN PRESIDENTIAL SYSTEM OF GOVERNMENT OF THE UNITED STATES

Note the clear separation of power between the main branches of government, which allows for a system of checks and balances against potential abuses of power.

Nevertheless, the respective roles of the legislative, executive, and judicial branches are significantly different, and their differences are rooted in our expectations for democratic government:

The legislative branch shall . . .
- represent the people and be accountable to them through periodic elections
- debate public issues and provide a forum for competition between political parties
- make laws
- approve government spending and make laws

The executive branch shall . . .
- implement the laws
- ensure that the public's business is carried out efficiently, accountably, and in accordance with the law
- be non-partisan at the bureaucratic level, such that non-elected officials faithfully carry out the policies of whatever party forms the government of the day

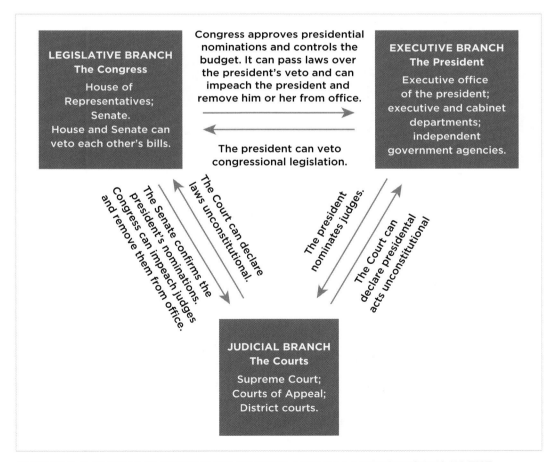

FIGURE 8.3 HOW THE SYSTEM OF CHECKS AND BALANCES WORKS IN THE UNITED STATES

Source: The Social Studies Help Centre, http://www.socialstudieshelp.com/Images/ChksBalnces.gif.

The judicial branch shall . . .
- be non-partisan and free from interference by the government
- interpret the law's meaning
- not substitute its preferences for those of elected public officials in matters of public policy, as distinct from legal and constitutional interpretation

These democratic expectations are not immutable. Today, many people expect that the bureaucracy should be representative of the population it serves, which may affect bureaucratic recruitment and promotion policies. Some argue that it is neither realistic nor desirable to expect non-elected officials to be politically neutral, and that accountability for policy (as distinct from its implementation) should be shared between politicians and bureaucrats. The elevated status of Canadian courts in the political process since the Charter of Rights and Freedoms was passed in 1982 has been welcomed by those who see judges as more likely than politicians to protect rights and promote democracy. Others, clinging to more traditional expectations, lament that the courts have come to trespass on turf that properly belongs to the people's elected and accountable representatives. The courts are also expected by many to be representative of Canada's diverse population, interests, and values.

In this chapter we discuss the main characteristics and roles of the institutions of Canadian government.

THE EXECUTIVE BRANCH

The Monarch and the Governor General

Canada is a **constitutional monarchy**: *a system of government with a monarch, as a formal head of state, that operates within a constitutional framework*. The monarch, currently Queen Elizabeth II, embodies the authority of the Canadian state. Any action of the government of Canada is taken in the Queen's name,[1] also known as the *Crown*. The monarch has a number of very important duties including giving royal assent to new legislation, the prorogation of Parliament, the appointing of the prime minister, and deciding when Parliament will be dissolved and a new election held. When she is not in Canada, which is of course most of the time, her duties are carried out by the Governor General, currently His Excellency the Right Honourable David Johnston. Although the Constitution suggests that the role of the monarch is a formidable one, most Canadians realize that the Queen and Governor General perform mainly symbolic functions. The real decision-making powers of the executive are exercised by the prime minister, who is the head of government and of cabinet.

Constitutional convention is far more important than the discretion of the monarch in matters such as the selection of the prime minister and the dissolution of Parliament. For example, the party that wins a majority of seats in an election gets to form the government, and the choice of prime minister is automatic. Even when no party has a majority, it is understood that the leader of the party with the most seats will be given the first opportunity to form a

CANADIAN SPOTLIGHT

BOX 8.1   How Responsible Government/ The Westminster Model Works in Canada

Named for the Palace of Westminster, the seat of Parliament in the United Kingdom, the Westminster system of government has these key features:

- A sovereign head of state (in Canada, the Queen's representative, the Governor General)
- A head of government (in Canada, the prime minister)
- The executive branch of government (in Canada, the ruling party's cabinet)

- The Opposition (in Canada, formed by the multiple parties that do not win a majority government)
- The legislature (in Canada, the elected House of Commons and the appointed Senate)
- Record of the legislature's activity (in Canada, these minutes take the traditional name of *Hansard*)

The operation of government in this model looks something like Figure 8.4.

The Government (Prime Minister and the Cabinet) is responsible to the House of Commons, and needs the support of a majority (50% plus one) of the duly elected members of parliament for all of its activities, legislation, and expenditures.

As occurred in April of 2011, the opposition parties can ask for a "vote of confidence" in the government.

→ If the Government does not get the required majority, then it is deemed to lack the "Confidence of the House of Commons" and the government must offer its resignation to the head of state or their representative (in Canada, the Governor General). The Prime Minister must then vist the Governor General and offer his or her government's resignation. The Prime Minister can recommend that parliament be dissolved, and that an election be held. The Governor General does not have to accept this advice.

→ The Governor General has one of two options:

Option 1: Accept the Prime Minister's resignation, dissolve Parliament, and sign the writs of election;

or

Option 2: Ask one of the other party leaders, usually the leader of the Loyal Opposition, to form a new government if they enjoy the confidence of the House of Commons.

FIGURE 8.4   HOW RESPONSIBLE GOVERNMENT/THE WESTMINSTER SYSTEM WORKS IN CANADA

government that has the support of a majority in the legislature. If, however, it is clear that the members of the other parties will not support a government led by this person, the Governor General may turn to the leader of another party. A Governor General cannot simply decide that there is no point in convening the legislature and that a new election should be held; a newly elected legislature must be given the opportunity to meet.

Likewise in the case of dissolving Parliament, the monarch's discretion is limited by constitutional conventions. The prime minister's request that Parliament be dissolved and a new

Listen to the "Who Is Canada's Head of State (and Does It Matter)?" podcast, available at www.oupcanada.com/BrooksConcise.

election held is usually granted automatically. It is conceivable, though improbable, that in circumstances of minority government the Governor General could refuse such a request and instead ask the leader of another party to try to form a government. The last time this happened was 1926, when Governor General Lord Byng refused Prime Minister Mackenzie King's request for a new election. This refusal provoked a minor constitutional crisis. Since then, the view of most constitutional experts has been that the monarch's representative is required to accept the "advice" of the prime minister.

The Byng precedent suddenly and rather unexpectedly became relevant several weeks after the federal election of 2008, which produced a Conservative minority government. Although the factors that precipitated the affair are disputed, the opposition parties agreed to bring down the government on a motion of non-confidence in the House of Commons, based on the government's financial statement ("mini-budget"). They also agreed to a coalition pact whereby the Liberals and NDP would form a **coalition government** (*a temporary agreement between two or more political parties to form a government*) for a period of at least two years, supported by the Bloc. But before this coalition could replace the Conservatives as the government, the Governor General would have to refuse Prime Minister Harper's request for a new election, and then call on Liberal leader Stéphane Dion to form a government. Constitutional experts were divided on the question of whether the Governor General would be breaking an unwritten rule of the Constitution in turning down such a request. In the end, the question became moot when Prime Minister Harper decided to request a **prorogation**, *a postponement of parliamentary activities without a dissolution of Parliament*, until late January 2009, when the government planned to introduce a new budget.

The monarch and Governor General play no significant role in setting the government's policy agenda or in the decision-making process. Royal assent to legislation is virtually automatic. It has never been withheld from a law passed by Parliament. The disallowance and reservation powers have been used by the monarch's provincial representatives, the lieutenant-governors, but this was almost always at the behest of the elected government in Ottawa.[2]

While the monarch's role today is primarily symbolic, the functions performed by the Queen, Governor General, and lieutenant-governors are important. The ceremonial duties of government must be performed by someone, and assigning them to an *impartial* head of state may reduce the association between the political system itself—the state—and the leadership of particular political factions within it. As James Mallory argues, "[the monarchy] denies to political leaders the full splendor of their power and the excessive aggrandizement of their persons which come from the undisturbed occupancy of the centre of the stage."[3] While there is no clear evidence that democracies are imperilled when these state functions are performed by an elected president, as is the case in the United States and France, it is worth noting that both the American and French political systems have *legislative checks* on executive power that do not exist in a British-style parliamentary system. Paradoxically, therefore, Mallory may be correct: having a non-elected head of state may in fact contribute to the protection of Canada's democratic social order.

Nonetheless, the monarchy has not always been an uncontroversial pillar of stability in Canadian politics. The monarch's status in Canada's system of government is *King* or *Queen of Canada*, not of the United Kingdom. But some perceive the institution as an irritating reminder of Canada's colonial ties to Britain and of the dominance of Anglo-Canadians in our politics. When French–English tensions run high, the issue of which groups in Canada are symbolically represented by the monarch resurfaces. But despite occasional imbroglios over royal visits, we should not exaggerate the institution's contribution to national disunity.

A new sort of controversy was associated with the position of Governor General during the tenure of Adrienne Clarkson (1999–2005). Clarkson's spouse, John Ralston Saul, a well-known philosopher-historian and author, made a number of pronouncements on contemporary issues that focused attention on the question of whether his relationship to the Governor General ought to have limited his forays into political matters. While his defenders noted that he was a private citizen, entitled to the same freedom of speech to which any other citizen is entitled, this was somewhat disingenuous. Like Governor General Clarkson, Saul was referred to as "His Excellency" and made use of the publicly financed staff and other facilities in the office of Governor General. Whether these circumstances ought to have limited his participation in the more controversial side of public life was a matter of disagreement.

Perhaps more important, Governor General Clarkson occasionally showed signs of wanting to reshape the boundaries of the office's role in public life. For example, in 2001 she sent a message of congratulations to a gay couple in Ontario who were wed in Toronto's Metropolitan Community Church, at a time when there was much public controversy over the legal definition of marriage. Critics charged that as a non-elected and non-partisan head of state, Clarkson should not have expressed views that could have been construed as critical of existing law and therefore as politically divisive. Nonetheless, Michaëlle Jean, Clarkson's successor as Governor

Listen to the "Who Should Represent Canada and Why?" podcast, available at www.oupcanada .com/BrooksConcise.

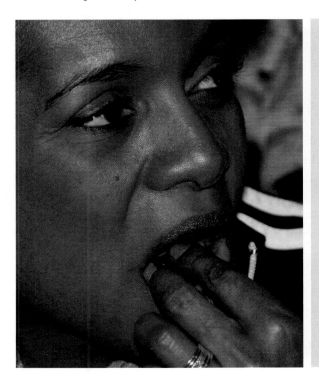

During her term as Governor General, Michaëlle Jean did not shy away from controversy. In an official visit to Nunavut in the Canadian North, Jean joined with community members in eating raw heart as part of the ancient and cultural tradition of the seal hunt, still practised in Rankin Inlet as a way of sustenance living off the land. Animal activists labelled the act "barbaric," but Jean said her detractors were "completely missing the reality of life here." After reading both sides of the story in the article at the link below, how would you either defend or condemn the Queen's representative and her actions? "Governor General Has a Heart—Raw Seal, That Is": http://www.thestar.com/news/canada/article/640335

General, was also not averse to wading into potentially controversial waters. For example, in a speech to Alberta's legislature in May 2006, Governor General Jean urged it to share the province's wealth: "Alberta's tremendous prosperity affords you the opportunity to make the most of this attitude of sharing. Surely a prime benefit to be derived from such communal wealth is the ability it gives us: to ensure that no one is left behind, and that each among us has a voice."[4]

The Prime Minister and Cabinet

Unlike the passive and principally symbolic roles of the monarchy, the prime minister (PM) and cabinet are at the centre of the policy-making process. The PM is the head of government in Canada. By convention, the PM is the leader of the dominant party in the House of Commons. One of the PM's first duties is to select the cabinet ministers. In the British parliamentary tradition, cabinet members are always drawn from the PM's political party. Cabinet ministers are almost always elected members of the House of Commons, but occasionally, a senator or two are appointed when there is little or no representation from a particular region, or because of the special abilities of a senator. In recent years, the size of the federal cabinet has ranged from a low of 20 to a high of almost 40 members. Provincial cabinets tend to be smaller.

The cabinet, also called the Privy Council, is under the leadership of the PM. The power of the PM and cabinet rests on a combination of factors, including section 11 of the Constitution Act, 1867, which states "There shall be a Council to aid and advise in the Government of Canada, to be styled the Queen's Privy Council for Canada." Section 13 goes even further to specify that the actions of the monarch's representative in Canada, the Governor General, shall be undertaken "by and with the Advice of the Queen's Privy Council for Canada." Although, formally, anyone who has ever been a member of cabinet retains the title of privy councillor after leaving government, only those who are active members of the government exercise the constitutional powers.

Cabinet dominates the entire legislative agenda of Parliament, including control over the budget. Section 54 of the Constitution Act, 1867 requires that legislation or other measures that involve the raising or spending of public revenue must be introduced by cabinet. MPs who are not members of the cabinet do have the right to introduce private members' bills; however, party discipline and the meagre time allocated to considering these bills combine to kill the prospects of most of these initiatives.

Although the position of prime minister is not mentioned in the written Constitution, the leader of the dominant party in the House of Commons has many powers:

- Appointing and removing cabinet ministers
- Determining when a new election will be held
- Setting out the administrative structure and decision-making process of government
- Making appointments to many positions including deputy ministers, judges of all federal and provincial courts, senators, members of federal regulatory agencies and of the boards of directors of federal Crown corporations, ambassadors, etc.

This list helps to explain why the PM is always the pre-eminent figure in Canadian government. The PM's pre-eminence is reinforced by constitutional conventions on accountability. Although individual cabinet ministers are separately accountable to Parliament for the actions of their departments, the entire cabinet is collectively accountable for government policy. The PM cannot avoid personal accountability for major policies and the overall performance of government. The opposition parties and the media ensure that the PM is held to account.

Responsible government is another constitutional convention that strengthens the power of the PM and cabinet. As we noted in Chapter 5, responsible government encourages party discipline. The government will fall if the members of the governing party break ranks. Consequently, the elected members of a party tend to act as a unified bloc on most matters, particularly when voting on budget measures and important government legislation. Party discipline, therefore, ensures that members of the governing party are normally docile in their support of the government's policies. When the government has a majority in both the House of Commons and the Senate the automatic support of the government party's **back-benchers** (*MPs who are not cabinet ministers*) enables the PM and cabinet to move their legislative agenda through Parliament without serious impediment.

The weakness of Canada's political party organizations also reinforces the dominance of the PM and cabinet. Parties, particularly Liberals and Conservatives, are geared primarily toward fighting election campaigns and are much more concerned with raising money, selecting candidates, and contesting elections than with formulating policy. Neither the Conservative Party nor the Liberal Party is considered a social movement party with ties to organizations and groups in civil society. A party usually has little influence on the policies adopted by its leadership when it forms the government. This stems from two main reasons. First, the parties try to attract a broad base of support, which requires that the party's leadership be allowed a large margin of manoeuvrability in communicating to different groups. Second, except for the NDP, parties tend not to have formal affiliations with organized interests. Since 1961 the NDP has been formally affiliated with the Canadian Labour Congress. Formal affiliations usually narrow a party's electoral appeal and increase the influence in a party's internal affairs of the affiliated group(s). But history shows that when in power, provincial NDP governments have been unwilling to tie themselves rigidly to the party's platform.

The constitutional and statutory foundations of prime ministerial and cabinet powers are reinforced by the relationship between the political executive and the media. This relationship is close and mutually dependent. The PM and members of cabinet regularly speak "directly" to the people or to targeted publics via the media. Even when presenting or defending the government's policies in the House of Commons, they are aware of the wider audience. For their part, journalists typically turn first to the PM and the responsible ministers when reporting on politics. In doing so, the media contribute to the personalization of politics and, more particularly, to the popular identification of government with the PM and cabinet.

Direct communications between the PM and cabinet and the public has undermined the role of the legislature and political parties. When public sentiment can be gauged through public opinion polls, and when the PM and cabinet ministers can speak to the general public or targeted groups via the media and personal appearances, there is less need to communicate through government MPs and the party organization. The result is that Parliament often seems to be little more than a procedural sideshow. This infuriates some constitutional purists, for whom Parliament is the proper conduit between the state and society. They argue that the practice of responsible government, the bedrock of the British parliamentary system, is subverted by direct communications between the government and the people. But the fact is that responsible government is already attenuated by party discipline.

The communications role of the PM and cabinet is related to their representative functions. From the beginnings of self-government in Canada, cabinet formation has been guided by the principle that politically important interests should be "represented" by particular cabinet ministers. Representation of different regions and particular provinces has always been considered important, as has representation of francophones. The numerical dominance of anglophones has always ensured that they would be well represented in any government. Representation from the business community—the minister of finance often has professional connections to either the Toronto or the Montreal corporate elite—and the inclusion of ministers perceived to be spokespersons for particular economic interests, particularly agriculture and occasionally labour, have significantly influenced appointments to particular cabinet positions. Some representational concerns, such as the inclusion of various religious denominations, have diminished in importance while others, such as the representation of women and non-French, non-British Canadians, have become significant.

Representational concerns also surface in the case of the PM, particularly when a party chooses its leader. Party members and the media look at candidates in terms of their likely ability to draw support from politically important regions and groups. An aspiring leader of a national political party cannot be associated too closely with the interests of a single region of the country. Given the numerical superiority of anglophone

Kiss me and the Liberal leadership is yours!

artizans.com

It was widely speculated that Conservative-turned-Liberal Belinda Stronach would seek the top spot during the Liberal Party's 2006 leadership campaign. Some members of the Canadian media suggested, however, that along with other issues her weak grasp of the French language would greatly hamper her bid. How important do you believe it is for otherwise qualified politicians to stay out of leadership races until they are fluent in both the country's official languages?

voters, it goes without saying that any serious leadership candidate must be able to communicate well in English. But he or she must be at least competent in French.

Being the leader of a national political party or even PM does not automatically elevate a politician above the factional strife of politics and accusations of favouritism from one region or the other. Despite holding a majority of that province's seats in the House of Commons between 1958 and 1962, Conservative prime minister John Diefenbaker (1957–63) was never perceived as being particularly sensitive to Quebec's interests. Similarly, Liberal prime minister Pierre Elliott Trudeau (1968–79, 1980–4) was never able to convince western Canada—not that he always tried very hard—that he shared their perspectives on Canadian politics. For westerners, Trudeau and the Liberals represented the dominance of "the East" and favouritism toward Quebec. Conservative prime minister Brian Mulroney (1984–93) may have been more successful than Trudeau in drawing support from all regions of the country. But he, too, came under attack for allegedly neglecting western interests in favour of those of central Canada, especially Quebec. Liberal prime minister Jean Chrétien was widely perceived as more successful than his predecessors in attracting the support of both French and English Canadians. In fact, however, under Chrétien's leadership the Liberal Party did less well in Quebec than during the Trudeau years.

A prime minister whose party's representation in the House of Commons from a key region is relatively weak can attempt to convey a message of inclusion by appointing a high-profile cabinet minister from that region. This is precisely what Conservative prime minister Stephen Harper did after the 2006 election. His party won only 10 of Quebec's 75 seats, but he moved immediately to appoint to the Senate and to cabinet Quebec's Michael Fortier. At the same time, Harper appointed four newly elected MPs from Quebec to his cabinet, three of these to the perennially important portfolios of industry, labour, and transport.

Setting the Agenda

Representation is about power. The PM and cabinet wield considerable power over the machinery of government, which is why representation in the inner circle of government is valued by regional and other interests. This power is based on the agenda-setting role of the PM and cabinet and on their authority within the decision-making process of the state.

Each parliamentary session begins with the Speech from the Throne, in which the Governor General reads a statement explaining the government's legislative priorities. This formal procedure is required by the Constitution.[5] Although a typical throne speech is packed with generalities, it also contains some specific indications of the agenda that Parliament will follow over the ensuing months.

Budgets are a second way for the PM and cabinet to define the policy agenda. Every winter, usually in late February, the minister of finance tables the estimates in the House of Commons. This is what students of public finance call the *expenditure budget*. It represents the government's spending plans for the forthcoming fiscal year (1 April–31 March; see Figure 8.5). Given that most public policies involve spending, changes in the allocation of public money indicate shifts in the government's priorities. The government can also use the expenditure budget to signal its overall fiscal stance. Increased spending may be part of an expansionary fiscal policy.

Spending restraint and cutbacks may signal the government's concern that public spending is damaging the economy.

From time to time, usually every two years, the minister of finance presents in Parliament either a **revenue budget** or a major **economic statement**. The former *outlines the government's plans to change the tax system.* The latter *provides the government's analysis of the state of the economy and where the government plans to steer it.* Both are major opportunities for the government to shape the economic policy agenda.

The government influences the policy agenda by deciding which initiatives are placed before Parliament, the priorities among them, and the strategies for manoeuvring policies through the legislature and communicating them to the public. Even when bills and budget proposals have originated in some part of the bureaucracy rather than the cabinet, or when they are reactions to politically or economically pressing circumstances, these initiatives must still be accepted and sponsored by the government. As Figure 8.5 shows, cabinet and cabinet committees such as the Treasury Board are central players in the budget-making process.

Setting the agenda is part of the decision-making process in government. It is a crucial part, the early stage during which public issues are defined and policy responses are proposed. The roles of the PM and cabinet at this and other stages of the policy process are institutionalized through the formal structure of cabinet decision making. The formal structure of cabinet decision making, including its committee structure, has never been more than an imperfect guide to who has influence over what within the government of the day. The one reliable rule of thumb is this: ministers are influential to the degree that the prime minister allows them to be influential and supports their favoured projects and initiatives. A minister who is thought to have the PM's ear and be part of the PM's favoured circle acquires enhanced status among his or her colleagues in Parliament and in the eyes of the media.

Other factors are important, too, such as a base of support within the party or being in charge of a powerful part of the bureaucracy, but the personal relationship between the PM and a minister is always a significant determinant of a minister's influence. The decision-making process in cabinet does not occur only through formal committee meetings. One-on-one conversations in the corridors of the Langevin Building (the location of the Privy Council Office), in the PM's office in the West Block, over the phone, or however and wherever they may take place have always been crucial in the decision-making process. No organization chart can capture this informal but crucial aspect of ministerial influence. Nor can it convey the extent to which the prime minister dominates this decision-making process. Political observers have long characterized the PM's status in cabinet as *primus inter pares*—first among equals. But as Donald Savoie notes, there is no longer any *inter* or *pares*. There is only *primus*, the PM, when it comes to setting the government's agenda and making major decisions.[6]

Ministerial control over the bureaucracy is another dimension of cabinet's decision-making authority, but the word "control" should be used carefully. Ministers are virtually never involved in the day-to-day running of the departments under their nominal control. Moreover, policy initiatives are more likely to be generated within the bureaucracy than from the responsible minister. There are, of course, exceptions. Stéphane Dion, when he was the federal minister of intergovernmental affairs, was the principal author of the 2000 Clarity Act, an idea that

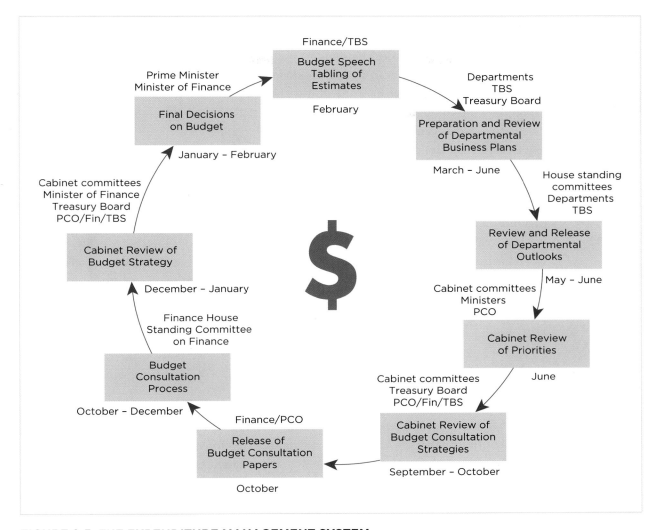

FIGURE 8.5 THE EXPENDITURE MANAGEMENT SYSTEM

Source: "The Expenditure Management System of the Government of Canada," at http://www.tbs-sct.gc.ca/Pubs_pol/opepubs/TB_H/images/figure1e.gif. Treasury Board of Canada, 2010. Reproduced with the permission of the Minister of Public Works and Government Services, 2012.

he had championed from the time of the 1995 Quebec referendum. Under the Conservative government of Stephen Harper, it appears that unelected advisers in and around the Prime Minister's Office have played a greater role in shaping the government's policy agenda. As well, the role of the permanent bureaucracy, which some argue is mistrusted by the Conservatives as too liberal, has been weaker than usual. Generally, however, most ministers act as cabinet advocates for the interests of their department and the groups that depend on them. But we should not succumb to the caricature of wily, powerful bureaucrats manipulating their hapless political "masters." Departments and other parts of the bureaucracy are created and restructured as a result of cabinet initiatives, and changes to their budgets and programs are often undertaken in spite of bureaucratic opposition.

Central Agencies

Cabinet has always been a decision-making body. But when John A. Macdonald and the first cabinet met in 1867, they dealt with a workload that was only a fraction of that which faces government today. In order to deal with the sheer volume of information that comes before cabinet and the hundreds of separate decisions that it makes annually, cabinet needs help. This help is provided by central agencies.

Central agencies are *areas of the bureaucracy whose main or only purpose is to support the decision-making activities of cabinet*. They provide cabinet with needed information, apply cabinet decisions in dealing with other parts of the bureaucracy, and communicate cabinet decisions and their implications to the public, provincial governments, or other organizations within the federal state. The general character of their policy role, their direct involvement in cabinet decision making, and their ability to intervene in the affairs of departments led political scientists Colin Campbell and George Szablowski to refer to the senior officials of central agencies as "superbureaucrats."[7] The main organizations usually considered to have central agency status are the Department of Finance, the Privy Council Office (PCO), the Treasury Board Secretariat, the Prime Minister's Office, and, within the PCO, Intergovernmental Affairs.

Department of Finance

The Department of Finance plays the leading role in formulating economic policy. Its formal authority is found in the Department of Finance Act, 1869 and in the Financial Administration Act. The authority that the law confers on Finance is reinforced by the department's informal reputation within the state. Although comparatively small (about 700 people), Finance has always been a magnet for "the best and the brightest" within the public service because of its unrivalled status in all aspects of economic policy making.

The Finance department has what amounts to almost exclusive authority over the preparation of the revenue budget, budget speeches, and economic statements delivered in Parliament by the finance minister. Whatever input other parts of the bureaucracy and interests outside of government have is at the discretion of the minister of finance and the department.[8] New initiatives in taxation and trade policy and in managing the level of government spending and debt will often be generated within Finance. Even when a new policy idea originates elsewhere, it is unlikely to reach the legislation stage if Finance is steadfastly opposed.

Finance officials can influence the entire spectrum of government policy through their role in the annual formulation of the expenditure budget. They are involved at the very beginning of the expenditure budget process, providing projections on the future state of the economy and the fiscal framework within which spending choices must be made. Finance's dominance was reinforced during the 1990s, once deficit reduction and debt management became Ottawa's overriding priorities. When Ottawa turned the corner on the deficit issue and began to accumulate considerable budget surpluses during the late 1990s, many believed that Finance's stranglehold on the government's agenda would loosen. In fact, however, Finance had lost none of its authority at the centre of the policy-making universe. The unrivalled status of Finance within the federal bureaucracy is one factor that effectively reinforces the power of the PM, who, along with his or her minister of finance, is the only member of the government to be intimately involved in the process that leads up to tabling a budget or economic statement in the House of Commons. As Donald Savoie observed:

> . . . the budget has come to dominate policy and decision-making in Ottawa as never before. This holds significant advantages for the centre of government. It enables the prime minister and the minister of finance to introduce new measures and policies under the cover of budget secrecy and avoid debate in Cabinet—and perhaps, more importantly, long interdepartmental consultations and attempts to define a consensus.[9]

Minister of Finance Jim Flaherty tries on new shoes prior to delivering the March 2012 budget. The reading of a new budget is a ceremonial affair in Ottawa, and though no one knows its origin, there is a long-standing tradition of the finance minister purchasing and wearing a new pair of shoes for the occasion.

Finance is directly responsible for only a handful of programs, but they are important, big-ticket ones. One of these is *fiscal equalization*, under which unconditional payments are made to the poorer provincial governments.

The Privy Council Office

The Privy Council Office (PCO) is the cabinet's secretariat and a principal source of policy advice to the prime minister. Donald Savoie characterizes it as "the nerve centre of the federal public service."[10] The PCO was formally created by order-in-council in 1940. The position of Chief Clerk of the Privy Council (CCPC) was made statutory in 1974, without any specification of the duties associated with this position. The authority of this person, who is the head of the public service, and the influence of the PCO derive mainly from their intimate and continuous involvement in cabinet decision making. The CCPC is a sort of deputy minister who reports directly and daily to the prime minster, and is one of the most influential people in the federal government.

In the first comprehensive study of central agencies, Campbell and Szablowski argue that the PCO is the lead agency for "strategic planning and formulation of substantive policy."[11] The PCO's role is strategic because it is situated at the confluence of all the various policy issues and decisions that come before cabinet.

The PCO is organized into a number of secretariats that provide support services for the various committees of cabinet. These services range from scheduling and keeping the minutes of committee meetings to activities that carry the potential for real influence, such as providing policy advice and dealing directly with government departments. Perhaps more than any other single component of the bureaucracy, the PCO can see "the big picture" of government policy. This picture embraces both policy and political concerns. A former head of the PCO, Gordon Robertson, has summarized the different roles of the PCO and the Prime Minister's Office in this way: "The Prime Minister's Office is partisan, politically oriented, yet operationally sensitive. The Privy Council Office is non-partisan, operationally oriented, yet politically sensitive."[12] As Donald Savoie observes, "the office briefs the prime minister on any issue it wishes, controls the flow of papers to Cabinet, reports back to departments on the decisions taken, or not taken, by Cabinet, advises the prime minister on the selection of deputy ministers . . . on federal–provincial relations and on all issues of governmental organization and ministerial mandates."[13] If the government of Canada is a railway, the PCO is Grand Central Station.

The Treasury Board Secretariat

The Treasury Board Secretariat (TBS) is an administrative adjunct to the Treasury Board, which in turn is the only cabinet committee that has a statutory basis, going back to 1869. The Treasury Board is, in a sense, guardian of the purse strings, but it performs this function in more of a micro fashion compared to Finance's macro authority in relation to spending matters. The Treasury Board is also the government's voice on employment and personnel matters and on administrative policy within the federal government. Its authority is, in a word, extensive. But although the responsibilities of the TBS are wide-ranging and important, it occupies the shadows of the policy-making and agenda-setting process compared to Finance and the PCO. Donald Savoie quotes a senior federal official who compares the roles of the three central agencies: "PCO looks after the broad picture and resolves conflicts between ministers and departments. Finance looks after the big economic and budgeting decisions. The Treasury Board looks after the little decisions."[14]

"Little," however, should not be confused with "unimportant." The TBS functions include conducting departmental audits, establishing and enforcing accounting standards in government, and evaluating particular programs. As government employer, the Treasury Board negotiates with federal public-sector unions, establishes the rules for recruitment and promotion, implements the terms of the Official Languages Act, and is responsible for setting rules for increasing the representation of women, visible minorities, disabled persons, and Aboriginals in the Canadian public service.

TBS officials formulate the expenditure outlook that, along with the economic outlook and fiscal framework developed by Finance, is the starting point in the annual expenditure budget exercise. The expenditure forecasts provided by TBS are used by cabinet in making decisions on the allocation of financial resources between competing programs. Along with the spending committees of cabinet, they assess the spending proposals and plans that departments are required to submit each year. Preparation of the main estimates, the detailed spending plans that the government tables in the House of Commons each winter, is the responsibility of the Treasury Board. Because the TBS has the deepest knowledge of government spending programs of all central agencies, the PCO and Finance often consult it for information and advice.[15]

The Prime Minister's Office

Unlike the other central agencies, the Prime Minister's Office (PMO) is staffed chiefly by partisan appointees rather than by career public servants. These officials are the prime minister's personal staff, performing functions that include handling the PM's correspondence and schedule; speech writing; media relations; liaison with ministers, caucus, and the party; and providing advice on appointments and policy. Gordon Robertson observes that the PMO is "partisan, politically oriented, yet operationally sensitive."[16] It serves as the PM's political eyes and ears, and can speak on behalf of the PM. The PMO is headed by the PM's chief of staff. No other non-elected official is in such regular contact with the PM.

Since the expansion in the PMO that took place under Pierre Trudeau nearly four decades ago, the size of the prime minister's staff has varied from about 80 to 120 people. Some may wonder what could possibly justify such a large staff, but the demands on the prime minister's time are enormous, and co-ordinating the PM's activities, providing him or her with briefing and advice, and dealing with the large volume of communications are daunting. The goal for all PMO staff, according to one former PMO staffer, is clear: "Our job is quite simple really, we make the PM look good."[17]

As an example of how PMO officials perform this job, let us consider the preparation that takes place before *question period* in the House of Commons, which takes place every day that the House is sitting. When the PM is in Ottawa, he or she is expected to attend to answer questions about the activities and policies of his or her government. Question period can be a political minefield, and it is well attended by journalists. Given the stakes, preparation of the PM and cabinet ministers is crucial. Within the PMO a handful of staffers arrive each day before sunrise to begin sifting through the day's newspapers and the broadcast media's coverage, identifying those issues that the opposition parties are most likely to pounce on during question period. They then craft responses to the anticipated questions, a process that involves considerable partisan and tactical thinking. The most successful response to an opposition member's question is, of course, one that turns the tables and puts the opposition on the defensive or in some way embarrasses the questioner and his or her party.

Protecting the prime minister and making him or her look good necessarily involve PMO officials in issues of policy, large and small. "Senior PMO staff," says Savoie, "will get involved in whatever issue they and the prime minister think they should."[18] It simply is not possible to separate the drafting of a speech for the prime minister, typically done in the PMO, and providing policy advice. But the extent that PMO officials are involved in shaping policy and influencing other central agency officials and departmental managers depends on the prime minister.

Intergovernmental Affairs (formerly the Federal–Provincial Relations Office)

Before the Federal–Provincial Relations Office (FPRO) was created in 1975, its functions had been carried out within the PCO. After its launch, and despite the prestige of Gordon Robertson, its first head, the FPRO never achieved the influence of other central agencies like Finance, the TBS, and the PCO. The precise functions performed by the FPRO during the 1980s and early 1990s depended on the PM. For example, the FPRO played a major role in the development of the Meech Lake Accord proposals. Its lesser stature among the central agencies was largely due to the fact that the FPRO did not hold a monopoly over advice on federal–provincial matters.

The FPRO was restructured under Prime Minister Chrétien after the Liberals returned to power in 1993. The functions of the FPRO were reintegrated into the PCO through its Intergovernmental Affairs office. Intergovernmental Affairs (IGA) provides policy advice to its minister and the prime minister on issues ranging from health and social programs to national unity and Aboriginal matters. The mandate of the office includes:

- Policy advice and strategic planning related to national unity, the broad federal–provincial–territorial agenda, constitutional and legal issues, and fiscal federalism. These files require close collaboration with a number of departments, including Finance, Justice, Treasury Board, and several others
- Liaison and advice on relations with the provinces and territories and the renewal of the federation
- Communications and parliamentary affairs support on issues and initiatives with important federal–provincial–territorial dimensions[19]

The influence of IGA waxes and wanes, depending largely on the stature of its minister, and on the nature of the issues it is permitted to deal with. "Permitted" is the key word, because whether IGA and its minister take the lead or a leading role on an issue will depend on the prime minister. For example, with Stéphane Dion as minister, IGA played an important role in the communications with Quebec over the terms of a future referendum on Quebec independence, which eventually produced the Clarity Act. Likewise, Dion and IGA played important roles in the federal–provincial negotiations that produced the 1999 Social Union Framework Agreement.

Prime Ministerial Government

Many have asked whether Canadian prime ministers have become more "presidential" in their stature and power. The question, however, is based on the false premise that an American president is more powerful in relation to the country's legislation and his own party than is a Canadian prime minister. In fact, there have always been fewer checks on the behaviour of a Canadian prime minister than on that of an American president.

Indeed, it is now widely recognized that the prime minister has far more clout in the Canadian system of government than the president has in the American system. Moreover, that power has become increasingly centralized in the hands of the PM and those around him or her. The counterweights to the PM's power are more plausibly found in the courts, the media, and in some provincial capitals than in Parliament. The centralization of power has advanced to such a degree that some of Canada's political commentators now characterize Canada's system of government as *prime ministerial* rather than *parliamentary*.[20] Donald Savoie and Jeffrey Simpson are among those who argue that not only has the influence of Parliament been effectively eclipsed by the growth of **prime ministerial government—***government where the executive is essentially dominated by the prime minister and the PMO*—but cabinet, too, has been marginalized in the policy-making process; it is now merely what Jeffrey Simpson calls a "mini-sounding board"[21] where decisions already approved by the PM and his advisers in key central agencies are rubber-stamped. As Savoie writes,

> Cabinet has now joined Parliament as an institution being bypassed. Real political debate and decision-making are increasingly elsewhere—in federal–provincial meetings of first ministers, on Team Canada flights, where first ministers can hold informal meetings, in the Prime Minister's Office, in the Privy Council Office, in the Department of Finance, and in international organizations and international summits. . . . The Canadian prime minister has little in the way of institutional check, at least inside government, to inhibit his ability to have his way.[22]

The greater influence of the prime minister within the Canadian system than the president in the American system is partly due to structural differences between these two governmental systems. But the high degree of centralization of power that commentators such as Savoie and Simpson argue has occurred under recent prime ministers—a trend that was not reversed when Stephen Harper came to power—may be explained by a combination of personal style and the political incentives to choose more rather than less centralization. Some prime ministers have preferred a more participatory process, such as Lester Pearson (1963–8) and Pierre Trudeau (1968–79, 1980–4). Marc Lalonde, one of the most influential ministers during the Trudeau era, described cabinet meetings under Trudeau as resembling university seminars. This is the decision-making style in which the prime minister has been depicted as *primus inter pares* or "first among equals." The historical evidence suggests that this style has been relatively rare. More common, certainly in recent times, has been a more centralized decision-making style in which priorities are effectively set and decisions are made by the prime minister and a relatively small group of advisers, only some of whom may be cabinet ministers.

The risks that a prime minister would take by adopting a more collegial approach are fairly easy to identify:

- The decisions or publicly expressed views of individual cabinet ministers might be perceived to conflict with other government actions.

A 21 May 2011 *Globe and Mail* editorial cartoon depicts Prime Minster Stephen Harper and his newly appointed cabinet ministers marching in step. What do you think cartoonist Brian Gable is saying about nature of this prime minister's leadership style?

- Ministers often have their own preferences on issues, and it is also well known that ministers often see their role at the cabinet table as that of defender of "their" department, programs, budget allocation, etc. The collegial approach to cabinet decision making probably has a built-in bias toward protection of the status quo and against change that might threaten their portfolios.
- A collegial approach is more likely to allow the emergence of powerful, high-profile cabinet ministers who may be seen as rivals to the prime minister.

The Bureaucracy

The original meaning of the word **bureaucracy** (*bureaucracie*, coined by the French writer Vincent de Gournay in the mid 1700s) is derived from the French word for "desk" (*bureau*), and was used to describe ***the political rule by unelected government officials***. Ever since, the study of bureaucracy has revolved around the study of the political power of unelected officials.

For policies to have an impact, they must be implemented. The Employment Insurance (EI) program, for example, depends on the administrative efforts of thousands of public servants employed in Canada Employment Centres across the country, hundreds of EI appeals commissioners, and the employees of the Employment Insurance Commission, which is responsible for making and applying regulations under the Employment Insurance Act. Similarly, educational policy is implemented through bureaucratic structures at the federal (student loans, support for research), provincial (ministries of education), and local (school boards) levels.

Policy implementation is the role of the bureaucracy. Implementation is not, however, an automatic process of converting legislative decisions into action. Unelected officials often wield enormous discretion in applying laws and administering programs. Moreover, their influence is not restricted to the implementation stage of policy making. It begins at the agenda-setting stage, when problems and possible responses are being defined. Bureaucratic influence is felt at numerous points in the decision-making process that precedes the actual introduction of a bill in Parliament. Often, the decision-making process has no parliamentary stage, or at least Parliament has minimal involvement in the process.

The Structure of Canadian Bureaucracy

The federal public sector employs roughly 486,000 people working in close to 400 different organizations (all figures as of 2007). Just over 60 per cent of them work directly for government departments and agencies. They are "public servants" in the narrow legal sense of this term. Their employer is the Treasury Board, and the organizations they work for fall directly under the authority of a cabinet minister. Close to 20 per cent are employed by federally owned Crown corporations and the remainder (another 20 per cent) work in the Canadian Forces; while these organizations receive all or part of their funding from the federal government, and are subject to its rules, there is some degree of autonomy.

Public-sector employment is even greater at the provincial, territorial, and local levels. In 2007, the combined employment of these governments came to about 753,000 persons. This figure does not include hospitals and other health-care facilities, schools, or enterprises owned by these levels of government, which together add another 1,986,000 employees to the public-sector total. If we define the public sector broadly to include those organizations that receive all or a major part of their operating revenues from one or more levels of government, then 20–25 per cent of Canadian workers fall within this sector. It includes nurses, teachers, fire-fighters, police officers, workers for Children's Aid Societies and at some women's shelters, and so on. According to interprovincial comparative analysis prepared by the Quebec Secretariat of Intergovernmental Affairs, the general trend for most governments in 2011 was to downsize the public service.[23] Despite such claims, the public sector remains quite extensive.

That part of it that is often labelled the "bureaucracy" may be divided into three main components: the public service (chiefly departments); independent and semi-independent agencies and tribunals; and Crown corporations.

- *Public service.* About half of the federal public sector falls into this category. It includes all statutory departments and other organizations whose members are appointed by the Public Service Commission (PSC) and are employees of the Treasury Board. This is the part of the bureaucracy most directly under the authority of cabinet.
- *Agencies and tribunals.* These organizations perform a wide variety of regulatory, research, and advisory functions, and have, in most cases, almost total independence from government. With few exceptions their members are not appointed by the PSC, nor are they employees of the Treasury Board. Among the most widely known federal regulatory agencies are the Canadian Radio-television and Telecommunications Commission (CRTC, which regulates communications and broadcasting), the National Transportation Agency (regulates air, water, and rail transportation), and the National Energy Board (regulates energy when it crosses provincial and international boundaries). Many important areas of regulation, including trucking, public utilities within provincial boundaries, and most labour relations, are controlled by provincial governments.
- *Crown corporations.* These are organizations such as Canada Post, that generally perform commercial functions and typically operate at "arm's length" from the government. They hire their own employees, determine their own internal administrative structures, and in many instances behave like privately owned businesses. Over the last couple of decades some of the largest of these corporations, notably Air Canada, Canadian National, and Petro-Canada, have been privatized.

The three categories do not cover the entire federal bureaucracy. Some relatively small but important parts of that bureaucracy, including the Auditor General's Office and the Commissioner of Official Languages, are independent of cabinet, reporting directly to Parliament. The Royal Canadian Mounted Police also has a distinct legal status, as does the Canadian Forces.

INSIDE POLITICS

BOX 8.2 | The Role of the Deputy Minister

The deputy minister's mission is to serve the minister in non-partisan fashion, competently, impartially, diligently and loyally. So as to optimize the management of the minster's time and to inform him in his decisions and projects, the deputy minister provides professional, non-partisan advice concerning the development and implementation of policies, prepares the tools that will enable the minister to take a discerning stand in public, and manages the compliance of the decisions he makes. On a daily basis, he ensures the sound operational management of the department.

The deputy minister also acts as the senior adviser to the minister concerning all the responsibilities exercised by him. In addition to having responsibility to Parliament for the agencies in his portfolio, the minister receives special mandates from the prime minister and Cabinet. The deputy minister acts as his chief adviser in all such matters.

. . .

Generally speaking, he comments on draft policies of the Council of Ministers and ensures that the agenda and priorities of the government are properly reflected in his department's action plan. He also ensures that all his department's employees act to fulfill the objectives of the government of the day. In addition, he organizes interministerial consultations on any issues liable to affect the general responsibilities of the other ministers. The manner in which the deputy minister supports his minister is another way of serving the government, overall; sound projects make the government look good, and timely cautions keep it from getting into trouble.

Source: *Restoring Accountability*, Research Studies: Volume 1 — Parliament, Ministers and Deputy Ministers, pp. 258 and 259. http://publications.gc.ca/site/eng/286124/publication.html. Privy Council Office, 2006. Reproduced with the permission of the Minister of Public Works and Government Services, 2012.

Together, this vast administrative apparatus has responsibility for implementing public policy. But the bureaucracy is not a uniform structure. One can identify several different functions performed by organizations within the administrative system. These include:

- Provision and administration of services to the public, often to narrow economic, social, or cultural clientele groups
- Provision of services to other parts of the bureaucracy
- Integration of policy in a particular field, or the generation of policy advice
- Adjudication of applications and/or interpretation of regulations (such as product safety standards, or the determination of what constitutes morally offensive scenes of sex or violence in films)
- Disbursement of funds to groups or individuals, as with the grants to artists and cultural organizations administered by the Canada Council
- Production of a good or the operation of a service that is sold to buyers

And these functions are not mutually exclusive. A large and organizationally complex department such as Transport Canada delivers services, regulates transport standards, and develops policy. Almost all government departments, regardless of their primary orientation, have a policy development capacity. During the 1970s this was formalized—although not necessarily enhanced—with the creation of policy analysis units, usually at the assistant deputy minister level. An informal policy advisory capacity, however, has always existed at the level of senior officials. This role is based on their expert familiarity with the programs administered by the department and on the fact that, typically, they remain within a particular policy field longer than their nominal superiors in cabinet. The turnover rate for deputy ministers and other senior bureaucrats has increased since the era of the "Ottawa mandarins," from the 1940s to the 1960s. The term **mandarin** usually refers to *powerful senior civil servants*. The more recent emphasis has been on senior officials as managers, whose management skills are transferable across policy fields. In fact, it would be more accurate to say that this power has become more diffuse. The days when a mere handful of key deputy ministers could dominate the policy-making process are gone. Today, bureaucratic influence is distributed more widely, largely because of the increased importance of central agencies like the Privy Council Office and the Treasury Board Secretariat, but also because a deputy minister rarely remains in charge of a particular department for more than a few years. Nevertheless, there is little doubt that senior bureaucrats continue to be key players in policy making.

The passing of the era of the Ottawa mandarins and the emergence of central agencies as an alternative source of expert policy advice to cabinet have not undermined the fundamental basis of bureaucratic influence on policy. This influence rests on the following factors:

- Ministers invariably depend on the permanent bureaucracy for advice on policy, and departments are repositories for vast amounts of information about programs (current and past) and their day-to-day operations.
- There is a relationship of a department to the social or economic interests that benefit from the programs it administers, and departments are an important target for professional lobbyists and interest-group representatives who wish to influence policy.
- "Ministers," observes Savoie, "do not manage."[24] Their deputy ministers perform this job. Given the competing pressures on a minister's time, the deputy minister inevitably assumes the job of senior manager of the department, and often the chief responsibility for policy direction.
- Most laws contain provisions delegating to bureaucrats the authority to interpret the general terms of the law in its application to actual cases. This is also true of other statutory instruments such as **orders-in-council**, which *are administrative orders (appointments, regulations, or legislative orders authorized by an existing act of Parliament) issued by cabinet and approved by the Governor General*.

On top of all the other expectations about bureaucracy, democratic societies also expect **representative bureaucracy**: *a concept and an expectation that the bureaucracy should "represent" the population and reflect in fair proportion certain demographic characteristics of society*. Affirmative action programs and quota hiring are the tools used in pursuit of this goal. The basic reasoning behind arguments for representative bureaucracy is threefold: first, it will have greater popular legitimacy; second, the services it provides will be sensitive to the values and aspirations of the governed, and third, it will help ensure that the advice bureaucrats give to politicians reflects these values and aspirations.

The idea and implementation of representative bureaucracy can be problematic. Which groups should be represented? What constitutes "fair proportion"? Is government efficiency compromised by equal representation? Can representative bureaucracy be politically neutral?

Problems aside, it is clear that a grossly unrepresentative bureaucracy can pose problems. The fact that comparatively few French Canadians were found at the senior levels of the federal bureaucracy was already controversial in the 1940s, 1950s, and 1960s, and led to major public service reforms and Canada's first policy of representative bureaucracy under Lester Pearson and Pierre Trudeau.

One thing is certain: governments that have instituted policies of affirmative action and quota hiring have done so chiefly for political reasons. Among the most important is national unity. It has long been recognized in Canada that the merit principle, which looks only at a candidate's job-related achievements and skills, should not interfere with what one writer called "a tactful balance of national elements."[25] Until fairly recently, this balancing act chiefly involved ensuring adequate francophone representation in the management ranks of the bureaucracy. Indeed, it is fair to say that until the 1970s this was the only serious representational factor taken into account in public service recruitment and promotion. John Porter's analysis of the senior federal bureaucracy during the 1950s showed that the British, French, and Jewish ethnic groups were significantly represented, and those of British origin were clearly dominant.[26] Women and visible minorities were almost completely absent at the senior levels.

As the ethnic composition of Canadian society has changed—people of non-British, non-French ancestry now constitute over one-quarter of the population—and especially as the discourse of collective rights and group identities has achieved greater prominence, the old concern with "fair" linguistic representation has been joined by efforts to recruit and promote women, visible minorities, Aboriginal Canadians, and the disabled.

THE LEGISLATURE

The legislature is a study in contrasts. Its physical setting is soberly impressive, yet the behaviour of its members is frequently the object of derision. Its constitutional powers appear to be formidable, yet its actual influence on policy is often much less than that of the cabinet and the bureaucracy. All major policies, including all laws, must be approved by the legislature, but the legislature's approval often seems a foregone conclusion and a mere formality—especially when the governing party holds a majority in the House of Commons and in the Senate.

The contradictions of the legislature have their source in the tension between traditional ideas about political democracy and the character of the modern state. *Representation*, *accountability* to the people, and *choice* are the cornerstones of liberal-democratic theory. An elected legislature that represents the population either on the basis of population or by region, or both, and party competition are the means by which these democratic goals are accomplished.

But the modern state, we have seen, is characterized by a vast bureaucratic apparatus that is not easily controlled by elected politicians. Moreover, while the prime minister's power has always been vastly greater than that of other members of Parliament, the concentration of power in and around the office of the prime minister appears to have reached unprecedented levels. As the scale and influence of the non-elected parts of the state have grown and prime ministerial government has been consolidated, the inadequacies of traditional democratic theory—centred on the role of the legislature—have become increasingly apparent.

There have been calls for reforms, such as a more representative and democratically responsive bureaucracy, to alleviate the problem of power without accountability. Reforms, however, cannot substitute for elections. If one begins from the premise that the free election must be the cornerstone of political democracy, the role of the legislature is crucial.

One way of ensuring that the legislature better performs its democratic functions is to improve its representative character. Possible ways include reforming the political parties' candidate selection process, instituting a proportional representation electoral system, or reforming the Senate. Another option is tightening the legislature's control over the political executive and the non-elected parts of the state. This may be done by increasing the legislature's access to information about the intentions and performance of the government and bureaucracy, providing opportunities for legislative scrutiny and debate of executive action, and enabling legislators to influence the priorities and agenda of government.

Canada has a **bicameral legislature:** *a legislature with two chambers—the House of Commons, which is democratically elected, and the Senate, with appointed senators.* Representation in the elected House of Commons is roughly according to population—roughly, because some MPs represent as few as 20,000 constituents, while others represent close to 200,000. Each of the 308 members of the House of Commons is the sole representative for a constituency, also known as a "riding."

Senators are appointed by the government of the day when a vacancy occurs. They hold their seats until age 75. As we see in Table 8.1, representation in the Senate is based on Canada's regions. In recent years there have been suggestions that senators be elected, and some have proposed that a certain number of Senate seats be reserved for women and Aboriginal Canadians.

TABLE 8.1 | REGIONAL REPRESENTATION IN THE SENATE

Region	Number of Senate Seats
Ontario	24
Quebec	24
Western Provinces: Manitoba, Saskatchewan, Alberta, British Columbia	24
Maritimes: Prince Edward Island, New Brunswick, Nova Scotia	24
Newfoundland and Labrador	6
Yukon, Northwest Territories, and Nunavut	3
Total	105

In law, the powers of the House of Commons and Senate are roughly equal. There are, however, a couple of important exceptions. Legislation involving the spending or raising of public money must, under the Constitution, be introduced in the House of Commons. And when it comes to amending the Constitution, the Senate can only delay passage of a resolution already approved by the Commons. But all bills must pass through identical stages in both bodies before becoming law (see Box 8.5 later in this chapter).

Despite the similarity of their formal powers, the superiority of the elected House of Commons is well established. For most of its history, the Senate has deferred to the will of the Commons. This changed, however, after the 1984 election of a Progressive Conservative majority in Parliament. On several occasions the Liberal-dominated Senate obstructed bills that had already been passed by the Commons. When the Senate balked at passage of the politically unpopular goods and services tax (GST), the Mulroney government used an obscure

The Senate continues to stir emotions in Canadian politics. This *Globe and Mail* editorial cartoon depicts the angry feelings of voters at the reappointment of three defeated Conservative candidates to the Senate (the "Red Chamber"), even though they had resigned their Senate seats to run in the May 2011 federal election.

constitutional power and appointed eight new Conservative senators, thereby giving the Conservatives a slender Senate majority. Under the Chrétien government the partisan balance in the Senate shifted back to a Liberal majority. The squabbles that often occurred after 1984, when the House of Commons was controlled by one party and the Senate by another, became increasingly rare from 1993 to 2006, when the Liberals formed the government and re-established a Liberal majority in the Senate through the filling of vacancies.

When this Liberal Senate majority posed a problem for the minority Conservatives of Stephen Harper, blocking and delaying legislation sent to it from the House of Commons, Harper allowed vacancies to accumulate, and then appointed 18 new senators in December 2008. This was done in spite of Conservative election promises to turn the Senate into an elected body. The Conservative government had been unable to win enough support in the House of Commons for such reform and, in any case, it was not clear that direct election and term limits for senators could be accomplished without changing the Constitution.

Democracy Watch

BOX 8.3 An Elected Senate?

The Senate currently has a few key roles in Canada's system of government: (1) Revising legislation, and (2) protecting linguistic and other minority groups—essentially acting as a "second sober thought" to all legislation moving through the system.

Some Arguments for an Elected Senate

- If elected, this body would acquire democratic legitimacy by being accountable to constituents.
- Elected senators could champion the issues most important to their regions.
- The public would have an opportunity not to re-elect a senator tied to any scandal or misconduct.

Some Arguments Against an Elected Senate

- Debate about whether or not the Constitution Act, 1982 would allow Parliament to reform the main functioning of the Senate is unresolved, and therefore current reform discussion are irrelevant.
- Using current demographics of the elected House of Commons as a guide, opening up Senate positions to election may result in fewer women and minorities serving in the Senate.
- It is the House of Commons' role to channel public opinion and table legislation; it is the Senate's role to scrutinize that legislation. Making senators beholden to constituents might interfere with their ability to look critically at legislation moving through the system.

Up for Debate

Consider these arguments for and against electing senators to their positions. Which argument makes the most sense for today's Canadians and their government? Why?

Functions of the Legislature

The legislature performs a number of functions that are basic to political democracy: the passage of laws by elected representatives, which includes the approval of budget proposals and new policy initiatives. The operation of party discipline ensures that bills tabled in the legislature are seldom modified in major ways during the law-passing process. However, Parliament's approval of the government's legislative agenda is not an empty formality. The opposition parties have opportunities to debate and criticize the government's proposals.

Robert Jackson and Michael Atkinson argue that those involved in the pre-parliamentary stages of policy making anticipate the probable reactions of the legislature and of the government party caucus before a bill or budget is tabled in Parliament.[27] While this may have been true in the past, recent evidence suggests that the PM and those who actually make policy decisions and draft legislation are more likely to pay attention to the results of surveys and focus groups than lose much sleep over how backbench MPs will react. On the influence of **caucus**, *the body of elected MPs belonging to a particular party*, Savoie states that "[government party MPs] report that they are rarely, if ever, in a position to launch a new initiative, and worse, that they are rarely effective in getting the government to change course. They also do not consider themselves to be an effective check on prime ministerial power."[28] In the words of one government party MP, "We simply respond to what Cabinet does, and there are limits to what you can do when you are always reacting."[29]

This being said, the legislature is far from being irrelevant in making policy. The legislature's functions include scrutiny of government performance, constituency representation, debate of issues, and legitimation of the political system.

Scrutinizing Government Performance

Various regular opportunities exist for the legislature to prod, question, and criticize the government. These include the daily question period in the House of Commons, the set-piece debates that follow the Speech from the Throne and the introduction of a new budget, and opposition days, when the opposition parties determine the topics of debate. Committee hearings and special parliamentary task forces also provide opportunities for legislative scrutiny of government actions and performance, although the subjects that these bodies deal with are mainly determined by the government. Party discipline is a key factor that limits the critical tendencies of parliamentary committees, particularly under a majority government.

While many have criticized the behaviour of MPs during question period, for better or for worse, it has become the centrepiece of Parliament's day, and the chief activity shaping most Canadians' ideas of what goes on in Parliament. The introduction of television cameras into the legislature in the late 1970s reinforced the stature of question period as the primary way that the opposition can hold the government to account on matters big and small. Question period is the opposition parties' main chance to influence the issues that will be discussed in the media as well as the way the issues are portrayed. In fact, journalists often react—although not always in the way that opposition parties may like—to the questions and lines of attack that opposition parties launch against the government. To what degree issues are driven by media rather than by the opposition parties is impossible to say. Critical scrutiny of the government clearly serves the interests of both the opposition parties, who wish to see the government embarrassed and its popular support drop, and the media, who know that controversy and the scent of wrongdoing attract more readers and viewers than do reports that all is well with the world.

Students of American politics know that the real action in Congress takes place in congressional committees, and that what enters the committee process may not bear much resemblance to what emerges from it. In Canada's Parliament, however, committees (whose membership is generally limited to about 20 MPs) usually only marginally modify what is placed before them and virtually never derail any bill that the government has introduced in the House. They may appear to be a forum for backbench MPs to acquire some expertise in particular policy areas that will enable them to assess the merits of legislation in a more informed and less partisan manner. However, evidence suggests otherwise. In his study of MPs' behaviour and perceptions of their jobs, David Docherty states that "several rookie Liberals indicated that the failure of their own executive to treat committee work and reports seriously was the single-most frustrating (and unexpected) aspect of their job as an MP."[30] Docherty found that frustration with House committees was not limited to government party members. Opposition MPs also expressed disappointment with the inability of committees to make more than a marginal and occasional difference.

Party discipline seems to be at the root of this dissatisfaction. Despite some attempts at reform over the last couple of decades, party discipline continues to operate in committees, just as it does on the floor of the House of Commons.

Senators argue that life is different in the Red Chamber. They point to the Senate's long string of committee and task force studies on topics ranging from corporate concentration in

INSIDE POLITICS

BOX 8.4 | Edmund Burke and the Role of Members of the Legislature

Edmund Burke was a member of the British House of Commons in the late 1700s. In his famous "Letter to the Sheriffs of Bristol," Burke explained why a member of the legislature—even one elected by the people—should not be overly concerned to ascertain and reflect the ideas and preferences of his constituents. Lawmakers should see themselves as trustees, he argued, not as the mere servants of public opinion. "Your representative owes you, not his industry only, but his judgment," said Burke, "and he betrays, instead of serving you, if he sacrifices it to your opinion."

Should Members of Parliament follow the will of their constituents, the will of their party, or their own conscience? Are Canadian senators, because they are appointed and not beholden to an electorate, more likely to act according to conscience?

Canada's media industries to the decriminalization of marijuana possession. Being appointed to serve until the age of 75, most of them argue, loosens the constraint of party discipline. Not having to worry about whether their party leader will sign their nomination papers at some future election and being unconcerned that their actions might affect their prospect of being appointed someday to cabinet, senators can behave far more independently than their House of Commons colleagues. While their committee reports have often influenced the contours of public debate on an issue—and the independence often associated with them could not have occurred in the House—there is no reason to believe that only the Senate as currently constituted could make this contribution to scrutinizing government policy, investigating important issues, and proposing legislative change. Indeed, the committee work that senators point to as their proudest accomplishment and chief raison d'être usually just covers the same ground that think tanks, academic studies, and government-commissioned studies have mapped. But how many Canadians know or care about this? The truth is that the media seldom report this side of the Senate, and, to senators' disappointment, few are paying attention but themselves.

Representation

The House of Commons is both symbolically and practically important as a contact point between citizens and government. Symbolically, the elected House embodies the principle of government by popular consent. The partisan divisions within it, between government and opposition parties, have the additional effect of affirming for most citizens their belief in *pluralism* and the competitive character of politics. At a practical level, citizens often turn to their elected representatives when they experience problems with bureaucracy or when they want to express their views on government policy.

Unlike the elected Commons, the Senate does not perform a significant representational role in Canadian politics, despite the fact that senators are appointed to represent the various provinces and regions of Canada. The unelected character of Canada's upper house and the crassly partisan criteria that prime ministers have usually relied on in filling Senate vacancies have undermined whatever legitimacy senators might otherwise have achieved as spokespersons for the regions. Provincial governments, regional spokespersons in the federal cabinet, and regional blocs of MPs within the party caucuses are more significant in representing regional interests.

Listen to the "Political Parties and the Parliamentary System" podcast, available at www.oupcanada.com/BrooksConcise.

Debate

The image that most Canadians have of Parliament is of the heated exchanges that take place across the aisle that separates the government and opposition parties. Parliamentary procedure and the physical layout of the legislature are based on the adversarial principle of "them versus us." At their best, debates in Parliament can provide a public forum for discussing national issues, as well as highlighting the policy differences between the parties. Unfortunately, the quality of parliamentary debate in Canada is often dragged down by the wooden reading of prepared remarks, heckling and personal invective, and occasional blatant abuses of either the government's majority or the opposition's opportunities to hold up the business of Parliament.

Generally, MPs' minds are made up when a measure is first tabled in Parliament. So why spend long hours criticizing and defending legislative proposals and the government's record? There are two reasons. First, outcomes are not always predictable. Even when the government party holds a commanding majority in Parliament, or when the policy differences between government and opposition are not significant, an issue is not always controlled by the government or by Parliament. Media coverage and opinion polls, as well as interventions by organized interests, other governments, and even individuals who have credibility in the eyes of the media and public, may also have a bearing on the trajectory of the debate.

Parliamentary debate is also important because it reinforces the popular belief in the open and competitive qualities of Canadian democracy. The stylized conflict between government and opposition parties, which is the essence of the British parliamentary system, often produces an exaggerated impression of the open and competitive qualities of Canadian politics. The adversarial nature of Canadian politics obscures the fact that these partisan disagreements take place within a fairly narrow band of consensus on basic values. As a result, parliamentary debate provides valuable support for the existing political system, and hides the obstacles that non-mainstream interests face in getting their concerns and views onto the public agenda.

Legitimation

As suggested above, Parliament is both a *legislative* and a *legitimizing* institution. Laws must pass through the parliamentary mill before being approved, and the legitimizing mechanisms of democratic accountability are embodied in the structure and procedures of Parliament. Parliament represents the people. It scrutinizes the actions of government and debates public issues. Along with elections and judicial review of the Constitution, Parliament appears to be one of the chief bulwarks against the abuse of power by a government.

How well Parliament performs its democratic functions is another matter. But the structures and procedures of the legislature are built around the ideas of open government and popular consent, and the constitutional requirement that the actions of government must be approved by Parliament. These factors help to legitimize the political system and the policies it produces. If most Canadians held the view that the legislature is a farce, then the legitimacy of the government would be undermined. This is not the case, however. Canadians may be cynical about the integrity of their politicians, but they appear to have faith in their parliamentary institutions.

Although the concentration of power in and around the prime minister has reached unprecedented levels, the legislature is not the helpless pawn of the executive. Witness the sanctioning of and the vote of non-confidence against the Conservative government that precipitated the May 2011 federal election. Using the rules of parliamentary procedure, opposition parties can prod, question, and castigate the government in front of the parliamentary press gallery and the television cameras in the House of Commons. The opposition's behaviour is usually reactive, responding to the government's proposals and policies. Nevertheless, the legislature's function

1	Speaker
2	Pages
3	Government Members*
4	Opposition Members*
5	Prime Minister
6	Leader of the Official Opposition
7	Leader of the Second Largest Party in Opposition
8	Clerk and Table Officers
9	Mace
10	Hansard Reporters
11	Sergeant-at-Arms
12	The Bar
13	Interpreters
14	Press Gallery
15	Public Gallery
16	Official Gallery
17	Leader of the Opposition's Gallery
18	Members' Gallery
19	Members' Gallery
20	Members' Gallery
21	Speaker's Gallery
22	Senate Gallery
23	T.T. Cameras

*Depending on the number of MPs elected from each political party, government Members may be seated on the opposite side of the Chamber with opposition Members (or vice versa).

a)

b)

FIGURE 8.6 LAYOUTS OF THE CANADIAN HOUSE OF COMMONS AND THE AMERICAN HOUSE OF REPRESENTATIVES

As this figure shows, the Canadian House of Commons (and the Senate) is designed for debate between opposing sides and is similar to parliaments around the world that use the Westminster model of parliamentary democracy (a). The semicircular design of the American House of Representatives in Washington, DC, suggests that representatives are gathered to listen and discuss (b).

Sources: a) "House of Commons," *The House of Commons Report to Canadians 2008*, p. 4, http://www.parl.gc.ca/About/House/ReportToCanadians/2008/HOC_RTC2008_E.pdf; b) © iStockphoto.com/GYI NSEA as a talking shop—the *parler* in "parliament"—enables it to draw attention to controversial aspects of the government's performance. MPs are not quite "nobodies," as Pierre Trudeau once labelled them. But they are far from having the policy influence of their American counterparts, who, because of loose party discipline and very different rules governing the law-making process, are often assiduously courted by interest groups and the president.

Earlier, we said that caucus, the body of elected MPs belonging to a particular party, generally has little influence on the party leadership, at least in the government party. When Parliament is in session, a party's caucus usually meets at least weekly. When they are in Ottawa, the prime minister and cabinet members regularly attend the government caucus. These meetings often amount to little more than what one MP describes as "bitching sessions," but almost never do MPs challenge the prime minister behind the closed doors of the party's weekly meeting.[31]

Some insiders argue, however, that the government caucus provides a real opportunity for backbenchers to influence government policy away from the peering eyes and listening ears of the media and the opposition. This may occasionally be true, but the limits on the influence of caucus are readily apparent from two facts. First, extremely unpopular policies or government priorities, such as the GST, are not affected by caucus opposition. The same is true of policies that create sharp divisions in a party's caucus, such as the Liberal government's 1995 gun control law. If the policy is a high priority, the prospect of a caucus revolt is extremely remote. Members who fail to toe the line are likely to experience the fate of those Liberal MPs who voted against the government's gun law in 1995: the loss of committee assignments. Expulsion from caucus is another sanction that may be used to punish recalcitrant backbenchers. Second, the caucus of the governing party—like the legislature as a whole—usually enters the policy-making process late, after much study, consultation, and negotiation have already taken place. The members of the government party caucus are thus asked to vote for a complex fabric of compromises and accommodations between government and interest groups, different agencies of government, or even Ottawa and the provinces. It is unlikely that the government would allow this fabric to unravel because of caucus opposition.

What Does an MP Do?

It is almost certainly true that most Canadians believe that their MPs are overpaid and underworked. Stories of "gold-clad" MPs' pensions and of senators who slurp at the public trough while living in Mexico help to fuel this widespread but generally unfair charge. Most backbench MPs work very long hours, whether in Ottawa or at home in their constituencies. The demands are even greater for members of the government and party leaders who are required to travel extensively in carrying out their jobs. But what does a typical MP do? For most MPs, the single largest block of their working day is devoted to taking care of constituency business. David Docherty reports that the MPs he surveyed from the thirty-fourth (1988–93) and thirty-fifth (1993–7) Parliaments claimed to spend just over 40 per cent of their working time on constituency affairs. The second largest block of time was spent on legislative work, such as committee assignments and attending question period and debates. These activities run a fairly distant second, however, to constituency work, as shown in Figure 8.7.

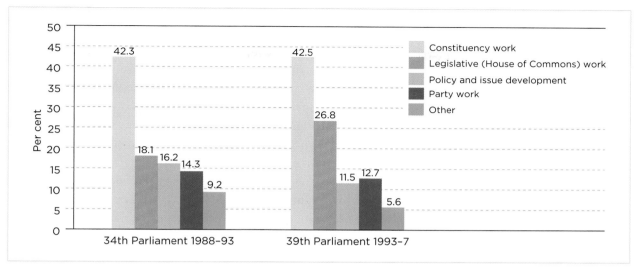

FIGURE 8.7 HOW AN MP SPENDS THE DAY (PERCENTAGE OF WORKING TIME DEVOTED TO DIFFERENT TASKS)

Source: Reprinted with permission of the Publisher from *Mr. Smith Goes to Ottawa: Life in the House of Commons* by David Docherty © University of British Columbia Press 1997. All rights reserved by the Publisher.

DAILY ORDER OF BUSINESSS

	Monday	Tuesday	Wednesday	Thursday	Friday
10:00–11:00		🍁 Routine	👥 Caucus	🍁 Routine	✍ Gov't Orders
11:00–11:15	🧍 Private				💬 Members'
11:15–12:00		✍ Gov't Orders		✍ Gov't Orders	Q Oral Questions
12:00–1:00					🍁 Routine
1:00–1:30	✍ Gov't Orders				✍ Gov't Orders
1:30–2:00					
2:00–2:15	💬	💬	💬	💬	🧍 Private
2:15–2:30	Q	Q	Q	Q	
2:30–3:00					
3:00–5:30	🍁 Routine	✍ Gov't Orders	🍁 📖 ✍	✍ Gov't Orders	
5:30–6:30	✍ Gov't Orders	🧍 Private	🧍 Private	🧍 Private	
6:30–7:00	⚖ Adjournment	⚖ Adjournment	⚖ Adjournment	⚖ Adjournment	

Time	Symbol
10:00–11:00	⚖ ADJOURNMENT PROCEEDINGS
11:00–11:15	👥 CAUCUS
11:15–12:00	✍ GOVERNMENT ORDERS
12:00–1:00	💬 MEMBERS' STATEMENTS
1:00–1:30	📖 NOTICES OF MOTIONS FOR THE PRODUCTION OF PAPERS
1:30–2:00	
2:00–2:15	Q ORAL QUESTIONS
2:15–2:30	🧍 PRIVATE MEMBERS' BUSINESS
2:30–3:00	🍁 ROUTINE PROCEEDINGS
3:00–5:30	

FIGURE 8.8 A TYPICAL WEEK IN THE HOUSE OF COMMONS

Source: Parliament of Canada, http://www.parl.gc.ca/About/Parliament/WeekInHouse/index-e.asp.

In performing their functions, all MPs are provided with a budget for hiring staff in Ottawa and in their riding office. They choose how these resources are allocated; however, most MPs opt to have two staffers in Ottawa and two in the constituency office. MPs are also provided with public funds to maintain their constituency office and are allowed an unlimited regular mail budget and four mass mailings to constituents—known as "householders"—per year. Although these resources are paltry compared to those at the disposal of US congressional representatives and senators, they are superior to those of legislators in many other democracies. And while they are adequate to enable an MP to carry out his or her constituency duties, they are not sufficient to pay for policy analysts and other research staff.

Docherty found that MPs who were new to Parliament tended to spend more time on constituency work than those who had been in the legislature longer. "[T]he longer members serve in office," he observes, "the less time they will devote to constituency work."[32] This shift from constituency to policy-oriented work does not, however, mean that a veteran MP's constituents are less well served than those of an MP who is new to Parliament. Docherty found that the Ottawa staffs of veteran MPs tended to make up the difference, spending more of their time on constituency business as their MPs' focus shifted to policy concerns. "No matter what stage of their career," Docherty states, "members of parliament see helping individuals as their most crucial duty."[33]

IS THERE A DEMOCRATIC DEFICIT IN CANADA?

During the 1990s it became increasingly popular to speak about a **democratic deficit** in Canadian politics, resulting from what critics believed to be *the excessive centralization of power in and around the prime minister and cabinet and the marginalization of the legislature.* In his book *The Friendly Dictatorship*, Jeffrey Simpson made the case for significant reform of the way in which Parliament conducts its business, as have many other political commentators. Even before becoming leader of the Liberal Party in 2003, Paul Martin started to speak out publicly on this issue, promising to change the way business is done in Ottawa.

Those who think that the prime minister should have a relatively unfettered hand in shaping and passing legislation do not think there is a democratic deficit. But revelations by the federal Auditor General, in her 2004 annual report to Parliament, seemed to illustrate at least one important dimension of the problem. Referring to what was later called the *Sponsorship Scandal*, she claimed that millions of dollars of taxpayer money were channelled to Quebec advertising agencies with Liberal Party connections for several years following the 1995 referendum, often for services that were not provided. There appeared to be no transparency in the awarding of the contracts, little public accountability for the spending of the money, partisan favouritism in its allocation, and a high probability of illegal behaviour on the part of many of those who distributed and received this money. Although there was no evidence that either Prime Minister Chrétien or his successor, Paul Martin, personally knew about or authorized any of these payments, the affair seemed to corroborate the view that corrupt practices were possible and that there were not enough checks on the actions of some public officials, particularly in the PMO.

In 2004 the Liberal government appointed the Commission of Inquiry into the Sponsorship Program and Advertising Activities under the direction of Justice John Gomery. The Gomery Commission's final report touched directly on the issue of this alleged democratic deficit, suggesting that the malfeasance and illegal activities were allowed to happen because of inadequate lines and methods of accountability, and an abdication of responsibility for subordinates' actions on the part of those at the top of the bureaucratic and political hierarchy. The problem was one of systemic failure, and not just or even primarily of bad people doing bad things. The research studies carried out for the Commission argued that the oversight of government programs by parliamentary committees is, most of the time, pathetically weak. The Commission made many recommendations including reforming the relationship of Parliament to the government and its public servants, increasing transparency in financial matters and program administration, and clarifying the roles and responsibilities of cabinet ministers and their deputies. Such recommendations, particularly those proposing a more robust role for Parliament, have been made before. The Conservative government elected in 2006 passed the Federal Accountability Act, which was influenced by the Gomery Commission's recommendations. Predictably, opinion is divided on the effectiveness of these reforms.[34]

THE JUDICIARY

Courts apply and interpret the law. They perform this role in matters ranging from contested driving offences to disputes over the most fundamental principles of the Constitution. As we have seen in previous chapters, the decisions of judges often have profound implications for the rights and status of individuals and groups, for the balance of social and economic power, and for the federal division of powers. It is therefore crucial that we understand the political significance of the judicial process and the methods of interpretation typically used by the courts.

Responsibility for Canada's judicial system is divided between Ottawa and the provinces. While the Constitution gives the federal government the exclusive right to make criminal law, it assigns responsibility for the administration of justice and for law enforcement to the provinces. Consequently, all provinces have established their own systems of courts that interpret and apply both federal and provincial laws.

The Constitution also gives Ottawa the authority to create courts. This authority was used in 1875 to create the Supreme Court of Canada. Since 1949 the Supreme Court has been Canada's highest court of appeal. Ottawa again used this constitutional power in 1971 to create the Federal Court of Canada. It has jurisdiction over civil claims involving the federal governments, cases arising from the decisions of federally appointed administrative bodies such as the Immigration Appeal Board, and matters relating to federal income tax, copyrights, and maritime law—all of which fall under the legislative authority of Ottawa. The structure of Canada's court system is shown in Figure 8.10.

The independence of judges is the cornerstone of the Canadian judicial system. Judges are appointed by governments. But once appointed they hold their office "during good

CANADIAN SPOTLIGHT

BOX 8.5   How a Law Is Passed

The law takes various forms. A statute passed by the House of Commons and the Senate, and given royal assent by the Governor General, is clearly a law. But decisions taken by cabinet that have not been approved in the legislature also have the force of law. These are called orders-in-council. Thousands of them are issued each year, and they are published in the *Canada Gazette*. The decisions of agencies, boards, and commissions that receive their regulatory powers from a statute also have the force of law. Finally, there are the regulations and guidelines issued and enforced by the departmental bureaucracy in accordance with the discretionary powers delegated to them under a statute. These also have the force of law.

In a strictly numerical sense the statutes passed annually by Parliament represent only a few of the laws promulgated each year. Nevertheless, virtually all major policy decisions—including budget measures and the laws that assign discretionary power to the bureaucracy—come before the legislature. The only exceptions have occurred when the normal process of government was suspended under the War Measures Act. This happened during World War I, again during World War II, and briefly in 1970 when Ottawa invoked the War Measures Act after two political kidnappings in Quebec by the Front de libération du Québec. The War Measures Act was replaced by the Emergencies Act in 1988.

During normal times the law-making process involves several stages and opportunities for debate and amendment. The steps from the introduction of a bill in Parliament to the final proclamation of a statute are set out in Figure 8.9.

There are two types of bills: private members' bills and government bills. Private members' bills

originate from any individual MP, but unless they get the backing of government they have little chance of passing. Government bills dominate Parliament's legislative agenda. When major legislation is being proposed, a bill is sometimes preceded by a **white paper**. This **is** *a report for discussion on proposed legislation, which is based on research by the bureaucracy and/or the legislature, and serves as a statement of the government's legislative intentions*. Major legislation may also follow from the recommendations of a **Royal Commission**, *a task force or some other consultative body that has been created by the government to study and make recommendations on an issue*.

Once a bill has been drafted by government, it may be introduced in the Senate, but is usually introduced in the House of Commons. Here, it is given *first reading*, which is just a formality and involves no debate. Then the bill goes to *second reading*, when the main principles of the bill are debated and a vote is taken. If the bill passes second reading it is sent to a smaller legislative committee, where the details of the bill are considered clause by clause. At this *committee stage*, amendments can be made but the principle of the bill cannot be altered. The bill is then reported back to the House, where all aspects, including any amendments, are debated. At this *report stage* new amendments also can be introduced. If a bill passes this hurdle it then goes to *third reading* when a final vote is taken, sometimes after further debate. Once a bill has been passed in the House, it is sent to the Senate where a virtually identical process takes place. If a bill was first introduced in the Senate, then it would now be sent to the House. Finally, a bill that is passed in both the House and the Senate can be given royal assent and become law.

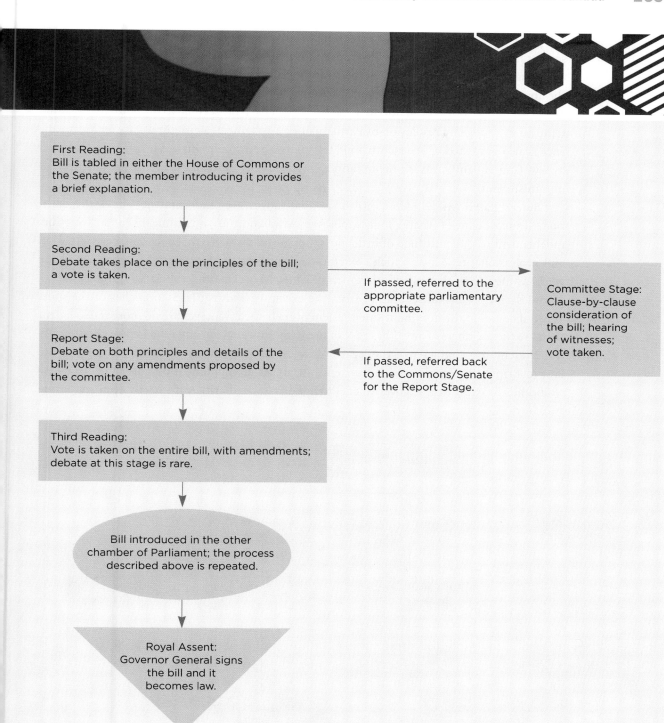

First Reading:
Bill is tabled in either the House of Commons or the Senate; the member introducing it provides a brief explanation.

Second Reading:
Debate takes place on the principles of the bill; a vote is taken.

If passed, referred to the appropriate parliamentary committee.

Committee Stage:
Clause-by-clause consideration of the bill; hearing of witnesses; vote taken.

Report Stage:
Debate on both principles and details of the bill; vote on any amendments proposed by the committee.

If passed, referred back to the Commons/Senate for the Report Stage.

Third Reading:
Vote is taken on the entire bill, with amendments; debate at this stage is rare.

Bill introduced in the other chamber of Parliament; the process described above is repeated.

Royal Assent:
Governor General signs the bill and it becomes law.

FIGURE 8.9 FROM BILL TO STATUTE

behaviour"[35]—or to age 75. What constitutes a lapse from "good behaviour"? A criminal or a serious moral offence could provide grounds for removal, as could decisions of such incompetence that they undermine public respect for the law and the judiciary. In such circumstances the appointing government may launch removal proceedings against a judge. In fact, formal proceedings have rarely been initiated and have never been prosecuted to the point of the actual removal of a judge by resolution of Parliament or a provincial legislature. Judicial independence is also protected by the fact that judges' salaries and conditions of service are established by law. Consequently, governments cannot single out any individual judge for special reward or punishment.

But as Ralph Miliband puts it, to say that judges are "independent" raises the question, "Independent of what?" Judges, observes Miliband, "are by no means, and cannot be, independent of the multitude of influences, notably of class origin, education, class situation and professional tendency, which contribute as much to the formation of their view of the world as they do in the case of other men."[36] Thus, to say that the judiciary is "independent" is to describe its formal separation from the executive and legislative branches of the state. When it comes to the dominant value system of their society, judges are no more independent than are the members of any other part of the state elite. Leaving aside the socio-economically unrepresentative character of the legal profession and the effects of formal training in the law, in British-style parliamentary systems all judges are appointed by governments.[37] One would hardly expect these governments to appoint radical critics of society, even supposing

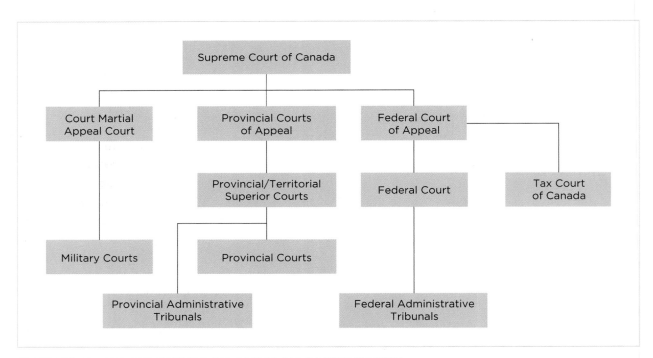

FIGURE 8.10 THE STRUCTURE OF CANADA'S COURT SYSTEM

Source: Canada's Court System 2011, http://www.justice.gc.ca/eng/dept-min/pub/ccs-ajc/page3.html, Department of Justice Canada, 2011. Reproduced with the permission of the Minister of Public Works and Government Services, 2012.

that many such individuals could be found within the more respected ranks of the legal profession. The fact that governments control promotion within the court system may also deter unconventional judicial behaviour.

Some argue that the socio-economic background of judges and the process of selection have introduced conservative tendencies into the judiciary. But these are not the only factors that may incline the courts toward protection of the status quo. The law itself is often a powerful conservative force. We are used to thinking of the law as simply "the rules made by governments" that "apply to everybody in society,"[38] but the law also represents values that have accumulated over a long time. The concepts, meanings, precedents, and interpretive rules that shape judicial decision making tend to inhibit sharp breaks with the past.

Judges work within the embedded premises of the law. Among the most important of these premises, in terms of their impact on the distribution of power in society, are the rights of the individual, the rights associated with private property, and the concept of the business corporation. Individualism is woven throughout the legal fabric of Canadian society. In practice, respect for individual rights tends to be more important for the privileged than for the disadvantaged. While this is obviously true in the case of property rights—protecting these rights matters more to those who have something to lose than to those who do not—it also tends to be true in matters like individual freedom of expression. For example, a series of court decisions handed down between 1983 and 2001 ruled unconstitutional sections of the federal Elections Act that prohibited advertising by organizations other than registered political parties during federal election campaigns. In the abstract this represented a victory for freedom of expression. Critics charge, however, that these victories mattered most to well-heeled organizations with the means to pay for such advertising, such as the ideologically conservative National Citizens Coalition that led the challenges to these restrictions. (In the end, these restrictions were upheld by the Supreme Court of Canada in a 2004 ruling.)

The powerful tug of *liberal individualism* on judicial reasoning was clearly demonstrated in a 1987 Supreme Court of Canada decision on the right to strike. A majority of the justices decided that "The constitutional guarantee of freedom of association . . . does not include, in the case of a trade union, a guarantee of the right to bargain collectively and the right to strike."[39] To put it very simply, economic rights were viewed as subordinate to political ones. The Court said as much: ". . . the overwhelming preoccupation of the Charter is with individual, political, and democratic rights with conspicuous inattention to economic and property rights."[40] But in practical terms "conspicuous inattention" meant that the existing balance of power and rights between employers and workers was considered to be correct, and that workers and unions could not count on the courts to defend their rights against governments intent on diminishing them.

On the other hand, judges are generally quite aware of the socio-economic and political consequences of their decisions. In his dissent from the majority decision in the 1987 right-to-strike case, Chief Justice Brian Dickson observed, "Throughout history, workers have associated to overcome their vulnerability as individuals to the strength of their employers. The capacity to bargain collectively has long been recognized as one of the integral and primary functions of associations of working people."[41] Collective bargaining, according to Dickson, requires that workers have the right to strike. Moreover, in a 1989 decision the Supreme Court rejected the traditional liberal notion of equality as *identical treatment before the law* in favour of what is sometimes called **substantive equality**, which means ***that individuals should be looked at in terms of their group characteristics and the possible advantages or disadvantages they may have experienced as a result of these attributes***.

Aspects of liberal individualism are also embedded in the judicial process. All judicial systems are adversarial: the plaintiff in civil cases or the prosecution in criminal cases brings an action against the defendant. Common-law systems like Canada's represent the most extreme form of this adversarial process. In civil cases the onus is placed on the individual parties—plaintiff and defendant—to make their respective cases before the court. In criminal proceedings the state is responsible for prosecuting the case against an individual or organization, but that individual or organization is responsible for the defence. In both civil and criminal proceedings, the role of the court is to hear and weigh the evidence, and the court does not participate in the development of either side of the action.

It is up to a plaintiff or defendant to make his or her most persuasive case. The ability of each to do so depends, in part, on his or her access to competent legal counsel. In criminal proceedings, the state pays for legal counsel for defendants who cannot afford to hire a lawyer. Legal aid is available in all provinces for those who cannot afford the legal costs of a civil action. But these forms of subsidized legal assistance by no means equalize access to effective legal counsel. High-priced legal professionals, which are beyond the means of most people, are backed up by the resources of a large law firm.

Although the judicial system is hardly a level playing field, it would be wrong to suggest that it serves only the interests of the wealthy and powerful. Indeed, particularly since the addition of the Charter of Rights and Freedoms to Canada's Constitution, groups representing women, Aboriginal Canadians, the disabled, gays and lesbians, and other interests that could hardly be described as being near the epicentre of power in Canadian society have frequently achieved successes in the courts that were not possible in legislative and electoral forums.

The era of judges deferring to the will of elected officials is over. The Charter was the catalyst for what both critics and supporters see as an enormous increase in the policy role of the courts. However, as Chief Justice Beverley McLachlin has argued (see Box 8.6), criticism of the courts in the Charter era too often has confused *outcome* (determination of social policy) with *process* (the impartiality of the courts as opposed to the partisan nature of the process by which governments and legislatures seek to establish social policy). Of course, some critics would challenge the Chief Justice's claim regarding the impartiality of judges and the judicial system.

Some argue that recourse to the courts to achieve ends that cannot be accomplished through the political process is fundamentally undemocratic and has weakened *parliamentary supremacy* in Canada. It is simply wrong, however, to conceive of the courts as being outside the political process. Even before the Charter, the courts were very much a part of politics and policy making in Canada. Their rulings on the federal–provincial division of powers and on all manner of policy questions have always been part of Canadian politics. Quebec nationalists have long complained that the Supreme Court of Canada has a pro-federal bias, a claim

INSIDE POLITICS

BOX 8.6 | Chief Justice McLachlin Defends the Court's Involvement with Questions of Social Policy

The fact that judges rule on social questions that affect large numbers of people does not, however, mean that judges are political. There is much confusion on this point in the popular press. Judges are said to be acting politically, to have descended (or perhaps ascended) into the political arena. Judges, on this view, are simply politicians who do not need to stand for election and can never be removed.

This misapprehension confuses outcome with process. Many judicial decisions on important social issues—say affirmative action, or abortion, or gay rights—will be political in the sense that they will satisfy some political factions at the expense of others. But the term "political" is used in the context to describe an outcome, not a process. While the outcomes of cases are inevitably political in some broad sense of the term, it is important—critical, even—that the process be impartial. It is inescapable that judges' decisions will have political ramifications. But it is essential that they not be partisan. In their final form, judgments on

social policy questions are often not all that different from legislation. It is the process by which the judgments are arrived at that distinguishes them. Legislation is often the product of compromise or conflict between various political factions, each faction pushing its own agenda. The judicial arena does not, and should not, provide simply another forum for the same kind of contests. Judges must *maintain the appearance and reality of impartiality*. It is impartiality that distinguishes us from the other branches of government, and impartiality that gives us our legitimacy.

—Remarks of the Right Honourable Beverley McLachlin, PC, Chief Justice of Canada, on "The Role of Judges in Modern Society," given at the 4th Worldwide Common Law Judiciary Conference in Vancouver, BC, on 5 May 2001. At: www.scc-csc.gc.ca/court-cour/ju/spe-dis/bm01-05-05-eng.asp. Supreme Court of Canada, 2001. Reproduced with the permission of the Minister of Public Works and Government Services, 2012.

that—true or not—reflects the inescapable involvement of the Court in the politics of federalism. The fact that by law three of the Supreme Court's nine judges must be members of the Quebec bar, and that by tradition three should be from Ontario, two from the West, and one from Atlantic Canada, shows that the essentially political issue of regional representation has been considered important for the judicial branch, just as it is important in the executive and legislative branches of government.

In recent years the issue of representation on the bench, particularly on the Supreme Court, has become even more politically charged. The death of Justice John Sopinka in 1997 and the retirement of Justice Peter Cory in 1999 unleashed flurries of behind-the-scenes lobbying and public advocacy on behalf of particular candidates for the vacancies on Canada's highest court. Gender and judicial ideology appear to have become more prominent criteria in the Supreme Court selection process, at least in the eyes of many advocacy and rights-oriented groups.[42] Many critics argue that the judicial selection process is mired in partisanship and a lack of transparency and should be reformed, including a public review of judicial appointees.

If we accept, then, that the courts are unavoidably part of the political process, is there any basis for the claim that recourse to the courts may be undemocratic? The short answer is "yes." Several decades before the Charter, James Mallory argued that business interests cynically exploited the federal division of powers in the British North America Act to oppose increased state interference in their affairs, regardless of which level of government was doing the interfering.[43] Respect for democratic principles and the Constitution was the cloak behind which business attempted to conceal its self-interest.

In the Charter era similar criticisms have been expressed. Charter critics like Rainer Knopff and Ted Morton argue that recourse to the courts by abortion rights advocates, gay and lesbian rights groups, and Aboriginals, among others, has produced rulings that often elevate the preferences of special interests over more broadly held values. These critics agree with Michael Mandel's argument that the Charter era has witnessed the "legalization" of Canadian politics.[44] Emboldened by the entrenchment of rights in the Constitution and the declaration of constitutional supremacy in section 52 of the Constitution Act, 1982, judges have been less deferential to governments and legislatures than in the past. Moreover, a network of rights-oriented advocacy

TABLE 8.2 | RECENT LANDMARK SUPREME COURT CASES

Date	Case	Decision
1988	R. v. Morgentaler	In a 5–2 decision, the Court declared that abortion, under the Criminal Code of Canada, violated a woman's right under section 7 of the Charter.
1989	Irwin Toy v. Quebec	The Court upheld a provincial law prohibiting advertising to children—this law did not infringe on the freedom of expression provision under section 2(b) of the Charter.
1990	R. v. Keegstra	The Court upheld the Criminal Code of Canada provisions against willfully promoting hated, and indicated that the violation of section 2(b) freedom of expression provisions was justified in this case.
1993	Rodriguez v. British Columbia	The Court (5–4) upheld the prohibition of assisted suicide under the Criminal Code of Canada.
1997	Delgamuukw v. British Columbia	The Court's unanimous decision on Aboriginal landownership produced a victory for the Gitksan and Wet'suwet'en peoples, and by extension for other Aboriginal communities claiming a historic right of occupancy and use to land not covered by a treaty, which years of political negotiation had not been able to achieve.
1998	Vriend v. Alberta	An Alberta college teacher was fired because he was a homosexual. The Supreme Court (8–1) determined that provincial human rights legislation should include a sexual orientation provision to prevent discrimination.
1999	R. v. Marshall	The Court decided that Donald Marshall, a Mi'kmaq, had treaty rights to fish and that he was exempt from certain fishing regulations.
2003	Miglin v. Miglin	In respect of re-opening negotiated settlements such as separation agreements, the Court supported the notion that negotiated settlements are final. It rejected a wife's request to re-open a separation agreement four years after the agreement was signed.
2004	Auton v. British Columbia	A group of parents claimed that the province's refusal to pay for certain treatment for their autistic children was discriminatory. The Court ruled that funding for "non-core" medical treatment was not protected under section 15 of the Charter.

groups, law professors, lawyers, journalists, and bureaucrats working within the rights apparatus of the state (from human rights commissions to the ubiquitous equity officers found throughout the public sector) has emerged; in the words of Morton and Knopff, it "prefers the policy-making power of the less obviously democratic governmental institutions."[45] The institutions they are referring to are the courts and quasi-judicial rights commissions and tribunals.

In spite of disagreements with specific decisions, Dalhousie law professor Wayne MacKay observes that most Canadians continue to respect the courts:

> Even when Canadians don't like a particular decision, the court still has high credibility. . . . We have come to accept that there is an important role for the courts in making, or at least, shaping, public policy. . . . Interest in the court is really quite astounding compared to the days before the Charter. These judges are significant players in the political-social landscape. It's important for people to be paying attention to what they are doing.[46]

SUMMARY

Those who teach and study Canadian parliamentary democracy often remark on its complexity. Yet our system of government has managed to work in Canada, in spite of its complexity and many societal cleavages, for over 140 years—longer than any other Commonwealth country, except the United Kingdom. The roles and the working relationships of the branches of government—the executive (including the bureaucracy), the legislature, and the judiciary—are based on the Westminster model. Unlike the republican–presidential model, the Westminster model provides no clear separation of powers between the branches of government. Nor is there a codified or formal system of legislative checks and balances to protect democracy. Instead, there is a set of principles, constitutional conventions, and institutional devices that have evolved over several hundred years to prevent any one person or branch of government from abusing power. These principles, conventions, and devices are at the heart of our democracy, in institutional features and concepts such as *constitutional monarchy, representative government* and *responsible government*, the *rule of law*, and *independent judicial review*.

Our system of government makes the monarch, and, in her absence, her representative, the Governor General, the formal head of state and the impartial head of the executive. The position has become mostly symbolic over the centuries, but it has retained some significant powers such as prorogation and dissolution of Parliament and legislative assent. Some experts have suggested that these powers could be used to protect Canadian democracy.

In practice, however, it is the prime minister who is the head of the executive, and at the same time, the head of the legislature. This makes the office of prime minister very powerful. In fact, the PM and cabinet essentially dominate the legislative agenda of Parliament. The leader of the party winning the most seats in a general election is given the first opportunity to form the government. In some ways, responsible government, which has evolved over centuries to prevent abuses of power by the prime minister and the cabinet, may in fact strengthen the PM's position, by requiring MPs to act as a disciplined bloc along party lines. Party discipline has diminished the role of the backbench MPs to the point where they tend to spend much of their time dealing with constituency matters, and less time with policy and legislative matters. Some pundits now wonder whether the office of prime minister has evolved to a point in Canada where the institutional and democratic checks against abuses of power no longer work effectively.

Cabinet ministers have a much greater say than backbenchers in policy matters and legislation. This is why cabinet positions are so desirable, and why it is important to a government's success that various regional interests and other special interests at least appear to be well represented in the cabinet. While ministers are also involved in the running of their departments, they rely heavily on public servants to manage day-to-day matters. The bureaucracy enters the policy process both early and late. Bureaucrats are the people who actually administer the programs established by law. In doing so they regularly exercise considerable discretion in policy and fiscal matters—a fact that often leads special-interest groups to focus at least part of their attention on the bureaucracy.

The judiciary has certainly played an important role in arbitrating disputes between Ottawa and the provinces, but the courts have also ensured that legislation and government policies are in keeping with the Constitution. Some critics have said that the Canadian courts have been the keepers of a proper balance between the powers of the state and the rights of the individual, while others have observed that unelected officials (judges) have become "political" and have supplanted the notion of parliamentary supremacy.

STARTING POINTS FOR RESEARCH

David Docherty, *Mr. Smith Goes to Ottawa: Life in the House of Commons* (Vancouver: University of British Columbia Press, 1997).

G. Bruce Doern, ed., *How Ottawa Spends 2007–2008* (Montreal and Kingston: McGill-Queen's University Press, 2007).

Christopher Dunn, ed., *The Handbook of Canadian Public Administration* (Toronto: Oxford University Press, 2002).

David Good, *The Politics of Public Money* (Toronto: University of Toronto Press, 2007).

David Johnson, *Thinking Government: Public Sector Management in Canada* (Toronto: University of Toronto Press, 2006).

Lydia Miljan, *Public Policy in Canada*, 5th edn (Toronto: Oxford University Press, 2008).

Donald Savoie, *The Politics of Public Spending in Canada* (Toronto: University of Toronto Press, 1990).

Donald Savoie, *Governing from the Centre: The Concentration of Power in Canadian Politics* (Toronto: University of Toronto Press, 1999).

CBC ARCHIVES AND TVO'S *THE AGENDA*

Visit the companion website for *Canadian Democracy: A Concise Introduction* to follow links to audio and video footage related to the main themes of the chapter: www.oupcanada.com/BrooksConcise.

RELEVANT WEBSITES

Visit the companion website for *Canadian Democracy: A Concise Introduction* to browse a collection of websites featuring material related to the key themes of the chapter, an excellent starting point for research.

REVIEW EXERCISES

1. Visit the government of Canada website (www.gc.ca). Click on "About Government," then "Departments and Agencies" (listed alphabetically). Choose a department or agency and find the following information about it:

    a. major programs or functions
    b. number of employees and budget
    c. cabinet minister responsible for the department/agency/Crown corporation

2. Develop a list of the checks on a prime minister's power and compare them to those of an American president.

3. List the various governmental organizations (federal, provincial, municipal) you have ever been in contact with and the reasons for the contact(s).

4. Most Canadians believe that public-sector organizations are less efficient than those in the private sector. Define "efficiency," and develop criteria you would use to measure the efficiency of private and public organizations. Can the same criteria be used for both?

Part IV

Participation in Politics

Politics does not stop at the doors of Parliament. It spills out onto the streets and into community halls and corporate boardrooms, involving citizens, organized interests, and the media. What is sometimes referred to as *civil society* both acts on and is itself acted on by the institutions of the state, making demands, organizing resistance, and providing support in various ways.

The participation of groups in civil society assumes many forms. Citizens play a role individually as voters and collectively through what is described as public opinion. Some are involved in more active ways, belonging to and working for political parties or groups that attempt to shape the political conversation and government policy. Organized interests often attempt to influence the actions of government, through a range of techniques that include lobbying, legal action, and attempting to shape public opinion. The media's specialized function involves reporting and framing the political conversation. Most of what we know about the political world is mediated by those whose job involves selecting information (i.e., news) for print and broadcast and then interpreting it.

In the following three chapters we will examine some of the most important forms of participation in Canadian politics.

9 Parties and Elections

Political parties and elections are essential features of modern democracy. After reading this chapter, you will be able to

1. Define the meaning of "political party," and explain the function of political parties in Canadian democracy
2. Explain the origins and the evolution of the party system in Canada
3. Outline the role of brokerage politics, particularly in the older Canadian political parties
4. Compare the Canadian first-past-the-post electoral system with the electoral systems used in other democracies
5. Discuss how political parties are financed and the potential for influence by special interests
6. Explain voting behaviour in Canada

Elections, and the political parties that contest them, represent the main contact points between most citizens and their political system. Most adult citizens vote at least some of the time, although perhaps not in every election and probably more often federally than provincially or locally. This may be, in fact, the extent of their participation in politics: short bursts of attention to candidates and their messages and occasional visits to the polls, interspersed around lengthier periods of inattention and political inactivity. Only about 6 of 10 eligible voters actually cast their ballots in the last few federal elections, but we can probably assume that even among those who did not vote most were at least aware that an election was taking place.

Elections remind us that we live in a democracy in which those who wish to govern must win the support of a considerable number of the governed. Elections are the cornerstone of democratic governance, yet many believe they have become meaningless and even farcical affairs in which political parties and their candidates serve up sound bites instead of sound policy in campaigns orchestrated by the same people who put together marketing campaigns for cars and deodorants. Political parties have for years ranked among the lowest of social institutions in public esteem. It would seem, therefore, that democracy's cornerstone suffers from some worrisome cracks.

Doubts about the democratic integrity of elections are not new. One of the oldest fears is that those with money are more likely to influence voter behaviour. For example, Hugh Allan essentially bankrolled the Conservative Party in the 1873 federal election in exchange for a promise from John A. Macdonald that Allan would be made president of the railroad company chartered to build a transcontinental railroad linking Ontario to the Pacific coast. Over a century ago Liberal cabinet minister Joseph-Israël Tarte remarked that "Elections are not won with prayers," a fact of political life that has become even truer in the age of television campaigning. But fact of life or not, if parties and votes can be purchased by those with deep pockets, this surely undermines the democratic credibility of the electoral process.

Political parties and candidates have also been criticized for avoiding important issues and framing electoral discourse in ways that deflect attention from major divisions in society, and for trivializing politics by replacing substance with style and image. Some have argued that the "dumbing down" of public life has been facilitated by the fact that modern elections are fought largely through the medium of television, which elevates images over ideas. But the claim that Canadian parties and candidates tend to avoid divisive issues and frame electoral discourse in ways that privilege specific interests is long-standing.

The problems of one-party states—ballot fraud, voter intimidation, and bribery—are routine in many countries. And when compared to the electoral systems of Zimbabwe, Haiti, or Russia, these criticisms of parties and elections in Canada seem petty. But Canadians are not used to comparing their democratic institutions and processes to those of undemocratic or failed regimes. We place the bar higher and measure the performance of our political parties and our electoral system against ideas of *equality* and *participation* that have evolved out of our liberal-democratic tradition. Critics may differ over the nature and extent of its shortcomings, but judged against these values, the Canadian experience is not perfect.

CANADIAN SPOTLIGHT

**BOX 9.1   What Do Canadians Get Worked Up About?
Single-Issue Elections in Canadian History**

As the 1891 general election poster below suggests, the issue of free trade has figured prominently in several Canadian general elections, and it has been the single-most important issue in three general elections since Confederation. In fact, free trade was an important issue before Confederation. One of the arguments used by the Fathers of Confederation in 1867 was that the trade created by Confederation would help replace the international trade lost when, in the 1850s and 1860s, Britain moved away from preferential trade with its colonies, and when, in 1866, the US cancelled the Reciprocity Treaty with the British North American colonies.

voters that *Reciprocity*—a policy of free trade with the United States proposed by the Liberals during the election—was tantamount to selling off Canada, and would eventually lead to the United States annexing Canada. Similar arguments were made by the Liberals and the NDP when Brian Mulroney's Progressive Conservatives made a free trade deal with the US the main issue of the 1988 general election.

A number of single-issue elections have been fought since Confederation, in which one issue, including free trade, has dominated the debate:

- 1891: Free trade with the United States
- 1896: The Manitoba schools question
- 1898: Free trade with the United States
- 1917: Conscription during World War I
- 1926: The role of the monarchy in Canadian politics
- 1945: Social programs and the welfare state
- 1957: One-party rule
- 1963: Foreign policy and nuclear weapons
- 1979: Central government power
- 1981: Central government power
- 1988: Free trade with the United States

In this 1891 campaign poster, John A. Macdonald and his Conservative Party were trying to persuade

What does a review of our media headlines tell us about current issues in Canadian politics? If a general election were held tomorrow, which issue(s) would be most likely to capture the Canadian public's attention today? Is there one particular issue that stands out above the others?

THE DEFINITION AND FUNCTIONS OF PARTIES

A **political party** may be defined as ***an organization that offers slates of candidates to voters at election time***. To this end, parties

- Recruit and select party candidates
- Raise money for their campaigns

- Develop policies that express the ideas and goals their candidates stand for
- Attempt to persuade citizens to vote for their candidates

In a democracy, parties are not created by nor are they agents of the state. They are, in Eugene Forsey's words, "voluntary associations of people who hold broadly similar opinions on public questions."[1]

It would be misleading to characterize political parties as organizations focused simply on the election of "governmental office-holders."[2] While most parties do hope to elect candidates to office, and perhaps enough candidates to form a government, some parties may contest elections as a means of making their ideas public. This is true of the Marijuana Party, whose stated mission is the decriminalization of cannabis, and the Marxist-Leninist Party, whose quixotic advocacy of global revolution by the proletariat has remained largely unchanged since the *Communist Manifesto* of 1848. The now defunct Rhinoceros Party, one that injected some welcome humour into elections—it stood for the repeal of the law of gravity, among other things—ran candidates in many Canadian ridings during the 1970s and 1980s, without any serious expectation of electing candidates.

John Meisel, one of Canada's foremost experts on parties and elections, identifies seven functions that political parties play in a democracy.[3]

1. *Integrating citizens into the political system*. Through voting for parties and thinking about public affairs in terms of the policies and ideologies represented by parties, citizens develop attachments to the political system more generally. This connection, Meisel argues, has weakened recently as political parties have fallen in public esteem and have come to be perceived by many as yet another distant and unaccountable institution.

2. *Developing policy*. In many democracies, political parties represent clear ideological and policy options. Moreover, the deliberations of the party membership are important

FIGURE 9.1 SOCIO-ECONOMIC VALUES AS REFLECTED BY CANADIAN POLITICAL PARTIES

sources of policies that a party will seek to implement once in power. Canada's historically dominant parties, the Liberals and the Conservatives, have seldom differed sharply from one another either in ideology or in their behaviour when in power. They have occasionally stood for different policies during election campaigns, as in 1988 when the Liberals opposed the Canada–United States Free Trade Agreement negotiated by a Progressive Conservative government. Also witness the Liberal government's refusal to either scrap or reform the Progressive Conservative government's GST after winning the 1993 election, in spite of policy initiatives from the party membership and a firm commitment to do so in the party's "Red Book" of election promises.

The New Democrats—and the Reform Party before it morphed into the present Conservative Party— have provided voters with clearer policy alternatives than the historically dominant parties. In fact, of all Canada's national parties, the NDP has seen the greatest involvement of the party membership in policy development.

3. *Elite recruitment.* With rare exceptions, those who run for and are elected to federal and provincial office in Canada do so as the official candidates of their parties. Parties choose their candidates and their leaders, and in doing so they determine the pool of persons from whom elected public officials, including members of the government, will be drawn. While the bar for selection of members, of electoral candidates, and of party leadership is set fairly low in most democracies, those with more formal education, higher incomes, and jobs of greater social status tend to participate more in the selection of party candidates and leaders, as well as being candidates themselves.

4. *Organization of government.* Governing parties propose; opposition parties oppose. This somewhat oversimplified formula expresses the fact that political parties play an important role in how governance occurs in democracies. Parties provide a partisan structure to the process of law-making and the debate of public affairs. Under the British-style parliamentary system that exists in Canada, this partisan structure is by design an adversarial one, from the physical layout of the legislature to the traditions and procedures observed in conducting the business of Parliament.

5. *Structuring the vote.* Just as parties lend structure to the activities of the legislature and allow for the identification of the government with a particular party (or coalition of parties in some democratic systems), they also serve to structure the vote in elections. The fact that only a handful of political parties are serious contenders for citizens' votes simplifies the information-gathering task facing voters. Each party represents, in a sense, a particular selection on a limited menu. Until the 1993 election it had been common to characterize Canada as having a two and one-half party system. With approximately 85 per cent of the popular vote between them, the Liberals and Progressive Conservatives had the most realistic chance of forming a government. The NDP accounted for the balance. This fairly stable structure to the vote and to the parliamentary status of the parties dissolved in 1993 with the arrival on the federal scene of the Bloc Québécois. The 2011 general election also proved to be an exception when the NDP gained enough seats to form the official opposition.

6. *Organizing public opinion.* Parties are often characterized as right wing, left wing, or centrist; as liberal, conservative, or socialist; or by some other set of labels signifying that they

occupy particular places on the ideological map. Parties reflect, but may also help create or at least reinforce, divisions within society.

Canada's two historically dominant political parties have used **brokerage politics**, which is *a strategic choice by a political party to avoid ideological appeals in favour of a flexible centrist style of politics*. They have avoided talking the language of class politics and have attempted to accommodate the preferences of major interests, regions, and communities through their flexible policy style. Of course, even the most centrist and waffling of parties cannot avoid taking positions on some divisive issues. Historically, language, religion, and region have been among the key issues distinguishing the Liberals from the Conservatives, the Liberals doing better among francophones and Catholics, and in the provinces east of Manitoba, and the Conservatives doing better among Protestants and western Canadians. These differences have helped to organize Canadian public opinion on religious (in the past), linguistic, and territorial lines. The NDP and its predecessor, the Co-operative Commonwealth Federation (CCF), have been the only significant parties presenting voters with a class-based definition of Canadian politics. In recent years the ability of the historically dominant parties to organize public opinion in ways that preserve their dominance was challenged by the Reform Party/Canadian Alliance, which emerged out of westerners' dissatisfaction with the older parties, and the Bloc Québécois, whose success in Quebec is testimony to the failure of brokerage politics to accommodate Quebec nationalism.

7. *Interest aggregation.* Organizations that represent secondary school teachers, gays, or wetlands conservationists may be influential in politics; however, the narrowness of their respective agendas and their population base mean that they could not hope to elect a Teachers' Party, Gay Rights Party, or Save-the-Ducks Party to power. Parties, especially parties that hope to form a government, must bring together a coalition of different interests sufficiently broad to win election. It is not always possible to satisfy all interests, and paradoxically, the practice of interest aggregation may reinforce regional division. In fact, history shows that it is seldom possible to avoid playing off one region against another in Canadian politics. The Liberal Party, the most successful of our national parties, has often formed a government with little representation from western Canada.

THE ORIGINS AND EVOLUTION OF CANADA'S PARTY SYSTEM[4]

The Nature of Brokerage Politics

The origins of Canada's two major political parties—the Conservatives and the Liberals—can be traced back to the shifting coalitions and alignments in the United Province of Canada in the 1840s and 1850s. Although these groups were much more amorphous and unstable than modern political parties, and would not really coalesce into cohesive organizations until the 1880s, they did represent distinct political tendencies. On the one hand was the governing coalition of Liberal–Conservatives (which would eventually drop the "Liberal" from its official name) under the leadership of Sir John A. Macdonald in Canada West and his French-Canadian counterpart, George-Étienne Cartier, in Canada East. It was a disparate organization encompassing a number of distinct groups. Many of these groups had potentially conflicting interests (Catholics and Protestants, French and English, urban and rural dwellers), but the organization was held together largely by the political dexterity of Macdonald and by the gradual development of a unifying vision, one based on the nation-building program eventually enshrined in the *National Policy* of 1878–9. The key elements of this program were the implementation of a protective tariff designed to promote the growth of domestic manufacturing in Ontario and Quebec, the encouragement of western settlement to open up a market for the products of central Canadian industry and to protect this territory from American encroachment, and the creation of a transcontinental railroad to ship the manufactured goods of the centre to the newly opened western territories.[5]

On the other side was an even looser opposition coalition, comprising the Clear Grits of Canada West and the *rouges* of Canada East. Both groups shared a common admiration for the republican and individualist ideas of the United States and both advocated free trade with the Americans. They also shared an unrelenting hostility to the commercial and banking interests linked to Macdonald's governing party. But the two groups made for a rather uneasy partnership and there was considerable ethnic and religious tension between the two groups. It was only when Wilfrid Laurier assumed the leadership of the Liberal Party in 1887 that these diverse elements were moulded into a relatively cohesive political organization.

It would be a mistake to make too much of the doctrinal differences between Liberals and Conservatives during these formative years of the party system (roughly 1880 to 1920). Admittedly, the Liberals were identified with free trade and provincial rights, and after 1885 (when Louis Riel was hanged for treason following the failed Northwest Rebellion) they appeared to be "more sensitive to the interests of French Canada" than the Tories.[6] They were also more sympathetic to the plight of the farmer than were the Conservatives. The latter, meanwhile, were generally thought of as the party of the British connection, the party of privilege—in the sense that its leading spokesmen claimed that all healthy and stable societies are ruled by a "natural governing" elite—the party of centralization and economic protection. But these ideological differences, far from constituting fundamental clashes of world outlooks, were almost always subordinate to the central preoccupation of Canadian politics: **patronage**, which is ***the distribution of favours by a governing politician (e.g., political appointments or government contracts) in exchange for political support.***

The scramble to control the distribution of government largesse was the dominant feature of Canadian politics during the 1860s and 1870s. A number of provisions in our electoral law have shaped our political life. For example, the use of the open ballot, whereby voters simply declared their choice at the polls in the presence of a government official (and anybody else who happened to be in the room at the time!), provided numerous opportunities for bribery, coercion, and intimidation. This made it difficult for anybody whose livelihood depended on government contracts to vote against candidates supported by the ruling cabinet. And the non-simultaneous, or staggered, elections permitted the government to call elections in safe ridings and forced candidates in many ridings to be *ministerialists*, so-called because their "politics were not to support a party but a ministry and any ministry would do."[7] This non-partisan stance was the surest way to provide for a steady flow of government patronage into the successful candidate's constituency.

The open ballot and staggered elections were eliminated by the late 1870s, and elections were gradually standardized across the provinces. However, this did not reduce the importance of patronage in federal politics. In fact, the federal parties continued to operate in a political environment characterized by the absence of civil service reform (the merit principle), a highly restricted franchise, and a weak working class (from an organizational and numerical standpoint). It has been suggested that these factors predisposed political parties to appeal to potential supporters through networks of *patron–client relations* (where votes are exchanged for certain "favours") rather than on the basis of *collectivist* or *solidaristic* appeals (class-based ideologies).[8] This is the situation described by the French political sociologist, André Siegfried, when he visited Canada just over 100 years ago. Siegfried complained that the preoccupation with questions of "material interest" and "public works" tended to "lower the general level of political life" in Canada. He also noted that Canadian politics was hardly lacking in substantive issues—rivalries between Catholics and Protestants, French and English, for example—that could have been addressed by the two major parties, but that the party leaders "prefer that they should not be talked about. The subjects which remain available for discussion are not numerous. In addition, the parties borrow one another's policies periodically, displaying a coolness in this process that would disconcert us Europeans."[9]

Siegfried's comments on the nature of party competition in Canada are still remarkably relevant. If Siegfried were somehow transported to present-day Canada, he would probably conclude that there have been few substantive changes in our party system since he published his work in 1906. The emphasis on accommodating the diverse interests—regional, linguistic, ethnic, class, religious—of the electorate through the prudent employment of "public works" and individual material incentives is still a characteristic feature of federal and provincial politics. Elections are usually preceded by a barrage of new government programs and spending initiatives in various parts of the country—ill-disguised attempts by the party in power to purchase electoral support in key ridings. As well, the nonchalant borrowing of elements of one party's program by another party is still going on today. These features of Canadian politics, as well as the many flip-flops by the older parties on key issues such as the GST and the like only serve to fuel the electorate's cynicism about politics in general and their distrust of politicians in particular.

The electoral opportunism exhibited by both the Liberals and the Tories in recent decades should not to be taken to mean that the two older parties have no principles or ideological commitments whatsoever. In recent times Canada's oldest parties have represented somewhat distinct traditions, particularly on matters concerning federalism and Canada–US relations. With the accession of Pierre Trudeau to the party leadership in 1968, the Liberals became identified in the minds of most Canadian voters with a strong central state (hence the ongoing battles between Ottawa and the provinces over control of natural resource revenues), with economic nationalism (Petro-Canada, the National Energy Program, the Foreign Investment Review Agency), and with "French power." The Tories, meanwhile, came increasingly to be associated with political decentralization: Joe Clark, when he was leader of the party and briefly prime minister in the late 1970s, described Canadian federalism as a "community of communities," which Trudeau sarcastically rejected as "shopping-mall" federalism. The Conservatives also came to embrace the notion of free trade with the United States; this represented a reversal of the party positions on the subject in the late nineteenth and early twentieth centuries, when the Liberals strongly advocated continentalist economic policies. Finally, the neo-conservatism of the 1980s, spearheaded by British prime minister Margaret Thatcher and US president Ronald Reagan, found its most receptive audience among the Conservatives during the Mulroney years. In recent years the federal Liberal Party has been associated with a somewhat more centralist vision of federal–provincial relations and a brand of mild to occasionally hotter anti-Americanism, while the Conservatives have branded themselves as more decentralist and more sympathetic to Washington.

Despite these apparent differences in the recent policy orientations of the two older parties, Siegfried's central contention about the Canadian party system remains indisputable. Our historically dominant parties have always been much more flexible, more opportunistic, more wary of ideological appeals to the electorate than those in most European nations, and, as Siegfried wrote, dominated by their leaders:

> . . . it is of the first importance to the success of a party that it should be led by someone who inspires confidence, and whose mere name is a program in itself. As long as the Conservatives had Macdonald for their leader, they voted for him rather than for the party. So it is with Laurier and the Liberals of today. If Laurier disappeared, the Liberals would perhaps find that they had lost the real secret of their victories. . . . Canadians attach themselves rather to the concrete reality than to the abstract principle. They vote as much for the man who symbolizes the policy as for the policy itself.[10]

The nature of our electoral system, and the norms that govern its party competition, are such that the Liberals and Conservatives can usually fight elections without having to worry too much about keeping their principles intact or consistent. Many observers of Canada's party system have called this type of mainstream or flexible, non-ideological party system a brokerage party system. That is, the two older parties at the federal level act as "brokers of ideas . . . middlemen who select from all the ideas pressing for recognition as public policy those they think can be shaped to have the widest appeal."[11] Each of the parties attempts to cobble together a winning coalition of voters at election time; the voting support for the two major parties, therefore, does not come from stable, well-defined social groups, as is the case in many Western European countries. Most important, politics in Canada lacks an obvious *class* dimension. Conflicts between the working class and capitalists over the political and economic rights of workers, and over the distribution of national wealth, take a back seat to other issues—those arising out of religious, ethnic, and regional rivalries, for instance.

This peculiarity of Canadian politics has led some observers to describe the Canadian party system as less developed or less modern than those of most other industrial nations. Robert Alford, for example, declared in his classic study of voting behaviour in four Anglo-American democracies (the United States, Canada, Great Britain, and Australia) that Canada had the lowest level of class voting among the nations he examined.[12] Alford's explanation of this situation echoed the one advanced by Siegfried almost 60 years earlier: "Class voting is low in Canada because the political parties are identified as representatives of regional, religious, and ethnic groupings rather than as representatives of national class interests, and this, in turn, is due to a relative lack of national integration."[13] Class divisions and antagonisms are certainly not absent in Canada, Alford observed, and he predicted that once the issue of national unity had been resolved, class voting would increase and Canada would come to resemble other modern democracies—Great Britain, for instance.

In the almost 50 years since Alford's book was written, his prediction has simply not come true: the issue of class is still subordinated to questions of national unity and regional or ethnic grievances. The two older parties do not normally appeal to specific class constituencies and still evade class issues when possible. Moreover, the self-described left-wing party in Canada, the NDP, receives nowhere near a majority of the votes of blue-collar workers.

Brokerage theory, then, makes two fundamental claims about Canada's two historically dominant political parties: first, they do not appeal to specific socio-economic groupings and they lack cohesive ideological visions, especially those based on class interests and identity; second, the parties are flexible and opportunistic because this sort of behaviour is necessary to preserve the fragile unity of the nation. This brings to mind Siegfried's observation that the prudent and cautious leaders do not want to discuss some of the pressing issues to be discussed for fear of inflaming group jealousies and thereby jeopardizing the stability of the country.

An alternative explanation of the absence of class politics in Canada is advanced by Janine Brodie and Jane Jenson in *Crisis, Challenge, and Change*.[14] They argue that brokerage theory tends to view political parties as more or less passive transmission belts for societal demands. The more important role of political parties in liberal democracies, however, is to create a *definition of politics*

> through which people make sense of their daily lives. Because issues are raised and choices provided in particular ways, this cultural construction defines the content and sets the limits of partisan politics. Social problems never included within the bounds of partisan political debate remain invisible and confined to the private sector or private life for resolution. From a myriad of social tensions the definition of politics identifies and selects those susceptible to "political" solutions. Political parties, in other words, by defining the political, contribute to the organization and disorganization of groups in the electorate.[15]

Brodie and Jenson argue that in the period immediately following Confederation, class, religion, language, and other social differences competed with each other as potential support bases for the two federal parties. Since both of these parties drew the bulk of their support from the same social group—the bourgeoisie—they tended to avoid the issue of class in their competition for votes.

Brodie and Jenson's explanation of the non-class nature of the Canadian party system is an important contribution. Nevertheless, it does seem somewhat overdrawn, since it appears to downplay or minimize the pre-eminence of religious and ethnic divisions in Canadian society in the late nineteenth century and to exaggerate the extent to which the parties have been able to play up the issues of language and culture for their own advantage. A large part of the explanation of the relative unimportance of class issues in Canadian politics must be found in the social organization of the working class itself, and not simply attributed to the major parties' manipulation of the definition of politics.

The Role of Minor Parties in the Brokerage System

By the summer of 1991, almost three years into its second mandate, the Progressive Conservative government of Prime Minister Brian Mulroney had sunk to historic lows in public opinion polls. In fact, the Conservatives were being rivalled in voter popularity by a fledgling organization that was beginning to capture a great deal of voter and media attention: the Reform Party of Canada. Under the leadership of Preston Manning, the son of the former Social Credit Premier of Alberta, Ernest Manning, the Reform Party was founded in late 1987 primarily as a vehicle for western discontent (its original slogan was "The West Wants In"). The Reform Party, which became the Canadian Alliance Party in 2000, was the latest in a string of Western protest movements that have tapped into the powerful feelings of economic and political alienation in the western provinces. The two major parties have been seen as co-conspirators in this vicious circle of exploitation, since they are beholden to the powerful economic interests in the metropolitan areas and are compelled to enact policies that favour those regions where the bulk of the seats are to be won in a federal election.

This deep-seated suspicion among westerners was briefly dispelled by the 1984 federal election. Although the new prime minister, Brian Mulroney, was himself a bilingual Quebecer, for the first time since the Diefenbaker interlude of the 1950s, a large number of westerners were placed in key cabinet positions. Western voters seemed to be saying that they were getting a government that would understand and respond to their concerns. Gradually, however, the guarded optimism gave way to disillusionment, as the Conservative government made a number of policy decisions that were viewed as detrimental to western interests. The most publicized instance of "biased" government decision making was Ottawa's awarding of a multi-million dollar maintenance contract for the CF-18 fighter aircraft to a Quebec-based firm, despite the fact that Bristol Aerospace of Winnipeg had presented what federal officials acknowledged was a technically superior bid. Many westerners concluded that the system itself—especially the "national" parties—was biased against the West. A new voice—a regionally based protest party like the Reform Party—was necessary to extract favourable policies from central Canada.

Although the Reform Party began its life as a strictly regional organization, it quickly capitalized on the public's growing disenchantment with so-called "traditional" political parties to make inroads into Ontario, the bastion of central Canadian power. The percentage of Canadians expressing "a great deal" or "quite a lot" of confidence in political parties had dropped from 30 per cent in 1979 to only 7 per cent in 1991.[16] Reform attacked existing political institutions as being unresponsive, unaccountable, and elitist, and attempted to portray itself as a *populist* movement rather than a political party. Rigid party discipline—which various governments had promised to relax, without much noticeable effect—was singled out by both voters and the Reform Party alike as one of the biggest culprits in driving a wedge between the individual citizen and the political system. Under the Mulroney Conservatives, two Tory backbenchers who were publicly critical of the GST found themselves expelled from the party's caucus. Likewise, and despite Jean Chrétien's promise to relax party discipline, those Liberal MPs who opposed the government's 1995 gun control law were stripped of their parliamentary committee assignments. Such incidents remind voters that elected MPs are expected to vote as the party brass decides, even if this collides with the desires of their constituents.

There is also a generalized suspicion, fuelled by occasional sordid conflict-of-interest scandals at the federal and provincial levels, that politicians have become overly concerned with furthering their own careers or lining their pockets, at the expense of their constituents. The issue of MPs' pensions is a lightning rod for this popular sentiment. The Reform Party made much of its commitment to

Preston Manning, who founded the Reform Party of Canada and led it from 1987 to 2000, helped to "fan the flames" on western regional and social conservative issues, forcing the country's dominant parties into ideological debates that would not have surfaced otherwise.

opt out of what it considered to be the unfairly generous terms of MPs' pensions, and in 1995 all but one of the party's MPs chose not to participate in the pension plan. Finally, there was a declining tolerance among voters for the kind of closed-door, elitist decision making that traditionally has characterized Canadian politics under Liberal and Conservative governments.

Responding to the widely held demands among the electorate for greater accountability and a more democratic political structure, the Reform Party and then the Canadian Alliance followed in the path of their populist predecessors, the Progressives of the 1920s and Social Credit of the 1930s and '40s, and called for a number of institutional reforms that would increase the individual citizen's control over his or her representatives. The Alliance advocated greater use of referendums and citizen initiatives, the right of constituents to recall their MPs, and relaxation of party discipline and more "free votes" in Parliament. The Reform/Alliance ideology was conservative, and it regularly found itself the sole political party advocating radical change to the policy status quo. For example, during the 1993 election campaign it was the only party to advocate a major reduction in Canada's annual intake of immigrants during times when the economy was weak. It was also the only party to insist that deficit reduction, to be achieved mainly through spending cuts, should be Ottawa's top priority (a policy that the Liberal government subsequently embraced). Reform Party MPs were the main critics in Parliament of the 1995 gun control law requiring the registration of all firearms. The party also stood alone in its opposition to official multiculturalism and bilingualism.

Although the Conservatives, Liberals, and NDP all initially tried to ignore or downplay the significance of the Reform Party, by the summer of 1991—when the report of the Spicer Commission was released, documenting the deep dissatisfaction of many Canadians with the functioning of their traditional democratic institutions, especially the political parties—this protest movement was simply too powerful to be casually dismissed.

"Minor" parties such as Reform/Alliance perform an important function in our brokerage party system: they provide a much-needed source of policy innovation, goading the major parties into acting on the concerns of regions, classes, or significant social groups that they have traditionally ignored or underestimated. This is exactly what happened during previous cycles of regional protest: the major parties were eventually compelled to head off the electoral challenge of a nascent protest movement (whether it was the Progressives, the CCF, or Social Credit) by endorsing policies that appealed to the new party's supporters. Walter Young, in his history of the national CCF, described the contribution of third parties to the Canadian political system:

> By providing . . . the kind of ideological confrontation which is typically absent in contests between the two major parties, [minor parties] have served to stimulate the older parties and reactivate their previously dormant philosophies. . . . Two parties alone cannot successfully represent all the interests or act as a broker— honest or otherwise. Attempts to represent a national consensus have been usually based on the assessment of a few with limited access to the attitudes of the whole. The result has been that the national consensus has in fact been the view of the most dominant voices in the old parties. And these are the voices at the centre; historically, the voices of the elite or the establishment.[17]

The Continuation of Brokerage Politics in Canada

Before the 1993 election it was common to speak of Canada's "two and one-half" party system. The Liberals and Progressive Conservatives were the parties that had a realistic chance of forming a government, while the NDP was a stable minority party on the federal scene, regularly winning 15–20 per cent of the popular vote and occasionally holding the balance of power during a period of **minority government**, *a government that depends on the support of another party's MPs in order to win votes in the legislature.*

The old certainties were shattered by the 1993 election results. The Liberals won a solid majority, taking 177 of the 295 seats in the House of Commons, with 41.3 per cent of the popular vote. Neither the Conservatives nor the NDP elected enough MPs to qualify for official party status, which guarantees the opportunity to speak in the House during question period as well as automatic funding for research staff. On the other hand, the Reform Party jumped from one seat to 52 seats. And the Bloc Québécois, created in 1990 by the defections of several Tory and Liberal MPs, went from seven to 54 seats. Not since 1921, when the Progressives came second to the Liberals, had the national party system received such a jolt from voters.

Neither the Reform party nor the Bloc gave signs of being interested in brokerage-style politics. Many interpreted the 1993 election results as a political realignment of voters as well as a display of voters' dissatisfaction with brokerage-style politics. This interpretation was greeted with some skepticism. Critics of the realignment argument pointed to such factors as the monumental unpopularity of former Conservative prime minister Brian Mulroney, the erosion of NDP support in Ontario where an unpopular NDP government was in power, a wave of western disaffection with the major parties, and the unusual and presumably passing phenomenon of the Bloc Québécois, spawned in the bitter wake of the 1990 defeat of the Meech Lake Accord.

The elements for a durable party realignment seemed to exist. One of these elements involved the low esteem in which parties and politicians were held by voters. The Royal Commission on Electoral Reform and Party Financing noted

> Canadians appear to distrust their political leaders, the political process and political institutions. Parties themselves may be contributing to the malaise of voters. . . . Whatever the cause, there is little doubt that Canadian political parties are held in low public esteem, and that their standing has declined steadily over the past decade. They are under attack from citizens for failing to achieve a variety of goals deemed important by significant groups within society.[18]

As may be seen in the summary of federal election results in Table 9.1, the wave of cynicism that has been building in the Canadian electorate has weakened attachments to the traditional parties.

A second element in the party realignment seemed to come from a so-called *shrinking centre* in Canadian politics. The traditional dominance of the Liberal and Progressive Conservative centrist parties, which differed very little from one another in terms of their principles and policies, depended on a broad popular consensus within the familiar confines of language, regionalism, and leadership. This popular consensus—in areas such as the welfare state, active economic management by the government, and official bilingualism—had become frayed and the traditionally dominant parties' ability to keep political conflict within "safe" boundaries was diminished.

Only the Liberal Party succeeded in continuing to practise the old brokerage-style politics. It emerged from the 1993 election as the only truly national party, electing members from every province and territory and receiving no less than one-quarter of the votes cast in any province. It became increasingly evident that the Progressive Conservative Party would have to reposition itself ideologically if it wanted to regain the votes that Reform/Canadian Alliance siphoned off in the 1993, 1997, and 2000 elections. It could not afford to remain a near-clone of the Liberal Party, especially since the Liberals in power created some distance between themselves and the Keynesian welfare state that they had been instrumental in building. The electoral success of

TABLE 9.1 | SUMMARY OF ELECTION RESULTS, 1965–2011

A. Percentage of Vote* and Candidates Elected by Political Party at Canadian General Elections, 1965–2011

Party	1965	1968	1972	1974	1979	1980	1984	1988
Liberal	40.2%	45.5%	38.5%	43.2%	40.1%	44.3%	28.0%	31.9%
	131	155	109	141	114	147	40	83
PC	32.4%	31.4%	34.9%	35.4%	35.9%	32.5%	50.0%	43.0%
	97	72	107	95	136	103	211	169
NDP	17.9%	17.0%	17.7%	15.4%	17.9%	19.8%	18.8%	20.4%
	21	22	31	16	26	32	30	43
Créditistes	4.6%	4.4%	—	—	—	—	—	—
	9	14	—	—	—	—	—	—
Social Credit	3.7%	0.8%	7.6%	5.0%	4.6%	1.7%	0.1%	***
	5	0	15	11	6	0	0	0
Reform/Alliance	—	—	—	—	—	—	—	2.1%
	—	—	—	—	—	—	—	0
Others	1.2%	0.9%	1.2%	0.9%	1.5%	1.7%	3.0%	2.6%
	2	1	2	1	0	0	1	0
Total valid votes	7,713,316	8,125,996	9,667,489	9,505,908	11,455,702	10,947,914	12,548,721	13,175,599
Total seats	265	264	264	264	282	282	282	295

Party	1993	1997	2000	2004	2006	2008	2011
Liberal	41.3%	38.5%	40.8%	36.7%	30.2%	26.2%	18.9%
	177	155	172	135	103	77	34
PC**	16.0%	18.8%	12.2%	29.6%	36.3%	37.6%	39.6%
	2	20	12	99	124	143	166
NDP	6.9%	11.0%	8.5%	15.7%	17.5%	18.2%	30.6%
	9	21	13	19	29	37	103
Bloc Québécois	13.5%	10.7%	10.7%	12.4%	10.5%	10.0%	6.0%
	54	44	38	54	51	49	4
Reform/Alliance	18.7%	19.4%	25.5%	—	—	—	—
	52	60	66	—	—	—	—
Green Party	—	—	—	4.3%	4.5%	6.8%	3.9%
	—	—	—	0	0	0	1
Others	3.6%	1.6%	2.2%	0.3%	1.0%	1.1%	1.0%
	1	1	0	1	1	2	0
Total valid votes	13,667,671	12,985,964	12,857,774	13,489,559	14,815,680	13,832,972	14,720,580
Total seats	295	301	301	308	308	308	308

Note:

*Columns may not add up to 100 per cent due to rounding.

**In 2003 the Progressive Conservative and Canadian Alliance parties merged to form the Conservative Party. The 2004 and 2006 election results for this party are reported at this line.

***Less than 0.1 per cent.

TABLE 9.1 | continued

| B. Percentage of Vote* and Candidates Elected by Party and Province, 2011 | | | | | | | |
Province	Liberal	Conservative	NDP	Green Party	Bloc Québécois	Others	Totals, Province
NL	37.9	28.4	32.6	0.9	—	—	215,874
	4	1	2	0			7
NS	28.9	36.7	30.3	4.0	—	—	451,330
	4	4	3	0			11
NB	22.6	43.9	29.8	3.2	—	—	388,437
	1	8	1	0			10
PEI	41.0	41.2	15.4	2.4	—	—	79,048
	3	1	0	0			4
Que.	14.2	16.5	42.9	2.1	23.4	—	3,798,430
	7	5	59	0	4		75
Ont.	25.3	44.4	25.6	3.8	—	—	5,531,288
	11	73	22	0			106
Man.	16.6	53.5	25.8	3.6	—	—	491,225
	1	11	2	0			14
Sask.	8.6	56.3	32.3	2.7	—	—	455,053
	1	13	0	0			14
Alta.	9.3	66.8	16.8	5.3	—	—	1,397,346
	0	27	1	0			28
BC	13.4	45.5	32.5	7.7	—	—	1,871,665
	2	21	12	1			36
Yukon, NWT, and Nunavut	26.4	36.4	27.7	9.2	—	—	39,881
	0	2	1	0			3
Totals, Party	2,783,175	5,832,401	4,508,474	576,221	889,788	130,521	14,720,580
	34	166	103	1	4	0	308

*Rows may not add up to 100 per cent due to rounding and the omission of candidates other than those of these five parties.

right-leaning Conservatives in Alberta and Ontario suggested that the future of the national party lay in this direction. In fact, the continued success of the Conservatives, culminating in a majority government in the 2011 general election, has proven that the Liberals can be replaced by the Conservatives the only true national party. Brokerage-style politics continues to be alive and well in Canadian politics.

A DIVIDED ELECTORATE: THE 2004, 2006, AND 2008 ELECTIONS

The 2004 Election

The 2003 merger of the Canadian Alliance and Progressive Conservative Party eliminated what many considered to be the conditions for permanent Liberal government in Canada. A united right could now make inroads in the Liberal stronghold of Ontario. There were reasons for opposition parties to feel optimistic when the 2004 election was called. In her annual report, the federal Auditor General, Sheila Fraser, had focused attention on what appeared to be inappropriate and probably unlawful misallocation of public dollars on advertising in Quebec. The Sponsorship Scandal, as it became known, exposed a network of shady dealings with and favouritism of Liberal operatives in Quebec. Money had gone to individuals and ad companies with little or nothing provided in exchange. This affair and subsequent investigation resulted in a sharp drop in Liberal support in Quebec and a corresponding boost in the popularity of the Bloc. The recently chosen Liberal leader, Prime Minister Paul Martin, attempted to distance himself from the scandal, but it cast a shadow and prevented the Liberals from achieving another majority government.

The new Conservative Party and the NDP also went into the 2004 election with new leaders. The stakes were different for these parties. In the case of the Conservatives, a breakthrough in Ontario was the goal. For the NDP, emergence from the near irrelevance that the party had experienced federally since the 1993 election was the objective. Both parties achieved their goals, but neither to the degree hoped for. The election produced Canada's first minority government in a quarter of a century. At one point, with opinion polls showing a steady deterioration in Liberal support in English Canada, it appeared that the Conservatives were on the cusp of sweeping into power with a minority government. However, a barrage of attack ads by the Liberals, which spoke of the Conservative "hidden agenda" to privatize health care, join American-led military ventures, and chip away at abortion rights, reinforced fears many voters held about the Conservatives.

The 2006 Election

Going into the 2006 campaign the polls placed the Liberals comfortably ahead of the Conservatives, but many voters were still undecided, ensuring that this, too, would be a campaign that would matter. The Liberals used a familiar strategy of relying on attack ads and tried to portray the Conservatives and their leaders as having a "hidden agenda" as they had done in 2004. The Conservatives countered with a disciplined campaign and a strategy of introducing a new policy promise each day. This placed the Liberals on the defensive, and the Conservatives were able to dominate the issue agenda and avoid the sorts of embarrassing and potentially damaging statements from candidates that had been used against them in previous campaigns. The Liberals saw their lead slip away. With significant gains in Ontario and a surprising breakthrough in Quebec, the Conservatives achieved a minority government.

The Conservative victory in 2006 was widely interpreted as a rightward shift in Canadian politics. However, several things suggest otherwise: the shift was not very large, as only 36 per cent of the electorate voted for Conservatives; Stephen Harper and his party were careful not to rely on ideologically polarizing language or messages; and the Liberals were handicapped by scandal and a widespread perception that they had become arrogant in power. The NDP increased both its share of the popular vote and its number of MPs back to levels that it had typically enjoyed before the party's collapse in the 1993 election.

The 2008 Election

The 2008 election failed to confirm this rightward shift. The Conservatives managed to increase their share of the popular vote by a couple of percentage points, mainly at the expense of sagging national support for the Liberal Party under the uncertain leadership of Stéphane Dion. The Bloc Québécois remained the dominant party in Quebec, denying the Liberals seats they had long counted on and preventing the Conservatives from capturing the seats that they needed to form a majority government. The centre-left of Canadian politics continued to be strong. But unlike the years before the 1993 election, the votes on the centre-left were distributed between the Liberals, NDP, the Bloc, and the Green Party. The Conservative Party controlled the centre-right of the political spectrum, but there did not appear to be enough votes in this electoral space to deliver the party a majority government.

REALIGNMENTS AND THE 2011 ELECTION

A **realignment** in a country's politics *occurs when an election or series of elections produces a durable change in the parties' bases of support*. In Canada, the 1896 election comes closest to deserving the realignment label, as French-Canadian Catholics, a voting bloc that had leaned toward the Conservative Party, shifted to the Liberals after the execution of the Métis leader Louis Riel and the selection of the francophone Wilfrid Laurier as the Liberal leader. The huge vote swings that occurred in 1958, when Quebecers shifted their support to the Conservative Party, and again in 1984, proved not to be durable, and were not realignments.

Canadian elections often produce changes in government, but only occasionally do they redraw the party map. The election of 1921 was one such case, when the Progressive Party, which had no seats in the House of Commons prior to the election, became the official opposition. By the 1926 election things were back to normal and the Liberal–Conservative duopoly in Canadian party politics had been re-established. The election of 1993, when the Conservative Party's support collapsed, and the Bloc Québécois and Reform Party surged into second and third place respectively was another case where the party map was dramatically redrawn.

No such surprises were expected when, on 26 March 2011, the fortieth Parliament was dissolved and an election was called. The conventional wisdom was that not very much was likely to change in the party standings. Most speculation involved whether the governing Conservative Party would manage to eke out a narrow majority this time. There were no clear issues dividing the parties and galvanizing voters, and another Conservative minority government was anticipated. Many thought that if this were to happen, the opposition parties would take the first opportunity to defeat the Conservatives in the House and install a coalition government.

And then, the unexpected happened. The election of 2 May 2011 was a jolting reminder that campaigns matter. No one predicted at the outset that the once mighty Liberal Party, Canada's "natural governing party," would fall to third place with the support of fewer than one out of five voters. Nor did anyone imagine that the NDP would vault into second place, winning more than twice as many seats as its previous election high of 43 in 1988 and doubling

Listen to "The 60/40 Country?" podcast, available at www.oupcanada.com/BrooksConcise.

its share of the popular vote. There were other surprises, including the startling almost total collapse of the Bloc in Quebec, and the emergence of NDP as Quebec's leading party, capturing 58 of the province's 75 seats.

Explanations for these seismic changes focused on two major factors: leadership and the Quebecers' apparent fatigue with the sovereignists and their goal of Quebec independence. The NDP leader, Jack Layton, was said to have caught the imagination of Canadians, including Quebecers, appearing confident, compassionate, and articulate—qualities some voters thought that he already showed in 2004, 2006, and 2008. But in 2011, his rivals for the centre-left vote, the Liberals' Michael Ignatieff and the Bloc's Gilles Duceppe, failed to connect with their usual supporters. The Conservatives won a clear majority nationally and the possibility of an NDP-led coalition melted away along with the last snow in the province of Quebec.

The 2011 election appeared to be all about change, but buried underneath the focus on the NDP surge, the Bloc collapse, and the Liberals' worst showing ever, there were two important

The public's perception of a political leader can be very difficult to change. Take a moment to think about the current leaders of Canada's main political parties. What three characteristics would you say are most strongly associated with each, and how do those characteristics influence how you feel about the party each leader represents?

elements of continuity. First, political issues appeared to take a back seat to the issues of leadership. As we saw earlier in this chapter, André Siegfried remarked upon this over 100 years ago—the tendency for Canadian elections to be contests between the parties' leaders rather than struggles between rival ideas and ideologies. It is not that ideas do not matter in Canadian elections, but rather that they become associated with and absorbed into voters' images of the party leaders.

Second, the election results demonstrated once again that Canada is a 60/40 country. In Canada, the balance of the electorate has tended to lean toward the centre-left of the Canadian political spectrum. The Conservative Party, the only party with a centre-right platform, won with about 40 per cent of the popular vote. The four centre-left parties, the Liberals being the most centrist of this group, together accounted for about 60 per cent of the vote. With the exception of the 1984 election, when the Conservatives won 50 percent of the popular vote, this has been the pattern for the past three decades. Otherwise the electorate has tended to divide ideologically on a 60/40 basis, with centre-left parties receiving the majority of the votes cast in these elections. In the eight elections from 1988 to 2011 the percentage of the vote received by centre-right parties has ranged between 29.6 per cent (2004) and 43 per cent (1988), averaging just over 37 per cent.

History will show whether the 2011 election results and the surge of the NDP is an actual realignment in the party system or a one-off affair. Some believe that victory for the left now requires that the centre-left parties unite, as the right united in the 2003 merger of the Canadian Alliance and the Progressive Conservative Party. While some prominent members of both the Liberal Party and the NDP have talked openly about a merger that would capitalize on the clustering of voters around the centre-left of the ideological spectrum, many Liberals and their supporters would be more comfortable under the Conservative Party banner than in a centre-left party that might be dominated by activists and supporters of the NDP. And as the dust settled after the 2011 election, it did not appear that a merger of any sort was imminent.

Selecting Party Leaders in Canada

When Wilfrid Laurier was chosen as the first French-Canadian leader of the Liberal Party in 1887, about 80 men did the choosing. They were the Liberal MPs in Canada's sixth Parliament. The rules for this leadership selection process were not written down in any formal document. It was simply understood that, following the British parliamentary tradition, it was the prerogative of caucus to choose who among its members would be the party leader.

When the Liberal Party of Canada chose Stéphane Dion as its new leader on 3 December 2006, 4605 delegates cast ballots. About 850 of them were *ex officio delegates*, men and women who because of their positions in the Liberal Party—including elected MPs and provincial legislators, senators, and party officials—automatically had the right to attend and vote at the party's leadership convention. All of these delegates cast their ballots on the final day of a five-day party convention that was covered on live television, choosing among a field of eight candidates. It took four ballots to select the party's new leader, following formal rules laid down in the 23-page Rules of Procedure for the 2006 Leadership and Biennial Convention.

INSIDE POLITICS

BOX 9.2 | Unite the Left?

"The lady doth protest too much, methinks." So says the Queen in Shakespeare's *Hamlet*, suggesting that the repeated protests of an actor whose performance she has just witnessed may in fact conceal exactly what she so insistently denies. Canadian politics is hardly the tragic drama that is *Hamlet*. But when former Ontario NDP leader and current Liberal MP Bob Rae was asked in June 2010 about rumours of high-level talks concerning a possible merger of the national NDP and Liberal Party, his categorical dismissal of such rumours sounded a bit like the lady's protests.

Whether or not party heavyweights had sat down in the same room to discuss the idea of a unite-the-left merger of the national Liberal Party and the NDP, the idea of such a marriage had been circulating since the 2006 election of the Conservative minority government. Former Liberal cabinet minister Lloyd Axworthy publicly

advocated such a merger after the 2008 election, arguing that it was necessary to defeat the Conservative Party led by Stephen Harper. Several former NDP politicians, including Roy Romanow, Ed Broadbent, and Lorne Calvert have spoken in support of the merger concept. No less a figure than former Liberal prime minister Jean Chrétien admitted in June 2010 to having had informal discussions with former NDP leader Ed Broadbent about ways of uniting the centre-left vote in order to defeat the Conservatives. And then there is the fact that the Liberals and the NDP, with the support of the Bloc, signed a formal agreement in 2008 to bring down the Conservative government on a confidence vote and support a Liberal government for an agreed period of time. Such an agreement was far from a merger, but it showed how desperate the parties were to find a way to dislodge the Conservatives from power, something that neither the Liberals

Not everyone, including some in the Liberal and NDP camps, is enthusiastic about the idea of a merger on the left. What do you see as the arguments for and against the Liberals and NDP uniting as a strategy for forming a federal government?

nor the NDP appeared capable of doing on their own at the polls.

On the face of it, a united left may appear to make sense. Axworthy, Broadbent, and others tirelessly point out that the Conservatives have governed since 2006 even though about 6 in 10 voters cast their ballots for candidates of parties further to the left. The bold and unpredicted decision of the British Conservative and Liberal-Democratic parties to form a coalition government after that country's May 2010 election seemed to make an inter-party merger in Canada a bit more credible, at least in the eyes of some.

So why don't the parties just merge? There are many reasons why such a step would neither be easy nor necessarily achieve the goals of those who advocate it. Here are three big ones:

- Some supporters of both the NDP and the Liberal Party hate the idea. Many NDP activists argue that it would pull their party away from what should be its proper left-wing agenda. From the Liberal side, not all activists and certainly not all Liberal voters are left of centre. Many are more comfortable with the ideas and

policies of the Conservatives than they are with those of the NDP.

- A merger of the parties cannot be achieved just because some leaders want it to happen. The parties operate under constitutions that require that their respective memberships be given a say in the matter, as happened in 2003 when the Canadian Alliance and Progressive Conservative parties merged to form the Conservative Party of Canada.
- Egos are at stake. Who would lead this new party? How would the career and leadership prospects of politicians and officials in the two parties be affected by a merger? Is their desire to defeat the Conservatives powerful enough for them to risk losing position and influence within their own party?

None of this means that a merger of the NDP and Liberal Party is impossible. Nor does it mean that some important people in the parties have not talked seriously about it. But the obstacles are huge and, even if overcome, there is no guarantee that the result would be the one that unite-the-left advocates would hope to see.

Shortly before the Liberals' 2006 leadership convention *Globe and Mail* columnist Jeffrey Simpson wrote a piece entitled "It's tough to be ahead."[19] And, indeed, in the wake of Michael Ignatieff's defeat and Stéphane Dion's unpredicted victory conventional wisdom quickly concluded that there are serious drawbacks to being the frontrunner. The scrutiny is more intense, the analysis and criticism of every word and action more unforgiving. Being an underdog, on the other hand, has the advantage of freeing a candidate from the media spotlight and, potentially, enabling him or her to profit from an "anybody-but-frontrunner-X" movement.

As plausible as all this sounds, it is also incorrect. If one looks at all the Conservative, Liberal, and NDP leadership conventions that required more than one ballot to choose the leader—16 in total—13 were won by the candidate who led on the first ballot. If there is a lesson to be drawn from the history of leadership conventions in Canada it is that there is a huge advantage to being the frontrunner heading into the convention vote.

Three Models for Selecting Party Leaders

The 2006 Liberal leadership convention involved a method for choosing party leaders that began in Canada in 1919. That year marked the transition from the *caucus model*, where party leaders were chosen by other elected MPs of their party, to the *convention model* (see Table 9.2). In some ways this transition was a simple product of circumstances. Wilfrid Laurier had called a national convention of the Liberal Party in 1919 to discuss policy at a time when the party was reduced to mainly Quebec representation in the House of Commons. Laurier died soon after the convention was called, and the party's national executive decided to use the Ottawa meeting as an opportunity to choose his successor. In doing so they were breaking new ground. In no other British-style parliamentary democracy were party leaders chosen in this manner. Presidential candidates in the United States were, of course, selected at conventions that brought together state delegations. In adopting the convention model for their party—a model that would also be followed by other Canadian parties—Liberals were aware of the American practice. But the Canadian convention model has always been different from the American one in important ways, from the process used to choose convention delegates to procedures on the convention floor.

Criticisms that the convention model was elitist and too easily dominated by money and backroom deal making were heard with increasing frequency after the 1960s. When the Reform Party began to choose its leaders through a direct vote of all party members the pressure on other parties to follow suit was difficult to resist. In 1997 the Bloc Québécois chose Gilles Duceppe as its leader using the *one member–one vote* (OMOV) model. The Progressive Conservative Party followed in 1998, choosing Joe Clark as its leader using the OMOV model, and today all parties except the Liberals use some variant of the OMOV model.

Whether the OMOV model produces better results than the caucus or convention is up for debate. The argument for OMOV is that it reduced the influence of elites within the party. Combined with limitations that all of the parties place on leadership campaign spending and the contribution limits and reporting requirements that have existed under Canadian law since 2004, this is expected to make leadership races more open.

Listen to the "Who Is Michael Ignatieff? What Our Leaders' Stories Say about Canadian Politics" podcast, available at www.oupcanada .com/BrooksConcise.

TABLE 9.2 | THREE MODELS OF LEADERSHIP SELECTION

Model	Participants	Procedures	Most Recent Federal Party Examples
1. Caucus Model	• Elected members (MPs)	Selection takes place behind closed doors without open competition between rival candidates.	• Liberals—Ignatieff in 2008 • Conservatives—Meighen 1941 • Bloc Québécois—Bouchard in 1990
2. Convention Model (Narrow)	• Party activists (narrow): Delegates to the leadership convention, elected by party members in their riding associations	Selection takes place at a party leadership convention, after several months of campaigning by candidates.	• Liberals—Dion 2006 • Conservatives—Mulroney in 1983 • NDP—McDonough in 2001 • Bloc Québécois—Bouchard in 1991
3. One Member–One Vote Model	• Party activists (broad) • Party members	Selection takes place by votes cast by party members. Some votes may take place at a fixed convention, but most votes are cast electronically elsewhere.	• Conservatives—Harper in 2004 • NDP—Layton in 2003 • Bloc Québécois—Duceppe in 1997

THE ELECTORAL SYSTEM AND ITS CONSEQUENCES

Many Canadians were shocked and even scandalized when George W. Bush was elected President of the United States in 2000, even though he received about one-half million fewer votes than Al Gore. What they did not realize is that such an outcome can happen and has happened in Canada. In 1979 the Liberal Party received about 4 per cent more of the popular vote than the Conservatives, but the Conservatives won 22 more seats and formed the government. Canadians who were scandalized by George W. Bush's victory in 2000 would do well to consider that Bush won a larger share of the eligible electorate than did Jean Chrétien's Liberal Party in the Canadian election of that same year. But no one seriously contested the legitimacy of Chrétien's victory.

There are many similar examples in Canadian federal and provincial elections of the electoral system not rewarding parties in *proportion* to their share of the popular vote. The Conservative Party garnered 39.6 per cent of the popular vote in the 2011 election and won 54 per cent of all seats in the House of Commons. Conversely, in the same election, the Bloc, with almost 6 per cent of the popular vote obtained in one province, Quebec, received less than 1 percent of the seats. In the same vein, the prize for apparent injustice was taken by the Green Party in the 2008 election when 6.8 per cent of the popular vote produced no seats in the House of Commons.

To understand what has happened in these elections, we must first describe the Canadian electoral system, whose principal features are the same at both the federal and provincial levels. It is based on the **single-member constituency**: *a system of electing representatives to legislatures in which each constituency (riding) gets one representative in the House of Commons (or provincial legislature)*. Canada has what some call a **plurality system** or a **first-past-the-post system,** *where the candidate who receives the most votes in a constituency election becomes the member of Parliament (or provincial legislature) for that constituency.* In other words, a majority of votes is not necessary for election and, given the fragmentation of votes between the three main parties, is the exception rather than the rule.

A political party's representation in the House of Commons depends, therefore, on how well its candidates fare in the 308 constituency races that make up a general election today. It regularly happens that the leading party's candidates may account for only about 40 per cent of the popular vote across the country and yet capture a majority of the seats in the Commons. Indeed, the advocates of the single-member, simple plurality electoral system point to this as the system's chief virtue. It manages, they claim, to transform something less than a majority of votes for a party into a majority of seats, thereby delivering stable majority government. However, the *winner-take-all* system's performance on this count has been rather mediocre: nine of the 18 general elections from 1957 to 2008 produced minority governments.

The **proportional representation** (PR) electoral system is the chief alternative to the single-member, plurality electoral system. PR is *a method of electing government representatives whereby a party's percentage of the popular votes translates into a corresponding share of seats in the legislature.* PR may sound eminently fair, but there are three significant criticisms:

1. PR promotes a splintering of the party system, by encouraging the creation of minor parties with narrow interests and by undermining the development of broad-based parties capable of bridging rivalries and differences.

2. PR is said to produce unstable government. The chances that any party will have a majority of seats is reduced, which necessitates the cobbling together and the maintaining of coalition governments. Inter-party deals may paralyze cabinet decision making, and elections, as illustrated in post–World War II Italy and Belgium, can be frequent. But the opposite is also true, as seen in the Netherlands and Germany.

3. PR electoral systems do tend to have more political parties than those with plurality systems, and the ideological distance between the extreme ends of the party spectrum will inevitably be greater than in plurality electoral systems such as Canada and the United States. As a result, PR systems can sometimes encourage ideological polarity and enable extremist parties to achieve representation in the legislature.

Canada's "winner-take-all" electoral system has its critics as well. In a classic analysis, Alan Cairns identifies several consequences that flow from the single-member, simple plurality system:[20]

- It tends to produce more seats than votes for the strongest major party and for minor parties whose support is regionally concentrated.
- It gives the impression that some parties have no or little support in certain regions, when in fact their candidates may regularly account for 15–30 per cent of the popular vote.
- The parliamentary composition of a party will be less representative of the different regions of the country than is that party's electoral support.
- Minor parties that appeal to interests distributed widely across the country will receive a smaller percentage of seats than votes.

Cairns concludes that the overall impact of Canada's electoral system has been negative. The system has, he argues, exacerbated regional and ethnolinguistic divisions in Canadian political life. There are many examples. For instance, the Conservative Party has been shut out in Quebec for most of the last century, which gives the impression that the Liberal Party was the only national party with support in French Canada. Cairns's article on the electoral system's effects was written in the late 1960s. If it were written today it would also mention distortions such as the gross under-representation of the Liberals in western Canada over the last couple of decades despite their receiving between one-quarter and one-third of western votes in most elections. As William Irvine observes, "the electoral system confers a spurious image of unanimity on provinces. By magnifying the success of the provincial vote leader, the electoral system ensures that party caucuses will over-represent any party's 'best' province."[21]

Along with the distortions that Canada's electoral system produces, another argument for reform is that the present system leaves many voters feeling disempowered and contributes to low levels of voter turnout. This view has become popular in recent years, and is reflected in what has become known as "strategic voting," whereby voters who do not support the frontrunner in their riding will cast their ballots not for the party or candidate of choice but for the party or candidate most able to defeat the frontrunner. This might be a compelling argument for reform of the electoral system, but those who study voting behaviour have been unable to find evidence that any significant number of Canadians vote strategically. On the

Democracy Watch

BOX 9.3 **First-Past-the-Post versus Proportional Representation**

Is it fair that a political party can form a majority government without winning the popular vote in an election? How efficient and productive is a government made up of many minority parties elected by proportion of their share of the popular vote?

These are two of the questions that arise when debating the pros and cons of the electoral systems a country can choose to implement. In Canada there is much debate about whether the first-past-the-post system is still the best way to form government, or if proportional representation is a better contemporary alternative. Let's recap the pros of each.

Pros of the First-Past-the-Post System

- Provides a clear choice for voters between major political parties
- Produces a single-party-rule government that is able to enact policy and legislation
- Produces a strong opposition to scrutinize the party in power (the official opposition)
- Prevents parties with narrow focus (and sometimes extreme views) from being represented in the legislature
- Encourages relationships between constituents and representatives based on geographical regions

Pros of Proportional Representation

- Encourages governments to compromise and build consensus, as the legislature is composed of voices from many parties instead of a single majority party
- Encourages diversity via the election of more minority and women representatives
- Makes it more likely that minority parties and independent candidates are represented
- Reduces the effects of "vote-splitting": a vote for a minority party in an area controlled by a majority party is not a "lost" vote
- Taps into a worldwide trend in democratic rule: most of the world's democracies use some form of proportional representation

Up for Debate

Would proportional representation be the best choice if Canada were to undertake election reform? Formulate your case for or against the country implementing this electoral system.

contrary, there appear to be many cases where labour groups have advocated such voting, without any indication that it works. Voter turnout in federal elections declined over the last several elections until 2006, reaching bottom at about 58 per cent of the eligible electorate in 2004. It rebounded to 65 per cent in 2006 but fell again to only 59 per cent in 2008. There is absolutely no definitive proof that people are deterred from voting because they think their vote will not make a difference in our current electoral system. There is stronger evidence that voter disillusionment with the choices on offer causes some to stay home on election day.

Irvine's point quoted above, that the electoral system tends to magnify the success of a province's most popular party and punish those parties whose share of the vote does not achieve some critical mass, has certainly been borne out by recent election results. Historically, the party standing to gain most from the replacement of Canada's electoral system by some form of proportional representation has been the CCF-NDP. It will be interesting, now that the NDP gained enough seats in the 2011 federal election to form the official opposition (33 per cent of the seats with 30.6 per cent of the popular vote), to see whether they will continue to champion electoral reform with some element of proportional representation.

Canadians probably will just have to live with the regionally divisive effects of the existing electoral system. The best hope for overcoming the negative consequences that Cairns, Irvine, and many others have pointed to may be reform of the Canadian Senate. An elected Senate whose members would be chosen according to some system of proportional representation within each province—so that a party's provincial share of Senate seats would be determined by its share of the popular vote in that province—could go some way toward compensating for the regional imbalance of parties' caucuses in the House of Commons. A Senate with greater legitimacy in the eyes of Canadians, and in which members felt free to vote on the basis of regional and other interests, free of the tight leash of party discipline, could be a step toward the better representation of the regions within the institutions of the national government. Little in our recent political history, and including Harper's 2011 foray into Senate reform, suggests that major reforms to the Senate are imminent. There are important obstacles to Senate reform in Canada; these include the reluctance of the major federal parties to encourage a serious institutional rival to the powers of the prime minister and the House of Commons.

VOTING BEHAVIOUR

When it comes to the voting behaviour of Canadians, few generalizations withstand the test of time. During the first couple of decades after Confederation, the Conservative Party did better than the Liberals among Catholics and French Canadians, but this changed after the 1885 execution of the Métis leader Louis Riel under a Conservative government and the 1887 selection of Wilfrid Laurier—a Catholic francophone from Quebec—as leader of the Liberal Party. For most of the following century the Liberal Party fared better than the Conservatives among francophones and Catholics, although their support among these groups temporarily weakened in the 1958 election and again in the 1984 and 1988 elections.

TABLE 9.3 | CANADIAN VOTER PARTICIPATION RATES OVER TIME

Election	Percentage of Voter Turnout
1988	75.3
1993	69.6
1997	67.0
2000	61.2
2004	60.5
2006	64.7
2008	59.1
2011	61.4

One of the criticisms of Canada's single-member, plurality electoral system is that it leaves many voters feeling disempowered and leads to low voter turnout. This table clearly shows that in the past eight general elections, voter participation has declined steadily, except for a slight increase in the 2011 election.

Source: Data compiled from Elections Canada

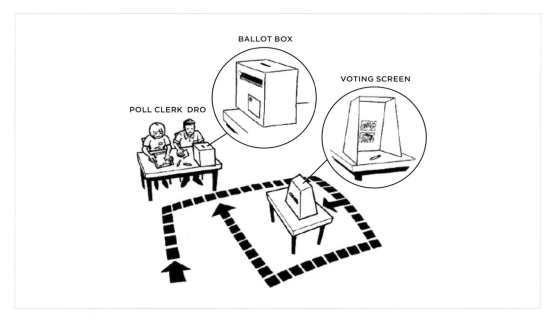

FIGURE 9.2 MAP FOR VOTERS ON ELECTION DAY

The tongue-in-cheek term "electile dysfunction" hints at the lack of excitement or engagement by the public on election day, leading many to stay away from the polls. Others believe that fear of the unknown could be another factor in low voter participation rates. One possible remedy for low voter turnout is a straightforward diagram, like this one, showing what a voter can expect on election day. Were you nervous the first time you had to vote? Would a diagram like this, showing exactly how the process unfolds, have helped you overcome your fears?

Source: Canada.com blog network: http://blogs.canada.com/2011/05/05/electile-dysfunction/

The West

Regionally, the Conservative Party began its long association with western voters in 1957 with the election of the Diefenbaker government. Conservative candidates outpolled Liberals in the West in most elections after 1957. This tendency was accentuated after the 1972 election, when the Liberal Party's western fortunes sank dramatically under the leadership of Pierre Trudeau and the region began to be regarded as mainly Conservative and NDP turf. The Reform Party, we have seen, became the vehicle for anti-Liberal resentment after many western voters became disappointed with the Conservative government of Brian Mulroney.

Quebec

Quebec was an electoral stronghold for the Liberal Party over most of the last century. But this association has been weakened since the emergence of the Bloc Québécois. The two-party competition between the Liberals and the Bloc between 1993 and 2004, and the continuing strong presence of the Bloc in subsequent elections, differentiated Quebec's situation from that

This cartoonist suggests that one of the greatest threats to Canadian democracy is low voter turnout. What strategies could improve voter turnout at the next federal election? What changes in the way elections campaigns are run can you suggest to better engage voters, particularly young people?

of the rest of Canada. The Bloc has outpolled the Liberals in five of the six general elections since 1993, and in 2006 a resurgent Conservative Party received more votes in Quebec than the Liberals and only two percentage points fewer in 2008, although winning fewer seats in both elections. The Quebec voting pattern was disrupted once again with the NDP winning most of the Quebec seats in the 2011 election, and the Bloc losing all but two of its 47 seats.

Class

In regard to social class, differences between voters for the Liberal and Conservative parties have never been very great and certainly have been less important than regional and ethno-linguistic differences. The NDP's formal affiliation with organized labour might have been expected to reflect a preference among working-class Canadians for that party. But class has never been a particularly strong political identity for most Canadians. Electoral studies carried out since the 1960s have shown that NDP support generally is stronger among voters who belong to unions than among most other segments of the electorate.

Gender and Rural/Urban Split

Two of the most widely accepted claims about the differences between Liberal and Conservative supporters are (1) women are less likely than men to prefer the Conservative Party and (2) urban Canadians prefer the Liberals while rural voters tend to favour the Conservatives. As Figure 9.3 indicates, the female vote was fairly evenly divided between the Liberals and Conservatives in 2006 (as it also was in 2004), but male voters were significantly more likely to have voted Conservative. Urban voters were evenly divided between the Liberals and Conservatives in 2006, with slightly more voting Liberal in 2004, but rural voters were much more likely to have voted Conservative.

This claim about the supposed rural/urban divide in Canadian politics seemed to hold true in the 2006 election. As evidence of this, the pundits—including many political scientists—pointed out that the Liberals did well in Toronto, Montreal, and Vancouver, while the Conservatives did not win a single seat from these three cities and received slightly fewer than half the number of votes cast for their Liberal rivals.[22]

In their rush to be interesting and insightful, pollsters, pundits, and political scientists sometimes allow sloppiness to creep into their analysis. It is not true that Canada's largest urban centres were unsympathetic to the Conservative Party in 2006. For example, the cities of Halifax, Calgary, Edmonton, Winnipeg, Ottawa, Hamilton–Burlington, and Waterloo–Kitchener–Cambridge all elected Conservative MPs. And of the three cities cited as proof of urban Canada's hostility to the Conservatives, the case of Montreal, arguably, had far more to do with language and a decades-old history of voting Liberal than it did with the urban condition. The idea that the conditions and demographics of big cities cause the values and partisan preferences of their residents to be significantly different from those who live in less urbanized settings seems reasonable and is certainly interesting, but the 2008 and 2011 elections put an end to this argument about urban hostility to the Conservative Party.

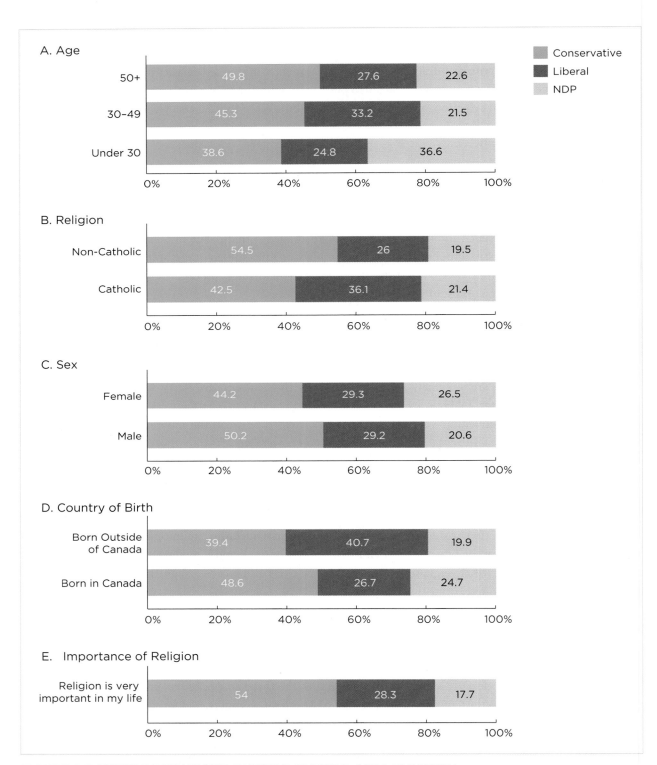

FIGURE 9.3 VOTING BEHAVIOUR OUTSIDE QUEBEC, 2008 ELECTION

Source: Data compiled from Elections Canada. Many thanks to Professor Lydia Miljan for generating these cross-tabulations.

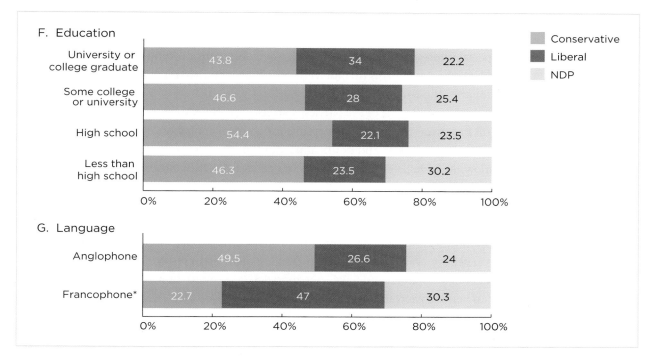

FIGURE 9.3 **continued**

PARTY FINANCES AND SPECIAL INTERESTS

Throughout their history, the Liberal and Conservative parties have relied heavily on corporate contributors to finance their activities. The NDP, by contrast, has depended mainly on contributions from individuals and on the financial support of affiliated trade unions. Corporate donations to the national NDP have always been minuscule.

It is difficult to attach precise numbers to party finances before 1974, for the simple reason that parties were not legally required to disclose their sources of revenue. A study done by Khayyam Paltiel for the federally appointed Royal Committee on Election Expenses (1966) estimated that, before the 1974 reforms, the older parties depended on business contributions for between 75 and 90 per cent of their incomes.[23] Not only were the Liberals and Conservatives dependent on business for all but a small share of their revenue, but most of this corporate money was collected from big businesses in Toronto and Montreal.[24]

Passage of the *Election Expenses Act, 1974* signalled a watershed in Canadian party finance. The Act included spending limits for individual candidates and political parties during election campaigns, changes to the Broadcasting Act requiring radio and television stations to make available to the parties represented in the House of Commons both paid and free broadcast time during election campaigns,[25] and a system of reimbursement for part of their expenses for candidates who receive at least 15 per cent of the popular vote. This last reform had the effect of subsidizing the three main parties at taxpayer expense, a consequence that can only be defended on the grounds that this public subsidy helps to weaken parties' financial dependence on special interests. As we will see below, the public subsidization of political parties was taken much further by reforms that took effect in 2004, and then removed by the Conservative government after the 2011 federal election.

But from the standpoint of the parties' sources of income, the most important reforms of the Election Expenses Act involved tax credits for political contributions and public disclosure requirements for candidates and political parties. On the first count, changes to the Income Tax Act allow individuals or organizations to deduct from their taxable income a percentage of their donation to a registered political party or candidate, up to a maximum tax credit of $650. Since 2007 the maximum amount that an individual may donate to a political party or candidate is $1,100 and the maximum tax credit is for a donation of $1,275. Second, since 2004 the law requires much more transparency in the parties' reporting of their annual and election campaign expenditures: parties and candidates are required to provide the chief electoral officer with a list of all donors who have contributed $200 or more in money or services in kind, as well as an itemized account of their expenditures.

Perhaps the most striking consequence of the 1974 reforms was the increase in the importance of donations by individuals. These contributions were always the mainstay of NDP finances. Spurred by the tax credit for political donations and the older parties' adoption of sophisticated direct-mail techniques of fundraising, contributions by individuals became a major source of income for all three political parties. In fact, contributions from individuals exceeded business contributions to both the PC and Liberal parties in many of the years after the tax credit came into effect. The same was true of candidates' revenue. The Reform Party/Canadian Alliance relied overwhelmingly on contributions from individuals, as did the Bloc Québécois. Figures 9.4 and 9.5 show the chief sources of revenue and expenditures in the 2008 general election.

Nevertheless, corporate donations continued to be a tremendously important source of revenue for the older parties. And NDP candidates received very little from corporate donors, but depended heavily on trade union contributions. The most important consequence of special-interest contributions to parties and individual politicians was almost certainly the access to policy makers it bought for contributors. Although cases of influence peddling came to light from time to time, it was usually erroneous to think of political contributions as payments offered in the expectation of receiving some particular favour. There were, no doubt, instances where firms that relied on government contracts for some part of their revenue, or that hoped to receive government business in the future, found it prudent to donate money to parties or candidates. But for most corporate contributors to the two older parties, there was no expectation of a specific quid pro quo.

So why did they bother? One explanation is that corporate political donations represented a sort of insurance premium. As the late Conservative strategist and political adviser Dalton Camp put it:

> For the wise donor, the financing of the political system may very well be a duty and an obligation to the system, but it is, as well, insurance against the unlikely—such as the ascendancy of socialism—or against occasional political aberration,

a Walter Gordon budget, say, or a Carter report on tax reform [both perceived to be anti-business policies]. When such contingencies arise, the price for access is modest indeed.[26]

In addition to helping finance a party system that is generally congenial to business interests, it was long understood that donations helped buy access. In the words of Dalton Camp: "Toronto money merely maintains access to the parties, keeping open essential lines of communication, corporate hotlines, so to speak, to the right ears at appropriate times."[27] In any given year about half of the largest 100 industrial firms in Canada did not even contribute to either of the two older parties. It would be ridiculous to conclude that their lack of generosity cut them off from direct access to political decision makers. But all things being equal, contributions probably opened the door a bit wider.

The link between party contributions and access became more controversial with the increasing prominence of *paid-access opportunities*: fundraising events such as dinners and cocktail parties where, for an admission price up to several thousand dollars, donors could rub shoulders with party leaders and possibly also members of the government. Money and the invitation list obviously act as filters in determining who can participate in such events.

These events have been supplemented by an American invention—special clubs for large contributors. For an individual contribution, a donor receives the chance to meet with important politicians. The Progressive Conservative Party was the first to establish this sort of exclusive donor network in Canada, the "500 Club," which has been succeeded by the Conservative Party's Leader's Circle. Membership costs $1,000. The national Liberal Party also has this sort of paid-admission elite network through its Laurier Club. Admission to the club costs $1,100—half that amount for those under 35. Donations buy the privilege of invitations to exclusive meetings with party leaders, opportunities that are particularly valuable when that party forms the government and the party leader is the prime minister. It must be said that since the entry bar was set much lower with the 2004 reforms to the Canada Elections Act, these special donor clubs are now less exclusive than they were.

Of course, paid-access opportunities raises ethical questions. At what point does the ability to pay for access to political decision makers subvert the democratic process, by favouring those with the money? Parties need funds to carry out their activities. Even with a tax credit for political contributions, only a small portion of all Canadian taxpayers contribute to parties or candidates. Paid-access opportunities represent the parties' search for stable sources of funds.

One alternative would be to impose severe restrictions on how much money parties can spend, so that individual contributions and the subsidies that candidates receive from the reimbursement provision of the Election Expenses Act would be sufficient.

Another alternative, one widely used in Western European democracies, is to increase the public subsidies that parties receive, which frees them from dependence on contributions from special interests. This is the model that Canada adopted in 2004. The major elements of the post-2004 model for party and campaign financing in Canada include:

- Donations by special interests, including corporations and trade unions, are banned.
- Individuals may donate up to $1,100 per year to a registered political party or candidate.

- Parties receive an annual public subsidy of $1.75 for every vote that they receive.
- Third parties—organizations and individuals other than registered political parties and their candidates—may spend no more than $172,050 in total, and no more than $3,441 in any single electoral district, on political advertising during an election.
- Candidates for the leadership of registered political parties must identify those who donate to their campaigns and, as of April 2006, no individual may contribute more than $5,400 in total to the contestants in any party leadership campaign. Corporate or union donations are not permitted. The amount that leadership candidates may spend on their campaigns is set by the parties, not by Canadian law.

Shortly after its re-election in 2008 the minority Conservative government rather imprudently proposed the abolition of this public subsidy system—"imprudently" because this proposal was important in galvanizing the opposition parties' resolve to try to bring down the government at the first possible opportunity. Only the Conservative Party's finances were in good shape at the time, owing to its superior ability to raise private contributions. The Conservative government discovered the truth of the old adage that it is unwise to kick a dog that is already down. But after the 2011 federal elections, the majority Conservative government finally abolished the public subsidy system.

There are restrictions on spending by political parties, groups, or individuals during periods other than elections. As a result, considerable money is spent on fundraising, polling, consultants, and pre-campaign advertising before an election is called. A clear example of such non-election advertising is the extensive negative ad campaign that the Conservatives launched as soon as Stéphane Dion was chosen as the Liberal leader, portraying Dion as indecisive and without leadership qualities. A similar negative campaign was also waged by the Conservative party against Michael Ignatieff almost immediately after he was chosen to replace Dion in late 2008. Some argue that this type of pre-campaign spending undermines the intent of the 2004 reforms. Certainly, the Conservatives' attack ads undermined both Dion's and Ignatieff's image among the Canadian public. Others maintain that the ability to spend money in order to craft a political message and communicate it to citizens is a basic democratic right that is already unjustifiably limited by these reforms. Whether legislation that restricts spending on political communications between election campaigns would be upheld by the courts is difficult to say. But as we saw in Chapter 6 in regard to the *Harper v. Canada* (2004) ruling by

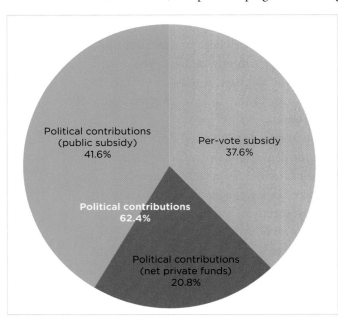

FIGURE 9.4 PRIMARY SOURCES OF PUBLIC AND PRIVATE FUNDING OF THE FEDERAL POLITICAL PARTIES IN 2009

Source: Data from Elections Canada

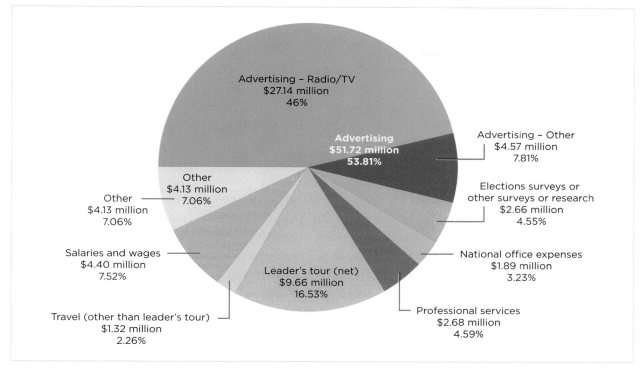

FIGURE 9.5 BREAKDOWN OF PAID ELECTION EXPENSES BY CATEGORY, 2008 GENERAL ELECTION

Source: Data from Elections Canada

the Supreme Court, the majority of Canada's top justices take the view that unequal spending power undermines the equality of citizens and skews the political conversation toward the interests and values of those with deep pockets.

Regardless of one's views on the rights implications of the 2004 *Harper* ruling, the fact remains that wealthier parties, candidates, private organizations, and individuals are able to purchase better-quality media advertising, and more of it. Given this potential for unequal access to the media, some believe that governments need to regulate who may purchase political advertising, when they may do so, and how much they may spend.

Some European democracies, such as France and Germany, ban paid political advertising on television and radio. Conversely, in the United States, efforts to introduce laws that would limit campaign spending on advertising are seen as a violation of the First Amendment's guarantee of free speech. Canada falls between these positions. Since the mid 1970s Canadian law has empowered the CRTC, Canada's telecommunications regulator, to require television and radio broadcasters to provide a certain amount of air time to registered political parties for their ads during election campaigns. As explained above, campaign spending by so-called "third parties" is sharply limited by Canadian election law. Federal law also limits the amount of money that registered political parties and their candidates may spend during campaigns, thus placing a ceiling on the amount of advertising a party can purchase. The communication activities of political parties via the Internet remain, so far, unregulated.

SUMMARY

Whether or not one lives in a democracy, political parties allow for the aggregation and the articulation of certain interests within the political system. And as we have seen, political parties offer voters a slate of candidates to choose from at election time. However, to paraphrase Eugene Forsey, in a democracy, people voluntarily join these political associations and participate in their activities because they share similar values and hold similar views about the role of government.

The origins of Canada's two major political parties—the Conservatives and the Liberals—can be traced back to the shifting coalitions and alignments in the United Province of Canada in the 1840s and 1850s. During this time, patronage appears to have played an important role in party politics. Mainstream political parties in Canada have traditionally avoided ideological and inflexible policy positions in favour of an adaptable, centrist style of politics. Our historically dominant parties have displayed certain characteristics that are not typical of other democracies: they are flexible and opportunistic, they tend to be dominated by their leaders, and they are wary of ideological appeals to the electorate.

For three generations Canada had what was often referred to as a two and one-half party system: two dominant brokerage parties competing to form a government and the CCF-NDP steadily winning enough votes and enough seats in the House of Commons to occasionally hold the balance of power during minority governments. In what some have called a "realignment election," the two and one-half party model fell apart in the 1993 election with the emergence of the Bloc Québécois as the official opposition. Another realignment appeared to take place in the 2011 federal election, when the Bloc lost all but two seats in the House of Commons and the NDP replaced the Liberal party as the official opposition.

Critics argue that our *single-member, simple plurality* electoral system has distorted political representation in our legislatures. It rewards the single-most popular party, as well as parties with regionally concentrated support, and it does not reward minor parties whose support is wide but not deep. Defenders of the system argue that it tends to produce stable majority governments. They also point to what they see as the faults of the alternative model: proportional representation.

Prior to the Election Expenses Act, 1974, there appears to have been little transparency, and most of the major parties' money came from big business. The NDP depended on union contributions and was the only party to receive many relatively small contributions from individuals. The Election Expenses Act, along with simultaneous changes to the Income Tax Act resulted in more transparency, tax credits, and paid and free broadcast time during campaigns. Although all parties increased their number of and their dependence on individual contributions after the 1974 reforms, the Liberal and Conservative parties remained largely dependent on corporate money, and the NDP on union contributions.

In the 2004 reforms to the Election Expenses Act, public subsidies were given to all of the parties based on the results of the previous election and private donations were strictly limited. There were also limits on spending by "third parties," groups that are not registered political parties, during election campaigns and limits on contributions to the contestants in party leadership campaigns. Paid-access opportunities to party leaders continue to be a source of income for parties, and raise the ethical question of whether wealth provides better access to politicians and governments.

STARTING POINTS FOR RESEARCH

R. Kenneth Carty and Munroe Eagles, *Politics Is Local: National Politics at the Grassroots* (Toronto: Oxford University Press, 2005).

William Cross, ed., *Political Parties, Representation, and Electoral Democracy in Canada* (Toronto: Oxford University Press, 2002).

Alain-G. Gagnon and Brian A. Tanguay, eds., *Canadian Parties in Transition*, 3rd edn (Toronto: University of Toronto Press, 2007).

Hans Michelmann, Donald Story, and Jeffrey Steeves, eds, *Political Leadership and Representation in Canada: Essays in Honour of John C. Courtney* (Toronto: University of Toronto Press, 2007).

John Pammett and Christopher Doran, eds, *The Canadian Election of 2006* (Toronto: Dundurn Press, 2006).

CBC ARCHIVES AND TVO'S *THE AGENDA*

Visit the companion website for *Canadian Democracy: A Concise Introduction* to follow links to audio and video footage related to the main themes of the chapter: www.oupcanada.com/BrooksConcise.

RELEVANT WEBSITES

Visit the companion website for *Canadian Democracy: A Concise Introduction* to browse a collection of websites featuring material related to the key themes of the chapter, an excellent starting point for research.

REVIEW EXERCISES

1. Using data available at the website of Elections Canada (www.elections.ca) for the last general election, look up the number of votes and percentage of the vote received by each political party across the country. Then calculate the number of seats each party would have received under a straight proportional representation system. Compare these results to the outcome in our first-past-the-post electoral system and draw some conclusions.

2. Visit the websites of two political parties represented in the House of Commons and compare the depth and breadth of information provided about each party's history, current leader, and present policies.

3. Debate which model shown in Table 9.2 is best for choosing a party leader.

Interest Groups

Politics does not stop between elections; much of the effort to influence the actions of government is channelled through interest groups. In this chapter we examine their characteristics and the role they play in Canadian politics. After reading this chapter, you will be able to

1. Define and identify "interest group," "lobbying," and "lobbyist"
2. Explain the role of interest groups in a democracy
3. Outline strategies for interest-group success
4. Examine the perspectives and biases of interest groups as well as the biases of the interest-group system
5. Explain the impact of federalism on interest groups

While elections are democracy's showpiece, the influence of elections on government is usually blunt and indirect. Policies are more likely to be determined by forces within the state, and by organized groups outside of it, than by elections. Indeed, special interests often seem to dominate the policy-making process in democracies. Their attempts to influence government are unremitting; their resources are impressive; and their access to policy makers is sometimes privileged. The influence of voters seems feeble in comparison.

Interest groups (or **pressure groups**) are *private organizations that promote their interests by trying to influence government rather than seeking the election of candidates to manage it*.[1] They arise from a basic fact of social life, the diversity in the interests and values of human beings. This diversity, in turn, gives rise to what James Madison called **political factions**: *groups of citizens whose goals and behaviour are contrary to those of other groups or to the interests of the community as a whole*.[2] If these factions or special interests appear to overshadow the public interest in democracies, there is a simple explanation: the tug of one's *personal interests*—as a teacher, farmer, or postal worker—tends to be felt more keenly than the nebulous concept of *public interest*. Arguments that appeal to interests such as consumer benefits or economic efficiency are unlikely to convince the farmer whose income is protected by the quotas and prices set by a marketing board. But economic interests are not the only factionalism in politics. Group characteristics like gender, ethnicity, and language may also provide the basis for the political organization of interests.

Economically based or not, interest groups are distinguished by the fact that they seek to promote goals that are not shared by all members of society. Paradoxically, however, their success in achieving these goals often depends on their ability to associate their efforts with the broader public interest.

CHARTING THE TERRITORY

The world of interest groups is characterized by vastness and variety. Although no unified reliable list of interest groups exists for Canada or any other democracy some idea of the sheer number may be had from a source like the directory *Associations Canada*.[3] In its 2009 edition, it lists some 20,000 organizations. some of which would not meet the criteria of "attempting to influence government." While many groups focus on non-political activities, several thousand regularly or occasionally perform political functions for their members.

Almost every imaginable interest is represented by an organization. There are several hundred women's associations across Canada, close to 1000 environmental groups, over 2000 business associations, perhaps 500 organizations representing agricultural interests, about 200 that focus on Aboriginal issues[4]—the range of organized interests and the sheer number of groups within each general category of interests are enormous. These figures do not include transitory groups that emerge briefly around a single issue. Nor do they include international organizations that may attempt to influence Canadian governments.

While it is impossible to say exactly which associations qualify as interest groups, no doubt many of them are politically active. One way to get a sense of this activity is to look at the list of groups that make representations to a legislative body or a government-sponsored commission. For example, well over 1000 groups made representations and submitted briefs to the Royal Commission on Aboriginal Peoples in six months of public hearings (1993). And the Commission on the Future of Health Care in Canada received submissions from 429 groups and associations during its public consultation phase (2001).

Alternatively, one may look at the composition of some politically active organizations. The Canadian Labour Congress is the umbrella organization for hundreds of unions, including provincial and federal federations of labour and 137 district labour councils that together represent about 3 million workers. The Canadian Chamber of Commerce, one of whose main functions is to influence government policies, represents over 500 community and provincial chambers of commerce and boards of trade, as well as close to 100 trade and professional associations and many international organizations.

THE BIAS OF THE INTEREST-GROUP SYSTEM

Obviously, some interest groups are more influential than others, but which are the most powerful and why? Is the interest-group system biased "in favour of a fraction of a minority"? Some, such as E.E. Schattschneider, claim that the interest-group system (the "pressure system") has a business and upper-class bias. "The notion that the pressure system is automatically representative of the whole community is a myth. . . . The system is skewed, loaded and unbalanced in favor of a fraction of a minority."[5]

Schattschneider observed about American politics in the early 1960s that business associations made up the single largest group of organized interests in American society; they were far more likely to lobby government and spend more money on attempting to influence policy makers than other interest groups. Moreover, Schattschneider's research demonstrated that "even non-business organizations reflect an upper-class tendency."[6] Persons with higher incomes and/or education were more likely to belong to organized groups than those lower down the socio-economic ladder. He explained that the business and upper-class bias of interest-group politics is a product of superior resources and of the relatively limited size and exclusive character of these special interests. "Special-interest organizations," he argued, "are most easily formed when they deal with small numbers of individuals [or corporations] who are acutely aware of their exclusive interests."[7] This awareness of special interests that are vital to one's material well-being or the well-being of one's organization is characteristic of trade associations like the Canadian Association of Petroleum Producers, or a more broadly based business organization like the Canadian Manufacturers & Exporters. It also characterizes producer and occupational groups like the Quebec Dairy Council and the Ontario Medical Association, but is less likely to characterize organizations that represent more general interests.

Most social scientists and political journalists agree with Schattschneider. Charles Lindblom argues that business occupies a "privileged position" in the politics of capitalist societies. In his book *Politics and Markets*,[8] Lindblom attributes this pre-eminence to business's superior financial resources and lobbying organization, greater access than other groups to government officials, and, most important, propagandistic activities that—directly through political advertising and indirectly through commercial advertising—reinforce the ideological dominance of business values in society.

One of the reasons most cited for the political superiority of business interests is the *mobility of capital*. Investors enjoy a significant amount of freedom to shift their capital between economic sectors and from one national economy to another. Transnational corporations, for instance, are organizations that span a number of national economies and often use their ability to move capital internationally as a lever in dealing with governments. In addition to being territorially mobile, investment capital also can expand or contract in response to investors' perceptions of the political-economic climate for business. Governments in capitalist societies tend to be aware of the levels of *business confidence* and are reluctant to take actions that might cause reduced investment or flight of capital. Politicians need to care about business confidence because of the very real possibility that they will not be re-elected if business's unwillingness to invest causes unemployment, falling incomes, and, in turn, popular dissatisfaction.[9]

Another factor that concerns governments is the state's financial dependence on business. A decline in the levels of investment profit is often felt as a drop in government revenues from corporate taxes, employment income taxes, payroll taxes, and consumption taxes. The problem of falling revenues is likely to be compounded by increased state expenditures on social programs, whose costs are sensitive to the levels of economic activity. Borrowing on the public credit is only a temporary solution. This can be both costly and subject to the confidence of international investors, who also influence the cost of borrowing.

No one would argue that business interests "win" all of the time. Nevertheless, theorists note that there has been a tendency to favour business interests over others because of the characteristics of capitalist societies. This is one of the few propositions about politics that cuts across the ideological spectrum. There are, however, dissenters. Some are likely to view business interests as being simply one set of interests in a sea of competing interest-group claims on government.[10]

Business historian Michael Bliss argues that whatever privileged access business people may have enjoyed in the corridors of political power had largely disappeared by the 1980s. "Groups with powerful vested interests," he writes, "including trade unions, civil servants, tenured academics, and courtesanal cultural producers, perpetuated a hostility toward business enterprise rooted in their own fear of competition on open markets."[11]

David Vogel argues that, on balance, "business is more affected by broad political and economic trends than it is able to affect them."[12] Although Vogel focuses on the United States, he develops a more general argument about the political power of business interests in capitalist democracies. Vogel says that popular opinion and the sophistication of interest groups are the key to understanding the political successes and failures of interest groups. He argues that business's ability to influence public policy is greatest when the public is worried about the economy and weakest when the economy is producing jobs and higher incomes.

The political organization of business interests is the second key to understanding the ebb and flow of business influence. Vogel maintains that the victories of environmental, consumer, and other public interest groups in the 1960s and 1970s were largely due to their ability to read the Washington map and work the levers of congressional and media politics. Business interests, by comparison, were poorly organized and amateurish. Today, in spite of very effective mobilization by business, divisions within the business community have generally checked its influence.

Another factor that has prevented business interests from dominating politics is what James Q. Wilson has called "entrepreneurial politics."[13] This involves the ability of politicians and interest groups to identify issues around which popular support can be mobilized in opposition to business interests. The opportunities for entrepreneurial politics are fewer in Canada than in the United States because of the tighter party discipline in Canada's legislature. Entrepreneurial politics is, however, practised by interest groups such as People for the Ethical Treatment of Animals (PETA) and Equality for Gays and Lesbians Everywhere (EGALE). Astute use of the media and adept packaging of a group's message so as to generate public awareness and support for its goals are essential to entrepreneurial politics.

Do business groups hold the higher ground in capitalist societies, or are their chances of victory the same as other interest groups? The conclusion reached by recent work on Canadian interest groups, what Paul Pross calls the *post-pluralism* (also called the *neo-institutionalist*) approach, suggests that neither view is accurate.

This approach is based on the observation that policy making generally involves the participation of a limited set of state and societal actors, a **policy community** that is centred on a sub-government; i.e., ***that set of state institutions and interest groups usually involved in making and implementing policy in some field***. Whether or not a group is part of the policy

PETA is known for evocative protests designed to mobilize popular public support. In this July 2010 protest, a participant is covered in red body paint to represent the blood shed during the annual seal cull in the Arctic. Have your opinions on a controversial issue ever been swayed by an interest group's message?

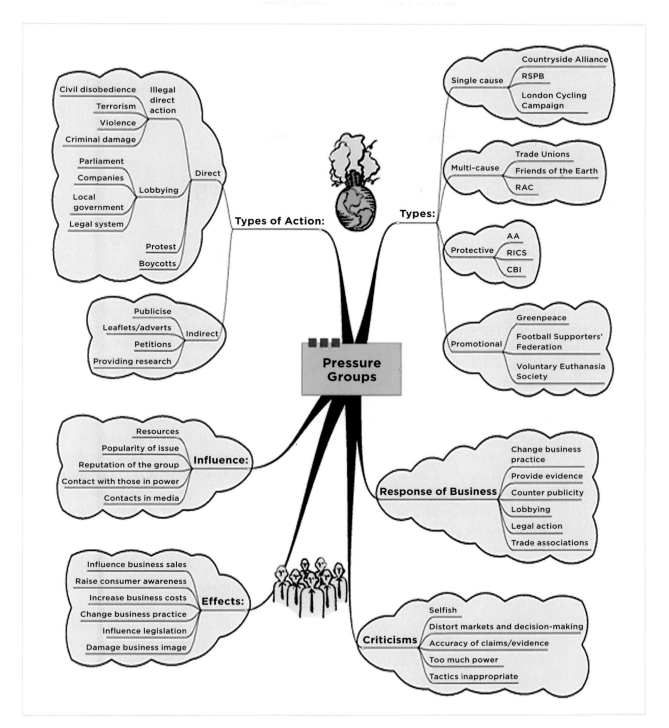

FIGURE 10.1 INTEREST GROUP MIND MAP

This mind map helps us understand just how complicated interest groups' activities and their consequences can be.

Source: Biz/Ed, http://www.bized.co.uk/educators/16-19/business/external/presentation/pressure1_map.htm

community, and its level of influence, depend on the particular policy field and on the configuration of interests in that community. Moreover, neo-institutionalists tend to emphasize the capacity of state actors to act independently of the pressures and demands placed on them by societal interests. This capacity will vary across policy sectors. But the bottom line of the neo-institutionalist approach is that state actors in some policy communities may be well able to resist the societal pressures as well as those from highly organized, well-financed business interests.

ANALYTICAL PERSPECTIVES ON INTEREST GROUPS

Pluralism Approach

In the pluralism approach, or group theory, organized interests are seen as the central fact of political life; this approach explains politics chiefly in terms of the activities of groups. It is a societal explanation of politics in that it locates the main causes of government action in the efforts and activities of voluntary associations, such as trade associations, labour unions, and churches, outside the state. Pluralist theory draws two main conclusions about the role and character of the state in democratic societies. First, the state itself is a sort of group interest— an assortment of different interests associated with various components of the state. Second, in spite of possible interests of its own, the state's chief political function is to ratify the balance of group interests in a society, and to enforce the policies that embody this balance of power. As Earl Latham put it: "The legislature referees the group struggle, ratifies the victories of the successful coalition, and records the terms of the surrenders, compromises, and conquests in the form of statutes."[14]

The purest embodiment of group theory is found in the work of Arthur Bentley, who argues that society can be understood only in terms of the groups that it comprises. He views government as a process of "groups pressing one another, forming one another, and pushing out new groups and group representatives (the organs or agencies of government) to mediate the adjustments."[15] This is an extremely reductionist approach. Other pluralists following Bentley,[16] while aware of the danger of squeezing too much explanation out of a single cause, have remained faithful to two basic elements of pluralist theory: one *empirical* and the other *normative*. The empirical element is the claim that politics is a competitive process where power is widely distributed, there is no dominant elite or class, and the interaction of organized interests outside the state is the chief force behind the actions of government. The normative element suggests that the outcome of this competitive struggle represents the public interest, and that this is the only reasonable way of understanding the public interest in democracy.

Pluralism begat *neo-pluralism*. The neo-pluralist assault took issue with both the empirical and normative claims of group theory. Writers like E.E. Schattschneider, Theodore Lowi, and Charles Lindblom showed that the interest-group system was much less open and competitive than argued by earlier pluralists. For example, Lowi argued "Interest group liberalism seeks pluralistic government, in which there is no formal specification of means or of ends. In pluralistic government there is therefore no substance. Neither is there procedure. There is only process."[17] Pluralists are also accused of misunderstanding the true character of political power. By focusing on group competition, their critics argue, pluralists are inclined to see political life as relatively open and competitive because they observe struggles between groups and the decisions of governments. But as Bachrach and Baratz suggest, "power may be, and often is, exercised by confining the scope of decision-making to relatively 'safe' issues."[18] Choosing not to make decisions, and to keep issues unformulated and off the public agenda, is a form of power. From this angle, the interest-group system appears much less competitive.

If special interests are, as pluralism theory suggests, a basic fact of political life, what does this cartoonist seem to be saying about the public's appetite for a system built to serve such groups?

Class Analysis Approach

Interest groups are discussed in the class analysis approach, but they are not as important as the class interests these groups are argued to represent. Some of the major works of contemporary Marxist scholarship do not even mention interest groups.[19] In Canada, in the class analysis approach, which is generally referred to as "political economy,"[20] interest groups are sometimes ignored entirely in preference for such categories as class fractions within subordinate and dominant classes. This is not to say that organized interests are denied or ignored entirely. Ralph Miliband's *The State in Capitalist Society* attempted to refute the pluralist model. He observes:

> Democratic and pluralist theory could not have achieved the degree of ascendancy which it enjoys in advanced capitalist society had it not at least been based on one plainly accurate observation about them, namely that they permit and even encourage a multitude of groups and associations to organize openly and freely and to compete with each other for the advancement of such purposes as their members may wish.[21]

Some of the Canadian political economy literature includes examples of how class analysis can coexist with a careful analysis of interest groups. Wallace Clement's *The Challenge of*

Class Analysis[22] and Rianne Mahon's study of Canada's textile industry fall into this category. Clement examines the complex network of unions, co-operatives, and associations in Canada's coastal fisheries in order to, in his words, "lend understanding to the material basis of class struggle."[23] In *The Politics of Industrial Restructuring*, Mahon develops an analysis of trade associations and labour unions in the textile sector, in terms of the fundamental class interests they represent, the organizational capacity of these interests, and their ideological characteristics.[24]

From the perspective of class analysis, classes are the basic units of society and political life, whereas organized groups are seen as the bearers of class interests and ideologies. This enables one to acknowledge the uniqueness of individual groups and associations while focusing on larger collective interests represented by individual groups. An association like the Canadian Council of Chief Executives, which represents 150 of the largest private-sector corporations in Canada, would be seen as a representative of "monopoly capital." And the Canadian Manufacturers & Exporters, representing over 3000 corporations in the manufacturing sector, is viewed as a voice for the manufacturing faction of the capitalist class. On the other hand, groups such as labour unions, and groups representing women, Natives or racial minorities, are viewed as representative of subordinate class interests and ideologies.

Corporatism Model Approach

Corporatism is a *political structure characterized by the direct participation of organizations representing business and labour in public policy making*. "In its core," states Jurg Steiner, "corporatism in a modern democracy deals with the interactions among organized business, organized labor, and the state bureaucracy. These three actors co-operate at the national level in the pursuit of the public good."[25] Such structures are associated to varying degrees with several of the capitalist democracies of Western Europe.

Compared to pluralism, which is characterized by an intensely competitive interest-group system that stands outside the state, a corporatist system is more consensus-oriented. It obliterates the barriers between the state and the societal interests represented through corporatist decision-making structures. The distinctiveness of corporatism as an interest-group system is based on three characteristics:

- The existence of *peak associations* for business and labour, which are organizations that can claim to represent all significant interests within specific communities, and have the ability to negotiate on their behalf
- A tripartite relationship with the formal integration of business and labour into the structures of state authority
- An ideology of social partnership between business and labour

How then does the corporatist model apply to interest groups in Canada? The peak associations of business and labour, necessary to make corporatism work, do not exist in Canada. The most inclusive of Canadian business associations, the Canadian Chamber of Commerce (CCC), is simply a loose federation of provincial and local chambers, individual corporations, and trade associations. The national organization exercises no control over its members, and the sheer range of interests represented within the CCC obliges it to focus on very general, broad consensus issues such as lower corporate taxation, cutting government spending, and reducing government regulation of business.[26] On the labour side, the ability of any association to claim to represent Canadian workers is weakened by the fact that fewer than 4 out of 10 members of the labour force belong to a union. The Canadian Labour Congress is the largest of Canada's labour associations, with close to 100 affiliated unions that represent about 2 million workers, or about 15 per cent of the total labour force. And unions representing mainly francophone workers have preferred to affiliate with the Confédération des syndicats nationaux.

The two other requirements for corporatism—tripartite decision-making structures bringing together the state, business, and labour, and an ideology of social partnership between business and labour—are also absent from the Canadian scene. Indeed, Gerhard Lehmbruch, one of the leading students of corporatism, places Canada in the group of countries having the fewest characteristics of corporatism.[27] While Canadian political scientist William Coleman agrees with this assessment, he notes that corporatist policy-making networks are found in the agricultural sector of the Canadian economy.[28]

Some observers claim to see elements of corporatism in some tripartite consensus-building efforts launched by governments in Canada and in the practice of inviting labour and business organizations to appoint representatives to public boards and tribunals. However, none of these has produced significant change in the economic policy-making process. The obstacles to corporatism in Canada are enormous: the parliamentary structures that centralize power in the hands of the PM and cabinet; the political culture that does not favour the interventionist planning associated with corporatism; the decentralization of authority that exists in both the business and labour communities; and the division of economic powers between Ottawa and the provinces. Whether or not corporatist-style interest mediation is desirable or not is a different question.[29]

Neo-Institutionalism Approach

New institutionalism, or **neo-institutionalism**, is *a perspective on policy making that emphasizes the impact of structures and rules, formal and informal, on political outcomes*. It is less a model of politics and policy making than a theoretical premise shared by a diverse group of perspectives. The premise is, quite simply, that institutions—their structural characteristics, formal rules, and informal norms—play a central role in shaping both the actions of individuals and of the organizations to which they belong. This "insight" is neither new nor very surprising. The founders of modern sociology knew very well the importance of institutions in determining behaviour, a relationship that is most pithily expressed in Robert Michels's aphorism, "He who says organization, says oligarchy."[30] Moreover, few of us would blink at the rather bland assertion that "where you stand depends on where you sit." How does this approach help us understand the behaviour and influence of interest groups? Let us begin by examining the diverse roots of the neo-institutionalist approach. They include economics, organization theory, and society-centred analysis.

Economics

Rational choice theory forms the bedrock of modern economics. In the 1950s and 1960s, economists began to systematically apply the concepts of individual (limited) rationality and market behaviour to the study of elections, political parties, interest groups, bureaucracy, and other political phenomena.[31] The economic theory of politics that has developed from this work emphasizes the role played by rules, formal and informal, in shaping individual choices and policy outcomes. In this perspective, "institutions are bundles of rules that make collective action possible."[32]

Organization Theory

Organization theory, *the study of how people act within an organization*, has been an important source of inspiration for the neo-institutionalist approach. One of the first to apply the behavioural insights of organizations theory to Canadian politics was Alan Cairns. In a 1977 speech to the Political Science Association, he relied heavily on organization theory in arguing that Canadian federalism is influenced mainly by state actors, the "needs" of the organizations they belong to, and the constitutional rules within which they operate.[33]

Society-Centred Analysis

The rising popularity of neo-institutional analysis can be attributed in part to a reaction against explanations of politics that emphasize the role of societal factors like interest groups, voters, and social classes. This reaction has produced an outpouring of work on the autonomy of the state (i.e., the ability of state actors to shape societal demands and interest configurations rather than simply responding to and mediating societal interests). Neo-institutionalism is not just a state-centred explanation of politics, but it takes seriously the structural characteristics of the state: the institutions, their structures, and their rules.

Neo-institutionalism deals intensively with the "interior lives" of interest groups: the factors responsible for their creation, maintenance, and capacity for concerted political action. James Q. Wilson identifies four categories of incentives that underlie the interior dynamics of interest groups:[34]

- *Material incentives*—money or other material benefits that have a monetary value
- *Specific solidarity incentives*—intangible rewards like honours and recognition
- *Collective solidarity incentives*—intangible rewards created by the act of associating together in an organized group—a collective sense of group esteem or affirmation
- *Purposive incentives*—intangible rewards derived from the satisfaction of a job well done

Economists have also tried to explain what Mancur Olson called the logic of collective action, including how the interior character of a group affects its capacity for political influence.

The relative importance of *societal* and *state* forces as determinants of political outcomes is often debated in neo-institutionalism. The concepts of **policy communities**—*the* *constellation of actors in a particular policy field*—and **policy networks**[35]—*the nature of the relationships between the key actors in a policy community*—are the building blocks of the neo-institutional approach. Embedded in them is the irrefutable claim that "the state" is in fact a fragmented structure when it comes to actual policy making. So, too, is society. The interests that are active and influential on the issue of abortion, for example, are very different from those that are part of the official-language policy community. Paul Pross's visual depiction of a policy community conveys a good sense of the complexity and potential for fluidity in the relations between interest groups and the state (see Figure 10.2).

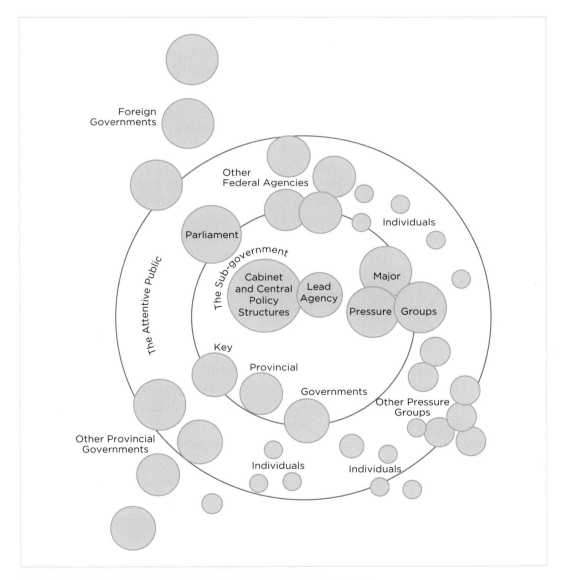

FIGURE 10.2 POLICY COMMUNITY "BUBBLE DIAGRAM"

Source: From Whittington, M.S. & Williams, G. *Canadian Politics in the 1990's*, 4E. © 1995 Nelson Education Ltd. Reproduced by permission. www.cengage.com/permissions

THE INGREDIENTS OF INTEREST-GROUP SUCCESS

There is no magic recipe for group influence, but it is possible to generalize. Successful strategies and appropriate targets depend on the issue, the resources and actions of other groups, the state of public opinion, and the characteristics of the political system. Business groups, and their dealings with government, seem to have these characteristics more than any other set of societal interests.

Organization

Organized interests are usually more influential than unorganized ones, probably because they are able to apply sustained pressure on policy makers. Writing to the prime minister, even a person of national stature is unlikely to have much of an impact. But tens of thousands of people writing and/or taking to the streets are more likely to get the prime minister's attention. This impact, however, is unlikely to be sustained without organizations that can credibly claim to speak on behalf of thousands of like-minded people and are skilled at media and government relations.

Paul Pross, a distinguished Canadian expert on interest groups, points to the character of modern government and the policy-making process in explaining why organization is crucial. Modern government, he observes, is a sprawling, highly bureaucratized affair where power to influence policy is diffused. Prior to the 1960s, government was smaller and the number of policies and programs were fewer, and power was concentrated in the hands of a small group of senior bureaucrats and cabinet. This was the era of the "mandarins," when a tightly knit group of deputy ministers dominated the process.[36] Groups did not need sophisticated organizational structures to deal with government. But as the scope of state involvement in economic and social matters deepened, it became desirable for groups to have the capacity to monitor and deal with those levels where the power resided.

The modern administrative state has resulted in a need to organize. A veritable explosion of associations representing business interests, environmental concerns, consumer interests, women, and so on, has taken place. Interest groups acquired prominence later in Canada than in the United States, and it was largely due to a defensive reaction against a state that was becoming more impenetrable and mysterious—not to mention hostile from the standpoint of those in the business community.

The increasing size and complexity of the public sector has spawned organized interests in another way. There was also an active role by government to promote the creation of associations that would represent and articulate specific interests. This phenomenon appears to have begun in World War I, when the federal Department of Trade and Commerce encouraged the creation of trade associations to represent corporations in the same industry.[37] Similarly, in the 1960s and 1970s, the Department of the Secretary of State was instrumental in creating a large number of organizations representing women, ethnic groups, and official-language minorities, particularly through providing core funding to finance the activities of these groups.[38]

The practice continues today in what appears to be a somewhat self-serving phenomenon. Government agencies have helped organize the interests that depended on their programs and budgets, thereby creating constituencies whose support could be useful to the bureaucracy in protecting its policy and budgetary turf.[39] For example, the Multiculturalism program of Citizenship and Immigration Canada funds ethnic, racial, religious, and cultural organizations in Canada, many of which lobby government officials or attempt to influence public opinion on matters that concern them. This is true of French language, Aboriginal, and human rights groups, who receive substantial funding from the Canadian government. Some women's and disadvantaged minority groups used to receive funding from programs like the Court Challenges Program and Women's Legal Education and Action Fund (LEAF). Women's groups were sometimes able to access funds to intervene in Charter cases involving alleged sexual discrimination. The Conservative government disbanded the Court Challenges Program in 2006 but resurrected part of it in 2008, through the Program to Support Linguistic Rights.

Sophisticated organization has become essential for maintaining influence. Paul Pross uses the term "institutional groups" to describe interests that possess the highest level of organization. Institutional groups have the following characteristics:

- Organizational continuity and cohesion
- Extensive knowledge and easy communication with sectors of government that affect their clients
- Stable memberships
- Concrete and immediate objectives
- Overall goals that are more important than any particular objective[40]

While many groups claim to have these characteristics, business associations are more likely to meet Pross's criteria for institutionalized groups. Indeed, the most organizationally sophisticated interest groups in Canada include associations such as the Canadian Council of Chief Executives, Canadian Manufacturers & Exporters, the Canadian Chamber of Commerce, the Conseil du Patronat du Québec, and the Canadian Federation of Independent Business.

Resources

Money is no guarantee of interest-group success, but it doesn't hurt. The most organizationally sophisticated groups, and the most successful, tend also to be well-financed. Money pays for the services that are vital for success. A permanent staff costs money; it may include lawyers, economists, accountants, researchers, public relations specialists, and others whose services are needed to monitor government activity and communicate both with the group's membership and with policy makers. And the services of public relations firms, polling companies, or professional lobbyists are usually too expensive for many interest groups.

Business groups tend to have more affluent and stable financial footings than other groups. Their closest rivals are major labour associations; some occupational groups, such as physicians, dentists, lawyers, university professors, and teachers; and some agricultural producer

TABLE 10.1 | INTEREST GROUPS, THEIR FUNDING, AND THEIR STAFF

Interest Group	Interest Focus	Budget	Approximate Staff Size in 2010	Advocacy
Ecojustice (formerly Sierra Legal Defence Fund)	Environment	$3.9 million (2009)	15	Examples of advocacy include "working to protect the environment and Ontarians from the risks associated with a plan to build several new nuclear reactors on the shore of Lake Ontario," and "working to ensure that the human rights of people living in one of Canada's most polluted communities—Sarnia's Chemical Valley—are recognized and protected."
Inuit Tapiriit Kanatami	Canada's Inuit population	$8.1 million (2010)	40	ITK "represents and promotes the interests" of 55,000 Inuit living in 53 communities across Canada on "a wide variety of environmental, social, cultural, and political, issues and challenges facing Inuit on the national level."
Canadian Federation of Independent Business	Small and medium-sized businesses	Over $25 million (2010)	–	The CFIB advocates for better tax laws and government regulations such as changes to employment insurance, pension plans, and labour policies.
Canadian Medical Association	Medical doctors	Over $25 million (2010)	165	The CMA advocates on behalf of Canadian physicians and the public about topical health care matters such as pharmaceutical issues, wait times and benchmarks, and public funding for health care.
Canadian Council of Chief Executives	Chief executive officers of approximately 150 major Canadian corporations	No data	12	The CCCE plays "a private sector leadership role in shaping fiscal, taxation, trade, competition, energy, environmental, education and corporate governance policies."
Canadian Bankers' Association	54 domestic banks, foreign bank subsidiaries, and foreign banks	Over $25 million (2010)	75	The CBA "provides governments and others with a centralized contact to all banks on matters relating to banking in Canada. The CBA advocates for effective public policies that contribute to a sound, successful banking system that benefits Canadians and Canada's economy."
Canadian Association of Petroleum Producers	Canadian oil and natural gas industry	No data	50	"CAPP's mission is to enhance the economic sustainability of the Canadian upstream petroleum industry in a safe and environmentally and socially responsible manner, through constructive engagement and communication with governments, the public and stakeholders in the communities in which we operate."

This table shows us that funding and staff size of interest groups may not be reliable indicators of their influence and effectiveness. Some groups, especially those backed by corporations, have corporate staff dedicated to working directly with the interest group.

Source: Compiled from Stephen Brooks, *Canadian Democracy*, 7/e (Toronto, OUP: 2012), pp. 354–56; and various organizations' websites.

groups. As Table 10.1 illustrates, budgets and personnel of some non-economic groups may also appear to be considerable; however, the size of the budget or the size of an association's staff is not always a reliable indicator of its probable influence with decision makers. There are three important differences between the monetary resources of major business interest groups and those of other organized interests:

1. The members of business interest groups tend not to rely on their collective associations for political influence to the extent that the members of other interest groups do. Large corporations usually have their own public affairs departments that, among other functions, manage the organization's relations with government. Moreover, corporations will often act on their own in employing the services of a professional lobbying firm or other services to help them influence policy makers. Corporations, more so than business associations, have traditionally been major contributors to the Liberal and Progressive Conservative parties. Prior to changes to the election Act covered in Chapter 9, "purchasing access" was another tactic seldom used by members of other types of interest groups.

2. The monetary resources of business and non-business associations relates to stability. Simply put, business groups rest on more secure financial footing, while many groups rely on the imminently less reliable financial support from government, or donations from "people on the street," or both.

INSIDE POLITICS

BOX 10.1 | King of the Interest Group Hill: The CCCE

The Canadian Council of Chief Executives (CCCE) was modelled after the Business Roundtable, created in the United States in 1974. The CCCE was created in response to the perception among the corporate elite that big business was under attack from consumers' groups, environmentalists, and governments wedded to tax and regulation policies. An organization was needed to articulate big business's points of view and to defend its interests.

The CCCE comprises the CEOs of 150 major companies operating in the Canadian economy. Most of them do some part of their business outside of Canada and many are truly international in their production and sales activities. The CCCE has never included a representative of a government-controlled firm. As of 2011, member companies of the CCCE controlled about $4.5 trillion in assets, had yearly revenues of more than $850 billion, and employed close to 1.4 million Canadians.

As the senior voice of Canadian big business, the CCCE takes positions on a range of public policy issues. For example, it supported the Charlottetown Accord in 1992. The CCCE is widely believed to have been instrumental in persuading the Conservative government to propose free trade talks to the United States in 1985. It focuses primarily on matters of trade and finance and strongly favours Canada–US economic integration and liberalized global trade.

3. A third difference involves the ability of business and non-business groups to raise money to deal with a "crisis" issue. The federal election campaign of 1988 was largely fought over free trade; business associations in favour of the Canada–US Free Trade Agreement outspent their opponents by a wide margin in an attempt to influence public opinion on the deal and to ensure the election of the Conservatives.

John Kingdon identifies several resources other than money that enable a group to influence what gets on (or stays off) the policy agenda and the options considered by policy makers. These include electoral influence, economic coercion, and group cohesion.[41]

Electoral Influence

The perceived ability to swing a significant bloc of votes is an important group resource as is the status or wealth of its members and their geographic distribution. Some groups' claims to speak on behalf of its membership are more credible others'. The distributional factor can cut two ways. With Canada's single-member constituency electoral system, the concentration of a group's members in a particular region may increase the political influence of that group. On the other hand, geographic dispersion of a group's membership may also be advantageous.

Economic Coercion

The ability to "down tools," close businesses, scale down investment plans, refuse to purchase government bonds, or in some other way inflict harm on the economy or public finances (or both!) can be a powerful group resource. It is a resource usually associated with business groups. Unions and occupation groups such as physicians and agricultural producers have a more difficult time using "economic blackmail" to influence policy makers for two reasons. First, when a group such as nurses, teachers, or postal workers attempts to tie up the economy or a public service by withholding their labour (striking or work to rule), their behaviour, and its social or economic consequences, is extremely visible and likely to be perceived by the public as a *special* interest working against the *public* interest. Public opinion is not likely to be favourable and may even be hostile. In fact, surveys regularly show that Canadians hold unions in very low esteem. Second, business interests have a cultural advantage over other economic interest groups in successfully using the threat of economic damage to pursue their objectives. In capitalist societies, the fundamental values that underpin the strength of business interests—the belief in private property, profit making, and in markets as the best mechanism for generating and distributing wealth—lend legitimacy to general business interests. A strike action by workers is often seen as irresponsible: but if a business refuses to invest in new machinery, lays off workers, or relocates off-shore, this is often seen by policy makers and the public as a failure of business confidence. Businesses are less likely to be accused of being irresponsible, because they are just acting in accordance with the rules of a system that most of us accept.

Group Cohesion

"United we stand, divided we fall" has been a sound rule of interest-group influence. An association's hand appears stronger to policy makers if it speaks with a single voice and genuinely represents its membership's views. This is not always easy. As we have seen, both labour and business interests are highly fragmented in Canada. There are numerous associations, and not one can credibly claim to speak on behalf of all labour or all business interests. This is true for many other collective interests in Canadian society such as agricultural producers, Aboriginals, and women. Aboriginals, for instance, are represented by many associations, the largest of which is the Assembly of First Nations. Its ability to speak on behalf of all Aboriginal groups is limited by the fact that it does not speak for Métis, non-status Indians, or Inuit, who are represented by their own associations.

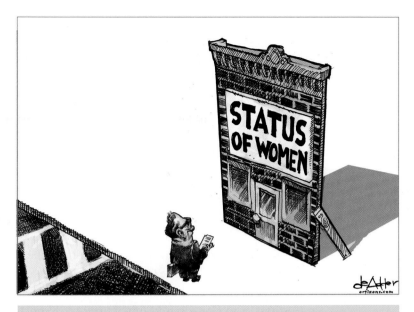

A cartoon appearing in the 2007 *Hill Times* notes how Status of Women Canada, an agency for women's equality, seemed to be on the verge of collapse even before government budget cuts were made. Should all interest groups be privately funded? Or should there be public money available for some causes? If so, which ones? What are the dangers to a democracy if only the wealthiest segments can afford to advocate through interest groups?

Cohesion once appeared to be greatest in the women's movement. In 1972, the National Action Committee (NAC) on the Status of Women was created by, and mainly financed by, the federal government. For many years, the NAC acted as a major umbrella association that represented about 700 smaller women's organizations. However, by the late 1980s, the NAC was increasingly beset by internal divisions, and some women's groups did not agree with the confrontational style that its leadership favoured. By 2004, the NAC was insolvent, and any claim that it was a voice for Canadian women's groups was no longer credible.

Group cohesion typically is less of a problem in a small organization of similar members. But this cohesion may, of course, be offset by the perception that an association represents a very narrow special interest. As well, it is easier to present a united front when an association is speaking on behalf of just one group. Alliances with associations representing other groups, however, may be politically useful. The downside, again, is the problem of submerging group differences in such a common front.

A rather different problem of cohesion involves the relationship between a group's leaders and its membership. A gap between the goals of leaders and those they purport to represent will undermine an association's credibility in the eyes of policy makers. A variation of this problem exists when an interest-group claims to speak on behalf of a collectivity that is largely unorganized, or where there are good reasons for doubting that the group actually expresses the views of those they claim to represent. For example, women's groups like the NAC have sometimes been accused of not expressing the views of a large part of Canada's female population. Labour unions' claims to speak on behalf of Canadian workers are weakened, in the eyes of some, by the fact that they represent fewer than 4 out of every 10 workers.

THE INTEREST-GROUP SYSTEM

If we turn now to the actual interest-group system, we find that business groups tend to be smaller than other interest associations. Indeed, some are quite small, particularly those that represent companies in oligopolistic industries—i.e. industries that control the size of the market and the prices of goods and services. For example, the Canadian Vehicle Manufacturers Association represents only four companies, the Forest Products Association of Canada has only 18 members, and the Canadian Bankers' Association has 54 member organizations. Some business associations, such as chambers of commerce, the Canadian Federation of Independent Business, and Canadian Manufacturers & Exporters, have much larger memberships. But it is also true that these organizations represent general interests of the business community, while the specific interests of corporations are represented through trade associations that have smaller memberships.

Business groups are not the only ones to rely on exclusive benefits and material incentives to attract, maintain, and motivate members. Labour unions, agricultural producer groups, and professional associations do as well. But one needs to remember that cohesion is only one group resource. Farmers' groups or labour unions may be as cohesive as business associations but still inferior to business in terms of the other resources at their disposal.

Safety in the Shadows

The Canadian public regularly sees the outward signs of interest-group activities such as demonstrations, full-page newspaper ads, or well-dressed spokespersons being interviewed outside of Parliament. These approaches may not be the most influential. Often, it is the absence of visible signs of interest-group activity that tells us most about the strength of organized interests. In the interest-group system, some seek safety in the shadows.

The fact that the status, privileges, or interests of some groups are not matters of public debate tells us something about these groups' power. As E.E. Schattschneider writes, "The very expression 'pressure politics' invites us to misconceive the role of special-interest groups in politics."[42] "Private conflicts," he argues, "are taken into the public arena precisely because someone wants to make certain that the power ratio among the private interests most immediately involved shall not prevail."[43] The point is obvious and yet profoundly important. Society's most powerful interests sometimes prefer to avoid the public arena where they have to justify themselves and respond to those who advocate changes that would affect their interests. They are safe in the shadows. But in the light of public debate they become prey to attacks from other groups. Conflict, Schattschneider notes, always includes an element of unpredictability. Indeed, when previously unquestioned interests reach the public agenda and are recognized as group interests, a loss of influence can result.

Federalism and the Interest-Group System

Hardly a corner of Canadian political life is unaffected by federalism, the interest-group system included. Because the Constitution divides political authority between two levels of government, an interest group must determine where jurisdiction lies or, as is often the case, how it is divided between the national and provincial governments. We will examine three of the more general propositions that emerge from the extensive work on federalism and interest groups in Canada.[44]

The first has been labelled the *multiple crack hypothesis*.[45] According to this interpretation, the existence of two levels of government, each of which is equipped with a range of taxing, spending, and regulatory powers, enables interest groups to seek from one government what they cannot get from the other. Business groups have been the ones most likely to exploit the constitutional division of powers, and have been the most successful.[46]

A second interpretation of federalism's impact on interest groups argues that a federal constitution tends to weaken group influence by reducing the internal cohesion of organized interests. According to this argument, divided authority on matters that affect a group's interests will encourage it to adopt a federal form of organization.[47] Federalism may reduce a group's ability to speak with a single voice and to persuade governments that its member organizations are capable of collective action. A group's influence may be weakened when the

Democracy Watch

BOX 10.2 Having an Impact: Politician or Special Interest?

It is common wisdom that politicians will at some point need to compromise on their strongly held convictions in order to make policy that is accepted by the mainstream. Members of special-interest groups, on the other hand, can devote their careers to further a cause they are passionate about—though they may never be successful in convincing politicians to translate that cause into actual political policy. Those choosing a career in public service will eventually make a decision to work either from within the system for incremental change or from outside the system for significant change.

Up for Debate

To have maximum effect in making changes that will benefit society, is it better to be a politician belonging to a party or a member of a special-interest group? Defend your choice with three examples.

two levels of government are in conflict, a situation that may create division within the group itself (for example, along regional lines) and between its representative associations.[48]

A third proposition, which might be called the *statist* interpretation, sees federalism as a constraint on rather than an opportunity for the influence of interest groups. According to this view, governments and their sprawling bureaucracies increasingly dominate the policy-making scene, particularly when jurisdictional issues are involved. Even societal groups with considerable resources may be frozen out of the process of intergovernmental relations. Alan Cairns's argument that modern Canadian federalism is mainly about conflicts between governments and their competing political and organizational goals[49] implies that this is so. Leslie Pal drew similar conclusions from his study of the historical development of Canada's Unemployment Insurance program. He found that the impact of societal groups on the original form of UI and on subsequent changes was minor compared to the role played by bureaucratic and intergovernmental factors.[50]

INTEREST-GROUP STRATEGIES

There are three basic strategies open to interest groups. One is to target policy makers directly (e.g., through personal meetings, briefs, and exchanges of information). This is the *lobbying* option. Another strategy is to target *public opinion* in the expectation that policy makers will be swayed by popular support for a group's position. The media play a crucial role here in communicating a group's message to the wider public. A variation on this strategy involves alliance-building. By building visible bridges with other groups on some issue, a group may convince policy makers that its position has broad support. A third strategy involves *judicial action*. This confrontational strategy involves a very public court challenge and an outcome that is likely to leave one a winner or a loser. For some groups, this tends to be an option of last resort. But for other groups, such as the Women's Legal Education and Action Fund (LEAF), EGALE, which advocates for lesbian, gay, bisexual, and transgender issues, Ecojustice (formerly the Sierra Legal Defence Fund), and the Canadian Civil Liberties Association, litigation is a basic weapon in their arsenal of pressure tactics.

These strategies are not mutually exclusive. A group may use more than one at once or switch from one strategy to another. A few generalizations are possible about which strategies to use and when:

- One of the keys to influence is early involvement in the policy-making process. Lobbying is the generally preferred strategy when policies are just being considered. Confrontation and visibility are relatively low, and the importance of thorough preparation and credible technical information is high.
- Well-established groups that are part of a policy community tend to prefer a lobbying strategy. Public and confrontational strategies have an element of risk and unpredictability and will be used only as measures of last resort.
- Less-established groups within a policy community are more likely to rely on confrontation, media campaigns, and other public strategies.

- Where a group's interests are significantly affected by regulation, lobbying strategies that supply research and technical information to the bureaucratic officials doing the regulating will be most successful.
- Even groups enjoying regular high-level access to policy makers now often find that lobbying is not enough.
- A successful influence strategy (e.g., hiring public relations or polling experts, or going to court) is usually quite expensive, and business groups tend to have deeper pockets.

Just what is the price of influence? It varies, but a legal challenge that makes its way to the Supreme Court can certainly cost millions of dollars in legal bills. If much of the legal work has been contributed on a *pro bono* basis, as it often is in sexual equality or same-sex discrimination cases, the costs may be considerably less. Large business corporations and industry associations have the financial means to defend their interests in court. For other groups, it is often necessary that a litigation-oriented advocacy group like Ecojustice or LEAF take on the burden of their representation.

A campaign directed at influencing public opinion can also be costly. For instance, the pro-FTA Canadian Alliance for Trade and Job Opportunities probably spent over $2 million even before the final blitz during the 1988 federal election campaign. This case may be a quarter of a century old, and the amount of money may sound paltry by today's standards, but it was in fact a catalyst for reform of the law on third-party spending during election campaigns. But groups outside of business interests also spend lavishly to shape public opinion. Quebec's Cree First Nations spent an estimated $500,000 on paid advertisements and the services of a New York public relations firm in an effort to stop the construction of the Great Whale hydroelectric project in Quebec. The public opinion target was the New York consumers of the power generated by Great Whale and exported to the US. In 2002 the provincial government dropped its plans for the project.

It is usually difficult to pinpoint the resources devoted to an advertising campaign to influence public opinion. Walmart is one of many companies that invest a significant amount of money in television and other ads intended to convey an image of a socially responsible company and valued member of the community where its stores are located. The beer and liquor industries likewise invest large amounts of money in advertising that aims to create a favourable public image, and to preclude the sort of regulation and product advertising limits that have been imposed on the tobacco industry. None of this spending is related to election campaigns, and therefore does not fall under the rules set by the Canada Elections Act.

Advocacy Advertising

The purchase of newspaper/magazine space or broadcast time to convey a political message is called **advocacy advertising**. As indicated above, business interest groups are not the only ones to buy advertising to influence public opinion on an issue. However, business groups use advocacy advertising most extensively. The crucial question raised by any form of advertising that carries a political message is whether the ability to pay for media time/space should

President Obama,
You'll never guess who's standing between us and our new energy economy...

Canada's Tar Sands: the dirtiest oil on earth.

President Obama travels to Canada on February 19. We hope he'll discuss his vision for a new energy future with leaders there. The US and Canada can revive our economies, create green jobs, and build a better future for our children.

This is the best path forward.

Right now, Canada is not on that path. Producing oil from Canada's Tar Sands releases massive greenhouse gas emissions, consumes huge amounts of energy, contaminates fresh water and fish, produces toxic waste and destroys vast forests along with their birds and wildlife. And now, downstream indigenous communities are suffering higher than normal rates of cancer.

Prime Minister Harper and the government of Alberta continue to turn a blind eye to these problems.

Your voice counts. Please let President Obama know that he should ask Canada to clean up the Tar Sands.

Take action online today.
Visit ForestEthics.org

MIKISEW CREE FIRST NATION

FORESTETHICS
VANCOUVER • TORONTO • SAN FRANCISCO • BELLINGHAM

ForestEthics teamed up with the Mikisew Cree and Athabasca Chipewyan First Nations to place this full-page ad in *USA Today*.

determine what views get expressed. The critics of advocacy advertising were quick to denounce the blitz of pro–free trade advertising by business during the 1988 election campaign. They argued that the deep pockets of the corporate interests ranged behind free trade made a sham of the democratic political process and totally undermined the intention of the statutory limits on election spending by political parties. The Royal Commission on Elections agreed. Its 1992 report recommended that spending by organizations other than registered political parties be limited during elections.

The defenders of advocacy advertising claim that it is a way for business to overcome the anti-business bias of the media and to bridge the "credibility gap" that has developed between business and the public. Mobil Oil, one of the pioneers of this advertising technique, has called it a "new form of public disclosure,"[51] thereby associating it with freedom of information. Business and economic issues are complex, and advocacy advertising—most of which is done through the print media—provides an opportunity for business to explain its actions and to counter public misconceptions. And in any case, argue corporate spokespersons, the biggest spender on advocacy advertising is government, whose justification for this spending is essentially the same as that of business![52] There is no doubt that strategies aimed at influencing public opinion have become increasingly important to interest groups. In fact, in discussing advocacy advertising we have only scratched the surface of these strategies.[53] Important as they are, however, strategies that target public opinion usually take a backseat to those that target policy makers directly. These are lobbying strategies.

Lobbying

Lobbying may be defined as ***any form of direct or indirect communication with government that is designed to influence public policy.***[54] Although the term conjures up images of smoke-filled rooms, "old boy networks," and sleazy deal making, this is a somewhat unfair caricature of lobbying on two counts. First, lobbying is a basic democratic right. When a group of citizens organizes to demand a traffic light at a dangerous neighbourhood corner and meets with their local city councillor to express their concerns, this is lobbying. When the president of a powerful business association arranges a lunch rendezvous with an official in the Prime Minister's Office with whom he went to law school, this, too, is lobbying. The fact that lobbying is often associated with unfair privilege, and even corruption, should not obscure the fact that it is not limited to organizations representing the powerful. Second, in principle there is nothing undemocratic about lobbying.

A second way in which the "sleaze" caricature of lobbying conveys a wrong impression is by associating it with practices that constitute only a small part of what lobbyists actually do. Direct meetings with influential public officials are certainly one aspect of lobbying. Likewise, there is no shortage of evidence that ethically dubious and sometimes illegal relations occasionally exist between lobbyists and policy makers. But lobbying is a broader set of activities than simply buttonholing cabinet ministers or their senior officials. Most professional lobbyists spend the better part of their time collecting and communicating information on behalf of the interests they represent. They monitor the political scene as it affects their client's interests. An effective lobbyist does not simply react, but instead acts like an early warning system, providing information about policy when it is still in its formative stages and tracking public opinion on the issues that are vital to a client's interests. The lobbyist may also provide advice and professional assistance in putting together briefs, press releases, speeches, and other communications, as well as public relations services such as identifying and targeting those segments of public opinion that influence policy makers on some issue (see Boxes 10.3 and 10.4). Helping to build strategic coalitions with other groups is another function of lobbyists.

While most interest groups lobby government on their own, wealthier groups may purchase the services of a professional lobbying firm. In 2012, the Ottawa *Yellow Pages* listed 22 firms under the heading of "Government relations." They range from large firms like Hill+Knowlton Strategies Canada (formerly Hill & Knowlton), which employ dozens of professional staff and have annual billings in the tens of millions of dollars (see Box 10.3), to smaller operations. In addition, many law firms and accounting companies, including such prominent ones as McCarthy Tetrault; Osler, Hoskins & Harcourt; and PwC, do lobbying work.

Since 1989, those who are paid to lobby federal public office holders have been required to register with a federal agency. The Lobbyists Registration Act provides for three categories of lobbyists:

- *Consultant lobbyists* are those who, for a fee, work for various clients.
- *Corporate in-house lobbyists* are those who work for a single corporation and who lobby federal officials as a significant part of their duties.

- *Organization in-house lobbyists* are the senior paid officers and other employees of organizations whose activities would include lobbying federal officials.

The majority of active lobbyists represent corporations and business associations. The clientele lists of Canada's leading government relations firms include major players in the Canadian and international corporate world. Hill+Knowlton Strategies Canada, for example (See Box 10.3) boasts that it represents such clients as Microsoft, SHL Systemhouse, De Beers, Rio Algom, Kraft, GlaxoWellcome, Deutsche Bank Canada, and Standard Life.

Box 10.4 lists some of Canada's most prominent consultant lobbyists and some of the clients they work for.

As the scope and process of governance have changed, so too, has the character of lobbying. The old model of lobbying as personal communications by a well-placed individual to a cabinet minister or high-ranking bureaucrat on behalf of a client morphed into an activity

INSIDE POLITICS

BOX 10.3 | What Does a Government Relations Firm Sell?

Public Affairs

Governments have a profound impact on the way business is conducted, especially when they make changes to policies and regulations with little or no public consultation. These changes can alter the competitive landscape for Canadian businesses, raise or lower taxes, and impact the investment climate for companies operating in Canada or abroad.

Hill+Knowlton Strategies national public affairs practice is dedicated to working with clients to ensure they are prepared for the ever-changing environment and are equipped to affect government decisions and processes in a meaningful manner.

Our public affairs practitioners are the best in the business. They have first hand experience with government decision-making structure and deep connections within government departments to assist their client's challenges. With years of experience, the PA team members have served in the offices of the Prime Minister and Premiers, at the executive branches of the public service, and as elected officials themselves, each consultant brings an in-depth understanding of how decisions are made, and how to engage in political debate in a meaningful way. Our strategic counsel and programs take into account the interplay between government departments, and the critical need to manage the internal and external debate through compelling arguments, strategically delivered—often through the inclusion of social media, outreach to key stakeholders, strategic media relations as well as political and bureaucratic influencers.

Whether it is securing a multi-billion dollar procurement contract, explaining opposition to a new tax, or mobilizing support for an infrastructure project, H+K's public affairs team helps clients succeed in every jurisdiction in Canada.

Hill+Knowlton Strategies is also able to provide clients with global representation as it draws on the resources of its parent company, Hill+Knowlton Strategies, a world leader in public affairs.

Source: Hill+Knowlton Strategies website: http://www
.hkstrategies.ca. Used by permission of Hill+Knowlton Strategies.

more akin to Sherpas guiding their climbers towards a destination. Key personal contacts continue to be a large part of what lobbying firms sell, but today, this is reinforced by extensive knowledge and intensive analysis of the policy matters in question. Allan Gregg of Decima Research played an important role in this transformation. Decima offered clients analysis of the public opinion environment in which their activities were situated and that affected the achievement of their goals. The *Decima Quarterly* provided clients with confidential and up-to-date information on public opinion. When Hill & Knowlton, a world leader in the lobbying industry, acquired Decima in 1989, a sort of one-stop-shopping model of public affairs advice and strategic communications was created. The new model fused public opinion expertise, marketing skills, and policy analysis with personal access to government officials. This remains the model in Canada, as practised by the heavyweights of the lobbying establishment.

The Lobbyists Registration Act requires that lobbyists identify the general subject matter of their activities as well as the government departments and agencies that they contact on behalf of those they represent. "Industry," "international trade," and "taxation and finance"

INSIDE POLITICS

BOX 10.4 | Who Do Government Relations Firms Represent?

Lobbyist	Company	Clients
Ronald Atkey	Osler, Hoskins & Harcourt	Time Canada Warner Brothers Viacom Canadian Motion Picture Distributors Association
Brian Mersereau	Hill+Knowlton Strategies	Eurocopter Northrop Grumman Amex Canada Rio Tinto General Dynamics
Charles King	Earnscliffe Strategy	Microsoft Canada Bell Canada Canadian Imperial Bank of Commerce General Motors Canadian Association of Broadcasters
David Angus	Capital Hill Group	Lockheed Martin Molson Canada Trillium Health Care Ducks Unlimited Royal Conservatory of Music Mackenzie Aboriginal Corp.

Source: Office of the Commissioner of Lobbying of Canada, online public registry. www.ocl-cal.gc.ca/eic/site/lobbyist-lobbyiste1 .nsf/h_nx00274.html. Reproduced with the permission of the Minister of Public Works and Government Services, 2012.

have, from the beginning of the registration system, been the most frequent subjects on which lobbyists have plied their trade. The subject of "Environment" has moved up the list and was ranked third in 2011–12. This reflects the increasing importance of environmental laws and regulations for corporations and business associations. Health policy matters have also been one of the most frequent subjects of lobbying in recent years. Lobbyists are also required to indicate the government institutions that they expect to contact, but not the names of the public officials they lobby. Among the most targeted institutions are the departments of Finance, Industry, Foreign Affairs and International Trade, as well as the PCO and the House of Commons.

SUMMARY

Interest groups are a very important feature of Canadian democracy. There are thousands of organized groups in Canada. While not all primarily aim to influence public policy and/or public opinion, many do. Other groups mobilize as a result of a specific issue or set of circumstances. Research has shown that the interest-group system is not representative of the whole community. And some have noted that business interests occupy a "privileged position" within this interest-group competition. It tends to be biased in favour of the wealthy, the educated, and the organized.

Public officials and policy makers do worry that their actions will affect business confidence mainly because corporations and the wealthy can stop investing in the economy or move capital out of the country. This is perhaps one of the greatest sources of influence for groups representing business interests. But interest groups also rely on other means of influence such as advertising, boycotts and other militant behaviour covered by the media, producing studies and disseminating their results and recommendations, celebrity endorsements of a position, and so on.

Certain analytical perspectives can be used to explain the behaviour and the effects of interest groups on society. These include the pluralism approach, which looks at the diverse and competitive nature of interest groups; the corporatism model, which sees a strong level of co-operation between the state, labour, and business; the class analysis approach, which stresses that social classes, not interest groups, are the basic units of society and political life; and the neo-institutionalism approach which deals with how institutions and their structures, norms, and rules shape the actions of individuals and of the organizations to which they belong.

A group's influence within a policy community will depend on its internal characteristics and on its external relationships to the larger political system and the state. Successful interest groups have a sophisticated organization that keeps pace with growing and increasingly complex governments, routine access to policy makers, access to resources (especially money), electoral influence, the capacity to affect the economy, and group cohesion.

Some experts have argued that federalism tends to strengthen interest groups by increasing the access to policy makers, and by making it possible to play one level of government against the other. Others maintain that federalism can also weaken groups by reducing the internal cohesion of organized interests. Lobbying, litigation, targeting public opinion, or taking to the streets are just some of the strategic options available to groups, and their use will depend on many factors. Some organizations, including business associations and labour unions, engage in direct lobbying. Others hire the services of government consulting/relations firms. The ability to lobby effectively and to pay for the services of specialized firms that lobby on behalf of clients is very unevenly distributed in the universe of interest groups.

Today's lobbyists are sometimes yesterday's politicians and bureaucrats. According to the Lobbyists Registration Act, 1989, individuals who are consultant lobbyists, corporate in-house lobbyists, or organization in-house lobbyists must register and keep records of contacts. The Federal Accountability Act of 2006 also sets some limits on the ability of public officials to lobby the government after leaving the public sector.

STARTING POINTS FOR RESEARCH

Robert Campbell, Michael Howlett, and Leslie Pal, *The Real Worlds of Canadian Politics*, 4th edn (Peterborough, Ont.: Broadview Press, 2004).

William Coleman, *Business and Politics: A Study of Collective Action* (Montreal and Kingston: McGill-Queen's University Press, 1988).

Geoffrey Hale, *Uneasy Partnership: The Politics of Business and Government* (Toronto: University of Toronto Press, 2006).

Leslie A. Pal, *Interests of State: The Politics of Language, Multiculturalism and Feminism in Canada* (Montreal and Kingston: McGill-Queen's University Press, 1993).

Donley T. Studlar, *Tobacco Control: Comparative Politics in the United States and Canada* (Toronto: University of Toronto Press, 2002).

CBC ARCHIVES AND TVO'S *THE AGENDA*

Visit the companion website for *Canadian Democracy: A Concise Introduction* to follow links to audio and video footage related to the main themes of the chapter: www.oupcanada.com/BrooksConcise.

RELEVANT WEBSITES

Visit the companion website for *Canadian Democracy: A Concise Introduction* to browse a collection of websites featuring material related to the key themes of the chapter, an excellent starting point for research.

REVIEW EXERCISES

1. Find a newspaper story that discusses an interest group and identify its name, the interests or associations it represents, the reason for it being in the news, and the group's demands or values.

2. Make a list of organized groups you have belonged to or contributed to in some way. If you are having trouble coming up with a list, just think about jobs that you may have had (were they unionized?), churches, clubs, or associations that you may have belonged to, causes you might have donated money to, petitions you may have signed, etc. Which of these do you think attempt to influence public opinion or policy?

3. Identify various political activities engaged in by various interest groups. Which activities do you consider to be strongly democratic, somewhat democratic, and undemocratic?

4. Visit http://www.ocl-cal.gc.ca/eic/site/012.nsf/eng/h_00010.html. Examine the rules that apply to politicians or civil servants who leave government to work for lobbying firms or interest groups. Discuss the potential for unethical conduct and whether the regulations go far enough.

The Media

Media impact on modern political life is profound. After reading this chapter, you will
be able to

1. Explain how the media shape the political agenda in Canadian democracy
2. Describe what the media produce
3. Determine what is a mass media product
4. Explain the many ways in which the media acts as a filter for much of the information we receive

Although most of you will not have personally met either the prime minister of Canada
or the president of the United States, virtually all of you will have ideas about these two
leaders, as well as strongly held views on their character, abilities, and performance. The
facts upon which we form our ideas and our judgments concerning these leaders, and
most of our knowledge and beliefs about our world, are based on third-hand information at best. Our information-saturated societies rely on the edited images and information offered on television screens, in newspapers, over the radio waves, and through
other electronic media.

If our ideas are based largely on third-hand information, then we should pay careful attention to those who communicate this information. For instance, a typical political story on the evening television news may involve about 60–90 seconds of images of the prime minister, other cabinet ministers, and opposition leaders and critics, probably in the House of Commons during question period or in the foyer near the entrance to the Commons, where journalists and cameras await their daily feeding by politicians exiting question period. The story may include brief segments featuring politicians, experts, and interest-group spokespersons commenting on the prime minister's remarks. Some portion of the story will consist of the reporter's own narration of what is happening and what it means. In short, the entire news clip may be described as "third-hand information" because it is the product of many choices by those who assign stories to reporters and those who edit and package the story at the television network's newsroom. Consequently, what the viewer ultimately sees has been influenced by a number of people whose choices contribute to what we call "the news."

Citizens' dependence on the media for much of their ideas and information is not a recent development. What is more recent is our awareness of the role of selection, distortion, and manipulation in the process of reporting the news. Long-standing fears that media might have a partisan bias or that propaganda might subvert democratic politics have been joined in recent years by worries that the biases of the media are more deeply rooted and insidious than ever before. The "seductions of language," says media expert Neil Postman, are trivial compared to the seductions and manipulative powers of the image-based media.[1]

The ability of those in the media to freely report on public affairs as they see fit—but within the limits of defamation laws, public disclosure laws, and national security and policy-making interests—is crucial to democracy. If broadcasters, Internet sites, or journalists can be shut down, censored, or punished because public officials do not like the information they convey, the free discussion of public issues is diminished, and democracy suffers. The founders of the American republic knew this, which is why freedom of the press, along with freedom of speech, religion, and assembly, was specifically mentioned in the First Amendment to the United States Constitution and in several of the state constitutions. Virginia's 1776 Bill of Rights states "That the freedom of the press is one of the great bulwarks of liberty, and can never be restrained but by despotick government."[2] Canada's founders devoted little attention to freedom of the press or other freedoms. They assumed that these would be adequately respected under the system of parliamentary government and that a democratic society had no need to explicitly state the principles that it lived by.

At the same time, all countries regulate the media system in some way. This is particularly true of broadcasting, where the airwaves have been defined as public property throughout the world and where there have been technological reasons for restricting the number of broadcasters in order to protect the quality of the television or radio signals reaching consumers. But this traditional argument for regulation has been challenged by newer technologies. The proliferation of websites and blogs on the Internet is the most recent culmination of these technological developments, resulting in more information and a more diverse range of perspectives being available to more people than at any time in human history. This flood of information means that state regulation of information is increasingly difficult.

The state regulation of the media may not be the only threat to freedom of the press and the health of democracy. A more serious threat, some critics argue, is the economic censorship that may result from the increasing monopolization of media ownership—when too few owners control too many media outlets. Critics also claim that most mass media outlets' dependence on advertising is a key factor in filtering out certain forms of controversial, critical, and non-mainstream coverage of political, economic, and social affairs.

Before we attempt to make sense of the controversial relationship between the media to politics, let us examine the mass media's role in social learning and the chief characteristics of Canada's media system.

"THE PICTURES IN OUR HEADS"

As creators and purveyors of images and information, the media play a role in **social learning**—*the process of acquiring knowledge, values, and beliefs about the world and ourselves.* Other agents of social learning include the family, schools, peer groups, and organizations that one belongs to. Studies of social learning have shown that the family is the most important agent of social learning. It has a crucial influence on the development of an individual's sense of self-esteem, trust, and disposition towards authority, all of which have been linked to political attitudes and behaviour. As well, the family typically has a major impact on one's acquisition of communication skills, class identification, and social attitudes (e.g., gender roles). Although none of this learning is about politics per se, it has important political consequences.

While the family and other agents of social learning contribute to what Walter Lippmann called "the pictures in our heads," none of them rival the media in their impact on the political agenda. "The only feeling that anyone can have about an event that he does not experience is the feeling aroused by his mental image of that event."[3] The contours of modern political discourse are largely determined by the mass media as they process and report on "reality." Moreover, when it comes to matters remote from one's personal experience and daily life—political turmoil in the Middle East, global pollution, or the latest Canadian federal budget—the media are the only source of images and information about the events, issues, and personalities involved. Politicians and generals realize the media's importance. This is why the first steps in any coup d'état are to seize control of broadcasting and to shut down or muzzle newspapers not sympathetic to the new regime.

It has been said that the media do not determine what we think so much as what we think about. This is a formidable power, which can shape the public consciousness by conveying certain images and interpretations and excluding others. The responsibility that accompanies such power is enormous. A "free press" has been viewed as a necessary ingredient of democratic politics since the American Revolution. The reasoning here is that because all groups and individuals are self-interested, they cannot be counted on to objectively assess their goals and actions. Too often their interests will be best served through concealment, deception, and manipulation, and by **propaganda**—*the dissemination of selected information and/or misinformation to the public as a means of spreading a particular ideology or doctrine.*

Many have argued that only the media have an interest in presenting the facts. They may perform their function imperfectly, and particular media outlets may have political biases, which reflect the values and prejudices of their journalists, editors, and readers, but competition ensures that significant points of view reach the public.

Is this an accurate picture of the media's role in a democracy? How well do the media cover all significant points of view? And what are the actual consequences of their behaviour on politics? Let us start by considering the "products" of the mass media.

WHAT DO THE MEDIA PRODUCE?

Despite the existence of a hard-core minority who tune in mainly or exclusively for news and public affairs, most programming aims to entertain rather than inform. Consequently, only a small portion of television and radio time is devoted to public affairs. The rest of the time is spent watching drama, comedy, game and talk shows, and sports, and listening to music. The

Anchors we watch on a daily basis (pictured here is Lisa LaFlamme of CTV National News) become a trusted source of news. After that relationship of trust has been formed, do we become less critical of content? When you watch a nightly newscast, do you think about the perspective from which the story is being told? Do you seek out other perspectives on that story? What might you discover if you watched reports from different broadcasters on the same news item?

English segment of Canada's television market has always been overwhelmingly dominated by American programming (see Figure 11.1) as evidenced by the top-ranked programs for any given week.

Private radio broadcasters account for about 90 per cent of the market, and most of what they offer is music. Although the Canadian Radio-television and Telecommunications Commission (CRTC), the industry's regulatory watchdog, requires all radio stations to carry news, only the largest privately owned stations generate any significant amount of news themselves. Most rely on information supplied by wire services, newspapers, and local sports and weather to meet their news quota. Only stations affiliated with the state-owned Canadian Broadcasting Corporation and Radio-Canada, its French-language counterpart, broadcast a significant amount of national and international public affairs programming that has been generated by their own staff.

Like most radio stations, newspapers are geared primarily to the local market. Although all dailies carry national and international news, studies suggest that newspapers are considered to be better than either television or radio as a source of community information, while television is believed to be the best source of information for international, national, and even provincial news. Television is also judged to be most up to date, fair and unbiased, believable, influential, and essential to the country. A 2007 survey conducted for the Information Technology Association of Canada found that this preference for television as the most important and trustworthy medium continues.[4] Newspapers are relied on by most readers chiefly as a source of local information. A few Canadian dailies, including the Toronto-based *Globe and Mail* and the *National Post*, do not conform to this community paper model, and they have the greatest national circulations among Canadian newspapers. Other dailies such as the *Toronto Star*, *Montreal Gazette*, *Ottawa Citizen*, and *Vancouver Sun* also include more coverage of national

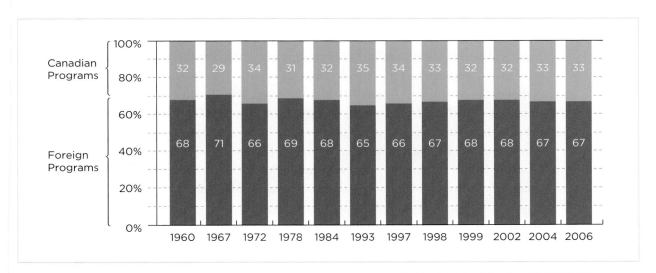

FIGURE 11.1 PRIME-TIME TV VIEWING IN ENGLISH CANADA, 1960–2006 (6 P.M.–MIDNIGHT)

Note: The domination of foreign, overwhelmingly American, programming is even more striking during the heart of prime time. The 6 p.m. to midnight period includes suppertime and late-evening news programming, which is popular with Canadian viewers.

Source: Canadian Media Research, "Trends in TV Audiences and Public Opinion, 1996–2006," 14 March 2007. Used with permission.

and international news than is typical of most dailies. The *Globe*'s long-standing reputation as English Canada's "national" newspaper—which the *Post* has challenged since it began in 1998—has been acquired in part because of high-calibre journalism. The political columnists and editorial writers of both the *Globe* and the *National Post* are influential players in defining the country's political agenda. Montreal-based *Le Devoir* plays a similar role in Quebec.

Print Media

Critics of Canadian newspapers have focused on a number of specific concerns relating to industry structure. First, concentrated ownership is seen as limiting the range of ideas and information that reach the public. However, the need to make profit and the organizational structure of news gathering and reporting seem to have more impact than competition within the industry.

Second, newspapers that are part of larger corporate networks that include non-media interests may be reluctant to cover stories and interpret events in ways that put their owners' other interests in a bad light. However, the empirical proof for this claim is weak. Incidents of owner interference or media self-censorship based on a sensitivity to an owner's interests occasionally happen.[5] But as Edward Herman and Noam Chomsky argue, it is too simplistic to look for direct correlations between ownership and the handling of particular issues or stories; instead, owners exercise their influence more diffusely through "establishing the general aims of the company and choosing its top management."[6]

Finally, ownership is said to produce a certain uniformity in the partisan orientations of newspapers within the chain. This claim is not supported by the evidence either. Studies carried out by researchers at the University of Windsor found no proof that chain ownership is associated with either the patterns of news reporting or editorial policy.[7] Differences between newspapers may have far more to do with readership characteristics than with ownership.

In the case of magazines, foreign ownership, rather than concentrated ownership, is the major political issue. Best-selling ones include scandal sheets like the *National Enquirer*, current affairs weeklies like *Newsweek*, *Time*, *Maclean's*, and *Sports Illustrated*, monthlies like *National Geographic* and *Reader's Digest*, and magazines directed mainly at a female readership such as *Ladies' Home Journal*, *Cosmopolitan*, *Elle*, and *Chatelaine*. All of these sell hundreds of thousands of copies monthly or weekly, but most are not oriented towards coverage of politics and public affairs, and in fact, several of the most popular ones are American-based. The "hard news" magazines with large circulations, such as *Time*, *Newsweek*, and *Maclean's*, occupy the conventional middle ground of Canadian and American politics.

Film

Compared to the media we have discussed so far, film may appear relatively insignificant. The average Canadian goes to the cinema only four or five times per year (city-dwellers more often). Some of the time Canadians spend in front of the television is spent watching films. Cable television, satellite broadcasting, pay-TV, DVD/Bluray players, and iPods have all increased the market penetration of films, allowing the film industry to bring its product directly into people's homes. New technology has enabled the film industry to recapture some of the prominence it held between the 1930s and the 1950s, before the advent of television.

Film is at the centre of the modern imagination. If a person has not read the book, they have probably seen its film adaptation. Indeed, we have seen in recent years the power of this visual medium to turn books into motion picture blockbusters like the *Lord of the Rings* trilogy and the Harry Potter films. The stories they tell, the characters they portray, and the stereotypes they convey shape and reflect our popular culture. The archetypes and icons of popular culture are more likely to be associated with movies than with any other mass medium. At the extreme, life may imitate art, as when in the 1999 Littleton, Colorado, massacre, teenage members of the "Trenchcoat Mafia" styled themselves after Leonardo DiCaprio's character in *The Basketball Diaries*. In the 1980s, US president Ronald Reagan borrowed from *Star Wars* to label the Soviet Union the "evil empire," and called for a "star wars" defence system (formally referred to as the Strategic Defense Initiative).

What does the film industry offer the viewing public? Hundreds of new releases every

Where film tends to reinforce dominant values and institutions, there is a trend in news satire shows that does the opposite. Canada's Rick Mercer, host of the award-winning *Rick Mercer Report*, offers a weekly take on current events that skewers and critiques mainstream politics. In the United States, similar shows like Jon Stewart's *The Daily Show* and Stephen Colbert's *The Colbert Report* offer this alternative view while also poking fun at the "infotainment" formats found on many news channels.

year from Hollywood studios, and thousands more from independents in the United States, Canada, and elsewhere, might lead one to assume that the industry produces a richly varied product. It does. But only a narrow band of the entire range of film production is backed up with the marketing resources of the studios that produce *commercial feature films*. The genre may vary, but what distinguishes such a film is the fact that it must appeal to a large mass audience to recoup the millions of dollars—sometimes hundreds of millions of dollars—spent on its production and marketing. Documentary and artistic films by contrast usually cost much less to make, and generate smaller revenues. They usually are made by small independent film companies or by state-owned filmmakers like Canada's National Film Board. Little is spent on marketing them, and public access to non-commercial films is limited; distributors do not want to show them and relatively few video rental stores stock them.

The images and stories purveyed by the commercial film industry are often disturbing and occasionally critical of "the system." Indeed, one of the most popular motifs of popular film has long been the lone good man versus the bad system. Bruce Willis, Denzel Washington, and Harrison Ford have been among the more successful in portraying this character. *It's a Wonderful Life* and *To Kill a Mockingbird* are classic examples of this simple theme, as are the archetypal westerns *Shane* and *High Noon*. More recent examples include *Places in the Heart*, *Silkwood*, *Grand Canyon*, and *Erin Brockovich*. But on balance, commercial film reinforces dominant values and institutions rather than challenging them. The economics of the industry make this inevitable.

Advertisement

Advertisements are another important part of the media product. Most people are exposed to hundreds of ads each day. Television and radio are heavily laced with them. Newspapers and magazines are bursting with them. Even films have become vehicles for advertising, with companies willing to pay thousands of dollars for *product placement*. Billboards, storefront signs, pamphlets, flyers, the cinema, Internet banners . . . there is no escape. The estimated amount spent on mass media advertising worldwide exceeds the value of Canada's GNP. The advertising assault is so massive and unremitting that the vast majority of it fails to pierce our consciousness. Advertisers have long been aware of this and search continually for ways to capture the attention of the public to whom they want to sell something.

While most advertising aims to affect our behaviour as consumers, some advertising aims to persuade people to vote or think in particular ways, or simply provides them with useful information. Much public service advertising by governments falls into this last category. But there is much more to commercial advertising than the message "buy product X." We are urged to buy because a high-consumption capitalist economy is sustained by the frenetic materialism that pervades our culture. This materialism is reinforced by the mass media through advertising and entertainment programming. When the message "buy this" is hurled at us hundreds of times a day from the time we are quite young, the cumulative impact is to instill and sustain a high-consumption mindset.

Another incidental but pervasive message communicated through commercial advertising is gender stereotyping and the use of sexual imagery and innuendo. The youthful, the slender, the muscular, the large-breasted, the extroverted, the materially successful, and the "cool" are far more likely to appear in mass media ads than are those who are deficient in these qualities. Who and what are excluded from visual advertising are as important as who and what are included. This includes the poor, visible minorities, men and women who do not conform to fairly traditional stereotypes, and so on (as defined by the marketers of popular culture). There are, of course, exceptions. But in general, advertisers find it more profitable to appeal to conventional beliefs and prejudices and to very basic emotional needs and insecurities. This aspect of commercial advertising has not changed since its birth on Madison Avenue, New York City, in the mid 1800s (see Box 11.1).

WHAT DETERMINES THE MASS MEDIA PRODUCT?

No one really believes that the mass media simply mirror reality. "The facts of modern life do not spontaneously take a shape in which they can be known. They must be given a shape by somebody."[8] Confronted with more information than can be conveyed, those who produce the media product must choose what stories, images, and "facts" to communicate to the public. What ultimately is offered to the consumer is a somewhat distorted version of a "reality" that is

MEDIA BEAT

BOX 11.1 | The Art of Selling

The principles underlying this [commercial advertising] are extremely simple. Find some common desire, some widespread unconscious fear or anxiety; think out some way to relate this wish or fear to the product you have to sell; then build a bridge of verbal or pictorial symbols over which your customer can pass from fact to compensatory dream, and from the dream to the illusion that your product, when purchased, will make the dream come true. "We no longer buy oranges, we buy vitality. We do not buy just an auto, we buy prestige.". . . In toothpaste, . . . we buy, not a mere cleanser and antiseptic, but release from the fear of being sexually repulsive. . . . In every case the motivation analyst has found some deep-seated wish or fear, whose energy can be used to move the consumer to part with cash and so, indirectly, to turn the wheels of industry. Stored in the minds and bodies of countless individuals, this potential energy is released by, and transmitted along, a line of symbols carefully laid out so as to bypass rationality and obscure the real issue.

Source: *Brave New World*, by Aldous Huxley. Copyright © 1932, 1946, by Aldous Huxley. Reprinted by permission of Georges Borchardt, Inc., on behalf of the Aldous and Laura Huxley Trust. All rights reserved. Excerpted from *Brave New World* by Aldous Huxley. Copyright © 1932, 1960 Aldous Huxley. Reprinted by permission of Random House Canada. Reprinted by permission of HarperCollins Publishers.

Democracy Watch

BOX 11.2 The Future of News Media

In our networked world, the way many people connect with news is changing rapidly. These changes will, in turn, reshape the way people engage with politics. Have a look at the following statistics, tracked by the Pew Research Center's Internet & American Life Project:

- Half of cellphone owners access news on their phone; two-thirds of smartphone users access news on their phone
- 20–40 per cent of consumers contribute to news (e.g., by joining comment threads when reading news online)
- The number of people who now check in on news periodically over the day rather than tuning at a specific time (e.g., watching a nightly newscast) has increased from 48 per cent in 2002 to 57 per cent in 2010
- From 1991 to 2010, the number of people who watch the news on TV has decreased by 10 per cent; who read hardcopy newspapers, 25 per cent; and who listen to radio news, 20 per cent. Meanwhile, the number of people who get their news from online sources has increased by 10 per cent, and the proportion of those who access the web for news through a mobile device currently sits at 44 per cent.

Source of statistics: Lee Rainie, Director, Pew Internet and American Life Project, "News in a Networked World," 27 April 2012: http://pewinternet.org/Presentations/2012/Apr/News-in-a-networked-world.aspx

Up for Debate

Given the statistics above, news consumed over the Internet will ultimately replace traditional media such as newspapers, radio shows, and nightly newscasts as citizens' primary source of political information. Is this good for democracy or bad for democracy? Why?

constructed in the process of being communicated. The choices made by those who contribute to the product are not random. Several factors influence how reality is processed and how news is reported by the media. These factors may be understood as a series of *filters* that are likely to let through certain information and images rather than others. To put it very simply, information and images that threaten the privileges of dominant social and economic groups are less likely to make it through these media filters than those that are orthodox and non-menacing. Most of us are conditioned to believe that the media are independent and frequently critical of the powerful. However, the media's role in politics is essentially conservative: they do much more to support the status quo than they do to erode it.

As we see below, economic pressures, regulatory requirements, the legal system, and the cultural norms have an important impact on what the mass media produce.

The Economic Filter

Most media outlets are privately owned, and are subject to the law of the marketplace: they must be able to sell a product that will attract enough subscribers, advertisers, buyers, or patrons to cover production costs and to make a profit. While no single media product needs to appeal to everyone, the high costs of producing a daily newspaper, magazine, television series, or movie requires a mass market. And when a marketplace is competitive, there is a tendency to avoid programming or content that has a limited appeal.

State ownership alters, but does not eliminate, the economic pressures to which the mass media are exposed. Publicly owned broadcasters must be sensitive to charges of elitism. This is particularly true of television broadcasting, where the costs of producing high-quality entertainment programming are great. Few politicians would risk losing votes over subsidies for programs that attract tiny audiences. Market influences are even greater when a public broadcaster must rely to some extent on revenues from advertising or viewer/corporate support.

The economic filter operates mainly through the influence of advertising and industry structure on the media product. Without advertising dollars, privately owned and even (to a lesser degree) publicly owned media companies are not economically viable. These media companies compete for the advertising patronage of business. The advertising base of a newspaper or radio broadcaster is typically more local than that of a television network, but the maxim still holds: in an ad-dependent medium, advertisers' preferences cannot be ignored. The media will tend to avoid reporting or programming that reduces their attractiveness in the eyes of advertisers.

How is this relevant to politics? First, dependence on advertising may reduce the likelihood that powerful economic interests will be portrayed in a negative light. Second, most television broadcasting and most viewing time are devoted to lucrative entertainment programming. As a result, economic pressure leads ad-dependent broadcasters to maximize the amount of high audience-appeal programming during prime-time hours, and to relegate public affairs programming to off-peak viewing times or to state-owned or viewer-supported broadcasters, and/or to adopt an entertainment format. The emergence of what has been called "infotainment" or "soft news"—news

The increase in the availability of electronic media and the merging of information and entertainment makes many wonder how well the media keep us informed about politics. What is your main source of news? Does the information in this chapter make you want to consider alternative sources?

that is packaged using an entertainment, celebrity journalist format—has become prevalent in the United States. The Canadian industry may not have gone as far in breaking down the traditional barriers between entertainment and public affairs programming, although the local news programming model developed by Rogers' "CityNews" is essentially the same as the soft news format pioneered in the United States. But as in the United States, the economics of broadcasting in Canada works against the viability of programming that does not attract a mass audience, and so the pressures to adopt the infotainment/celebrity newsreader format are great.

State-owned media outlets like the CBC, TV Ontario, and Télé-Québec in Canada and the viewer-supported Public Broadcasting System (PBS) in the United States are not immune from the influence of advertising. Both the CBC and Télé-Québec rely on advertising for part of their revenue. Viewer-supported broadcasters like TV Ontario and the American PBS rely on government subsidies (directly and through the tax system) and corporate sponsorship of programs for part of their revenue needs. Some critics have argued that corporate sponsorship, like advertising, tends to filter out socially divisive and controversial programming.

Dependence on state subsidies does not necessarily remove all constraints on media content. Public broadcasters must constantly be sensitive to charges of bias and ideological favouritism. Over the years CBC television programs such as *This Hour Has Seven Days*, *the fifth estate*, *Marketplace*, *The Passionate Eye*, and the various programs hosted by environmentalist David Suzuki, notably *The Nature of Things*, have been accused of having a leftist political bias and of being anti-business. The in-house monitoring of CBC broadcasting for "fairness" has reached unprecedented levels of sophistication. Much of this, as during election campaigns, is intended to ensure that the CBC is even-handed in its treatment of the major political parties and their leaders. In the world of public broadcasting, "culturecrats" and politicians' aversion to controversy may substitute for the check that dependence on advertising imposes on private broadcasters.

Industry structure is the second component of the economic filter. As the costs associated with producing a newspaper have increased, competition has suffered. The daily newspaper industry in Canada (as in the United States) is characterized by local monopoly. In only nine Canadian cities (Halifax, Quebec City, Montreal, Ottawa, Toronto, Winnipeg, Calgary, Edmonton, and Vancouver) is there competition between same-language, mass-circulation dailies that have different owners. Chain ownership is a feature of both the English- and French-language markets.

Television and radio markets, to say nothing of the Internet, are much more fragmented than the newspaper market. The days are long past when a handful of American broadcasters, plus the CBC, dominated television broadcasting. Cable and satellite technology, and the development of the Internet, have created unprecedented opportunities for niche programming targeted at smaller audiences than was required previously to ensure profitability. The economics of electronic media are significantly different from those of print media, such that concentrated ownership is not as prominent an issue in broadcasting as in newspaper markets.

Instead, the ownership issue in broadcasting and new media like the Internet is framed chiefly as an issue of American penetration into Canadian markets. There may indeed be hundreds of television stations that Canadian viewers have access to through direct broadcast satellite (DBS), cable technology, or the Internet, but the fact remains that the most popular ones either originate in the United States or rely extensively on American-produced programming. Issues of ownership in the United States and abroad are thereby imported into Canada.

One of these issues involves the new corporate convergence in mass media, particularly in electronic media industries. As the nationalist Friends of Canadian Broadcasting puts it, "large media multinationals are getting larger, concentrating their market power, crossing over into new lines of [media] business and crossing national borders with unprecedented ease."[9] Critics argue that multi-media convergence and the growth of giants like Time Warner, Sony, and Disney (corporate empires that span every kind of media including books, music, magazines, television, films, and pay-per-view TV) will accelerate the erosion of national cultures like that of Canada.

The trend towards the monopolization of media production and distribution is not likely to provide much opportunity for the expression of distinctively Canadian values, perspectives, and stories. Or is it? There is, after all, little doubt that more Canadian programming is produced and available today than ever before. This has been largely due to government regulation and subsidies, to which we now turn.

The Legal/Regulatory Filter

Unlike radio and television broadcasters and cable system companies, the print media in Canada and in most other democracies are basically free from direct regulation by government. They essentially regulate themselves through press councils created and operated by the industry. These councils receive and investigate complaints but do not systematically monitor performance. Calls for greater state regulation of their behaviour invariably provoke cries of censorship from those in the newspaper and magazine business.

Nonetheless, indirect forms of regulation may affect the content of print media. Most of these involve measures whose ostensible aim is to promote Canadian values through newspapers and magazines. For example, the federal Income Tax Act permits advertisers to deduct from their taxable income only the cost of ads placed in newspapers or magazines that are at least 75 per cent Canadian-owned. This explains why foreign ownership of Canadian newspapers has never been an issue. But it is doubtful that the provisions of the Income Tax Act favouring Canadian-owned publications has much of an impact on newspaper content. As indicated previously, with the exceptions of the *Globe and Mail*, the *National Post*, and *Le Devoir*, newspapers are geared mainly to local markets. Therefore, the content and their profitability will depend on a large local readership that they can "sell" to local advertisers and not on the nationality of their owners.

One might argue that the owner's nationality could influence a newspaper's coverage of national and international news, or of sports and comics, but even Canadian-owned papers, for economic reasons, depend on news purchased from foreign news agencies like the Associated Press, particularly for international news and sports. Most comic strips and cartoons, which are important reinforcers and purveyors of values, are produced by American cartoonists. In the end, the Income Tax Act almost certainly does more to promote Canadian ownership than Canadian culture.

The Canadian ownership provisions of the Income Tax Act also apply to magazines, but the English-Canadian market is dominated by American magazines and split-run publications: magazines that incur most of their editorial and other production costs outside of Canada, and a mostly non-Canadian readership. Split-run editions could be produced at a very low cost by importing the American version via satellite and then adding a few pages of Canadian content, thereby qualifying for the lower Canadian advertising rates that Canadian magazines are able to offer advertisers. This was done in 1993 by Time Warner's immensely popular *Sports Illustrated*, which in turn triggered changes in Canadian tax law to halt the practice.

In 1997 the World Trade Organization, responding to an American complaint, ruled that laws subsidizing Canadian magazines and treating foreign periodicals differently in terms of taxation and postal rates violated Canada's international trade obligations. The federal government responded with Bill C-55, which proposed heavy fines for any magazine publisher selling ads in Canadian editions of foreign magazines, a measure that was clearly targeted at the highly profitable split-run issues of US magazines. When American publishers protested loudly, Canadian advertisers and the American government reached a compromise in 1999 requiring that split-run editions include a majority of Canadian content in order to sell advertising space at the lower Canadian rate.

The split-run issue encapsulates the essential regulatory dilemma for Canadian policy makers grappling with preserving Canadian culture and promoting domestic cultural industries. It boils down to this: the much larger American market enables US magazine publishers to produce a glossier product and pay better rates for articles at a lower cost than their small-market Canadian counterparts. Moreover, Canadians essentially like what American magazines offer. An estimated 80 per cent of the magazines on Canadian newsstands are American. Availability of Canadian magazines is not the problem. According to the Canadian magazine industry's own figures there are roughly 1500 magazines published in Canada. But with no language barrier and low cultural barriers between English Canada and the United States, American magazines do not seem to be foreign in the way that British or other English-language ones do.

State regulation is much more intrusive in the case of the electronic media. The original reason for treating broadcasting differently from print media was the need to prevent chaos on overcrowded airwaves. Controlling entry in a market through the licensing of broadcasters seemed the only practical solution to this potential problem. At the same time, however, broadcasting policy has always been based on the assumption that only extensive state intervention can prevent complete American domination of the Canadian market.[10]

The content regulations for both radio and television constitute one of the pillars of Canadian broadcasting policy. The CRTC establishes and enforces a complicated set of content guidelines that all licensed broadcasters must observe. The idea behind them is to ensure that more Canadian content reaches the airwaves (see Box 11.3).

As for television, the economics of the recording industry encourages products that are marketable outside of Canada. Radio stations typically deal with Canadian content requirements by relying heavily on recordings by performers like the Barenaked Ladies, Céline Dion, Nelly Furtado, and Avril Lavigne, whose music seems as at home in Boston as Toronto, and, to the degree that regulations permit, by marginalizing much of their Canadian content to

MEDIA BEAT

BOX 11.3 | What Is Canadian Content?

Media	CRTC Canadian Content Requirements
Radio	Musical selections qualify if they meet any two of the following criteria:

- The music is composed entirely by a Canadian.
- The lyrics are written entirely by a Canadian.
- The music is or lyrics are performed principally by a Canadian.
- The live performance is performed wholly in Canada and broadcast live in Canada or recorded wholly in Canada.
- The musical selection was performed live or recorded after 7 September 1991, and a Canadian who has collaborated with a non-Canadian receives at least 50 per cent of the credit as composer and lyricist.

At least 35 per cent of all music aired must meet the above definition. Other requirements include:

- In recognition of FM radio's diversity of formats, the CRTC allows different levels of required Canadian music content.
- The quota is as low as 7 per cent for ethnic radio stations.
- At least 65 per cent of the music played on French-language radio stations must have French vocals—a quota that drops to 55 per cent between 6:00 a.m. and 6:00 p.m.

Television To be considered Canadian, a television program must have:

- A Canadian producer and must earn a minimum 6 of a possible 10 points. Points are awarded when the duties of certain positions are performed by Canadians.
- There are additional criteria regarding financial and creative control for programs involving foreign production partners.
- Canadian programs must be used to fill at least 60 per cent of the overall schedules of both public and private television broadcasters.
- Canadian content must fill at least 50 per cent of evening programming hours for private broadcasters and 60 per cent for public broadcasters.

off-peak hours. The advent of satellite radio has presented Canadian regulators with a new version of the old challenge of Canadians' apparent appetite for American products over homegrown competitors.

Governments also affect the content of Canadian film and television productions through subsidies and through their direct participation in the industry as broadcasters and film-makers. The Canadian content quotas are, in the case of television, met largely through sports, news, and public affairs programming. However, most viewing time is spent watching enter-tainment programs, few of which are Canadian, because American-made products are made at a fraction of the production costs. In English-speaking Canada only the CBC broadcasts a significant amount of Canadian-made entertainment programming. To compensate for the unfavourable economics of domestic production, Ottawa offers subsidies, which is done mostly through Telefilm Canada for Canadian-made feature films, television programs, docu-mentary films, and animation, and also international co-productions.

While the publicly owned CBC, Radio-Canada, TV Ontario, and Télé-Québec have been among the major recipients of money provided through Telefilm Canada over the years, private television and film producers have also drawn on this source of public money. Fears have long been expressed that private producers typically use these subsidies to produce films and television programs that are as far as possible unrecognizable as Canadian productions so as not to alienate potential American audiences. There are economic pressures to turn out an exportable product in order to recoup costs through foreign (usually American) sales. In the case of feature films, the problem is largely that the sole major distribution chain, Cineplex Galaxy, does little to promote Canadian-made films. And the companies producing films do not have the resources to advertise widely to generate audience interest.

In spite of the unfavourable economics and a system of subsidies that appears to have a limited impact, recognizably Canadian programs and films do get produced. In the end, it falls to public broadcasters and the National Film Board to show Canadians what is distinctive about their society and culture. Under the Broadcasting Act, the CBC is required to be "a balanced service of information, enlightenment and entertainment for people of different ages, interests and tastes covering the whole range of programming in fair proportion." The CBC, through its English- and French-language divisions, has done far more to Canadianize the airwaves than any other broadcaster. Its ability to do so, however, is threatened by budget cuts that began in the late 1970s.The CBC has responded by increasing its dependence on advertising, which places it between a rock and a hard place. On the one hand, the CBC must rely on Canadian programming. On the other hand, it is increasingly dependent on the revenues from the sale of advertising time, which requires that programming achieve audience ratings that will attract and retain advertisers.

The NFB's mandate is to "interpret Canada to Canadians and the rest of the world" (Film Act). For 70 years the NFB has done this to critical and international acclaim, turning out documentaries and serious drama that the private sector has been unwilling to invest in, produce, distribute, or show. As in the case of the CBC, the burden of showing Canadians images of themselves falls to a publicly owned corporation.

Media content is also affected through federal and provincial laws dealing with obscenity, pornography, and what is called *hate literature*. None of these terms is defined very precisely in Canadian law, but the federal Criminal Code and the Customs Act, as well as provincial statutes dealing with hate literature, restrict the sorts of printed matter and films that may enter Canada or be distributed here, as well as the media products that individuals may possess.

The issue of when and how to restrict media content raises issues of censorship, individual privacy, freedom of expression, public morality, and the safety of certain groups, such as the children who become fodder for pornographic films, magazines, and Internet sites. These issues have become increasingly complex, and traditional methods used to regulate media content have been challenged by the newer media of satellite communications and the Internet. Proposals to regulate media content on the Internet have ranged from making service providers responsible for the content of their websites and email carried over their networks to a law that would require the labelling of all online information to identify the degree of adult content. To this point, however, regulation of the Internet remains relatively slight in Canada and other democracies. Nonetheless, websites and those who communicate via cyberspace, and who fall under the jurisdiction of Canadian governments, are subject to the provisions of the Criminal Code and federal and provincial human rights laws, just as those who communicate through traditional media are.

Not surprisingly, countries in which traditional media are state-controlled have been unwilling to let their populations have full and open access to web-based sources of information. Political authorities in China and some countries of the Middle East routinely attempt to control and restrict access to websites that they deem unacceptable.

The Technological Filter

Few things date more quickly than news. The technology of broadcasting is instantaneous and that of newspapers involves a matter of hours. Indeed, we generally expect that the media will communicate what is happening now. Current events can be reported in the context of the larger background against which they unfold. However, the practical problem is that stories must be edited down to a length suitable for inclusion in a 30-minute news program or the pages of a newspaper.

It is often said that one picture is worth a thousand words. This is doubtless true—sometimes. But it is often the case that the moving images on the screen capture only the surface of events, and this substitutes for an explanation that is more complicated and *non-visual* than the medium can deal with. Of course, people can turn to newspapers, magazines, and books to fill in those parts of the picture that are not covered well by television. But there are good reasons for believing that most do not. We mentioned earlier that a clear majority of Canadians rely on television for their knowledge of national and international affairs and, furthermore, believe this medium to be the most unbiased and believable. In other words, they count on what they see before their eyes. The visual character of television lends itself to the personalization of reality—an emphasis on individuals and personalities at the expense of broad social forces that are not captured by the camera. Consequently, the media, and in particular the technology of television, are disposed towards the personal, the immediate, and the concrete. Reality becomes a constantly shifting pastiche of images, as though those who produce the news assume that the average viewer has an attention span that lasts a minute or two at best. Entertainment programming tends to assume the same faster-than-life character. According to Morris Wolfe, this is due to what he calls the First Law of Commercial Television: "Thou shalt give them enough jolts per minute (JPMs) or thou shalt lose them."[11] Too few JPMs and viewers will lose interest, ratings will suffer, and advertising revenue and profits will fall.

But what are the consequences for politics if the networks simply give the viewers what they want, and, in Wolfe's words, "all television increasingly aspires to the condition of the TV commercial"?[12] He also argues that "a steady diet of nothing but high JPM television tends to condition viewers' nervous systems to respond only to certain kinds of stimulation. Their boredom thresholds are frequently so low that TV viewers find it difficult to enjoy anything that isn't fast-paced."[13]

Politicians and others who regularly come under the eye of the camera have long understood the biases of the visual medium. Photo opportunities and highly structured, controllable events are among their ways of using television's need for the immediate, the personal, and the visual to their

Television spot ads—usually only 20–30 seconds long—are one of the main vehicles for political communication during election campaigns. Some worry that the medium debases the message, dumbing down the political conversation. Do you take the accusations in attack ads seriously, or do you dismiss them?

own advantage. Television has had an enormous impact on how elections are fought, how special interests attempt to influence public policy, and how public officials communicate with the people. One of the masters of the medium, the American social activist Jesse Jackson, remarked over three decades ago on the importance of speaking in short memorable sentences—"sound bites" as they are called today. They conform to the needs of television technology, whereas long, complex statements do not (see Box 11.4).

The visual character of television introduces two significant biases. First, there is a dependence on what Walter Lippmann called a "repertory of stereotypes." He argued that newspaper reporting consisted largely of fitting current news to these stereotypes. There are cultural reasons for this that we will discuss later. But in the case of a visual medium, there are also technological reasons for this dependence. "Viewers' interest," observes Edward Jay Epstein, "is most likely to be maintained through easily recognizable and palpable images, and conversely, most likely to be distracted by unfamiliar or confusing images."[14]

And secondly there is an *emphasis on confrontation*. From the standpoint of a visual medium, confrontation has two virtues: it involves *action*, which is a requirement of most television news and public affairs coverage, and it involves *conflict*, which helps present a story in a way that viewers can easily grasp. Epstein notes that "Situations are thus sought out in network news in which there is a high potential for violence, but a low potential for audience confusion."[15]

The Organizational Filter

News gathering and reporting are carried out by organizations. The needs and routine procedures of these organizations influence the content of the news, both what is reported and how it is covered. The organization's difficulty is that news developments are often not predictable, and no organization can be everywhere or cover all stories equally well. News organizations rely on various strategies to deal with this problem. In the case of television, several criteria help make the news credible to the public.

Newsworthiness

Those who have a reputation for being influential or who occupy official positions are more likely to make the news than those who do not. Much depends on the eyes of the news gatherers who automatically confer on them a mantle of credibility. The newsworthy include: prime ministers, premiers, and the leaders of opposition parties; mayors and leading councillors when the news is local; spokespersons for what are considered to be important organizations (e.g., the Canadian Council of Chief Executives, the Canadian Labour Congress, EGALE, and the Catholic Church).

Government officials and powerful private interests understand the routines and operational requirements of news organizations. For instance, the evening news needs to have the film footage ready by a certain hour to allow time for editing. And if one wants to influence public opinion, then accommodating the media's needs through well-timed press conferences, photo opportunities, news releases or staged events—what Daniel Boorstin has called "pseudo-events"—is essential. This practice has been called news management. Governments, public affairs departments, and media relations specialists may not able to control the news agenda, but they are able to influence news reporting.

Publicly acknowledged experts will also be sought out by the media. What makes one a "publicly acknowledged expert"? A specialty and an affiliation with a respectable institution such as the C.D. Howe Institute, the Canadian Centre for Policy Alternatives, or a university—particularly a university located in a city where a network has production facilities—is one of the key determinants of this status. Spokespersons for marginal groups and unconventional views are much less likely to be deemed newsworthy.

The mass media's demand for the ideas and information generated by experts is based on a combination of factors. One of these is the media's self-image as dispenser of the news, reporter of the facts. A second factor is the media's need for low-cost information and instant analysis. To conduct their own analysis would be expensive and time-consuming, and most journalists are in any case not professionally trained as economists or epidemiologists or political scientists. Third, in order to protect themselves against charges of bias and lawsuits, media organizations and reporters need information "that can be portrayed as presumptively accurate."[16] Expert knowledge meets this requirement. In fact, the media's need for expert opinion and information helps to confer this social respectability on individuals and institutions, and in many instances probably serves to reinforce the political status quo.

Predictability

Predictability is important in determining what becomes "news." Any news organization operates within the framework of a budget and the limited resources. Other things being equal, it makes sense to concentrate organizational resources (e.g., researchers, camera crews, and journalists) where news is most likely to happen: Parliament Hill, the provincial capitals, Toronto, Montreal, and internationally as resources permit. The unplanned and unexpected happenings are less likely to be covered than scheduled events that take place near where a news crew is stationed. As Epstein puts it, "The more predictable the event, the more likely it will be covered."[17]

Visual Appeal

Television obviously needs pictures. But some subjects are more telegenic than others. Epstein writes:

> . . . priority is naturally given to the story in a given category that promises to yield the most dramatic or visual film footage, other things being equal. This means, in effect, that political institutions with rules that restrict television cameras from filming the more dramatic parts of their proceedings are not routinely assigned coverage.[18]

Canadians see much more of what is happening in the House of Commons, particularly question period, than they do of the Supreme Court. Yet the Court's decisions have an enormous impact on public policy and in many instances more so than the fairly predictable antics of parliamentarians. Likewise, closed meetings of first ministers or of the institutions of the bureaucracy generally are either inaccessible to cameras or lack the sort of *visual spice* considered crucial to televised news. The result, therefore, is to overemphasize the importance of those actors and individuals who can be filmed in action—action that is often stage-managed by the actors themselves—and to underemphasize the significance of those who are more reclusive, less confrontational, or less visually sensational.

A news organization's need for stories that are newsworthy, predictable, and visually appealing produces a situation where "the news selected is the news expected."[19] Along with the other filters that we have discussed, the organizational one creates biases that affect media content. Simple dramatized confrontation, familiar players and issues, and a relatively narrow range of locales where most news happens are among these biases.

The Ideological Filter

Those who report the news are often accused by conservatives and business people of having liberal-left and anti-business biases. They are more likely, it is argued, to favour stories and groups that challenge established authority. The CBC in general and some of its programs in particular have occasionally been accused of ideological bias against conservatism and big business (especially American business). Similar charges have been heard in the United States, where Republicans, conservatives, fundamentalist Christians, and business interests have often accused the major networks, and journalists generally, of having liberal biases.

Studies seem to confirm these claims. An early American study that looked at the social backgrounds, personality traits, ideologies, and world views of business and media elites found that media respondents typically gave more liberal responses to such statements as "Government should substantially reduce the income gap between rich and poor."[20] The researchers concluded that "leading journalists seem to inhabit a symbolic universe which is quite different from that of businessmen, with implications for the manner in which they report the news to the general public."[21] Several American studies have confirmed that those in the media, particularly the electronic media, tend to be more liberal than members of the general population. A study of CBC radio, directed by Barry Cooper, concluded that "on the whole, [the CBC] adopted a left-wing, rather than right-wing critical stance."[22]

This conclusion is reinforced by what is probably the most systematic study of Canadian journalists' values and beliefs to date.[23] Based on a survey of electronic and print journalists and a sample of the general public, Barry Cooper and Lydia Miljan draw two main conclusions. First, English-Canadian journalists tend to be more left of centre than the general public. Second, the left-leaning tendencies of journalists affect the way news stories are reported, which challenges the media's credo of objectivity. The media differ from their audiences and readerships in the following ways:

- Journalists are less religious than the public.
- Although they tend to agree with the general public's ideas of private-sector journalists on the desirability of capitalism, free markets, and private property, the views of the public-sector CBC journalists are significantly to the left.
- The public is more conservative on social issues than those in the media.
- Journalists are considerably more likely than the general public to vote for the NDP.

Cooper and Miljan also note that French-Canadian journalists are closer to their audience/readership in their political and social views than are English-Canadian journalists to theirs, which may reflect a more secularized, libertarian, and left-leaning society in Quebec.

BECAUSE 'TRUTH' IS A SUBJECTIVE TERM

MEDIA BIAS

AND 'FACTS' ARE WHAT YOU MAKE THEM

A number of media watchers have noted that the quality of political coverage and discourse in the media may be deteriorating. What makes democracies particularly vulnerable to the quality of the political coverage in the media? How does the quality of the information we get in the media affect our quality of life? What might be some of the consequences to the political process if the average person cannot rely on quality coverage by their trusted media networks?

The ideological gap between the media's left-of-centre views and Canadian society needs to be understood in the context of what "left" and "right" mean in Canadian society. "Left" does not mean fundamental opposition to the basic institutions of the capitalist economy. On the contrary, in the predominantly liberal societies of Canada and the United States, left has always implied ambivalence about business: distrust of excessive concentrations of economic power and the belief that business must be regulated, while accepting the superiority (in most circumstances) of private property and the market economy.

News and public affairs reporting often focuses on conflict and controversy that involves government officials and powerful private interests. This may give the impression that those in the media are anti-establishment critics. However, only a minority of those in the mass media have strong left-wing or right-wing commitments. This is certainly true in Canada. Those on the right, such as David Frum, George Jonas, and Mark Steyn, and those on the left, such as Linda McQuaig, David Suzuki, and Judy Rebick, are the exceptions rather than the rule. Most Canadian journalists are typically in the middle of the ideological spectrum and generally accommodate themselves to the needs of the organization they work for. "They mostly 'say what they like,'" says Ralph Miliband, "but this is mainly because their employers mostly like what they say, or at least find little in what they say which is objectionable."[24]

It should not be assumed that the entertainment and information products of the media industry carry no political messages or ideological biases. They do, both through the images, themes, and interpretations they communicate and through their silences. If the mass media are "more important in confirming or reinforcing existing opinions than they are in changing opinions,"[25] as studies generally suggest, this is partly due to the ideological orthodoxy of most writers, producers, editors, and others who have an influence on the media product.

THE MEDIA AND DEMOCRACY

> In regard to propaganda the early advocates of universal literacy and a free press envisaged only two possibilities: the propaganda might be true, or it might be false. They did not foresee what in fact has happened, above all in our Western capitalist democracies—the development of a vast mass communications industry, concerned in the main neither with the true nor the false, but with the unreal, the more or less totally irrelevant. In a word, they failed to take into account man's almost infinite appetite for distractions.[26]

The media often appear to have few friends except themselves. Politicians, business people, and those on the right of the political spectrum regularly accuse the media of having liberal-left biases, of irresponsible scandal-mongering, and of being inherently and unfairly opposed to established authority. The political left are no less critical of the media. They are apt to view the media as the servile handmaidens of powerful, usually economic interests. Both right and left critics accuse the media of having strong anti-democratic tendencies. Conservatives argue that those in the media tend to be more liberal-left than society as a whole, but that they foist their interests and perspectives on the public behind a smokescreen of journalistic integrity. Left-wing critics claim that the media help to "manufacture consent"[27] for a social system that operates mainly in the interests of a privileged minority: i.e., a *false consciousness* of the dominant ideology.

In this chapter we have argued that the behaviour of the mass media is shaped by a number of filters. These filters cumulatively determine the sort of "product" that is likely to reach the consuming public. Our conclusion is that the products of the mass media generally support established values and institutions whose interests are best served by the status quo. And while it would be ludicrous to claim that the media avoid all criticism of powerful interests, it is easy to prove that the bulk of what appears in the media conforms to mainstream values.

On the other hand, the gains made in recent years by socially marginal, politically weak interests, such as women, Aboriginal Canadians, and environmental activists, have been largely due to media coverage of their demands and spokespersons. The media have helped raise public consciousness of the issues and discourse such as "equal pay for work of equal value," "Aboriginal self-government," and "sustainable development." Moreover, it can hardly be denied that the media usually do a better job of scrutinizing and criticizing government actions, to say nothing of those of powerful societal groups, than do the opposition parties. Indeed, it is precisely the critical and even irreverent tone of much public affairs journalism that contributes to the widespread belief in the mass media's independent and anti-establishment character.

Most of what the mass media offer does not have this character. Frank Lloyd Wright's description of television as "chewing gum for the eyes" is a fairly apt characterization of much

MEDIA BEAT

BOX 11.4 | Editorializing through Public Opinion Polls

"According to an Environics Research Group survey, 57 per cent of Canadians believe that gays and lesbians should be allowed to marry. The results are based on a telephone survey of 1,500 people and are considered to be accurate within a margin of error of plus or minus 2.5 per cent, 19 times out of 20."

Statements like the one above are reported on a daily basis. In fact, polling results have become an indispensable part of media coverage of public affairs, along with the observations and analysis of "experts." Poll results, perhaps even more than the words of interviewed experts, seem to carry a sort of authority that is widely respected. For this reason, it is worth paying attention to why they are conducted, who pays for them, and where they are reported.

It turns out that public opinion polling sometimes shades into editorializing when surveys of public opinion are deliberately used to push the public conversation on an issue in a particular direction. Political parties, governments, and private organizations may commission surveys that are designed to tell a particular story about public opinion. These poll results are inconsequential until they are reported and commented on in the media. And not all polls and polling firms are treated by the media in the same way. Indeed, it has become routine for particular television broadcasters, newspapers, and magazines to have a special relationship to a particular survey research firm. For example, *The Toronto Star*'s pollster of choice is Ekos; the *National Post* and Global Television regularly commission polls carried out by Compas Research; and *Maclean's* magazine has a similar relationship with Environics.

Political parties also have their preferred pollsters for determining the levels of support on issues or for framing and sending messages or images they wish to convey about themselves or their opponents. These polling data will be kept either private or public depending on the strategic and campaigning purposes. All of this requires that some journalists, producers, and news outlets provide access for the public to learn what it is the party wants them to know.

of the electronic and print media. Wright's judgment was basically an aesthetic one. But Aldous Huxley's argument that the "mass communications industry is concerned in the main neither with the true nor the false, but with the unreal, the more or less totally irrelevant," expresses a political judgment about the mass media. Huxley suggested that the media—particularly their entertainment and advertising components—help foster a false consciousness among the public, the sort of pacified somnolence that characterizes the masses in his *Brave New World*. This may seem harsh, but Huxley is certainly right in suggesting that one should not assume that only news and public affairs reporting has political consequences.

SUMMARY

What do the media produce and what do citizens consume? The general public's ideas and images of politics are based on information and interpretations provided by the media. And so, the process of deciding what to cover and how to cover it has important consequences for the interpreters of political news. Several factors influence how reality is processed and how news is reported by the media. These factors may be understood as a series of filters—economic, regulatory, and ideological—that let through certain information and images but not others.

On balance, the media do an uneven job in providing Canadians with the information needed to make informed judgments about their society and its political issues. The biases of the mass media are towards familiar images and stories—what Lippmann called a "repertory of stereotypes"—oversimplified conflict, the personalization of events, drama and action, and reliance on established opinion leaders. As we have seen, even media products that are not explicitly political may nonetheless include images, ideas, and messages that have social and political significance. These biases support much more than threaten the status quo. At the same time, citizens cannot avoid shouldering some of the responsibility for whatever information deficit they experience and ill-founded views they hold. For all the problems surrounding the quality of information that beset the Internet, there is also no doubt that it has put within the reach of almost everyone an enormous range of information and interpretation concerning matters all the way from our own communities to the global community. Reliance on the same old sources of news and public affairs is a choice, not an inevitability.

STARTING POINTS FOR RESEARCH

Lydia Miljan and Barry Cooper, *Hidden Agendas: How Journalists Influence the News* (Vancouver: University of British Columbia Press, 2003).

Paul Nesbitt-Larking, *Politics, Society, and the Media: Canadian Perspectives*, 2nd edn (Toronto: University of Toronto Press, 2007).

Florian Sauvageau, David Taras, and David Schneiderman, *The Last Word: Media Coverage of the Supreme Court of Canada* (Vancouver: University of British Columbia Press, 2005).

Stuart Soroka, *Agenda-Setting Dynamics in Canada* (Vancouver: University of British Columbia Press, 2002).

CBC ARCHIVES AND TVO'S *THE AGENDA*

Visit the companion website for *Canadian Democracy: A Concise Introduction* to follow links to audio and video footage related to the main themes of the chapter: www.oupcanada.com/BrooksConcise.

RELEVANT WEBSITES

Visit the companion website for *Canadian Democracy: A Concise Introduction* to browse a collection of websites featuring material related to the key themes of the chapter, an excellent starting point for research.

REVIEW EXERCISES

1. Keep a two-day record of your typical media consumption (e.g., television, films, radio, newspapers, magazines, books and the Internet), then answer the following:

   a. Which categories does your daily media consumption fall under: entertainment, news and public affairs, or other?

   b. Which medium do you rely upon most for news?

   c. If you pick up a newspaper, which section do you read first? What else do you look at in the newspaper?

   d. Do you read news on the Internet? How often do you click on news stories? Do you rely on blogs or particular websites to keep you informed? Are they Canadian?

2. Watch the late-evening television news broadcast of one of the main Canadian broadcasters (CBC, CTV, or Global). Make a list of those stories where experts are interviewed, and record the positions and affiliations of the experts. Are there other sorts of experts or organizations that could have been contacted for these stories?

3. Find an example of poll results in the media.

   a. Who published the poll?

   b. Who paid for the poll to be conducted?

   c. Was the poll shaped by a political party or a group sympathetic to it or a news outlet sympathetic to its policies?

   d. What is the poll intended to tell the public? Is this information, manipulation, or both?

Part V

Canadian Political Issues

Sometimes, the institutions and processes of Canadian democracy are best understood by examining the issues that roil the waters of politics. For example, the long-standing conflict between French and English Canadians has been played out within the framework of particular institutions and managed through certain processes that have evolved for more than 200 years. These institutions and processes have affected the relationship between the two communities, but the values, demographic characteristics, and circumstances of these communities have also shaped the laws, constitutional changes, and processes that influence their relations.

The text's final two chapters focus on several important issues in Canadian politics, all of which are crucial to understanding what might be described as the Canadian condition. Chapter 12 looks at three issues: language politics and Quebec, the oldest continuing conflict in Canadian politics; diversity, and how various forms of pluralism have affected Canadian political life; and an issue that in many ways is just as old as the ethnolinguistic conflict, that of Aboriginal Canadians and their relationship to other citizens and governments in Canada. The final chapter examines Canada's relations with the rest of the world with a particular emphasis on Canada–US relations. Together, the study of these issues helps us to understand how Canadian democracy has evolved.

12 Language, Diversity, and Aboriginal Politics

It is helpful to look at the challenges and issues faced daily by Canadians as a way to understand Canadian democracy—what it has been and what it is today. After reading this chapter on contemporary issues in Canadian political life, you will be able to

1. Understand why language and the status of Quebec are such prominent issues in Canada
2. Examine the politics of diversity in Canada, with special attention on multiculturalism and gender
3. Explore Aboriginal politics and its core issues, such as landownership and discrimination

LANGUAGE POLITICS

Lord Durham's words, written some 170 years ago, still ring true today: Canada is "two nations warring in the bosom of a single state." The "Quebec question," with demands for changes to Quebec's constitutional status and for language rights, has surfaced repeatedly in Canadian politics. The "Quebec question" might just as fairly be called the "Canada question." Even if Quebec were to separate from Canada, practical matters related to language and economic relations with the rest of Canada would still have to be addressed. Why are Quebec and language so central to Canadian politics? Why has nationalism always been the key to unlocking the mysteries of Quebec politics? And what does Quebec want from the rest of Canada, and the rest of Canada from Quebec? Answers to these questions have been elusive.

History and the Demographics of Language Politics

When New France was formally placed under British control in 1763, francophones outnumbered anglophones by about eight to one. Forty years later, the two groups were of roughly equal size. The wave of immigrants from the British Isles in the 1800s was such that by the 1871 census, Canadians of French origin made up about one-third of the population.[1] The extraordinarily high birth rate among French-Canadian women enabled francophones to hold their own until the end of the 1950s. The end of ***la revanche des berceaux*** ("revenge of the cradle")—***the high birth rate that for close to a century enabled French Canada to maintain its numerical strength***—coupled with the fact that the vast majority of immigrants had chosen to speak English, finally led to a decline in the francophone share of the Canadian population by the early 1960s. The key factor in shifting the linguistic balance of Quebec was immigration. By the 1960s, immigration became the sole reason for provincial population growth; the fertility rate had fallen below the replacement levels.

The francophone share of Canada's population has nudged down to its present all-time low of about 22 per cent.[2] More worrisome to Quebec governments has been the fact that demographers began to predict a fall in the francophone share of that province's population, particularly in Montreal where most new immigrants chose to establish themselves. Except for the relatively few immigrants whose native tongue was French, all other groups (known as **allophones**—*a term used by Canadian demographers for those whose native language is neither English nor French*) have overwhelmingly adopted English for themselves and their children. The possibility that francophones would become a minority in Quebec has often been raised by Quebec nationalists,[3] and has provided the impetus for provincial language laws intended to stem this tide.

French Outside Quebec

Outside Quebec the language picture looks very different. Except in New Brunswick and Ontario, the francophone populations of the other provinces are tiny. In fact, in certain provinces and in all but a handful of Canada's major metropolitan areas outside Quebec, some of the non-official-language communities are considerably larger than the French-speaking minority. In all provinces except Quebec, the French language communities have been experiencing **assimilation**: *the absorption of the minority culture into the majority (English) culture*. By contrast, the rate of language retention among native English-speakers is high everywhere in Canada. This is not a recent development.

In *Languages in Conflict*, Richard Joy carefully documented the trend toward the assimilation of francophones outside Quebec.[4] Only in what Joy called the *bilingual belt*, the narrow region running from Moncton, New Brunswick, in the east, to Sault Ste Marie, Ontario, in the west, was the rate of assimilation among all generations significantly lower. Joy's prediction was that the failure to retain young francophones would contribute to the steady erosion of the community's base. The reason, of course, was that the ability to shop, work, go to church, and so on in one's own language are the things that keep a language alive; francophones were losing this ability. And a number of studies suggest that a combination of aging populations, low birth rates, marriage to non-francophones, and the general lack of supportive social and economic milieux for French speakers will lead to the collapse of many francophone communities outside of Quebec within a generation or two. This is no doubt the reason why René Lévesque once referred to the French-Canadian communities outside of Quebec as "dead ducks."

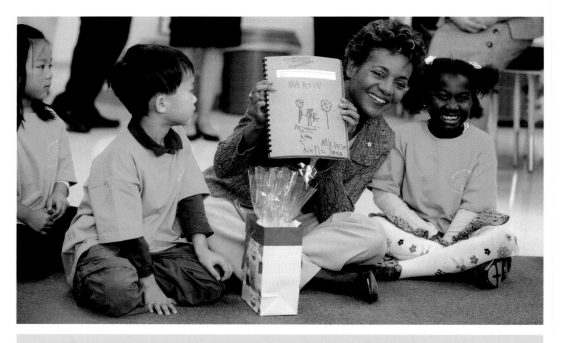

In 2008 a new French immersion public elementary school named after former Governor General and Quebec resident Michaëlle Jean opened in Richmond Hill, Ontario, a community just north of Toronto. If you had children, would you send them to French immersion so that they could become bilingual or receptively bilingual? To what extent do you feel it is important for citizens to be fluent in both official languages?

Some point to statistics that suggest bilingualism outside of Quebec has been increasing in recent years. Immersion education has been heralded by some as a guarantee that bilingualism will survive outside of Quebec. For example, there has been a rapid expansion of French immersion schools since the 1980s, particularly in Ontario, which accounts for over half of all immersion students in Canada. However, many are skeptical. The fact that increasing numbers of those whose mother tongue is English are "functionally fluent" in French does not mean that French will be used more often in the home, the workplace, at the pub, and wherever else communication takes place. Indeed, there is a good deal of evidence suggesting that three decades of French immersion education[5] has produced a wave of **receptive bilinguals—***people who are capable of responding to French communications but do not themselves initiate conversations in French, consume French language media, or seek out opportunities to live in their acquired second language*. There is certainly nothing wrong with this and, indeed, much that is good about the expansion of bilingualism, receptive or otherwise! But the claims made for and conclusions drawn from the immersion experience should be viewed with a certain amount of caution. In fact, the most recent census found that the level of bilingualism among anglophones outside Quebec has declined in recent years. The bottom line is that the social and economic milieux outside Quebec have not become more supportive for francophones.

From French-Canadian to Québécois Nationalism

French-Canadian nationalism, Pierre Trudeau writes, was originally a system of self-defence. Conquered by arms, the French-speaking people of New France found themselves subordinated to an anglophone minority about one-eighth their size. English was the language of the new political and commercial elites. The *Conquest* left French a second-class language within Quebec, and francophones were largely excluded from the colony's structures of power. Three chief factors can explain why French Canadians did not assimilate in Quebec as they did in Louisiana after it too passed from French control.

First, the British colonial authorities in New France, by the terms of the Quebec Act, 1774, granted formal protection to the status of the Roman Catholic religion and the *code civil*, the basis of civil law in New France.[6] The recognition of the rights of the French-Canadian population may have been motivated chiefly by the desire to ensure the allegiance of the clerical and civil leaders of that population at a time when the British were facing a rebellion in the Thirteen Colonies, which two years later would successfully declare their independence from Britain. Regardless, these significant accommodations officially recognized the rights of the francophone Catholic majority and reinforced the leadership role of that community's clerical elite.

Second, French speakers in the south of the United States were quickly swamped by a rapidly growing anglophone population. Although the immigration of Loyalists from the United States and English-speakers from the British Isles eventually tipped the linguistic balance in Canada toward English by the early nineteenth century, the high fertility rate among French Canadians enabled them to hold their ground at about one-third of Canada's population between Confederation and the 1950s.

Third, the defensive posture characteristic of French-Canadian nationalism enabled French Canada to resist the pressures of assimilation. The clerical elite's leading social role was strengthened when anglophones occupied the political and commercial elites of the colony, and French Canada met the challenge of English domination by remaining loyal to traditional values and institutions.

Traditional French-Canadian nationalism was guided by the idea of ***la survivance—survival against the pressures of a dominant culture that was anglicizing, Protestant, materialistic, liberal democratic, and business oriented***. In other words, this dominant anglophone culture was all the things that French Canada, according to the spokespersons for this ideology, was not and should not become. While liberal voices of dissent were occasionally heard,[7] the chief characteristics of the dominant nationalist ideology in French Canada during the nineteenth century to the middle of the twentieth century were:

- French Canada formed a distinct nation, whose chief characteristics were the Catholic religion and the French language. The preservation of these was considered inseparable.[8]
- French Canadians had a special vocation as a people. Their mission was to remain faithful to their roots, and to resist the lure of materialistic, English, Protestant pressures. The democratic belief in the separation of church and state (secularism) was a lamentable heresy spawned by the French Revolution and the American Constitution.
- The character of the French-Canadian people was most secure in the province of Quebec, but French Canada was not restricted to the boundaries of that province.

The traditional nationalism came under mounting pressure during the middle of the twentieth century. The emigration of hundreds of thousands of French-speaking Quebecers to the northeastern United States during the 1800s clearly demonstrated the weakness of the traditional nationalism. There simply was not enough arable land to support the rural parish lifestyle that the ideologues of the traditional nationalism clung to so tenaciously. By the early twentieth century the "typical" Québécois lived in a city or town, worked in a factory, store, or office, and had family members who had left the province in search of employment opportunities.

Quebec's path of modernization produced a political side effect of enormous importance. This was the increasing realization that francophones, despite accounting for about four-fifths of the Quebec population, were largely shut out of the centres of economic decision making and controlled relatively little of the province's wealth. "Is there any inherent or unavoidable reason why," asked Abbé Lionel Groulx in 1934, "with 2,500,000 French Canadians in Quebec, all big business, all high finance, all the public utilities, all our water rights, forests and mines, should belong to a [mostly English-speaking] minority of 300,000?"[9] Between the 1930s and 1950s, many raised the same issue in arguing that educated francophones needed to rid themselves of their apparent distaste for careers in industry and finance.[10]

In these decades emerged the first serious challenge to the conservative ideology since the crushed rebellion of 1837. A diverse group of university professors and students, journalists, union activists, liberal politicians, and even elements within the Catholic Church, were united in their opposition to the so-called "unholy alliance" of the Catholic Church, anglophone capital, and the Union Nationale party of Maurice Duplessis—and, of course, to the conservative nationalism that sought to justify French Canadians' marginal economic status. It contested the traditional elites' monopoly over power in the province and what was argued to be their backward characterization of French-Canadian society and culture. Its goal was to recoup lost ground; to bring Quebec's society, economy, and government up to date; a goal that became known in Quebec as *rattrapage* ("catching up").

This challenge to the conservative establishment and ideology centred on the Faculty of Social Sciences at Laval University; the intellectual revue *Cité libre*, founded by such figures as Pierre Trudeau and Gérard Pelletier; and the provincial Liberal Party. As the political party attempting to depose Duplessis, the Quebec Liberal Party naturally attracted the energies of those who saw the Union Nationale under his leadership as one of the principal obstacles to reform. The ideologically conservative Union Nationale managed to hold on until the 1960s, largely because of the tight web of patronage politics that Duplessis used to keep the party in power between 1945 and his death in 1959. The Liberal Party's election victory in 1960 probably owed as much to disorder within the Union Nationale as to popular support for change. Regardless, the opportunity for reform had come.

The Quiet Revolution

Duplessis's death in 1959, and the election of the provincial Liberals under Jean Lesage in 1960, opened the way to ***many socio-political reforms and changes, and a turning point in the history of Quebec*** known as the **Quiet Revolution**. At the heart of these reforms lay an increased role for the Quebec state, which replaced the authority of the Catholic Church in social services and education and also acquired a vastly broader range of economic functions. The provincial state was seen as the prime mover of Quebec's break with the past, its attempt to modernize, and the focus of nationalist energies.

Nationalism is always based on some concept of the nation: who belongs to it and who does not. The traditional nationalism, defined by such people as Abbé Lionel Groulx, went beyond the territory or the powers of the Quebec state. For reasons that had to do with Catholicism and an extended role for the Church, and the *anti-statist* quality of the traditional nationalism, the boundaries of *la nation* extended beyond Quebec to embrace French Canadians throughout Canada. Traditional nationalism was an ideology of *conservation*. It emphasized preservation of the *patrimoine*—the language, the faith, the mores of a community whose roots went back to New France, as well as a leading role for the Church in articulating these values and controlling these structures (i.e., the schools, hospitals, labour unions, etc.) The modern welfare state threatened this dominant social role of the Church.

Although traditional nationalists insisted on constitutional protection for the province's exclusive right to make education policy and put limits on Ottawa's ability to interfere with social affairs in the province, they did not expect that the Quebec state would actively occupy these fields. Traditional nationalism attached no particular value to the Quebec state, except insofar as its powers could be used to maintain the status of conservative values and the power of the traditional elites: the clergy, anglophone business leaders, and provincial politicians. The survival of the nation did not depend on the Quebec state, but on those institutions that were crucial to the continuation from generation to generation of the French language and the Catholic religion—family, school, and parish. And although the schools were under the constitutional jurisdiction of the provincial state, their control was mainly left in the hands of the Church until the early 1960s.

Instead of defining *la nation* in terms of language and religion, the nationalism of the Quiet Revolution developed an understanding of Quebec's history, economy, and social structure that was based on language and dependency. The dependency perspective portrayed Quebec as a society whose evolution had been shaped and distorted by the economic and political domination of English Canadians. This secularized version of French-Canadian history, and more particularly of francophone Quebec, suggested that if the problem was that *Québécois* were dominated economically and politically by English Canada, then the solution required that they take control of their economic and political destiny through a newly assertive use of the Quebec state. The Quiet Revolution saw reforms by the state such as the creation of a provincial ministry of education, the nationalization of hydroelectric companies, the creation of Crown corporations like la Caisse de dépôt et placement du Québec, and the passage of the Quebec Pension Plan.

The replacement of the traditional nationalism by the state-centred nationalism of the Quiet Revolution was not uniform or as abrupt as history might suggest. It quickly became apparent that the new nationalism forces shared little more than a common antipathy toward the old order. They were divided on at least three main levels. First, there was a split between the federalists and those who advocated either a special status or independence for Quebec. The federalists included Pierre Elliott Trudeau, Jean Marchand, and Gérard Pelletier, who entered federal politics through the Liberal Party in 1965. Leadership of the Quebec autonomy side would fall on René Lévesque, formerly a popular television journalist who masterminded the nationalization of the hydroelectric industry in the Lesage government, and who later became the first leader of the Parti Québécois in 1968. The second division concerned the size and functions of the Quebec state. Even within the reformist Liberal government of Jean Lesage, there were sharp differences over the role of the provincial state in Quebec society and over the extent of the nationalization policies. Third, Quebec separatists were divided on ideological lines: those who, like René Lévesque, Jacques Parizeau, and Claude Morin, were ideologically liberal; and those for whom Quebec independence was linked to the overthrow of what they saw as a (predominantly English) bourgeois state.

Two developments indicate that a state-centred nationalism emerged out of the Quiet Revolution. First, the identification of French Canada with the territory of Quebec was a view shared by most nationalists. Indeed, the entry of Trudeau and his fellow federalists into national politics was chiefly a reaction to this Quebec-oriented nationalism. The provincial Liberals' 1962 campaign slogan, *Maîtres chez nous* ("Masters of our own house"), captured a nationalist consensus that ever since has been an accepted tenet of Quebec politics. Second, key institutional reforms of the Quiet Revolution, such as the Caisse de dépôt et placement, Hydro-Québec, and the jurisdictional terrain that the Quebec government wrested from Ottawa in social policy, immigration, and taxation, have left an important mark on Quebec nationalism.

The Unilingual Approach of Quebec

The origins of present-day language policy in Canada lie in developments in Quebec during the 1960s. With the election of the Quebec Liberal Party in 1960, the political obstacles to change were largely removed and the outdated character of the traditional ideology was exposed. It was replaced by an emphasis on catching up with the level of social and economic development elsewhere. The state, traditionally viewed as a second-class institution in a province where most social services were controlled by the Church and government was associated with crass patronage, became the focus of nationalist energies. The fact that the new nationalism of the Quiet Revolution focused on the provincial government, and that francophones were unquestionably in the majority in Quebec, reinforced the identification of French Canada with the territory of Quebec.

The ideology of *rattrapage* and the identification of French Canada with Quebec had important consequences for language policy in that province. In its new role as the instrument for economic and social development, the Quebec state expanded the scope of its economic

Language laws have stirred up demonstrations in Quebec on both sides of the argument. (above) A war veteran makes his views known outside the Quebec Language Commission in 1987. (right) A supporter carries a sign (translation: "In Quebec, everything in French and in French only") in a 2007 march in favour of Bill 101. Do you think Bill 101 is an infringement on civil liberties or a necessary tool for the preservation of the French language?

activities. In doing so it provided career opportunities for the growing number of educated francophones graduating from the province's universities. Access to high-paying managerial and technical jobs in the private sector, however, remained blocked by anglophone domination of the Quebec economy.[11] This situation ran directly counter to the goals of the Quiet Revolution and became an important political issue.

Demographic trends also shaped provincial language policy in Quebec. Immigrants to the province overwhelmingly adopted the English language. This fact, combined with the dramatically lower birth rate among francophones, made it seem possible that francophones might eventually become a minority even within Quebec.

These trends formed the basis for the policy recommendations of the 1972 Quebec Royal Commission of Inquiry on the Situation of the French Language and on Language Rights in Quebec. It recommended that the provincial government pass laws to promote the use of French in business and in education. Following these recommendations the Quebec Liberal government introduced the Official Language Act[12] and the subsequent Parti Québécois government passed the *Charte de la langue française*[13] (Bill 101). There are three principal features of Quebec language policy since the passage of Bill 101:

- In spite of a 1979 decision by the Supreme Court of Canada that this section of Bill 101 violated section 133 of the BNA Act, which guarantees the co-equal status of the French and English languages at the federal level and in the province of Quebec,[14] the principal language of provincial government services and the courts in Quebec is French. Many provincial and local services are not available in English in much of the province.

- Through a requirement that businesses with 50 or more employees receive a *francization* certificate as a condition of doing business in the province, the Quebec government seeks to increase the use of French as a working language of business in the province. Despite some initial resistance from the anglophone business community, this has generally been accepted by employers. More controversial have been the provisions requiring that public signs and advertisements be in French only. Certain provisions were relaxed to make exceptions for "ethnic" businesses, and because of a 1988 Supreme Court ruling that Bill 101 violated the freedom of expression guaranteed in the Charter.[15]

- The provisions of Bill 101 that initially excited the most controversy were those restricting access to English-language schools in Quebec. Under this law, children could enroll in an English school only if certain conditions were met, and these conditions would not apply to most immigrants. The intent was obviously to reverse the overwhelming preference of immigrants for the English language. The Supreme Court was unwilling to accept the Quebec government's argument that the demographic threat to the position of the French language justified this restriction on language rights. In 1993 the education provisions of Bill 101 were brought into conformity with section 23 of the Charter.

Despite some setbacks in the courts, the principles on which Quebec's language policy rests have remained substantially unchanged since the passage of Bill 101. If one looks at its

MEDIA BEAT

BOX 12.1 Do English-Language Posters in Pubs Threaten the French Language in Quebec?

Quebec's French-language watchdog is investigating a popular Montreal pub, which is cluttered with classic Irish signage and English-only posters. The owner of McKibbin's received a letter from the Office québécois de la langue française (OLF) earlier this month inquiring about the use of English signs inside. The wall hangings include vintage advertisements for Guinness and the St James Gate brewery in Dublin, posters the owners say add to the charm and ambience of their downtown establishment. An OLF inspector ruled McKibbin's bilingual menu, bar service and vintage posters do not respect article 58 of Quebec's language charter.

McKibbin's owner Rick Fon told CBC News he will not take the posters down because they serve as decoration, not to advertise beer.

The language office understands and will withdraw its order for McKibbin's to remove some of the posters, Montreal's *La Presse* newspaper reported. It quoted a spokesperson as saying the office accepts that most of the posters are decorative and therefore not covered by language laws. However, three posters are still considered to be ads and will be ordered to be taken down, the paper said.

"What we asked them were what measures would be taken to ensure that service would be offered in French, because we received two complaints," Gérald Paquette, a spokesman for the language watchdog, said on Friday.

"If the business says some of those pictures are decorative to give the pub an Irish flavour, it is certain we would exempt them," Paquette said. "But there were other posters also, notably ones about contests and events, that were in English only."

The brewhaha has prompted the pub's co-owners to extend an invite to Quebec Premier Jean Charest to stop by for a hearty meal and a pint and inspect the signs himself. Dean Laderoute and Rick Fon said they'll remove the posters if Charest believes they violate Quebec's language laws, which require French to be predominant on most commercial signs.

"An Irish pub without these decorations is just an empty box," Fon said in an interview. "It's the decor, the pictures, the clutter—it creates the warmth."

Fon also said they have bilingual menus and that his regulars, including a considerable French clientele, all agree the complaints are ridiculous.

"It makes no sense. It's silly," regular Suzette L'Abbé said.

"The staff, if not French-speaking to begin with, get by in French," L'Abbé added.

The pub could face fines as high as $1,500 for each infraction.

Source: CBC News, "Quebec Language Police Pressure Montreal Bar over Posters," 14 February 2008. Reprinted by permission of CBC and the Canadian Press.

main objectives of increasing French language use in the Quebec economy and stemming the decline in the francophone share of the provincial population, Bill 101 must be judged a success.

In the past decade, the debate over immigration in Quebec has shifted somewhat from the impact of immigrants on the French language to the integration of newcomers into its culture and society. Tensions in the province were crystallized in the highly publicized case of Hérouxville, a small town north of Montreal whose local government adopted a declaration of cultural standards that newcomers were expected to respect.[16] This apparently xenophobic resolution from the heart of rural Quebec—the former bastion of traditional Quebec nationalism—targeted Muslims, Sikhs, North Africans, South Asians, and Middle Eastern Arabs. It stated that immigrants were unwelcome in their community of less than 2000 if they covered their faces, carried weapons to school, practised genital mutilation, or stoned or burned women to death. The furor over this code of behaviour—the story was widely covered throughout the world—led the Quebec government to appoint the Bouchard–Taylor consultative commission on "reasonable accommodation." The commission's report seemed to some to recommend that the Quebec government and Quebec citizens adopt a form of provincial multiculturalism similar to that of the federal government.

> Our deliberations and reflections have firmly convinced us that integration through pluralism, equality and reciprocity is by far the most commendable, reasonable course. Like all democracies in the world, Québec must seek to reach a consensus against a backdrop of growing diversity, renew the social bond, accommodate difference by combating discrimination, and promote an identity, a culture and a memory without creating either exclusion or division.[17]

The report's reception was not enthusiastic. Most French-speaking Quebecers felt that the emphasis in the Bouchard–Taylor report leaned too far toward accommodation and openness to change on the part of old-stock Québécois—sometimes called *les québécois de souche*—and not enough on the need for newcomers to adapt and accept not only the language of the French majority, but their culture and mores as well. Premier Jean Charest's response to the report was to take a middle path, which included the following measures:

- Reinforce francization prior to the arrival of immigrants.
- Provide for a signed statement by potential immigrants committing to the common values of our society.
- Develop a mechanism to help decision makers handle questions of *accommodation* while respecting the secular character of our institutions.
- [And] . . . adopting Bill 63, which would amend the Charter of Rights and Freedoms to affirm the equality of men and women.[18]

The Bilingual Approach of Ottawa

A very different approach to language policy—one based on a conception of French and English Canada that cuts across provincial borders—has been pursued by successive federal governments since the 1960s. In response to the new assertive nationalism of the Quiet Revolution, including the placing of bombs in mailboxes and at public monuments, as well as demands for more taxation powers and less interference by Ottawa in areas of provincial responsibility, the Liberal government of Lester Pearson established the *Royal Commission on Bilingualism and Biculturalism* (the B and B commission). As Eric Waddell writes, "The federal government was facing a legitimacy crisis in the 1960s and 1970s and had the immediate task of proposing a Canadian alternative to Quebec nationalism."[19] The Commission was a first step toward Ottawa adopting a policy of official bilingualism. This policy was partly intended to defuse the *indépendantiste* sentiment building in Quebec by opening career opportunities in Ottawa to rival the Quebec public service.

As expressed in the federalist philosophy of Pierre Trudeau, Ottawa offered an alternative in which language rights would be guaranteed to the individual and protected by national institutions. This meant changing the overwhelmingly anglophone character of the federal state so that francophones would not feel excluded. These changes have been carried out on two main fronts. First, a change in Canadian symbols has been implemented since the 1960s, including adopting a new flag, proclaiming "O Canada" to be the official national anthem, and changing the names of some federal institutions, documents, and celebrations to make them more language-neutral. A deliberate attempt was made to create symbols that did not evoke Canada's colonial past and British domination. Second, with a view to redress the under-representation of French Canadians in the federal civil services as well as the level of services to the French-speaking populations, the Official Languages Act (1969) made the policy of bilingualism into law. The Act established the Office of the Commissioner of Official Languages as a "watchdog" agency to monitor the three main components of language equality: (1) the public's right to be served by the federal government in the official language of their choice; (2) the equitable representation of francophones and anglophones in the federal public service; and (3) the ability of public servants of either language group to work in the language of their choice.

Evidence on recruitment to the federal public service and upward mobility within it demonstrates that the linguistic designation of positions has indeed worked to the advantage of francophones. But as the Commissioner of Official Languages regularly observes, increased representation of francophones should not be taken as an indication that the French and English are approaching greater equality as *languages of work* in the federal state. Outside of federal departments and agencies located in Quebec, the language of work remains predominantly English. And inside Quebec, the ability of anglophone public servants to work in English is often limited. In short, fluency in French has become a valuable attribute from the standpoint of career advancement, without French becoming a working language on a par with English.[20]

Ottawa's language policy acquired two additional thrusts in the 1970s. First, it has given financial assistance to organizations and individuals seeking to defend or expand the rights of official-language minorities and to local francophone cultural organizations outside of Quebec. Second, it has given financial assistance for second-language instruction and minority-language schools controlled by the provinces, including French immersion schools and summer immersion programs. French immersion education has become steadily more popular over the last two decades, fuelled by non-francophone parents' perception that bilingualism will give their children an edge in the future competition for good jobs.[21]

As we noted earlier, studies of immersion graduates demonstrate that the experience tends to produce "receptive" bilinguals—people who neither initiate conversations in French nor consume French-language culture after leaving immersion. Bilingualism has become a badge of social distinction rather than a part of their lifestyle.

A Distinct Society?

Listen to "The Reasonable Accommodation of Cultural Difference: The Case of Quebec" podcast, available at www.oupcanada .com/BrooksConcise.

It is a fair bet that few Canadians had heard of "distinct society" before the late 1980s, when the Meech Lake Accord came to grief over a proposal to recognize Quebec as a distinct society. Does Quebec comprise a **distinct society**—*a society noticeably different than other provinces*? And is this distinction necessary or desirable? In spite of much study and debate, most Canadians are probably no wiser today about the meaning of distinct society. What is clear is that the demand for constitutional recognition of Quebec as a distinct society has been a non-negotiable requirement for Quebec's political elite since the late 1980s.

Whether or not Quebec is a distinct society depends on what criteria we use in comparing Quebec to the other provinces. In terms of how people in Quebec make a living, the films they watch, the popular novels they read, how and where they spend their vacations, and most other aspects of their lifestyle, they are not remarkably different from Canadians in other regions of the country. However, if we look at the social, historic, and regional characteristics, as well as values and belief systems, there are characteristics that distinguish Quebec from Canada's other regions and provinces.

If the distinct-society clauses of Meech Lake and Charlottetown are merely statements of demographic and cultural reality, why the fuss? What probably bothers English-speaking Canadians more than anything else is their gut sense that distinct-society status for Quebec undermines their ideas about national unity and of Canada as an egalitarian society. Many English Canadians believe that a "distinct society" recognition would give Quebec legislative powers not possessed by other provinces. And some worry that minority rights—of non-francophones in Quebec and of francophones outside the province—would suffer.

In an unarticulated way, English Canadians sense that distinct society recognition for Quebec is a sort of Trojan horse for a *two-nations* conception of Canada: a theory that has been very popular in certain political parties and among anglophone political scientists. This offends against a particular understanding of equality that—again, while usually inarticulate—objects to the idea that there are categories of Canadians instead of Canadians, period. Former Conservative prime minister John Diefenbaker probably expressed this best when he inveighed against what he called "the Anglo-phonies, the Franco-phonies, and all the other phonies" whose insistence on defining Canada in linguistic and ethnic terms, he believed, undermined national unity.

Although many of Canada's national political elite have for years denied that the "one Canada" aspirations of most English Canadians conflict with the recognition of Quebec as a distinct society, Québécois political leaders suffer from no illusions on this count. The report of the Commission on the Political and Constitutional Future of Quebec made it clear that the "one Canada" and "dual societies" conceptions have become irreconcilable since the passage of the Charter and other constitutional reforms of 1982. According to the commission, from Quebec's point of view, "Canada's federal system was founded . . . on Canadian duality [French/English] and the autonomy of the provinces. Canadian duality, which rests on the relationship between the French-Canadian and English-Canadian peoples . . . is a 'pact' which exists between these two peoples that may only be changed with the consent of each of these parties."[22] The Commission argued that the Constitution Act of 1982 was based on three principles that are fundamentally opposed to the idea of Quebec as a distinct society:

- The equality of all Canadian citizens, from one ocean to the other, and the unity of the society in which they live
- The equality of all cultures and cultural origins in Canada
- The equality of the 10 provinces of Canada

The fact remains that Quebec is a province *pas comme les autres* ("unlike the others") and one that continues to attract special attention from federal politicians. In 2006, the House of Commons passed a resolution affirming that the Québécois are a "nation within the nation of Canada." One of the politically significant ways in which this difference may be seen is in French-speaking Quebecers' weaker attachment to Canada, particularly among younger citizens. A 2006 survey found that young francophones were far less likely than anglophones to believe that independence would harm Quebec's economy (29 versus 72 per cent).[23]

And so, whatever a distinct society clause in the Constitution might mean in practice, there can be no doubt that the Quebec elites expect it to make a difference. Distinct society is, in their eyes, a corrective against the centralizing implications of the Charter and, moreover, represents a return to the founding spirit of Canada. However, distinct society status and a veto over constitutional change may no longer be enough. For their part, the PQ and the Bloc have been determined to shift the debate away from a federalist framework—the one over distinct society and constitutional vetoes—onto a debate over political independence and economic association.

Listen to the "Does Quebec Separatism Have a Future?" podcast, available at www.oupcanada .com/BrooksConcise.

DIVERSITY AND POLITICS

Diversity is nothing new in Canada: it has always been a pluralistic society. For example, the official recognition of group rights goes back at least as far as the 1774 Quebec Act, under which the British authorities recognized the religious rights of French Canadians. What is relatively new, however, is the level of awareness of diversity and the idea that it should be recognized, protected, and even nurtured by the state.

The group composition of Canadian society has changed significantly over time. Canada has moved away from the concepts of "two nations" or "two founding peoples" to the concept of **multiculturalism**: *the idea that cultural diversity is not only good for society, it should* *also be encouraged*. Some would go so far as to say that diversity has become *the pre-eminent Canadian cultural trait*, a quality that more than any other defines what Canada is about, and differentiates it from those of other countries, particularly the United States. Canada is, as former Prime Minister Joe Clark once put it, "a community of communities."

The very idea that there is such a thing as a "Canadian ethos"—that Canada is a democracy built around tolerance, accommodation, respect, the recognition of group rights, and a belief in the equal dignity of different cultures—is comparatively recent. Today, many Canadians see Canada as a pluralistic society par excellence, and a model of cultural coexistence.

This image of Canada is not without its ironies and skeptics. Foremost is the fact that separatist sentiment in Quebec is far from extinguished and challenges this rosy picture of

The City of Burnaby's Celebrating Diversity Quilt Project brought together students, teachers, community members, and families to create 380 quilt pieces that together created a design depicting self-expression and the unique components that make up contemporary society. Name five elements that you feel helps to create the unique diversity we recognize in today's Canadian society.

Canada as a model of cultural coexistence. Some skeptics maintain that the diversity-centred image of Canada, and of its policies and institutions, undermines rather than strengthens Canadian unity. Others question whether multicultural democracy can work at all, in Canada or elsewhere, except in special circumstances. They note the resurgence of ethnicity-based nationalism in the modern world and the breakup or instability of many countries that combine different cultures.

From Founding Nations to Multiculturalism

The Canada that we know today was built upon two pillars: the displacement and marginalization of Aboriginal Canadians, and the settlement and development of what would become Canada by European immigrants. The overwhelming majority of the immigrants who settled in Canada during the country's formative years were of French and British Isles origins (although many of the latter came to Canada via the United States in the wave of Loyalists who left America after the War of Independence). The languages that they established were mainly French and English. With very few exceptions their religions were Christian (Roman Catholic or Protestant). For much of Canada's history, they would be referred to as the *founding nations* or *charter groups*: one French and Catholic and the other English and mainly Protestant. The image of Canada as a partnership—albeit an unequal one—of two European charter groups survived well into the twentieth century.

It was not until the 1960s and the work of the Royal Commission on Bilingualism and Biculturalism that the two-nations image of Canada was questioned. Ukrainian spokespersons, among others, were critical of the two-nations, bicultural image. They stopped short of demanding equality of status with English and French for their groups and languages. But what they won was official recognition of Canada as a *multicultural society*, not a bicultural one. This was achieved through the 1971 passage of the Multiculturalism Act and the creation of a ministry responsible for multiculturalism. Today, responsibility for multiculturalism falls under Citizenship and Immigration Canada.

The challenges launched by the critics and groups that wanted biculturalism to be replaced with multiculturalism would not have had much effect were it not for the changes to Canada's population that were underway by the 1960s and have accelerated since then. New waves of immigration that were neither French nor from the British Isles presented even greater challenges to the older notions of Canadian pluralism than those first launched in the 1960s. Immigrants from Eastern and Southern Europe became increasingly important within Canada's overall immigration picture between the 1950s and 1970s. They have been joined in recent decades by increasing numbers of non-European immigrants, many of whom come from non-Christian cultures. As Figures 12.1 and 12.2 show, the ethnic composition of Canadian society has changed significantly over the last half-century, particularly in Canada's largest metropolitan areas, where the new Canadians of neither British nor French ethnic origins have clustered, and where the visible minority population has increased significantly in recent years.

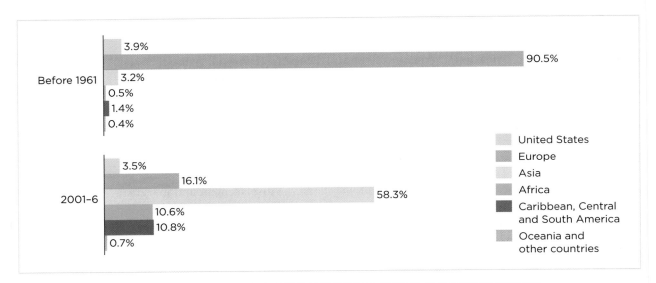

FIGURE 12.1 ETHNIC ORIGINS OF THE CANADIAN POPULATION, SELECTED YEARS

Source: Human Resources and Skills Development Canada, " Canadians in Context—Immigration"; Data source: Statistics Canada. *Immigration in Canada: A portrait of the Foreign-Born Population, 2006 Census.* Ottawa, Statistics Canada, 2007. (Cat. No. 97-557-XIE).

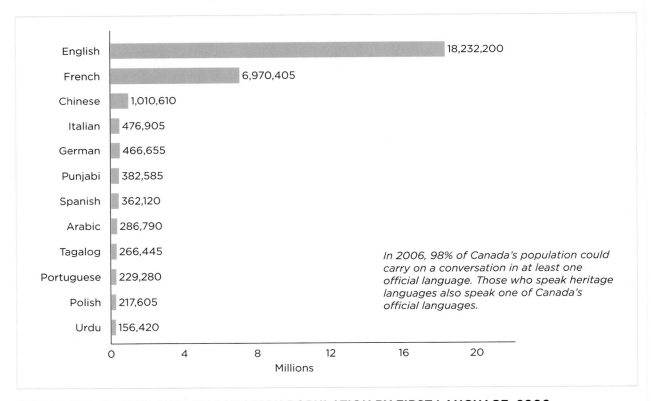

FIGURE 12.2 BREAKDOWN OF CANADIAN POPULATION BY FIRST LANGUAGE, 2006

Source: *Annual Report on the Operation of the Canadian Multiculturalism Act 2008–2009*, Citizenship and Immigration Canada, 2010. http://www.cic.gc.ca/english/resources/publications/multi-report2009/part2-2.asp. Reproduced with the permission of the Minister of Public Works and Government Services, 2012.

Canada remains a predominantly Christian society in spite of the recent waves of immigration from non-European countries. However, Canadian society has become much more secular than it was even a couple of generations ago, and religion tends not to be a particularly important factor in politics. People belonging to non-Christian religions constitute a rather small minority, at about 6 per cent of the population. About four out of five Canadians claim an affiliation with either the Catholic Church or a Protestant denomination. This is down from all but a sliver of the population at the time of Confederation, and even represents some small slippage since 1971. This slippage is due to a recent sharp increase in the number of people without a religious affiliation.

The growth of the non-European and non-Christian elements of Canadian society has not been entirely free from tensions and unease on the part of some. Most people appear to accept the changes taking place in their society, but a 2004 survey of attitudes toward cross-cultural and interracial marriage found that a significant minority of the population is uneasy with the idea of their children mixing with members of certain groups. Tolerance is greater among younger age cohorts.[24]

Along with greater diversity in the ethnic, religious, and racial composition of Canada, the demographic picture has become more recognizably varied in other ways, too, including family composition, sexual orientation, and disability.

- *Families.* Families tend to be smaller today than they were a generation ago and considerably smaller than they were two generations ago. There are many more single-parent families and many more couples who choose not to marry. Same-sex couples are also more frequent.
- *Sexuality.* Sexual diversity is much more apparent today. The ratio of heterosexuals to those who are gay or lesbian has probably not changed, but what has changed is the willingness of non-heterosexuals to proclaim openly their sexuality and the readiness of a growing number of Canadians to accept this in many, if not all, circumstances. The struggle over the legal definition of marriage as excluding same-sex unions was seen by many as the last major legal barrier to the equality of gays and lesbians with heterosexuals. A combination of court rulings and legislation passed by Parliament in 2005 extended full legal status to same-sex marriages, but polls show that Canadians remain divided on this issue.
- *Disability.* According to statistics, a greater proportion of the population is disabled today than at any point in Canada's history. Health Canada reports that about one in eight Canadians claims to experience either a mental or a physical disability. It is doubtful whether the actual incidence of Canadians suffering from various forms of disability is greater today than in the past. What has changed, however, are our society's ideas about what constitute disabilities and the legal definition of what counts as a disability for purposes of pensions, workers' compensation, social assistance, employment, housing, and other matters. The recognition of disability has increased and, moreover, it has become one of the diversity criteria used by governments in making public policy.

Official Recognition and the Institutionalization of Diversity

In 1972, multiculturalism was given its own minister. But the official recognition of groups according to their group characteristics and the institutionalization of diversity go back much further. We have already mentioned that the Quebec Act of 1774 represented the first official confirmation of the status and rights of a particular group, in this case French-speaking Catholics. But the distinction of "first" probably belongs to the Royal Proclamation of 1763, which recognized the presence and rights of "the several Nations or Tribes of Indians with whom we are connected, and who live under our protection." Aboriginal Canadians were recognized by the Proclamation as distinct rights-bearing peoples under the protection of the British Crown. This relationship continues to the present day with the Canadian state, perpetuated and institutionalized through the Indian Act and section 35 of the Constitution Act, 1982, which embeds the treaty rights of Aboriginal peoples in Canada.

Until the 1960s, the official recognition of groups extended principally to the French- and English-language communities (s. 133 of the Constitution Act, 1867), the Catholic and Protestant religions for schooling purposes (s. 93 of the Constitution Act, 1867), and Aboriginal Canadians. This changed in the 1960s and 1970s as a result of the emergence of feminism and the increasing popularity of multiculturalism and group-oriented thinking about rights.

CANADIAN SPOTLIGHT

BOX 12.2 *Little Mosque on the Prairie*

From 2007 to 2012, *Little Mosque on the Prairie*, a CBC sitcom about a makeshift mosque in a small Canadian prairie town, was praised by critics for raising the issue of accommodation for cultural minorities. The premise of the show was straightforward: Muslims are different in terms of their religious beliefs and practices, some of which translate to lifestyle differences, but these differences are insignificant compared to the values that they share with other Canadians.

Actors from the cast of *Little Mosque on the Prairie* joke with their director during a rehearsal. What other popular television shows or films can you think of that play on the theme of showcasing different cultures' similarities despite their obvious differences?

Leslie Pal argues that the institutionalization of diversity in Canadian public life was leveraged from the late 1960s to the 1980s by the activities of the Citizenship Branch within the Department of Secretary of State (SOS).[25] The grants were disbursed through a variety of programs that helped finance thousands of organizations. The programs and the dollars may have been small, but their enduring significance, Pal argues, was to help reshape the structures of government and the relationship of the state to groups of citizens in ways that institutionalized diversity.[26]

In addition to this, human rights commissions at both the federal and provincial levels have played an important role in expanding the concept of minorities. The emphasis on language, religion, and ethnic origins has shifted in recent years to such non-racial and non-cultural forms of minority status as gender, sexual orientation, dependence on alcohol and drugs, and social conditions. Human rights commission officials, as R. Brian Howe and David Johnson argue, have been at the forefront of the movement to extend the recognition of diversity through expanding the number of rights-bearing groups.[27]

At the federal level, the activities of the CBC, the National Film Board, and Telefilm Canada all have contributed to the public projection of images of Canadian society that reflect the diversity of the country's population and history. This is also true of the Department of Canadian Heritage which has inherited the functions pioneered by the Citizenship Branch, providing grants to an enormous array of groups and operating as the leader within government for the promotion of Canadian pluralistic identity.

Diversity and Political Representation

The 1878 cabinet of Sir John A. Macdonald had 14 members. All but one were born in Canada. About 80 per cent (11 of 14) had British Isles ethnic origins and the others were of French ethnic origin. All were either Catholic (4 of 14) or Protestant.

The 2010 cabinet of Stephen Harper was not as different from Sir John A.'s government as one might have expected, given the enormous demographic shifts that have occurred in Canadian society. Of its 32 members, only a couple were born outside Canada. The vast majority, about 85 per cent, had French or British ethnic origins. The religious affiliation of MPs is today more difficult to ascertain from public records than it was in the past, but only one or two of the members of cabinet may have had a non-Judeo-Christian religious affiliation. It is probable that a handful had no religious affiliation. On the whole, however, the demographic composition of Harper's 2010 cabinet was more similar to than different from the Macdonald cabinet of 1878, except in one striking respect. The Harper government included seven women and one Aboriginal Canadian, whereas Macdonald's included none.

Forty years ago John Porter remarked that Canada's political elite had been slow to change, failing to reflect the increasing ethnic diversity of the country. It was, he said, still an elite dominated by males from the two charter groups. Members of these groups continue to be disproportionately represented, at least in the federal cabinet.

The situation is not different in the case of the judicial elite and the highest ranks of the federal bureaucracy. If we look at the 74 individuals who have been members of the Supreme

Court since its creation, all but three have had British or French ethnic origins and all have had Judeo-Christian backgrounds. The same, broadly speaking, is true of the ranks of deputy ministers in Canada, although members of non-charter groups have made somewhat greater inroads into this elite. The main change to have occurred in both of these elites is the increased presence of women.

We are not suggesting that the continuing dominance of these elites by members of the French and British charter groups is evidence of discrimination against those who come from other backgrounds. A couple of factors need to be taken into account. First, it takes time for demographic change to work its way through to the top of a political system. For example, most of the decline in the share of Canada's population claiming either French or British Isles ethnic origins has occurred since the 1970s. We might expect to see more elite representation by non-charter group Canadians as the number of such people with the qualifications and other necessary attributes grows. Second, a growing number of Canadians have mixed ethnic origins and a considerable share of the population now rejects the traditional ethnic identities, preferring to describe themselves as being "Canadian." Consequently, it may be more accurate to say that the elites in Canada are dominated by persons of French, British, and Canadian origins.

The Under-Representation of Women

Women constitute about 52 per cent of the Canadian population and a slightly larger percentage of the electorate. Despite their numerical superiority, the number of women who have been elected to the leadership of political parties in Canada and have achieved high public office can be counted on the fingers of a couple of hands. There are, however, some signs of change. The percentage of female candidates nominated by the major political parties has never been as high as it is today.

A similar pattern of under-representation is found in the case of non-elected positions within the state. A relatively small percentage of judges in Canada are women. Somewhat deeper inroads have been cut into the senior ranks of the bureaucracy. Women account for about 30 per cent of senior managers in the federal public service, and their presence is no longer rare at the top of the bureaucratic ladder (deputy ministers and equivalent positions). While women often are appointed to the boards of directors of Crown corporations and hold officer positions in these companies—approximately 27 per cent of senior positions in federal Crowns were held by women as of 2010[28] (compare this to the 20 per cent average of senior officer positions held by women, as reported in the top 500 Canadian companies in 2010)—few women have ever been the CEOs of major commercially oriented Crowns at either the federal or the provincial level. While there has been some improvement in recent years, Crown corporations have simply mirrored the pattern of female exclusion in Canada's corporate elite. The reasons behind female under-representation are, however, more easily explained than are its consequences. Let us begin with the relatively uncontroversial part.

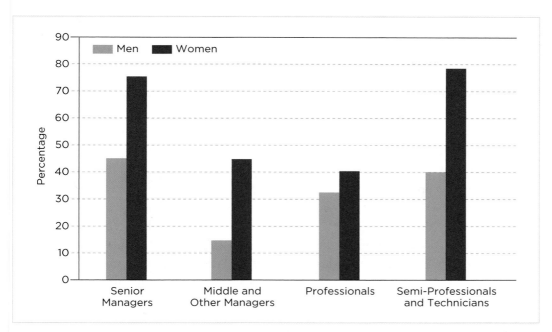

FIGURE 12.3 GROWTH OF SELECTED OCCUPATIONAL GROUPS OF WOMEN IN THE WORKFORCE, 1996–2006

This figure shows how women have made some important strides in many sectors of the workforce, but they continue to hit a glass ceiling when it comes to the upper echelons of management.

Source: *2006 Employment Equity Data Report*, Human Resources and Skills Development Canada, 2012. http://www .hrsdc.gc.ca/eng/labour/equality/employment_equity/tools/eedr/2006/data_reports/page08.shtml. Reproduced with the permission of the Minister of Public Works and Government Services, 2012.

Why Aren't More Women Involved in Political Life?

Superficially, the riddle of women's under-representation in public life appears simple: they have been less interested than men. Female participation levels have long been about the same as men's for political activities like voting and campaigning, but much lower for more demanding activities, such as holding office in a political party and running for office. "The higher, the fewer" is how Sylvia Bashevkin describes the political participation gap between males and females.[29] This gap has narrowed over time, but it continues to exist. What explains different levels of interest? The answer lies in social learning.

Traditionally, females learned from the world around them that politics was a predominantly male occupation. The prime minister/president and cabinet ministers were men, and leadership or active involvement beyond the family and the neighbourhood were associated with masculinity. The influence of social learning was reinforced by the sexual division of labour in society, particularly in the family but also in the workplace. The traditional male breadwinner–female homemaker family and the more contemporary two breadwinner–female homemaker household are universally acknowledged by feminists as important sources of female subordination to males, including their comparatively marginal status in politics. This subordination and marginalization operates on two main levels:

- *Psychological.* Child-rearing and housework are necessary activities, but society's attitude toward them is ambivalent. In brief, the traditional roles of mother and homemaker are not likely to generate the motivations, interests, and personal resources for political activism.
- *Status and professional achievements.* Traditionally, women have been under-represented in those occupations from which political office-holders tend to be drawn: law, business, and the liberal professions. Their formal educational attainments have tended to be less than those of men and their numbers have been low in fields like finance, economics, and engineering—important professional backgrounds for many senior positions in the public service. Even when women made "non-traditional career choices," they were expected to take primary charge of household duties and nurturing of the children.

Women in Politics

Women were active in politics before being entitled to vote and run for office. Much of this activity was aimed at achieving full citizenship rights for women. But this was far from being the sole concern of women's groups during the pre-suffrage era. They were also active in demanding a long list of social reforms ranging from pensions for widowed mothers, to non-militaristic policies in international relations. By contemporary standards, however, the early women's movement was small and politically weak. Moreover, its demands and values— although radical in the context of the times—today appear to have been quite moderate and sometimes even reactionary. In tracing the history of women's political involvement in Canada, we will focus on the social and ideological forces, as well as the issues, organizations, strategies, and accomplishments that have characterized the movement at different points in time.

Phase One: Industrialization and Democracy

Feminist writings and occasional incidents of women mobilizing around particular events or issues before the nineteenth century were quite rare. The overthrow of absolute monarchy in Britain (1688) and the American (1776) and the French revolutions (1789) generated some agitation for equality of political rights, but its consequences were negligible. In matters of law and property, a woman was subsumed under her father and, after marriage, her husband.

The origins of the women's movement usually are located in the mid nineteenth century. As Sheila Rowbotham writes, "Feminism came, like socialism, out of the tangled, confused response of men and women to capitalism."[30] The progress of capitalism produced both affluence and misery. As more and more people crowded into the cities whose growth was spawned by factory production, a new set of social problems arose. The cheap labour of working-class women and children made several industries very profitable, but the poor sanitation,

CANADIAN SPOTLIGHT

BOX 12.3   Timeline: Dates in Women's Progress toward Legal and Political Equality

1916   Alberta, Saskatchewan, Manitoba give vote to women.

1918   Women given franchise in federal elections.

1921   Agnes Macphail first woman elected to Parliament.

1928   Supreme Court rules women are not "persons" and cannot be appointed to Senate.

1929   Judicial Committee of the British Privy Council overturns Supreme Court decision.

1931   Cairine Wilson first woman appointed to the Senate.

1940   Quebec gives vote to women.

1947   Married women restricted from holding federal public service jobs.

1955   Restrictions on married women in federal public service removed.

1957   Ellen Fairclough sworn in as first female federal cabinet minister.

1967   Royal Commission on Status of Women established.

1971   Canada Labour Code amended to allow women 17 weeks' maternity leave.
About one-third of university graduates are female.

1973   Supreme Court upholds section of Indian Act depriving Aboriginal women of their rights.
Supreme Court denies Irene Murdoch right to share in family property.

1977   Canadian Human Rights Act passed, forbidding discrimination on basis of sex.

1981   Canada ratifies UN Convention on the Elimination of All Forms of Discrimination against Women.
Just under half of university graduates are female.

1982   Bertha Wilson becomes the first woman appointed to the Supreme Court of Canada.

1983   Affirmative action programs mandatory in the federal public service.

1984   Twenty-seven women elected to Parliament, six appointed to cabinet.

1985   Section 15 of Charter of Rights and Freedoms comes into effect.
Employment Equity legislation passed.

1988   *Morgentaler* decision strikes down Canada's abortion law.

1989   Indian Act amended to remove discrimination against Aboriginal women.
Andrews decision introduces the concept of "substantive equality" in applying section 15 of the Charter.
Audrey McLaughlin chosen to lead the national NDP.

1991   Ontario passes pay-equity law that applies to the private sector (repealed in 1995).

1993   Kim Campbell becomes Canada's first female prime minister.

1995   Alexa McDonough chosen to lead the national NDP.

1997   Sixty-one women elected to House of Commons, eight appointed to cabinet.

2000   Right Honourable Beverley McLachlin appointed Chief Justice of the Supreme Court of Canada.

2001   Just under 60 per cent of university graduates are female.

2002   Justice Marie Deschamps appointed to the Supreme Court of Canada.

2004   Justices Rosalie Abella and Louise Charron appointed to the Supreme Court of Canada, bringing the number of female judges on the nine-person court to four.

2008   Sixty-nine women elected to the House of Commons; seven appointed to cabinet.

overcrowding in improperly ventilated housing, and improper diet combined to produce low life expectancy and high infant mortality. The harshness of early industrialization as manifested in child labour, poverty, and alcohol abuse became central issues in the early women's movement because of their perceived impact on the family and on prevailing standards of decency. The Woman's Christian Temperance Union (WCTU), the Young Women's Christian Association (YWCA), and the Federated Women's Institutes that sprang up across Canada starting in the late nineteenth century advocated for social reforms and urged governments to protect women and the family from what they saw as the corrosive influences of industrial life.

Early feminism was not, however, merely a response to the contradictions that industrialization created for women. Democracy was also full of contradictions. The arguments used to deny political rights for women were intellectually flabby and often amounted to nothing more than "nice women do not want the vote" or "my wife doesn't want the vote."[31] But the logic of democratic rights is universal, and the exclusion of the female half of the population from the enjoyment of these rights was one of the major contradictions of most democracies until well into the twentieth century.

The early women's movement focused mainly on three sets of issues: political rights, legal rights, and social reform. The demands made by organizations like the WCTU and YWCA and by prominent feminists like Nellie McClung were based on traditional values and middle-class morality of the times and the perceived threats to the security of women and the family.

The dominant middle-class morality could, and eventually did, accommodate itself to political rights for women. "Respectable" feminists were those who consented to play by the rules of the game. The mainstream of the women's movement was represented by organizations like the WCTU, the YWCA, and the Women's Institutes. They were politically moderate organizations, fundamentally conservative in their goals and their strategies for attaining them. Even Nellie McClung, who was considered a firebrand, did not in the least suggest that the social roles of "man the provider" and "woman the nurturer" be changed. Instead, most leaders of the early women's movement wanted to put women's role on a more secure material footing. The political tactics employed by mainstream women's groups hardly ever strayed beyond the familiar bounds of accepted practice. Unlike their sisters in Great Britain and the United States, Canadian *suffragists* did not resort to confrontational methods such as resisting the police or hunger strikes. Instead, they relied on petitions to government and efforts to persuade public opinion.

After 40 years of campaigning, women achieved the right to vote provincially and federally between 1916 (Manitoba) and 1940 (Quebec), and federally in 1917–18. The right to hold office in the House of Commons was granted in 1918, although women appeared to be barred from the non-elected Senate and other appointive public offices, such as judgeships, as they were not considered "persons," as this term was understood in law.

Absurd though it may seem, the personhood of women was thought dubious in the years following their enfranchisement.[32] After a couple of provincial rulings in their favour, the question was placed before the Supreme Court of Canada in 1927. Feminists were shocked when the Court ruled that the legal meaning of "persons" excluded female. This decision was reversed on appeal by the Judicial Committee of the Privy Council (JPNC).

Phase Two: After the Vote, What?

"Is Women's Suffrage a Fizzle?" asked a 1928 article in *Maclean's*. Little, it seemed, had changed. Men still dominated the political process. The issues that interested women's groups, except for prohibition, were no more prominent than before women's suffrage. And women were still viewed as a not-quite-appropriate oddity in public life. Those who spearheaded the fight for women's suffrage believed—wrongly as it turned out—that the vote would be the tool that women would use to change the world.

It is usual to treat the period from suffrage to the new feminism that gained momentum in the 1960s as one long hiatus in the women's movement.[33] A few women did run for pub-

lic office, and even fewer won election. The break-throughs and accomplishments of the few stood in sharp contrast to the unchanged status of the many. Among the plausible reasons for this lack of change were the nature of early feminism, the party system, and societal attitudes. Early mainstream feminism was a weak force in Canadian politics, and hard-core feminism barely scratched the surface of public and political discourse.

Why social attitudes were slow in changing is a complex issue. However, the ability of women to better control their reproductive role and to choose to stay in school or participate in the workforce longer was a chief factor contributing to this change. Reproductive choice was a crucial material condition for *women's liberation* in other aspects of life.

The birth control pill made it possible but not inevitable that a second wave of feminism would arrive in the 1960s: there were other factors such as sexuality, secularism, and economics. *Sexuality*, a topic shrouded in mystery and taboo before the 1960s, was publicly debated in such matters as reproductive rights and women's control of their bodies, pornography's impact on violence against women, and sexual stereotyping in education and the media. Conventional beliefs about female passivity, maternal instincts, and home-centredness were now deemed to be the structural foundations of women's political subordination. *Secularism* was a second factor that contributed to the changed character of second-wave feminism. Traditional religious values regarding the family, procreation,

Nellie McClung was one of the leading figures in advancing feminist causes of her day. Name a woman in politics whose work you feel has made a contribution to contemporary Canadian society.

and appropriate behaviour, as well as the patriarchal authority structures of most churches, became targets of feminist criticism.

With respect to *economics*, the two conventional beliefs—that women should only take jobs not held by men and that outside employment was fine for single but not for married women—began to weaken during the 1950s and 1960s. Women's share of the total labour force also increased sharply. The falling real family incomes and the introduction of labour-saving household appliances might account for some of these trends, but the fact was that women wanted more than a husband, children and a home.[34] The service industries also underwent a remarkable expansion after World War II, which in turn increased the supply of low-wage jobs that were deemed to be "female" employment. However, their segregation into low-pay, low-prestige occupations[35] became less and less palatable to women as their participation in the wage economy increased.

Phase Three: The Personal Is Political

The 1950s was like the quiet before the storm. Once women had achieved political rights, it seemed that equality was no longer an issue. Post-war economic growth and the "baby boom" combined to reinforce traditional gender roles and stereotypes. Television sitcoms, films, and popular magazines almost unfailingly portrayed the male breadwinner–female homemaker family as the pinnacle of human happiness.

The syrupy bliss of the era, it turned out, was an illusion. By the early 1960s voices of discontent were being increasingly heard. Women were challenging the deep-seated beliefs and social structures that limited their participation in the male-dominated world. The "problem that has no name" was being named, and the name was **sexism**, *a term coined in the 1960s as a label for behaviour that treated males and females unequally for no better reason than their sex*. Sexism became the target of the women's movement that emerged during these years.

The revival of the women's movement was the result of several factors. Intellectually, writers like Simone de Beauvoir, Germaine Greer, and Gloria Steinem were developing a powerful analysis that went far beyond the earlier feminist concerns of political and legal rights and social reform, and exposed the social, cultural, and economic roots of inequality. This was also the era of the civil rights movement in the United States. Student radicalism, anti-war or anti-establishment protest marches, sit-ins, and occasional violence were the visible signs of a reaction against the status quo. While the feminist movement did not spearhead the 1960s protest movements, it profited from the way these movements saw all established power relations as unjust. American civil rights advocates argued that *affirmative action* programs were necessary to provide real equality of opportunity for blacks, and women in many countries borrowed the same arguments and policies. Although Canada had no first-hand experience with racially based affirmative action policies before the 1960s, the logic of affirmative action was not foreign to Canada. Language policies, in Quebec and nationally, incorporated elements of such an approach by the mid 1970s. As such, the logic and machinery of targeting groups for preferred treatment was already embedded in the Canadian state.

Organizing for Influence

Women have long been active in Canadian politics and several important women's organizations date from the pre-suffrage era. But contemporary feminism is different from the first wave of the women's movement, when female suffrage and social reform were the key issues. The organizational network of women's groups is much more developed, and new strategies distinguish it from its predecessor. Moreover, the political parties have provided a channel—though not a very effective one—for women's participation in political life. Over the last three decades these organizations have been joined by hundreds more, as the organizational network of the women's movement has proliferated. This proliferation has generated, in response, new state structures to deal with "women's issues" and the groups expressing them.

Although it is common to refer to the women's or feminist movement, there is an enormous range of perspectives within feminism: the world of women's organizations reflects diversity rather than a monolithic bloc. Perhaps the most prominent and arguably the most crippling

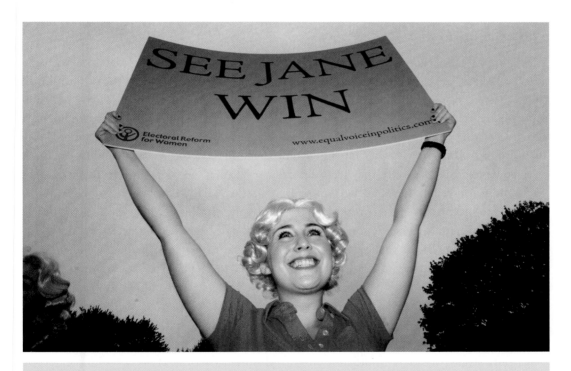

A member of Equal Voice, a group advocating for the election of more women at all levels of government, demonstrates at the Ontario legislature in 2007. Organizations such as Equal Voice strive to break down the barriers to women's participation in politics through such avenues as recruiting and training, working to create family-friendly work environments, advocating for electoral reform, and running public awareness campaigns. Give three reasons why you think there are not more women representatives in municipal, provincial, and federal politics.

recent division within the Canadian women's movement has been between the predominantly white middle-class feminists who have led the movement since the 1960s and the non-white feminists of less privileged ethnic groups and classes. This second group emphasizes race and class as central themes of their feminist vision. At the extreme, some segments of the feminist movement like the *National Action Committee on the Status of Women* (NAC) have argued that white middle-class feminists are incapable of truly understanding and representing the circumstances and aspirations of women who are black, Aboriginal, poor, or from some other historically oppressed group. This claim has generated considerable controversy. And this division appears to have made it easier for governments to question whether the NAC truly represented the concerns and values of a majority of Canadian women. By 2004, this once influential voice no longer had enough money to staff a permanent office and answer its phones. The organizations that had traditionally been voices for women—the National Council of Women of Canada, women's teacher and nursing associations, and others—were pushed aside by groups such as the Canadian Abortion Rights Action League and the Women's Legal Education and Action Fund.

Strategies

"There are fifty-six whooping cranes in Canada and one female federal politician."[36] So began a 1971 article by Barbara Frum in *Chatelaine*. Half a century after winning the same political rights as men, women's inroads into Canada's political parties were pitiful. Their participation was still channelled into mostly social, administrative, fundraising, and campaigning activities by the very women's auxiliaries/associations that modern feminism condemned. The 1970 Royal Commission on the Status of Women recommended that separate women's associations be abolished because they were a barrier to women's participation in party politics. The trend since the late 1960s has been to replace these associations with new women's groups dedicated to increasing women's representation and policy influence.

But as Sylvia Bashevkin notes, the transition has not been frictionless,[37] and the internal structures of political parties are no longer to blame. Most major parties are disinclined to alienate voters and organized interests who object to elements of the feminist agenda such as unrestricted abortions, affirmative action in hiring, and publicly subsidized daycare. Consequently, the women's movement has sought socio-political change by using other strategies.

As discussed later on in this chapter, litigating in support of sexual equality claims has long been a strategy used by Canadian women to eliminate barriers. However, with the notable exception of the 1929 *Persons* case, in which the JCPC overruled Canadian courts in determining that women were persons in law, most pre-Charter litigation on sexual equality has resulted in defeats for women's claims.[38] Given the dismal pre-Charter track record, plus the high cost of litigation, this strategy was seldom chosen by women.

The Charter was expected to make it easier for women to challenge these barriers. Indeed, women's groups fought hard and successfully for the inclusion of section 28 of the Charter, which states that "the rights and freedoms referred to in [the Charter] are guaranteed equally to male and female persons." Their efforts had already ensured that the equality section of the Charter (s. 15) proscribed discrimination based on sex. With sections 15 and 28 in hand, it appeared that women's groups would turn to the courts as never before. Results have been mixed. Feminists have argued that the sexual equality guarantees of the Charter are under-mined by two aspects of judicial interpretation. One is the courts' unwillingness to elevate equality rights over other rights and freedoms guaranteed in the Charter. Second, and more serious according to feminists, is the tendency of judges to interpret equality in *formal* rather than *substantive* terms: judges will be satisfied that no discrimination has occurred if laws treat similarly persons who are similarly situated. According to feminists, this "equality before the law" approach fails to understand the mechanisms through which discrimination occurs.[39]

Activist Penney Kome identifies several political strategies, including legal action, that are open to women's groups. Few financial resources and little personal access to carry on effective behind-the-scenes lobbying have encouraged women's organizations to resort to very public and sometimes confrontational strategies intended to generate media coverage. They make extensive use of political action strategies such as grassroots organizing to deal with emergencies (e.g., a rash of sexual assaults in a neighbourhood) or chronic local problems (e.g., inadequate public transportation or pollution), representations through official channels, lob-bying campaigns directed at decision makers and potential supporters, and courting media coverage.[40] The NAC and other women's groups have made several representations over the years to the United Nations Committee on Economic, Social and Cultural Rights. And inter-national meetings on women's issues have also often received considerable media attention in Canada. Such strategies do not guarantee success, but they can maintain public awareness of feminist demands. On the other hand, attempts to embarrass governments through public reproaches and protests can backfire, as the NAC discovered in the 1990s when its revenues fell by 40 per cent largely due to cuts in federal government grants.

Achievements

The achievements of modern feminists can be grouped into three types of change: legislative reform, changes in the decision-making process, and the material and social conditions of women. Together these add up to a mixed record of success and failure.

Legislative Reform

Some of the most celebrated achievements of the women's movement have been in changes to the law. Sex was not one of the proscribed grounds of discrimination in the draft Charter proposed by the Liberal government in 1981. It became part of the Charter after women's groups made vigorous representations before the Special Parliamentary Committee on the Constitution. Likewise, the section 28 guarantee of legal equality for men and women was a direct product of intense lobbying by women's groups.[41] And in a major victory, and perhaps the most publicized of court decisions on the Charter, in 1988 the Supreme Court of Canada struck down the section of the Criminal Code dealing with abortion. Several other legislative changes and judicial rulings are also seen as victories:

- 1970: Maternity leave provisions are written into the Canada Labour Code
- 1983: Amendments to the Unemployment Insurance Act eliminate discrimination against pregnant women; pay-equity laws are passed by Ottawa and the provinces
- *Blainey* (1986): An Ontario Court of Appeal decision that opened boys' sports leagues to girls
- *Daigle* (1989): A Supreme Court ruling that the father of a fetus cannot veto a woman's decision to have an abortion
- 1998: A Canadian Human Rights Tribunal pay-equity decision found that the federal government owed $5 billion in back pay to female public servants
- *Ewanchuk* (1999): A Supreme Court ruling that no defence of implied consent to sexual assault exists under Canadian law

Human rights codes and commissions to enforce them exist nationally and in all the provinces. They have provided opportunities to challenge discriminatory employment and commercial practices in the private sector, which falls outside the ambit of the Charter.

In spite of these advances, women's groups point to inaction or government's inadequate responses to such issues as daycare, affirmative action, female poverty, pay equity, and pornography. And more recently, many feminists argue that a popular backlash has enabled governments to roll back some of the gains made in the past.

Decision-Making Structures of the State

Among the striking characteristics of the modern women's movement are its financial and organizational links to government. The 1970 report of the Royal Commission on the Status of Women was followed by the creation of the Canadian Advisory Council on the Status of Women, now called Status of Women Canada (SWC), and the creation of a women's portfolio in the federal cabinet. Similar advisory councils have been created by all provinces, and some have also established special cabinet positions. Within government departments and agencies it is now common to have special divisions devoted to "women's issues" or affirmative action.

Financially, the women's movement, which from the early 1970s until the mid 1990s was led by the NAC, has been dependent on money provided by government. Ottawa's cutbacks on social spending and transfers to the provinces affected grassroots women's groups that depend on public money. Those on the left wing of the women's movement have often criticized the organizational and financial ties between women's groups and the state, arguing that such ties have the effect of co-opting feminists into the state.

Material and Social Conditions

The record of achievement in equality, material circumstances of women, and social attitudes is mixed. Social attitudes regarding appropriate roles and behaviour for males and females have changed over the last two generations. Most Canadians believe that a woman could run any business as well as a man, and most claim that the sex of a political party leader does not influence their likelihood of voting for that party. On such issues as abortion and equality of job opportunities, there is little evidence of a significant gender gap. Canadians' attitudes

toward gender equality are more progressive than those of the populations of most other affluent democracies.[42]

Nevertheless, considerable sexism persists. These signs include gender characterizations in
commercial advertising and entertainment programming; the child-rearing practices of many,
indeed probably most, parents; the unequal division of domestic responsibilities between men
and women; and the rarity of women's career choices taking precedence over men's even in
this age of two-earner households. The 2001 Canadian census reported that women were twice
as likely as men to say that they spent 15 hours or more each week on housework and almost
twice as likely as men to say that they spent at least 15 hours per week on unpaid child care.[43]

Despite the fact that there are today more women lawyers, professors, accountants, and
even engineers than in the past, and that females are more likely than males to attend university (among university graduates in 2008, 60 per cent were female and 40 per cent were
male), the breakthroughs made by middle-class women have not been matched by their less
privileged sisters.

The continuing exclusion of women from Canada's corporate elite, while their participation in the political elite has been increasing, may thwart some of the gains achieved by the
women's movement. According to a report by CBC News, by 2011 only three of the Fortune 500
companies had at least half of their executive officer posts occupied by women.[44]

The belief that more women in the corporate elite would make a difference in the decisions made by major corporations may also be mistaken. As economies become international-
ized, domestic politics matters less and business matters more. Increasingly, decisions with
major social implications are made by the corporate elite, from which women are still largely
excluded. The general opposition of the women's movement to globalization is certainly influenced by the realization that the decline in the power of the "state" relative to that of transnational corporations and markets has reduced the political clout of women's groups.

Materially, women are still less well off than men despite the legal reforms and changed
social attitudes that have been produced by the women's movement. Poverty and economic
dependence undermine individuals' ability to control their lives and to grasp the opportunities promised by formal legal and political equality. So far as women are concerned, Canadian
democracy remains flawed. Nevertheless, and to a significant degree the feminist movement,
in Canada as elsewhere, pioneered the modern discourse of diversity politics: that real democracy cannot be achieved without recognizing the different circumstances experienced by
members of different groups, and that justice requires laws and institutions that recognize
these different group experiences in its treatment of them.

ABORIGINAL POLITICS

For most of Canada's history Aboriginal affairs were relegated to the dim corners of public
life. Politicians and most Canadians paid them little attention. This has changed. Aboriginal
groups have become much more sophisticated in their political strategies and tactics, and the
issues that concern them, from landownership to abuse and discrimination, have become part
of the political conversation in Canada.

The opulence of the Grand Hall at the Canadian Museum of Civilization stands in stark contrast to a group of unidentified Innu youth in Sheshatshiu, Labrador, openly sniffing gas in their community in 2004. As you read this section, think about some of the gaps between the symbols we use to acknowledge the Aboriginal peoples of Canada and the reality of their everyday lives in this country. What are some factors that contribute to the creation of those gaps?

The 2004 reports of gas-sniffing by teenagers and young children in the Innu community of Sheshatshiu, Labrador, and the 2011 housing crisis in Attawapiskat First Nation, Ontario, stand in stark contrast with the celebration of Aboriginal symbols and culture in places like the Museum of Civilization in Gatineau, Quebec. Many Canadians are puzzled that circumstances like those at Sheshatshiu and Attawapiskat exist. After all, government expenditures per Aboriginal person in Canada are estimated to be about 50 per cent more than that for all Canadians.[45] Canadians are also perplexed by news stories of continuing tensions and occasionally outbreaks of violence between some Aboriginal communities and their neighbours or the political authorities. Why, they wonder, after years of treaties, legislation, government programs, inquiries, apologies, and financial settlements, do so many issues remain unresolved?

Aboriginal Demographics: Who and How Many?

Aboriginal Canadians are those who can trace their ancestry back to before the arrival and permanent settlement of Europeans in what would become Canada. The actual size of this population is uncertain. Estimates range from half a million to 3 million (1.6 to 9 per cent of the national population).

Statistics Canada defines "Aboriginal" as a person that self-identifies as North American Indian, Métis, or Inuit. According to the 2006 census:

- 1,678,200 people (5.4 per cent of Canada's population) identify themselves as North American Indian, Métis, Inuit, or a combination of one of these and another ethnic origin.
- 1,172,790 people (4 per cent of Canada's population) identify with an Aboriginal group.

- 763,555 (2 per cent of Canada's population) are status Indians, i.e., those to whom the Indian Act applies. Slightly more than half of these people live on reserves or in other recognized Aboriginal settlements.

The regional distribution of those who identify themselves as Aboriginal Canadians is shown in Figure 12.4.

The social and economic conditions of Aboriginal Canadians tend to be considerably less favourable than those of the general population. This is regularly brought home by news reports of substance abuse or high rates of suicide among young Aboriginal Canadians living in isolated communities. Statistics confirm that Aboriginal Canadians are less well off than their fellow Canadians. For example, an Aboriginal working full-time earns on average about three-quarters of what a non-Aboriginal Canadian earns. Government transfer payments make up about one-fifth of Aboriginal income, compared to about one-tenth of income for non-Aboriginal Canadians. According to the 2006 census, about one-third of Aboriginal Canadians aged 25 to 64 have not completed high school (about 50 per cent among those living on reserves), compared to 15 per cent of other Canadians, and only 8 per cent have graduated from university, compared to 23 per cent of other Canadians.

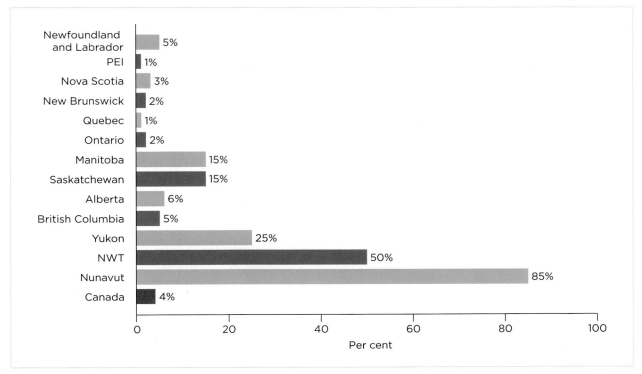

FIGURE 12.4 ABORIGINAL IDENTITY POPULATION AS PERCENTAGE OF TOTAL POPULATION, PROVINCES AND TERRITORIES, 2006

Source: Statistics Canada, Census of Population, 2006, Figure 1, http://www12.statcan.ca/census-recensement/2006/as-sa/97-558/figures/c1-eng.cfm.

The Language of Aboriginal Politics

The words used to describe those who trace their ancestry back before the arrival of Europeans provide a useful starting point for understanding the politics of Aboriginality. For most of Canada's history these people and their communities were only marginally acknowledged in the official life of the country and were barely visible in mainstream interpretations of Canadian history and society. The terms "Indian," "Métis," and "Eskimo," were used to describe various segments of the Aboriginal population. The legal meanings and implications of these terms were sometimes contested in the courts. Until the 1960s, there was little controversy over the terms used to characterize the Aboriginal population of Canada and virtually no sense that the language made a difference.

By the 1960s, labels and concepts that had been considered acceptable and appropriate were brought into question because of changing Western thought. **Communitarianism—** *the belief that communities and communal identities are essential to individual dignity and the maintenance of truly democratic societies*—was gaining ground. At the street level, this belief system was embodied in elements of the black civil rights movement, in echoes of Quebec nationalism from books like Pierre Vallières' *Nègres blancs d'Amérique* (*White Niggers of America*), and to René Lévesque's insistence that Quebecers needed an independent state in order to have a free and democratic society. During these years black, ethnic, and women's studies emerged at universities across North America.

An additional and crucial feature of the communitarian model involved *inequality*. Virtually all calls for greater group self-awareness and demands for official recognition of this collective identity were linked to an analysis and historical narrative of discrimination, exploitation, and unjust treatment—in brief, inequality—in relations between the group in question and the state. This was a challenge to what had been thought of as progressive liberal thinking in the decades after World War II. Liberal opinion leaders now aimed at eradicating poverty, socio-economic inequality, and discrimination. The path to progress involved the full and equal integration of all people, as individuals, into society and the dismantlement of laws, norms, and practices that treated people differently on the basis of skin colour, ethnicity, or religion—that officially recognized and institutionalized differences.

In the case of Aboriginal Canadians, the first step was to reject the mid-twentieth-century language of *integration* and *liberal notions of equality*: these ideas were leading to assimilation and cultural genocide. Despite the obvious misnomer applied by the early European explorers to native North Americans, the term "Indian" was not immediately rejected. Indeed, "Indian" continues to be used by community members and their leaders today.

By the late 1970s and 1980s, "Indian," which carried the historical baggage of conquest, displacement, and subordination, was being replaced by "Native," "Aboriginal," and "First Nations." This shift was both intellectual and political. Intellectually, the change reflected a reappropriation of Aboriginals' identities and histories. Politically, the term *First Nations* carried connotations of prior claims as well as communal status and rights. The language of *nationalism* and the *claims of nations*, particularly nations that had been colonized by foreign powers, became familiar and powerful. The dismantlement of European colonial empires and the 1960 UN Declaration on the Granting of Independence to Colonial Countries and Peoples reinforced nationalist claims and the idea that "all peoples have the right to self-determination."

Quebec nationalist intellectuals enthusiastically supported this doctrine of national self-determination. If Québécois could make such nationalist claims, then why not Aboriginal Canadians as well? Indeed, it is difficult to argue that Aboriginal peoples are somehow less deserving of nation status than the Québécois. They certainly can make a more compelling case for having experienced "alien subjugation" and "domination", terms used in the UN Declaration.

Whether Aboriginal communities are "nations" is disputed. The same question arises about the Québécois nation. More important is whether the widespread acceptance of terms like "First Nations" and "Indigenous peoples" can have consequences with respect to legitimacy and a group's claims. Relations between Aboriginal communities and the Canadian state were long about treaty obligations and reserves. Consequently, the language of treaty obligations continues to be important and reserves still exist. Several other terms and associated issues have become part of the conversation on Aboriginal affairs: "sovereignty," "self-government," "self-determination," and "nation-to-nation." The new vocabulary reflects an enormous change over the last three decades in the scope and nature of Native demands in Canada—demands that now rest on an increasingly influential *communitarian ethos*.

Who Is an Indian?

It has become unfashionable in some circles to use the word "Indian." However, practically speaking, the word "Indian" must be used in a discussion of government policies toward Aboriginal peoples. Under Canada's Indian Act (1876), a person who qualifies as an Indian under the law has certain entitlements that do not apply to others. Moreover, Indian bands that live on land referred to in law as Indian *reserves* are subject to special legal provisions such as individual landownership and transfer, a prohibition against mortgages on reserve land, and numerous restrictions on economic activities. Until the Indian Act and the legal status of "Indian" are abolished, any analysis of Aboriginal policies cannot avoid using these terms.

In law, an Indian or status Indian is anyone who has been or is entitled to be registered under the Indian Act, including those who belong to communities covered by treaties. The defining characteristics are both biological and social. The Indian Act of 1876 stipulated that an Indian was any male person of Indian blood who belonged to a band recognized by the federal government, any child of such a person, or any woman married to such a person.

An Indian woman who married a non-Indian lost her legal status as an Indian and the entitlements associated with that status. This discriminatory section of the Act was changed by the federal government in response to pressure from Aboriginal women and to conform to the UN International Covenant on Civil and Political Rights, and the Charter of Rights and Freedoms.

Ancestry is not the only criterion determining who is an Indian under the law. Indeed, the courts have recognized that a person's "associations, habits, modes of life, and surroundings" may weigh more heavily in the balance than the ethnicity of one's forebears in determining legal status as an Indian.[46] Canadian law also recognizes the Métis and Inuit as two other categories of Aboriginal peoples of Canada. The Inuit and Métis are grouped with the Indian people of Canada by section 35 of the Constitution Act, 1982, which recognizes and affirms the "existing aboriginal and treaty rights of the aboriginal peoples of Canada."

The Reserve System

There are over 2700 Indian reserves in Canada. They cover about 10,000 square miles, an area roughly half the size of Nova Scotia. Some have called Indian reserves Canada's own system of apartheid. Superficially, the apartheid label seems a fair one. The reserve system was created to provide a sort of fixed homeland for Indians and the vast majority of those residing on reserves today are status Indians. Average life expectancy and incomes of those who live on reserves are significantly lower than the Canadian norms. Rates of suicide, alcoholism, violent death, unemployment, crowded housing conditions, and infant mortality are all higher, sometimes dramatically higher, than the Canadian average.

The enormous disparity between life on reserves and mainstream society combined with the racial basis for the physical segregation of Indians does sound like apartheid. But when the Liberal government's 1969 White Paper proposed the abolition of reserves along with all the other legal and paternalistic structures that have treated Indians differently, the leaders of Canada's Aboriginal communities responded with a vehement "No." Why then is this apparent form of apartheid not rejected outright by the very people who are its "victims"? To understand why, we must look at the origins and operation of Indian reserves in Canada as well as the goals of today's Aboriginal leaders.

The Indian Act of 1876 defines a reserve as ". . . any tract or tracts of land set apart by treaty or otherwise for the use or benefit of or granted to a particular band of Indians, of which the legal title is in the Crown, but which is unsurrendered, and includes all the trees, wood, timber, soil, stone, minerals, metals, or other valuables thereon or therein." Central to this definition and to the quandary of the reserve system is the *guardianship* relationship between the federal government and Indians living on reserves. Reserve land belongs to the Crown, but the land and all its resources must be managed for the "use or benefit" of the band. In practice, this meant that virtually all legal or commercial transactions by Indians living on a reserve required the permission of the federal Department of Indian Affairs (now Aboriginal Affairs and Northern Development). Restrictions have been eased somewhat recently. When critics speak of the Indian Act's paternalism, they may be referring to the fact that band members may not sell any part of the reserve, or use the land as security for loans, and that the federal government has the ultimate authority to grant timber-cutting licences.

Roughly 400,000 Indians live on reserves, but about three-quarters of all reserves are uninhabited, since many bands have leased their reserve land to non-Indians for various economic and recreational uses. A vast majority of reserves are in rural and remote areas, with populations that vary from two to just under 20,000 people. Most reserves have fewer than a thousand inhabitants. This has important social and economic consequences. Job opportunities are fewer, and many who want secondary or post-secondary education must leave home.

Physical isolation impedes the integration of reserve populations into the rest of society. However, as Harvey McCue explains, not everyone considers physical isolation a bad thing:

> To many Indians, reserves represent the last visible evidence that they were the original people of this country. The reserve nurtures a community of "Indianness" and reinforces spiritual unity among Indians. Despite the manifest poverty, ill health, poor housing and lack of services, the life-style on reserves, traditional values, kinship affiliations and the land itself all contribute to an Indian's identity and psychological well-being.[47]

As McCue suggests, the pressure on Aboriginal Canadians to assimilate is powerful. Language loss is one of the key indicators of assimilation. Only three of Canada's roughly 53 Aboriginal languages—Cree, Inuktitut, and Ojibwa—continue to be spoken by significant numbers of Aboriginal Canadians. While there still is cause for concern, however, in the first years of the twenty-first century, fluency in some Aboriginal languages was holding steady, indicating that there is renewed interest in keeping these languages alive.[48]

Assimilation, Integration, Self-Determination

Although some major components of present-day Aboriginal policy have been in place since pre-Confederation, the principles underlying federal policy have undergone important transformations.

Under French colonial rule two key principles underlay Aboriginal policy in New France: the non-recognition of any Aboriginal proprietary rights in the lands claimed by France, and assimilation. France laid claim to territory in the New World by right of discovery and conquest. As well, conversion of the Aboriginal population to Christianity was a central objective of French colonial policy. Notably, French policy did not consider the Aboriginal population to be subhuman and beyond redemption. In fact, the 1627 Charter of the Company of One Hundred Associates declared that a converted Aboriginal had the status and rights of a naturalized French citizen.

The transfer of French territories in Canada to the British laid the foundation for Aboriginal policies for the next two centuries. The *Royal Proclamation of 1763* and the treaties between the colonial authorities and Indian tribes were clearly based on the assumption that Aboriginals had fallen under the protective stewardship of the British state. Unlike the French, the British acknowledged a proprietary Aboriginal interest in the land, but within the broader context of British sovereignty and the colonial authorities' expectations that European settlement would continue to expand onto land traditionally occupied by Aboriginal peoples. Moreover, as both the Royal Proclamation and early dealings between the British and Indians show, the British believed that they were required to compensate the Aboriginal population for land through treaties and purchase agreements. And unlike the French, the British were much less concerned with the state of Aboriginals' souls than with ensuring that the Indigenous population did not impede the colonies' growth. To this end, the policy of reserving certain lands for occupation and use by Indians was practised by the British—a policy that was continued after Confederation.

Under the BNA Act (now called the Constitution Act, 1867), Ottawa assumed exclusive legislative authority over Indian affairs. Within a decade, the federal government passed the Indian Act: a sweeping piece of legislation that consolidated the dependency relationship that already had been developing between Aboriginals and the state. Under the Act, Indians living on reserves were placed under the almost total control of the Superintendent-General of Indian Affairs, whose god-like powers would be exercised by federal bureaucrats in Ottawa and by powerful officials in the field, referred to as Indian agents.

The Indian Act made it impossible for Indians living on reserves to assume responsibility and control over their social and economic development. Unlike many Aboriginal traditions of governance that involved traditional and inherited leadership, the Act conferred extremely limited powers of self-government to elected reserve bands.

Until well into the latter half of the twentieth century it was widely believed that Aboriginal Canadians would gradually abandon their language and culture and be absorbed into Euro-Canadian society. The 1884 ban on the potlatch ceremony and on religious ceremonies exemplifies the sanctions used to stamp out Aboriginal traditions. The prohibition on using

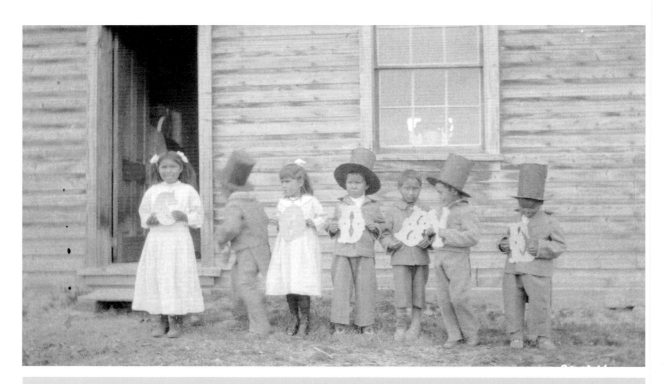

Aboriginal children at Fort Simpson Indian Residential School. The residential system was an attempt at assimilating Aboriginal communities into mainstream Canadian society, as evidenced by the European-style clothing. Can you name some of the long-lasting negative effects of these kinds of attempts as assimilation?

Aboriginal languages in the federal government's residential schools was another attempt at assimilating Aboriginal people into mainstream society. The goal of assimilation is especially apparent in the sections of the Indian Act that set out procedures whereby an Indian could *request* to become a Canadian citizen. While enfranchisement was automatic for Indians who acquired a certain education or social rank, full Canadian citizenship was not granted to all Aboriginal people until the Act was amended in 1960.

The extension of voting rights to Aboriginals brought their political status closer to that of other Canadians, but their legal and social status, and their civil rights, remained distinct. Moreover, instead of disappearing, as many had hoped, Indian reserves continued to exist as islands of shame within an affluent and democratic society.

The government of Pierre Trudeau set out to change this. In 1969, Trudeau's Minister of Indian Affairs, Jean Chrétien, introduced the 1969 **White Paper** (*a report for discussion on a major piece of legislation being proposed by government*) on Aboriginal reform, which proposed dismantling the Indian Affairs bureaucracy, an end to the reserve system, the abolition of different status for Indians under the law, as well as a transfer of responsibility for the education, health care, and social needs of Aboriginal citizens, like other Canadians, to the provinces. These proposed changes were in keeping with the ideas of the civil-rights movement of the 1950s and 1960s, which proposed *inclusive integration* as a remedy—barriers to the full economic, social, and political participation of historically disadvantaged minorities would be abolished.

The reaction of Canada's Aboriginal leadership to the 1969 White Paper was swift and overwhelmingly negative. And although its authors certainly did not intend such interpretations, some critics equated its "liberal integrationist" vision with assimilation, "cultural genocide" and "extermination."[49] Nothing galvanized Aboriginal opposition more than its proposals concerning treaty obligations and land claims. The very concept of a treaty between one part of society and the government of all the people was morally and philosophically repugnant to Pierre Trudeau, and the government argued that while it recognized its lawful obligations, treaties should not be expected to define in perpetuity the relationship between Aboriginals and the government of Canada.

This vision and its premises survive today in some of Canada's political and intellectual elites. They have been refuted by numerous court decisions on treaty rights and Aboriginal land claims. Since the ill-fated 1969 White Paper, the government appears to have recognized, in the law and in the Constitution, the separate and distinct status of Aboriginal communities within Canadian society. Although most have little idea of what it might involve, a concept of *self-government* for Aboriginal communities has emerged. It is now endorsed by the Assembly of First Nations, and accepted as both fair and desirable by many Canadians.

The self-government vision for Aboriginal Canadians was set forth in the 1996 report of the *Royal Commission on Aboriginal Peoples*. The philosophical premises and policy proposals of the Royal Commission could hardly have been further from those of the 1969 White Paper. The Commission started from the premise that Aboriginal Canadians constitute First Nations whose sovereignty should be respected by the government of Canada. Among other things, it called for an official admission of the wrongs done to Aboriginal people; the creation of an Aboriginal third order of government (an Aboriginal parliament) based on the acknowledgement of the inherent right to self-government as a treaty right guaranteed by the Constitution of Canada; a form of *dual citizenship* for Aboriginal Canadians; negotiations with Métis representatives on self-government and the allocation to the Métis people of an adequate land base; and more money for Aboriginal programs. In short, historical land claims must be acknowledged, and Aboriginal peoples' continuing right to a land base and self-government must be embedded in the Constitution. Moreover, Aboriginal cultures must be protected and survival ensured through policies that recognize Aboriginal people as distinct communities with special rights and powers.

The problem with previous federal policies is that they had not provided the Aboriginal population with the decision-making autonomy or financial resources to escape the cycle of dependency that the Indian Act and the reserve system have perpetuated. Some of the Commission's recommendations have been acted on:

- Various forms of self-government have been set up in many Aboriginal communities, and some innovative models have been developed (e.g., Nunavut).

CANADIAN SPOTLIGHT

BOX 12.4   Chief Matthew Coon Come Compares Canada to South Africa under Apartheid

At the end of August 2001, Matthew Coon Come, at the time the National Chief of the Assembly of First Nations, spoke at the World Conference Against Racism in Durban, South Africa. His words, and the significance of this global gathering, soon were overshadowed by the terrorist attacks on the United States of 9/11 and subsequent events.

Canadians, and the government of Canada, present themselves around the world as upholders and protectors of human rights. In many ways, this reputation is well-deserved. In South Africa, the government of Canada played a prominent role in isolating the apartheid regime. In many other countries, Canada provides impressive international development assistance.

However, at home in Canada, the oppression, marginalization, and dispossession of Indigenous peoples continue.

Every year, the Canadian government's own federal Human Rights Commission draws attention to this discriminatory situation, one that stunts and takes the lives of thousands and thousands of people. Yet little progress is made in addressing the fundamental, underlying cause of our poverty, hopelessness, and despair.

This root cause is the one that the South African anti-apartheid representative described [to us] over 20 years ago: landlessness, dispossession, and the social marginalization and exclusion of our peoples.

The lesson for me is that colonial and discriminatory policies and practices are not restricted to less developed parts of the world. They are also to be found in Australia, Canada, New Zealand, the United States, and Scandinavia, to name a few examples. Indigenous peoples everywhere are being "pushed to the edge of extinction"—even in Canada, where the plentiful land, resources, and capacity exist to correct these ongoing injustices.

—From "Remarks of National Chief, Matthew Coon Come," World Conference Against Racism, Durban, South Africa, 30 August 2001. Used with permission

- Reparations have been paid to thousands of Aboriginal survivors who experienced mistreatment and abuse in residential schools.
- In June 2008 Prime Minister Stephen Harper issued a formal apology to the victims of the residential schools.

However, the federal government has been unwilling to concede the division of sovereignty that seemed to be at the heart of the Commission's approach to reform—a notion of self-government premised on the idea that Aboriginal sovereignty must exist alongside and equal to the sovereignty that Ottawa and the provinces enjoy under the Constitution.

Land Ownership and Sovereignty

Disputes over land—who owns it, and who can live on it, benefit from it, and make laws that apply within its boundaries—are among the most intractable. Aboriginal Canadians have come to realize that the crux of their demands involves land. Phrases like "self-government for Canada's Aboriginal peoples" have inoffensive and even positive associations for many Canadians until they are linked to exclusive Aboriginal ownership of land and political sovereignty in territory that the majority of Canadians assumed was part of Canada. One of the chief differences between Aboriginal and European-based cultures is said to be how each culture views the land and their relationship to it. Clearly, the land was crucial to the traditional lifestyles of Aboriginal peoples. Aboriginal hunting and fishing rights recognized in the treaties between Aboriginals and non-Aboriginals were important to the Aboriginal peoples, but were often restricted or ignored by federal and provincial governments and private citizens. In contrast, and somewhat more controversial, are claims to control mineral or other resources that are important to the lifestyles and economic activities of Europeans cultures, but traditionally have had little or no relationship to Aboriginal cultures. This is an issue that Canadian courts have addressed in recent years.

Ownership of a particular parcel of land does not exempt a person or group from the obligation to obey the law of the sovereign country in which their land is located. But many leaders within Canada's Aboriginal communities deny the sovereignty of the Canadian state over them and their land. Former Assembly of First Nations (AFN) national chief Ovide Mercredi's comment is fairly typical: "We will not allow some other society to decide what we can do and determine the limits of our authority."[50] Nonetheless, while virtually all Aboriginal spokespersons express support for the principles of *Aboriginal self-government* and Aboriginal rights, most advocate some form of self-determination that would be realized within the context of the Canadian state.

The issues of sovereignty and landownership are obviously intertwined and much in dispute. These are matters that have been contested and determined largely through the courts, based on the interpretation of treaties. Indeed, those who make the case for Aboriginal sovereignty often begin with the Royal Proclamation of 1763. The Proclamation dealt with the North American territories that were formally surrendered by France to England under the terms of the Treaty of Paris. It included detailed provisions regarding relations between the British and the Aboriginal inhabitants. Aboriginal leaders generally view the Royal Proclamation as an affirmation of their existing right to the lands they occupied. It is not entirely clear, however, that the Royal Proclamation of 1763—which was formally incorporated into the Canadian Constitution through section 25 of the Charter of Rights and Freedoms—recognizes Aboriginal sovereignty. What is clear, however, is that the Proclamation speaks of the "Sovereignty, Protection, and Dominion" of the Crown in relation to the Aboriginal inhabitants who "live under our protection."

That the Royal Proclamation recognizes Aboriginal rights is indisputable. However, a ruling by the Judicial Committee of the Privy Council in 1888 stated that the Proclamation did not explicitly recognize Indian sovereignty. Perhaps there is an implicit recognition of Aboriginal sovereignty in the Proclamation. This seems to be the argument of those who characterize it as a *nation-to-nation* agreement. The restriction on the use of what the Proclamation calls "Lands of the Indians" might be interpreted as an acknowledgement of Aboriginal sovereignty. It seems to establish an Indian right to compensation for land transferred by them to the Crown.

A number of land issue cases, including *St Catherine's Milling and Lumber Company v. the Queen* (1888), *Calder et al. v. Attorney General of British Columbia* (1973), *Hamlet of Baker Lake et al. v. Minister of Indian Affairs* (1980), *and Regina v. Sparrow* (1990), set the stage for the *Delgamuukw v. Attorney General of British Columbia*, which worked its way through the courts from 1987 to 1997. In *Delgamuukw*, the issue of Aboriginal title was addressed head-on. A group of Gitksan and Wet'suwet'en chiefs argued that they owned an area in British Columbia roughly the size of Nova Scotia. The stakes could hardly have been greater. Following rejection of the claim by the British Columbia Supreme Court in 1991, and an upholding of this judgment on appeal, the Supreme Court of Canada in 1997 ruled that the Gitksan and Wet'suwet'en are the owners of the land to which they lay historical claim. Where Aboriginal title to land has not been extinguished by the terms of a treaty—and this would include most of British Columbia as well as parts of Atlantic Canada—Aboriginal communities able to prove that they historically occupied and used the land continue to have property rights.

The *Delgamuukw* decision generated more questions than answers. What is clear, however, is that the Court's interpretation of Aboriginal title means that Aboriginal communities have a right to compensation for land determined to be theirs by historical right, and that the oral historical accounts of a people are now admissible in court as proof of land occupancy and use. The ruling strengthened the hand of Aboriginal groups who can now say that they have a constitutionally protected right of ownership that can be extinguished only through the terms of a treaty with the Crown. Landownership issues aside, the Supreme Court's 1997 decision did not establish a constitutional right to self-government for Aboriginal communities.

The essential character of treaties between Aboriginal peoples and the Crown is another matter that has arisen in the courts. Some have argued that the treaties and other agreements are tantamount to international treaties. If this is so, then it would follow that these Aboriginal peoples have been recognized as sovereign nations capable of entering into agreements with other nations on a basis of legal equality. But even in their generally sympathetic treatment of Aboriginal rights, Peter A. Cumming and Neil H. Mickenberg say that historically and legally there is little basis for interpreting treaties as international treaties. They note that the Supreme

Court of Canada has expressly rejected this view of treaties. Moreover, they note that "the Government did not consider the Indians to be independent nations at the time the treaties were made . . . and both the Government representatives and the Indian negotiators indicate that they considered the Indian peoples to be subjects of the Queen."[51]

The courts may have lacked sympathy for the interpretation of Indian treaties as international agreements, but Aboriginal spokespersons and some governments have insisted that treaties be viewed in this light. On the issue of treaties with European powers, Georges Erasmus and Joe Sanders write, "Our people understood what the non-native people were after when they came amongst our people and wanted to treaty with them, because they had done that many times amongst themselves."[52] Not only are treaties agreements between sovereign nations, according to this view, they are emphatically not real-estate transactions. This point is crucial, because the position taken by the courts and most governments in Canada has been that any Aboriginal right to ownership of the land covered by the terms of a treaty is *extinguished* by such an agreement. The nation-to-nation view of treaties denies that any extinguishment occurred, on the grounds that this was not how treaties were understood by the Aboriginals who agreed to them. That non-Aboriginals understood these agreements differently does not, Aboriginal leaders argue, mean that their view, rather than that of Aboriginal people, should be considered the correct one. The courts have, however, recognized that Indian treaties constitute a rather unique sort of contractual agreement, and have tended to interpret any ambiguous terms of treaties in favour of Aboriginal rights.

According to Cumming and Mickenberg, however treaties were viewed by the Aboriginal people, there is little doubt that colonial officials and subsequent Canadian authorities used the "language of real property law" and interpreted the treaties as a way of ". . . extinguishing Indian title in order that lands could be opened to white settlement. The treaties, therefore, can be best understood . . . when considered as agreements of a very special nature in which the Indians gave up their rights in the land in exchange for certain promises made by the Government."[53]

The question of how treaties negotiated centuries ago should be interpreted today—treaties negotiated by parties who spoke different languages, written in the language of only one of the parties, and operated from very different cultural premises—has arisen on numerous occasions. For instance, in *R. v. Marshall* (1999), the Supreme Court made two controversial rulings. In the first ruling, the court stated that according to 1760s treaties with Britain, the Mi'kmaq Indians had the right to catch and sell fish, and that federal fisheries regulations infringed on those rights. In the second ruling, the Court indicated that Aboriginal treaty rights were still subject to treatment under Canadian law.

The Institutionalization of Aboriginal Affairs

The treaties and the federal Indian bureaucracy that has existed since and even before the Indian Act (1876) would ensure that Aboriginal affairs were embedded in the activities of the Canadian state. Government transfers to Aboriginal communities under the terms of treaties, which were administered through the Indian agents, and transfers to individual Aboriginals through welfare spending (Aboriginal Canadians living off reserve are about three times more likely than other Canadians to receive social assistance) created a web of financial dependency on the state that continues to exist. The institutionalization of Aboriginal affairs into the structure and activities of the Canadian state has also created and perpetuated dependency relations. Dependency continues in spite of some important reforms designed to break the cycle.

Some, like former Liberal minister of Indian affairs, Hugh Faulkner, have argued that the motive behind his government's deliberate policy of funding selected interest groups, including Aboriginal organizations, was progressive and intended to strengthen the political voice of such groups.[54] Others, like Noel Starblanket of the National Indian Brotherhood, accused Ottawa of using money as part of a divide-and-conquer strategy for dealing with Aboriginal groups.[55] Roger Gibbins and Rick Ponting agree that the potential for the co-optation and control of Aboriginal organizations certainly existed as Ottawa became increasingly involved in the funding of these groups.

The leading organizational voices for Aboriginal Canadians continue to depend on public funding mainly from Aboriginal Affairs and Northern Development Canada (AANDC). However, there is little evidence that this dependence has muted their criticisms. For example, the criticisms from various leaders of the Assembly of First Nations and other groups, sometimes at international forums, have frequently been scathing. And money spent on legal proceedings against the Canadian state, and for lobbying and advertising campaigns to influence public opinion on policy, has come, at least in part, from the state.

The institutionalization of Aboriginal affairs and identity within the Canadian state has also occurred through broadcasting. Many initiatives for Aboriginal-language television and radio programming were launched between 1960 and the mid 1990s, but the consensus is that the major impact of broadcasting to the North, where most viewers and listeners were Aboriginal Canadians, was to "accelerate the process of cultural and language loss, particularly among the young."[56] The airwaves in Aboriginal communities continue to be dominated by English programming and the use of Aboriginal languages continues to decline.

Another way in which Aboriginal concerns and issues have been institutionalized through the Canadian state involves employment. Aboriginal representation in the federal public service, negligible for most of Canada's history, today is about proportional to the size of the Aboriginal identity population of the country. Aboriginal Canadians make up about 3 per cent of the public service in the National Capital Region, but closer to one-quarter in the combined territories of Yukon, the Northwest Territories, and Nunavut. About 40 per cent of all Aboriginal federal employees work in the North or in western provinces. The largest employer of Aboriginal Canadians is the AANDC. Almost one-third of its employees are Aboriginal, ensuring that the organizational culture of AANDC is sensitive to the values and backgrounds of those it serves.

Second Thoughts or Citizens Plus?

In 2000, two of Canada's leading political scientists, Alan Cairns and Thomas Flanagan, offered two very different perspectives on where Aboriginal policy ought to go, based on their rather different readings of the past and current state of Aboriginal peoples' relations with government and the rest of Canadian society. They agree that some sort of Aboriginal sovereignty that excludes or overshadows Canadian citizenship is a bad idea. Aboriginal policy should be crafted, they concur, so as to ensure that Aboriginal Canadians are part of the wider Canadian community. Beyond that, however, their analyses and recommendations widely diverge.

Flanagan's *First Nations? Second Thoughts* staked out what would be described as the "conservative" position on Aboriginal policy, attacking the idea of a distinctive and separate status for Aboriginal Canadians as both doomed to failure and unjust, and proposing instead a return to the sort of *integrationist* philosophy and model that informed the ill-fated 1969 White Paper. This was once considered a progressive approach to Aboriginal policy that emphasized values of universalism, equality before the law, and removal of barriers to the movement of marginalized groups into society's mainstream. But as liberalism has morphed into a more group-oriented ideology that sees universalism as an obstacle to the equal participation and status in society of historically disadvantaged minorities, Flanagan's position and those who share it are generally labelled conservative. His writings have been called "antiquated, ill-informed, regressive and offensive." And Prime Minister Harper has been asked to distance himself, and his party, from his friend and sometimes political adviser.

Within months of Flanagan's broadside launched at what he called "the Aboriginal orthodoxy," Cairns weighed in with his book, *Citizens Plus*. Cairns put forward an analysis and proposals for reform that are in the spirit of the *communitarian liberalism* that Flanagan rejects. He accepts the argument that Aboriginal Canadians deserve to be treated as Indigenous nations

Democracy Watch

BOX 12.5 **Speak Up for Your Most Important Contemporary Issue**

This chapter explores three of the most prominent issues in contemporary Canadian political life. These are not the only contemporary issues of importance to Canadians, however.

Some people in this country are very concerned about the erosion of ethics in government, particularly after events like the Liberal Sponsorship Scandal and the two prorogations of Parliament by the Conservatives. Others point to major problems with the relationship between the country's municipal governments and the federal government, which have an enormous impact on factors such as immigration, housing, and welfare programs. Still others worry about youth and their employment prospects in a country whose job demographics have shifted away radically from their roots in industry and manufacturing.

Up for Debate

In your opinion, what is the most important contemporary issue in Canadian politics? Why is it important to you, and why should it be important to everyone else?

with a sort of *dual citizenship* status within Canada. At the same time he rejects the view of many in the Aboriginal community that Aboriginal nations can or should exist as fully sovereign communities outside of the Canadian constitutional and citizenship umbrella. "*Citizens plus*" is Cairns' formula for satisfying Aboriginal Canadians' demands for a restoration of dignity through their simultaneous recognition as Canadian citizens and as rights-bearing members of Aboriginal communities. Cairns notes that this is already the situation for many Aboriginal Canadians, and lists examples of "the positive recognition of difference":

- State funding of Aboriginal organizations
- Legal recognition of Aboriginal title to lands that they have traditionally occupied
- Entrenchment of Aboriginal rights in the Constitution Act, 1982
- Court-acknowledged Aboriginal rights relating to land use, fishing, hunting, etc.
- The creation of Nunavut
- The use and acceptance of the term "First Nations" to describe Aboriginal communities

SUMMARY

From our discussion of the contemporary issues of language, diversity, and Aboriginal politics, a number of observations can be made about the nature and the evolution of Canadian democracy.

First, history should teach us not to be complacent about Quebec's relationship with Canada. One of the most enduring facts of this situation is the gap between the vision of one Canada (the dominant view outside of Quebec that insists on the equality of the provinces and on multiculturalism) and the insistence by Quebec's politicians and opinion leaders (federalists and separatists alike) that Quebec must be considered a province *pas comme les autres*. The art of national unity involves finding ways to bridge gaps such as this one.

Second, while diversity has become one of the central values associated with Canadian democracy, there is no corresponding community belief system or pan-Canadian nationalism—as in the United States—that supersedes ethnicity, religion, and culture. Some Canadians worry that this is a recipe for division, resentment, and preferential treatment. Others believe it is a model of equality worthy of emulation by democracies around the world.

Third, the impact of the politics of diversity has been most profound in gender relations. In a little more than a generation, the Canadian political, social, and economic scenes now provide women with many more choices and opportunities than existed previously. Today, the same ideas form the basis for political demands of groups that include Aboriginal Canadians, visible minorities, gays and lesbians, and the disabled.

And finally, as we saw in the discussion on Aboriginal politics, the relationships between these groups and the Canadian state are being re-defined.

STARTING POINTS FOR RESEARCH

Language

Ramsay Cook, ed., *French Canadian Nationalism: An Anthology* (Toronto: Macmillan, 1969).

Alain-G. Gagnon, ed., *Quebec: State and Society*, 3rd edn (Toronto: University of Toronto Press, 2004).

Raffaele Iacovino, *Federalism, Citizenship, and Quebec* (Toronto: University of Toronto Press, 2007).

Kenneth McRoberts, *Quebec: Social Change and Political Crisis*, 3rd edn (Toronto: Oxford University Press, 1999).

Garth Stevenson, *Community Besieged: The Anglophone Minority and the Politics of Quebec* (Montreal and Kingston: McGill–Queen's University Press, 1999).

Charles Taylor, *Reconciling the Solitudes: Essays on Canadian Federalism and Nationalism* (Montreal and Kingston: McGill–Queen's University Press, 1993).

Diversity

Yasmeen Abu-Laban and Christina Gabriel, eds, *Selling Diversity: Immigration, Multiculturalism, Employment Equity and Globalization* (Peterborough, Ont.: Broadview Press, 2002).

Neil Bissoondath, *Selling Illusions: The Cult of Multiculturalism in Canada* (Toronto: Penguin, 2002).

Raymond Breton and Jeffrey Reitz, *The Illusion of Difference: Realities of Ethnicity in Canada and the United States* (Toronto: C.D. Howe Institute, 1994).

Will Kymlicka, *Multicultural Odysseys: Navigating the New International Politics of Diversity* (Toronto: Oxford University Press, 2007).

Jacquetta Newman and Linda White, *Women, Politics, and Public Policy: The Political Struggles of Canadian Women* (Toronto: Oxford University Press, 2006).

Manon Tremblay and Linda Trimble, eds, *Women and Electoral Politics in Canada* (Toronto: Oxford University Press, 2003).

Aboriginal Politics

Yale D. Belanger, *Aboriginal Self-Government in Canada: Current Trends and Issues*, 3rd edn (Saskatoon: Purich Publishing, 2008).

Olive Patricia Dickason, with David T. McNab, *Canada's First Nations: A History of Founding Peoples from Earliest Times*, 4th edn (Toronto: Oxford University Press, 2009).

Paul Robert Magocsi, ed., *Aboriginal Peoples of Canada: A Short Introduction* (Toronto: University of Toronto Press, 2002).

Joe Sawchuck, *The Dynamics of Native Politics* (Saskatoon: Purich Publishing, 1998).

CBC ARCHIVES AND TVO'S *THE AGENDA*

Visit the companion website for *Canadian Democracy: A Concise Introduction* to follow links to audio and video footage related to the main themes of the chapter: www.oupcanada.com/ BrooksConcise.

RELEVANT WEBSITES

Visit the companion website for *Canadian Democracy: A Concise Introduction* to browse a collection of websites featuring material related to the key themes of the chapter, an excellent starting point for research.

REVIEW EXERCISES

1. What circumstances do you think would have to exist for a referendum on Quebec independence to succeed?

2. How bilingual is your community? Make an inventory of the indications that French (or English, if you are in Quebec) language rights are protected and the French language promoted.

3. Debate: Statistics Canada has sometimes asked Canadians to declare their sexual orientation in a national survey. Do you think this information should be collected?

4. How many women or members of visible minorities hold public office on your municipal council or as your provincial or federal representative?

5. Research how the status and conditions of Aboriginal Canadians compare with their counterparts in the United States or Australia.

6. Debate: Should the Charter of Rights and Freedoms apply to all Aboriginal communities in all respects and at all times? Or should Aboriginal rights and the concept of self-government be construed so that they take precedence over the Charter in some circumstances?

Canada in the World

Political pundits often say that a proper understanding of Canada's place on the world scene requires a proper understanding of its domestic politics. This may be true to a certain extent, but the study of **international relations**—*a branch of political science that studies the relationships between states and the international system of governance*—is more complex than that. It requires a multidisciplinary approach that draws on many areas of knowledge other than politics, such as geography, psychology, and history. A multidisciplinary approach to understanding Canada's international relations is necessary in an era when many aspects of social, political, economic, and cultural life have become integrated, and when the globalized environment has made it difficult for governments around the world to control their domestic affairs.

While our discussion of Canada on the world scene is by necessity too brief to be comprehensive, after reading this chapter you will be able to

1. Explore how Canadians view themselves and examine how these perceptions have often affected Canada's behaviour internationally
2. Identify historical trends in Canada's relations with our most important neighbour, the United States, as well as with other countries
3. Develop a sense of Canada's place in a globalized, and always-changing, world scene

CANADA'S CENTURY: THE TWENTIETH OR THE TWENTY-FIRST?

"The twentieth century will belong to Canada." This was the bold prediction of Sir Wilfrid Laurier, Liberal prime minister of Canada from 1896 to 1911. Laurier made his forecast of greatness for Canada against the backdrop of the enormous growth that had occurred in the United States over the previous century. In the heady years of the early 1900s, as the nation-building strategy launched by Sir John A. Macdonald in 1879 appeared to be fulfilling its promise and about 200,000 immigrants arrived in Canada each year, Laurier's prediction appeared possible.

Over 100 years later, it is clear that the twentieth century did not "belong" to Canada. The friends and foes of the United States would probably agree that it was the American century, for better or worse. The sheer economic, cultural, and military dominance of the United States was unprecedented. Its global influence was such that the term "hyperpower" entered the modern lexicon. Notwithstanding the United States' one-time status as the world's only superpower, some Canadians believe that their country has achieved the greatness predicted by Laurier, though not in a form that he imagined. Canada is, according to many of its opinion leaders, the cosmopolitan, multicultural, equality-oriented, internationalist face of the future. "For generations," says philosopher Mark Kingwell, "we have been busy creating, in [the shadow of the United States], a model of citizenship that is inclusive, diverse, open-ended and transnational. It is dedicated to far-reaching social justice and the rule of international law. And we're successfully exporting it around the world . . . by seeing [the UN] for the flawed but necessary agency it is."[1] Is the "Canadian model" the real achievement of the last century? And is it the one most likely to shape the direction of history in the twenty-first century?

Perhaps so, although Canadians might be surprised to learn that the world does not think of the Canadian model when it thinks of the future of democracy. John Ralston Saul, a prominent Canadian intellectual, argues that "Canada is above all an idea of what a country could be, a place of the imagination . . . it is very much its own invention."[2] Canada is, he has argued, a successful model of accommodation and flexible ways of thinking about citizenship. Indeed, not only our American neighbours, but other national populations as well, appear to know hardly anything about us (except that we are like the Americans in some ways).

Most Canadians view themselves, and their country as having the following characteristics:

- We are a peace-loving people.
- We are respected, listened to, and admired abroad.
- We stand for multilateralism and reliance on the UN to solve global conflicts.
- We "punch above our weight" in international affairs.

In addition to these national characteristics, most Canadians probably would agree that their idea of citizenship is quite dramatically different from that of our southern neighbours. And as definers of the Canadian identity and interpreters of Canada's role in the world such as John Ralston Saul and Mark Kingwell argue, this Canadian idea of citizenship is perhaps our greatest contribution to world history.

Democracy Watch

BOX 13.1 Our Vision of Ourselves as Canadians

As the text points out, many Canadians would say that as a people we are

- Peace-oriented
- Respected and admired abroad
- Supporters of co-operative global relationships
- Major players in international affairs

Up for Debate

Is this list of Canadian characteristics accurate? Name examples that would contradict each of these Canadian traits.

For the most part, Canadians tend to be complacent. We feel very good about ourselves, our lives, and the state of the country. In a 2002 survey and report by the Pew Global Attitudes Project,[3] only Guatemalans expressed a higher level of satisfaction with their lives. Canadians were also far more likely than Americans and the citizens of several other wealthy nations to express satisfaction with the state of their country. When asked what the top ten biggest problems in our country were, "corrupt political leaders" was the highest. And yet, according to Transparency International, corruption in Canadian government and business is quite low.

Complacency and self-congratulations may be appropriate in some circumstances, but when thinking about the hard realities of Canada's relations with and influence in the world, Canadians' understanding is flawed in many important ways.

GLOBALIZATION AND CANADA

Globalization is *the political, economic, and social integration that comes from the increased international flow of goods, people, capital, and ideas.* Canada's economy has always been integrated into greater patterns of trade and shaped by forces beyond its borders. From the arrival more than 500 years ago of European fishermen off the coast of Newfoundland until the middle of the twentieth century, Canada's economic prosperity depended on the exploitation and export of a succession of natural resources to markets abroad, and on the import of people, capital, and finished goods.

At some point, however, there developed a hope and an expectation that Canada would shake off this dependence and become the master of its economic destiny. One sees this in Sir John A. Macdonald's ambitious National Policy of 1879; the first and only coherent and explicit economic development strategy that Canada had known before the decision in the late 1980s to embrace free trade, and therefore dependence, as the Canadian fate. One sees it also in Sir

Wilfrid Laurier's optimism and in the rise of economic nationalism in Canada, particularly from the 1950s to the early 1980s, the path of which was marked by a series of policies and institutions designed to limit American influence in the Canadian economy and promote indigenous capital.

Some nationalistic hopes still survive today, but they seem increasingly out of step in a world with unprecedented levels of economic, political, and social interconnectedness. The current debate is not about whether the forces of globalization can be rolled back, but how to control them. In Canada, the question of globalization is inseparable from that of its relationship to the United States. For Canada, at least, globalization has meant an enormous intensification in economic and other ties to the world's only superpower. Whether this is a good thing is one of the leading issues in Canadian public life.

Globalization and Anti-Globalization in Canada

The consequences of globalization have been the subject of enormous debate. In some ways, globalization may appear to be a very old phenomenon; one that is millennia old, like the Silk Road that increased the flow of goods across the eastern Mediterranean, the Middle East, and Asia, 2000 years ago. A characteristic of today's globalized world is the unprecedented volume and speed of economic exchanges. According to economist Jeffrey Sachs, in 1980 about one-quarter of the world's population and half of global production was linked by trade. Two decades later, almost 90 per cent of the world's population is so linked.[4]

Economists point to two chief factors that have driven globalization in recent decades. One factor is new transportation, telecommunications, and manufacturing technologies. The other factor—now made possible and profitable by the first—is the integration of global production and sale of goods and services. Witness the increased transnational flows of investment capital, leading to greater integration of financial markets as banks, investment funds, and companies spill across national borders.

It is also important to note that politicians and business leaders around the world have encouraged this integration through international agreements like the North American Free Trade Agreement (NAFTA) and the European Union. These deals were designed to reduce trade barriers and open up markets to stimulate economic growth. A more comprehensive agreement, the World Trade Organization (WTO), has now formalized and institutionalized trade liberalization. National subsidies and various forms of protectionism are still practised by all governments, but the overall thrust of Canada's trade policy, as elsewhere, has been toward export-led industrialization and more open markets. The dismantling of the Canadian Wheat Board in 2011 is an example of the push by the Conservative government to open markets to international trade.

Globalization is a complex phenomenon involving numerous trends that may or may not be new: the unprecedented global movement of people; the exchange of ideas and cultural values; the rapid and widespread diffusion of diseases; new cross-border security concerns; the introduction of invasive or detrimental animal and vegetable species into ecosystems; and the emergence of the virtual global village via telecommunications. And not all aspects of globalization are seen as positive. While liberalized trade may have become the fashion among many elites in developing and developed countries, there has been dissent. Note the violent clashes between protesters and police that accompanied negotiations such as the 1999 Seattle meeting of the WTO, the 2001 G8 meetings in Genoa and in Rostock, Germany, and the 2010 G20 protests in Toronto.

Protests in the streets have been joined by other forms of anti-globalization. These range from intellectual attacks, to political parties, to social movements and interest groups for whom the critique of globalization is a central ideological principle, or even the central principle. Indeed, the chief characteristic of the 2011 *Occupy movement*, in which protesters occupied public spaces in cities around the world, was that participants saw their concerns as "global."

In Canada, the anti-globalization message may come from diverse sources: many who teach in the social sciences, a significant part of the country's media elite, much of the leadership of the labour movement, the NDP, many religious organizations, environmental groups, and nationalist groups like the Council of Canadians. Their criticisms of globalization receive considerable media and classroom coverage. Indeed, the criticism of globalization is widely known to most Canadians.

Protesters march along Queen Street in downtown Toronto during the 2011 Occupy movement. Do you agree with the demonstrators' message, that capitalism—the dominant system of private ownership of businesses that create goods or services for profit—is at the root of many of the problems attributed to globalization? Why or why not?

In many ways the anti-globalization movement and its analysis have tended to be ideological, and go back to the critique of capitalism developed by Karl Marx in the middle of the nineteenth century. Marx made several claims that sound familiar today. Globalization is blamed for exacerbating the income gap between the rich and the poor, for widening the economic divide between the developed and underdeveloped world, for undermining indigenous cultures, for weakening the ability of governments to regulate business in the public interest, and for reducing governments' willingness and ability to finance social programs. Degradation of ecosystems, child labour, international conflict (e.g., the 1991 Gulf War and the 2003 Iraq War), and the rise of global terrorism can be added to this list.

Many, if not all, of these claims are difficult to prove with certainty. For instance, while globalization may explain some aspects of income inequality, other causes may be at play, such as government policies, shifting demographic patterns, or economic restructuring. The pros and cons of globalization cannot be sorted here, but these issues are hotly debated in Canadian politics, and the broader consequences of globalization do affect many Canadians as well as the international system of which Canada is a part.

Globalization and the Canadian Economy

Few would disagree, however, that the worldwide recession triggered by the 2008 "subprime crisis" in American financial markets revealed important weaknesses of globalization. The new post-industrial model spawned by globalization is all about outsourcing. At the extreme, huge companies like communications equipment manufacturer Cisco Systems and computer manufacturer Dell "exert a sort of post-industrial 'Command Control' over [a] vast network of outsourced production,"[5] depending on minimal parts inventories to keep costs down. Cisco Systems and Dell are not particularly exceptional, differing from such important companies operating in Canada as Research in Motion, Bombardier, Chrysler, and Magna only in the extent of their dependence on a complex chain of outsourcing that extends across the world.

The problem with this model, argues Barry Lynn, is that it introduces *vulnerability* in the economies of rich countries that could be far more significant than dependence on foreign sources of oil. A disruption at a crucial link in the supply and distribution network of a globalized economy, argues Lynn, could bring entire industries to a screeching halt because of the high degree of *specialization* in the globalized supply chain. Lynn's argument is that our exposure to disruptions and the amplitude of their consequences are greater these days than in the past. Canadians had a glimpse of the scenarios that Lynn argues have become increasingly possible after the terrorist attacks of 11 September 2001.

Globalization and Canada–US Relations

The Chrysler minivan that rolls off the assembly line at Windsor, Ontario, appears to be the very embodiment of what economic globalization is about; the vans are assembled in Canada by a Canadian workforce; parts and component systems come from the United States, Mexico, and China; plastics and metals in these parts come from an even broader set of countries; and the design and marketing decisions are made principally at Chrysler headquarters in Michigan.

Globalized production, sourcing, and investment have forced us to rethink what were, until fairly recently, firmly established ideas about what is "Canadian." Products exported from companies operating in Canada routinely include foreign content, and vice versa. Moreover, every Canadian provincial economy, with the exception of PEI, does more business with economies outside of Canada than it does with the rest of Canada. Thus, the very notion of a Canadian economy, let alone the concept of "Made in Canada," seems outdated.

In fact, Canada's economic globalization has really meant greater integration with and dependence on the American economy. With the FTA in 1989, and NAFTA in 1994, the trading relationship has reached unprecedented levels of intimacy. The total value of Canada–US trade in merchandise, services, and investment makes it the largest bilateral trading relationship in the world (although the China–US relationship is poised to surpass it in the near future). About 80 per cent of Canadian exports go to the United States, accounting for close to 30 per cent of Canada's total GDP. Only a slightly lower share of Canada's substantial import trade comes from the United States, at about three-quarters of total imports. Canada has been the major export market for American goods for over half a century and is today the leading export market for about three-quarters of all state economies. The United States has long been the largest source of foreign investment in Canada, currently accounting for close to two-thirds of all foreign investment, and is the location for about half of all Canadian direct investment abroad.

The trading relationship is both huge, and hugely asymmetrical, affecting Canada's vital interests far more than those of the United States. For example, when the Canadian media were full of stories about American duties on Canadian softwood lumber imports in 2005, there was barely any mention in the American media. But still, Canada has some leverage in this relationship. After all, Canada—not Saudi Arabia!—is the single largest source of energy imports to the United States, and is the destination for over half the value of all US automotive exports. The Canadian economy is extremely important, and even strategically important, to the United States. But the influence that this might give Canadians in trade disputes with Washington is diluted by Canada's far broader dependence on the American economy.

The enormous imbalance in the Canada–US trade relationship was one of the chief arguments put forward by Canadian advocates of free trade in the 1980s. Major manufacturers, but also important exporters of natural resources such as wood products, oil and gas, and

TABLE 13.1 | AN ASYMMETRICAL ECONOMIC RELATIONSHIP, 2009

	Canada (%)	United States (%)
1. Exports to the other country as a share of total GDP	25	2
2. Investment from the other country as a share of total stock of foreign investment	53 (1st)	10 (4th)
3. Share of total exports going to the other country	75	19
4. Share of total imports coming from the other country	51	14

Source: Compiled from CIA Fact Books: https://www.cia.gov/library/publications/the-world-factbook/geos/us.html; https://www.cia.gov/library/publications/the-world-factbook/geos/ca.html

hydroelectricity, recognized that their growth prospects depended on access to the American market. A growing wave of protectionist sentiment in the American Congress during the 1980s seemed to lend urgency to Canadian free traders' case. Even among many of those who were dubious about some of the economic claims made for free trade, the political argument that this would help shield Canadian industries from Congress's protectionist moods was persuasive.

The Canada–US Free Trade Agreement (FTA) (1989) and NAFTA (1994) created an architecture of dispute settlement rules, agencies, and monitoring requirements that have not taken the politics out of trade disputes, but provided forums for their resolution. The older forums and channels still matter, as does the World Trade Organization. But on the whole, the rules and the dispute settlement mechanisms created under the FTA and NAFTA make it more difficult for member governments to pursue protectionist trade policies.

The asymmetry in the Canada–US economic relationship is not helped by the fact that most Americans are simply unaware of, and (perhaps worse) harbour certain misconceptions about Canada's economic importance to the United States. A 2001 *Time*/CNN poll found that 64 per cent of those surveyed believed that Mexico, not Canada, had more of an impact on the US economy.[6] Ignorance may sometimes be benign. In this case, however, it may be a liability for Canada.

As Allan Gotlieb, Canada's ambassador to the United States from 1981 to 1989, observed, part of Canada's problem in its trade relations with the United States is getting the attention of those who matter in Washington.[7] He argued, however, that the answer may not lie in government-financed media blitzes or in Canadian efforts to lobby US interests. "Like it or not," Gotlieb said, "in the US political system a foreign country is just another special interest. And not a very special one at that. It lacks the clout of a domestic special interest because it cannot contribute to political campaigns or deliver votes." Gotlieb suggested two approaches: first, influence aimed at and a good rapport with the highest level of the American administration (the president and top advisers); and second, a tighter formal integration across the Canada–US border. He advocated a "grand bargain" with the United States, establishing a North American community of law.[8] Canada's 2011 seamless cross-border agreement, with tighter security measures and sharing of information between security agencies in both countries, is proof that this second strategy has now been adopted by the Canadian government.

THE CANADIAN DILEMMA IN FOREIGN AFFAIRS

The Canadian dilemma boils down to a choice between maintaining foreign policy independence and maintaining a good relationship with an economic, cultural, and military giant. This dilemma has occupied centre stage in debates over Canadian foreign policy since the end of World War II, and since the emergence of the United States as the unchallenged leader of the Western world. Former Canadian prime minister and Nobel Peace Prize winner Lester B. Pearson, one of the chief architects of Canadian foreign policy, acknowledged Canada's particular dependence on the United States "brought us anxiety as well as assurance."

The policy implications of this dilemma on Canada's participation in world affairs can hardly be overstated. The asymmetrical relationship between Canada and the United States, overlain by structures of policy integration that operate through agreements such as NORAD and NAFTA, leave Canada with little room to maneuver in conflicts with its American neighbour. "One of the great foreign policy challenges facing Canada," observes Michael Ignatieff, "is staying independent in an age of [American] empire."[9]

For several decades successive Canadian governments—the Progressive Conservative government of Brian Mulroney (1984–93) excluded—have searched for and supported counterweights to American dominance. Chief among these has been the United Nations and multilateralism more generally. **Multilateralism** involves *the resolution of international differences and conflicts through structures and processes that represent many states.* The United Nations has been the most prominent structure for multilateralism in the post–World War II

Mike Baldwin / artizans.com

One editorial cartoonist's elephant-and-the-mouse interpretation of the asymmetrical relationship between Canada and the United States. Do you think there are more pros or more cons to Canada's tight policy integration with its neighbour to the south?

era. There are, however, many other international organizations to which Canada belongs, including the North Atlantic Treaty Organization (NATO), the World Bank, the Organization for the World Trade Organization, the Commonwealth, la Francophonie, and so on.

Some of these multilateral organizations are dominated by the United States, and therefore can hardly be said to serve as counterweights to its might. NATO, for example, has almost never blocked or modified the military objectives of American administrations. Influence in the International Monetary Fund's decision making is weighted, based on the size of member-state contributions, and the United States is its major contributor. In fact, multilateralism may not always dilute American influence: it may actually provide greater political legitimacy to American goals by including other countries in the decision-making process.

Multilateralism is not always a convenient cover for the ambitions and interests of a single member state. States must be willing to accept some limitations on their national sovereignty. Canada's governing elites and opinion leaders "have a vision of a multilateral world in which . . . sovereignty is not unconditional, but limited and bound by human rights agreements, or multilateral engagements which limit and constrain the sovereignty of states in the name of collective social goods."[10] There are many examples of Canada's support of multilateralism and its leadership role: the creation of the International Criminal Court, the Ottawa Process, which led to the international treaty banning landmines, and its ratification of the Kyoto Protocol. Canada has often supported the UN as the proper forum for the discussion of issues of war and peace and the authorization of the use of force. Not all Canadians accept this multilateral vision of the world—note the 2011 withdrawal of Canada from the Kyoto Accord by the Conservative government—but recent history suggests that it has broad popular support. As with many other allies of the United States, Canada has also experienced the United States' lack of enthusiasm for multilateralism. This has occasionally produced outcomes that set Canada seriously at odds with its southern neighbour.

One of the great ironies of Canadian politics in recent times is that Canada's greater economic integration with the United States, under the FTA and NAFTA, may well have created the political space for Canada to pursue a more independent foreign policy than was available before. Critics of NAFTA have suggested that Canadian sovereignty would be vaporized by tighter economic integration. However, there are several instances of Canada being at loggerheads with the United States over global warming, landmines, an International Criminal Court, continental missile defence, and, most important, the formal refusal of the Canadian government to join the American-led coalition in the 2003 invasion of Iraq without approval from the UN. Free trade may have loosened the leash somewhat, because some forms of retaliation are no longer available to Congress and the White House or could be challenged under the terms of the free trade agreements.

Of course, the 2006 Canadian federal election brought to office a minority Conservative government intent on improving relations and influence with the United States. This is exemplified by the new government's aim to boost military spending and bolster the image of the Canadian military in Washington, DC. The successful negotiation of a resolution to the two-decades-old softwood lumber dispute in April 2006 was hailed by the Conservative government and its supporters as proof that its new approach was paying off. These celebrations were toned down in 2011 when American claims of unfair lumber subsidies were upheld by an international court.

There have long been limits to how far and in what circumstances Canadian foreign policy can depart from that of the United States. Canada's refusal to support the war on Iraq did not damage the security interests and military goals of the United States. Canada's absence virtually went unnoticed when other countries, including the United Kingdom, Japan, and Australia, joined in the Iraq military action. Canada was less able to avoid the "war on terrorism" launched after the terrorist attacks of 11 September 2001. The policy actions taken by the American government involved matters that directly affected Canada, like border security, air travel, and immigration. Given the amount of trade and the enormous number of jobs and investments that depend on the smooth flow of goods and people across the border, the Canadian government has had little choice but to coordinate its policies with those of the American government. By late 2011, this coordination had evolved into the creation of a common security perimeter around Canada and the United States—a concept that required that Canadian immigration policy be in line with American policy.

From 1993 to 2006, during the years of the Chrétien Liberal government, the dominant paradigm for Canadian foreign policy was what is known as **soft power:** *a term coined by Harvard's Joseph Nye, which refers to international influence based on intangible or indirect factors that include culture, values, and a sense of legitimacy ascribed to a nation's international aims.* Soft power operates through "the complex machinery of interdependence, rather than . . . expensive new weapons systems."[11] Nye identified Canada and the Scandinavian countries as examples of countries whose governments have successfully exercised soft power, "punching above their weight" as a former Canadian Minister of Foreign Affairs, Lloyd Axworthy, liked to say.

It is easy to see the appeal of the doctrine of soft power for many Canadians. It suggests that their country could make a difference internationally and maintain its values and its reputation as a good global citizen, without having to spend much on the latest military technology or to be combat-ready. Indeed, despite significant increases over the last several years, Canada spends less on defence, at about 1.2 per cent of GDP, than most of the countries in NATO.

Some have argued, however, that this self-image is an illusion. Although Canadians never hear this from those who govern them, by 2003 Canada had fallen to thirty-fourth in the world in terms of countries' contributions to UN peacekeeping. Bangladesh and India were first and second, and the United States was ahead of Canada. Michael Ignatieff, writing in 2003 as a Harvard professor, before he was leader of the federal Liberal Party from 2008 to 2011, argued that Canadians' belief in multilateralism is laudable, but that international influence requires three national attributes: moral authority as a good global citizen, a military capacity, and an international assistance capability. Canadians' image of themselves as "honest brokers" and good global citizens are not false. But, Ignatieff argues, "The disagreeable reality for those who believe in human rights is that there are some occasions when war is the only real remedy for regimes that live by terror. This does not mean that the choice is morally unproblematic."[12]

WHAT NOW WITH THE UNITED STATES?

More than virtually any other country, Canada is caught in a vice on the question of whether to support our most important ally and trading partner, or chart an independent course. Events since 9/11 have brought home to Canadians and people throughout the world the remarkable lopsidedness of the world's power structure, dominated by the United States, and have forced them to think hard about what this means. American decisions relating to "homeland security" and in the name of combatting terrorism—for example, requiring passports for Canadians entering the United States since June 2009, the elimination of regimes deemed to pose a threat to American security, and the creation of a Canada–US security zone in 2011—carry costs. These costs affect individual liberties, such as personal privacy and equality rights, that may be jeopardized by practices like ethnic profiling.

Yet another dilemma arises for Canada about whether to support multilateralism and UN-sanctioned policies and missions to deal with threats to human rights and peace, or to

Listen to the "Who Owns the Arctic?" podcast, available at www.oupcanada. com/BrooksConcise.

CANADIAN SPOTLIGHT

BOX 13.2   Timeline: Canada in the World

Late 1400s–early 1500s
Fishing by Basque, English, Portuguese, French, and Spanish ships on the Grand Banks off the east coast of Newfoundland, and whaling off the Labrador coast and in the Strait of Belle Isle—the first economic exploitation of Canadian resources by Europeans.

Late 1500s
Trade in beaver pelts and other furs begins, providing the basis for the eventual extension of trading routes from Quebec all the way to the north of Saskatchewan and Alberta.

1603–8
Samuel de Champlain makes two visits to Canada, establishing the city of Quebec in 1608 on his second voyage; European colonization of Canada begins.

1759–63
The war between Britain and France spills over into a rivalry in the New World, British troops defeating French forces at Quebec in 1759. The formal transfer of New France to Britain takes place in 1763 under the Treaty of Paris.

Early 1800s
Canada becomes a major supplier of white pine for British ships.

1812–14
The War of 1812 between Britain and the United States produces many battles on Canadian territory and the shared waters of the Great Lakes.

1820s
In an effort to dilute the influence of American-born residents of Canada, the colonial authorities encourage immigration from the British Isles. The arrival of tens of thousands of immigrants from Ireland during the potato famine of the 1840s marks the significant beginning of ethnic pluralism that went beyond the French and English communities.

1854
The first Reciprocity Treaty with the United States is signed, abrogated by the US government in 1865.

1867
The creation of Canada as a sovereign state is prompted by fears that the United States might have designs on parts of British North America and by Britain's unwillingness to continue to pay for the defence of Canadian territory.

1870–1
The vast territories controlled by the Hudson's Bay Company are transferred by Britain to Canada in 1870, and British Columbia becomes the fifth province in 1871, after which Canada stretches from the Atlantic to the Pacific Oceans.

1879
The National Policy is adopted by the Conservative government. It includes a sharp increase in tariffs on manufactured goods to protect fledgling Canadian producers from American competition, but which also encourages US-based companies to operate in Canada. This leads to high levels of foreign ownership and lower levels of productivity as a result of foreign-owned corporations that produce only for the small Canadian market.

1909
The International Boundary Waters Treaty between the United States and Canada takes effect, creating the International Joint Commission (IJC) (see 2009, below).

1911
The Canadian general election is fought largely on the issue of reciprocity in trade with the United States. The pro-reciprocity government of Wilfrid Laurier is defeated.

1914–18	World War I: Canada is a junior partner in the alliance against Germany; Canadian troops fall under the command of British officers.
1919	Canada becomes a founding member of the League of Nations.
1920	Canada passes from the economic orbit of Great Britain into that of the United States: American investment now officially exceeds the value of British investment.
1921	Canada's prime minister, Mackenzie King, sees multilateralism as a way to assert Canada's independence from Great Britain in international affairs.
1931	Under the Statute of Westminster, Canada acquires the authority to negotiate and sign foreign treaties in its own right.
1939–45	Canada participates in World War II, but no longer as a subordinate of Great Britain. Canada emerges from the war as one of the world's leading economies.
1945	Canada becomes a founding member of the United Nations. The UN and multilateralism are seen as counterweights to the influence of the United States on Canadian foreign policy.
1947	Canada is a founding member of the General Agreement on Tariffs and Trade (GATT) and the North Atlantic Treaty Organization (NATO).
1950–3	Canada participates in the Korean War under a UN Security Council resolution.
1956	Suez Crisis: Canada sides with the United States against the Franco–British invasion of Egypt, and Canadian foreign minister Lester Pearson, who brokers a settlement to end the crisis, is awarded the Nobel Peace Prize.
1957	The North American Air Defense Command (NORAD) is created, a partnership of Canada and the United States against the possibility of a Soviet missile attack. Early warning radar stations are established on Canadian territory: the Pinetree Line across southern Canada in 1954, and the Mid-Canada Line, at the fifty-fifth parallel, and the Distant Early Warning (DEW) line, along the seventieth parallel, in 1957.
1960s	Under Lester Pearson, the Canadian government becomes critical of US involvement in the Vietnam War, even though Canadian companies continue to profit from the production of defence-related exports. Under Quebec premier Daniel Johnson, that province becomes more assertive in its demands for representation and an independent voice abroad. Canadian dependence on the United States becomes a prominent political issue as American ownership in resources and manufacturing reach unprecedented levels.
1962	The Kennedy administration requests that the Canadian government permit, under the NORAD and NATO agreements, nuclear warheads on missiles on Canadian territory. The request is refused by the Diefenbaker government, creating a major rift in Canada–US relations. The Liberal government elected in 1963 complies with the request.
1973	The Liberal government of Pierre Trudeau announces the "Third Option" policy of diversifying Canadian trade, but by the end of the decade the total export and import trade tied to the American economy is at an all-time high.

BOX 13.2 Continued

1976 The G7, the annual meeting of the leaders of the world's seven largest capitalist democracies, is created when Canada joins the G6 countries.

1985 The Macdonald Royal Commission on the Economic Union and Development Prospects for Canada recommends free trade with the United States. The Conservative government of Brian Mulroney approaches the Reagan administration to open free trade talks.

1989 The Canada–US Free Trade Agreement takes effect.

1994 The North American Free Trade Agreement (NAFTA) among Canada, Mexico, and the United States takes effect.

1997 Canada signs the Kyoto Accord, later ratified in 2002. A decade after signing, Canada's CO_2 emissions exceed the Accord's targets by about 25 per cent.

2000 Over 80 per cent of Canada's imports and exports are tied to the United States and about one-third of Canada's GDP depends on trade with the United States.

2001 After the terrorist attacks of 11 September 2001, movement across the Canada–US border becomes a major issue. As a member of NATO, Canada supports the American-led invasion of Afghanistan to replace the Taliban regime. Eventually, Canada becomes a major contributor of combat forces in Afghanistan.

2003 The Liberal government of Jean Chrétien decides not to join the Anglo-American alliance that invades Iraq. Massive opposition to the war in Quebec, and in the Liberal Party's Quebec caucus, is a factor in the government's decision to withhold significant support.

Early 2000s As the possibility of a shipping passage through the Arctic and exploitation of resources increases, the issue of Arctic sovereignty assumes greater urgency. Canada's claim to full sovereignty in the waters of the High Arctic is not

support the Americans as globo-cops. The presidency of Barack Obama was greeted by many Canadians and others with high expectations. The emphasis on diplomacy and multilateralism, and the intention to shift American troops and resources from Iraq to Afghanistan were viewed positively by most Canadians and their leaders. The announcement that the new president, unlike his predecessor, would resume the long-standing practice of making Canada his first foreign visit was greeted with enthusiasm by Canadians.

The fact remains, however, that while Canadians have probably found life with Obama to be more agreeable than life with Bush, the substance of the Canada–US relationship has changed relatively little. There is little reason to think that the Obama administration will take a different line on Canadian claims of sovereignty over the Arctic. Canadian manufacturers and exporters are concerned that the White House and Congress will be more protectionist over trade. Although Canadian exporters of oil, gas, and hydroelectric power thought they had little to fear, Obama's 2011 postponement of the Keystone XL oil pipeline project was a reminder that American administrations continue to be more concerned with domestic politics than with good Canada–US relations.

Listen to the "Pipeline Politics" podcast, available at www.oupcanada .com/BrooksConcise.

accepted by other nations with a direct Arctic presence.

2005   Canada, Mexico, and the United States agree to the Security and Prosperity Partnership, an agreement that appears to pave the way toward greater policy coordination among the three countries.

2008   Canada has roughly 2500 troops stationed in Afghanistan and plays a major combat role within the NATO mission fighting the resurgent Taliban. Canadian public opinion remains divided on Canada's involvement as the number of Canadians killed exceeds 100.

2009   The hundredth anniversary of the Boundary Waters Treaty between Canada and the United States, which created the IJC. Despite some high expectations associated with the treaty and IJC, most policy experts agree that environmental governance now operates largely through agreements and networks of subnational governments.

2009   Barack Obama assumes the presidency of the United States. Canadians have high expectations for the president and his policies. Prime Minister Harper's office announces that the president's first official visit outside the United States will be to Canada.

2010   In March the Conservative government announces the withdrawal of Canadian troops from Afghanistan.

2011   The Conservative government announces Canada's withdrawal from the Kyoto Accord and agrees to form an integrated security zone with the United States. Canada fails to win a seat on the UN security council and Canada participates in a nine-month military mission to help end a civil war in Libya.

SUMMARY

The 2012 federal budget signalled a further move away from multilateralism, with cuts of $319 million in foreign aid and $170 million from Foreign Affairs and International Trade. The selling off of foreign residences, the closing of consulates, and the cutting back of consular staff were also included in the budget.[13] And, notwithstanding its participation in the military missions of Afghanistan (2001–2014) and of Libya (2011), Canada's contributions to peace-keeping activities have been declining for many years. In a 2010 ranking of ranking of military and police contributions to UN operations, Canada ranked fiftieth.[14] One wonders therefore how much longer Canadians can continue to believe that they are purveyors of human rights values, peace, and international collaboration, when their profile in these matters has been steadily diminishing.

With respect to Canadian democracy's place in the world, the boundaries separating Canadian politics from events and influence from the rest of the world have always been porous, but never so much as they are today in this era of globalization. This truth was brought to Canadians in a fundamental way with the terrorist attacks on the United States on 11 September 2001, and again with popular uprisings in 2011 against despotic regimes in the Arab states of North Africa and the Middle East.

The constant apparent dilemma in Canadian politics and in our foreign policy is whether to support multilateralism and the UN policies and mission to deal with international threats to human rights and peace, or to support the Americans as global peacekeepers and enforcers. Questions about what promotes and what threatens democracy do not stop at Canada's borders. This becomes clear when Canadians ask themselves what sort of world, governed in what way, is most likely to guarantee the values and interests they cherish.

STARTING POINTS FOR RESEARCH

Robert Bothwell and Jean Daudelin, eds, *Canada Among Nations 2008: 100 Years of Canadian Foreign Policy* (Montreal and Kingston: McGill–Queen's University Press, 2008).

Mark Brawley, *The Politics of Globalization: Gaining Perspective, Assessing Consequences* (Peterborough, Ont.: Broadview Press, 2002).

Paul Cellucci, *Unquiet Diplomacy* (Toronto: Key Porter, 2007).

Stephen Clarkson, *Uncle Sam and Us: Globalization, Neoconservatism, and the Canadian State* (Toronto: University of Toronto Press, 2002).

Tom Keating, *Canada and World Order: The Multilateralist Tradition in Canadian Foreign Policy*, 3rd edn (Toronto: Oxford University Press, 2013). A very good historical survey and thematic interpretation of Canadian foreign policy.

Stephen Randall and John Herd Thompson, *Canada and the United States: Ambivalent Allies*, 3rd edn (Athens: University of Georgia Press, 2002).

CBC ARCHIVES AND TVO'S *THE AGENDA*

Visit the companion website for *Canadian Democracy: A Concise Introduction* to follow links to audio and video footage related to the main themes of the chapter: www.oupcanada.com/BrooksConcise.

RELEVANT WEBSITES

Visit the companion website for *Canadian Democracy: A Concise Introduction* to browse a collection of websites featuring material related to the key themes of the chapter, an excellent starting point for research.

REVIEW EXERCISES

1. Canada participates in a large number of international organizations such as the OECD, NATO, the WTO, and the International Criminal Court. Explain each organization's mandate, Canada's participation, and the leading issues faced by the organization in recent years.

2. How dependent is your community on international trade? To find out, identify the five or six leading employers in your area. Find out how much of their goods or services they export and to what countries, and how many people they employ.

3. Debate whether the Canadian mission in Afghanistan was worth the effort, the resources, and loss of life.

Glossary

Aboriginal rights   recognition and a set of guarantees by the state that Indigenous peoples have certain entitlements or rights such as civil rights, and the rights to land, to preservation of culture, and to self-government

advocacy advertising   purchase of newspaper/magazine space or broadcast time to convey a political message

alienation   apathy, estrangement from the political system, or the belief that politics is systematically biased against one's interests and values

allophones   Canadian demographers' term for those whose native language is neither English nor French

anarchy   chaos and civil strife

assimilation   absorption of a minority culture into a majority culture

asymmetrical federalism   constitutional recognition of differences in the status and powers of provincial governments

authority   form of power that is used to enforce obedience and that lies in the recognition that a person or organization issuing a command has the right to do so and should be obeyed

backbenchers   members of Parliament who are not cabinet ministers

bicameral legislature   legislature with two chambers: in Canada's case, the House of Commons, which is democratically elected, and the Senate, with appointed senators

block funding   program funding where Ottawa's financial contribution is geared to the previous year's subsidy plus an amount calculated on the basis of growth in the recipient province's gross product

brokerage politics   strategic choice by a political party to avoid ideological appeals in favour of a flexible centrist style of politics

bureaucracy   political rule by unelected government officials

Canadian Bill of Rights   statutory declaration of rights passed by the Canadian Parliament on 10 August 1960

caucus   body of elected MPs belonging to a particular party

central agencies   areas of the bureaucracy whose main or only purpose is to support the decision-making activities of cabinet

centre   mainstream of a society's politics

Charlottetown Accord   second round of reforms from 1990 to 1992 called the "Canada round", attempted by the federal government after the Meech Accord failed in 1987; this second attempt also failed

civil liberties or civil rights   terms sometimes used to refer to all the basic rights and freedoms of citizens; human rights has become the more commonly used term

class analysis   theoretical approach that sees the state in capitalist societies as an instrument through which small minorities control wealth to maintain their social and economic dominance

classical conservatism   ideology based on the importance of tradition and social order. It accepted human inequality—social, political, and economic—as part of the natural order of things

classical liberalism   liberalism as understood until the middle of the nineteenth century and associated with freedom of religious choice and practice, free enterprise and free trade in the realm of economics, and freedom of expression and association in politics

classical socialism   ideology based on the principle of equality of condition and radical egalitarianism

coalition government   temporary agreement between two or more political parties to form a government

codified constitution   formal, written constitution found in a unified document

coercion   changing or controlling people's actions or behaviours by threat of or use of force

communitarianism   belief that communities and communal identities are essential to individual dignity and the maintenance of truly democratic societies; the public mobilization of resources to fulfill group objectives; the belief that real human freedom and dignity are possible only in the context of communal relations that allow for the public recognition of group identities and that are based on equal respect for these different identity-groups

conservatism   ideology based on the belief that traditions and social order are important and that gradual change is best

constitution   set of fundamental rules that govern political life in a particular territory

constitutional amendments   changing some aspect(s) of the existing constitution, leaving the basic constitutional structure intact

constitutional conventions   practices that emerge over time and are generally accepted as binding rules of the political system

constitutional monarchy   system of government with a monarch, as a formal head state, that operates within a constitutional framework

constitutional supremacy   concept that the constitution (the law of laws) is above all else, even the Parliament. The Constitution Act, 1982 states that "The Constitution of Canada is the supreme law of Canada, and any law that is inconsistent with the provisions of the Constitution is, to the extent of the inconsistency, of no force or effect."

constitutionalism   principle that involves predictable governance that has its source in written rules rather than the arbitrary wills of individuals

co-operative federalism   concept that federalism can be a decentralized and possibly an unequal sharing of power and financial resources

corporatism   political structure characterized by the direct participation of organizations representing business and labour in public policy making

coup d'état   illegal overthrow of a government by violence or threat of violence

cross-border regions (CBRs)   distinct grouping of neighbouring and nearby provinces and states whose economic, cultural, and institutional linkages create commonalities between the members of this binational (Canada–US) grouping and set it apart from other regions

cultural hegemony   ability of society's dominant class to have its values and beliefs accepted as the conventional wisdom in society at large

democracy   political system based on the formal political equality of all citizens, in which there is a realistic possibility that voters can replace the government, and in which certain basic rights and freedoms are protected

democratic deficit   term used in Canadian politics to describe the excessive centralization of power in and around the prime minister and cabinet and the marginalization of the legislature

democratic right   right of all adult citizens to vote in periodically held elections and stand for public office

direct democracy   government of the citizens by the citizens

distinct society   a society (Quebec) noticeably different than other provinces

economic statement   provides the government's analysis of the state of the economy and where the government plans to steer it

equality rights   rights that embody the rule of law principle that everyone should be treated equally under the law

equalization payments   grants paid to provincial governments whose per capita tax revenues fall below the average of the two most affluent provinces

executive federalism   term sometimes used to describe the relations between cabinet ministers and officials of the two levels of government

federal system   form of government with a constitutional division of law-making powers between a national government and regional governments; the constitutional authority to make laws and to tax is divided between a national government and some number of regional governments

feminism   theoretical approach that views the state as an inherently patriarchal (male-dominated) institution, where politics are not neutral or gender-free

first-past-the-post system   electoral system where the candidate who receives the most votes in a constituency election becomes the member of Parliament (or provincial legislature) for that constituency; also known as **plurality system**

fundamental freedoms   basic individual political rights that include freedom of religion, belief, expression, the media, assembly, and association

globalization   political, economic, and social integration that comes from the increased international flow of goods, people, capital, and ideas

government   organization of the state and the system of institutions and agencies used to exercise its authority. It can also refer to those who have been elected to power

human rights   term that refers to all the basic rights and freedoms of citizens; also known as **civil liberties** or **civil rights**

ideology   set of interrelated values and beliefs about how society is organized and how it ought to function

influence   changing people's actions or behaviours by persuasion; convincing them that a particular action is reasonable or otherwise in their best interests

interest groups   private organizations that promote their interests by trying to influence government rather than seeking the election of candidates to manage it; also **pressure groups**

international relations   branch of political science that studies the relationships between states and the international system of governance

intra-state federalism   representation and accommodation of regional interests within national political institutions

judicial independence   ability of judges to be free from any and all interference in their decision making

judicial restraint   legal concept expressed in the Charter and related to "reasonable limits," that judges should defer to the legislature when exercising their judicial power.

language (linguistic) rights   guarantees by the state that an individual or a group has the right to choose a particular language for use in private or in public, and to use that language in a given jurisdiction, for example in the educational system, in the government, or in the courts of a given territory

left   in politics, refers to collectivist and social justice ideas, ideologies, and political parties that advocate social reform

left-wing   label used to classify the political ideas that lie behind an action, opinion, or statement; see **left**

legal rights   procedural rights intended to ensure the fair and equal treatment of individuals under the law

legitimacy   rules and institutions that comprise the state, and which determine how governments are chosen, are accepted by most people as being reasonable

liberalism   ideology based on the belief that the state must protect individual liberty, personal choice, and the right to private property

libertarianism   ideology that believes that individuals should be allowed the largest possible margin of freedom in all realms of life, including moral choices

lobbying   any form of direct or indirect communication with government that is designed to influence public policy

majoritarianism   belief that the opinion of the majority should almost always be considered in decision making; may also refer to "tyranny of the majority"

mandarin   powerful senior civil servant

Manifest Destiny   nineteenth-century American belief that the United States was destined to expand and include all of North America

materialism   ideology that places greater stress on economic security and material well-being than on human needs for belonging, self-esteem, and personal fulfillment

Meech Lake Accord   1987 attempt by the federal government and some provincial governments to reform Canada's constitution that, among other things, would have recognized Quebec as a "distinct society"

ministerial responsibility   entails the obligation of a cabinet minister to explain and defend policies and actions carried out in his or her name

minority government   government that depends on the support of another party's MPs in order to win votes in the legislature

mobility rights   right of citizens to move freely within a country's borders

multiculturalism   idea that cultural diversity is not only good for society, it should also be encouraged.

multilateralism   resolution of international differences and conflicts through structures and processes that represent many states

national standards   Canada-wide standards in the delivery of social programs linked to federal transfer payments to the provinces, and designed to make social services uniform from province to province and create a "national social union"

nationalism   patriotic feelings, values, and beliefs that are translated into a public policy or program; that which defines a community by its language, ethnic origins, traditions, or unique history; the values and beliefs shared by the people of a territory or a community translated into a public policy or agenda

neo-institutionalism   perspective on policy making that emphasizes the impact of structures and rules, formal and informal, on political outcomes

notwithstanding clause   feature of the Charter of Rights and Freedoms that enables either Parliament or a provincial legislature to declare that a law shall operate even if it violates the fundamental freedoms, legal rights, or equality rights sections of the Charter. Such a declaration must be renewed after five years; otherwise the Constitution reasserts its supremacy.

orders-in-council   administrative orders (appointments, regulations or legislative orders authorized by an existing act of Parliament) issued by cabinet and approved by the Governor General

organization theory   study of how people act within an organization

parliamentary supremacy   principle that Parliament's authority is superior to that of all other institutions of government, and that the courts will not second-guess the right of Parliament to pass laws on any subject

party discipline   tradition of British parliamentary government according to which the MPs of a party generally vote as a unified block in the legislature

patrimoine   language, the faith, and the mores of a community whose roots went back to New France

patronage   distribution of favours by a governing politician (e.g., political appointments or government contracts) in exchange for political support

peace, order, and good government of Canada (POGG)   important constitutional principle and emergency powers, written in the first sentence of section 91 of the Canadian Constitution Act, 1867, which provide the constitutional basis for federal actions and lawmaking in special circumstances, but that cannot be used to justify federal laws during "normal" times

plebiscite   direct vote of citizens on important public question

pluralism   society in which there are several centres of power; also a theoretical approach that sees politics as being fundamentally a competition between different interests

plurality system   electoral system where the candidate who receives the most votes in a constituency election becomes the member of Parliament (or provincial legislature) for that constituency; also known as **first-past-the-post system**

policy community   that set of state institutions and interest groups usually involved in making and implementing policy in some field; the constellation of actors in a particular policy field

policy networks   nature of the relationships between the key actors in a policy community

political community   shared sense of belonging to a country whose national integrity is worth preserving

political culture   characteristic values, beliefs, and behaviours of a society's members in regard to politics

political efficacy   people's sense of whether their participation in politics matters

political factions   groups of citizens whose goals and behaviour are contrary to those of other groups or to the interests of the community as a whole

political party   organization that offers slates of candidates to voters at election time

politics   activity by which rival claims are settled by public authorities

populism   ideology based on the belief that power should be returned to the common people, and that economic and political elites are too powerful and unsympathetic to the people's interests

post-materialism   ideology that attaches comparatively greater importance to human needs for belonging, personal fulfillment, self-esteem, and quality-of-life issues such as the environment, human rights, and group equality, than on economic security and material well-being

postmodernism   theoretical approach that views the state as an essentially oppressive and even repressive institution

poverty line   point at which more than 55 per cent of income (20 percentage points above the national average) is spent on food, clothing, and shelter

power   ability to influence what happens

pressure groups   private organizations that promote their interests by trying to influence government rather than seeking the election of candidates to manage it; also **interest groups**

prime ministerial government   government where the executive is essentially dominated by the prime minister and the PMO

Privy Council   that part of the executive, made up of the Crown's advisers, in which the power of the monarch resides; formally includes all members of the present and past cabinets

propaganda   dissemination of selected information and/or misinformation to the public as a means of spreading a particular ideology or doctrine

proportional representation   method of electing government representatives whereby a party's percentage of the popular votes translates into a corresponding share of seats in the legislature

prorogation postponement of parliamentary activities without a dissolution of Parliament

province building political administrative needs of governments are reinforced by the demands of province-oriented economic interests; the phenomenon of powerful provincial governments using the constitutional, legal, and taxation levers to increase their control within their provincial borders and, consequently, their stature vis-à-vis Ottawa

public agenda matters that have been identified by opinion leaders in the media and in government as ones that warrant some policy response

Quality of Life Index (QOL) measures social and economic prosperity using a combination of objective and subjective determinants

Quiet Revolution many socio-political reforms and changes that occurred in Quebec during the 1960s—a turning point in Quebec's history

realignment occurs when an election or a series of elections produces a durable change in the parties' bases of support

reasonable limits reasonable legislative limits can be placed on human rights by legislation if it can be established that they are in the best interest of a free and democratic society

receptive bilinguals people who are capable of responding to French communications but do not themselves initiate conversations in French, consume French language media, or seek out opportunities to live in their acquired second language

red Tories conservatives who believe that government has a responsibility to act as an agent for the collective good, and that this responsibility goes far beyond maintaining law and order

referendum direct vote of citizens on an important public question

representation by population also known as "rep by pop," is based on the principle of "one person–one vote," where all elected members of the legislature should represent approximately the same number of voters

representative bureaucracy concept and an expectation that the bureaucracy should "represent" the population and reflect in fair proportion certain demographic characteristics of society

representative democracy government carried out by elected legislatures that represent the people

resources things we need for survival or desire for comfort

responsible government constitutional principle that the prime minister and cabinet require the confidence (majority support) of the elected members of Parliament in the House of Commons in order to govern; the governor, himself chosen by the British Colonial Office, was obliged to select cabinet ministers who were members of the elected legislature

revanche des berceaux, la "revenge of the cradle"; the high birth rate that for close to a century enabled French Canada to maintain its numerical strength against English Canada

revenue budget outlines the government's plans to change the tax system

reverse discrimination policies that shift the burden of injustice onto the shoulders of the qualified members of advantaged groups who are not personally responsible for the injustices suffered by minority groups

right (1) something that a person is entitled to; (2) in politics, refers to ideas and ideologies that advocate social order, protection of private property, economic freedom and support for capitalism

right-wing label often used to classify the political ideas that lie behind an action, opinion, or statement; see **right**

Royal Commission task force or some other consultative body that has been created by the government to study and make recommendations on an issue

rule of law constitutional principle that guarantees that all public authority must be exercised in accordance with the law and that there will be one law for all persons; no public official has the legitimate right to exercise any powers other than those assigned to his or her office by the law

secularization decline in the belief that religion and religious authorities should be looked to for guidance about behaviour and an increase in the social, cultural, and political influence of elites whose expertise is not based on religious faith

sexism term coined in the 1960s as a label for behaviour that treated males and females unequally for no better reason than their sex

shared-cost programs provincially administered programs where Ottawa's financial contribution is geared to what a province spends

single-member constituency system of electing representatives to the legislatures, in which each constituency (riding) gets one representative in the House of Commons and/or provincial legislature

social capital political culture approach concept that is used to the fabric of connections between members of a community such as the norms of interpersonal trust, a sense of civic duty, and a belief that one's involvement in politics and in the life of the community matters; the fabric of connections between members of a community

social learning process of acquiring knowledge, values, and beliefs about the world and ourselves

socialism ideology based on the collective or state ownership of the means of production and the belief in the state's ability to provide social justice, redistribute wealth, and fix social problems

socio-economic mobility ability of individuals, families, and groups to move from one social or economic position to another

soft power term coined by Harvard's Joseph Nye that refers to international influence based on intangible or indirect factors that include culture, values, and a sense of legitimacy ascribed to a nation's international aims

sovereignty ability of a person or entity to act independently without outside interference

sovereignty-association term generally understood to mean a politically sovereign Quebec that would be linked to Canada through some sort of commercial union or free trade agreement

state set of institutions that manage power and conflict for a society within a geographically defined territory

statism political tradition characterized by a relatively strong political executive and by a population that tends to be deferential towards those in power

substantive equality legal principle by which individuals are looked at in terms of their group characteristics and the possible advantages or disadvantages they may have experienced as a result of these attributes

survivance, la French-Canadian concept of survival against the pressures of a dominant culture that was anglicizing, Protestant, materialistic, liberal democratic, and business oriented

systemic discrimination discrimination inherent in traditions, customary practices, rules, and institutions that have the effect of favouring the members of one group over another

Tory person who believes that the organization of society along class lines is a natural and desirable state of affairs

totalitarianism system of government that suppresses all dissent in the name of some supreme goal

uncodified constitution powers of government, as well as the limits to government power, are unwritten, or based on precedents, or are embedded in the country's laws, conventions, and traditions

unitary state system form of government where sovereignty or competence resides exclusively with the central government, and regional or local governments are legally and politically subordinate to it

value personal belief in what is right or wrong, important or not important, valuable or not valuable, etc.

welfare gap gap that exists between the income that social assistance provides and the cost of living

western alienation awareness in western Canada that the public realm—whose voices are heard and what counts as legitimate political discourse—belongs to others

white paper report for discussion on a major piece of legislation being proposed by government, which is based on research by the bureaucracy (and sometimes the legislature as well), and serves as a statement of the government's legislative intentions

Notes

PART I | INTRODUCTION

1 | An Introduction to Political Life

1. Leger Marketing, annual survey of Canadians' trust in professions, 2005.
2. World Values Survey, 2000, www.worldvaluessurvey.org.
3. Charles Merriam, *Public and Private Government* (New Haven: Yale University Press, 1944).
4. Bertrand Russell, *Power: A New Social Analysis* (London: Unwin and Allen, 1938), 10, 11.
5. The full exchange may be viewed online at www.cbc.ca/archives/categories/politics/civil-unrest/the-october-crisis-civil-liberties-suspended/just-watch-me.html.
6. Leo Panitch, "State," in *The Canadian Encyclopedia*, 2nd edn (Edmonton: Hurtig, 1988), vol. 4, 2071.
7. Victor Davis Hanson, talk at Woodrow Wilson Center, 2 June 2005, Washington, DC.
8. C.B. Macpherson, *The Real World of Democracy* (Toronto: CBC Enterprises, 1965).
9. Gabriel A. Almond and Sidney Verba, *The Civic Culture* (Princeton, NJ: Princeton University Press, 1963).
10. Quoted in Henry Steele Commager, *Living Ideas in America* (New York: Harper, 1951), 556.
11. Neil Postman, *Amusing Ourselves to Death* (New York: Viking, 1985), 107.
12. "The people get it right, on the whole," *The Economist*, 7 Nov. 1998, 24.
13. Freedom House, World Democracy Audit, www.worldaudit.org.
14. Eugene Forsey, *How Canadians Govern Themselves*, 6th edn (Ottawa: Library of Parliament, Public Information Office, 2005), 32.

PART II | THE SOCIETAL CONTEXT OF POLITICS

2 | Political Culture

1. "In Search of the Canadian Dream," *The Atlantic* (Dec. 2004).
2. R. Kirk, *The Conservative Mind* (London: Faber & Faber, 1953).
3. David Bell and Lorne Tepperman, *The Roots of Disunity* (Toronto: McClelland & Stewart, 1979), 23.
4. Fernand Ouellet, *Histoire économique et sociale du Québec, 1760–1850* (Paris: Fides, 1966).
5. William Christian and Colin Campbell, *Political Parties and Ideologies in Canada*, 2nd edn (Toronto: McGraw-Hill Ryerson, 1982), 23–5; Gad Horowitz, "Conservatism, Liberalism and Socialism in Canada: An Interpretation," *Canadian Journal of Economics and Political Science* (1966).
6. Kenneth McRae, "The Structure of Canadian History," in Louis Hartz, ed., *The Founding of New Societies* (New York: Harcourt, Brace & World, 1964), 235.
7. Bell and Tepperman, *The Roots of Disunity*, 76–7.
8. Horowitz, "Conservatism, Liberalism and Socialism."
9. Seymour Martin Lipset, *Continental Divide* (Montreal: C.D. Howe Institute, 1989), 1.
10. Bell and Tepperman, *The Roots of Disunity*, 61–2.
11. Reg Whitaker, "Images of the State in Canada," in Leo Panitch, ed., *The Canadian State* (Toronto: University of Toronto Press, 1977), 30.
12. Patricia Marchak, *Ideological Perspectives on Canada* (Toronto: McGraw-Hill Ryerson, 1975), 115.
13. Pierre Trudeau, "Some Obstacles to Democracy in Quebec," in Trudeau, *Federalism and the French Canadians* (Toronto: Macmillan, 1968).
14. In 1951, 80 per cent of Quebec's workforce was in secondary industries (manufacturing and construction) and the service sector, a percentage that was higher than for Canada as a whole (78 per cent).
15. See Kenneth McRoberts, *Quebec: Social Change and Political Crisis*, 3rd edn (Toronto: McClelland & Stewart, 1988), 90–100.
16. W.L. Morton, "The Dualism of Culture and the Federalism of Power," in Richard Abbott, ed., *A New Concept of Confederation*, Proceedings of the Seventh Seminar of the Canadian Union of Students (Ottawa, 1965), 121.
17. Donald Smiley, *The Canadian Political Nationality* (Toronto: Methuen, 1967).
18. All of these statements are based on the rankings in Charles Lewis Taylor and David A. Jodice, *The World Handbook of Political and Social Indicators*, 3rd edn, vol. 2, *Political Protest and Government Change* (New Haven: Yale University Press, 1983); see also Judith Torrance, *Public Violence in Canada 1867–1982* (Toronto: University of Toronto Press, 1986), 57–66.

19. See the analysis of Oka in Robert Campbell and Leslie Pal, "Feather and Gun," *The Real Worlds of Canadian Politics*, 2nd edn (Peterborough, Ont.: Broadview Press, 1991), 267–345.

20. Simon Langlois and Leger Marketing, cited in A. Brian Tanguay, *The Stalled Realignment: Quebec's Party System After the 2003 Provincial Election*, (Department of Political Science, Wilfrid Laurier University, Waterloo, Ontario), a paper prepared for the conference Quebec and Canada in the New Century, Institute of Intergovernmental Relations, Queen's University, Kingston, Ontario, 31 Oct.–1 Nov. 2003, http://www.queensu.ca/iigr/conf/Arch/03/03-1/10.pdf.

21. McRoberts, *Quebec*, 239.

22. En collaboration, *Québec un pays incertains. Reflexions sur le Québec post-referendaire* (Montréal: Québec/Amérique, 1980), 170–2.

23. Status Indians are those registered under the Indian Act.

24. Graham Fraser, "PM Unveils Indian Agenda Program to Tackle Land, Self-Rule," *Globe and Mail*, 26 Sept. 1990, A1.

25. Lipset, *Continental Divide*, 136.

26. Pierre Berton, *Why We Act Like Canadians* (Toronto: McClelland & Stewart, 1982), 16.

27. Paul M. Sniderman et al., *Liberty, Authority, and Community: Civil Liberties and the Canadian Political Culture* (Berkeley: Survey Research Center, University of California, 1988), Figures 9A–9D.

28. Stephen Brooks, "A Tale of Two Elections: What the Leaders' Rhetoric in the 2000 Elections Tells Us about Canada–US Differences," in Rick Farmer et al., eds, *The Elections of 2000: Politics, Culture, and Economics in North America* (Akron, Ohio: University of Akron Press, 2006), 136–66.

29. Frank Graves, "The Shifting Public Outlook on Risk and Security," in Karlyn Bowman and Frank Graves, *Threat Perceptions in the United States and Canada: Assessing the Public's Attitudes toward Risk and Security*, One Issue, Two Voices Series, Issue Four (Washington: Canada Institute, Woodrow Wilson Center, Oct. 2005), 10–15.

30. Robert Kudrle and Theodore Marmor, "The Development of Welfare States in North America," in Peter Flora and Arnold J. Heidersheimer, eds, *The Development of Welfare States in Europe and America* (New Brunswick, NJ: Transaction Books, 1981), 110.

31. Gerard Boychuk, "National Health Insurance in Canada and the United States: Race, Territorial Integration and the Roots of Difference," paper presented at the annual meeting of the Canadian Political Science Association, Vancouver, June 2008.

32. See the summary of studies in Lipset, *Continental Divide*, 155–8.

33. Michael Ignatieff, *True Patriot Love* (Toronto: Viking, 2009).

34. Lipset, *Continental Divide*, 156.

35. Lars Osberg and Timothy Smeeding, "Fair Inequality? An International Comparison of Attitudes toward Pay Differentials," working paper, Russell Sage Foundation, 2005, 31, www.russellsage.org/research/reports/fair-inequality.

36. World Values Survey, 2000, www.worldvaluessurvey.org.

37. Canada, Constitution Act, 1982, s. 27.

38. Canada, Constitution Act 1982, s. 15(2).

39. Neil Bissoondath, *Selling Illusions: The Cult of Multiculturalism in Canada* (Toronto: Penguin Books, 1994).

40. Reginald Bibby, *Mosaic Madness: The Poverty and Potential of Life in Canada* (Toronto: Stoddart, 1990).

41. Jeffrey Reitz and Raymond Breton, *The Illusion of Difference* (Toronto: C.D. Howe Institute, 1994), 133.

42. Berton, *Why We Act Like Canadians*, 16–17.

43. Charles Taylor, "Deep Diversity and the Future of Canada," www.uni.ca/taylor.html.

44. Peter C. Newman, *The Canadian Revolution, 1985–1995* (Toronto: Penguin Books, 1995), 12–13.

45. Neil Nevitte, *The Decline of Deference: Canadian Value Change in Cross-National Perspective* (Peterborough, Ont.: Broadview Press, 1996).

46. World Values Survey, www.worldvaluessurvey.org.

47. Michael Adams, *Fire and Ice: The United States, Canada and the Myth of Converging Values* (Toronto: Penguin, 2003).

48. Philip Resnick, *The European Roots of Canadian Identity* (Peterborough, Ont.: Broadview Press, 2005).

49. Christian Boucher, "Canada–U.S. Values: Distinct, Inevitably Carbon Copy, or Narcissism of Small Differences?," *Horizons* 7, 1 (2004): 46.

3 | The Social and Economic Setting

1. International Bank for Reconstruction and Development, *2008 World Development Indicators* (World Bank, Washington D.C., Apr. 2008), http://data.worldbank.org/sites/default/files/wdi08.pdf.

2. Statistics Canada, Labour Force Survey, Dec. 2010, http://www.statcan.gc.ca/daily-quotidien/120706/dq120706a-eng.htm.

3. United States Department of Labor, Monthly Employment and Unemployment: News Releases, (Bureau of Labor Statistics, Dec. 2010), http://www.bls.gov/bls/newsrels.htm#OEUS.

4. Statistics Canada, Labour Force Survey, June 2012, "Employment by class of worker and industry—Seasonally adjusted," http://www.statcan.gc.ca/daily-quotidien/120706/t120706a002-eng.htm.

5. See, for example, Stephen Cohen and John Zysman, *Manufacturing Matters* (New York: Basic Books, 1987).

6. Gregg Easterbrook, "Life Is Good, So Why Do We Feel So Bad?", *Wall Street Journal*, 13 June 2008; *The Progress Paradox: How Life Gets Better While People Feel Worse* (New York: Random House, 2003).

7. John Porter, *The Vertical Mosaic* (Toronto: University of Toronto Press, 1965), 3–4.

8. Dana Flavelle, "Why the gap between rich and poor in Canada keeps growing," *Toronto Star*, 5 Dec. 2011, http://

www.thestar.com/business/article/1097055--why-the-gap-between-rich-and-poor-in-canada-keeps-growing.

9. Barrie McKenna, "Gap between rich and poor won't be closing any time soon," *The Globe and Mail*, Ottawa, 3 Oct. 2010, http://www.theglobeandmail.com/report-on-business/rob-commentary/gap-between-rich-and-poor-wont-be-closing-any-time-soon/article4327920/.

10. Keith Jones, "Canada's richest 1 percent grabbed one-third of all income growth since 1987," World Socialist website, 9 Dec. 2010, http://www.wsws.org/articles/2010/dec2010/cana-d09.shtml.

11. National Council of Welfare, *A New Poverty Line: Yes, No or Maybe?* (Ottawa: Minister of Public Works and Government Services Canada, 1999), 1.

12. John A. Price, "Native People, Economic Conditions," *The Canadian Encyclopedia*, 2nd edn (Edmonton: Hurtig, 1988), vol. 3, 1449.

13. Statistics Canada, *Income in Canada 2006* (Ottawa: Statistics Canada Catalogue no. 75-202-X, 2008), 15.

14. Monica Boyd et al., *Ascription and Achievement: Studies in Mobility and Status Attainment in Canada* (Ottawa: Carleton University Press, 1985).

15. Miles Corak, "Getting Ahead in Life: Does Your Parents' Income Count?" and Patrice de Broucker and Laval Lavallée, "Getting Ahead in Life: Does Your Parents' Education Count?," *Canadian Social Trends* (Ottawa: Supply and Services, Summer 1998), 6–10, 11–15.

16. Jo Blanden, Paul Gregg, and Stephen Machin, *Intergenerational Mobility in Europe and North America* (London: The Sutton Trust, Apr. 2005).

17. Miles Corak, *Intergenerational Earnings Mobility among the Children of Canadian Immigrants* (Bonn: Institute for the Study of Labor, 2006).

18. Porter, *The Vertical Mosaic*; Wallace Clement, *The Canadian Corporate Elite* (Toronto: McClelland & Stewart, 1975).

19. World Values Survey, 2000, www.worldvaluessurvey.org.

20. Jan van Dijk et al., *Criminal Victimisation in International Perspective* (Tilburg, Netherlands: Tilburg University and United Nations Office on Drugs and Crime, 2007), 132, Figure 28.

21. Michael Tjepkema, *Alcohol and Illicit Drug Dependence* (Ottawa: Statistics Canada, 2004).

22. Food Banks Canada, *Hunger Count 2011*, http://www.foodbankscanada.ca/getmedia/dc2aa860-4c33-4929-ac36-fb5d40f0b7e7/HungerCount-2011.pdf.aspx.

23. National Council of Welfare, "Welfare Incomes 2004," Revised (Ottawa: Government of Canada, Aug. 2005), 35, http://www.ncw.gc.ca/l.3bd.2t.1ils@-eng.jsp?lid=126.

24. Statistics Canada and Department of Foreign Affairs and International Trade, *State of Trade 2004* (Ottawa, 2005).

25. Canada, Royal Commission on Newspapers, *Newspapers and Their Readers* (Ottawa: Supply and Services, 1981), 26, table 19; Pew Research Center, *What the World Thinks in 2002* (Washington: Pew Research Center for the People and the Press, Dec. 2002), www.people-press.org. The Pew study found that Canadians, by a 2:1 ratio, relied on television instead of newspapers as their main source of information about national and international affairs.

26. Ministry of Canadian Heritage, *Canadian Music Industry—2006 Economic Profile*, (Gatineau, Quebec: Ministry of Government of Public Works, 2006), http://www.pch.gc.ca/pgm/fmusc-cmusf/pubs/prfl/102-eng.cfm.

27. Jim Stanford, quoted in Lawrence Martin, "Divided against Ourselves," *Globe and Mail*, 15 May 2012, A11.

4 | Regionalism and Canadian Politics

1. Richard Simeon and David Elkins, "Regional Political Cultures in Canada," *Canadian Journal of Political Science* 7, 3 (Sept. 1974): 397–437.

2. Centre for Research and Information Canada, *The Charter: Dividing or Uniting Canadians?* (Apr. 2002), 30, www.cric.ca.

3. Michael Ornstein and Michael Stevenson, *Politics and Ideology in Canada* (Montreal and Kingston: McGill–Queen's University Press, 1999), ch. 5.

4. Ibid., 206.

5. Debora VanNijnatten, "Canada–US Relations and the Emergence of Cross-Border Regions," 4, Briefing Notes, Government of Canada, Policy Research Initiatives, 2006, at: www.policyresearch.gc.ca.

6. Stephen Brooks and Barry Rabe, eds, *Transboundary Environmental Governance between Canada and the United States: The Second Century* (Washington: Woodrow Wilson Center, 2009).

7. Roger Gibbins and Sonia Arrison, *Western Visions: Perspectives on the West in Canada* (Peterborough, Ont.: Broadview Press, 1995), 45.

8. W.L. Morton, "The Bias of Prairie Politics," *Transactions of the Royal Society of Canada* series 3, 49 (June 1955): 66.

9. George Woodcock, *Confederation Betrayed: The Case against Trudeau's Canada* (Vancouver: Harbour Publishing, 1981).

10. Barry Cooper, "Western Political Consciousness," in Stephen Brooks, ed., *Political Thought in Canada: Contemporary Perspectives* (Toronto: Irwin, 1984), 230.

11. Patrick Boyer, *Direct Democracy in Canada: The History and Future of Referendums* (Toronto: Dundurn Press, 1992).

PART III | THE STRUCTURES OF GOVERNANCE

5 | The Constitution

1. Canada, Constitution Act, 1982, s. 16(1).

2. Pierre Trudeau, *Federalism and the French Canadians* (Toronto: Macmillan, 1968), 187.

3. Constitution Act, 1867, preamble.

4. Constitution Act, 1867, s. 121.
5. Constitution Act, 1867, s. 145 (repealed in 1893).
6. Constitution Act, 1982, s. 36.
7. Supreme Court of Canada, *Reference re Secession of Quebec*, Aug. 1998, at p. 18 of online decisions.
8. *Reference re Secession of Quebec*, 19.
9. Ibid., 20.
10. Ibid., 21.
11. Ibid., 22.
12. Supreme Court of Canada, *R. v. Oakes*, 1986, 1 S.C.R. 103, 136.
13. *Reference re Secession of Quebec*, 22.
14. Ibid., 23.
15. Ibid.
16. Ibid., 25.
17. Constitution Act, 1982, s. 6(3)(6).
18. Constitution Act, 1982, s. 6(4).
19. Supreme Court of Canada, *Morgentaler, Smoling and Scott v. The Queen* (1988), 37 C.C.C. (3rd) 449.
20. Constitution Act, 1982, s. 15(1).
21. Constitution Act, 1982, s. 15(2).
22. Pierre Elliott Trudeau, "P. E. Trudeau: 'Say good-bye to the dream' of one Canada," *Toronto Star*, 27 May 1987, A7.
23. Constitution Act, 1867, ss. 96–100.
24. *The Queen v. Beauregard* (1986), 2 S.C.R. 56.
25. This was the basis of a 1986 court action brought against the Quebec government by several Provincial Court judges and the Chief Justice of the Quebec Superior Court.
26. From "Remarks at a Conference on Globalization, Citizenship and Identity", 26 October 2004, http://www.scc-csc.gc.ca/court-cour/ju/spe-dis/bm04-10-26-eng.asp.
27. Philip Resnick, *Parliament vs. People* (Vancouver: New Star Books, 1984), 19.
28. Ibid., 25.
29. Section 91(1). Repealed by the Constitution Act, 1982.
30. Section 92(1). Repealed by the Constitution Act, 1982.
31. Supreme Court of Canada, *Re Constitution of Canada* (1981), 125 D.L.R. (3rd) 1.
32. *Re Attorney General of Quebec and Attorney General of Canada* (1982), 140 D.L.R. (3rd) 385.
33. Cited in Paul Gerin-Lajoie, *Constitutional Amendment in Canada* (Toronto: University of Toronto Press, 1950), 241.
34. Cited ibid., 234.
35. See "Federal Referendum Legislation" in *Referendums in Canada: The Effect of Populist Decision-Making on Representative Democracy*, http://publications.gc.ca/Collection-R/LoPBdP/BP/bp328-e.htm#A.%20Federal.
36. *Reference re Secession of Quebec*, 26.
37. Ibid., 19.
38. Ibid., 27.
39. Ibid., 35.
40. Ibid., 4.

6 | Rights and Freedoms

1. These are the words used in the "anti-hate" section of Canada's Criminal Code.
2. Walter S. Tarnopolsky, "Human Rights," in *The Canadian Encyclopedia*, 2nd edn (Edmonton: Hurtig, 1988), vol. 2, 1024.
3. United States Constitution, 14th amendment, 1868.
4. Although many now consider the term "Indian" to be inaccurate and even offensive, it is still used in the Indian Act. See Chapter 12 for a discussion of the term.
5. *R. v. Drybones* (1970), S.C.R. 282.
6. *Ottawa Roman Catholic Separate School Trustees v. Mackell* (1917), A.C. 62; *Protestant School Board of Greater Montreal v. Minister of Education of Quebec* (1978), 83 D.L.R. (3d) 645.
7. *Attorney General of Quebec v. Blaikie* (1979), 2 S.C.R. 1016 (Supreme Court of Canada).
8. *R. v. Oakes* (1986), 26 D.L.R. (4th) 20 (Supreme Court of Canada).
9. Roy Romanow et al., *Canada . . . Notwithstanding: The Making of the Constitution 1976–1982* (Toronto: Carswell, 1984), 211.
10. Alan Borovoy, *When Freedoms Collide: The Case for Our Civil Liberties* (Toronto: Lester & Orpen Dennys, 1988), 211–12.
11. Ibid., 389.
12. *Retail, Wholesale & Department Store Union, Local 580 et al. v. Dolphin Delivery Ltd.* (1986), 33 D.L.R. (4th) 174.
13. Quoted in Mandel, *Charter of Rights*, 204.
14. *Reference re Public Service Employee Relations Act* (Alberta), quoted in F.L. Morton, Rainer Knopff, and Peter Russell, *Federalism and the Charter* (Ottawa: Carleton University Press, 1989) 496.
15. Quoted in Michael Mandel, *The Charter of Rights and the Legalization of Politics in Canada*, 2nd edn (Toronto: Thompson Educational Publishing, 1994). 193.
16. *Dunmore et al. v. Attorney General for Ontario and Fleming Chicks* (2001), S.C.C. 94.
17. *Morgentaler, Smoling and Scott v. The Queen* (1988), 37 C.C.C. (3d) 449.
18. *R. v. Keegstra*, [1990] 3 S.C.R. 697.
19. *Harper v. Canada*, [2004] 1 S.C.R. 827.
20. *WIC Radio Ltd. v. Simpson* (2008), S.C.C. 40.
21. Peter Hogg, *Constitutional Law of Canada*, 2nd edn (Toronto: Carswell, 1988), 786.
22. *Law v. Minister of Human Resources Development*, [1999] 1 S.C.R. 497.
23. See, for example, the majority and dissenting judgments in the right to strike case, *Re Public Service Employees Relations Act* (1987), and in the Ontario Roman Catholic high school funding case, *Reference re An Act to Amend the Education Act* (1987).
24. See www.scc-csc.gc.ca/AboutCourt/judges/speeches/index_e.asp.

25. John Ibbitson, "Charter That Reshaped Canada Becomes a Model to the World," *Globe and Mail*, 16 Apr. 2012, A1.

26. Kirk Makin, "Why This Year May Prove To Be the Charter's Most Controversial," *Globe and Mail*, 16 Apr. 2012, A4.

7 | Federalism

1. Pierre Elliott Trudeau, "Federalism, Nationalism and Reason," in Trudeau, *Federalism and the French Canadians* (Toronto: Macmillan, 1968), 195.

2. The term is a translation of "rois-nègres," coined by André Laurendeau, in "A Search for Balance," *Canadian Forum* (Apr. 1963): 3–4.

3. Donald Smiley, *The Canadian Political Identity* (Toronto: Methuen, 1967), 30–1.

4. Profiles of Canada 2005, www.cric.ca.

5. Roger Gibbins, *Regionalism: Territorial Politics in Canada and the United States.* (Toronto: Butterworths, 1982), 178.

6. Ernest Renan, *What is a Nation?*, (Toronto: Tapir Press, 1996), 48.

7. Peter Waite, *The Life and Times of Confederation 1864–1867* (Toronto: University of Toronto Press, 1962), 96.

8. The diversity of expectations was reflected in newspaper accounts of the Confederation agreement. See ibid., 111.

9. There are some exceptions. In *Citizens Insurance Co. v. Parsons; Queen Insurance Co. v. Parsons* (1881), the Judicial Committee of the Privy Council ruled that Ottawa's trade and commerce power did not take pre-eminence over enumerated provincial powers. Why? In the words of Sir Montague Smith, "[The founders] could not have intended that the powers exclusively assigned to the provincial legislature should be absorbed in those given to the dominion parliament." Reproduced in Peter H. Russell, ed., *Leading Constitutional Decisions*, 4th edn (Ottawa: Carleton University Press, 1987), 35.

10. Ibid., 527, Re Constitution of Canada (1981).

11. *Amicus curiae* concerning Certain Questions Relating to the Secession of Quebec, 31 Jan. 1998.

12. See the discussion in Keith G. Banting, *The Welfare State and Canadian Federalism*, 2nd edn (Montreal and Kingston: McGill–Queen's University Press, 1987), 52–4.

13. *Attorney General of Ontario v. Attorney General of Canada* (Local Prohibition case), 1896, in Russell, *Leading Constitutional Decisions*, 59.

14. *Re Board of Commerce Act and Combines and Fair Prices Act*, 1919, 1922, ibid., 75.

15. See Peter Russell, "The Anti-Inflation Case: The Anatomy of a Constitutional Decision," *Canadian Public Administration* 10, 4 (Winter 1977).

16. Constitution Act, 1867, s. 91(2).

17. Constitution Act, 1867, s. 92(13).

18. Russell, *Leading Constitutional Decisions*, 39.

19. *Ontario Farm Products Marketing Reference*, [1957] S.C.R. 198; *R. v. Klassen* (1959), 20 D.L.R. (2nd) 406 (Manitoba Court of Appeal); *Caloil v. A.G. of Canada*, [1971] S.C.R. 543.

20. Russell, *Leading Constitutional Decisions*, 194.

21. Ibid., 199.

22. *General Motors of Canada Ltd. v. City National Leasing*, [1989] 1 S.C.R. 641.

23. Trudeau, "Federalism, Nationalism and Reason," 198.

24. Henri Bourassa, "The French Language and the Future of Our Race," in Ramsay Cook, ed., *French Canadian Nationalism* (Toronto: Macmillan, 1969), 141.

25. Kenneth McRoberts, *Quebec: Social Change and Political Crisis*, 3rd edn (Toronto: McClelland & Stewart, 1988), 214.

26. See Richard Simeon, *Federal–Provincial Diplomacy* (Toronto: University of Toronto Press, 1972), 115–22.

27. Quoted in George Woodcock, *Confederation Betrayed!* (Vancouver: Harbour Publishing, 1981), 8.

28. This argument is developed by Barry Cooper in "Western Political Consciousness," in Stephen Brooks, ed., *Political Thought in Canada* (Toronto: Irwin, 1984), 213–38.

29. James Bickerton, *Nova Scotia, Ottawa, and the Politics of Regional Development* (Toronto: University of Toronto Press, 1990).

30. G.V. LaForest, *Disallowance and Reservation of Provincial Legislation* (Ottawa: Department of Justice, 1955).

31. Ottawa ceded control to Manitoba in 1930.

32. Alberta and Saskatchewan also acquired these powers in 1930.

33. Doug Owram, "Reluctant Hinterland," in Larry Pratt and Garth Stevenson, eds, *Western Separatism* (Edmonton: Hurtig, 1981), 61.

34. Alan Cairns, "The Governments and Societies of Canadian Federalism," in Cairns, *Constitution, Government, and Society in Canada* (Toronto: McClelland & Stewart, 1988), 153–4.

35. Two of the major works using this concept are John Richards and Larry Pratt, *Prairie Capitalism* (Toronto: McClelland & Stewart, 1979), and McRoberts, *Quebec*.

36. R.A. Young, Philippe Faucher, and Andre Blais, "The Concept of Province-Building: A Critique," *Canadian Journal of Political Science* 17, 4 (Dec. 1984): 785.

37. Donald Smiley, "An Outsider's Observations of Federal–Provincial Relations," in R.D. Olling and W.M. Westmacott, eds, *Perspectives on Canadian Federalism* (Scarborough, Ont.: Prentice-Hall Canada, 1988).

38. Constitution Act, 1867, s. 118.

39. Ibid., s. 111.

40. Paul Boothe and Derek Hermourtz, "Paying for ACCESS: Province by Province," paper delivered before the Political Economy Research Group, University of Western Ontario, 24 Oct. 1997, Figure 3b.

41. Department of Finance Canada, *Budget 1995: Key Actions and Impacts*, unpaginated.

42. Ibid.

43. France St-Hilaire, "Fiscal Gaps and Imbalances: The New Fundamentals of Canadian Federalism," paper presented at Queen's University, Institute of Intergovernmental Relations, 12–14 May 2005, 11.

44. Roy Romanow, Linda Silas, and Steven Lewis,"Why Medicare Needs Ottawa," *Globe and Mail*, 16 Jan. 2012, http://www.theglobeandmail.com/commentary/why-medicare-needs-ottawa/article1358545/.

8 | How Parliamentary Government Works in Canada

1. "The Executive Government and Authority of and over Canada is hereby declared to continue and be vested in the Queen." Constitution Act, 1867, s. 9.

2. In the provinces, the Crown's authority is exercised through the lieutenant-governors, who are appointed by the Governor General to serve five-year terms.

3. James R. Mallory, *The Structure of Canadian Government*, rev. edn (Toronto: Gage, 1984), 42–3.

4. "Her Excellency the Right Honourable Michaëlle Jean Speech on the Occasion of the Official Welcoming Ceremony at the Legislative Assembly," 4 May 2006, www.gg.ca/media/doc.asp?lang=e&DocID=4750.

5. Constitution Act, 1867, s. 54.

6. Donald Savoie, *Governing from the Centre: The Concentration of Power in Canadian Politics* (Toronto: University of Toronto Press, 1999), ch. 6.

7. Colin Campbell and George Szablowski, *The Super-Bureaucrats: Structure and Behaviour in Central Agencies* (Toronto: Macmillan, 1979).

8. See David A. Good, *The Politics of Anticipation: Making Canadian Federal Tax Policy* (Ottawa: School of Public Administration, 1980).

9. Savoie, *Governing from the Centre*, 189.

10. Ibid., 109.

11. Campbell and Szablowski, *The Super-Bureaucrats*, 29.

12. Gordon Robertson, "The Changing Role of the Privy Council Office," *Canadian Public Administration* 14 (Winter 1971): 506.

13. Savoie, *Governing from the Centre*, 109.

14. Ibid., 195.

15. Ibid.

16. Robertson, "The Changing Role of the Privy Council Office," 506.

17. Savoie, *Governing from the Centre*, 101.

18. Ibid., 103.

19. Privy Council Office, "Role and Structure of IGA," http://www.pco.gc.ca/aia/index.asp?lang=eng&page=about-sujet&sub=structure&doc=structure-eng.htm.

20. Both Donald Savoie in *Governing from the Centre* and Jeffrey Simpson in *The Friendly Dictatorship* (Toronto:

McClelland & Stewart, 2001) make the case for this characterization.

21. Simpson, *The Friendly Dictatorship*, 248.

22. Savoie, *Governing from the Centre*, 362.

23. ENAP, "Canadian Governments Compared," http://etatscanadiens-canadiangovernments.enap.ca/en/nav.aspx?sortcode=2.0.0.

24. Savoie, *Governing from the Centre*, 248.

25. Alexander Brady, *Democracy in the Dominions* (Toronto: University of Toronto Press, 1947), 82.

26. John Porter, *The Vertical Mosaic* (Toronto: University of Toronto Press, 1965).

27. Robert J. Jackson and Michael A. Atkinson, *The Canadian Legislative System*, 2nd edn (Toronto: Gage, 1980), 22.

28. Savoie, *Governing from the Centre*, 91.

29. Ibid., 92.

30. David C. Docherty, *Mr. Smith Goes to Ottawa: Life in the House of Commons* (Vancouver: University of British Columbia Press, 1998), 234.

31. Savoie, *Governing from the Centre*, 91–2.

32. Docherty, *Mr. Smith Goes to Ottawa*, 204.

33. Ibid., 206.

34. C.E.S. Franks, "From Gomery to the Accountability Act: The Devil Is in the Details," *Policy Options* (June 2006): 46–52.

35. See the Constitution Act, 1867, s. 99(1). This phrase, or reference to "misbehaviour," is found in the federal and provincial statutes that govern the removal of judges.

36. Ralph Miliband, *The State in Capitalist Society* (London: Quartet Books, 1973), 124.

37. Judges of county courts and all higher courts are appointed by Ottawa. Provincial court judges are appointed by the provinces. See Figure 8.10 in the text.

38. Canada, Department of Justice, *Canada's System of Justice* (Ottawa: Supply and Services, 1988), 7.

39. *Reference re Public Service Employment Relations Act* (Alberta) (1987), 38 D.L.R. (4th) 161.

40. Ibid., 232.

41. Ibid., 200.

42. See Tonda MacCharles, "Top Court Speculation Begins Anew," *Toronto Star*, 19 Jan. 1999.

43. James Mallory, *Social Credit and the Federal Power* (Toronto: University of Toronto Press, 1954).

44. Michael Mandel, *Charter of Rights and the Legalization of Politics in Canada* (Toronto: Thompson Educational Publishing, 1994).

45. Rainer Knopff and Ted Morton, *Charter Politics* (Toronto: Nelson Canada, 1992), 79.

46. Dalhousie law professor Wayne MacKay, quoted in Kirk Makin, "Consensus-driven Supreme Court under the Microscope," *Globe and Mail*, 5 June 2011, http://www.theglobeandmail.com/news/national/time-to-lead/consensus-driven-supreme-court-under-the-microscope/article598631/?page=all.

PART IV | PARTICIPATION IN POLITICS

9 | Parties and Elections

1. Eugene A. Forsey, *How Canadians Govern Themselves* (Ottawa: Supply and Services Canada, 1982), 32.

2. Leon Epstein, *Political Parties in Western Democracies* (New Brunswick NJ: Transaction Books, 1980 [1967]), 9.

3. John Meisel, "Decline of Party in Canada," in Hugh G. Thorburn, ed., *Party Politics of Canada*, 4th edn (Scarborough, Ont.: Prentice-Hall, 1979).

4. This section was co-authored by Professor A. Brian Tanguay, Wilfrid Laurier University.

5. George M. Hougham, "The Background and Development of National Parties," in Hugh G. Thorburn, ed., *Party Politics in Canada* (Toronto: Prentice-Hall, 1963), 3.

6. Ibid., 13.

7. Escott Reid, "The Rise of National Parties in Canada," in Hugh G. Thorburn, ed., *Party Politics in Canada*, 5th edn (Scarborough, Ont.: Prentice-Hall, 1985), 12. See also Norman Ward, *The Canadian House of Commons* (Toronto: University of Toronto Press, 1950), 157–62.

8. See, in particular, Martin Shefter, "Party and Patronage: Germany, England, and Italy," *Politics and Society* 7, 4 (1977): 403–51; Epstein, *Political Parties in Western Democracies*, ch. 5.

9. André Siegfried, *The Race Question in Canada* (Toronto: McClelland & Stewart, Carleton Library Edition, 1966 [English translation first published 1907]), 114.

10. Siegfried, *The Race Question in Canada*, 136.

11. J.A. Corry, *Democratic Government and Politics*, 2nd edn (Toronto: University of Toronto Press, 1951), 22. Variations on this theme can be found in R.M. Dawson and Norman Ward, *The Government of Canada*, 5th edn (Toronto: University of Toronto Press, 1987), 430–3, and Hugh G. Thorburn, "Interpretations of the Canadian Party System," in Thorburn, ed., *Party Politics in Canada*, 5th edn (Scarborough, Ont.: Prentice-Hall, 1985), 20–40. For a critique of the adequacy of brokerage theory, see Janine Brodie and Jane Jenson, *Crisis, Challenge and Change: Party and Class Revisited* (Ottawa: Carleton University Press, 1988), ch. 1.

12. Robert Alford, *Party and Society* (Westport, Conn.: Greenwood Press, 1963), 250–1. Alford computed his index of class voting by subtracting the percentage of non-manual workers voting for left parties (in Canada, the Liberals and the NDP, according to Alford) from the percentage of manual workers voting for the left parties, on the assumption that a party of the left should receive the bulk of its support from the traditional blue-collar (manual) occupations. See the discussion ibid., chs 4 and 5. Obviously, Alford's index leaves a great deal to be desired and has been subjected to substantial criticism over the years. Many critics of his work are particularly exercised by his classification of the Liberal Party of Canada as a party of the "left."

13. Ibid., 251.

14. Brodie and Jenson, *Crisis, Challenge and Change*.

15. Janine Brodie and Jane Jenson, "Piercing the Smokescreen: Brokerage Parties and Class Politics," in Alain G. Gagnon and A. Brian Tanguay, eds, *Canadian Parties in Transition: Discourse, Organization, and Representation* (Scarborough, Ont.: Nelson, 1989), 28.

16. Canadian Institute of Public Opinion, *The Gallup Report*, "Confidence in Political Parties Declines," 1 Feb. 1989, and "Government Increasingly Becoming Object of Scorn among Canadians," 20 Feb. 1991.

17. Walter Young, *The Anatomy of a Party: The National CCF, 1932–61* (Toronto: University of Toronto Press, 1969), 298, 300.

18. Canada, Royal Commission on Electoral Reform and Party Financing, *Reforming Electoral Democracy*, vol. 7 (Ottawa: Supply and Services Canada, 1991), 221.

19. Jeffrey Simpson, "It's Tough to be Ahead," *Globe and Mail*, 28 Nov. 2006, http://www.theglobeandmail.com/news/politics/its-tough-to-be-ahead/article733087/.

20. Alan Cairns, "The Electoral System and the Party System in Canada, 1921–1965," *Canadian Journal of Political Science* 1, 1 (Mar. 1968): 55–80.

21. William P. Irvine, *Does Canada Need a New Electoral System?* (Kingston, Ont.: Institute of Intergovernmental Relations, Queen's University, 1979), 14.

22. See, e.g., Paul Nesbitt-Larking, cited in Tara Brautigam, "Conservative Urban Shutout Deepens Divide," www.canada.com, 24 Jan. 2006; Allan Gregg, cited in David Warren, "The Urban Angle," *Ottawa Citizen*, 26 Jan. 2006, online edition.

23. See Khayyam Paltiel, *Political Party Financing in Canada* (Toronto: McGraw-Hill Ryerson, 1970), 19–75.

24. According to Khayyam Paltiel, "For the 1972 [national] election half the funds raised in Ontario by the Liberal Party were collected personally by the chairman of the party's Treasury Committee from 90 large corporations." "Campaign Financing in Canada and Its Reform," in Penniman, ed., *Canada at the Polls: The General Election of 1974* (Washington: American Enterprise Institute, 1975), 182.

25. The number of hours per network and the division of time between the parties are determined by the CRTC. In deciding how much time each party receives, the CRTC is guided by a formula weighted according to each party's share of the seats and popular vote in the previous election.

26. Dalton Camp, *Points of Departure* (Toronto: Deneau and Greenberg, 1979), 91.

27. Ibid.

10 | Interest Groups

1. V.O. Key, *Politics, Parties, and Pressure Groups*, 4th edn (New York: Crowell, 1958), 23.
2. James Madison, *The Federalist Papers*, no. 10 (New York: New American Library, 1961).
3. *Associations Canada: An Encyclopedic Directory* (Mississauga, Ont.: Canadian Almanac & Directory Publishing Co., 2008).
4. Estimates based on ibid.
5. E.E. Schattschneider, *The Semi-Sovereign People* (New York: Holt, Rinehart and Winston, 1960), 35.
6. Ibid.
7. Ibid.
8. Charles E. Lindblom, *Politics and Markets* (New York: Basic Books, 1977), especially chs 13–16.
9. Bruno S. Frey, *Modern Political Economy* (New York: John Wiley & Sons, 1978), ch. 11.
10. Business's ideological and academic spokespersons adopt an essentially pluralistic position on the matter of interest-group influence. William Stanbury's remarks are typical: "The relationship between business firms and governments in either positive or normative terms cannot be characterized in a single phrase. It is inevitably plural and diverse. Depending upon the industry, the time, the other issues on the public policy agenda, the individuals involved, and what each 'side' is seeking to do vis-à-vis the other, the relationship might be characterized as adversarial, cooperative, symbiotic, supportive, or protective." Stanbury, *Business–Government Relations in Canada* (Toronto: Methuen, 1986), 9.
11. Michael Bliss, *Northern Enterprise: Five Centuries of Canadian Business* (Toronto: McClelland & Stewart, 1987), 578.
12. David Vogel, *Fluctuating Fortunes: The Political Power of Business in America* (New York: Basic Books, 1989), 193.
13. James Q. Wilson, "The Politics of Regulation," in Wilson, ed., *The Politics of Regulation* (New York: Basic Books, 1980), 370.
14. Earl Latham, *The Group Basis of Politics* (New York: Octagon Books, 1965), 35.
15. Arthur F. Bentley, *The Process of Government* (Evanston, Ill., 1935), 208.
16. David B. Truman, *The Governmental Process* (New York: Alfred Knopf, 1951); Robert Dahl, *Who Governs?* (New Haven: Yale University Press, 1961); John Kenneth Galbraith, *American Capitalism: The Concept of Countervailing Power* (Boston: Houghton Mifflin, 1952).
17. Theodore Lowi, *The End of Liberalism* (New York: W.W. Norton, 1969), 97.
18. P. Bachrach and M. Baratz, "Two Faces of Power," *American Political Science Review* 56, 4 (1962): 948.
19. This is true of Nicos Poulantzas, *Political Power and Social Classes* (London: New Left Books, 1973); Fred Block,

Revising State Theory (Philadelphia: Temple University Press, 1987); Bob Jessop, *The Capitalist State* (New York: New York University Press, 1982). Interest groups are given some passing mention in James O'Connor, *The Fiscal Crisis of the State* (New York: St Martin's Press, 1973); Claus Offe, *Contradictions of the Welfare State* (Cambridge, Mass.: MIT Press, 1984). Among the leading Marxist intellectuals, it is perhaps fair to say that only Ralph Miliband has very much to say on interest groups: see *The State in Capitalist Society* (London: Quartet Books, 1973).
20. The term "political economy" includes three separate streams or meanings today: the Canadian tradition of political economy, which, after Harold Innis's early work, moved squarely to the left; the political economy in the Downs–Buchanan tradition, with a centre of gravity in the United States and a pro-market orientation; and the political economy work among those in international relations, whose focus is globalization and its discontents and whose orientation is more often than not on the left.
21. Miliband, *The State in Capitalist Society*, 131.
22. Wallace Clement, *The Challenge of Class Analysis* (Ottawa: Carleton University Press, 1988), chs 7 and 8.
23. Ibid., 132.
24. Rianne Mahon, *The Politics of Industrial Restructuring: Canadian Textiles* (Toronto: University of Toronto Press, 1984).
25. Jurg Steiner, *European Democracies* (New York: Longman, 1986), 221.
26. It occasionally happens, however, that the CCC is capable of taking a firm position on issues that are more divisive in the business community. Its support for the Canada–US Free Trade Agreement was an example of this.
27. Gerhard Lehmbruch, "Concentration and the Structure of Corporatist Networks," in John Goldthorpe, ed., *Order and Conflict in Contemporary Capitalism* (Oxford: Clarendon, 1984), 65–6.
28. William D. Coleman, *Business and Politics: A Study of Collective Action* (Montreal and Kingston: McGill-Queen's University Press, 1988), ch. 6.
29. William Coleman is among those who have argued that such structures would benefit Canada economically. See Coleman, *Business and Politics*, ch. 13.
30. Michels's argument was that the specialization of function that accompanies organization inevitably results in domination of the organization by a minority and, therefore, creates the likelihood that the goals pursued by the organization will more closely reflect those of its leadership than its membership. Robert Michels, *Political Parties* (London: Jarrold, 1915).
31. Some of the classics of this literature include Anthony Downs, *An Economic Theory of Democracy* (New York: Harper and Row, 1957); Mancur Olson, *The Logic of Collective Action* (Cambridge, Mass.: Harvard University

Press, 1965); James M. Buchanan and Gordon Tullock, *The Calculus of Consent* (Ann Arbor: University of Michigan Press, 1965); Anthony Downs, *Inside Bureaucracy* (Boston: Little, Brown and Company, 1967).

32. Michael Atkinson, "How Do Institutions Constrain Policy?," paper delivered at the conference "Governing Canada: Political Institutions and Public Policy," McMaster University, 25 Oct. 1991, 8. A good introduction to this approach and its application to politics is provided by Queen's University economist Dan Usher in *Political Economy* (London: Blackwell, 2003).

33. Alan Cairns, "The Governments and Societies of Canadian Federalism," *Canadian Journal of Political Science* 10, 4 (Dec. 1977): 695–725.

34. James Q. Wilson, *Political Organizations* (New York: Basic Books, 1973), 3–4.

35. These definitions are the ones used in William D. Coleman and Grace Skogstad, "Introduction," in Coleman and Skogstad, eds, *Policy Communities and Public Policy in Canada* (Toronto: Copp Clark Pitman, 1990). They are not, however, agreed upon by everyone who mines this vein.

36. J.L. Granatstein, *The Ottawa Men* (Toronto: Oxford University Press, 1982).

37. O. Mary Hill, *Canada's Salesman to the World: The Department of Trade and Commerce, 1892–1939* (Montreal and Kingston: McGill–Queen's University Press, 1977), 172.

38. Leslie A. Pal, *Interests of State* (Montreal and Kingston: McGill–Queen's University Press, 1992), ch. 6.

39. A. Paul Pross, *Group Politics and Public Policy* (Toronto: University of Toronto Press, 1986), 68–9.

40. Ibid., 114–16.

41. John W. Kingdon, *Agendas, Alternatives, and Public Policies* (Boston: Little, Brown and Company, 1984), 54–7.

42. Schattschneider, *The Semi-Sovereign People*, 37.

43. Ibid., 38.

44. This literature is brought together in Hugh G. Thorburn, *Interest Groups in the Canadian Federal System*, vol. 69 of the research studies for the Royal Commission on the Economic Union and Development Prospects for Canada (Ottawa: Supply and Services, 1985).

45. Richard J. Schultz, *Federalism, Bureaucracy and Public Policy: The Politics of Highway Transport Regulation* (Montreal and Kingston: McGill–Queen's University Press, 1980), 148.

46. See, for example, M.W. Bucovetsky, "The Mining Industry and the Great Tax Reform Debate," in A. Paul Pross, ed., *Pressure Group Behaviour in Canadian Politics* (Toronto: McGraw-Hill Ryerson, 1975), 89–114.

47. The long-accepted claim that Canada's federal Constitution has led most associations to adopt a federal form of organization is not supported by the facts—at least not in the case of business associations. A survey by William Coleman finds that about three-quarters of business associations have unitary structures. Coleman's conclusion is that Canada's industrial structure has a far greater impact on how business

associations organize themselves than does the Constitution. See Coleman, *Business and Politics*, 260.

48. See Schultz, *Federalism, Bureaucracy and Public Policy*, especially ch. 8.

49. Alan Cairns, "The Governments and Societies of Canadian Federalism," in Cairns, *Constitution, Government, and Society in Canada* (Toronto: McClelland & Stewart, 1988), 167.

50. Leslie A. Pal, *State, Class, and Bureaucracy* (Montreal and Kingston: McGill–Queen's University Press, 1988).

51. Quoted in Duncan McDowall, ed., *Advocacy Advertising: Propaganda or Democratic Right?* (Ottawa: Conference Board of Canada, 1982), v.

52. For example, a former federal Minister of Justice defended his government's advertising on proposed constitutional reforms by saying, "Government is too complex nowadays to rely on policy by press release. Programs must be explained—not by reporters but by people who created them." Ibid., 7. On the subject of government advertising, see Jonathan Rose, *Making "Pictures in Our Heads": Government Advertising in Canada* (Westport, Conn.: Greenwood Publishing Group, 2000).

53. Privately funded think tanks like the C.D. Howe Institute, the Fraser Institute, and the Conference Board of Canada are another way of promoting group interests, in this case the general interests of business, by producing studies and funding experts whose perspectives and options for public policy are favourable to business interests. Direct-mail campaigns, targeted at selected groups whose opinions and actions may, in turn, affect policy makers is another technique employed mainly by business groups.

54. A fascinating though somewhat dated account of lobbying in Canada is John Sawatsky, *The Insiders: Government, Business, and the Lobbyists* (Toronto: McClelland & Stewart, 1987).

11 | The Media

1. Neil Postman, *Amusing Ourselves to Death: Public Discourse in the Age of Show Business* (New York: Penguin, 1985).

2. Henry Commager, ed., *Documents of American History*, 8th edn (New York: Appleton, Century, Crofts, 1968), 104.

3. Walter Lippmann, *Public Opinion* (New York: Harcourt, Brace and Company, 1922), 13.

4. "ITAC Media Choice & Trust Poll," www.itac.ca.

5. The Royal Commission on Newspapers expressed this view, although only the case of newspapers owned by the Irving family in New Brunswick was cited explicitly. See also the comments of the former Premier of Saskatchewan, Allan Blakeney, in Diane Francis, *Controlling Interest: Who Owns Canada?* (Toronto: Macmillan, 1986), 316.

6. Edward Herman and Noam Chomsky, *Manufacturing Consent* (New York: Pantheon, 1988), 8.

7. Walter I. Romanow et al., "Correlates of Newspaper Coverage of the 1979 Canadian Election: Chain Ownership,

Competitiveness of Market, and Circulation," study done for the Royal Commission on Newspapers (Ottawa: Supply and Services, 1981).

8. Lippmann, *Public Opinion*, 345.

9. Friends of Canadian Broadcasting, "Split Screen," www. friends.ca/Resource/Publications/publications11019201.

10. See the discussions in Frank Peers, *The Politics of Broadcasting 1920–1951* (Toronto: University of Toronto Press, 1969); and Marc Raboy, *Missed Opportunities: The Story of Canada's Broadcasting Policy* (Montreal and Kingston: McGill–Queen's University Press, 1990).

11. Morris Wolfe, *Jolts: The TV Wasteland and the Canadian Oasis* (Toronto: James Lorimer, 1985), 14.

12. Ibid., 16.

13. Ibid., 18.

14. Ibid., 262.

15. Ibid.

16. Herman and Chomsky, *Manufacturing Consent*, 19.

17. Edward Jay Epstein, *News from Nowhere: Television and the News* (New York: Random House, 1973),146.

18. Ibid., 147.

19. Ibid., 199.

20. Stanley Rothman and S. Robert Lichter, "Personality, Ideology and World View: A Comparison of Media and Business Elites," *British Journal of Political Science* 15, 1 (1984): 36.

21. Ibid., 46.

22. Barry Cooper, *Sins of Omission: Shaping the News at CBC TV* (Toronto: University of Toronto Press, 1994), xi.

23. Lydia Miljan and Barry Cooper, *Hidden Agendas: How the Beliefs of Canadian Journalists Influence the News* (Vancouver: University of British Columbia Press, 2003).

24. Ralph Miliband, *The State in Capitalist Society* (London: Quartet Books, 1969), 211.

25. Leon Epstein, *Political Parties in Western Democracies* (New York: Praeger, 1967), 237.

26. Aldous Huxley, *Brave New World Revisited* (New York: Harper & Brothers, 1958), 44.

27. The term is used by Herman and Chomsky in their analysis of the political role of the American media. They, in turn, borrow it from Walter Lippmann, who had in mind, however, government's use of propagandistic techniques to cultivate popular acceptance of their rule.

PART V | CANADIAN POLITICAL ISSUES

12 | Language, Diversity, and Aboriginal Politics

1. Information on mother tongue was first collected with the census of 1931. Before then, the census only asked about ethnic origin. Demographer Jacques Henripin suggests that French ethnic origin was probably a good surrogate measure for language group at the time of Confederation.

2. F.H. Leacy, ed., *Historical Statistics of Canada* (Ottawa: Supply and Services, 1983), R1-22, R81-87.

3. Henripin estimated that at the rate of decline experienced in the early 1970s, Quebec would still be 77 per cent French-speaking by 2001.

4. Richard Joy, *Languages in Conflict* (Toronto: McClelland & Stewart, 1972), 58, Table 25.

5. The first experience with immersion education was in 1975 in St Lambert, Quebec.

6. See Peter C. Waite, *Pre-Confederation* (Toronto: Prentice-Hall, 1965), 54–5.

7. These voices included such figures as Gonzalve Doutre, Errol Bouchette, and Olivar Asselin, and the activities of the Institut Canadien.

8. Henri Bourassa, *La langue, guardienne de la foi* (Montreal: Bibliothèque de l'action française, 1918).

9. Quoted by Pierre Trudeau in "Quebec on the Eve of the Asbestos Strike," in Ramsay Cook, ed., *French Canadian Nationalism* (Toronto: Macmillan, 1969), 35–6.

10. Victor Barbeau, *Mesure de notre taille* (1936); Barbeau, *Avenir de notre bourgeoisie* (Montréal: Editions de l'action canadienne française, 1939); Jacques Melançon, "Retard de croissance de l'entreprise canadienne-francaise," *L'actualité économique* (jan.–mars 1956): 503–22.

11. See Melançon, "Retard de croissance."

12. Lois du Quebec, 1974, c. 6.

13. Lois du Quebec, 1977, c. 5.

14. See *Attorney General of Quebec v. Blaikie et al.* (1979), 101 D.L.R. (3d) 394 (Supreme Court of Canada).

15. *Ford v. Attorney General of Quebec* (1988), Supreme Court of Canada.

16. See municipalite.herouxville.qc.ca/Standards.pdf.

17. From Consultation Commission on Accommodation Practices Related to Cultural Differences (Bouchard–Taylor Commission), *Building the Future: A Time for Reconciliation*, 2008.

18. From a speech by Premier Jean Charest, 22 May 2008, www.premier-ministre.gouv.qc.ca/salle-de-presse/discours/2008/mai/2008-05-22-en.shtml.

19. Eric Waddell, "State, Language and Society: The Vicissitudes of French in Quebec and Canada," in Alan Cairns and Cynthia Williams, eds, *The Politics of Gender, Ethnicity and Language in Canada*, vol. 34 of the research studies for the Royal Commission on the Economic Union and Development Prospects for Canada (Toronto: University of Toronto Press, 1985), 97.

20. "Francophones in the National Capital Region represent over 35 per cent of the Public Service population but, on average, they work more than 60 per cent of their time in English. In bilingual areas of Ontario the corresponding figures are 23 per cent and 66 per cent; roughly one-quarter of all employees are thus working two-thirds of their time in their second language." Commissioner of Official Languages, *Annual Report 1985* (Ottawa: Supply and Services, 1986), 54.

21. Commissioner of Official Languages, *Annual Report 1985*, 172.

22. Québec, Commission sur l'avenir politique et constitutionnel du Québec, *Rapport* (Québec, 1991), 17.

23. CRIC Quebec Youth Survey.

24. Environics Poll conducted for the Department of Canadian Heritage, 29 Mar.–18 Apr. 2004.

25. Leslie A. Pal, *Interests of State: The Politics of Language, Multiculturalism, and Feminism in Canada* (Montreal and Kingston: McGill–Queen's University Press, 1993).

26. Ibid., 281.

27. R. Brian Howe and David Johnson, *Restraining Equality: Human Rights Commissions in Canada* (Toronto: University of Toronto Press, 2000).

28. Janet McFarland, "Women Still Scarce in Top Ranks of Canada's Biggest Companies," *Globe and Mail*, 3 March 2011.

29. Sylvia Bashevkin, *Toeing the Lines* (Toronto: University of Toronto Press, 1985).

30. Sheila Rowbotham, *Hidden from History* (London: Pluto Press, 1974), 47.

31. Nellie McClung, "Hardy Perennials," in McClung, *In Times Like These* (Toronto: University of Toronto Press, 1972), 56.

32. See the discussion in Penny Kome, *Women of Influence* (Toronto: Doubleday Canada, 1985), ch. 2.

33. See, for example, Bashevkin, *Toeing the Lines*, 20–3.

34. Ibid., 32.

35. Pat Armstrong and Hugh Armstrong, *The Double Ghetto: Canadian Women and Their Segregated Work*, 3rd edn (Toronto: McClelland & Stewart, 1994), 42–3.

36. Barbara Frum, "Why There Are So Few Women in Ottawa," *Chatelaine* 44 (Oct. 1971): 33, 110.

37. Bashevkin, *Toeing the Lines*, 110–19.

38. See the summaries of landmark judgments in National Action Committee on the Status of Women, *Women and Legal Action* (Oct. 1984), 8–27.

39. Canadian Advisory Council on the Status of Women, *Canadian Charter and Equality Rights for Women: One Step Forward or Two Steps Back?* (Sept. 1989), 19.

40. Canadian Advisory Council on the Status of Women, *Every Voice Counts: A Guide to Personal and Political Action* (Ottawa, 1989), 39–58.

41. Penney Kome, *The Taking of Twenty-Eight: Women Challenge the Constitution* (Toronto: Women's Press, 1983).

42. 2002 International Social Survey Program, World Values Survey 2000, www.worldvaluessurvey.org.

43. Statistics Canada, "The Changing Profile of Canada's Labour Force," Catalogue no. 96F0030XIE2001009, 11 Feb. 2003.

44. CBC News, "Female Execs on Wane at Fortune 500 Firms" (Canadian Broadcasting Corporation, 14 Dec. 2011), http://www.cbc.ca/news/business/story/2011/12/14/biz-catalyst-study-women-fortune-500.html.

45. The RCAP estimated the difference at 49 per cent for 1992–3. In a study for Infometrica's *Monthly Economic Review* 15, 7 (28 Nov. 1996), a former policy coordinator for the RCAP put the difference at 57 per cent for that same year.

46. *Regina v. Howson* (1894), 1 Terr. L.R. 492 (S.C.N.W.T.), 494.

47. Harvey McCue, "Indian Reserve," *The Canadian Encyclopedia*, 2nd edn (Edmonton: Hurtig, 1988), vol. 2, 1056.

48. Statistics Canada, "Share of First Nations People Who Speak an Aboriginal Language Holds Steady, Even among Younger Generation," 2006 Census: Aboriginal Peoples in Canada in 2006: Inuit, Métis and First Nations, 2006 Census: First Nations People, http://www12.statcan.ca/census-recensement/2006/as-sa/97-558/p19-eng.cfm.

49. Harold Cardinal, *The Unjust Society* (Edmonton: Hurtig, 1969), 1.

50. Quoted in Melvin H. Smith, *Our Home or Native Land?* (Toronto: Stoddart, 1995), 143.

51. Peter A. Cumming and Neil H. Mickenberg, eds, *Native Rights in Canada* (Toronto: General Publishing, 1972), 55.

52. Ibid., 4.

53. Cumming and Mickenberg, eds, *Native Rights in Canada*, 53.

54. J. Hugh Faulkner, "Pressuring the Executive," *Canadian Public Administration* 25 (Summer 1982): 248.

55. Ninth annual presidential address to the National Indian Brotherhood, Fredericton, New Brunswick, Sept. 1978.

56. Gary Granzberg et al., "New Magic for Old: TV in Cree Culture," *Journal of Communication* 27, 4 (1977): 155–77; Gary Granzberg, "Television as Storyteller: The Algonkian Indians of Central Canada," *Journal of Communication* 32, 1 (1982): 43–52.

13 | Canada in the World

1. Mark Kingwell, "What Distinguishes Us from the Americans," *National Post*, 5 Mar. 2003, A16.

2. John Ralston Saul, *Reflections on a Siamese Twin: Canada at the End of the Twentieth Century* (Toronto: Penguin, 1997), 171.

3. The Pew Research Center for the People and the Press, "What the World Thinks in 2002," part of the Pew Global Attitudes Project, www.people-press.org.

4. Jeffrey Sachs, "Nature, Nurture and Growth," *The Economist*, 14 June 1997, 19–22.

5. Barry Lynn, "Unmade in America: The True Cost of a Global Assembly Line," *Harper's* (June 2002): 37.

6. *Time*, 11 June 2001, 30.

7. Allan Gotlieb, "Getting Attention," *National Post*, 17 May 2002, A17.

8. Allan Gotlieb, "A Grand Bargain with the U.S.," *National Post*, 5 Mar. 2003, A16.

9. Michael Ignatieff, "Canada in the Age of Terror—Multilateralism Meets a Moment of Truth," *Policy Options* (Feb. 2003), www.irpp.org.

10. Ibid.

11. Joseph Nye, "The Misleading Metaphor of Decline," *The Atlantic* (Mar. 1990): 86–94.

12. Michael Ignatieff, "The Burden," *New York Times Magazine*, 5 Jan. 2003, www.nytimes.com/2003/01/05/magazine/05EMPIRE.html.

13. Jeffrey Simpson, "Canada is 'back' on the world stage? Hardly," *Globe and Mail*, 13 Jun. 2012, http://www.theglobeandmail.com/commentary/canada-is-back-on-the-world-stage-hardly/article4254018/.

14. UN, "Ranking of Military and Police Contributions to UN Operations," http://www.un.org/en/peacekeeping/contributors/2010/sept10_2.pdf.

Credits

PHOTOS AND CARTOONS

Page iii: (top) Jeff Chevrier/iStockphoto; **Page iv:** (top left) © iStockphoto.com/Sergey Ivanov; (top right) Bradcalkins / Dreamstime.com / GetStock.com; **Page v:** (top left) Mark Tomalty / Aurora Photos / GetStock; **Page vi:** (top centre) © Government of Canada. Reproduced with the permission of the Minister of Public Works and Government Services Canada (2013). Source: Library and Archives Canada/Credit: Robert Cooper/National Archives of Canada fonds/e002852801; (bottom centre) Katherine Welles/iStockphoto; **Page vii:** (bottom right) Julie de Leseleuc/iStockphoto; **Page viii:** (top left) Paul McKinnon/ iStockphoto; (top centre) © ZUMA Wire Service / Alamy; (bottom right) Shaun Lowe/iStockphoto; **Page ix:** (top left) 1000words / Dreamstime.com / GetStock.com; **Page x:** **(top left)** TinaFields/iStockphoto; (top right) Lucas Oleniuk/Toronto Star / GetStock. com; **Page xxii:** © iStockphoto.com/Keith Binns; **Page 2:** © iStockphoto.com/Shaun Lowe; **Page 3:** © Dale Cummings/Artizans; **Page 8:** © Steve Russell/GetStock.com; **Page 14:** (left) © Pictorial Press Ltd / Alamy; (right) topham Picturepoint ©1999 / GetStock.com; **Page 23:** © Michael de Adder/Artizans; **Page 28:** © iStockphoto.com/Stacey Newman; **Page 30:** © Chris Cheadle/ Alamy; **Page 32:** © Joseph Rank/www.cartoonstock.coml; **Page 42:** © Simon Fraser University/John Larter; **Page 46:** © Richard Lautens/GetStock.com; **Page 53:** (left) © Library and Archives Canada/C-006859; (right) © CP Photo 1955 (Montreal Gazette); **Page 57:** (left) © The Canadian Press/Shaney Komulainen; (right) © CP Photo/Hamilton Spectator—Sheryl Nadler; **Page 63:** (left) © Doukhobors/Library and Archives Canada/C-005849; (right) © Tak Toyota/Library and Archives Canada/C-046350; **Page 67:** (top left) © iStockphoto.com/Visual Field; (top right) © iStockphoto.com/Uschools University Images; (bottom left) © iStockphoto. com/Shunyu Fan; (bottom right) © Canada. Dept. of Interior/Library and Archives Canada/PA-034374; **Page 74:** © Bill Casselman, http://www.billcasselman.com/casselmania/mania_eh.htm.; **Page 77:** © Design Pics Inc./Alamy; **Page 79:** © Brain Gable/Globe and Mail/CP; **Page 89:** © Glen Le Lievre/www.cartoonstock.com; **Page 93:** © Oakland Ross/GetStock.com; **Page 99:** Courtesy Magazines Canada, www.magazinescanada.ca; **Page 104:** © Inudstrykb/Alamy; **Page 107:** © Michael de Adder/Artizans; **Page 111:** © Cindy Hopkins/Alamy; **Page 124:** © Roy Peterson/Artizans; **Page 128:** © Jiawangkun/Dreamstime.com; **Page 130:** © Canada Post Corporation 1982. Reproduced with Permission.; **Page 135:** Library and Archives Canada, Acc. No. 1988-243-517 © Estate of Leonard Norris; **Page 139:** Brent Lynch/© Simon Fraser University; **Page 152:** © CP Photo/Jonathan Hayward; **Page 159:** Bob Bierman/© Simon Fraser University; **Page 166:** © CP Photo/Fred Chartrand; **Page 170:** © The Canadain Press/Fred Chartrand; **Page 176:** © Baloo (Rex May)/www.cartoonstock.com; **Page 178:** © Sneuro/www.cartoonstock.com; **Page 179:** © CP Photo/Peter McCabe; **Page 187:** © Baloo (Rex May)/www.cartoonstock.com; **Page 191:** © Yvon Sauvé/Alamy; **Page 197:** George P. Roberts/ Library and Archives Canada/C-000733; **Page 205:** © McCord Museum; **Page 207:** © McCord Museum; **Page 209:** (left) © CP Photo/stf—Tom Hanson; (right) © CP Photo/stf—Jacques Bossinot; **Page 211:** © Roy Peterson/Artizans; **Page 221:** © Roy Peterson/ Artizans; **Page 226:** © CP Photo/Tom Hanson; **Page 233:** © The Canadian Press/Sean Kilpatrick; **Page 236:** © Bado/Artizans; **Page 241:** © The Canadian Press/Fred Chartrand; **Page 246:** © Brian Gable/The Globe and Mail/CP; **Page 253:** © Brian Gable/ The Globe and Mail/CP; **Page 259:** © iStockphoto.com/GYI NSEA; **Page 274:** © Adrien Veczan/GetStock.com; **Page 276:** © The Canadian Press/John Woods; **Page 278:** Library and Archives Canada, Acc. No. 1983-33-1102; **Page 287:** © Simon Fraser University/ Bob Krieger; **Page 294:** © Brian Gable/Globe and Mail/CP; **Page 296:** © Graeme MacKay/Artizans; **Page 304:** © Greg Perry; **Page 314:** © Louie Palu/The Globe and Mail; **Page 318:** © Ray Tang/Rex Features [2005]. All rights reserved.; **Page 321:** © Harley Schwadron/www.cartoonstock.com; **Page 331:** © Michael de Adder/Artizans; **Page 336:** © ForestEthics, www.forestethics.org; **Page 343:** © Mark Blinch/Reuters; **Page 346:** © ZUMA Wire Service/Alamy; **Page 349:** © Kevin Van Paassen/The Globe and Mail; **Page 353:** © David Donar; **Page 360:** © Roy Peterson/Artizans; **Page 363:** © Sad Hill News; **Page 368:** © mauritius images GmbH/ Alamy; **Page 370:** © Rick Rudnicki/Alamy; **Page 372:** © Toronto Star/GetStock.com; **Page 377:** (left) © CP Photo/Bill Grimshaw; (right) © CP Photo/Peter McCabe; **Page 384:** Shelley Twist. Used with the permission of the City of Burnaby.; **Page 388:** © AP Photo/Christopher Brown; **Page 395:** Library and Archives Canada/Credit: Cyril Jessop/Canadian Intellectual Property Office fonds/ PA-030212; **Page 397:** © Toronto Star/GetStock.com; **Page 402:** (left) Courtesy Canadian Museum of Civilization; (right) © CP Photo/Ted Ostrowski; **Page 408:** © J.F. Moran/Library and Archives Canada, PA-102575; **Page 419:** © Finbarr O'Reilly/Reuters/ Corbis; **Page 423:** © Rick Eglinton/GetStock.com; **Page 427:** © Mike Baldwin/Artizans

Index